About the Authors ...

B. W. JOHNSON

Barton W. Johnson was born in 1833. In his eighteenth year he commenced to study at Walnut Grove Academy, which later became Eureka College —here he attended two years. After teaching in the College one year he went to Bethany College in 1854. At that time the College was presided over by Alexander Campbell, aided by such professors as R. Milligan, W. K. Pendleton, R. Richardson, and others. In 1856 he graduated in a class of twenty-seven, the honors of which were divided between him and W. A. Hall of Tennessee. In 1857 he took a position in Eureka College, where he remained seven years—for two years as its president. For two years he taught in Bethany College. For sixteen years he was editor of the weekly periodical THE EVANGELIST—later THE CHRISTIAN EVANGELIST.

DON DEWELT

Since 1957 he has been a professor in the Ozark Bible College of Joplin, Mo. For fourteen years prior to this he taught in the San Jose Bible College of San Jose, California. He received his education at Pacific Bible Seminary, San Jose Bible College, Abilene Christian College, and San Jose State College. He has earned the degrees of Bachelor of Theology and Bachelor of Divinity.

The author has a constant interest in evangelism. He has held scores of evangelistic meetings during his years of training and teaching. He was minister of the Maricopa Church of Christ in California and at Carterville, Missouri.

He is the author of: *Sacred History and Geography; Acts Made Actual; Romans Realized; Paul's Letters to Timothy and Titus; The Church in The Bible; If You Want to Preach; If You Want to Be a Soulwinner; If You Want to Write For Christ; The Power of The Holy Spirit.*

"And they bri ... ent in his speech; and they bes ...

—Mark VII:32

THE GOSPEL OF MARK

Other Books in the

BIBLE STUDY TEXTBOOK SERIES

- ACTS MADE ACTUAL
- SACRED HISTORY AND GEOGRAPHY
- THE CHURCH IN THE BIBLE
- ROMANS REALIZED
- HELPS FROM HEBREWS
- THE GLORIOUS CHURCH OF EPHESIANS
- THE GOSPEL OF JOHN
- GUIDANCE FROM GALATIANS
- THE GREATEST WORK IN THE WORLD
- PAUL'S LETTERS TO TIMOTHY AND TITUS
- SURVEY COURSE IN CHRISTIAN DOCTRINE VOL. I
- SURVEY COURSE IN CHRISTIAN DOCTRINE VOL. II
- LETTERS FROM PETER
- THINKING THROUGH THESSALONIANS
- STUDIES IN FIRST CORINTHIANS
- THE SEER, THE SAVIOUR, AND THE SAVED IN THE BOOK OF REVELATION
- SURVEY COURSE IN CHRISTIAN DOCTRINE VOL. III & IV
- STUDIES IN LUKE
- JAMES AND JUDE

BIBLE STUDY TEXTBOOK

THE GOSPEL OF MARK

B. W. Johnson
and
Don DeWelt

A New . . .

- Commentary
- Workbook
- Teaching Manual

Both the *Authorized King James Version* of 1611 and *American Standard Translation* of 1901 are used in the *TEXT of this book*

College Press, Joplin, Missouri

DEDICATION

To the one who teaches
by life and word the
Life of our Lord — Seth Wilson

ACKNOWLEDGEMENTS

In 1889 B. W. Johnson (author of *People's New Testament; Vision of the Ages; The Gospel of John*) wrote a *Lesson Commentary* on 277 verses of the gospel of Mark. There are 678 verses in Mark. The editor has written *Thought Questions* for all 678 verses, as well as *Fact Questions* for the entire Gospel. The *Outline* and *Analysis* for the 401 verses B. W. Johnson did not discuss in his *Lesson Commentary* are also the work of the editor. The *Explanatory Notes* on the 401 verses are compiled by the editor from the following writers:

1. Lyman Abbott—*An Illustrated Commentary on the Gospel According to Mark and Luke,* New York; A. S. Barnes & Company, 1877.
2. J. A. Alexander—*Commentary on the Gospel of Mark,* Grand Rapids; Zondervan Publishing House, 1955—reprint of 1864.
3. Henry Alford, *New Testament for English Readers,* 4 volumes in one, Chicago, Moody Press—reprint.
4. W. C. Allen, *The Gospel According to Saint Mark,* New York; Macmillan Co., 1915—Oxford Church Biblical Commentary.
5. Samuel J. Andrews, *The Life of Our Lord Upon Earth,* Grand Rapids; Zondervan Publishing House, 1954—reprint of revised edition of 1891.
6. Albert Barnes, *Notes on the New Testament, Explanatory and Practical,* Grand Rapids; Baker Book House, 1949—reprint of 1832.
7. J. V. Bartlet, *St. Mark* in the *Century Bible*—Edinburgh; T. C. and E. C. Jack, 1922.
8. John Albert Bengel, *Gnomon of the New Testament,* Philadelphia; Perkin, Pine & Higgins, 1860.
9. E. Bickersteth, *St. Mark: Exposition,* in the *Pulpit Commentary*—Grand Rapids: Wm. B. Eerdmans Publishing Co., 1950 (Reprint)
10. David Brown, *Matthew—John* in Vol. V of *A Commentary Critical Experimental and Practical*—by Robert Jamieson, A. R. Fausset, and David Brown, Grand Rapids; Wm. B. Eerdmans, 1948 (reprint).
11. John Henry Burn, *A Homiletical Commentary on the Gospel according to St. Mark* in the *Preacher's Homiletical Commentary,* New York; Funk and Wagnalls, 1896.
12. Madam Cecilia, *The Gospel According to St. Mark,* London; Kegan Paul, Trench, Trubner, & Co., Ltd., 1904.
13. G. A. Chadwick, *The Gospel According to St. Mark* in the *Expositor's Bible,* Grand Rapids; Wm. B. Eerdmans Pub. Co. (reprint).
14. W. N. Clarke, *Commentary on the Gospel of Mark—An American Commentary.* American Baptist Publishing Society, 1881.

15. F. C. Cook—*Mark's Gospel*—in *The Speaker's Commentary* Vol. I, New York; Charles Scribner's Sons, 1896.
16. Joseph S. Excell—*The Biblical Illustrator*—Grand Rapids; Baker Book House—(reprint) 1953.
17. Edward Hastings—*Speaker's Bible:* Mark 2 vols. Aberdeen, Scotland; 1962, Baker Book House—reprint of 1929.
18. John Peter Lange—*Mark* in *Commentary on the Holy Scriptures,* Grand Rapids, Zondervan—(reprint).
19. Alexander Maclaren—Expositions of Holy Scriptures: *St. Mark*—Grand Rapids; Wm. B. Eerdmans Pub. Co., 1944 (reprint).
20. J. W. McGarvey, *Commentary on Matthew and Mark,* Delight, Ark.; Gospel Light Pub. Co., 1875. (reprint)
21. James Morison—*A Practical Commentary on the Gospel According to St. Mark,* London—Hodder and Stoughton, 1889.
22. Matthew Riddle, *The Gospel According to Mark in the International Revision Commentary on the New Testament,* New York; Charles Scribner's Sons, 1881.
23. J. C. Ryle, *Expository Thoughts on the Gospels,* 4 vols., Grand Rapids; Zondervan Publishing House (reprint).
24. M. F. Sadler, *The Gospel According to St. Mark,* London; George Bell & Sons, 1892.
25. Henry Barclay Swete, *The Gospel According to St. Mark,* London; MacMillan & Co., 1898.
26. E. W. Thornton and Edwin R. Errett, *Notes on the International Sunday School Lessons,* Cincinnati; Standard Publishing Co., 1918.

GOSPEL OF MARK

A Complete List of Authors
From Which Quotations are
Made in this Text

1. Lyman Abbott
2. J. A. Alexander
3. Dean Alford
4. W. C. Allen
5. Samuel J. Andrews
6. W. Arnot
7. Albert Barnes
8. J. V. Bartlett
9. Richard Baxter
10. John Albert Bengel
11. Beza
12. E. Bickersteth
13. David Brown
14. Bunyan
15. Burckhardt
16. John Henry Burn
17. John Calvin
18. Madam Cecelia
19. G. A. Chadwick
20. Chrysostom
21. Adam Clark
22. G. W. Clark
23. W. N. Clarke
24. F. C. Cook
25. Cumming
26. Dante
27. Don Dewelt
28. Diodorus
29. Dodd
30. Ralph Earle
31. Ellicott
32. Edwin R. Errett
33. Ewald
34. Joseph S. Excell
35. Farrar
36. A. R. Faussett
37. Thomas Fuller
38. Cunningham Geikie
39. Godet
40. Godwin
41. Gordon
42. Greenleaf
43. H. B. Hackett
44. Hanna
45. Edward Hastings
46. Matthew Henry
47. Dean Hook
48. Hort
49. Howson
50. Hurlburt
51. Jacobus
52. Robert Jamison
53. Jerome
54. B. W. Johnson
55. Josephus
56. Kitto
57. John Peter Lange
58. Lenski
59. Lightfoot
60. Lindell and Scott
61. Luthardt
62. Martin Luther
63. George MacKenzie
64. Alexander Maclaren
65. Maclear
66. J. W. McGarvey
67. Meyer
68. Mimpliss
69. G. Campbell Morgan
70. James Morison
71. Muir
72. Peloubet
73. Petler
74. Plato
75. Plumptre
76. Quesnel
77. Matthew Riddle
78. F. W. Robertson
79. Robinson
80. Rose
81. J. C. Ryle
82. M. F. Sadler
83. St. Gregory
84. Schaff
85. Sporgeon
86. Stalker
87. Stanley
88. Stier
89. Stock
90. Swete
91. Swieton
92. Theophrastus
93. Tholuck
94. Thomas
95. Thomson
96. E. W. Thornton
97. Tischendorf
98. Trench
99. Tristram
100. Tyng'
101. Wells
102. Westcott
103. Whedon
104. Seth Wilson

Contents and Analytical Outline

SPECIAL STUDIES

by Seth Wilson

SUMMARY OUTLINE OF THE LIFE OF CHRIST

Noting Places, Periods of Time and Events

— Seth Wilson —

THIRTY YEARS PREPARATION

1. Bethlehem—Birth, Lk. 2
2. Jerusalem—Presented in the Temple, Lk. 2
3. Bethlehem—Wisemen found Him, Mt. 2
4. Egypt—Fleeing from Herod's decree, Mt. 2
5. Nazareth—Boyhood home, Mt. 2
6. Jerusalem—Passover, age 12, Lk. 2
7. Nazareth—Grew up until about 30 years of age, Lk. 2
8. Jordan in Wilderness of Judea—Baptized by John, Mt. 3; Mk. 1; Lk. 3
9. Wilderness—Tempted of Satan, Mt. 4; Mk. 1; Lk. 4
10. Bethabara—Pointed out by John, obtained first disciples, Jn. 1
11. Cana of Galilee—Wedding; first miracle, Jn. 2
12. Capernaum—With family and disciples—"Abode not many days" Jn. 2

FIRST YEAR OF MINISTRY

EARLY JUDEAN MINISTRY (8 or 9 months)

13. Jerusalem—FIRST PASSOVER; cleansed temple; first public presentation, Jn. 2
14. Judea—Period of about 8 or 9 months, Jn. 3
    Miracles ("no man can do these things . . .")
    Preached to Nicodemus New Birth and Eternal Life, Son lifted up
    Making and baptizing more disciples than John
15. Sychar in Samaria—Women at well; all city came out; abode two days, Jn. 4 (4 months to harvest)

GALILEAN MINISTRY (1 year and 3 or 4 months)

16. Cana of Galilee—Spoke the word and the son at Capernaum healed, Jn. 4
17. Nazareth—Read and taught in synagogue; first rejection there, Lk. 4
18. Capernaum—Called four fishermen; healed many. Mt. 4; Mk. 1; Lk. 5
19. Galilean tour (first)—Great crowds; miracles, Mt. 4; Lk. 4; Mk. 1
    Leper healed, Mt. 8; Mk. 1; Lk. 5. Paralytic (through roof) Mt. 9; Mk. 2; Lk. 5
    Call of Matthew, feast of publicans, Mt. 9; Mk. 2; Lk. 5
    Controversies over eating and fasting, Mt. 9; Mk. 2; Lk. 5

SECOND YEAR OF MINISTRY

20. Jerusalem—SECOND PASSOVER: Lame man at pool; controversy about Sabbath healing; sermon on Deity and credentials, Jn. 5
21. Galilee—Controversy over Sabbath Reaping, Mt. 12; Mk. 2; Lk. 6
    Healed withered hand on Sabbath in synagogue (Capernaum?) Mt. 12; Mk. 3; Lk. 6
    Thronging crowds from far and near, Many miracles, Mt. 12; Mk. 3; Lk. 6
    Named twelve "Apostles," Mt. 3; Lk. 6
    Sermon on the Mount, Mt. 5,6,7; Lk. 6
    Healed centurions servant (Capernaum) Mt. 8; Lk. 7
22. Nain—Raised Widow's son, Lk. 7
23. Capernaum—Question from John the Baptist; sermon on John, Mt. 11; Lk. 7
    Condemnation of unrepentant cities; the great invitation, Mt. 11
    in house of Simon the Pharisee; Penitent woman forgiven, Lk. 7
24. Galilean tour (second)—Charge of league with Satan, Mt. 12;
    Sign sought; sign of Jonah; judgment of this generation, Mt. 12
    Mother and brethren try to interrupt, Mt. 12; Mk. 3; Lk. 8
    Sermon in parables, Mt. 13; Mk. 4; Lk. 8
    Challenge of high cost to would-be followers, Mt. 8; Lk. 9
25. On Sea of Galilee—Stilled the tempest, Mt. 8; Mk. 4; Lk 8
26. Gergesa—Demoniacs and swine, Mt. 8; Mk. 5; Lk. 8
27. Capernaum—Healed woman with flow of blood and raised Jairus' daughter, Mt. 9; Mk. 5; Lk. 8
    Healed two blind men and a dumb demoniac, Mt. 9
28. Nazareth—Apparently last visit; unbelief; some miracles, Mt. 13; Mk. 6
29. Galilean tour (third)—Twelve sent out in pairs, Mt. 10; Mk. 6; Lk. 9
    Herod's fear of Jesus, Mt. 14; Mk. 6; Lk. 9
    (Tour ends at Capernaum; multitudes greatly aroused.)
30. Across the Sea, near Bethsaida Julias—THIRD PASSOVER NIGH —Day of teaching; fed 5000; refused crown; night of prayer— Mt. 14; Mk. 6; Lk. 9; Jn 6

THIRD YEAR OF MINISTRY

RETIREMENTS AND TRAVELS WITH THE TWELVE (6 months)

31. On the Sea—(in the night) Walked on water; stilled tempest, Mt. 14; Mk. 6; Jn 6

32. Gennesaret—Miracles, Mt. 14; Mk. 6
33. Capernaum—Sermon on the Bread of Life, Jn. 6. Many forsake Him.
    Controversy with Pharisees about traditions (washing) Mt 15; Mk. 7
34. Phoenicia—Retirement with apostles; healed the demonized daughter of the Syro-Phoenician woman, Mt. 15; Mk. 7
35. Decapolis—Healed deaf stammerer and many others, Mt. 15; Mk. 7
    Fed 4000 (Considerable public ministry implied) Mt. 15; Mk. 8
36. Magadan—Pharisees and Sadducees demand sign from heaven, Mt. 16; Mk. 8
37. On the Sea—Crossing in boat; warned disciples against influence of popular leaders and parties, Mt. 16; Mk. 8
38. Caesarea Philippi—Question of Jesus' identity; Peter's confession, Mt. 16; Mk. 8; Lk. 9
    First plain prediction of His death, Mt. 16; Mk. 8; Lk. 9
39. An exceeding high mountain (Hermon?) Transfiguration, Mt. 17; Mk. 9; Lk. 9
    Healed Demoniac boy, Mt. 17; Mk. 9; Lk. 9
    Further prediction of cross, Mt. 17; Mk. 9; Lk 9
40. Capernaum—Peter and the temple tax, Mt. 17
    Discussion of who shall be greatest, Mt. 18; Mk. 9; Lk. 9
    The unknown worker of miracles, Mk. 9; Lk 9
    Discussion of stumbling blocks, mistreatment, forgiveness, Mt. 18; Mk. 9
    Advice of His unbelieving brethren, Jn. 7
41. Journey through Samaria—Sons of Thunder would call down fire, Lk. 9

LATER JUDEAN MINISTRY (about 3 months)

42. Jerusalem—FEAST OF TABERNACLES: Confused opinions about Him; Attempt to arrest Him; Water of Life, Jn. 7
    Sermon on the Light of the world; freedom; Abraham's seed, Jn. 8
    Healing the man born blind; controversy, Jn. 9
    The Good Shepherd and the Door of the Sheep, Jn. 10
    The seventy sent out; discussion on their return, Lk. 10
    A lawyer's question; parable of good Samaritan, Lk. 10
43. Bethany—Jesus and Mary and Martha, Lk. 10
44. Place of Prayer—Discourse on Prayer, Lk. 11

45. Place Unknown—Controversy about demons and league with Satan, Lk. 11
    Signs and the judgment of this generation, Lk. 11
46. Pharisee's house—Invited to dinner; Denounced Phariseeism, Lk. 11
47. Before a multitude of many thousands—Great evangelistic appeals; Lk. 12 & 13
    (1) Warning against hypocrisy & fear of men
    (2) Against covetousness: parable of rich fool
    (3) Against anxiety for worldly needs: trust God
    (4) Urged watchfulness and preparedness for day of account; parables of waiting servants and wise steward
    (5) Christ the burning issue: no neutrality
    (6) Settle with God "out of court"
    (7) No difference, *all* must repent
    (8) Parable of fig tree: 3 chances, one more, then cut down.
48. In a synagogue—Woman bowed double; controversy about Sabbath healing, Lk. 13
    Parables of the kingdom: mustard and leaven, Lk. 13
49. Temple in Jerusalem—Feast of Dedication; attempts to kill Jesus for blasphemy; Jesus' claims:—the door, the good shepherd, one with God, the Son of God. Jn. 10

LATER PEREAN MINISTRY (about 3 months)

50. Perea—Retirement to place of His baptism, Jn. 10
51. Cities and villages—Journeys and discussions in Perea: few saved, Herod the fox. Lk. 13
52. Home of a Pharisee—On the Sabbath, healed dropsy and discussion; Conduct at feasts: chief seats, whom to invite; Parable of great feast, slighted invitation, excuses. Lk. 14
53. Before a great multitude—Sermon on cost of discipleship. Lk. 14
54. Place unknown—Parables of lost sheep, coin and son. Lk. 15
    Parable of the unjust steward, Lk. 16
    The rich man and Lazarus, Lk. 16
    Stumbling blocks; forgiveness; unprofitable servants, Lk. 17
55. Bethany—Raising of Lazarus, Jn. 11
    Rulers in Jerusalem plot to kill Jesus, Jn. 11
56. Ephraim (city)—"Tarried" with the disciples, Jn. 11
57. Trip through borders of Samaria, Galilee, and Perea to Jerusalem, Lk. 17
    Healing ten lepers.

Sermon on the time of the coming of the kingdom.
Teaching on prayer: the unjust judge; Pharisee & Publican, Lk. 18
Teaching on divorce (in Perea) Mt. 19; Mk. 10
Jesus and the little children, Lk 18; Mt. 19; Mk. 10
Rich young ruler; peril of riches; apostles' reward, Mt. 19; Mk. 10; Lk. 18
Parable of laborers in the vineyard, Mt. 20
Plain prediction of the crucifixion, Mt. 20; Mk. 10; Lk. 18
James and John ask chief honors, Mt. 20; Mk. 10

58. Jericho—Blind men healed (Bartimaeus), Mt. 20; Mk. 10; Lk. 18
Zacchaeus, Lk. 19
59. Road to Jerusalem—Parable of the Pounds, Lk. 19

LAST WEEK IN JERUSALEM AREA

60. Bethany—Reception; Many anoints Jesus, Mt. 26:6-13; Mk. 13:3-9; Jn. 12:1-11
61. Jerusalem—"Triumphal" entry (probably Sunday), Mt. 21; Mk. 11; Lk. 19; Jn. 12
62. Bethany—"Night's lodging, Mt. 21:17
Next day cursed fig tree on way to Jerusalem, Mt. 21; Mk. 11
63. Jerusalem—Second cleansing of the temple (Monday?), Mt. 21; Mk. 11; Lk. 19
64. "Every evening He went out of the city" (to Bethany most likely), Mk. 11:19
65. Jerusalem—(Tuesday?) Day of discussions
Question of Jesus' authority, Mt. 21; Mk. 11; Lk. 20
Parable of two sons, Mt. 21
Parable of the vineyard, Mt. 21; Mk. 12; Lk. 20
Parable of the wedding garment, Mt. 22
Question of tribute to Caesar, Mt. 22; Mk. 12; Lk. 20
Question of the resurrection, Mt. 22; Mk. 12; Lk. 20
Question of the greatest commandment, Mt. 22; Mk 12
Question about the Son of David, Mt. 22; Mk. 12; Lk. 20
Denunciation of Scribes and Pharisees, Mt. 23; Mk. 12; Lk. 20
Widow's mite, Mk. 12; Lk. 21
Sermon on significance of life and death, Jn. 12
Predictions of end of Jerusalem and of the world; His second coming, Mt. 24; Mk. 13; Lk. 21
On judgment: ten virgins; talents; judgment scene, Mt. 25
Prediction of Jesus' death, Mt. 26; Mk. 14; Lk. 22
(Wednesday?) Judas' plot to betray Jesus, Mt. 26; Mk. 14; Lk. 22

FOURTH PASSOVER

Thursday, 1st day of unleavened bread; made ready Passover, Mt. 26:17-19; Mk. 14:12-16; Lk. 22:7-13

The Upper Room—After night (Jewish Friday) Passover meal; feet washed; disciples warned; Judas departed; Lord's supper instituted; farewell discourse with the apostles, Mt. 26; Mk. 14; Lk. 22; Jn. 13,14

Out in the night—Parting instructions and predictions: parable of the vine; Holy Spirit promised, Jn. 15 & 16

Great intercessory prayer, Jn. 17

Gethsemane—Agony and prayer; angels come; betrayal and arrest, Mt. 26; Mk. 14; Lk. 22; Jn. 18

Court Rooms—Trials before Annas, Caiaphas, Sanhedrin, Pilate, Herod, Pilate: tortures, Mt. 26 & 27; Mk. 14 & 15; Lk. 22 & 23; Jn. 18

Golgotha—Crucifixion and burial (Friday, day of preparation) Mt. 27; Mk. 15; Lk. 23; Jn. 19

FORTY DAYS AFTER THE RESURRECTION

In a garden outside the city—(Sunday) The resurrection; appearances to Mary, other women, (Peter I Cor. 15:5) Mt. 28; Mk. 16; Lk. 24; Jn. 20

66. Trip to Emmaus—Appearance and teaching to two disciples, Lk. 24
67. Jerusalem—(same night) Appearance to the ten, Mk. 16; Lk. 24; Jn. 20

    (8 days later) Appearance to the eleven, Jn. 20; (I Cor. 15:5)
68. Galilee—Appearance to seven by the sea, Jn. 21

    To the disciples on a mountain; great commission, Mt. 28

    To more than 500 brethren, I Cor. 15:6
69. Jerusalem—Appearance to James; to the apostles (I Cor. 15:7; Acts 1), Lk. 24
70. Near Bethany—The ascension, Mk. 16; Lk. 24; Acts 1.

INTRODUCTION TO MARK

by J. W. McGarvey

1. THE AUTHORSHIP.

If we were to transcribe from our Introduction to the book of Matthew, what we have written on the subject of its authorship, almost every word would be equally appropriate to the book of Mark. There is the same uniformity in the testimony of early writers; the same absence of doubt among both ancient and modern scholars; the same improbability that the authorship could have been attributed in early times to the wrong person, and the same or even greater certainty, that if a fictitious authorship had been assumed for the book by the early Christians, it would have been attributed to some one supposed to have a higher claim to credibility and to the reverence of the disciples. It would certainly have been attributed to some one of the apostles.

2. QUALIFICATIONS OF THE WRITER.

Mark was not an apostle, nor is there any evidence that he was at any time a personal attendant of Jesus. He was not, then, an eye-witness of the scenes, at least of the chief part of the scenes, which he describes. In this respect he was like Luke (Luke 1:2), but unlike Matthew and John. This fact, connected with the circumstance that Mark is nowhere said in express terms, to have been an inspired man, has given prominence to the question, whether he was qualified to write an infallible account of incidents in the life of Jesus. In order to a right judgement on this question, we should consider, first, his natural opportunities for information, and second, the evidences of his inspiration:

1. John Mark was the son of a woman named Mary, who was a prominent disciple in the city of Jerusalem at the time of the death of James and the imprisonment of Peter, and whose dwelling in that city was a well known place of resort for the disciples. All of this appears from the incident recorded in Acts 12:12-17. The house was so well known as a place of resort for the brethren, that when Peter was released from prison by the angel, though it was the dead of night, he at once repaired thither to give notice of his release, and to send word to the surviving James and other leading brethren. Mary was also a sister to Barnabas (Col. 4:10); which fact would in itself render her somewhat conspicuous; for Barnabas became at a very early period one of the most noted men in the Jerusalem Church. (See Acts 4:36, 37; 9:26, 27; 11:22-24). The land which Barnabas had owned in the island of Cyprus, and which he sold for the benefit of the poor, points to the probability that his sister Mary, besides owning a residence in Jerusalem,

was possessed of other property. The indications are that she was a widow in easy circumstances, full of hospitality, and intimately associated with the apostles and the other leaders of the Church in Jerusalem. Thus it appears that from the very beginning of the Church, if not during the life of Jesus, John Mark enjoyed the company of the apostles in his own home, where their conversations with one another and with inquiring friends, must have perfected that knowledge of Jesus which, in common with the masses of the people, he acquired by listening to their daily discourses in the temple court. Had he been, then, but an ordinary youth, with a disposition to remember facts and to record them, he might have written from what he heard the inspired witnesses relate, an account which would have been fallible only in so far as he used his own words instead of theirs.

But besides these opportunities, Mark spent some years in most intimate association with Paul and Barnabas, laboring as their "minister," or assistant (Acts 12:25, 13:5; 15:37-39); at a later period he was associated in a similar way with Peter (1 Peter 5:13); and then again with Paul (Col. 4:10; 2 Tim. 4:11).

During these associations, Mark must have heard the inspired preachers, in preaching to different communities and different individuals, rehearse many hundreds of times the leading events in the life of Jesus; and he must have been an exceedingly inattentive listener, if these events, in the very language of the apostles, were not indelibly imprinted on his memory. It is impossible, then, for Mark to have enjoyed better natural opportunities than he did, except by having, in addition to these, the opportunity of witnessing for himself the events of which he writes. He could truly have said with Luke: "Forasmuch as many have taken in hand to set forth in order a declaration of those things which are most surely believed among us, even as they delivered them unto us, who from the beginning were eye-witnesses and ministers of the word; it seemed good to me also, having obtained perfect understanding of all from the beginning, to write." (Luke 1:1-4). Those, then, who are disposed to regard the gospel narrative as nothing more than uninspired records, should abate nothing from the credibility of Mark's narrative on the ground of his want of information; for surely no uninspired writer ever had better facilities for informing himself with entire accuracy concerning events of which he had not been an eye-witness.

2. As we have intimated before, there is no express statement in the Scriptures of the fact that Mark was an inspired man; yet there are various facts which force us to the conclusion that he was. In the first place, it was a custom of the apostles to impart spiritual gifts to prominent men in the churches, and especially to their traveling companions

and fellow-laborers. Thus Philip, Barnabas, Simeon, Lucius, Manaen, Silas, Judas, and Timothy, enjoyed miraculous gifts (Acts 8:6; 13:1; 15:32; 2 Tim. 1:6) and individuals in the churches in Samaria, Ephesus, Corinth, Rome, Galatia, etc. enjoyed similar gifts. (Acts 8:14-17; 19:6; 1 Cor. 1:4-7; Rom. 15:14; Gal. 3:5). Now to assume that Mark, who was, at different times, and for many years, a companion and fellow-laborer of two apostles, was overlooked in the distribution of these gifts, would be unwarrantable and even absurd. In the second place, there are evidences that Mark was regarded as especially fitted for labors which were usually performed by men possessed of miraculous gifts. He was chosen by Paul and Barnabas as their assistant on their first tour among the Gentiles (Acts 12:25; 13:5); and although, on their second tour, Paul declined his company, Barnabas still preferred him and separated from Paul rather than separate from Mark. (15:36-39). At a later period he was sent by Paul on important missions among the churches (Col. 4:10); and he was sent for by Paul during the last imprisonment of the latter, because he was profitable to him for the ministry. (2 Tim. 4:11). Finally, if a tradition preserved by Papias, who wrote in the first half of the second century, has any foundation in fact, the apostle Peter had some connection with the labors of Mark in preparing his gospel, and it is highly improbable that he would have allowed him to undertake such a work without imparting to him the Holy Spirit if he were not already endowed with the requisite gifts. The words of Papias as quoted by Eusebius, are these: "This also the elder (John) said: Mark, being the interpreter of Peter, wrote down exactly whatever things he remembered, but yet not in the order in which Christ either spoke or did them; for he was neither a hearer nor a follower of the Lord's, but was afterward, as I (Papias) said, a follower of Peter." See Smith's Dictionary, Art. Mark; and on the value of this and some similar traditional statements see Alford's Introduction to Mark, Section II.

From these considerations we think there can be no reasonable doubt, that in addition to Mark's free and long continued access to original and infallible sources of information, he enjoyed such direct aid from the Holy Spirit as must have guarded him absolutely against errors of every kind in the composition of his narrative.

3. CHARACTERISTICS OF THE NARRATIVE.

Mark's narrative is distinguished from Matthew's, which it resembles more than it does either Luke's or John's, by several striking peculiarities, of which we mention the following:

1. While Matthew begins with the genealogy of Jesus, intended to show that he was a son of Abraham through David, and follows this with a brief account of his childhood, Mark, omitting all the ground

covered by the first two chapters of Matthew, announces Jesus at once as the Christ, the Son of God (1:1), hurriedly touches the ministry of John and the temptation of Jesus, and enters on his main theme with the commencement of the ministry in Galilee. He also omits other passages of the history which Matthew treats at considerable length, such as the sermon on the Mount, the denunciation of the scribes and Pharisees found in the 23rd chapter of Matthew, and the prophetic discourse found in the 25th chapter.

2. In his treatment of the material which is common to himself and Matthew, he is, on the whole, more brief, but at times is much more elaborate; and his arrangement of the matter is often widely different.

For an illustration of the difference in arrangement, we refer the reader to the note headed "Difference from Matthew," at the end of chapter first. His more elaborate treatment of some passages results from his peculiar treatment of the argument from miracles. While Matthew mentions a large number, Mark selects those which are the more striking, and describes them with greater minuteness.

3. Throughout the portions in which the matter of the two narratives is the same, there is constantly occurring an identity of thought accompanied by variety of expression, and especially by a more graphic style, showing clearly that Mark is an independent writer even in those passages which have been erroneously regarded as extracts from Matthew.

4. Another peculiarity is that of selecting from a group of persons acting in a given scene, or from a group of miracles wrought on a given occasion, a single one which is described particularly, while nothing at all is said of the others.

All of these peculiarities combine to prove what is now almost universally believed by critics, that neither is Mark's narrative an abridgement, as some have thought, of Matthew's and Luke's; nor are theirs, as others have thought, expansions of Mark's. Each evidently wrote without having seen the manuscript of either of the other two.

4. APPARENT DISCREPANCIES.

In many passages in which Mark treats of matter common to himself and the other historians there are various appearances of discrepancy, which have been regarded by some as irreconcilable contradictions. Each of these which is regarded as worthy of notice at all, has been treated in the body of this text, and we think it is there made to appear that in none of them is there a real contradiction. We allude to them here because of the argument which has been based on them to disprove the plenary inspiration of the writers.

It has been argued, that if the Holy Spirit guided the inspired writers not only in the thoughts which they should express, but also in their choice of words, there would be none of these appearances of discrepancy, but the same thought would always be expressed in about the same words. Indeed, it is argued that on this supposition we ought to find a uniform style pervading the writings of all the inspired men, seeing that it was not they but the Holy Spirit who spoke and wrote. But all such reasoning is fallacious in two particulars: first, in assuming that the Holy Spirit either would not or could not vary his style to suit the peculiar mental organization of each writer; and second, in assuming that there is not a style common to all the writers of Sacred History. Both of these assumptions are illogical, and the latter is contradicted by facts. There are characteristics of style common to all the historical writers of both the Old Testament and the New, which distinguish them from all uninspired historians, and which mark their style as that of the Holy Spirit. We can not here elaborate this proposition, but we mention first, the purely dramatic form in which they depict the characters of men, allowing them to act their respective parts without a word of comment, without an expression by the historian, of approbation or disapprobation, and utterly without those attempts at analysis of character which all other historians have found indispensable. Second, the unexampled impartiality with which they record facts, speaking with as little reserve concerning the sins and follies of their own friends, as of the most cruel deeds of their enemies—as freely, for example, of Peter's denial, as of the high-priest's malice and cruelty. Third, the imperturbable calmness, the utter freedom from passion, with which they move along the current of history, relating with as little apparent feeling the most wonderful and exciting events as those the most trivial. The final sufferings of Jesus, for example, are described with as much calmness, as the fact of his taking a seat on Peter's fishing boat to address the people. This characteristic of the inspired historians has been noticed by every appreciative reader of the sacred volume, and fixes the primary authorship unmistakably in Him,

"Who sees with equal eye, as God of all,
A hero perish, or a sparrow fall;
Atoms or systems into ruin hurled,
And now a bubble burst, and now a world."

As it was desirable that the Bible should touch every cord in every human soul, it was needful that the presentation of truth should be characterized by very great diversities of style. While preserving, then, as it does, those characteristics which mark it as divine, God has wisely chosen, in order to secure the needed variety, that its various parts should be written by men of great diversity of mental peculiarities, and that each of these should leave the impress of his own style of thought and expression on his composition. As the light which starts from the sun in passing through a cathedral window takes on the many hues of the stained glass, allowing each pane to impart its own particular hue, and spreads them all in delightful harmony on the objects within, so the truth that came down from heaven was allowed to pass through the minds of many men ere it reached the written page, bearing with it the impress of each without being changed from truth to error. In this way alone can all of the peculiarities of this book of books be accounted for.

5. FOR WHAT READERS INTENDED.

We think that there are no conclusive evidences that Mark intended his narrative for any special class of readers. From his omission of the genealogy of Jesus, and of all references to the prophecies fulfilled in the career of Jesus, it is inferred that he did not, like Matthew, write especially for Jewish readers; but the evidences commonly relied on as proof that he wrote especially for Gentiles, are, we think, inconclusive. True, he translates into Greek, some Hebrew or Aramaic terms which he employs, but Matthew does the same almost as often, and the only apparent reason why Mark does so more frequently is because he introduces two words more which need translation than does Matthew. (Comp. Mark 5:41; 5:11, 34; 15:22, 34 with Matt. 1:23; 17:33, 46). In neither writer, however, should this be regarded as an adaptation to Gentile readers; for they were writing in the Greek language, and it is but compliance with an ordinary rule of composition, that foreign terms introduced are accompanied by a translation. Moreover, Jews as well as Gentiles, in that age, seldom read any other language than the Greek. The argument in favor of the proposition that Mark wrote especially for Gentile readers, depends, when fairly stated, on nothing more than the fact that in one instance (7:3, 4) he explains a custom which Jews, at least those who resided in Palestine, well understood. But this only shows that he was not unmindful of his Gentile readers, not that he wrote with especial reference to them. I conclude that while Matthew wrote especially for Jews, and Luke especially for the Gentiles, Mark, whose evangelical labors had been divided between the two classes, wrote without especial reference to either, but with both classes constantly before his mind.

CHRONOLOGICAL TABLE OF THE LIFE OF CHRIST (FROM ANDREWS)

Annunciation to Zacharias	October	6 B.C.
Annunciation to Mary	April	5 B.C.
Mary visits Elizabeth, and remains three months	April-June	5 B.C.
Birth of John the Baptist	June	5 B.C.
Jesus Born at Bethlehem	December	5 B.C.
The Angel and the shepherds	December	5 B.C.
Presentation of Jesus	February	4 B.C.
Coming of the Magi	February	4 B.C.
Flight of Jesus into Egypt	February	4 B.C.
Return to Nazareth and sojourn there	May	4 B.C.
Jesus, at twelve years of age, attends the Passover	April	8 A.D.
John the Baptist begins his labors	Summer	26 A.D.
Baptism of Jesus	January	27 A.D.
Jesus tempted in the Wilderness	January-	
Deputation of priests and Levites to the Baptist	February	27 A.D.
Jesus Returns to Galilee	February	27 A.D.
Wedding at Cana of Galilee	February	27 A.D.
First Passover of Jesus' ministry; cleansing of Temple	April	27 A.D.
Jesus begins to baptize (by his disciples)	May	27 A.D.
Jesus departs into Galilee, through Samaria	December	27 A.D.
A few weeks spent by Jesus in retirement	January-	
The Baptist Imprisoned	April	28 A.D.
The second Passover; healing of impotent man	March	28 A.D.
Jesus begins his ministry in Galilee	April	28 A.D.
Calling of the four disciples and healing at Capernaum	April-May	28 A.D.
First circuit in Galilee; healing of the leper	May	28 A.D.
Return to Capernaum, and healing of the paralytic	Summer	28 A.D.
Plucking the corn, and healing the man with the withered hand	Summer	28 A.D.
Choice of Apostles, and Sermon on the Mount	Summer	28 A.D.
Healing of centurion's servant at Capernaum	Summer	28 A.D.
Journey to Nain, and raising of the widow's son	Autumn	28 A.D.
Message to Jesus of the Baptist	Autumn	28 A.D.
Jesus anointed by the woman, a sinner	Autumn	28 A.D.

Healing at Capernaum of the blind and dumb possessed; charge of the Pharisees that he cast out devils by Beelzebub	Autumn	28 A.D.
Teaching in Parables, and stilling of the tempest . Healing of demoniacs in Gergesa, and return to Capernaum	Autumn	28 A.D.
Matthew's Feast; healing of woman with issue of blood, and raising of Jairus' daughter . Healing of two blind men, and a dumb possessed; Pharisees blaspheme	Autumn	28 A.D.
Second visit to Nazareth; sending of the twelve . .	Winter	29 A.D.
Death of the Baptist; Jesus returns to Capernaum	Winter	29 A.D.
Crossing of the Sea, and feeding of the five thousand; return to Capernaum	Spring	29 A.D.
Discourse at Capernaum respecting the bread of life	April	29 A.D.
Jesus visits the coasts of Tyre and Sidon: heals the daughter of the Syro-Phoenician woman; visits the region of Decápolis; heals one with an impediment in his speech; feeds the 4,000	Summer	29 A.D.
Jesus returns to Capernaum; is tempted by the Pharisees; reproves their hyprocrisy; again crosses the sea; heals blind man at Bethsaida	Summer	29 A.D.
Peter's confession that he is the Christ; the transfiguration	Summer	29 A.D.
Healing of lunatic child	Summer	29 A.D.
Jesus journeys through Galilee, teaching the disciples; at Capernaum pays the tribute money; goes up to the feast of tabernacles	Autumn	29 A.D.
He teaches in the temple; efforts to arrest him . .	October	29 A.D.
An adulteress is brought before him; attempt to stone him; healing of a man blind from birth; return to Galilee	October	29 A.D.
Final departure from Galilee; is rejected at Samaria; sending of the seventy	November	29 A.D.
Jesus is attended by great multitudes; parable of the good Samaritan	November	29 A.D.

Healing of a dumb possessed man; renewed blasphemy of the Pharisees; dining with a Pharisee, Jesus rebukes hypocrisy; parable of the rich fool	November	29 A.D.
Jesus is told of the murder of the Galileans by Pilate; parable of the fig tree; healing of a woman eighteen years sick	December	29 A.D.
Feast of Dedication; visit to Mary and Martha; the Jews at Jerusalem attempt to stone him; he goes beyond Jordan	December	29 A.D.
Jesus dines with a Pharisee, and heals a man with dropsy; parables of the great supper, of the lost sheep, of the lost piece of silver, of the unjust steward, of the rich man and Lazarus	December	29 A.D.
Resurrection of Lazarus; counsel of the Jews to put him to death; he retires to Ephraim	December	29 A.D.
Sojourn in Ephraim till passover at hand; journeys on the border of Samaria and Galilee; healing of ten lepers; parables of the unjust judge, and of Pharisee and publican; teaching respecting divorce; blessing of children; the young ruler, and parable of laborers in the vineyard	January-February	30 A.D.
Jesus again announces his death; ambition of James and John	March	30 A.D.
Healing of blind men at Jericho; Zaccheus; parable of the pounds; departure to Bethany	March	30 A.D.
Supper at Bethany and anointing of Jesus by Mary	Saturday April 1	30 A.D.
Entry into Jerusalem; visit to the temple and return to Bethany	Sunday, April 2	30 A.D.
Cursing of the fig-tree; second purification of the temple; return to Bethany	Monday, April 3	30 A.D.
Teaching in the temple; parables of the two sons; of the wicked husbandmen; of the king's son; attempts of his enemies to entangle him; the poor widow; the Greeks who desire to see him; a voice from heaven; departure from the temple to the Mount of		

Olives; discourse respecting the end of the world; return to Bethany; agreement of Judas with the priests to betray him	Tuesday, April 4	30 A.D.
Jesus seeks retirement at Bethany	Wednesday,	
Sending of Peter and John to prepare the paschal supper	Thursday,	
Events at paschal supper	Thursday	
After supper Jesus foretells the denial of Peter, speaks of the coming of the Comforter, and ends with prayer	evening April 6 Thursday evening	30 A.D.
Jesus in the Garden of Gethsemane	Thursday evening	
Jesus is given into the hands of Judas	Thursday midnight	
Jesus is led to the house of Annas, and thence to the palace of Caiaphas; is condemned for blasphemy	Friday 1-5 A.M. Friday	
Mockeries of his enemies; he is brought the second time before the council, and thence taken before Pilate	5-6 A.M. Friday 6-9 A.M.	
Charge of sedition; Pilate attempts to release him, but is forced to scourge him, and give him up to be crucified	Friday 9-12 A.M.	
Jesus is crucified at Golgotha	Friday	
Upon the cross is reviled by his enemies; commends his mother to John; darkness covers the land; he dies; the earth shakes, and rocks are rent	12 P.M. 3 P.M. Friday 3-6 P.M.	
His body taken down and given to Joseph, and laid in his sepulchre	Friday 3-6 P.M.	
Resurrection of Jesus, and appearance to Mary Magdalene	Sunday A.M. April 9	30 A.D.
Appearance to the two disciples at Emmaus; to Peter and to the eleven at Jerusalem	Sunday P.M.	
Appearance to the apostles and Thomas		
Appearance to seven disciples at Sea of Tiberias, and to 500 at mountain in Galilee	April-May	30 A.D.
Final appearance to the disciples at Jerusalem, and ascension to heaven	Thursday— May 18	30 A.D.

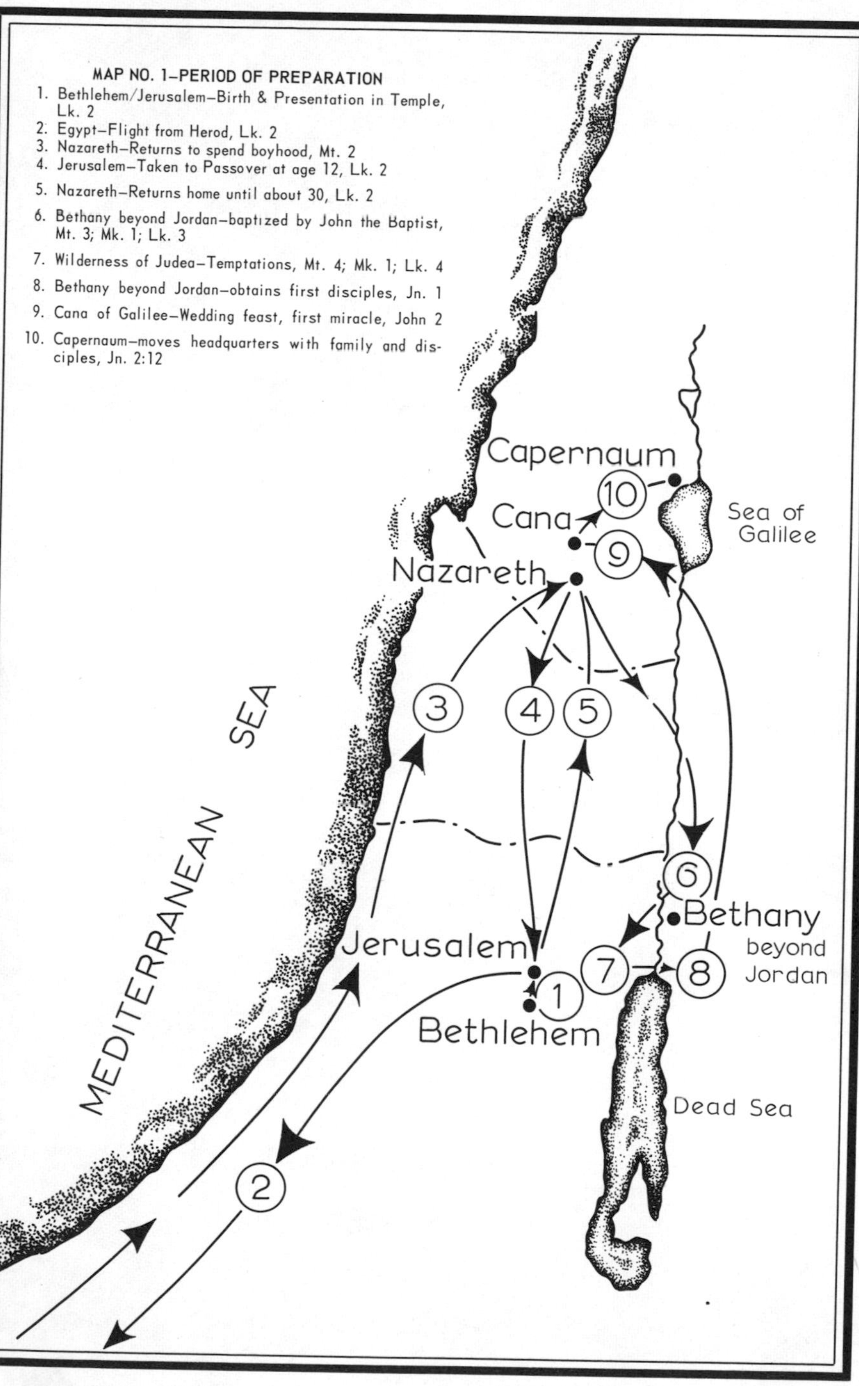

MAP NO. 1–PERIOD OF PREPARATION
1. Bethlehem/Jerusalem–Birth & Presentation in Temple, Lk. 2
2. Egypt–Flight from Herod, Lk. 2
3. Nazareth–Returns to spend boyhood, Mt. 2
4. Jerusalem–Taken to Passover at age 12, Lk. 2
5. Nazareth–Returns home until about 30, Lk. 2
6. Bethany beyond Jordan–baptized by John the Baptist, Mt. 3; Mk. 1; Lk. 3
7. Wilderness of Judea–Temptations, Mt. 4; Mk. 1; Lk. 4
8. Bethany beyond Jordan–obtains first disciples, Jn. 1
9. Cana of Galilee–Wedding feast, first miracle, John 2
10. Capernaum–moves headquarters with family and disciples, Jn. 2:12
Capernaum
Cana
Nazareth
Sea of Galilee
MEDITERRANEAN SEA
Jerusalem
Bethlehem
Bethany beyond Jordan
Dead Sea

I. THE PREPARATION PERIOD 1:1-13

A. THE MISSION OF JOHN THE BAPTIST.— Mark 1:1-11.

TEXT 1:1-11

The beginning of the gospel of Jesus Christ the Son of God. Even as it is written in Isaiah the prophet. Behold, I send my messenger before thy face. Who shall prepare thy way; The voice of one crying in the wilderness. Make ye ready the way of the Lord. Make his paths straight; John came, who baptized in the wilderness and preached the baptism of repentance unto remission of sins. And there went unto him all the country of Judaea and all they of Jerusalem; and they were baptized of him in the river Jordan, confessing their sins. And John was clothed with camel's hair, and had a leathern girdle about his loins, and did eat locusts and wild honey. And he preached, saving. There cometh after me he that is mightier than I, the latchet of whose shoes I am not worthy to stoop down and unloose. I baptized you with water; but he shall baptize you with the Holy Ghost. And it came to pass in those day, that Jesus came from Nazareth of Galilee, and was baptized of John in the Jordan. And straightway coming up out of the water, he saw the heavens rent asunder, and the Spirit as a dove descending upon him; and a voice came out of the heavens, Thou art my beloved Son, in thee I am well pleased.

THOUGHT QUESTIONS 1:1-11

1. In what sense are we to understand the word "beginning" as used in verse 1?
2. Why refer to the work of our Lord as "good tidings"? Please be specific.
3. In what two Old Testament references do we find the prophesy quoted in verse 2?
4. What was the primary work of John the Baptist?
5. In what way did John accomplish his work?
6. In what wilderness did John baptize? How could he do this?
7. Could you estimate the crowd who came to hear John? 1,000?, 5,000? 10,000?
8. To whom did certain confess their sins? Why do so?
9. Was John's baptism for the washing away of sins?

10. Why did John dress as he did? Why did he live where he did?
11. Why would anyone want to loose the latchet of someone else's shoe?
12. Why mention the baptism in the Holy Spirit? Please read Acts 1:5. Did the persons who heard John understand the promise of the Holy Spirit and baptism?
13. How far did Jesus walk to be baptized? Why?
14. Did John baptize "with" the Jordan, "in the Jordan" or "into the Jordan"?
15. What is meant by the expression—"The heavens rent asunder"? At what particular moment was this seen?
16. Why was the Holy Spirit in the form of a dove? Where did He go? i.e. the Holy Spirit?
17. At what two other occasions did God speak from heaven?

COMMENT

TIME—John the Baptist was born about B.C. 5; Jesus was born about B.C. 5; the preaching of John the Baptist was during the summer and autumn of A.D. 26; the baptism of Jesus by John in January, A.D. 27; the temptation in the wilderness in January and February, A.D. 27.

PLACES—The preaching of John the Baptist was in the wilderness of Judea,—a wild, hilly, thinly-inhabited region (not a desert) lying west of the Dead Sea and the Lower Jordan. John's ministry extended as far north as Enon, near Salim, two-thirds of the way up the Jordan from the Dead Sea. The baptism of Jesus was, it is supposed, at the fords of the Jordan, called Bethabara, five miles northeast of Jericho. The temptation occurred probably in the northern part of the wilderness of Judea, between Jerusalem and Jericho on the west and the Jordan and the upper part of the Dead Sea on the east. Tradition places it in Mount *Quarantania,* near the Jordan, so named because Jesus is supposed to have passed his forty days fasting in one of its caves.

While tradition and general opinion place the baptism of Christ at the fords of the Jordan near Jericho, it is proper to say that all we can certainly know was that it was in the Jordan at a place called Beth-abarah, or the House of the Ford. Lieut. Conder states that there are about forty fords of the Jordan and he locates Beth-abarah farther north at Abarah (the Ford) above Bethshean and near the borders of Galilee.

CONNECTING HISTORY—Mark, passing by the accounts of the births of John and Jesus, leaps at once into the midst of events, and begins with the preaching of the great Forerunner. In the history given by the other Evangelists we have:

B.C. 6. The Annunciation to Zacharias.

B.C. 5. The Annunciation to Mary and the Births of John and Jesus.

B.C. 4. The flight to Egypt and return to Nazareth.

A.D. 8. Jesus attends the Passover at Jerusalem and converses with the Doctors.

A.D. 26. John the Baptist begins his work. We have followed the chronology of Andrews.

PARALLEL ACCOUNTS—The ministry of John in the wilderness (verse 1-8) is described also in Matt. 3-1-12, and Luke 3:1-18. The baptism of Jesus (verse 9-11) in Matt. 3:13-17, and Luke 3:21-23. The temptation of Jesus (verse 12, 13) in Matt. 4:1-11, and Luke 4:1-13. A view of the whole ministry of John from another standpoint is given in John 1:5-51.

OUTLINE—1. *Prophecy of the Forerunner.* 2. *John's Ministry.* 3. *The Baptism of Jesus.*

ANALYSIS

I. THE PROPHECY OF THE FORERUNNER — Vs. 1-3.
   1. The Prediction of the Messenger. Mark 1:2; Matt. 3:3; Isa. 40:3.
   2. The Voice in the Wilderness. Mark 1:3; Matt. 3:3; Luke 3:4.

II. JOHN'S MINISTRY— Vs. 4-8.
   1. The Preacher in the Wilderness. Mark 1:4; Matt. 3:1; Luke 3:3.
   2. The Nation Moved by his Voice. Mark 1:5; Matt. 3:5.
   3. The Baptism of Repentance. Mark 1:5; Matt. 3:6; Luke 3:3.
   4. The Raiment of the Prophet. Mark 1:6; Matt. 3:4.
   5. The Coming One. Mark 1:7; Matt. 3-11; Luke 3:16.
   6. The Baptism of the Holy Spirit. Mark 1:8; Matt. 3:11; Luke 3:16.

III. THE BAPTISM OF JESUS — Vs. 9-11.
   1. Jesus Baptized in Jordan. Mark 1:9; Matt. 3:16; Luke 3:22.
   2. Anointed from On High. Mark 1:10; Matt. 3:16; Luke 3:22.
   3. The Voice from Heaven. Mark 1:11; Matt. 3:17; Luke 3:22.

INTRODUCTION

At the date when John the Baptist began preaching, Tiberius Caesar, the successor of Augustus Caesar, was the emperor of the Roman Empire, and had been ruling for over twelve years. Judea was a Roman province with Pontius Pilate for governor. The Roman Empire held sway over nearly all the known world. It was a general time of peace, with slight wars only on the frontiers. Greece was subject to Rome politically, but ruled still intellectually, the school of literature and art. She was crowded with temples and statues, and her schools of philosophy and rhetoric were flourishing. It was the period of the greatest intellectual activity during the entire scope of Roman history. Horace, Virgil, Livy, Ovid, Strabo and Seneca were all living when Christ was born, and Cicero died only a few years before. It was, however, an age of extreme moral depravity.

For a hundred years not a single Roman is named, whose domestic history is known, who had not divorced his wife. The picture given in the first chapters of Romans is fully confirmed by the admissions of the Greek and Roman writers of the time. Mark does not begin his history, like Matthew and Luke, with the birth of Christ, or of John, but with the beginning of their public ministry. His object was to portray the *official* life of our Lord and he omits all that is not essential to this purpose.

EXPLANATORY NOTES

I. THE PROPHECY OF THE FORERUNNER — 1. *The beginning of the gospel.* This verse is a kind of title to the outline of the Lord's ministry Mark is about to give. The gospel begins its development with the preaching of John; it is more fully unfolded during our Lord's ministry, but not developed in its fullness until he suffers on the cross and rises from the dead. Then his apostles are commanded to preach his gospel, finished, perfect, to all nations. His gospel began with the preaching of the forerunner and his own baptism; it was fully developed when he died, was buried, and rose again. *The gospel.* Gospel means "good tidings." The best tidings the world has ever had is that we have a Savior who is able and willing to save us from sin and death. *Of Jesus Christ the Son of God.* Matthew, writing with reference to Jews, shows that Jesus is the son of David and of Abraham; Mark, writing for Gentiles, pays no attention to a matter so important to Jews, but at once declares him to be the Son of God.

2. *As it is written in the prophets.* The Revision says, "in Isaiah the prophet," which has the support of the best manuscripts, but Mark's reference is to two prophets, Isaiah 40:3 and Malachi 3:1. It is often the case that the New Testament writers quote from more than one prophet, while naming only one. Verse 2 is quoted from Malachi, and verse 3 from Isaiah. If the Revised reading is preferred, Mark names Isaiah, because he is the great prophet and the quotation from him is the essential one in this place. Let it be noted that John the Baptist as well as Christ was a subject of Old Testament prophecy. He is the only New Testament character save the Son of God of whom the prophets spoke. *Behold I send my messenger before thy face.* This passage is found in Mal. 3:1, and undoubtedly refers to the Messiah King. It was and still is a custom in oriental countries to send messengers to see that all is prepared before the king takes a journey. So John was sent to prepare the way for Christ by preaching repentance, baptism, and the coming kingdom of which Christ should be king.

3. *The voice of one crying in the wilderness.* Quoted from Isaiah 40:3. See how strangely this prediction, made seven hundred years before, was fulfilled. All other New Testament teachers, and indeed all Bible teachers, sought the towns and cities; John, the wilderness. After his birth we see him no more until the strange, startling, voice is heard in the wilderness of Judea, preaching a strange message with such power as to call all Isreal to rush into the wilderness to hear him. He describes himself (John 1:23) as a Voice. He organized no body of followers, established no system, but broke up the old stagnation, aroused a ferment of thought, and filled men with the expectation of the Coming One. He is well described as a Voice in the wilderness.

II. JOHN'S MINISTRY—4. *John did baptize in the wilderness.* Mark has quoted the predictions of the prophets concerning the work of John, and he now turns to the fulfillment in John's ministry. In order to read a fuller account than Mark gives, see Matthew, chap. 3 and John, chapter 1. This John was called the *Baptist,* because he baptized those who repented under his preaching. He was the son of Zacharias and Elizabeth, of the priestly order, a relative of Jesus, born in the summer of B.C. 5, and consequently now (A.D. 26) about 30 or 31 years old. "The year during which John began his ministry was probably a *sabbatic year* (Exod. 23:11). If this year was now observed by the Jews, according to its original intent, it was a most appropriate time for the Baptist to begin his labors, the people having no burdensome agricultural tasks to occupy them, and being thus at liberty to attend upon his instructions." *Andrews' Life of Christ,* p. 139. *Baptize in the wilderness.* The "wilderness of Judea" was bounded on the east by the river Jordan which was the place where John baptized at this time (see verse 5). At a later period he moved farther northward to the borders of Samaria and Galilee and "baptized at Enon because there was much water there" (John 3:23). *Preach the baptism of repentance.* John preached as well as baptized. The preaching came first. There must be a moral preparation before one was a fit subject of baptism. That preparation was a repentance, or a purpose to leave off sin and lead a better life. This preparation is always a prerequisite to scriptural baptism. See Matt. 3:7, 8 and Acts 2:38. *For the remission of sins.* This declares the end or object to be sought in repentance and baptism. These are steps leading to the pardon of sins. God does not pardon sins on baptism alone, nor on repentance alone, but upon the baptism of repentance, or of a pentinent subject. See Acts 2:38.

5. *Went out to him.* That which, no doubt, drew the whole population in such crowds to the desert shores of the Jordan, was the mysterious yet

distinct assertion that the "kingdom of heaven was at hand;" that kingdom of which the belief was as universal as of the personal coming of the Messiah. "The nation was daily expecting the appearance of the wise and perfect prophet, who should restore the tribes of Israel, reprove the times, and appease the wrath of God, before it broke out in fury."—*Geikie. All the land.* The word is used in a free and easy and popular way; and yet, it must mean more than *many,* namely, the great bulk and body of the population. It included representatives of every class, Pharisees and Sadducees (Matt. 3:7), tax-gatherers (Luke 3:12,) soldiers (Luke 3:14,) rich and poor (Luke 3:10.) *In the river Jordan.* We hear of him at Bethabara, the fords about five miles north-east of Jericho, where Jesus was baptized, and at Enon, near Salim, some 35 miles farther north. *Confessing their sins.* From the form and expression this does not seem to have been merely "showing a contrite spirit" "confessing themselves sinners," but a particular and individual confession; not, however, made privately to John, but before the people.

6. *John was clothed with camel's hair.* He was, like his great prototype of the Old Testament, Elijah, a hairy man, garbed like an ascetic and eating the food furnished by the wilderness. His robe of camel's hair was well adapted to an open air life to protect against cold or rain, and from the fact that it did not absorb water, suited for a Baptist. This mantle was fastened around him by a leathern girdle,a style still followed by the Arabian children of the wilderness. *Did eat locusts and wild honey.* Locusts were permitted as an article of food (Lev. 11:21, 22). The common brown locust is about three inches in length, and the general form is that of a grasshopper. Thomson's *Land and Book*, states that though tolerated as an article of food, only by the very poorest people, locusts are still eaten by the Bedouin. Burckhardt mentions having seen locust-shops at Medina and Tayf. After being dried in the sun, the locusts are eaten with butter and honey. Sometimes they are sprinkled with salt and either broiled or roasted. Sometimes they are ground and pounded, and then mixed with flour and water, and made into cakes. Thomson adds that *wild honey*, i. e., honey made by wild bees, is still gathered from trees in the wilderness and from rocks in the wadies.

7. *Preached, saying.* Mark omits the details of John's preaching given by Matthew, but gives the great central thought, the announcement of the coming Christ. To *preach* is to proclaim like a herald. He was the King's herald. *Cometh one mightier than I.* Like all true preachers of Christ, John points away from himself to the Lord. He hides behind the Master. The preacher who exalts himself is not worthy of Christ. *The latchet of whose shoes.* The shoe latchet was a shoe lace or thong that bound the sandal on

the foot. To bear, to fasten or to loose the sandals of a great personage was the work of a menial slave. John uses this comparison to show how far he was below Christ. His language shows how exalted were his ideas of the dignity of Christ.

8. *I indeed have baptized you with water.* It should read *in* water, and so the American revisers of the Revised Version rendered it. The Greek preposition is *en,* from whence the Latin and English *in.* He describes the baptism he had administered in Jordan. *He shall baptize you with (in) the Holy Ghost.* This higher baptism of the soul neither John, nor an apostle, or any other human being could administer. Such a baptism was a proof of divinity. John's words are equivalent to the saying that the Coming One is divine. When the first baptism of the Holy Spirit, the one on the day of Pentecost took place, Peter declared that the crucified Christ "had shed forth the things you do see and hear."

III. THE BAPTISM OF JESUS—9. *In those days.* While John was preaching and baptizing in the Jordan. It is supposed that he had been preaching about six months when Jesus came to him, as he was six months older than Christ, who was baptized when he was thirty years old, and in accordance with Jewish customs, John would be likely to begin his work when he was thirty. *Jesus came from Nazareth of Galilee.* This mountain town had been his home ever since the return from Egypt. It was about 70 miles north of Jerusalem and probably 80 from where John was baptizing, situated on one of the foot hills of the Lebanon range. It is not named in the Old Testament, was a considerable village in the time of Christ, having a synagogue, and now has about 6,000 population. It lies just north of Samaria and overlooks the valley of Esdraelon. *And was baptized of John in Jordan.* These words plainly show how Christ was baptized, but if the *eis* of the Greek, here rendered in, had been properly rendered *into,* which is its primary meaning, it would have been still plainer. Matthew tells of John's reluctance to baptize one so much higher and purer, of the demand of Jesus, of his declaration that it thus became them to fulfill all righteousness. Our Lord came to set us a perfect example, hence it was needful for him, having taken the form of a man and a servant, to set us an example of obedience. He was baptized, not unto repentance, for he had no sins, but to fulfill all righteousness, and thus to show us how every disciple ought to do.

10. *Straightway coming up out of the water.* As the eunuch and Philip in Acts 8:38, so Jesus and John went down into the Jordan, John baptized him and then Jesus "came up out of the water." We learn from Luke 3:21 that our Lord came up praying. *He saw.* Behold a marvel! John saw

the heavens rolled back, and then the Holy Spirit descending in a visible form, like a dove, and resting upon Jesus where it disappeared within him. Like the gentle, harmless dove it descended, not like a consuming fire. Christ came to save, not to destroy.

11. *A voice from heaven.* It is noteworthy that the great event of the Lord's baptism was emphasized by the presence of three Divine persons. The Son was the subject; the Holy Spirit descended upon him, and the Father from heaven spoke in acknowledgment of Jesus as his Son. It is also noteworthy that the three Divine persons are present in the baptismal formula of every person baptized. They are baptized "into the name of the Father, and of the Son, and of the Holy Spirit," and God acknowledges baptized penitents as children by sending his Spirit into their hearts. See Acts 2:38 and Rom. 8:14, 15. *Thou art my beloved Son, in whom I am well pleased.* This is the first formal acknowledgment of Christ as the Son. It follows his act of obedience, and has therefore a special significance. If the Father was pleased with the Son when he thus obeyed, is he not also pleased when men yield their wills to his and humbly obey? Three times during Christ's ministry is the Divine voice heard; first at the baptism; second at the Transfiguration; thirdly in the temple during the Savior's last week on earth. (John 12:28).

FACT QUESTIONS 1:1-11

1. Give the approximate date of the birth of both Jesus and John.
2. When did John preach? Year and months?
3. When was Jesus baptized? Year and month? When was Jesus tempted by Satan? Year and month?
4. Locate on the map the place where John preached—how far north did he go in his preaching? Locate.
5. At what place on the Jordan River was Jesus baptized?
6. According to tradition where was Jesus during the forty day fast?
7. List the five events Mark leaves out of his narrative.
8. Where do we find the parallel accounts of the events of Mark 1:1-11?
9. Who was the emperor when John started preaching? Who was the governor?
10. Who ruled the world of intellectualism and art?
11. Name three great artists, poets or philosophers of this period.
12. Show indications of how intellectualism, poetry or art fail to make man moral.
13. What chapter in the New Testament well describes the moral conditions when Christ was born?

14. What was the object of Mark's gospel?
15. When was the gospel developed in its fullness? Cf. I Cor. 15:1-4.
16. What two prophets are cited as speaking of John the Baptist?
17. In what sense was John a messenger?
18. Why was the place of John's preaching strange?
19. Why did men rush out to hear John?
20. Why called John "the Baptist"? Does this mean there could only be one?
21. What was said of the "sabbatic year" and the work of John the Baptist?
22. Why preach repentance? What connections does repentance have to baptism?
23. Could sins be remitted without the blood of Jesus? Explain.
24. What was the "kingdom of God" as it related to the Messiah?
25. Name three classes represented in the audience to whom John spoke.
26. How did they prepare the locusts for eating?
27. What proof of divinity was indicated by John?
28. How long had John been preaching when Jesus came to be baptized?
29. Does the text show us *how* Christ was baptized? Explain.
30. Why was Jesus baptized?
31. What happened to the dove after it descended from heaven?
32. In what sense are the three divine persons (The Trinity) present at the time every person is baptized?

SIDE-LIGHTS

1. Jesus was *anointed* by the Holy Spirit at his baptism and thus became the Lord's Anointed or the Christ. So too the Lord promises us the gift of the Holy Spirit at baptism (Acts 2:38), or that we shall receive the unction of the Spirit.

2. John's preaching. — Everything was new, startling, impressive — the wilderness, the stream, the solemn hills. A prophet appearing after more than five hundred years; his words, his baptismal symbol, the kingdom he preached; the Messiah whom he announced as at hand, the very multitudes assembled, the visible emotion, the evident good effected, the contrition of the most sunken classes—the publicans and harlots—all showed that the whole nation believed in him.—Geikie.

LESSONS

1. The true man of God, whether preacher or teacher, should be a Voice, always hiding behind the Cross, and pointing to the Master.

2. Every preacher of Christ should seek to prepare the way of the Lord. If he can make the rough ways smooth and the crooked ways straight, lead

men to repentance, honesty of heart, and submission, then the Lord will enter.

3. All true repentance is accompanied by a confession of sin. Scriptural baptism, a burial into the death of Christ is a humble confession of sin.

4. Christ is the WAY, our perfect example; he says "Follow me" and he does not command us to do anything where he has not shown the way. Hence, he submitted to the baptismal rite, though he had no sin. Let all humbly follow the Lord.

POINTS FOR TEACHERS

1. Note that this lesson treats of preparation for Christ. Let every teacher be a John the Baptist in this respect. Notice that his first message was *Repent.* Let it be a chief end to prepare for Christ by leading to repentance. 2. John was a preacher, but not a dull preacher. His audiences listened. So too you are preachers. Be like him in dead earnest, but not prolix or prosy. "Would you urge the scholars to come to Jesus with every lesson?" asked a teacher at a convention. "Not by saying over 'Come to Jesus,' with every lesson," was the sensible reply. "The best way of preaching," said an old and successful preacher, "is to preach every way." See to it that you are no more monotonous in your preaching than was John the Baptist. He was a model preacher in his day. 3. Impress upon your pupils that the way of the Lord in their hearts is prepared, not by repentance alone, but by confession and obedience. These will relieve the life of crookedness and make the crooked paths straight. 4. Note the example of John, his place of preaching, his life, his devotion, his baptism, its significance. 5. Note the coming of Jesus, where, what for, why he was baptized, the incidents, the dignity given to his baptism. 6. Note how, in our baptism, the three Divine persons are present, as in Christ's. Note that the lesson divides into four branches. (1) *The command to prepare* (vers. 1-3) as expressed in these two prophets. (2) *Preparation by Repentance* (vers. 4-6). John and his preaching; how repentance prepares for Christ; why confession as well as repentance. (3) *Preparation by pointing to Christ* (verse 7, 8). Note the two ways in which John shows the superiority of Christ. (4) *Christ's preparation for his work.* This again divides into three: (1) *by his baptism,* profession of religion; (2) *by receiving the Holy Spirit;* (3) *by being tempted,* and gaining the victory.

B. THE TEMPTATION OF JESUS 1:12, 13

TEXT 1:12, 13

And straightway the Spirit driveth him forth into the wilderness. And he was in the wilderness forty days tempted of Satan; and he was with the wild beasts; and the angels ministered unto him.

THOUGHT QUESTIONS 1:12, 13

18. "Straightway" after what? Why is it important that we notice the time of our Lord's temptation?
19. Are we to conclude the Holy Spirit led Jesus into temptation? Explain.
20. What does the word "driveth" mean to you?
21. Was Jesus tempted during the entire forty days? Cf. Matt. 4:1-11; Luke 4:1-13.
22. Are we to understand there were actual animals with Jesus in the wilderness? Discuss.
23. Just what was the ministry of the angels to Jesus?

COMMENT

TIME—January and February, A.D. 27.
PLACE—In the northern part of the wilderness of Judea, between Jerusalem and Jericho on the west, and the upper part of the Dead Sea on the east. Tradition places it in Mount *Quarantania,* near the Jordan—Jesus is supposed to have passed forty days fasting in one of its caves.
PARALLEL ACCOUNTS—Read Matt. 4:1-11; Luke 4:1-13.
OUTLINE—1. Driven by the Spirit into the wilderness.
2. The duration of the temptation.
3. Associates in the temptation.

ANALYSIS

I. DRIVEN BY THE SPIRIT INTO THE WILDERNESS. Vs. 12
1. Immediately after His baptism.
2. "Cast out" or "thrust out" by the Holy Spirit.
3. The wilderness—a wild, barren, desolate place.

II. THE DURATION OF THE TEMPTATION. Vs. 13
1. Only Mark indicates that He was tempted during the entire period.
2. Tempted by an outside force—not purely subjective but objective.
3. Satan the great "adversary"—Luke and Matthew use "devil"—accuser but not Mark.

III. THE ASSOCIATES IN THE TEMPTATION.
1. Wild beasts—panther, bear, wolf, hyena, lion.
2. Angels—Cf. Matt. 4:11; Luke 4:10.

EXPLANATORY NOTES

I. DRIVEN BY THE SPIRIT INTO THE WILDERNESS.—12

And straightway—The next event after the baptism was the temptation. What a strange thought it is to read of the Holy Spirit anointing Jesus and filling Jesus and then immediately driving Him into the wilderness to be tempted of Satan. This is to teach us that God's ways are not our ways.

The Spirit driveth him into the wilderness. The Holy Spirit did not lead Jesus into temptation, "The strong urge of the Spirit met the consent of Jesus." The Spirit thrust Him out into the wilderness where Satan tempted Him.

II. THE DURATION OF THE TEMPTATION. Vs. 13.

. . . *forty days tempted of Satan;* Mark says nothing of the fasting mentioned by the other writers. Mark is the only one to indicate the temptation extended over the whole forty day period "Satan alone caused this continuous temptation. None of it arose from the thoughts and desires in Jesus heart about either his Sonship or his Messiahship." (Lenski)

He was with wild beasts; Mentioned only in this gospel. This seems to suggest the desolation and danger of the temptation period. The very thought of suggesting that the beasts were friendly to Jesus and here we have Paradise reproduced is so out of context with the temptation scene as to scarcely be worthy of mention.

The angels ministered unto him. Matthew 4:11 also mentions this blessed aid of these ministering spirits. Of just what this ministering consisted we are not told—it must have indeed been a source of comfort and strength to our Lord in his need. Every Christian is promised such comfort and help; and from the same source. Cf. Heb. 1:14.

SUMMARY OF 1:1-13
(by J. W. McGarvey)

In this section Mark has set forth three facts which have an important bearing on his proposition that Jesus is the Son of God: First, that the prophet John, with direct allusion to him, announced the speedy appearance of one so much more exalted than himself that he was not worthy to stoop and loosen his shoe; second, that when Jesus was baptized, God himself, in an audible voice, proclaimed him his Son; and third, that immediately after this proclamation, Satan commenced against Him such a warfare as we would naturally expect him to wage against God's Son in human flesh.

FACT QUESTIONS 1:12, 13

33. At what time of the year did this temptation probably take place? What year?
34. How long did the temptation last? When were the three offers of Satan made?
35. What part did the Holy Spirit have in the temptation of Jesus?
36. Did Jesus ever doubt or question His purpose or mission?
37. Why mention wild beasts? What did they do?
38. Why mention angels? What did they do?

II. THE GALILEAN MINISTRY 1:14—9:50

A. THE FIRST PERIOD 1:14—3:12

1. THE BEGINNING OF HIS MINISTRY 1:14, 15

TEXT 1:14, 15

Now after John was delivered up, Jesus came into Galilee, preaching the gospel of God, and saying, The time is fulfilled, and the kingdom of God is at hand: Repent ye, and believe the gospel.

THOUGHT QUESTIONS 1:14, 15

24. What events occurred between the temptation in the wilderness and the imprisonment of John the Baptist? Cf. John chapters two through five.
25. Into what particular part of Galilee did Jesus come?
26. In what sense did Jesus preach the gospel? i.e. What was the good news He preached?
27. Why repentance before faith?
28. What time was fulfilled?
29. What is the Kingdom of God?

COMMENT

TIME—April, A. D. 28. We shall consider the incidents in detail in a later section. Suffice to say here that there was a year and one half lapse of time between the temptation of Jesus and the imprisonment of John the Baptist.

PLACE—Probably Nazareth and Capernaum. Cf. Luke 4:14; also Luke 4:16-32; Matt. 4:12-17.

PARALLEL ACCOUNTS—Read Matt. 4:12-17; Luke 4:14, 15; John 4:1-3, 43-45.

OUTLINE—1. Jesus preaches. 2. His message.

ANALYSIS

I. JESUS PREACHES. VS. 14A
   1. The time of His preaching.
   2. The place of His preaching.

II. HIS MESSAGE. 14B, 15
   1. Gospel of God.
   2. Time fulfilled.
   3. Kingdom of God is at hand.
   4. Repent and believe.

EXPLANATORY NOTES

I. JESUS PREACHES—14A

Mark omits the marriage at Cana—our Lord's first Passover— his discourse with Nicodemus and John's testimonies of him,—passing promptly to our Lord's public, official ministry.

Do not fail to note that Christ begins to preach when John ceases.

Galilee. The light of his gospel was to spring up upon the borders of Zebulon and Naphtali. See Matt. 4:13. He would also go out of the jurisdiction of Herod, who had imprisoned John. Galilee was the northern division of Palestine, and was divided into Upper and Lower Galilee—the former called also "Galilee of the Gentiles."

Preaching the gospel, etc. How beautifully Mark here describes our Lord's first preaching, as distinct from John's, which was under the law, and a mere heralding of something better to come. The substance of this discourse was the good tidings of the kingdom having come, as spoken of by Daniel, 2:44. And this is the very message which Isaiah sees the messenger publishing, as he comes with beautiful (or timely) feet upon the mountains, (Isa. 52:7) viz. the advent of the kingdom of God. Christ preached the "good news" of his kingdom of grace—the new dispensation in which he was to reign. They had other ideas of his kingdom, that it was temporal and consisted in earthly power and show.

15. *The time, etc.* The period mentioned by the prophets when Christ was to appear. The nation had expectations of the Messiah about this time. The seventy weeks of Daniel (or 490 years) were now accomplished. The time and place of our Lord's birth agreed with the interpretations of prophecy common among the Jews.

Repent ye, etc. John preached repentance. So did Christ, but not without the gospel as the burden of his preaching. He preached repentance and faith. They were commanded to turn from sin and from all their false views, and to embrace the gospel.

FACT QUESTIONS 1:14, 15

39. At what approximate date did the preaching of Jesus occur?
40. What was the time lapse between the temptation of Jesus and His preaching in Galilee?
41. In what towns of Galilee did He preach?
42. What prophecy was fulfilled in His preaching in Galilee? Cf. Matt. 4:13.
43. How did Daniel 2:44 and Isa. 52:7 relate to the message of Jesus?
44. What is repentance? How did it relate to the persons who heard Christ's message? i.e. of what did they repent?

2. THE CALL OF THE FISHERMEN. 1:16-20

TEXT 1:16-20

And passing along by the Sea of Galilee, he saw Simon and Andrew the brother of Simon casting a net in the sea; for they were fishers. And Jesus said unto them, Come ye after me, and I will make you to become fishers of men. And straightway they left the nets, and followed him. And going on a little further, he saw James the son of Zebedee, and John his brother, who also were in the boat mending the nets. And straightway he called them: and they left their father Zebedee in the boat with the hired servants, and went after him.

THOUGHT QUESTIONS 1:16-20

30. Was this the first time Jesus had seen Simon and Andrew? Cf. John 1:25-35.
31. In what specific manner did Jesus keep His promise to make fishers of men? i.e. what elements were involved in the process?
32. Compare Luke 5:1-11 and tell why these two were so willing to immediately leave their nets and follow him.
33. Please notice the type of men called by Jesus to be his followers, and later his apostles. Does this give hope to us?
34. Why did these men leave their business to follow one who offered them no money?

COMMENT 1:16-20

TIME—April, A. D. 28

PLACE—Along the sea of Galilee near Capernaum.

PARALLEL ACCOUNTS—Read Matt. 4:18-22; Luke 5:1-11

OUTLINE—1. The place and persons of the call of the master vs. 16. 2. The call to man-fishing vs. 17. 3. The immediate response vs. 18. 4. Two more to answer the call. vs. 19. 5. They left the nets to others and they went after him. vs. 20.

ANALYSIS

I. THE PLACE AND PERSONS OF THE CALL. VS. 16.
   1. By the shore of the sea of Galilee.
   2. Simon and Andrew—fishermen.

II. THE CALL TO MAN-FISHING, VS. 17.
   1. From Jesus personally.
   2. Obtain by following Him.

III. THE IMMEDIATE RESPONSE. VS. 18.
   1. Left nets.
   2. Followed Him.

IV. TWO MORE TO ANSWER THE CALL. VS. 19.
   1. Just a little way from where He called Simon and Andrew.
   2. Not fishing but mending nets.

V. NETS LEFT TO OTHERS—THEY WENT AFTER HIM. VS. 20.
   1. Immediate answer to an immediate (urgent) call.
   2. Left father and work (and money) to follow Him.

EXPLANATORY NOTES

Observe the Harmony. The fact of our Lord's first gaining disciples when John first points him out to two of his followers, is recorded in John 1:25-35. Simon and Andrew were then first made acquainted with Christ, and this explains their prompt compliance here. After their first call, they had continued in their worldly business. This is the further call to attend upon Christ in his ministry, leaving all and following him wheresoever he went. There is still a further call to the Apostleship, with ordination, ch. 3:14. The accounts in Matthew and Mark are almost in the same words. Luke is more full, and gives us the narrative of a miracle which Christ wrought at this time; which throws light upon Mark's more brief statement here. It is worthy of note, that this miracle, so full of meaning, was twice wrought by our Lord; both now, when he called them to their work, and at the last, when he was about to leave them. John 21:6. And in both cases, he would show by it how he could and would make their work successful. See Eze. 47:10; Jer. 16:16. He who could make them from *fishermen* to become *fishers of men,* could make them catch men in their new work as easily and abundantly as now he could make them catch fish. So our Lord uses the figure of a net. Matt. 13:41.

20. *Hired servants.* This would intimate that they were not of the poorest class.

FACT QUESTIONS 1:16-20

45. When and where did the calling of the four occur?
46. Read carefully Matt. 4:18-22 and Luke 5:1-11 and see if these are indeed parallel accounts—some feel they are not—what do *you* believe?
47. Read John 1:25-35 and show how it relates to this incident.
48. State the *three* calls of Christ to these men.
49. Why the miracle of the draught of fish? Why given twice? Cf. John 21:6.
50. Why mention the hired servants as in vs. 20?

3. A SABBATH IN THE LIFE OF JESUS 1:21-34

TEXT 1:21-34

And they go into Capernaum; and straightway on the sabbath day he entered into the synagogue and taught. And they were astonished at his teaching: for he taught them as having authority, and not as the scribes. And straightway there was in their synagogue a man with an unclean spirit; and he cried out, saying, what have we to do with thee, Jesus thou Nazarene? Art thou come to destroy us? I know Thee who Thou art, the Holy One of God. And Jesus rebuked him, saying, Hold thy peace, and come out of him. And the unclean spirit, tearing him and crying with a loud voice, came out of him. And they were all amazed, insomuch that they questioned among themselves, saying, What is this? a new teaching! With authority he commandeth even the unclean spirits, and they obey him. And the report of him went out straightway everywhere into all the region of Galilee round about.

And straightway, when they were come out of the synagogue, they came into the house of Simon and Andrew, with James and John. Now Simon's wife's mother lay sick of a fever; and straightway they tell him of her and he came and took her by the hand, and raised her up; and the fever left her, and she ministered unto them.

And at even, when the sun did set, they brought unto him all that were sick, and them that were possessed with demons. And all the city was gathered together at the door. And he healed many that were sick with divers diseases, and cast out many demons; and he suffered not the demons to speak, because they knew him.

THOUGHT QUESTIONS 1:21-34

35. Who went into Capernaum?
36. Why use the word "straightway" in vs. 21?
37. How did Jesus have such ready access to teaching in the synagogue?
38. From what did Jesus teach?
39. Didn't everyone teach from the same source of authority? Why then the astonishment?
40. How did the scribes teach without authority?
41. When did the possessed man cry out? i.e. How soon?
42. Why did the demon cry out?
43. In what sense was the evil spirit "unclean"?
44. In what sense could Jesus destroy the evil spirit? Aren't they immortal?
45. Why did Jesus rebuke the evil Spirit? Wasn't the testimony of the demon true?
46. What is meant by the expression "tearing him"?
47. Who cried with a loud voice,the demon or the man?
48. Why refer to casting out of the evil spirit as a teaching?
49. Upon what basis was the popularity of Jesus built?
50. Did Jesus have a home in Capernaum? Why go to the house of Simon and Andrew?
51. Please note the miraculous elements in the raising of Peter's mother-in-law. List them.
52. Why wait until the setting of the sun to bring the sick?
53. What percent were healed?
54. Why not let the demons speak?

COMMENT

TIME—The incidents of this lesson are assigned by the best authorities to May A.D. 28, in the second year of the Lord's ministry. Mark does not adhere to the chronological order.

PLACE—At Capernaum, on the northwest shore of the Sea of Galilee, a city of about 30,000 inhabitants, called the Lord's "own city," because he made his earthly home there. It has disappeared so completely that even its site is unknown, some identifying it with the ruins of Tel Hum on the north, and others at Khan Minyeh on the west of the sea.

CONNECTING HISTORY—According to Andrews the interval in the ministry of Christ between the Baptism and the present section contains the following events:

January, A.D. 27. The fast in the wilderness and the temptation.

February, A.D. 27. Jesus returns from the wilderness of temptation to Bethabara, where John bears testimony to him (John 1:15-37).

February, A.D. 27. Here Jesus gains his first disciples, Philip, Andrew, and Peter, who belonged in Bethsaida of Galilee, and all return to Galilee (John 1:38-51).

March, A.D. 27. Jesus performs his first miracle at Cana (John 2:1-11).

March, A.D. 27. Goes to Capernaum for a few days (John 2:12, 13).

April 11-18, A.D. 27. Goes to Jerusalem to the first passover of his public ministry.

April, A.D. 27. Drives the money-changers from the temple (John 2:14-35).

April, A.D. 27. Conversation with Nicodemus (John 3:1-21).

May to September, A.D. 27. Preaching and baptizing in Judea (John 4:2).

Autumn, A.D. 27. Driven from Judea by Pharisees, he leaves for Galilee (John 4:1-3).

December, A.D. 27. Going through Samaria, he talks with the woman by Jacob's well (John 4:4-42.) Heals nobleman's son (John 4:46-54).

January to March, A.D. 28. Period of retirement in Galilee. John the Baptist imprisoned (Matt. 4:12).

March 30 to April 5, A.D. 28. Attends Passover at Jerusalem. Cure of the impotent man at the pool of Bethesda (John 5).

April, A.D. 28. Returns to Galilee (Luke 4:14. Matt. 4:12); preaches at Nazareth, his early home; but being rejected there (Luke 4:16-32), he goes to Capernaum, where he makes his home (Matt. 4:12-17). Then follows the incident of our present study.

PARALLEL ACCOUNTS—The general view of Christ's ministry given (vers. 14, 15) is related also in Matt. 4:17, and Luke 4:14, 15. Then come in the accounts of his Galilean ministry found in John 4:46-54, followed by Luke 4:16-31. Vers. 16-20 are reported in Matt. 4:18-22, Luke 5:1-11; and vers. 21-28 in Luke 4:31-37.

OUTLINE—1. *Teaching in the Synagogue.* 2. *The Unclean Spirit Cast Out.* 3. *The Great Healer at Work.*

ANALYSIS

I. TEACHING IN THE SYNAGOGUE. VS. 21, 22.
  1. The Great Teacher in the Synagogue. Mark 1:21; Luke 4:33.
  2. Astonished at His Doctrine. Mark 1:22.

II. THE UNCLEAN SPIRIT CAST OUT. VS. 23-28.
  1. The Man with the Unclean Spirit. Mark 1:23; Luke 4:34, 35.
  2. The Demon Obeys His Voice. Mark 1:26, 27; Luke 4:35.
  3. The People Amazed. Mark 1:27, 28; Luke 4:36, 37.

III. THE GREAT HEALER AT WORK. VS. 29-34
  1. Heals in Peter's House. Mark 1:29-31; Matt. 8:14, 15; Luke 4:38.
  2. The Multitudes Healed. Mark 1:32-34; Matt. 8:16, 17; Luke 4:40.

INTRODUCTION

After a year's preparatory teaching, the Savior began the selection of the disciples who were to become his apostles, calling Simon and Andrew from their nets (verse 16), also James and John from the same calling (verse 17) and Matthew from his place at the receipt of custom in Capernaum. Following these incidents we have an account of how the Lord passed Saturday, the Jewish Sabbath, in that city. Indeed, by comparing the other accounts we seem to have a full account of one day's ministry in the life of our Lord, and as there were no doubt many other days like it, it gives us a vivid picture of his work on earth.

EXPLANATORY NOTES

I. TEACHING IN THE SYNAGOGUE—21. *And they went into Capernaum.* Christ was now attended by the disciples whom he had just called from their nets and boats upon the sea of Galilee. (Henceforth, as long as his earthly ministry continues, they attend his footsteps. They were called upon a week day, while at work, and probably all came on Friday into Capernaum, in order to attend the synagogue service upon the Sabbath. It is well to keep in mind that the Lord, during his Galilean ministry, made Capernaum his home, as far as he had one on earth. Its position on the northwest coast of the sea enabled him to reach easily all the populous towns on its shores and all parts of Galilee. Brought up in Galilee, this was always his favorite portion of Palestine, and all his apostles but Judas, the traitor, were Galileans. *Straightway on the Sabbath.* On Saturday, the Jewish day of rest and worship. Our Lord " born under the Law," kept the law of Moses blamelessly, was even circumcised, attended the feasts and observed the Jewish Sabbath, but at the same time proclaimed himself Lord of the Sabbath day. *Entered the synagogue.* This was our Lord's usual custom on the Sabbath and the apostle Paul in his missionary labors followed the same custom. It gave an opportunity to teach a Jewish audience. *The synagogue.* There is no mention of synagogues in the law of Moses, or in the prophets. They are supposed to have been introduced during the Captivity, on account of the need of special teaching, and to have been continued ever afterwards wherever Jews were found. As we sometimes use the word *church* to denote the congregation, and sometimes the building, so the word synagogue was sometimes used in this double sense. The arrangements of a Jewish congregation, as well as the construction of the synagogue, seem to have resembled those of a modern Christian church. The people in the front part of the building sat facing the pulpit or desk on a platform which was occupied by the reader or speaker. Behind the pulpit were ranged high seats of honor, "chief seats," where the scribes and Pharisees loved to sit facing the people. A chest or ark was near the pulpit, in which the Scriptures of the Old Testament were deposited. From the pulpit the Scriptures were read; and the reader, or some other person, expounded, taught, or preached. Prayers were also offered; and at the close a solemn benediction was pronounced, and the people responded Amen, and dispersed. These exercises took place every (Saturday) *Sabbath. And taught.* It was the custom in the synagogue to invite members of the congregation or visitors of note to make remarks. It is obvious that in the synagogues of Palestine this was the safety-valve, the open sphere, the golden opportunity for any fresh teaching to arise—*Stanley.* Christ preached in many synagogues, for there was always opportunity given to a distinguished Jewish teacher. Only once in the synagogue at Nazareth, Luke 4:16, is he represented as reading the Scriptural lesson. The reason of this is that the lesson was never read by a stranger but always by a member of the synagogue.

22. *They were astonished at his doctrine.* Never had such a teacher stood before them. There was no lifeless droning over dry traditions or idle ceremonies, but his teaching was fresh as the morning, original, going to the root of things, authoritative, and burning with Divine fire. It is not strange that the great Teacher whose doctrines have revolutionized the earth, astonished the audiences who listened to him in Judea and Galilee. Taught as one who had authority. He taught with the authority of one who knows all the facts and all their bearings. Being Divine he knew all about heaven and hell and the way there, all about God and the truths he had revealed to the Jews, and all his plans and purposes for his kingdom in the future. It was this perfect knowledge that gave him the authority with which he spoke, and gives superiority to the

Bible over all philosophical systems and attempts at religious systems. He never was in doubt, nor had he ever to lean on the authority of others, because he knew all things. *And not as the scribes.* The *scribes* were the learned men of the Jewish nation, the men who had to do with *letters.* Almost all the writing that was required in the nation would be done by them; most of the reading, too. The transcribing of the Scriptures would devolve on them. Hence the interpretation of the Law and Prophets, in the synagogues, would devolve chiefly on them. They also engaged in idle discussion and differed among themselves.

II. THE UNCLEAN SPIRIT CAST OUT—23. *A man with an unclean spirit.* The address of the great Teacher was interrupted by a piteous cry of a demoniac. In the audience was a man with an unclean spirit. He had evidently remained silent until Jesus was nearly done, and then his cry arose. *An unclean spirit.* Some have held that the possession of unclean spirits and of demons was only a way of described epilepsy or lunacy. *Abbot* well says: "That there is described here, not a case of physical and mental disease, but rather a real and actual possession of the soul by a fallen spirit is, I think, clear, both from the tenor of the narrative here, and from parallel passages in the New Testament. How could a lunatic know Christ to be the Holy One of God, when as yet he was unknown even to his disciples? How could he fear that Christ would destroy him, who came to heal the sufferer, but to destroy the Devil? How could lunacy be said to come out of him, or to cry with a loud voice?" In order that I may add as much light as space will permit upon a difficult and controverted subject, I quote from *Dean Alford* and *Dr. Clark.* "What was this demoniacal possession? But we may gather from the Gospel narrative some important ingredients for our description. The demoniac was one whose being was strangely interpenetrated by one or more of those fallen spirits, who are constantly asserted in Scripture (under the name of demons, evil spirits, unclean spirits, their chief being the Devil, or Satan) to be the enemies and tempters of the souls of men. He stood in a totally different position from the abandoned wicked man, who morally is given over to the Devil. This latter would be a subject for punishment, but the demoniac for deepest compassion. There appears to have been in him a double will and double consciousness—sometimes the cruel spirit thinking and speaking in him, sometimes his poor crushed self crying out to the Savior of men for mercy; a terrible advantage taken, and a personal realization, by the malignant powers of evil, of the fierce struggle between sense and conscience in the man of morally divided life. It has been not improbably supposed that some of these demoniacs may have arrived at their dreadful state through various progressive degrees of guilt and sensual abandonment. Lavish sin, and especially indulgence in sensual lusts, superinducing, as it would often, a weakness in the nervous system, which is the especial bond between body and soul, may have laid open these unhappy ones to the fearful incursions of the powers of darkness.—*Alford.* To the frequent inquiry, How comes it that similar possessions do not occur at the present day? it may be answered: (1) It cannot be proved that they do not sometimes occur even now. It cannot be said that in many cases of insanity, and in some cases of spiritualism, the malady may not be traced to the direct agency of demons. (2) But, admitting that such possessions are not common, yet there was a reason in our Savior's day for the external manifestation of Satan's power. The crisis of the moral history of the world was at hand. The Devil was allowed to exercise unusual power in temptation on the souls and bodies of men, in order that Christ might meet him openly, and manifest his power in his victory over him. When God was manifested in the flesh, then demons may have been permitted to manifest themselves specially among men.—*Clark.*

24. *What have we to do with thee?* The Savior had not, so far as appears, been formally interfering by any specific action; but his very presence on the scene was felt to be interference. There emanated from him, round about, an influence that went in upon men blissfully, counter-working all evil influences. The unclean spirit felt the power, and resented it as an interference,—an interference, not with itself in particular, but with the entire circle of kindred spirits. "What hast thou to do with *us?" Art thou come to destroy us?* Note the *us,—Camest thou to destroy us?" Is it the intent of thy mission to put down all demonic power?* Note the word *destroy.* It has no reference to the annihilation of being. *I know thee.* Not as an acquaintance, but by fame and report. Earth has not recognized her King, has not seen him through his disguise; but heaven and hell alike bear witness unto him. *The Holy One of God.* Such is Christ, both morally and officially. This term expresses the character in which this being recognized his deadly enemy. Christ is the exact opposite of the unclean spirits, being holy, and producing holiness in others.

25. *And Jesus rebuked.* The original word is very peculiar, and strictly means *rated.* Our Savior *chides* the evil spirit. He never on any occasion gave any quarter to anything demonic. *Hold thy peace.* The word translated Hold thy peace is exceedingly graphic. *Be muzzled.* It is a word for a beast. He silences the devils, even when they spake the truth, lest he should seem to approve of witnesses who were liars by nature. It was to bring the truth itself into suspicion and discredit, when it was borne witness to by the spirit of lies. *Come out of him.* Two distinct person-

alities are here recognized. The demon is treated as a person as much as the man. The one was just as much a disease or a principle as the other, no more, and no less.

26. *The unclean spirit had torn him.* Thrown him into convulsions. *Cried with a loud voice.* The evil spirit seems to have resisted to the last obedience to the Master's command.

27. *Amazed . . . questioned.* Each turned to his neighbor in astonishment, to ask his opinion, Saying, What is this? New teaching with authority! And he commandeth the unclean spirits, and they obey him! Such is, apparently, the correct reading and rendering of the abrupt remarks which the astonished people made to one another.—*Morison. Doctrine* is, as elsewhere, the teaching taken as a whole, including manner as well as substance.—*Ellicott. With authority.* The authority with which he taught found its guaranty in the authority backed by power with which he forced the devils themselves to render obedience. Christ's cures differed from the pretences of the exorcists, just as his teaching did from that of the scribes.—*Godet.*

28. *His fame.* Literally, the *report* of him. *Spread abroad.* Flew, as it were, on the wings of the wind, into all the surrounding district of Galilee.

III. THE GREAT HEALER AT WORK.—29. *And forthwith.* The day's work was not nearly ended. As soon as they left the synagogue, the Lord comes in contact with a case of suffering. *Entered the house of Simon Peter.* Peter and Andrew now lived in Capernaum, though their former home had been at Bethsaida.

30. *Simon Peter's wife's mother.* Peter, though the Romanists claim him as the first of the Popes, was a married man. Many years after this, Paul (1 Cor. 9:3) speaks of Peter as then having a wife and traveling with him. *Lay sick of a fever.* Malarious fevers of a malignant type are common in the vicinity of Capernaum. In the very imperfect medical language of that day, fevers were simply divided into little and great fevers. Luke, who was a physician, characterizes this as a "great fever." That she was entirely prostrated by it, is evident by the language here, "laid and sick of a fever."—*Abbott.* The quantity of marshy land in the neighborhood, especially at the entrance of the Jordan into the lake, has made fever of a very malignant type at times the characteristic of the locality.—*Geikie.*

31. *He came.* Observe all the graphic touches in this verse: the Lord (1) *went to the sufferer,* (2) *took her by the hand,* (3) *lifted her up,* and (4) *the fever, rebuked* by the Lord of life (Luke 4:39), *left her* and (5) she began to *minister unto them.*

32. *And at Even, when the sun did set,* i. e., the close of the sabbath, which, amongst the Jews, ended with the setting sun. There are two reasons why the time should be thus specified. (1) It was natural that the sick should be brought in the cool of the evening, rather than in the scorching heat of the afternoon. (2) It was the sabbath, and the feeling which made the Pharisees question the lawfulness of a man's carrying the bed on which he had been lying (John 5:10) on the sabbath, would probably have deterred the friends of the sick from bringing them as long as it lasted. *They brought to him.* The news that he was in the city, and of his healing power had not time to spread. *All that were diseased.* The term *diseased* in its current modern acceptation, is perhaps a trifle too strong to represent the import of the original expression; but when looked at etymologically, *dis-eased,* that is *sundered from ease,* or *ill at ease,* and thus *unwell,* it is all that could be desired. *Possessed with devils.* With demons or evil spirits. It is no doubt a correct enough description; but the word *devil* or *devils* is never used in the original, when demoniacs are spoken of. It is always the word *demon* or *demons,* or the generic term *spirit* or *spirits.*

33. *All the city.* The effect was to rouse and gather the entire population of the city, to obtain healing for themselves or friends, or at least to see and hear the new teacher. *At the door,* of Peter's house where Jesus was.

34. *He healed many . . . cast out many devils.* Jesus came as the great Healer. Disease is the result, the outgrowth, the representative, of sin; and Christ's healing of the maladies of the body is an exhibition of his power and willingness to heal the maladies of the soul.—*Dean Howson.* Matthew says (8:17) that here was fulfilled the prophecy "which was spoken by Isaiah the prophet, saying, Himself took our infirmities, and bare our sicknesses" (Isa. 53:4, 5). How did he bear the infirmities of the sick? Not literally. He removed them from others, but did not become diseased himself. Neither in removing sins from others does he become stricken with sin himself. *Suffered not the devils to speak.* The reasons for this prohibition are suggested in the comments on verse 25.

FACT QUESTIONS 1:21-34

51. What advantage was there in making Capernaum His headquarters during His Galilean ministry?
52. Why attend the synagogue?
53. When did the synagogue originate? In what two senses is the word synagogue used? How does this relate to the word church?
54. Why didn't Christ read the lesson in the synagogues?

55. Did the manner or the content astonish those in the synagogue?
56. Was the man with the unclean spirit in the assembly or did he run in from the outside?
57. Is demon possession just another way of describing insanity? Explain.
58. Give one thought each from Clark and Abbott as quoted here.
59. Why was the evil spirit so unhappy with Christ?
60. Why did Christ rebuke the evil spirit?
61. Is there some difference in the amazement here and that spoken of in vs. 21?
62. How could Peter be the first Pope and yet have a wife?
63. What type of fever is here mentioned?
64. How did so many folk know of the whereabouts of Jesus?
65. Read Isa. 53:4, 5 and show its fulfillment here.

SIDELIGHTS

1. *Teaching with authority.* Whoever *knows* any subject can teach it with *authority.* Some men are authorities on science, some on literature, some on medicine: because they know more about these subjects than others do. But Christ is the only one who has ever been into the other world, and returned to this; and therefore he is *authority* upon the future life. He *knows* the final result of sin, and the glory of heaven, and the way to it. And because he is *divine,* and knows all things, there can be no mistake about what he says: he speaks with perfect authority.—P.

2. *Synagogue worship.* I attended the Jewish worship at Jerusalem, and was struck with the accordance of the ceremonies with those mentioned in the New Testament. The sacred roll was brought from the chest or closet where it was kept; it was handed by an attendant to the reader; a portion of it was rehearsed; the congregation rose and stood while it was read, whereas the speaker, and all others present, sat during the delivery of the address which formed a part of the service.—*H. B. Hackett.*

3. *Devils Bearing Witness.*—They were ready to speak *because* they knew his nature and work. The mere belief of the facts and doctrines of Christianity will never save our souls. "The devils believe, and tremble." Let us take heed that ours is a faith of the *heart* as well as of the head. "The life of Christianity," says Luther," consists in possessive pronouns." It is one thing to say, *Christ is a Savior,* it is quite another to say, *Christ is my Savior and my Lord.* The devil can say the first: the true Christian alone can say the second.—*Ryle.*

LESSONS

1. The true way to keep God's holy day is to follow Christ to church; to rest from labors and to worship in the sanctuary.

2. We should have such an experience of religion that we may be able to speak to men with authority.

3. We can trust Christ perfectly, because all he says is with the authority of one who knows.

4. It is safe to follow one who has power over the principalities and powers of evil.

5. Every disciple of Christ should be a helper and a healer. He should minister to the afflicted, whether in body or mind. He should cast out unclean spirits by the power of the love of Christ.

POINTS FOR TEACHERS

There are two great thoughts in this lesson, and both concentrate in Christ. First, *Christ, the Great Teacher,* and second, Christ, the Great Healer. Note 1. How he teaches by example; he is in the house of worship on God's holy day; 2. he leads his disciples there; 3. Observe him teaching, (1) in solid earnest, (2) no idle speculation, (3) he teaches what he knows. 4. Hence he teaches with authority. What we know we can teach with authority. His was the authority of absolute knowledge; we can teach with the authority of faith. He next appears as the Great Physician who heals not only sicknesses but sins. Observe (1) He healed a dear friend of his disciples (verse 29-31), as he is glad to heal those we love, if we bring them to him. (2) Then he healed great multitudes (verse 32-34), showing the nature of his religion to heal and to help. We should note also that Christ refused the aid, testimony or any compromise with devils, and we should learn by his example (1) never to compromise with sin, (2) to decline all aid tendered by the devil, or in his name, (3) seek to overcome the devil and all his works.

4. HEALING OF THE LEPER—1:35-45

TEXT 1:35-45

And in the morning, a great while before day, he rose up and went out, and departed into a desert place, and there prayed. And Simon and they that were with him followed after him; and they found him; and say unto him, All are seeking thee. And he saith unto them, Let us go elsewhere into the next towns, that I may preach there also; for to this end came I forth. And he went into their synagogues throughout all Galilee, preaching and casting out devils. And there cometh to him a leper, beseeching him, and kneeling down to him, and saying unto him, If thou wilt, thou canst make me clean. And being moved with compassion, he stretched forth his hand, and touched him, and saith unto him, I will; be thou made clean. And straightway the leprosy departed from him, and he was made clean. And he strictly charged him, and straightway sent him out, and saith unto him, See thou say nothing to any man: but go thy way, shew thyself to the priest, and offer for thy cleansing the things that Moses commanded, for a testimony unto them. But he went out, and began to publish abroad the matter, insomuch that Jesus could no more openly enter into a city, but was without in desert places: and they came to him from every quarter.

THOUGHT QUESTIONS: 1:35-45

55. Are we to understand that this incident occurred after the busy sabbath of 1:21-34?
56. Did Jesus have a particular reason for prayers? If so, what was it?
57. Why get up so early?
58. Why not pray in his room?
59. What needs did Jesus have that could be satisfied in prayer?
60. Why did Simon follow Jesus? Who was seeking Jesus? For what reason?
61. Did Jesus come to heal or to preach? Does Jesus say in vs. 38 that He was sent from heaven to preach?
62. How did Jesus have such ready access to the synagogues?
63. Was there a crowd about Jesus when the leper came to Him? Cf. Matt. and Luke.
64. Give three characteristics of the leper.
65. Do our physical and emotional infirmities "move with compassion" our Savior? Cf. Heb. 4:14, 15.
66. Why touch the leper?
67. Why didn't Jesus inquire of the Father's will in the healing?
68. How long did it take to effect a complete cure of the leprosy?
69. Why be so stern when He has just been so tender?
70. Why go to the priest? To whom was "the testimony" (vs. 44) to be given?
71. Why did the leper disobey Jesus?

COMMENT 1:35-45

TIME—April-June, A.D. 28. The healing of Peter's wife's mother occurred immediately after the same sabbath on which Jesus' teaching in the synagogue was interrupted by the demoniac. After this he began his first missionary tour of Galilee. The healing of the leper was toward the latter part of the tour, in May or June. This was in the fifteenth year of the reign of Tiberius Caesar, Emperor of Rome; Pontius Pilate was now Governor of Judea and Herod Antipas Tetrarch of Galilee.

PLACES—Capernaum, and the towns and cities of Galilee. This was Jesus' first missionary circuit of Galilee. The sea, or lake of Galilee, was 13 miles long, from 4 to 6 miles wide, was 165 feet deep in the deepest part, and lay 700 feet below the level of the Mediterranean Sea. Its western and northern shores were at this date densely inhabited, and five populous cities, Bethsaida, Chorazin, Capernaum, Magdala and Tiberias, stood upon or near its bank. It was on the direct route between the great city of Damascus and the Mediterranean, and was hence an appropriate center for the Lord's missionary labors. Its shores are now desolate, and the boats that once covered its surface have almost entirely disappeared. The rule of the Turks, the lawlessness, and the raids of the Bedouin, have desolated one of the fairest spots on the earth.

PARALLEL ACCOUNTS—The healing of Peter's wife's mother and others (vers. 29-34) is recorded also in Matt. 8:14-17, and Luke 4:38-41. The first circuit of Galilee (vers. 35-39), also in Luke 4:42, 44 followed by Matt. 4:23-25. The healing of the leper (vers. 40-45), also in Matt. 8:2-4, and Luke 5:12-16.

OUTLINE—1. *The Lonely Prayer.* 2. *Seeking to Save the Lost.* 3. *Healing the Leper.*

ANALYSIS

I. THE LONELY PRAYER. VS. 35-37.
   1. Prayer in the Secret Place. Mark 1:35; Luke 4:42.
   2. Sought by the Disciples. Mark 1:36, 37; Luke 4:42.

II. SEEKING TO SAVE THE LOST. VS. 38, 39.
   1. The First Missionary Tour. Mark 1:38; Matt. 4:23; Luke 4:43.
   2. Preaching in the Synagogues. Mark 1:39; Matt. 4:23; Luke 4:44.

III. HEALING THE LEPER. VS. 40-45.
   1. The Leper's Appeal. Mark 1:40; Matt. 8:2; Luke 5:12.
   2. The Lord Hears and Heals. Mark 1:41, 42; Matt. 8:3; Luke 5:13.
   3. Leper spreads Abroad the Story. Mark 1:45; Luke 4:15.

INTRODUCTION

The Sabbath service in the synagogue had been interrupted by the outcry of the demoniac while Jesus was preaching. After his cure, and the close of the public services, Jesus with his four disciples retires to the modest home of Peter and Andrew, where he works a miracle, the beginning of a series which leads to the height of his fame and popularity and success through Galilee. The leper was healed on the first missionary circuit of Galilee, not long after the preaching of the Sermon on the Mount.

EXPLANATORY NOTES

I. THE LONELY PRAYER.—35. *And in the morning.* On Sunday morning, immediately after the busy Sabbath day, Mark graphically brings the scene before our eyes. The previous day had been a long day of conflict with and victory over the kingdom of sin and death. He now retires to refresh himself in the haven of prayer, in communion with his Father. He prepares himself in the desert for a second great mission of love, this time accompanied by his first four disciples. *A great while before day.* Our Lord always prepared himself for special work or for trial by solitary prayer. See Matt. 14:23; Mark 6:46; Luke 5:16; 6:12; 22:41. It is possible that his night was sleepless because of his anxiety for others; and he arose from his sleepless couch to pray for strength. We may learn from his example (1) that when we are restless and anxious the best relief is found in prayer; (2) the prayer most efficacious, when we have a special burden, is solitary prayer, the prayer of the closet. Christ was wont to seek *solitude* for special occassions of prayer. *Solitary place.* Not merely *solitary,* for a garden might be solitary, but *desert, desolate,* as the word in all other places is rendered. "A remarkable feature of the lake of Gennesaret was that is was closely surrounded with desert solitudes. These "desert places" thus close at hand on the table lands or in the ravines of the eastern and western ranges, gave opportunities of retirement for rest or prayer. 'Rising up early in the morning while it was yet dark,' or 'passing over to the other side in a boat,' he sought these solitudes, sometimes alone, sometimes with his disciples. The lake in this double aspect is thus a reflex of that union of energy and rest, of active labor and deep emotion which is the essence of Christianity, as it was of the life of Him in whom that union was first taught and shown."—*Stanley's Sinai and Palestine. And there prayed.* The original word does not simply denote asking. Prayer, says Petler, is a holy conference with God. Prayer gave him power. The gate to heaven is prayer. No man is strong enough or spiritual enough to be able to neglect it. By daily food the body lives and is able to perform its functions. By daily prayer the soul lives, and only by prayer performs its work of grace. Christ communed in the wilderness with his own soul and with the Father for forty days before he began his ministry, and here he waits before the Lord before beginning his special work in Galilee.

36. *Simon, and they were with him.* The Simon here named is Simon Peter, the apostle, to whose house the Lord had gone after the discourse at the synagogue on the day before. The others with him were probably Andrew his brother, and James and John, who had now left their secular business to attend the Savior. Peter, impetuous, abrupt, impulsive, did not hesitate to intrude himself on the Lord's retirement. He is always the same, wherever he appears in the four gospels; self-confident, generous, bold, often making mistakes from his impulsiveness, and always ready to correct them. On this occasion he, no doubt, acted as the leader in the search after the praying Savior. *Morison* says: "When they awoke in the morning, and found him gone, they seemed to have got alarmed

lest he should have left them, betaking himself to some other sphere of labor. So, too, the inhabitants of the little city in general seem to have felt. Hence the haste and eagerness of Simon and his companions (Andrew, James and John, see vers. 29), as indicated by the strong verb employed: they pursued him, as if he were fleeing from them. Peter was the leader of the pursuing party, thus giving early indication of the impulsive ardor of his nature."

37. *And they found him.* Search and uncertainty is implied, since he had retired to an unfrequented spot. *They said unto him.* Peter said this to induce him to return and the crowd besought him to stay. The will of the multitude did not govern him, as they supposed, hence the reply in the next verse. *All seek thee.* That is, though indefinitely, all the people (in Capernaum.) The people in general had no sooner risen in the morning than they thought of the wonderful preacher and healer and demon-expeller. (Luke 4:42). They wanted still to hear more, and to see more; and hence they came, one after another to the house where he had been lodging in quest of him. The emphasis is on the word *seek.*

II. SEEKING TO SAVE THE LOST.—38. *Let us go into the next towns.* The disciples had pressed the Lord to return to Capernaum, because all men there were seeking for him, but he replies by a request for them to attend him to other cities. In Luke (4:43) he says. "I must preach the kingdom of God in other cities also." *Towns.* The word so translated means village cities, country towns, imperfectly enclosed towns, and unenclosed villages. Josephus says, concerning the two Galilees, Upper and Lower, "The cities lie thick; and the multitude of villages are everywhere full of people, in consequence of the richness of the soil, so that the very least of them contains about 15,000 inhabitants" (War, 3:3, 2). "Christ had no ambition to be a metropolitan preacher. Having awakened spiritual desires in the people of Capernaum, he went elsewhere that he might awaken them in others also."—*Abbott. For therefore came I forth.* To preach. He wrought miracles, but these were mainly to arrest attention and to induce people to give a ready ear to his preaching. *Preached.* The form of Jesus' preaching was essentially Jewish. It was concise, epigrammatic, oracular, so pointed as to stick in the mind like an arrow. It swarmed with figures of speech. He thought in images, pictures. The qualities of the preacher were (1) authority; (2) boldness; (3) power; (4) graciousness.—*Stalker's Life of Our Lord.* The places of preaching were the synagogues in each city, and the times, the Sabbath days. Besides, he was constantly teaching and healing during the week. *Throughout all Galilee.* Throughout the whole region, as well as the nearest towns (Matt. 4:23). Josephus says that in his day "there were

240 towns and villages in Galilee" (Life, 45). Galilee, the northernmost province of Judea, was the scene of Christ's most abundant labors; all the apostles except Judas Iscariot were Galileans; its inhabitants were simple-minded and comparatively free from the control of the priestly class, which ruled in Judea, and from the bigotry and intolerance of the Jews who dwelt about Jerusalem. The greater part of Mark's Gospel is confined to our Lord's ministry in Galilee. *Cast out devils.* Referred to again and again as the most remarkable exhibition of his power, being utterly incurable and unmanageable by men; and as the best type of his whole work on earth, casting out all evil, all that mars this world, and fitting the world for the kingdom of heaven. For a discussion of devils or demons and demoniacs, see the preceding section. The Lord not only cast out demons and thus delivered men from their power, but he came to destroy the power of the devil.

III. HEALING THE LEPER—40. *There came a leper to him.* This account is also given in Matthew 8:2-4, and in Luke 5:12, 13. Matthew places it after the Sermon on the Mount, but he does not aim to follow the chronological order closely, and we are only to infer that it came soon after the descent from the mountain, after he entered "a certain city" and before his return to Capernaum. Luke says that the leper was healed at a "certain city" but does not say what one. Luke says, "A man full of leprosy" (Luke 5:12). This disease is nothing short of a foul decay, arising from the total corruption of the blood. It was a living death, as indicated by bare head, rent clothes, and covered lip. In the middle ages, a man siezed with leprosy was "clothed in a shroud, and the masses of the dead sung over him." In its horrible repulsiveness it is the gospel type of sin.—*Farrar.* Leprosy began with little specks on the eyelids and on the palms of the hands, and gradually spread over different parts of the body, bleaching the hair white wherever it showed itself, crusting the affected parts with shining scales, and causing swellings and sores. From the skin it slowly ate its way through the tissues, to the bones and joints, and even to the marrow, rotting the whole body piecemeal. The lungs, the organs of speech and hearing, and the eyes, were attacked in turn, till at last consumption or dropsy brought welcome death. The dread of infection kept men aloof from the sufferer; and the law proscribed him as above all men unclean. The disease was hereditary to the fourth generation.—*Geikie. The leprosy.* We find that nearly everywhere the disease is most common on the seashore, and that, when it spreads inland, it generally occurs on the shores of lakes or along the course of large rivers.—*Medical Press.* Is the leprosy contagious? A review of the evidence led the speaker to the conclusion that this disease was not contagious by ordinary contact; but it may be transmitted by the blood and secretions. It is a well-established fact that when leprosy has once gained for itself a foothold in any locality, it is apt to remain there and spread. Being the worst form of disease, leprosy was fixed upon by God to be the especial type of sin; and the injunctions regarding it had reference to its typical character. It was accompanied by the emblems of death. (Lev. 13:45, comp. with Num. 6:9. Ezek. 24:17). It involved ceremonial uncleanness (see Num. 19:13. Ezek. 45:25); and the exclusion of the leper from the congregation (Lev. 13:44-46. Num. 5:1-3; 12-14, 15. 2 Chron. 24:19-21) strikingly typified the separation of the sinner from God's presence. *Kneeling down.* Not an act of worship, but a gesture of entreaty. There is no contrivance of our body but some good man in Scripture hath hallowed it with prayer. The publican standing, Job sitting, (Job. 2:8,) Hezekiah lying on his bed, (2 Kings 20:2,) Elijah with his face between his legs, (1 Kings 18:42.) But of all postures give me St. Paul's: "For this cause I bow my knees to the Father of our Lord Jesus Christ." Eph. 3:12; Acts 7:60.—*Thomas Fuller. If thou wilt, thou canst.* If thou art willing, thou art able. The leper had faith in the miraculous power of Jesus, but had a doubt about his willingness to exercise it on such an object as him, on one so unclean. Here was (1) a thorough consciousness of his own misery and helplessness; (2) he knew it was not too bad for Christ's power. It has been well said that the language of faith always is, not if thou canst, but if thou wilt. He is willing to leave the whole matter in Christ's hands. (3) Let us pause on this little word IF. "If" embodies doubt; and faith, in its earlier stages, almost always involves doubt, but, when the soul can use "if," it has made great progress in faith. *Cleanse me.* He felt the impurity of his disease, not merely ceremonial, but actual,—as we should feel the impurity of sin, and pray not merely, forgive, but cleanse.

41. *Moved with compassion.* Jesus felt for the leper what he and his Father feel for all sinners, an unutterable compassion and love. *Touched* him—To have touched him was, in the eyes of a Jew, to have made himself unclean, but he had come to break through the deadly externalism that had taken the place of true religion, and could have shown no more strikingly how he looked on mere rabbinical precepts than by making a touch, which, till then, had entailed the worst uncleanness, the means of cleansing. Slight though it seemed, the touch of the leper was the proclamation that Judaism was abrogated henceforth.—*Geikie.* His hand became not unclean from the leprosy, but the leprous body was made clean by his holy hand.—*Chrysostom.*

42. *The leprosy departed.* At the touch and command, the leprosy immediately departed and the man was well.

43. *Straitly charged him.* Strictly and positively charged him.

44. *Say nothing to any man.* Our Lord almost uniformly repressed the fame of his miracles, for the reason given in Matt. 12:15-21, that, in accordance with prophetic truth, he might be known as the Messiah, not by wonder-working power, but by the great result of his work upon earth. See chap. 12:16-19. Thus the apostles always refer primarily to the resurrection, and only incidentally, if at all, to the wonders and signs. Another reason, perhaps, was that the Lord wished him to obtain the legal certificate of cleanness from the priest before too much was said. It might be refused through prejudice. *Show thyself to the priest.* At Jerusalem. *Those things which Moses commanded.* Viz., (1) two birds, "alive and clean" (Lev. 14:4); (2) cedar wood, (3) scarlet, (4) hyssop; this was for the preliminary ceremony (Lev. 14:4-7). On the eighth day further offerings were to be made—(1) two he-lambs without blemish, (2) one ewe-lamb, (3) three tenth deals of fine flour, (4) one log of oil. If the leper was poor, he was permitted to offer one lamb and two doves or pigeons, with one-tenth deal of fine flour. The law was still in force and the Lord strictly enjoins that it be observed.

45. *Began to publish.* Where men ought to publish Christ, alas! how silent are they. Here, when the great Savior commanded silence, this man will publish the cure. Thus our Lord's work was hindered. How many from ill-timed zeal prevent much good! *Could no more openly enter into the city.* Not the city of Capernaum, but any city or town. He was compelled to go into the desert places. He was unable, because, the moment that his presence was recognized in a town, he was liable to be surrounded and hemmed in by a surging crowd of ignorant, and ignorantly expectant, gazers, wonderers and volunteer followers. One sees now how wise it was to tell the leper to hold his tongue. *And they came to him from every quarter.* The people kept coming to him, notwithstanding the difficulty of reaching him, and the inconvenience connected with a sojourn, even for a very limited period, in an unpopulated district.

FACT QUESTIONS 1:35-45

66. Give the time for this section—i.e. date, the name of the emperor, governor and tetrarch.
67. State three places involved in these verses—i.e. 1:35-45.
68. What is the condition of Capernaum today?
69. Please read Matt. 8:14-17; Luke 4:38-41 for a parallel account of part of the record in Mark. Read Luke 4:42-44; Matt. 4:23-25; also Matt. 8:2-4 and Luke 5:12-16 for the rest of the account.

70. Mention again the purpose of prayer in the life of Jesus. Read Matt. 14:23; Luke 5:16; 6:12.
71. What one lesson can we learn from the praying of Jesus?
72. What is meant by the word "solitary" in reference to the place of prayer?
73. What more than mere petition was involved in the praying of Jesus?
74. Why did Peter so urgently, eagerly seek for Jesus?
75. Why did the multitude of Capernaum seek Jesus? Why didn't He return?
76. What was the possibility for preaching in Galilee—i. e. how many towns, how many people?
77. Mention two qualities of the preaching of Jesus.
78. Why especially mention casting out demons?
79. Where and when in the ministry of our Lord was the leper healed?
80. How serious was the leprosy of the one healed?
81. Why did the leper kneel to Jesus?
82. Why the question of "If thou wilt"?
83. Did the leper doubt the power of Christ?
84. How deeply was Jesus moved with the need of the leper? Why touch him?
85. Why go to the priest if he was already healed?

SUMMARY 1:14-45

In this section Mark has furnished a striking exhibition of both the divine authority and the divine power of Jesus. Such was the authority which he could exercise over men, that when he commanded the four fishermen to follow him, they left all they had on earth, without a question or a moment's delay, and followed him. And such was the authority with which he commanded demons, that although these wicked spirits were not willingly obedient, they instantly departed from their victims at his bidding. Such, too, was his power, that at his touch the malignant fever, the incurable leprosy, and all the maladies which afflict the body, were instantly healed. Such, finally, was his unexampled meekness, that amid these displays of divine authority and power, when popular applause ran high, he retired by night to pray, or wandered away into desert places. His meekness was as high above the capacity of a merely human being, as were his miracles. *McGarvey.*

DIFFERENCE FROM MATTHEW

One of the characteristic differences between Mark and Matthew, their difference in regard to arrangement, is conspicuous in their modes of treating the subject-matter of the preceding section. Mark uses almost the same material with Matthew, but how differently he arranges it! They both begin with the removal of Jesus to Galilee, after the imprisonment of John, and follow this with the call of the four fishermen; but Matthew next introduces the general statement of the preaching throughout Galilee (iv. 23-25), which Mark reserves until after the cures at Simon's house (i. 39); he next devotes considerable space to the sermon on the mount, which Mark omits; then he introduces as his first mentioned miracle the cure of the leper (viii. 1-4), which is the third miracle mentioned by Mark (i. 40-45); his second miracle is the cure of the centurion's servant (viii. 5-13), of which Mark says nothing; his third is that of Simon's mother-in-law, which is the second with Mark; and finally, they unite in following this last miracle with the cures at Simon's door. This difference alone is sufficient proof that Mark's narrative is not an abridgement of Matthew's.—*McGarvey*

SIDE-LIGHTS

1. *The Leprosy.*—Wandering a little way outside the walls of the city we came upon the dwellings of the lepers. The place is separated from all other human habitations, and consists of a rude court or enclosure, containing about twenty huts or kennels. At the sound of our voices and footsteps the lepers came out into the sunlight, clamoring with most unearthly sounds for charity. Death was visibly eating them away. Some were of a liver color, others white as snow—all deformed. Handless arms were held out to us; half-consumed limbs obtruded; countenances woefully defaced and eyeless were turned up to us, and cries came out from palateless mouths that were wildly imploring and inhuman. The old law which prohibited the leper from touching or drawing near to a clean person, was scrupulously regarded by them, so that, even when they begged, they stretched out to us little iron cups into which we might drop our alms.—*Thompson.*

2. *Leprosy as a Type.*—Thus sin affects the soul, rendering it unclean, separating it from God, producing spiritual death; unfitting it forever for heaven and the company of the holy, and insuring its eternal banishment, as polluted and abominable. Some, as they look on infancy, reject with horror the thought that sin exists within. But so might any one say who looked upon the beautiful babe in the arms of a leprous mother. But time brings forth the fearful malady. New-born babes of leprous parents are often as pretty and as healthy in appearance as any; but by and by its presence and workings become visible in some of the signs described in the 13th chapter of Leviticus.—*Land and Book*, 11:519.

3. How to be Healed.—(1) We must see Jesus, inquire after him, acquaint ourselves with him. (2) We must humble ourselves before him, as this leper, seeing Christ, fell on his face; we must be ashamed of our pollution, and, in the sense of it, blush to lift up our faces before the holy Jesus. (3) We must earnestly desire to be cleansed from the defilement and cured of the disease of sin, which renders us unfit for communion with God. (4) We must firmly believe in Christ's ability and sufficiency to cleanse us. Lord, thou canst make me clean, though I be full of leprosy. No doubt is to be made of the merit and grace of Christ. (5) We must be importunate for pardon and grace: He fell on his face and besought him. They that would be cleansed must reckon it a favor worth wrestling for. (6) We must refer ourselves to the good will of Christ: Lord, if thou wilt, thou canst .—*M. Henry.*

LESSONS

1. We cannot save sinners, but we can bring them to Christ, the Savior.

2. Every one, like Christ, needs seasons of retirement and prayer. Spiritual growth comes from activity in Christian work, and seasons of restful communion with God.

3. The hardest work in the world is casting out the devils of sin. Building cities and ruling empires are nothing in comparison.

4. Sin is like leprosy—incurable, loathsome, contagious, hereditary, painful, all-pervasive, from small beginnings; shameful, separating from others.

5. Learn from the leper how the sinner should come to Jesus and be saved. He felt his disease; despaired of human help; believed in the power of Jesus; he came with his leprosy and submitted to the will of Jesus.—*Clark.*

6. In the services we are called to render one another, we fail far oftener from want of will than want of power. We fail to use many opportunities, not because we cannot, but because we will not, use them. —*Howson.*

7. The healed by Christ are his living witnesses that he can save men. Even enemies must acknowledge the change. Every transformed sinner is a living witness of Christ's power to save.

POINTS FOR TEACHERS

1. Review the Sabbath day's work, the wonderful discourse, the admiring multitude, the demoniac healed, all Capernaum stirred, the woman healed, the throngs that gather at the house of Peter, the multitude of miracles. 2. Observe the Savior at rest in the darkness of night, rising to pray before the dawn, possibly praying to be saved from popularity, in lonely prayer in the morning twilight. 3. Note the eager search led by

Peter, their triumphant assurance of his popularity, all men seeking for him, his rejection of the popular breeze, and determination to go elsewhere. 4. Observe his missionary circuit and his work: (1) Preaching in the synagogues, (2) teaching daily, (3) healing the distressed and diseased or sin-laden. 5. Note the healing of the leper, his awful disease, a type of sin, unclean, banished from men. 6. Observe *how* he is healed: (1) He wants to be healed, (2) believes that Christ can heal him, (3) comes to Christ, (4) falls before him and implores mercy, (5) the Lord has compassion, (6) touches and heals. Thus every sinner by faith and coming to Christ can be healed of his sins. The lesson sets forth Christ as the great Healer. (1) He prepared for his great labors by solitary prayer (v. 35), as we need the more to commune with God, and get strength from heaven, the more we have to do. (2) He made his first missionary tour through Galilee (vs. 36-39); and on this tour (3) he healed a leper—the type of sin and its cure (vs. 40-45,) a most helpful illustration of the evil of sin, and of the way of salvation by going to Christ to be saved.

5. FORGIVENESS AND HEALING—2:1-12

TEXT 2:1-12

And when he entered again into Capernaum after some days, it was noised that he was in the house. And many were gathered together, so that there was no longer room for them, no, not even about the door: and he spake the word unto him. And they come, bringing unto him a man sick of the palsy, borne of four. And when they could not come nigh unto him for the crowd, they uncovered the roof where he was: and when they had broken it up, they let down the bed whereon the sick of the palsy lay. And Jesus seeing their faith saith unto the sick of the palsy, Son thy sins are forgiven. But there were certain of the scribes sitting there, and reasoning in their hearts, Why doth this man thus speak? he blasphemeth: who can forgive sins but one, even God? And straightway Jesus, perceiving in his spirit that they so reasoned within themselves, saith unto them, Why reason ye these things in your hearts? Whether is easier, to say to the sick of the palsy, Thy sins are forgiven; or to say, Arise, and take up thy bed, and walk? But that ye may know that the Son of man hath power on earth to forgive sins (he saith to the sick of the palsy), I say unto thee, Arise, take up thy bed, and go unto thy house. And he arose, and straightway took up the bed, and went forth before them all; insomuch that they were all amazed, and glorified God, saying, We never saw it on this fashion.

THOUGHT QUESTIONS 2:1-12

72. What had occurred between the healing of the leper and entering

back into Capernaum?

73. In which house in Capernaum was Jesus staying?
74. Why so much interest in the words of Jesus?
75. Was Jesus preaching to the people or merely conversing with them?
76. Why bring the palsied man to Jesus—why not just tell Jesus about him and let His power operate over the distance?
77. Wasn't it wrong to destroy property to see Jesus? Why didn't Jesus rebuke them?
78. Was there some connection between the sickness of the palsied man and sin in his past life? What?
79. Just what was involved in "speaking blasphemy"?
80. Why didn't Jesus heal the sickness first and then forgive sins?
81. This was the first step of our Lord toward Calvary—show how this was true.

COMMENT

TIME—May-June, A. D. 28. The paralytic was cured some days after the healing of the leper on Jesus' return from his first tour of Galilee. The calling of Matthew was not very long after. But Matthew's feast was probably several weeks later, in the autumn, A.D. 28, following Mark 5:21. See *Andrew's Life of Christ,* pp. 277-283.

PLACE—The paralytic was cured at Capernaum. Matthew's place for the receipt of custom was at Capernaum, probably, upon the Damascus road near its entrance into the city. The road from Damascus to the cities along the coast passed by "Jacob's Bridge" over the Jordan, and thence along the shore of the lake—*Andrews.* The feast of Matthew was also at Capernaum.

PARALLEL ACCOUNTS—The healing of the paralytic (Matt. 9:2-8; Luke 5:17-26).

LESSON OUTLINE—1. *Coming to Christ in Faith.* 2. *The Accusation of the Scribes.* 3. *The Power of the Son of Man.*

LESSON ANALYSIS

I. COMING TO CHRIST IN FAITH. Vs. 1-4.
   1. The Lord Preaching in Capernaum. Mark 2:2; Luke 5:17.
   2. The Palsied Man Brought. Mark 2:3; Matt. 9-2; Luke 5:18.
   3. Faith Overcomes Difficulties. Mark 2:4; Luke 5:19.

II. THE ACCUSATION OF THE SCRIBES. Vs. 5-9.
   1. Sins Forgiven. Mark 2:5; Matt. 9:2; Luke 5:20.
   2. The Charge of Blasphemy. Mark 2:7; Matt. 9.3; Luke 5:21.
   3. The Lord's Reply. Mark 2:8, 9; Matt. 9:4, 5; Luke 5:22, 23.

III. THE POWER OF THE SON OF MAN. Vs. 10-12.

1. Power to Forgive Sins Asserted. Mark 2:10; Matt. 9:6; Luke 5:24.
2. The Power to Forgive Sins Demonstrated. Mark 2:11, 12; Matt. 9:6; Luke 5:25.

INTRODUCTION

The return to Capernaum and the healing of the paralytic followed, after a short period, the history of which is not recorded, the healing of the leper. The incident narrated in this text occurred at the close of our Lord's first missionary circuit of Galilee. His labors were now devoted to this northern district of Palestine, where prejudices and bigotry were not so intense as in Judea. He was now at the most popular period of his earthly ministry. He had shown his divine power by many miracles, healing the nobleman's son at Capernaum, bringing myriads of fish to the disciples' net on the Sea of Tiberias, and restoring the demoniac in the synagogue. Though rejected at Nazareth, he was received with honor at Capernaum. His teachings, whether on the hill top, or beside the lake, or in the house of worship, were heard by wondering throngs, and his steps throughout Galilee were attended by multitudes, drawn by the fame of his miracles and the fascination of his words. The Pharisees and leaders, though suspicious, were not yet openly his enemies, and the unthinking masses followed him with blind expectation of a new Judean kingdom which was to transform the Romans at once from masters to slaves, and bend the world in homage. Just at this hour occurred two significant miracles: the one silently asserting Jesus as superior to all ceremonial regulations, the other calmly claiming for him the divine prerogative of forgiving sin.

EXPLANATORY NOTES

I. COMING TO CHRIST IN FAITH—1. *Again he entered Capernaum.* Matthew says, "he entered his own city," the city he made his home, in which some have supposed that his mother now dwelt. It was "after days," some time having been occupied in his teaching and healing tour of Galilee. The excitement that followed his displays of divine power, and especially the healing of the leper, had rendered seclusion necessary until it should subside and he had remained "without in desert places" for a time. He evidently entered Capernaum quietly, but the tidings soon spread that he was in the house, probably either the home occupied by his mother and brethren, or the home of Peter, where we recently found him. His own house, as far as he had one, was now in Capernaum (Matt. 4:13).

2. *Many were gathered together.* Luke (5:17) says, there were present Pharisees and doctors of the law from Galilee, Judea and Jerusalem.

They had evidently gathered by a concerted arrangement to examine into the claims of a teacher who was creating so profound a sensation, and were moved by hostile purposes. This is the first time the antagonism of these classes shows itself. Hence, as he taught the throng that crowded the house, they sat by as spectators, censors, and spies, to pick up something on which to ground a reproach or accusation. How many are there in the midst of our assemblies where the gospel is preached that do not *sit under* the word, but *sit by!* It is to them as a tale that is told them, not as a message that is sent them; they are willing that we should preach before them, not that we should preach to them. *And he* preached the word to them. The simple language of Mark outlines the picture so that we can almost see the eager throngs filling the house, crowding around the door on the outside until there was no more entrance, stretching their heads over each other in order to see and hear, and the Lord, without any formality, declaring the word of the kingdom. *Preached.* It is not the same Greek word that is found in Mark 1:39. That means to announce as a herald; thus simply to speak, as rendered in the Revision. The Savior was in a private house, and sat *talking* to the people. Such is the import of the term. It is almost always rendered *speak* in the Common Version, sometimes *talk* (or *say* or *utter*); never *preach,* except here and in four or five places in the Acts of the Apostles, and in all of these it would be better to render it *speak.*

3. *They come . . . bringing one sick of the palsy.* Four persons bear the invalid, who was perfectly helpless, to the house while Christ was engaged in teaching. Albert Barnes, in his notes (Matt. 4:24), classifies the infirmities which, in the New Testament, are included under the general name of palsy: (1) The paralytic shock affecting the whole body; (2) a stroke affecting only one side, or a part of the body; (3) paraplegy, affecting all the system below the neck; (4) catalepsy, caused by a contraction of the muscles in the whole or a part of the body (5) the cramps, a fearful and common malady. The disease, in its worst forms, was incurable. *Borne of four.* Borne on his pallet or bed, with one person at each corner.

4. *Could not come nigh unto him for the press.* The crowd. Here, then, we have a reason, as one has observed, why it was "expedient that our Lord should depart," and that "the Comforter should come." The throng of multitudes crowding after the bodily presence of Christ was a hinderance to the gospel; while many could not "get at him by reason of the press," and even some, for a season, might go "empty away." His body was necessarily limited by space, but the spirit of the Lord is in all places. *Uncovered the roof.* Unable to enter the house, they climbed to its roof, either by an outside staircase, a ladder, or from the roof of an adjoining

house. The following from *Thompson* will make the account easily understood: "The houses of Capernaum, as is evident from the ruins, were like those of modern villages in this same region, very low, with flat roofs reached by a stairway from the yard or court. The roof is only a few feet high, and by stooping down and holding the corner of the couch, merely a thickly-padded quilt, as at present in this region, they could let down the sick man without any apparatus of ropes or cords to assist them. I have often seen it done, and done it myself, to houses in Lebanon, but there is always more dust than is agreeable. The materials now employed for roofs are beams about three feet apart, across which short sticks are arranged close together and covered with thickly-matted thorn-bush, called *bellan.* Over this is spread a coat of stiff mortar, and then comes the marl, or earth, which makes the roof. Now, it is easy to remove any part of this without injuring the rest. No objection, therefore, would be made on this account by the owners of the house. They had merely to scrape back the earth from a portion of the roof over the *lewan,* take up the thorns and short sticks, and let down the couch between the beams at the very feet of Jesus. The end achieved, they could easily restore the roof as it was before." *The bed.* This was a small, low couch or bed of the commonest description, such as was used by poor people, having a mere network of cords stretched over the frame to support the mattress. Sometimes merely a sheepskin, used for the service of the sick, or as a camp-bed.

II. THE ACCUSATION OF THE SCRIBES—5. *When Jesus saw their faith.* Their faith was shown by their action. A living faith is always a power that moves. It is not a strong conviction of any docrine *about* Christ, but a strong trust *in* Christ. These men had no theories about Jesus, but had confidence in him as the great Healer and sought to come to him *Matthew Henry* quaintly says: "When the centurion and the woman of Canaan were in no care at all to bring the patients they interceded for into Christ's presence, but believed that he could cure them at a distance, he commended their faith. But though in these there seemed to be a different notion of the thing, and an apprehension that it was requisite the patient should be brought into his presence, yet he did not censure and condemn their weakness, did not ask them, 'Why do you give this disturbance to the assembly? Are you indeed under such a degree of infidelity as to think I could not have cured him though he had had been out of doors?' But he made the best of it; and even in this he saw their faith. It is a comfort to us that we serve a Master that is willing to make the best of us." The palsied man had faith as well as his bearers, for they would not bring him against his will. *Thy sins be forgiven thee.* Matthew says, "Be of good cheer," etc. The Jews held that all disease was a punishment for sin (John 9:2), and in a deeper sense, all evil of every kind is the fruit of sin. Nor is it unlikely that in this case the paralysis was really the punishment of his special sins (probably of sensuality). Accordingly, he first of all promises forgiveness, as being the moral condition necessary to the healing of the body; and then, having by forgiveness removed the hinderance, he proceeds to impart that healing itself by an exercise of his supernatural power.

6. *Certain of the scribes.* The doctors of the law that Luke says had come from Judea and Jerusalem. They had come to criticise and condemn, and hence had eyes and ears open to discover a fault. Not long before Jesus had startled the theologians at Jerusalem when he attended the passover, and hearing of his wonderful popularity in Galilee they had come to scent out heresy. *Reasoning in their hearts.* Matthew says, "within themselves". They did not speak out, but Christ read their hearts.

7. *Why doth this man thus speak?* Another reading adopted by the revisers and the critical editors. *Tischendorf, Hort* and *Westcott* is even more forcible: "Why doth this man speak thus? He blasphemeth." *Speak blasphemies.* "Blasphemy", says George Mackenzie, in his *Laws and Customs of Scotland in Matters Criminal* (Tit. iii., 1), "is called in law, *divine lese majesty or treason;* and it is committed either (1) by denying that of God which belongs to him as one of his attributes, or (2) by attributing to him that which is absurd and inconsistent with his divine nature," or, as it may be added (3), by assuming one's self, or ascribing to others, what is an incommunicable property or prerogative of God. It is with a reference to this third form of the offense that the word is used in the passage before us. *Who can forgive sins but God only?* Christ had not yet said that he forgave sins; only that his sins were forgiven. Nor could he claim to forgive sins, were he only a man, without blasphemy, and when he asserts the power to forgive sins he declares that he is the Son of God. Says *Geikie*: "His claim of this divine power was the turning point in the life of Christ, for the accusation of blasphemy, muttered in the hearts of the rabbis present, was the beginning of a process that ended after a time on Calvary, and he knew it."

9. *Whether is it easier to say, . . . Thy sins be forgiven thee.* To say, "Thy sins be forgiven thee," was easy, for no visible result could test the saying. To say, "Take up thy bed and walk," was not apparently so easy, for failure would cover with confusion. He said the last, leaving the inference—If I can do the most difficult, then, of course, I can do the easier. Here we have the true character of a miracle; it is the outward manifestation of the power of God, in order that we may believe in the power of God in things that are invisible.—*F. W. Robertson.* As much as

the soul excels the body does the forgiveness of sin rise above the cure of bodily sickness. But Christ adapts his mode of speech to their capacities, who in their carnal minds felt more influence by outward signs than by the whole putting forth of his spiritual power as availing to eternal life. —*Calvin.*

III. THE POWER OF THE SON OF MAN.—10. *That ye may know.* By doing that which is capable of being put to proof, I will vindicate my right and power to do that which in its very nature is incapable of being proved. By these visible tides of God's grace I will give you to know in what direction the great under-currents of his love are setting, and that both are obedient to my word. *The Son of man* cannot simply mean *a man*, or a mere man, for this would be untrue in fact, since the powers in question do not belong to men as such, nor could any reason be assigned for this circuitous expression of so simple an idea. The true sense is determined by Daniel 7:13, where the phrase is confessedly applied to the Messiah, as a partaker of our nature, a description which itself implies a higher nature, or, in other words, that he is called the Son of man because he is the Son of God. This official application of the term accounts for the remarkable and interesting fact that it is never used by any other person in the gospel, nor of Christ by any but himself. *Hath power on earth to forgive sins.* "Authority" is a better rendering than "power," and it is so given by the American Revision Committee. He had "authority" from the Father who had sent him, and who had committed judgment to his hands on earth. Not merely authority while on the earth to forgive sins, nor authority to forgive sins committed on the earth, but authority to exercise the function of forgiveness of sins upon the earth; that is, that ye may know that this is the Messiah's earthly mission. Bengel finely remarks: "This saying savors of heavenly origin." The Son of man, as God manifest in man's flesh, has on man's earth that power which in its fountain and essence belongs to God in heaven.—*Alford.* Sins are against God, and therefore only God can forgive them; for in the nature of things only he can forgive against whom the offense has been committed.

11. *Arise, take up thy bed.* A light mattress. Other men brought him on the bed; he can now carry himself away, bed and all. Christ's argument here affords a fair test of all priestly claims to absolve from sin. If the priest has power to remit the eternal punishment of sin, he should be able, certainly, to remit the physical and temporal punishment of sin. This Christ did; this the priest does not, and cannot do. Any popish priest can say, "Thy sins be forgiven thee," and the credulous may believe that a miracle of pardon is performed; but it is not quite so easy to perform the bodily miracle.

12. *Insomuch that they were all amazed.* Amazed at the high claims of Jesus and at the demonstration that his claims were well founded. The scribes had whispered in their hearts the charge of blasphemy, but the people saw a manifestation of divine power and glorified God, because, as Luke says, "God had given such power to men." They looked upon Jesus, not as Divine, but as the commissioned agent of the Divine will.

IV. POWER TO FORGIVE SINS.—This whole incident illustrates: (1) The difference between the spiritual authority of Christ and that of his apostles, none of whom assumed to forgive sins. See Acts 8:22-24. (2) It affords a test for all claims of priests or bishops to pardon sin, or to officially pronounce the absolution of sin. If they possessed the power to absolve from sin they should be able, like Christ, to relieve from the temporal consequences of sin. Romish priests claim a prerogative that was never claimed by Peter or the other apostles, which belongs to the Lord alone, and which it is not only presumption but blasphemy for any man or set of men to claim who cannot manifest divine credentials to confirm their claims.

FACT QUESTIONS 2:1-12

86. When did the healing of the paralytic occur?
87. What was the incident immediately before this? The one soon after?
88. Where was this incident in relation to His first circuit of Galilee?
89. Mention two miracles which promoted the popularity of Jesus. Where had He been rejected?
90. What evidence do we have that the mother of Jesus and His brothers lived in Capernaum?
91. Who came to the house from Judea and Jerusalem? Cf. Luke 5:17. Why were they there?
92. Mark 1:39 and 2:2 both speak of the preaching of Jesus but they use two different words—what are they?
93. Name three infirmities classified under the general heading of palsy.
94. Explain the reason why the crowd suggested the need for the comforter.
95. Discuss the procedure used in uncovering the roof. Was this neccessarily destructive?
96. How did Jesus "see" their faith?
97. Show how Jesus "made the best" out of the failure of the four.
98. In what way were the words of Jesus concerning the forgiveness of sins appropriate to the belief of the Jews? Cf. John 9:2.

99. Did Jesus intend to teach His deity by His actions and words with the palsied man? Why didn't the scribes believe Him?
100. Why use the word "easier" in reference to the forgiveness of sins?
101. Explain the true character of a miracle?
102. Read Daniel 7:13 and show its application in this connection.
103. "In the nature of things only he can forgive against whom the offense has been committed."—how had the palsied man sinned against Jesus?
104. What proof have we of the failure of present day priests to forgive sins?
105. Who was amazed? Who were incensed? Why?
106. This incident shows the difference between the spiritual authority of Christ and that of his apostles—in what manner?

SIDELIGHTS

MORAL PARALYSIS—In one of our city hospitals a young woman of beautiful face and form had lain motionless for many months. Except for the brightness of her face, and the action of the hands, her body was apparently dead. Yet she spoke with great confidence of her restoration to health at some future time, and was enthusiastic in planning good works then to be executed. A physician remarked that it was the saddest case he had ever witnessed. It was a paralysis, not of the flesh, but of the mind: it was a *moral paralysis.* The will itself had lost its power of action. She could plan for the future, but not *will* anything at the present moment. After a few months the inactivity bred fatal disorder and she passed away. This is a picture of the moral paralysis of many. They mean to be Christians at some time; they do not determine to do it *now.*—Anon.

LESSONS

1. Sin is like paralysis—a weakness and torpor of the conscience, and the will to do good.

2. It is our privilege to bring those to Christ who cannot or will not come of themselves.

3. Difficulties are in the way of the sinner's cure, to prove and strengthen faith. Faith will find or make a way to come to Christ.

4. Christ forgives and saves only on condition of faith; for the faith that loves and chooses God is the beginning of heavenly life in the soul. It is useless to forgive those who immediately plunge into sin again.

5. The first need of the soul is forgiveness; then follows the healing of the soul from its sinful nature.

6. Christ knows our inmost thoughts and motives—a terror to the bad, but a comfort to the good.

7. THE LESSON.—This may be regarded as an enacted parable of sin and redemption. The paralytic typifies the sinner by his original helplessness (Isaiah 40:30; John 6:44; 15:5), faith, by his earnestness to come to Christ in spite of obstacle (Ps. 25:15; 86:2, 7), a common Christian experience, by the delay he suffers between his repentance and faith, and his cure (James 5:7, 8) and the power of divine grace, in the ability to obey Christ's command, received in the very attempt to comply with it (Phil. 4:13).—*Abbott.*

POINTS FOR TEACHERS

1. Consider Christ's return, from whence, and to what place and how received. 2. Note the evidences of strong faith in the palsied man and his bearers. 3. Bring out the circumstances; Christ teaching in a house, crowds around, no way to reach him, the palsied man, helpless, brought on a couch by four men, no other way and they open the flat roof and let the sick man down to Christ. 4. Observe the language of Christ, the complaint of the scribes, and the answer of Christ. 5. Consider who forgives sins, blasphemy for a man to make such a claim, why Christ had power. 6. Point out how he demonstrated his power, as no pope or priest ever does. 7. Observe that we have in this lesson an "ENACTED PARABLE OF SIN AND REDEMPTION," together with Christ's example in dealing with sinners. (1) The paralytic—a type of sinners (vs. 1-3). (2) He is brought to Christ (vs. 3, 4), as we must bring sinners by our labors and our prayers. (3) He comes in faith and finds forgiveness (v. 5). (4) Forgiveness is proved and followed by healing (vs. 6-12), as renewed lives follow and prove the forgiveness of our sins. (5) Then sinners, even of the worst class, are called to be the disciples of Christ.

6. THE CALL OF MATTHEW AND HIS FEAST 2:13-17

TEXT 2:13-17

And he went forth again by the seaside; and all the multitude resorted unto him, and he taught them. And as he passed by, he saw Levi the son of Alphaeus sitting at the place of toll, and he saith unto him, Follow me. And he arose and followed him. And it came to pass, that he was sitting at meat in his house, and many publicans and sinners sat down with Jesus and his disciples: for there were many, and they followed him. And the scribes of the Pharisees, when they saw that he was eating with the sinners and publicans, said unto his disciples, He eateth and drinketh with publicans and sinners. And when Jesus heard it, he saith unto them, They that are whole have no need of a physician, but they that are sick: I came not to call the righteous, but sinners.

THOUGHT QUESTIONS 2:13-17

82. Why did Jesus do most of His teaching outside?

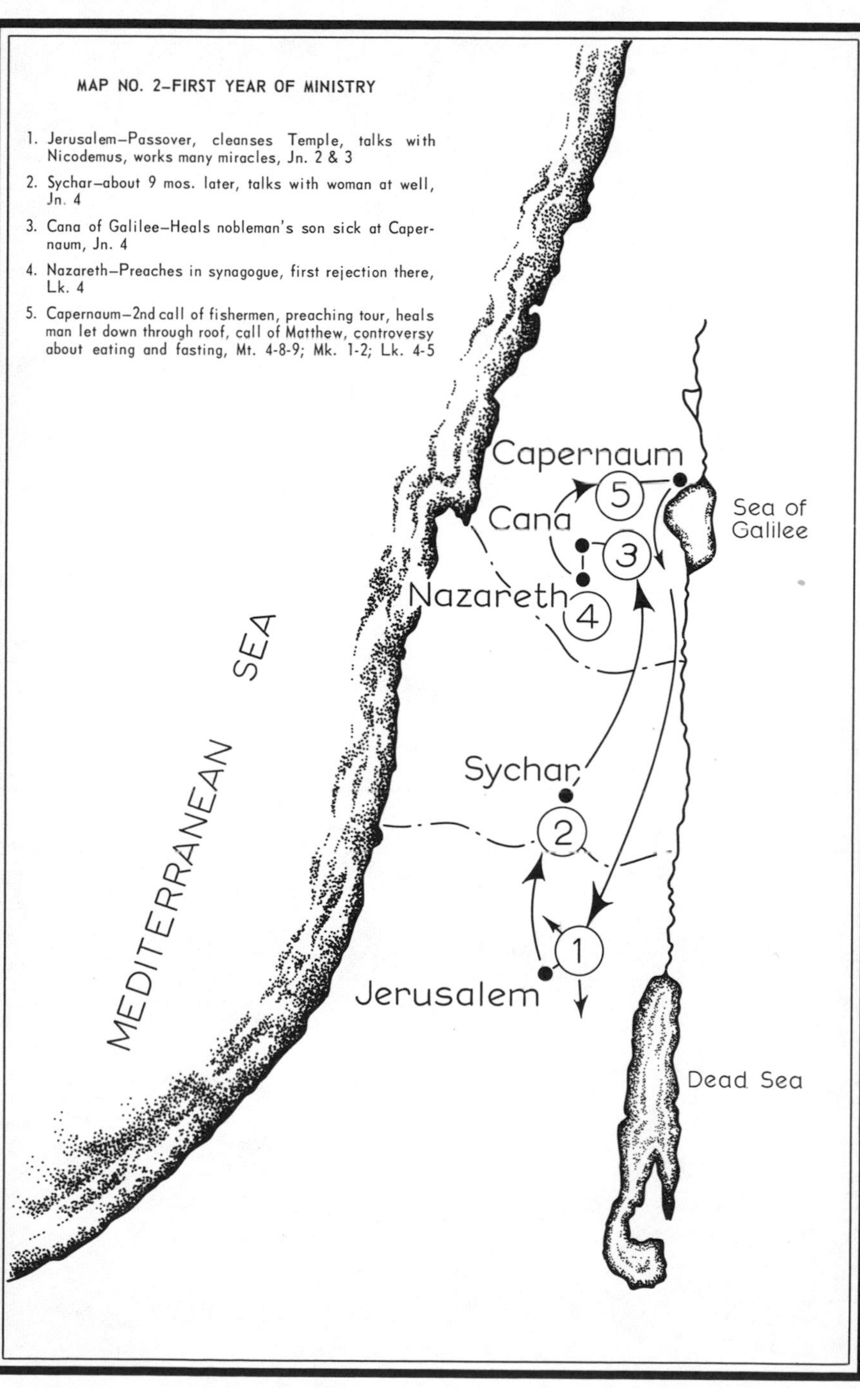

MAP NO. 2–FIRST YEAR OF MINISTRY
1. Jerusalem—Passover, cleanses Temple, talks with Nicodemus, works many miracles, Jn. 2 & 3
2. Sychar—about 9 mos. later, talks with woman at well, Jn. 4
3. Cana of Galilee—Heals nobleman's son sick at Capernaum, Jn. 4
4. Nazareth—Preaches in synagogue, first rejection there, Lk. 4
5. Capernaum—2nd call of fishermen, preaching tour, heals man let down through roof, call of Matthew, controversy about eating and fasting, Mt. 4-8-9; Mk. 1-2; Lk. 4-5
Capernaum
5
Cana
3
Nazareth
4
Sea of Galilee
MEDITERRANEAN SEA
Sychar
2
1
Jerusalem
Dead Sea

83. Isn't it rather strange to read of a tax collector working by the Sea of Galilee? Explain.
84. Was this the first meeting of Jesus with Matthew? How account for the immediate response?
85. Why did Jesus go to eat at the home of Matthew? Be specific.
86. Are we to conclude that the publicans and sinners were at the feast only because they followed Jesus?; or did they come by invitation?
87. What was wrong with eating and drinking with publicans and sinners?
88. Why ask the disciples—why not ask Jesus?
89. In the answer of Jesus was He being ironical in His reference to the well and the sick?

COMMENT 2:13-17

TIME—Early Summer A.D. 28.

PLACE—Near the northern shore of Galilee—on the road from Damascus as it entered Capernaum.

PARALLEL ACCOUNTS—Matt. 9:9; Luke 5:27, 28.

OUTLINE—1. Teaching the multitude by the seaside, vs. 13. 2. Matthew called from his work to follow Jesus, vs. 14. 3. The feast in the home of Levi, v. 15. 4. The criticism of eating with sinners; the answer of Jesus, v. 16, 17.

ANALYSIS

I. TEACHING THE MULTITUDE BY THE SEASIDE, V. 13.
   1. The place where He had taught before.
   2. A great crowd present because of previous miracles.

II. MATTHEW CALLED FROM HIS WORK TO FOLLOW JESUS. VS 14-17
   1. The place of toll was noticed by our Lord.
   2. Immediate response.

EXPLANATORY NOTES

I. TEACHING THE MULTITUDES BY THE SEASIDE, V. 13.

13. *By the seaside.* Our Lord often is found in the open air preaching to the multitudes—especially was this true beside the Sea of Galilee. There were many villages from which came the many people to hear Him.

II. MATTHEW CALLED FROM HIS WORK TO FOLLOW JESUS. VS. 14-17

14. *He saw Levi*—There were many who fished in the lake—There were many more who came in and out of the city—from all of these would Levi collect taxes. Jesus had already healed one leper—he is about to heal another—a social leper of the society of His day. Here was a Jew hired to collect taxes of his own people for the despised Romans. If such tax collectors were paid a common wage for their work it would have been scorned as an occupation—but when all knew they assessed beyond

the amount prescribed and kept the overcharge for themselves it became a position of utter contempt. "By Mark alone is he called the son of Alphaeus. There is no reason to suppose that this was any other Alphaeus than the one referred to in all the lists of the apostles where we have "James, the son of Alphaeus." In three of the lists he stands next to Matthew and Thomas. Matthew and James are thus presumably brothers; and if, as is almost certain, Thomas was the twin brother of Matthew, Alphaeus was the father of three of the twelve. If the word "brother" is rightly supplied before "of James" in Luke 6:16 ("Judas the brother of James"), he may have been the father of four."

We have no record of a previous acquaintance of Jesus on the part of Levi. We can assume the following: (1) He could have heard the preaching of vs. 13. (2) One of his brothers could have introduced Jesus to him. (3) He could have been among the other publicans who were baptized by John (Luke 3:12, 13: 7:29). (4) Peter said the apostles were followers of Jesus from the baptism—or baptizing of John (Acts 1:21,22).

We must conclude that when the words of Jesus *Follow Me* fell on his heart it was one prepared to receive them. Here was a hungry soul in the most unlikely of circumstances—but then our Lord found several of these—we think immediately of the woman at the well (John 4:7-38).

15. *Jesus* (he) *sat at meat in his house*—Luke tells us the feast was prepared by Matthew for Jesus (Luke 5:29). We are not to conclude this event happened immediately after the calling of Levi—no time element is indicated. We ought to mark the difference in the readings of the King James Version and the American Standard. The name "Jesus" is supplied by the translators—it is much more natural to refer this to Levi ——who here in his own house is reclining at the table in the presence of Jesus and many others. Evidently Matthew wanted all publicans to hear and see what he had heard and seen. The publicans were at the feast by invitation as were undoubtedly the disciples of Jesus.

16. *The scribes and Pharisees*—a better translation would read "the scribes of the Pharisees." "This is the first mention of the Pharisees in Mark's Gospel. They were a sect of separatists. The group began in the Maccabean period, in the second century before Christ. The Pharisees were trying to withstand the rising tide of Hellenism in Palestine. They stood strongly for close adherence to the law, including strict observance of all the ceremonial requirements. But like all such groups, the sect became more and more legalistic in its emphasis." (Earle) These scribes stood outside the house to ask this question of the disciples.

17. *They that are whole* (strong). This was used ironically by Jesus to describe the Pharisees' attitude about himself—since he felt self suffi-

cient—he need not concern himself over the work of the great physician.

They that are sick—surely even at the risk of contagion the physician must minister to the sick. If the Pharisees felt these publicans and sinners so much in need they could not object if someone attempted to help them.

not to call the righteous but sinners. Jesus plainly states His purpose—His work, His concern would be among sinners—His call—His healing would be for them—if this offended the Pharisees so be it!

FACT QUESTIONS 2:13-17

107. Who would hear Jesus by the Sea of Galilee i. e. besides a few fishermen?
108. Why did Levi have his place of toll by the Seaside? Why was he hated?
109. Who were the brothers of Matthew?
110. What are the possibilities of previous contact of Matthew with Jesus?
111. Why was Levi so ready to follow?
112. Who prepared the feast—in whose house?
113. Why did the Pharisees criticize Him?
114. How did Jesus attempt to show the Pharisees their sin?
115. Did Jesus infer there were some men who could not be helped?

7. DISPUTE ABOUT FASTING 2:18-22.

TEXT: 2:18-22

And John's disciples and the Pharisees were fasting: and they come and say unto him, Why do John's disciples and the disciples of the Pharisees fast, but thy disciples fast not? And Jesus said unto them, Can the sons of the bride-chamber fast, while the bridegroom is with them? as long as they have the bridegroom with them, they cannot fast. But the days will come, when the bridegroom shall be taken away from them, and then will they fast in that day. No man seweth a piece of undressed cloth on an old garment: else that which should fill it up taketh from it, the new from the old and a worse rent is made. And no man putteth new wine into old wine-skins: else the wine will burst the skins, and the wine perisheth, and the skins: but they put new wine into fresh wineskins."

THOUGHT QUESTIONS 2:18-22

90. Was there something wrong about the fasting of John's disciples or of the fasting of the Pharisees? Why did they fast?
91. Was Jesus saying that He and His disciples were as happy as a bridal party? If not what did He say in vs. 19?
92. Are we living in the day when the bridegroom has been taken away? If so are we to fast? If so why do we fail to do it? Cf. Acts 13:1, 2.
93. What is represented by the undressed cloth in the figure of speech Jesus used? What was the old garment?

94. What worse rent would be made? What was the point of the parable?
95. Was the point the same in the figure of new and old wine skins?

COMMENT

TIME—(Same as the call of Levi—Early Summer A.D. 28.)

PLACE—Many feel this conversation took place around the table in Matthew's house.

PARALLEL ACCOUNTS—Matt. 9:14-17; Luke 5:33-39.

OUTLINE—1. The question of John's disciples, v. 18. 2. The answer of the bridegroom, vs. 19, 20. 3. The answer of the garment, v. 21. 4. The answer of the wine skins, v. 22.

ANALYSIS

I. THE QUESTION OF JOHN'S DISCIPLES, 18.
   1. Asked during a fast by John's disciples and the Pharisees.
   2. Why do John's disciples fast and the disciples of Christ fail to fast?

II. THE ANSWER OF THE BRIDEGROOM, 19, 20.
   1. The joy of the bridal party prevents fasting.
   2. When the bridegroom is gone there will be fasting.

III. THE ANSWER OF THE GARMENT, 21
   1. New cloth cannot patch old clothes.
   2. The results prevent such action.

IV. THE ANSWER OF THE WINE SKINS, 22.
   1. New wine cannot go in old skins.
   2. Results prevent such action.

EXPLANATORY NOTES

I. THE QUESTION OF JOHN'S DISCIPLES, 18.

18. *John's disciples and the Pharisees were fasting.* Perhaps they chose the very time of the feast for a fast. This would indeed produce a contrast and conflict. We believe John's disciples were sincere in their questions and offered no criticism. We could not say the same of the disciples of the Pharisees. The law of God prescribed only one fast—the great Day of atonement—(Lev. 23:27). During the captivity of the Jewish nation fasting was practiced by many. Fasting undoubtedly was associated with the repentance John preached.

II. THE ANSWER OF THE BRIDEGROOM, 19, 20.

19. *Sons of the bride-chamber.* What a beautiful way to describe the attitude of our Lord for His work! Jesus was as happy as a bridegroom—His disciples shared His joy. How could they be sad or fast when they had just made the greatest discovery in time and eternity? It was time to rejoice, they had found the Messiah!

20. *Then they will fast in that day.* We now live in that day. We look for the coming of the bridegroom for His bride—there are many oc-

casions when we need to fast. The church in Antioch fasted (Cf. Acts 13:1, 2). This is not a legal requirement but it can be a wonderful spiritual exercise. There are mental, emotional, physical and spiritual benefits for the sons of the bride-chamber who will commit themselves to a period of prayer and fasting. The immediate reference here is probably to His crucifixion and the sorrow felt at that time. It can have a more far-reaching application as we have indicated.

III. THE ANSWER OF THE GARMENT, VS. 21

21. . . . *a piece of undressed cloth or an old garment.* This is an answer to question about fasting. Jesus is saying His mission is entirely new. It will not be added to that of the law as reflected so poorly through the Pharisees, nor even a part of the work of John—which was only a preparation for the new kingdom. The Messiah was not sent to patch up the old but to offer an entirely new garment. "The garment of praise for the worn-out garment of law."

IV. THE ANSWER OF THE WINE SKINS, VS. 22

22. *New wine in old wine-skins*—This is a Hebrewistic manner of presenting parables—two with the same point for emphasis. "The point in the use of the 'parables' is that the using of the ill-chosen patch and the unsuitable bottles defeats the purpose of him who resorts to it, and the purpose is defeated because of an unwise uniting of the new with the old. The new is the living, expanding, divinely-vigorous kingdom of Christ; the old is that which pertains to the Jewish dispensation, which was decaying and ready to vanish away (Heb. 8:13)" (W. N. Clarke)

FACT QUESTIONS 2:18-22

116. At what time and place did this question of fasting occur?
117. What was the probable motive behind the question?
118. Why call the disciples of Jesus "sons of the bride-chamber?"
119. In what day did Jesus promise that His followers would fast?
120. What is represented by the piece of undressed cloth? What is the garment?
121. What is represented by the new wine?

SIDELIGHTS

"Vers. 13-22.—Levi's feast: the moral questions it occasioned. 1. Vers. 13-17. *Eating with publicans and sinners.* In calling Matthew (Levi) from the receipt of custom, our Saviour made him relinquish all his old pursuits and companions, and conferred upon him an unexpected honour. The feast given by him was, therefore, partly a farewell, partly a celebration. In overstepping the boundary line of Jewish religious and social etiquette, the Lord performed an act of great significance, which was sure to call forth remark.

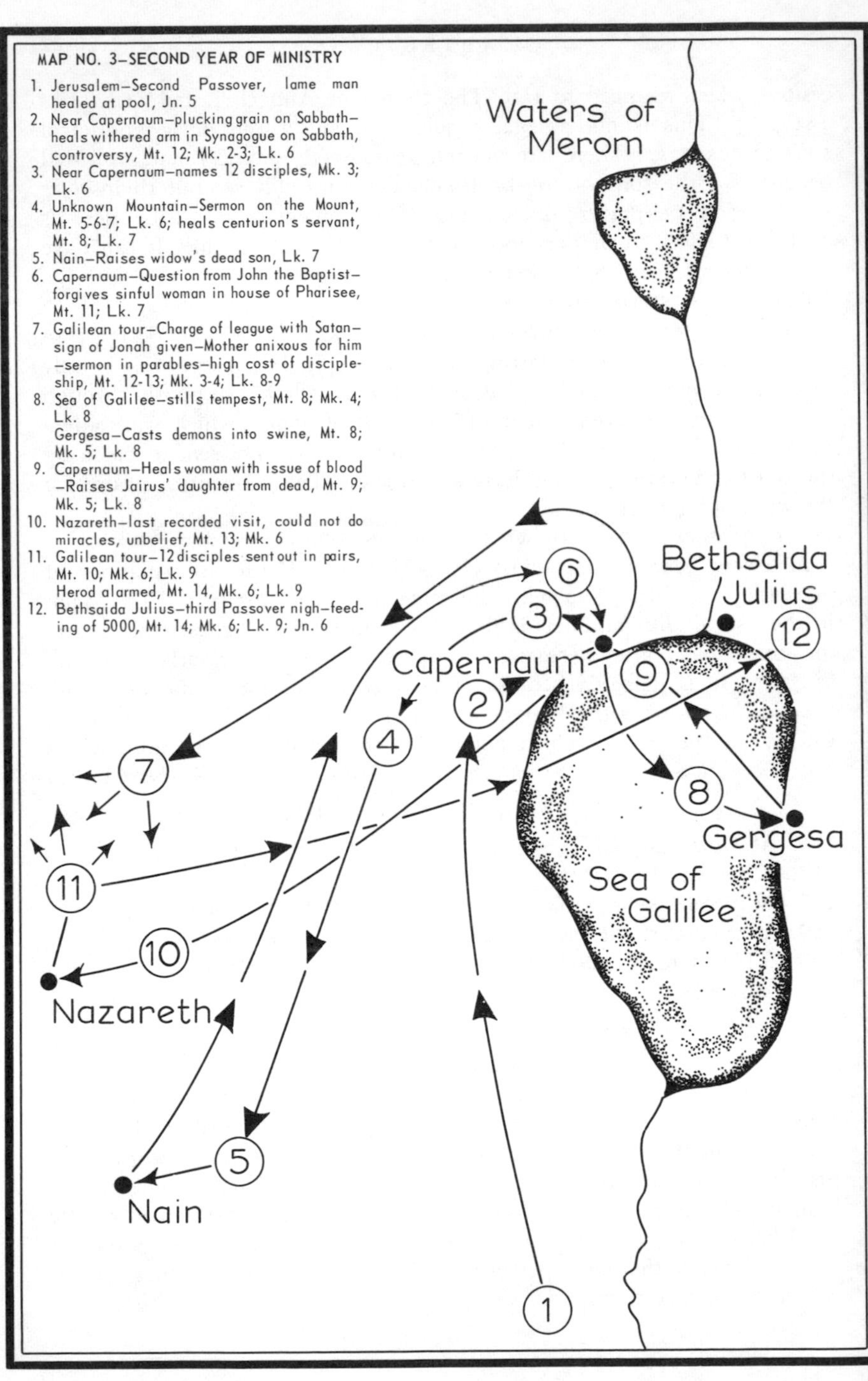
MAP NO. 3–SECOND YEAR OF MINISTRY
1. Jerusalem–Second Passover, lame man healed at pool, Jn. 5
2. Near Capernaum–plucking grain on Sabbath–heals withered arm in Synagogue on Sabbath, controversy, Mt. 12; Mk. 2-3; Lk. 6
3. Near Capernaum–names 12 disciples, Mk. 3; Lk. 6
4. Unknown Mountain–Sermon on the Mount, Mt. 5-6-7; Lk. 6; heals centurion's servant, Mt. 8; Lk. 7
5. Nain–Raises widow's dead son, Lk. 7
6. Capernaum–Question from John the Baptist–forgives sinful woman in house of Pharisee, Mt. 11; Lk. 7
7. Galilean tour–Charge of league with Satan–sign of Jonah given–Mother anixous for him–sermon in parables–high cost of discipleship, Mt. 12-13; Mk. 3-4; Lk. 8-9
8. Sea of Galilee–stills tempest, Mt. 8; Mk. 4; Lk. 8
Gergesa–Casts demons into swine, Mt. 8; Mk. 5; Lk. 8
9. Capernaum–Heals woman with issue of blood–Raises Jairus' daughter from dead, Mt. 9; Mk. 5; Lk. 8
10. Nazareth–last recorded visit, could not do miracles, unbelief, Mt. 13; Mk. 6
11. Galilean tour–12 disciples sent out in pairs, Mt. 10; Mk. 6; Lk. 9
Herod alarmed, Mt. 14, Mk. 6; Lk. 9
12. Bethsaida Julius–third Passover nigh–feeding of 5000, Mt. 14; Mk. 6; Lk. 9; Jn. 6
Waters of Merom
Bethsaida Julius
Capernaum
Gergesa
Sea of Galilee
Nazareth
Nain
1
2
3
4
5
6
7
8
9
10
11
12

I. *Superficial knowledge, when linked with malice, will put the worst construction upon the best actions.* Conventional morality was invoked to condemn Christ in mingling with the publicans. No trouble was taken to ascertain the true character of the feast. By their criticism the Pharisees exposed their own hollowness and unspirituality. They condemned themselves in seeking to condemn Christ. For such judgements men are responsible. The greatest care and most spiritual view should be taken ere judgement is passed upon the actions of others, especially when their character is known to be good.

II. *It is the motive which is the true key to the nature of actions.* 1. This applies absolutely in the case of actions in themselves indifferent, or only conventionally forbidden; but in all actions it is an indispensable canon of ultimate judgment. Even where the external nature of an action is unmistakable, the utmost care should be taken in forming an opinion. Absolute and unqualified judgment is for God alone. 2. When challenged for our conduct it is well to explain the principle upon which we act. Christ at once makes known his motives, and with no anger. Yet in so doing he judged his accusers. They pretended to be whole, and so could not object to him doing good to those who required his aid. Why were they dissatisfied, if not from secret disquietude with their own condition and attitude? Irony proceeding fromdeepest spiritual discernment!

III. *The holiest sought out and companied with sinners that He might make them holy.* "It is only by sympathy, and by appeals to their highest nature, that sinful men can be won to God."—(Muir)

LESSONS

1. Jesus was first, last, and always a teacher. No occasion went by unimproved for teaching.
2. If we do not speak to all we meet about Christ how shall we discover the hungry hearts like Levi?
3. Could we have dinners for sinners and introduce Jesus to them at the meal? It has been done with good success.
4. We should not be surprised at criticism—much of it unfounded—this is part of the price of progress.
5. How glad we should be to take the particular prescription the Great physician gives for us.
6. We should be as happy in our labors for Christ as a bride and groom on their honeymoon.

POINTS FOR TEACHERS
The Calling of Matthew

(A wonderful lesson for every teacher—)

We know three things about him:

(1) He was a Hebrew.
  a. Justifiable pride.
  b. Understandable narrowness.

(2) He was a publican.
  a. A consciousness of an authority under which he served.
  b. Responsible for accuracy in keeping of records.

(3) A profoundly religious man.
  a. His remarkable familiarity with the Scriptures of the Hebrew people. No less than 99 references in his gospel.
  b. He applied his knowledge.

How our Lord dealt with this man:

1. Found him in the *midst of work.*
   a. "All the brooding of his mind lay behind the outward activity of the tax collector."
   b. Perhaps he knew very much about Jesus since his place of work was at Capernaum.
   c. The decisive moment—the command of Jesus.
2. Jesus asked for *submission.*
3. He promised *fellowship.*
4. He called Matthew into an *enterprise.*

The results are self-evident in the gospel he wrote. (G. Campbell Morgan)

8. THE SABBATH DISPUTE 2:23—3:6
a. Eating on the Sabbath. 2:23-28

TEXT 2:23-28

And it came to pass, that he was going on the Sabbath day through the cornfields; and his disciples began, as they went, to pluck the ears of corn. And the Pharisees said unto him, Behold, why do they on the sabbath day that which is not lawful? And he said unto them, Did ye never read what David did, when he had need and was an hungered, he and they that were with him? How he entered into the house of God when Abiathar was high priest, and did eat the shew-bread, which it is not lawful to eat save for the priests, and gave also to them that were with him? And he said unto them. The sabbath was made for man, and not man for the sabbath: so that the Son of man is lord even of the sabbath."

THOUGHT QUESTIONS 2:23-28

96. To where were Jesus and His disciples going as they went through the grain fields?
97. Why were his disciples plucking the ears of grain? Wasn't this stealing?
98. Of what did the Pharisees accuse the disciples?
99. How could Jesus use the example of David when David lied to the priest in getting the shewbread?
100. In what sense was the sabbath made for man?
101. Is Jesus saying the Sabbath law was subject to man not man to the Sabbath law? Explain.
102. In what sense is the Son of man Lord of the Sabbath?
103. Wouldn't this arouse anger in the hearts of the Pharisees and therefore be wrong?

COMMENT 2:23-28

TIME—Early summer of A.D. 28.

PLACE—In a grain field near Capernaum.

PARALLEL ACCOUNTS—Matt. 12:1-8; Luke 6:1-5.

OUTLINE—1. Walking on the sabbath, 23. 2. The criticism of the Pharisees, 24. 3. Jesus' answer, 25, 26. 4. The application, 27, 28.

ANALYSIS 2:23-28

I. WALKING ON THE SABBATH 23
   1. Through the grain-fields with His disciples.
   2. As they went the disciples plucked the grain and ate it.

II. THE CRITICISM OF THE PHARISEES. 24.
   1. Careful to watch for mistakes.
   2. Objected to harvesting grain on the sabbath.

III. JESUS' ANSWER. 25, 26.
   1. They were unaware of the record and meaning of the scripture.
   2. David's exception would surely allow for theirs.

IV. THE APPLICATION. 27, 28.
   1. The true purpose of the sabbath.
   2. The claim to Divine prerogative.

EXPLANATORY NOTES

I. WALKING ON THE SABBATH. 23.

23. . . . *on the sabbath . . . his disciples began to pluck the ears.* Matthew mentions the hunger of the disciples as the cause for plucking the grain. Both Jesus and His disciples had been so pressed with work that they had not time for eating. Deut. 23:25 makes provision for the poor and permits eating a few ears from the neighbor's field. We do not know if this was a wheat field or a barley field.

II. THE CRITICISM OF THE PHARISEES. 24.

24. . . . *why do they on the sabbath day that which is not lawful?* The Pharisees were accusing the disciples of working on the sabbath—actually of harvesting on the sabbath. The law was Exodus 20:10. The infraction of the law was a matter of legalistic interpretation.

III. JESUS' ANSWER. 25, 26.

25, 26. "The reply, as given by all three evangelists, cites a violation on the ground of necessity, and one in which the necessity, as now, is that of hunger. The sanctity is not that of the Sabbath alone, but also that of the shew-bread in the tabernacle. The reference is to 1 Sam. 21:1-6: "In the days of Abiathar, the high priest;" the mention of the name is peculiar to Mark, and is not without difficulty. The high priest who is mentioned in the original narrative is not Abiathar, but Ahimelech, his father. Abiathar succeeded his father in office not long after, and was high priest during David's reign; so that his name is constantly associated with that of David in the history. Various attempts have been made to reconcile the difference, some supposing that Abiathar was already assistant to his father at the time of David's visit and was present when he came, although this can be nothing but conjecture; others, that our Lord or Mark was content with mentioning the name of the chief high priest of David's time, and the one that was chiefly associated with David's name, which is the same as to say that absolute accuracy was not aimed at; others, that the name of Abiathar stands in the text of Mark as the result of a copyist's error. The law of the shew-bread is given at Lev. 24:5-9. Our Lord's argument is again, as so often, an *argumentum ad hominem*—an appeal to the Pharisees on their own ground. The visit of David to the tabernacle was on the Sabbath, for the previous week's shew-bread was just being changed for the fresh, and this was done on the Sabbath (1 Sam. 21:6 with Lev. 24:8). So David violated the sanctity of the Sabbath (if the Pharisees were right), and at the same time the law that gave the sacred bread to the priests alone. Here was a double violation on the ground of necessity, and the Scriptures nowhere condemned it; nor would the Pharisees really condemn it. David was no Sabbath-breaker, as they all knew; neither were his disciples Sabbath-breakers for gathering and eating the ears of grain. In Matthew a second illustration is added—of the priests laboring in the temple on the Sabbath without sin; also a second citation of the Scripture quoted in verse 13—"I will have mercy, and not sacrifice"—as appropriate to this case also. The principle throughout is that higher requirements subordinate lower; the application of the principle, that necessity and mercy are of higher rank than any ceremonial or formal duties. The requirement of "mercy" was a rebuke to the spirit of the fault finders, who were very tender of the Sabbath, but cared nothing for the supplying of the needs of their fellow-men. The principle of Paul, "Love worketh no ill to his neighbor, therefore love is the fulfilling of the law" (Rom. 13:10), was to them utterly unknown.—

IV. THE APPLICATION. 27, 28

27, 28. "*sabbath was made for man.*—These verses contain an argument not reported by either Matthew or Luke. That the Sabbath was made for man, and not man for the Sabbath, implies that when the welfare of man conflicts with the observance of the Sabbath, the letter must give way. But of this, man himself is not to judge, because he can not judge with impartiality his own interests. No one is competent to judge in the case who does not know all that pertains to the welfare of man, and this is known only by the Lord. For this reason Jesus adds, "Therefore the Son of man is Lord also of the Sabbath;" that is, as the Son of man came to provide for man's welfare, and as the Sabbath law might need modification or even abrogation for the highest good of man, therefore lordship over the Sabbath was given to the Son of man. The passage teaches, then, not that man might violate the law of the Sabbath when their welfare seemed to them to demand it, but that Jesus could set it aside, as he afterward did, when his own judgment of man's welfare required him to do so. He made it clear on this occasion that said law was not to be so construed as to prevent men from providing necessary food on the Sabbath-day." (J. W. McGarvey)

FACT QUESTIONS 2:23-28

122. Why did the disciples eat the grain?
123. Why go through the field? Why not use the road?
124. Was it wrong to eat the grain? What law provides for this?
125. What law did the Pharisees imagine the disciples had violated?
126. Please explain the difficulty in referring to Abiathar as the high-priest—what explanation seems best?
127. What principle was involved in the action of David which was also a part of the action of the disciples?
128. In what sense was the sabbath made for man? When?
129. Explain the point in saying the Son of Man is Lord of the sabbath.

b. Healing On The Sabbath 3:1-6

TEXT 3:1-6

And he entered again into the synagogue; and there was a man there which had his hand withered. And they watched him, whether he would heal him on the sabbath day; that they might accuse him. And he saith unto the man that had his hand withered, Stand forth. And he saith unto them, Is it lawful on the sabbath day to do good, or to do harm? to save a life, or to kill? But they held their peace. And when he had looked round about on them with anger, being grieved at the hardening of their heart, he saith unto the man, Stretch forth thy hand. And he stretched it forth: and his hand was restored. And the Pharisees went out, and straightway with the Herodians took counsel against him, how they might destroy him.

THOUGHT QUESTIONS 3:1-6

104. On what sabbath did this event occur? Please read Luke 6:6 before answering.
105. Just what is meant by "a withered hand"?
106. Who was watching Jesus to accuse Him?
107. Why call the man to stand forth in the midst?
108. Was the question of Jesus in vs. 4 based on scripture? Why ask the question?
109. In what sense was Jesus angry with the Pharisees?
110. Please explain in your own words the heart action described in vs. 5.
111. Did the willingness of the cripple relate to the healing? If so, how?
112. Why the decision to kill Him? Why made at this particular time?
113. Who were the Herodians?

COMMENT

TIME—Early Summer A.D. 28—although on a different sabbath than the one on which the disciples plucked the grain yet in the same summer.
PLACE—Capernaum—in the synagogue of this city.
PARALLEL ACCOUNTS—Matt. 12:9-14; Luke 6:6-11.
OUTLINE—1. The place of the healing, vs. 1. 2. The critics of the healing, vs. 2. 3. The man to be healed, vs. 3. 4. The question of the purpose of healing and the sabbath, vs. 4. 5. The attitude of Jesus and the healing, vs. 5. 6. The sad reaction of the healing on those who refused to learn, vs. 6.

ANALYSIS

I. THE PLACE OF THE HEALING, VS. 1.
   1. At Capernaum in the synagogue.
   2. In the midst of the Jewish worshippers in the synagogue.

II. THE CRITICS OF THE HEALING, VS. 2.
   1. The Pharisees and perhaps the Herodians.
   2. They were there to spy not to worship or learn.

III. THE MAN TO BE HEALED, VS. 3.
   1. An adult with a hand which was "dried up."
   2. He was asked to arise so he could be seen by all in the service.

IV. THE QUESTION OF THE PURPOSE OF HEALING AND THE SABBATH, V. 4.

1. Some were worried about the purpose of the sabbath—Jesus asked if they really knew what should or should not be done on this day?
2. They refused to answer the obvious question.

V. THE ATTITUDE OF JESUS AND THE HEALING, VS. 5.

1. Searching the faces and hearts Jesus was grieved at what He saw.
2. In the face of opposition and danger Jesus "does good" on the sabbath by healing.

VI. THE SAD REACTION OF THE HEALING ON THOSE WHO REFUSED TO LEARN, VS. 6.

1. Left with their minds made up.
2. Immediately agreed with their enemies to destroy Jesus.

EXPLANATORY NOTES

I. THE PLACE OF HEALING, VS. 1.

1. "*And he entered again into the synagogue; and there was a man there which had a withered hand.*

Mark records another charge of Sabbath-breaking, probably to show how various were the outward occasions of such opposition; to illustrate the variety of Christ's defenses; and mark the first concerted plan for his destruction. *Again,* that is, on a different occasion from the one referred to in 2:21. The *synagogue,* most probably the one there mentioned, which was in Capernaum. Here, as in 2:23, the absence of any more specific note of time shows that exact chronological order was of small importance to the author's object. There is somewhat more precision as to this point in the parallel accounts of Luke (6:11) and Matthew (12:9). There is no ground in the text of either gospel for the conjecture of some writers, that the presence of this sufferer had been contrived in order to entrap Christ. The constant application for his healing aid precludes the necessity of such supposition, and indeed suggests that this was only one of many miracles performed at this time, and is recorded in detail on account of its important bearing on the progress of Christ's ministry. *Withered,* literally, *dried* or *dried up,* elsewhere applied to liquids (5:29. Rev. 16:12), and to plants (4:6. 11:20. James 1:11), but also to the pining away of the human body. The passive participle adds to the meaning of the adjective (dry) employed by Matthew and Luke, the idea that it was not a congenital infirmity, but the effect of disease or accident, the more calamitous because it was the right hand that was thus disabled (Luke 6:6). A similar affliction, preternaturally caused, was that of Jeroboam (1 Kings 13:4-6)."

II. THE CRITICS OF THE HEALING, VS. 2.

2. "*And they watched him, whether he would heal him on the sabbath-day; that they might accuse him.*

We have here a striking indication that the opposition to our Saviour was becoming more inveterate and settled, so that his enemies not only censured what he did, but watched for some occasion to find fault with him. *Watched*, i. e. closely or intently, as suggested by the compound form of the Greek verb, both here and in Acts 9:24. *Whether he would,* literally, *if he will,* a form of speech which represented the scene as actually passing. The motive of their watching was not simply curiosity, but a deliberate desire to entrap him. *That they might accuse him,* not in conversation merely, but before the local judges, who were probably identical with the elders or rulers of the synagogue, or at all events present at the stated time and place of public worship. The subject of the verb is not expressed by Mark and Matthew, although easily supplied from the foregoing context (2:24. Matt. 12:2), and from the parallel account in Luke (6:7), where the scribes and Pharisees are expressly mentioned."

III. THE MAN TO BE HEALED, VS. 3.

3. "*And he saith unto the man which had the withered hand, Stand forth!*"

This direction to the patient is placed by Matthew (12:13) after the address to his accusers, but without asserting that it was not given sooner, as would seem to be the case from the accounts of Mark and Luke, who represent it as a sort of prepartion for the subsequent discourse, which would be rendered more impressive by the sight of the man standing *in the midst,* i.e. among them, and no doubt in a conspicuous position, but not necessarily in the exact center of the house or assembly. This phrase is omitted in our version, or included in the phrase *stand forth.* The Greek verb is the same with that in 1:31. 2:9. 11:12, and strictly means to rouse another or one's self, especially from sleep. (Compare Matt. 8:25. Luke 8:24.)"

IV. THE QUESTION OF THE PURPOSE OF HEALING AND THE SABBATH, VS. 4.

4. "*And he saith unto them. Is it unlawful to do good on the sabbath-days, or to do evil? to save life, or to kill? but they held their peace.*

Before proceeding to perform the miracle, he appeals to them as to the question of its lawfulness, retorting the same question which they had already put to him (Matt. 12:10), as if he had said, 'answer your own question; I will leave it to yourselves, and will abide by your decision, not however as expressed in words alone, but in your actions' (Matt. 12:11,

12). *Is it lawful,* not right in itself, but consistent with the law of Moses, and with your acknowledged obligation to obey it. *To do good* and *to do evil* may, according to etymology and usage, mean *to do right* and *to do wrong* in the general (1 Pet. 3:16, 17. 3 John 11), or *to do good* and *to injure* in particular (Acts 14:17). On the former supposition the meaning of the sentence is, 'You will surely admit that it is lawful to do right in preference to wrong on the Sabbath, as on any other day.' But as this is little more than an identical propostion, or at least an undisputed truism (namely) that what is right is lawful), most interpreters prefer the other explanation, according to which our Lord is not asserting a mere truism, which his hearers were as ready to acknowledge as himself, but pointing out their obvious mistake as to the nature of the action which they had condemned beforehand. Stripped of its interrogative form, the sentence contains two distinct but consecutive propositions. The first is that it must be lawful, even on the Sabbath, to confer a favor or to do a kindness, when the choice lies between that and the doing of an injury. Even if not absolutely lawful, it would certainly become so in the case of such an alternative. The next proposition is that this rule, which is true in general, is emphatically true when the alternative is that of life and death. To this may be added, as a tacit influence, not formally deduced, but left to be drawn by the hearers for themselves, that such a case was that before them, in which to refuse help was virtually to destroy. This is not to be strictly understood as meaning that unless the withered hand were healed at once the man would die, but as exemplifying that peculiar method of presenting extreme cases, which is one of the most marked characteristics of our Saviour's teaching. As in the Sermon on the Mount and elsewhere, he instructs us what we must be prepared to do in an extreme case, thus providing for all others; so here he exhibits the conclusion, to which their reasoning naturally tended, as a proof that it must be erroneous. If the rest of the Sabbath was not only a divine requisition, but an intrinsic, absolute necessity, to which all human interests must yield, this could be no less true in an extreme case than in any other, so that life itself must be sacrificed to it. This revolting conclusion could be avoided only by admitting that the obligation of the Sabbath rested on authority, and might by that authority be abrogated or suspended. This implies that such authority belonged to him, that he was not acting as a mere man, or a prophet, but as the Son of man, and as such lord of the Sabbath; so that, although his answer upon this occasion is in form quite different from that before recorded, it amounts to the same thing, and proceeds upon the same essential principle. Thus understood, the sentence may be paraphrased as follows: 'You consider me a breaker of the law, because I heal upon the Sabbath; but you must admit that where the choice is between doing good and evil, for example, between saving life and killing upon that day, we are bound to choose the former. There is therefore some limit or exception to the obligation which you urge upon yourselves and others, not indeed to be decided by your own discretion or caprice, but by the same authority which first imposed it. Now that authority I claim to exercise, a claim abundantly attested by the very miracles on which your charge is founded, for no man can do such things unless God be with him.' (Compare John 3:2.)"

V. THE ATTITUDE OF JESUS AND THE HEALING, VS. 5.

5. *And when he had looked round about on them with anger, being grieved for the hardness of their hearts, he saith unto the man, Stretch forth thine hand. And he stretched (it) out: and his hand was restored whole as the other.*

We have here an instance of what some regard as characteristic of this gospel, and ascribe to Peter's influence upon it, to wit, the occasional description of our Saviour's feelings, looks and gestures, most of which details we owe exclusively to Mark. Three such particulars are here recorded, one external, two internal. *Looking round upon* (or at) *them* is an act mentioned by Luke also (6:10), with the addition of the strong word *all.* But Mark tells what feelings were expressed by this act, or at least accompanied it. One was *anger,* a passion belonging to our original constitution, and as such not sinful in itself, and therefore shared by the humanity of Christ, in whom it was a holy indignation or intense displeasure at what really deserves it, unalloyed by that excess or that malignity which renders human anger almost always sinful. The absence of the quality last named in this case is apparent from the other feeling mentioned, that of grief or sorrow. *Grieved with* is in Greek a compound verb, admitting of two explanations, one of which makes the particle in composition refer to the anger previously mentioned, *being grieved* (in conjunction or at the same time) with that anger. But the classical usage of such writers as Plato. Theophrastus, Diodorus, is in favour of referring the particle in question, not to the anger, but to those who caused it, so as to express a sympathetic sorrow. Looking round with anger and yet grieving (sympathizing) with them. In the very act of condemning their sin, he pitied the miserable state to which it had reduced them. The specific object of this sympathetic grief or pity was the *hardness of their heart,* including intellectual stupidity and insensibility of feeling. The first Greek word is less exactly rendered *blindness* in the margin of our Bible, and in the text of Rom. 11:25. Eph. 4:18. But the figure, although not suggested by the Greek word, is expressive of two things which it denotes, a state of mental and spiritual apathy or insensibility. There is here no mention of external contact (as in 1:31, 41), nor of any other order or command than that to stretch out the hand, which could only be obeyed when the miracle was wrought, and is therefore not required as a previous condition. This is often and justly used to illustrate the act of faith, which is perfomed in obedience to divine command and by the aid of the same power which requires it. *Whole* (or sound) *as the other,* though expunged in this place by the critics as a mere assimilation to Matt. 12:13 (compare Luke 6:10), may be used to illustrate Mark's laconic phrase, in which it is really implied."

VI. THE SAD REACTION OF THE HEALING ON THOSE WHO REFUSED TO LEARN, VS. 6.

6. *"And the Pharisees went forth, and straightway took counsel with the Herodians against him, how they might destroy him.*

One of the most important circumstances of this case, for the sake of which it was perhaps recorded (see v. 1), is the effect which it produced upon the Pharisees or High-Church Jewish party, whose religious tenets brought them into constant opposition to the Sadducees or latitudinarians, as their political or national exclusiveness arrayed them against the Herodians or followers of Herod, and as such defenders of the Roman domination, of which the Herods were the instruments and agents. Herod the Great, created king by the Romans, and enabled by their aid to take possession of his kingdom, was devoted to their service both from interest and inclination; and although upon his death his dominions were divided, and his eldest son Archelaus had been superseded in Judea by Roman procurators, two other sons of Herod were still reigning (Luke 3:1), Antipas in Galilee, Samaria, and Perea, and Philip in Trachonitis and Iturea. Even in Judea, the Herodian interest and party still existed, as the most extreme political antithesis to that of he Pharisees. It is therefore a clear proof of growing hatred to our Saviour, that these opposite extremes should now begin to coalesce for his destruction, an alliance which appears to have continued till its object was accomplished. *Going out* (from the synagogue) *immediately,* as soon as the miracle was wrought, and therefore in full view of the proof which it afforded of our Lord's divine legation; a conclusive confirmation of that hardness and judicial blindness which had excited his own grief and anger. *Took counsel* is a phrase peculiar to Matthew (12:14. 22:15. 27:1. 28:12), Mark's equivalent to which is *made counsel,* i.e. consultation. *How they might destroy him,* not for any past offenses, but how they might take advantage of his words or acts to rid them of so dangerous an enemy. The motives of this concerted opposition were no doubt various, religious, political, and personal, in different degrees and cases.

That it should have been deliberately organized, at this time, out of such discordant elements and in the face of such conclusive evidence, can only be ascribed to the infatuation under which they acted (Luke 6:11)." (J. A. Alexander)

FACT QUESTIONS 3:1-6.

130. What possible purposes were there in the record of Mark of the Sabbath healing?
131. Was the cripple "planted" there to entrap Christ? Prove your answer.
132. How did the man come to have a withered hand?
133. In what manner and in what attitude did the Pharisees watch Jesus?
134. How would the accusations of the enemies of Jesus be carried out?
135. At what particular time in the action did Jesus ask the man to stand forth? What is meant by "Stand forth"?
136. Why did Jesus ask the question of vs. 4? Cf. Matt. 12:10.
137. Was our Lord stating a truism?
138. If this was not a truism what two propositions were involved in the statement?
139. In what reference do some see the influence of Peter upon the writer Mark?
140. How could Jesus look upon certain persons with anger and yet not sin?
141. With whom was Jesus grieved? I thought He was angry with them? Explain.
142. What was included in the expression "hardness of heart"?
143. Was there any act of faith on the part of the man healed? Explain.
144. How does vs. 6 indicate the purpose for verses 1-6?
145. Who were the Herodians? Why did the Pharisees want their help?

SIDELIGHTS

2:23-28

"We see from these verses, what extravagant importance is attached to trifles by those who are mere formalists in religion.

The Pharisees were mere formalists, if there ever were any in the world. They seem to have thought exclusively of the outward part, the husk, the shell, and the ceremonial of religion. They even added to these externals by traditions of their own. Their godliness was made up of washings and fastings and peculiarities in dress and will-worship, while repentance and faith and holiness were comparatively overlooked.

The Pharisees would probably have found no fault if the disciples had been guilty of some offense against the moral law. They would have winked at covetousness, or perjury, or extortions, or excess, because they were sins to which they themselves were inclined.

We see, in the second place, from these verses, the value of a knowledge of Holy Scripture.

Our Lord replies to the accusation of the Pharisees by a reference to Holy Scripture. He reminds His enemies of the conduct of David, when "he had need and was an hungered." "Have ye never read what David did?" They could not deny that the writer of the book of Psalms, and the man after God's own heart, was not likely to set a bad example.

Let us observe in these verses, how our Lord Jesus Christ was watched by His enemies. We read that "they watched Him, whether He would heal him on the Sabbath Day, that they might accuse Him."

What a melancholy proof we have here of the wickedness of human nature! It was the Sabbath Day when these things happened. It was in the synagogue, where men were assembled to hear the Word and worship God. Yet even on the day of God, and at the time of worshipping God, these wretched formalists were plotting mischief against our Lord. The very men who pretended to such strictness and sanctity in little things, were full of malicious and angry thoughts in the midst of the congregation. (Prov. 5:14).

Let us observe, in the last place, the *feelings which the conduct of our Lord's enemies called forth in His heart.* We are told that "He looked round about on them with anger, being grieved for the hardness of their hearts."

This expression is very remarkable, and demands special attention. It is meant to remind us that our Lord Jesus Christ was a man like ourselves in all things, sin only excepted. Whatever sinless feelings belong to the constitution of man, our Lord partook of, and knew by experience. We read that He "marvelled," that He "rejoiced," that He "wept," that He "loved,' and here we read that He felt "anger."

It is plain from these words that there is an "anger" which is lawful, right, and not sinful. There is an indignation which is justifiable, and on some occasions may be properly manifested. The words of Solomon and St. Paul both seem to teach the same lesson. "The north wind driveth away rain, so doth an angry countenance a backbiting tongue." "Be ye angry and sin not." (Prov. 25:23; Eph. 4:26)." (J. C. Ryle)

LESSONS

1. Jesus did not remove Himself or His disciples from the ordinary

course of life—it was in the grain field and the synagogue He taught His lessons.

2. Jesus never ate the grain—whereas He defended the actions of His disciples He was above reproach—so should the teacher be.
3. The sabbath was indeed made for man—for the Jewish man in Palestine—there are numerous persons who could not observe it because of the length of the day in the area where they live—most of all because God commanded no one but the Jews to observe it. Cf. Deut. 5:15.
4. How many withered hands do we have in the church today? Jesus is commanding them to stand forth and be healed.
5. We can expect some people to intentionally misunderstand and misinterpret all the good we do. A servant is not above His Master.

POINTS FOR TEACHERS

1. How many of the Ten Commandments are reproduced in the New Testament? Give references.
2. Is there any commandment in the New Testament to observe the Lord's Day? Why do we observe it?
3. Make a contrast between the sabbath and the Lord's Day.
4. Name some things we should do on Sunday.
5. Is it right to keep drug stores and other stores open on Sunday?
6. If a man works all day on Sunday and gives what he earns on that day to the Lord's work, does that excuse him for working?
7. What are some of the things causing the American people to misuse the Lord's Day?
8. Show how the forces of evil today are united.
9. Show how the forces of good are divided.
10. What is the unpardonable sin?

9. THE FAME OF JESUS 3:7-12

TEXT 3:7-12

"And Jesus with his disciples withdrew to the sea: and a great multitude from Galilee followed: and from Judea, and from Jerusalem, and from Idumaea, and beyond Jordan, and about Tyre and Sidon, a great multitude, hearing what great things he did, came unto him. And he spake to his disciples, that a little boat should wait on him because of the crowd, lest they should throng him: for he had healed many; insomuch that as many as had plagues pressed upon him that they might touch him. And the unclean spirits, whensoever they beheld him, fell down before him, and cried, saying, Thou art the Son of God. And he charged them much that they should not make him known."

THOUGHT QUESTIONS 3:7-12

114. Did the opposition of the Pharisees prompt the move to the beach of Galilee?
115. Where was Idumaea? What is meant by "beyond the Jordan"?
116. What number is estimated in the expression "a great multitude"?
117. Why were the crowds so interested?
118. What was Jesus going to do with "the little boat"?
119. What was physically wrong with the persons with "plagues"?
120. Did Jesus have any "failures" in healing? Specify.
121. Why the testimony of the demons?
122. Why so urgently caution the demons?

COMMENT 3:7-12

TIME—Midsummer—A.D. 28.

PLACE—The beach of the sea of Galilee, not far from Capernaum.

PARALLEL ACCOUNTS—Matt. 12:15-21.

OUTLINE—1. Jesus withdraws to the Sea, vs. 7. 2. A multitude follows, vs. 8. 3. The little boat requested, vs. 9. 4. Healing and casting out demons, vs. 10-11.

ANALYSIS

I. JESUS WITHDRAWS TO THE SEA. VS. 7.
   1. His disciples are with Him.
   2. He is accompanied by a great multitude.

II. A MULTITUDE FOLLOWS. VS. 8.
   1. From Jerusalem and Judea.
   2. From Idumaea and beyond Jordan.
   3. From round about Tyre and Sidon.

III. A LITTLE BOAT REQUESTED. VS. 9.
   1. Asked disciples for the boat.
   2. Feared lest He be thronged.

IV. HEALING AND CASTING OUT DEMONS. VS. 10-12.
   1. So many were healed others pressed toward Him for just a touch.
   2. Unclean spirits cast out and caused to acknowledge His divinity.
   3. Jesus wanted no testimony from an evil source—and most especially when it was given before He wanted it known.

EXPLANATORY NOTES

I. JESUS WITHDRAWS TO THE SEA. VS. 7.

"But Jesus withdrew himself with his disciples to the sea." "His hour was not yet come; so He went with His disciples to the borders of the lake of Galilee, where, if pursued, He could the more easily take ship, and escape to some other part, out of the reach of His persecutors.

II. A MULTITUDE FOLLOWS. VS. 8.

"And a great multitude from Galilee followed him," We should put a full stop after "followed him," and read the two verses thus: "And a great multitude from Galilee followed him. And a great multitude from Judea, and from Jerusalem, and from Idumaea, and from beyond Jordan, and about Tyre and Sidon, hearing what great things He did, came unto Him." The multitude from the neighbouring Galilee, in which He had been preaching and healing, *followed* Him; the multitude from Judea, and Jerusalem, and from all the regions bordering on the Holy Land, attracted by the fame of His miracles, "came" to Him. Notice how, though He is rejected by the leaders both in Church and State, the people from all parts seem to accept Him. I say "seem," for the Evangelist is careful to inform us that they were attracted, not by His preaching, but by His miracles.

Let the reader notice how here, as before, this Evangelist loves to dwell upon the widespread popularity of the Lord."

III. A LITTLE BOAT REQUESTED. VS. 9.

"And he spake to the disciples, that a small ship should wait on him," The word "wait" does not give the full meaning of the original, which is the same word as that used in the Apostolic precept, "continue instant in prayer," of Romans 12:12. It means that the ship should be always at His beck and call, so that, by escaping the pressure of the multitude, He should not be unduly hindered in the exercise of His ministry."

IV. HEALING AND CASTING OUT DEMONS. VS. 10-12.

"For he had healed many: insomuch that they pressed upon him," "Pressed upon him" should rather be rendered *"fell upon him,"* as if there was a rush towards Him of all who had plagues—plagues (literally "scourges") describing the painfulness and distress of disease, as if it were a scourging inflicted on man as a punshment for his sin.

"To touch him." It was the Lord's will most frequently to heal men by contact with His body. He makes communication with His body the means by which virtue flows from Himself to those whom He wills to benefit. The reader will understand.

"And unclean spirits, when they saw him, fell down before him." The uniformity of action on the part of all evil spirits in the presence of the Lord, in that they should fall down and confess Him, is exceedingly remarkable (Matt. 8:29; Mark 1:23, 24). These fallen beings seem to be under a law that they should thus acknowledge the Son of God. I cannot think that this is to be explained, as so many attempt to do, on the ground of diabolical cunning. It seems as if they were compelled to fall down,

and confess their Maker, even though they had made it the one object of their existence to oppose and thwart Him.

"And he straitly charged them that they should not make him known." On this Bede remarks, "A sinner is forbidden to preach the Lord, lest any one listening to his preaching should follow him in his error, for the devil is an evil master, who always mingles false things with true, that the semblance of truth may cover the witness of fraud. But not only devils, but persons healed by Christ and even Apostles (Mark 8:9) are ordered to be silent concerning Him before the Passion, lest by the preaching of the majesty of His Divinity, the economy of His Passion should be retarded." (M. F. Sadler)

FACT QUESTIONS 3:7-12

146. Why did Jesus withdraw to the borders of the lake of Galilee?
147. Who *followed* Jesus and who *came* to Him?
148. What is meant by the word "wait" in reference to the boat?
149. What would be a better translation of "pressed upon him"?
150. Why did the sick want to touch him?
151. Why did the demons seem compelled to fall down before Jesus?
152. If demons told the truth why not accept it?

B. THE SECOND PERIOD 3:13-7:23

1. Friends and Foes 3:13-35

a. The appointment of the twelve 3:13-19

TEXT 3:13-19

"And he goeth up into the mountain, and calleth unto him whom he himself would: and they went unto him. And he appointed twelve, that they might be with him, and that he might send them forth to preach, and to have authority to cast out devils: and Simon he surnamed Peter; and James the son of Zebedee, and John the brother of James; and them he surnamed Boanerges, which is, Sons of thunder: and Andrew, and Philip, and Bartholomew, and Matthew, and Thomas, and James the son of Alpheus, and Thaddeus, and Simon the Cananean, and Judas Iscariot, which also betrayed him."

THOUGHT QUESTIONS 3:13-19

123. Please read Matt. 10:1-4 and Luke 2:12-16 as parallel accounts of this important event.
124. What did Jesus do before He went into the mountain to choose the twelve?
125. What mountain?; is it the mount of the sermon on the mount?
126. Why were the disciples so willing to go after Him?
127. What was the two-fold purpose of appointing the twelve?
128. Why the authority to cast out demons?
129. Why the surname for Peter and the two sons of Zebedee?

130. Read the list in Matthew and Luke and explain the use of the name Thaddaeus.

131. Is the term "Cananaean" the same as "Zealot"—compare accounts. (Acts 1:13)

COMMENT 3:13-19

TIME—Midsummer, A.D. 28.

PLACE—On a mount at no great distance from Capernaum.

PARALLEL ACCOUNTS—Matt. 10:1-4; Luke 6:12-16.

OUTLINE—1. The place where He called the twelve, 13a. 2. The actual call of the twelve, 13b. 3. Their appointment, 14. 4. Sent with authority, 15. 5. The names, 16-19.

ANALYSIS

I. THE PLACE WHERE HE CALLED THE TWELVE, 13a.
   1. Near Capernaum and the sea of Galilee.
   2. A place of prayer—probably the mount from which we have the sermon on the mount. Cf. Matt. 10:1-4; Luke 6:12-16.

II. THE ACTUAL CALL OF THE TWELVE, 13b.
   1. From among the multitude.
   2. Made by the power of Jesus' will.
   3. They left all to follow Him.

III. THEIR APPOINTMENT, v. 14.
   1. The word appoint sometimes translated "ordained."
   2. That they might be with Him.
   3. That He might send them out to preach.

IV. SENT WITH AUTHORITY, v. 15.
   1. Over demons.
   2. With His message.

V. THE NAMES, 16-19.
   1. The first four—Peter, James, John and Andrew.
   2. The second four—Philip, Bartholomew, Matthew, Thomas.
   3. The third four—James, Thaddaeus, Simon, Judas.

EXPLANATORY NOTES

I. THE PLACE WHERE HE CALLED THE TWELVE, 13a.

"*The Chosen Twelve* (vs. 13-19a).—It is evident that the bitter opposition and plots of the rulers must, in no long time, put an end to Jesus' earthly work. He can not hope to do more than start the work, to break the ground and commence scattering the seed. Jesus had summoned to his side a few of the Baptist's disciples (John 1:35-51). Later, by the seaside, he had attached four of these more distinctly to him, to travel with him. But there was yet to be formed a compact, organized body of disciples commissioned to teach his doctrines.

But ere he did it, he withdrew into the mountain, doubtless the "Horns of Hattin," and there spent an entire night in prayer (Luke 6:12).

II. THE ACTUAL CALLING OF THE TWELVE. 13b

When dawn came, he called out of the disciples about him twelve whom he ordained (1) to "be with him"—that is, especially and continuously with him; (2) to be sent forth to preach as his special apostles, and (3) to have power to exercise his authority over demons. These, Luke informs us, he named apostles. "Apostle" means "one sent," and is very close in meaning to our words "ambassador" and "missionary.' It was a necessary condition of this apostleship that the apostles should have been with Jesus, and so be qualified to tell of his words and actions, particularly of the resurrection (Acts 1:8, 21, 22; 1 Cor. 9:1; Acts 22:14, 15). The apostles can therefore have no successors.

III. THEIR APPOINTMENT, V. 14

The number twelve was evidently with purpose, for they were to be tribal judges of the twelve tribes of Israel (Luke 22:30), and were, according to Paul, ministers to the twelve tribes, or to the circumcision, rather than to Gentiles (Gal. 2:7-9).

The lists in the four gospels are different, but the first four names, the second four and the last four in each are the same in all groups. The first name in each four is the same, and the traitor, Judas Iscariot, is always last. This seems to signify that the apostles were so banded as groups of four, each with a leader.

V. THE NAMES, 16-19.

Because he was first to publicly confess Christ, and because the Lord saw in him peculiar gifts of bold, aggressive leadership, Peter was given the right to open the doors of the kingdom of heaven. But after he had done this in the two sermons to Jews and Gentiles (Acts 2:14-41; 10:34-48), there is no evidence of Peter's having any authority above that of the other apostles. Christ never so stated; Peter never so claimed; the Apostles never so owned. Jesus, on the other hand, specifically placed them on a level, with himself as their only Master (Matt. 23: 8-11). Peter claims only equal position with other officers in the church (1 Pet. 5:1, 4). Paul names James first (Gal. 2:9, 11-14). See Matt. 18:18; 19:27, 28: 20:25-27; John 20:21; Acts 1:8. Peter was but one of the apostles, one of the "pillars" of the church (Gal. 2:9).

Jesus had prophesied that Simon should be called Peter when Simon was first brought to him by Andrew (John 1:41, 42). The name signifies a piece of stone broken from mother-rock, and indicates Jesus' prophetic insight into his character. Probably because of their vigor and zealous, stormy dispositions (Luke 9: 51-56; Mark 9:38), James and

John were surnamed "Sons of thunder." James' vigorous character probably led to Herod's slaying him, and John's vigor sustained him to a ripe old age—between ninety and one-hundred. John's writings, too, reveal this vigor; he denounces sin in strong terms, such as "liar," "antichrist," "deceiver," "children of the devil" and "murderer" (1 John 1:6; 2:4, 22; 3:15; 2 John 3-11). James and John were sons of Zebedee and Salome (Matt. 27:56; Mark 15:40) and perhaps cousins of Jesus (cf. John 19:25).

Philip, like the four preceding disciples, was a native of Bethsaida, and became allied to Jesus on the latter's return from temptation to Galilee (John 1:43, 44). He brought to Jesus Nathanael, who is generally identified with the Bartholomew here named, because John always names Philip and Nathanael together, while the Synoptists name Philip and Bartholomew. Philip seems to have been of practical turn of mind (John 6:5-9). Nathanael was "the Israelite in whom is no guile" (John 1:47).

Matthew is Levi, and alone of all the Synoptists, describes himself in the list of apostles as "the publican," as if recalling the depth from which grace had raised him (Mark 2:14).

Thomas is also called Didymus (John 11:16). Both words mean "twin," the first being Aramaic and the second Greek. His attachment to Jesus was deep (John 11:16), but a tendency to misgiving and despondency probably accounts for his doubting the news of Christ's resurrection, until the sight of his beloved Master brought that explosion of affection, "My Lord and my God!"

James called "son of Alphaeus" and "James the Less" (Mark 15: 40), to distinguish him from James the son of Zebedee, must not be confused with James the Lord's brother, who became a leader in the Jerusalem church (Gal. 1:19: 2:9-12: 1 Cor. 15:5-7; Acts 15: 6-9; 21:18), and wrote the Epistle of James.

Thaddaeus is called Judas, son of James, in the two later Gospels—Luke and John. He may have been known as Thaddaeus in the early days to distinguish him from Judas Iscariot. He is not the author of the epistle of Jude, written by the Lord's brother.

The cognomen "Cananaean" means "the Zealot" (used by Luke and John).

Judas, famed for his infamy, is called Iscariot, from his native city Kerioth, in Judea; he was the only one of the twelve not from Galilee. He was treasurer of the group. Much speculation has been wasted upon the reason for his choice as an apostle; suffice it to note that Jesus called "whom he himself would."

It is a strikingly human group, possessed in varying degrees of fear, ambition, rivalry, impetuosity, vows, weakening faith, yet real loyalty—a group of men, and not supermen, with common virtues and common faults, to do an uncommon work with divine power and under divine guidance." (*Standard Bible Lesson Quarterly*, Jan., Feb., March 1918.)

FACT QUESTIONS 3:13-19

153. What was the purpose in the appointment of the twelve?
154. Who were the first disciples to follow Jesus? (Cf. John 1:35-51).
155. Why spend the whole night in prayer?—please think on this question.
156. In what sense were the twelve to be "with Him"—in what special sense were they to represent Him?
157. What is the meaning of the word "apostle"?
158. What were the necessary conditions of apostleship? Why twelve apostles?
159. Why in three groups of four?
160. What right did Jesus give Peter?
161. Give three lines of evidence to indicate Peter was on a level with the other apostles. Give the meaning of the name "Peter."
162. State indications that James and John had "stormy dispositions."
163. Give two historical facts about each of the following: (1) Philip (2) Matthew (3) Thomas (4) James, son of Alphaeus (5) Thaddaeus (6 Judas)

B. OPPOSITION 3:20-27

(1) From Friends 3:20,21

TEXT 3:20-21

"And he cometh into a house. And the multitude cometh together again, so that they could not so much as eat bread. And when his friends heard it, they went out to lay hold on him: for they said, He is beside himself."

THOUGHT QUESTIONS 3:20-21

132. In whose house did this incident occur?
133. Why such a large crowd? Is Mark complaining about the inability to eat?
134. Who were the friends making this complaint?
135. What particular circumstances seemed to disturb His friends? What did they want to do?
136. Were they accusing Jesus of being insane?

(2) From enemies 3:22-27

TEXT 3:22-27

"And the scribes which came down from Jerusalem said, He hath Beelzebub, and, By the prince of the devils casteth he out the devils. And he called them unto him, and said unto them in parables, How can Satan cast out Satan? And if a kingdom be divided against itself, that kingdom cannot stand. And if a house be divided against itself, that house will not be able to stand. And if Satan hath risen up against himself, and is divided, he cannot stand, but hath an end. But no one can enter into the house of the strong man, and spoil his goods, except he first bind the strong man; and then he will spoil his house."

THOUGHT QUESTIONS 3:22-27

137. What authority had the scribes to pass judgment on the miracles of Jesus?
138. Who was Beelzebub?
139. Jesus did not evade opposition i.e. on this occasion—show indications this is true.
140. What is meant by the expression "said unto them in parables"?
141. Knowing something of the deceitfulness of Satan why wouldn't Satan on some occasions "cast out Satan?"
142. Did Jesus infer there was an evil kingdom over which Satan rules? In what sense would this kingdom be divided?
143. Who is the head of the house? In what sense divided? Is there a lesson in this parable for us?
144. What is meant by the expression "hath an end" in vs. 26?
145. Who is "the house"? who "the strong man"? What are the goods "to be spoiled?—who is the one stronger than the strong man?

COMMENT 3:20-27

TIME—Midsummer and Autumn, A.D. 28.

PLACE—In the house of Jesus in the city of Capernaum.

PARALLEL ACCOUNTS:—Matt. 12:22-30.

OUTLINE—1. Opposition from friends, 20, 21. 2. Opposition from enemies, 22-27.

ANALYSIS 3:20-27

I. OPPOSITION FROM FRIENDS, 20, 21.
   1. This occurred at home in Capernaum.
   2. The occasion of opposition was the inability to eat.
   3. The form of the opposition was to bodily remove Him from His labors.
   4. The reason—they feared for His sanity.

II. OPPOSITION FROM ENEMIES, 22-27.

1. Jesus is accused of being in league with Satan.
2. Jesus answers in parables:
   (1) A kingdom divided cannot stand.
   (2) A house divided cannot stand.
   (3) Satan casting out himself is defeating himself—this would end in his own complete loss.
   (4) There must be someone stronger than Satan to cast out Satan.

EXPLANATORY NOTES

I. OPPOSITION FROM FRIENDS, 20, 21.

"20. As soon as he had returned the crowd was about him again.—the vivid description is peculiar to Mark. *So that they could not so much as eat bread.* So at chap. 6:31. The activity on our Lord's own part is left to be inferred, but it must have been an intense activity of teaching and healing, continued we know not how long.

21. *His friends* of verse 21 are "his mother and his brethren" of verse 31. Their coming and calling for him is narrated by Matthew and Luke as well as by Mark, but Mark alone tells of their setting out in search of him and of their motive. Considerably later his brethren did not believe on him (John 7:5), and probably they persuaded his mother on this occasion, playing, perhaps, upon the anxiety of maternal love. These "brethren" appear to be the "James and Joses and Juda and Simon" of Mark 6:3. The question, What was their relation to Jesus? will probably never be settled with unanimous consent. The data being insufficient to furnish a positive decision, temperament and feeling, as well as theological prepossessions, will always be elements in the formation of opinions on the subject. The theories are: (That they were children of Joseph and Mary, younger than Jesus; (2) That they were children of Joseph by a former marriage; (3) That they were cousins, probably orphaned, and in some way adopted into the family. The first is rejected by all Roman Catholic interpreters, by all who share their feeling as to the superior holiness of virginity, and by some besides who feel that reverence is best satisfied by regarding the Only-begotten of God as also the only offspring of his mother. Yet the scriptural argument for it is very strong (see it stated at length by Alford, on Matt. 13-55), and its adherents claim—probably correctly—that no other view would ever have been thought of but for unscriptural ideas of our Lord's mother. If the first theory is rejected, there is no choice between the second and the third.—His friends heard *of it*—of the great throng that was about him and of the busy life he was living—and *went out* from their home in Nazareth, where they were all living, mother, brothers, and sisters, a little later,

when Jesus visited the place (chap. 6:1-6). The news reached them there, and brought them down to Capernaum, a distance of perhaps twenty miles. They came *to lay hold on him*—i. e. by force, as one who was not fit to take care of himself. They said, *He is beside himself*, insane—a conclusion from the excited life that he seemed to them to be living; perhaps the more plausible from the quietness and placidity of the years that he spent with them at Nazareth. Strangers misapprehended him thus (John 10:20), but so did his nearest friends. Unbelief will misapprehend whether its opportunities be small or great. Even the "mother and brethren" cannot know Jesus except they be true "mother and brethren."

II. OPPOSITION FROM ENEMIES, 22-27.

22. Mark omits the occasion of this conversation, which is carefully given by Matthew and Luke—namely; the healing of the blind and dumb demoniac (Matt. 12:22), which caused many to inquire, "Is not this the Son of David?"—i.e. the Messiah. The scene is still "at home," and most probably in the house of Peter. "Pharisees" are present (Matthew), and so (Mark) are *the scribes which came down from Jerusalem*. This language distinctly indicates an embassy, men who had come on purpose to watch and harm him. It is not to be assumed that they were the same as the men mentioned at Luke 5:17, for some time had elapsed and meanwhile Jesus had been absent from Capernaum. But, whether the same or not, these were spies.—Indignant at the suggestion that this was the Christ, they were ready with their explanation of his mighty works, the reality of which they thus explicitly admitted. *He hath Beelzebub*, or, as the best manuscripts agree, "Beelzebul." The name has been variously interpreted. The name from which it came was Baalzebub, "lord of flies," the god of the Philistines worshipped at Ekron (2 Kings 1:2) and consulted as an oracle. The god was named, doubtless, from his supposed control over the swarms of flies and similar insects that torment the East. After a time the Jews, thinking all heathen deities to be evil spirits, adopted this name as a title of the chief of evil spirits, but changed it by one letter, making Beelzebub into Beelzebul. Some think that in this change they intentionally degraded and insulted it, even as a word, by turning it into a name which meant "lord of dung" or "of the dunghill." But others, apparently with better reason, make it mean "lord of the mansion" or "of the dwelling"—i.e. lord of the place in which evil spirits dwell, or, substantially, "head of the family of evil spirits," he who rules them as a man rules his household. This sense best corresponds to the form of the word (Meyer) and best suits the allusions in the New Testament. So here: "He hath Beelzebul" means "he is possessed by the spirit who is lord of all the rest, and who orders them in and out at his

pleasure, as a man commands his servants."—Thus the second clause of their charge is the application of the first. *By the prince of the devils casteth he out devils,* or demons. In the Greek the use of the recitative *hoti* ("that") before each of these clauses seems to indicate that two separate remarks are quoted. One says, "that he hath Beelzebul." Another, "that by the prince of the demons casteth he out demons." Luke adds that others, tempting him, asked of him a sign from heaven.

23-26. The whole twenty-third verse is peculiar to Mark. He *called them*—the scribes from Jerusalem—bespeaking their attention and bringing them face to face with himself and their own words. The wonderful calmness and self-control of this reply cannot be too distinctly noticed in connection with the fearful charge that had just been brought against him. No more terrible accusation than this was possible; it was the direct charge of a positive and practical league with infernal powers. But he, "when he was reviled, reviled not again: when he suffered, he threatened not" (1 Pet. 2:23).—*He said unto them in parables.* In illustrative comparisons. The word does not require a narrative, such as we often associate with it. The point lies in the fact of a comparison. But here the fact to be confirmed is given in the first question (verse 23); it is then confirmed and illustrated by two comparisons, of the kingdom and the household, in verses 24, 25 and it is restated directly in verse 26.—*How can Satan cast out Satan?* The principle is that no intelligent power works against itself and defeats its own purposes. Observe what is here assumed: it is assumed that the dominion of Satan is an intelligent dominion, with character and purposes; that the kingdom of evil is one intelligent kingdom, managed by one mind who knows what he is doing. The individual spirits that torment men are not identified personally with Satan, but they are identified morally with him; so that their presence is his presence, and when they are cast out he is cast out. Now, it is said that in a kingdom there must be unity of counsel, illustrated first by the case of a kingdom among men. It is notorious that divided counsels, going into action, are the ruin of a state; divided counsels or, more exactly, contradictory counsels—not between rulers and subjects, but in the government itself. How, then, if the kingdom of "the prince of the demons" be thus divided against itself and act against its own purposes? Illustrated next by the case of a household, regarded, not as made up of individuals, who may disagree, but as under the rule of a "householder," "goodman of the house," "lord of the mansion." If it acts against the character and counsels that govern it, it will be a failure. How, then, if the "lord of the mansion" be thus divided against himself, acting for the defeat of his own work? And now is made the application. If Satan were casting out demons, he would be rising up against himself. His sole purpose is to injure men. If he brings in health, calmness, purity, reason, godly gratitude, piety, to the souls of men, and if he sets them free from the bondage by which they are held away from these blessings, he will be acting directly against his own nature. Such a work as that of Jesus cannot possibly be attributed to him, any more than demoniacal possession can be attributed to God. Judge a work by its moral affinities. If it is good, it is not of the devil, for he never delivers men from evil. If such a rising up of Satan against himself as the work of Christ would be were proved real, there would be more than danger to his kingdom. *He cannot stand, but hath an end,* would be the true word. A kingdom so broken would be no kingdom at all.

27. More than this does Christ's work mean. The verse should begin with "but"—But *no man can enter*, etc. Not only does Christ's merciful and holy work prove him to be no ally of Satan, but if Satan's kingdom is being taken away from him, the fact proves the presence of Satan's conqueror. No one can plunder the property of a strong "lord of the mansion" until he has bound the "lord of the mansion" himself; so, if Jesus is doing a great triumphant work of mercy in setting men free from the inferior agents of Satan's kingdom, he must already be master over Satan himself. The defeat of the Lord precedes the defeat of the servants; if the master were at liberty and had the power, he would not suffer his goods to be spoiled.—Perhaps there is a special touch of triumph in the closing words. *And then he will spoil his house*; as if Jesus were regarding the end as absolutely sure and the work as actually begun. Compare John 12:31: "Now is the judgment of this world; now shall the prince of this world be cast out." Here speaks, in Jesus, the consciousness that he is absolutely the conqueror and destroyer of Satan's kingdom. Here, as a transition to the solemn words that Mark adds immediately, Matthew and Luke insert, "He that is not with me is against me; and he that gathereth not with me scattereth abroad." There are only two sides in this conflict, and they are the side of the "strong man armed" and the side of the "stronger than he." Not to be with the conqueror of Satan is to be with Satan." (*W. N. Clarke*)

FACT QUESTIONS 3:20-27

164. In whose house was Jesus living at this time?
165. What were Jesus and His disciples doing instead of eating?
166. Just who was involved in the effort to restrain Him?
167. Why would those who knew Him best think Him fanatical in His work?
168. How could it be said the scribes came "down" from Jerusalem when they traveled north?

169. Why did Jesus call the scribes to Him to deliver His answer to their criticism?
170. Does the use of the term "parable" here fit your previous use of the form? Explain its use here. How many parables are used?
171. Discuss the king, dominion, subjects, and expansion of Satan's kingdom.
172. In what sense does Satan have a house?
173. Jesus said Satan was divided—explain.
174. I thought Satan was an immortal being—in what sense has he an "end"?
175. What glorious victory is indicated in vs. 27?

C. THE UNPARDONABLE SIN 3:28-30

TEXT 3:28-30

"Verily I say unto you, All their sins shall be forgiven unto the sons of men, and their blasphemies wherewith soever they shall blaspheme: but whosoever shall blaspheme against the Holy Spirit hath never forgiveness, but is guilty of an eternal sin: because they said, He hath an unclean spirit."

THOUGHT QUESTIONS 3:28-30

146. What is meant by the word "blaspheme"?
147. Why use the expression "verily I say unto you"? What does it mean?
148. Is Jesus saying the sins of men *will* be forgiven them or *could* be forgiven?
149. When Jesus warned concerning it, had anyone committed the eternal sin?
150. Why is it impossible to forgive this sin? (Please attempt an answer of *your own*).

COMMENT

TIME—Autumn of 28 A.D.

PLACE—At home in Capernaum.

PARALLEL ACCOUNTS—Matt. 12:31-37.

OUTLINE—1. Forgiveness promised, vs. 28. 2. One exception, vs. 29. 3. The cause of such a severe warning, vs. 30.

ANALYSIS 3:28-30

I. FORGIVENESS PROMISED, VS. 28.
   1. Promised with great certainty.
   2. To all the sons of men.
   3. All sins and blasphemies.

II. ONE EXCEPTION, VS. 29.
  1. Applies to all.
  2. The blasphemy against the Holy Spirit.
  3. An eternal sin with no forgiveness.

III. THE CAUSE OF SUCH A SEVERE WARNING, VS. 30.
  1. The Pharisees and scribes involved.
  2. The words, "He hath an unclean spirit" caused the warning.

EXPLANATORY NOTES

I. FORGIVENESS PROMISED, VS. 28.

"28,29,30. "I say unto you, All sins shall be forgiven . . . He hath an unclean spirit." We learn clearly from this place in what this fearful sin consists; the only one of all the evils which the sons of men commit which will not be forgiven. Those with whom the Lord was now remonstrating were in danger of committing it, "*because* they said, He hath an unclean spirit." This was, in point of fact, almost equivalent to their calling the Lord an Incarnation of Satan.

II. ONE EXCEPTION, VS. 29.

In order to see something of the wickedness of this sin we must realize that all our Lord's teaching was on the side of God and goodness, and all His miracles, especially that of the expulsion of evil spirits, were done to enforce such teaching, and to set forth the character of God—the God Who sent Him, as at once a holy and benevolent God, desirous to free men from the yoke of all moral and spiritual as well as of all physical evil. To call the Spirit of such an One as our Lord an evil spirit was the extremest form of that wickedness denounced by the prophet when he said: "Woe unto them that call evil good and good evil; that put darkness for light, and light for darkness" (Is. 5:20). For a man to have a mind which could deliberately ascribe such a spirit to the Saviour is, as far as man can, to cut himself off from redemption—to make the acceptance of redemption impossible to him. This will be more clearly seen if we remember certain words said on this occasion by the Lord, which are only given in St. Matthew, "Whosoever speaketh a word against the Son of Man it shall be forgiven him, but whosoever speaketh against the Holy Ghost it shall not be forgiven him." A man might, through prejudice, speak against the claims of Jesus to be the Messiah. He might not be the Messiah whom he expected. He might be led away by false hopes of an earthly temporal Messiah, to reject the true one. Such an one might continue in infidelity, but the door of repentance and faith would be open to him, because, as Saul of Tarsus, what he did in rejecting Christ he did ignorantly and in unbelief. But if such an one had an opportunity of observing the Spirit of Christ—the Spirit of goodness and love displayed in all His character and discourses, and enforced by His mighty deeds, all on the side of benevolence and holiness, and yet deliberately called such a Spirit the Spirit of Evil, then there was nothing left in him for Redemption to take hold of. He was reprobate in the deepest sense of the word. He had first given himself over, and then he was given over by God, to a reprobate mind—that is, to his own evil, absolutely evil, self. But if a person thus ascribed the works of Christ to the power of evil, would that not be blaspheming against the Son of Man—not against the Holy Spirit? No, we are told that both the teaching and the mighty works of Christ were done by the Spirit (Acts 1:2; Matt. 12:28). Christ taught very emphatically that He did nothing of Himself. He must, consequently, act by some spiritual power not His own. Was that power Divine or diabolical? Of God, or of God's enemy? If a man deliberately said it was from God's enemy he displayed an intensity of perverse and malicious wickedness almost incredible.

III. THE CAUSE OF SUCH A SEVERE WARNING, VS. 30.

Some of the most acute observations on this difficult subject are to be found in Calvin's "Commentary on the Synoptics." "Shall any unbeliever curse God? It is as if a blind man were dashing against a wall. But no man curses the Spirit, who is not enlightened by Him, and conscious of ungodly rebellion against Him; for it is not a superfluous distinction, that all other blasphemies shall be forgiven, except that one blasphemy which is directed against the Spirit. If a man shall simply blaspheme against God, he is not declared to be beyond the hope of pardon, but of those who have offered outrage to the Spirit it is said that God will never forgive them. Why is this but because those only are *blasphemers* against the Spirit, who slander His gifts and power contrary to the conviction of their own mind?"

Two observations on all this may not be out of place:

1. It is clear that no one can have committed the sin against the Holy Ghost who desires the influence of the Holy Ghost to deliver him from sin, and make him love God, for such an one must believe that the power exhibited in Christ was on the side of God and goodness. He must believe that Christ was actuated and impelled by a holy and good spirit, which must be from God.

2. Looked at in the light of this one exception to the forgiving power of God, how exceedingly broad and large is the promise implied in the 28th verse, "Verily, I say unto you, ALL sins shall be forgiven unto the sons of men." The one exception proves the universality of the rule. If any sinner has a mind to lay hold on the Divine mercy, no memory of past sin need deter him; and the state of mind which he has towards sin, and his desire of deliverance, forbids the idea that he has committed the one unpardonable sin." (*M. F. Sadler*).

FACT QUESTIONS 3:28-30

176. What was meant by saying of the Lord, "He hath an unclean spirit"?
177. What helps us to realize something of the wickedness of this sin?
178. Show how the man who would attribute the work of the Holy Spirit to Satan is "reprobate in the deepest sense of the word."
179. Would not speaking against the works of Christ be speaking "against the Son of Man" instead of against the Holy Spirit? Explain.
180. What did Calvin's comments add to your understanding of this subject?
181. When can one know he has not committed this sin? Could the sinner know he had committed this sin? Explain.

D. THE HOUSEHOLD OF CHRIST 3:31-35

TEXT 3:31-35

"And there come his mother and his brethren; and, standing without, they sent unto him, calling him. And a multitude was sitting about him; and they say unto him, Behold, thy mother and thy brethren without seek for thee. And he answered them, and saith, Who is my mother and my brethren? And looking round on them which sat round about him, he saith, Behold, my mother and my brethren! For whosoever shall do the will of God, the same is my brother, and sister, and mother."

THOUGHT QUESTIONS 3:31-35

151. Are we to associate this incident with the one in 3:21? If so how?
152. How many half-brothers did Jesus have? (Cf. Matt. 13:56; Mark 6:3)
153. Why had His mother and brothers come?
154. Did Mary or the brothers speak to Jesus personally?
155. What was the purpose behind the reply of Jesus?
156. Did Jesus ignore the request of His mother? What impression did this make upon the multitude?; upon His mother?; upon His brothers?

COMMENT

TIME—Autumn A.D. 28.

PLACE—At home in Capernaum or on hill outside the city.

PARALLEL ACCOUNTS—Matt. 12:46-50; Luke 8:19-21.

OUTLINE—1. The arrival from Nazareth of His mother and brothers, vs. 31. 2. The message relayed to Jesus, vs. 32. 3. The response of Jesus to the visit, vs. 33-35.

ANALYSIS 3:31-35

I. THE ARRIVAL FROM NAZARETH OF HIS MOTHER AND BROTHERS, VS. 31.
   1. They stood without the door of the house.
   2. They requested an audience with Him.

II. THE MESSAGE RELAYED TO JESUS, VS. 32.
   1. Word sent in to the house from the family to the multitude.
   2. Someone told Jesus—probably one of His apostles.

III. THE RESPONSE OF JESUS TO THE VISIT, VS. 33-35.
   1. Answered with a question.
   2. He was now speaking with His family.
   3. Their needs were met in doing the will of God.

EXPLANATORY NOTES 3:31-35

I. THE ARRIVAL FROM NAZARETH OF HIS MOTHER AND BROTHERS, VS. 31.

"31, 32. They had come "to take him." (See note on verse 21). Mark has meanwhile described the scene in which they found him and the conversation in which he was engaged. He graphically shows them coming, standing without, and sending their message in through the crowd which they could not penetrate.

II. THE MESSAGE RELAYED TO JESUS, VS. 32.

A multitude sat about him. Not "the multitude." Some manuscripts (and Tischendorf, not the revisers) read, "Behold, thy mother and thy brethren and thy sisters without are seeking thee." The sisters are mentioned at Mark 6:3, but we know nothing of their names or history. His mother, coming as his mother, would doubtless have been welcomed; but an intrusive coming of his kindred to interfere with his work was quite another matter. Now that he was fully "about his Father's business," it was even more necessary than at the beginning of his work (John 2:4) that his mother should leave him to his Father's guidance. The moment, too, was a solemn one; he had just been speaking of the deadly opposition between the two kingdoms, and was in a frame of mind to prize most highly those who were "with him" and were not "scattering abroad." Any attempt to "scatter abroad," to weaken his work, would then be especially painful to his soul, and the more if it came from those who ought to know him well. Yet in their coming, (at least, we may be sure, in his mother's) there was kindness, but kindness how ignorant and mistaken! With what faults of friends he had to bear, as well as with evil in enemies! Not without pain, however, can he have given to his mother this rebuff. It was necessary; but he was a genuine son, and had a son's grateful and loyal heart toward his mother. His dying act of care for her (John 19:26) was a more congenial act to his heart.

III. THE RESPONSE OF JESUS TO THE VISIT, VS. 33-35.

33-35. *Who is my mother, or my brethren?* As if he did not know any from without who might appeal to him in that name.—*He looked round about on them which sat about him.* Literally, "in a circle about him." A graphic touch of Mark, to which Matthew adds another "Stretching out his hand toward his disciples." The gesture impressed one beholder, the look another. Very full of tenderness and solemnity must the look have been, accompanying such words, for here is the adoption of the obedient. —*Behold* (these are) *my mother, and my brethren! for whosoever shall do the will of God, the same is my brother, and my sister, and my mother.* In Luke, "My mother and my brethren are these, who hear and do the word of God." Compare "Every one that heareth these sayings of mine and doeth them" (Matt. 7:24). The center of his true kindred is not the mother, the brother, or the sisters, but the Father. This, he says, is the *only* center; there is no true unity with him except through spiritual harmony with the will of God: "Whoever would be a brother to me must be a child to him." Without this even natural kinship is as nothing. This, he also says, is the *real* center—the center of an actual unity; whoever is doing the will of God is united to Jesus by a tie stronger than any tie of flesh and blood: "Whoever is my Father's own is my own, one of my true kindred, in the closest bonds." Does he not even imply that the relation is as close and tender on one side as on the other?—toward the true brother, sister, and mother as toward the Heavenly Father? Do not God and they that do the will of God thus come into one family for Jesus, in which one and the same love reaches out in both directions? He said elsewhere, "As the Father hath loved me, so have I loved you;" and this is almost saying, "As I love my Father, so do I love you." Does this passage make God (or the doing of the will of God) the way to Christ, rather than Christ the way to God? Yes, in a sense. Whoever comes to Christ does the will of God in doing so, and it is in (not by the merit of) the doing of what God appoints that Christ accepts him. In all this Jesus did not disown the ties of kindred or put any slight upon them; rather did he show how highly he esteemed them. What must the natural relations be to him if he can make them the illustration of his relations both to God who sent him and to the people whom he saves?—Notice that the two mis-statements respecting Jesus, "He is beside himself" and "He hath Beelzebul," are morally very far apart. One was a misunderstanding of his work—an ignorant, mistaken misrepresentation in which there was at least room for the anxiety of affection, and in which he was regarded as unfortunate. It implied spiritual ignorance, but not malignity. The other was a malignant refusal to see good in him, and a spontaneous judgment that his highest good was highest evil. The one corresponds to "speaking a word against the Son of man;" while the other at least approaches the unpardonable sin of blasphemy against the Holy Spirit.—It is a satisfaction to find that after the resurrection of Jesus, Mary, the mother of the Lord, and his brethren were with the apostles in the upper room, where they waited for the fulfillment of Jesus' promise (Acts 1:14)." (W. N. Clarke)

FACT QUESTIONS 3:31-35

182. Who probably instigated the visit of the family?
183. Read Mark 6:3 and John 19:26 and notice the expression "son of Mary" as in contrast to the way the brothers are mentioned.
184. Why did Jesus commit the care of his mother to John if He had brothers?
185. Is there any contradiction in the accounts concerning the message of Mary and His brothers—Cf. Matt. 12:47; Luke 8:20; Mark 3:31.
186. What type of rebuke did Jesus give to His relatives? Show how this was needed.
187. Why "look round about Him" and "stretch forth His hand"?
188. Please explain how doing the will of God makes us brothers and sisters to Christ.

SUMMARY

2:1—3:35

There are three facts set forth in the preceding section, which have an important bearing on the claims of Jesus. The first is the fact that he had authority to forgive sins. This was demonstrated in the case of the paralytic (ii. 1-12), and it is the one fact which proves Jesus adapted to the highest demands of human salvation. Sins being forgiven, all other blessings follow as a consequence.

In the second place, it is shown that his conduct as a man was irreproachable. He was attacked in reference to the company he kept (ii. 13-17); in reference to his neglect of fasting (ii. 18-22); and in reference to Sabbath-keeping (ii. 23-28; iii. 1-6); but in all these matters he vindicated his conduct, and put his accusers to shame. That they made no more serious attacks on his conduct, proves that they could not, and that in morals he was irreproachable.

In the third place, it was demonstrated by his discussion with the Jerusalem scribes, that the power by which he cast out demons, and, *a fortiori,* the power by which his other miracles were wrought, was not, as they alleged, satanic, but divine. Finally, his answer to the people, in reference to the call of his mother and his brothers, is in perfect keeping with the character and position which the text assigns him. It is a singular infatuation which has led the Roman Catholic Church to attribute to Jesus even in heaven, a subserviency to his mother which he so expressly repudiated while on earth. (J. W. McGarvey).

2. THE PARABLES OF JESUS 4:1-34

a. The parable of the sower 4:1-9

TEXT 4:1-9

"And again he began to teach by the sea side. And there is gathered unto him a very great multitude, so that he entered into a boat, and sat in the sea; and all the multitude were by the sea on the land. And he taught them many things in parables, and said unto them in his teaching, Hearken: Behold, the sower went forth to sow: and it came to pass, as he sowed, some seed fell by the way side, and the birds came and devoured it. And other fell on the rocky ground, where it had not much earth; and straightway it sprang up, because it had no deepness of earth: and when the sun was risen, it was scorched; and because it had no root, it withered away. And other fell among the thorns, and the thorns grew up, and choked it, and it yielded no fruit. And others fell into the good ground, and yielded fruit, growing up and increasing; and brought forth, thirtyfold, and sixtyfold, and a hundredfold. And he said, Who hath ears, let him hear."

THOUGHT QUESTIONS 4:1-9

157. At what other time in Mark's account had Jesus taught by the seaside?
158. When did this teaching take place? Cf. Matt. 13.1.
159. How far out do you imagine the boat was from the shore?
160. How many in a great multitude? 10,000? 20,000? 36,000?
161. Why teach in parables?
162. What was the method of sowing to which Jesus referred? Why was the sower sowing?
163. Why was there a path in the midst of the field?
164. Why spring up soon in the rocky ground? What does this indicate about the fields of Palestine?
165. Why were there thorns in a field plowed for sowing?
166. Notice the plural word "others" in vs. 8 as contrasted with "other" in vs. 5 and vs. 7.—why?
167. What is meant by thirty-fold—sixty-fold—hundred-fold?

COMMENT

TIME—On the same day of the visit of the relatives of Jesus. Autumn A.D. 28.

PLACE—At the Sea of Galilee near Capernaum.

PARALLEL ACCOUNTS—Matt. 12:1-9; Luke 8:4-8.

OUTLINE—1. The place and the people for teaching, vs. 1. 2. The type of teaching, vs. 2. 3. The parable of the sower, vs. 3-9.

I. THE PLACE AND PEOPLE FOR TEACHING, VS. 1.
   1. By the seaside.
   2. A very great multitude.

II. THE TYPE OF TEACHING, VS. 2.
   1. In parables.
   2. They must give close attention to understand.

III. THE PARABLE OF THE SOWER, VS. 3-9.
   1. Some seed by the wayside, its fate.
   2. Some seed on rocky ground, its fate.
   3. Others in good soil, its fate.

EXPLANATORY NOTES

I. THE PLACE AND PEOPLE FOR TEACHING, VS. 1.

"1. Like Luke (8:4) and Matthew (13:1), Mark records, as a sort of epoch or important juncture in his history, the beginning of our Saviour's parabolical instructions, as a part of the preparatory process by which he contributed to the reorganization of the Church, although he did not actually make the change during his personal presence upon earth, because, as we have seen, it was to rest upon his death and resurrection as its corner-stone. The other part of his preparatory work consisted in the choice and education of the men by whom the change was to be afterwards effected. *Began*, as in 1:45, 2:23, is not superfluous, but indicates the opening of some new series or process, which was to be afterwards continued. *Again*, on the other hand, suggests that this was not the commencement of his teaching ministry, but only of one form of it. He had already taught the people publicly with great effect, but now began to teach them in a peculiar manner, with a special purpose to elucidate the nature of his kingdom, for the benefit of those who were to be his subjects, but without a too explicit and precipitate disclosure of his claim to the Messiahship. *By the sea-side*, or *along the sea*, i.e. the lake of Tiberias or Galilee, not only near it, but upon the very shore. *Was gathered*, or, according to the oldest text, *is gathered* (or *assembled*), a more graphic form, exhibiting the scene as actually passing. Another emendation by the latest critics is the change of the positive (*great*) to the superlative (*greatest*), either in reference to all former gatherings, or absolutely in the sense of the *very great. Multitude*, or *crowd*, the Greek word indicating not mere numbers, but promiscuous assemblage. The situation is like that described in 3:9, where we read that he directed a small vessel to be ready, if the crowd should be so great as to prevent his standing on the shore with safety or convenience. Here we find him actually *entering into* (or *embarking in*) the boat, no doubt the one already mentioned as in readiness, and *sitting in the sea*, i.e. upon the surface of the lake, while his vast audience was *on the land* (but) *at* (or *close to*) the sea, a stronger expression of proximity than that in the first clause. The scene thus presented must have been highly impressive to the eye, and still affords a striking subject for the pencil.

II. THE TYPE OF TEACHING, VS. 2.

2. *Taught* is in the imperfect tense, and according to Greek usage properly denotes continued or habitual action, *he was teaching* or he *used to teach.* This yields a good sense, as the writer is undoubtedly describing one of our Lord's favorite and constant modes of teaching. But the use of the aorist by Matthew (13:3) and Luke (8:4), and the specific reference by Mark himself (in v. 1) to a particular occasion, seem to forbid the wider meaning, unless it be supposed that he made use of the imperfect (as of the verb *began*) to intimate that, although this was the first instance of such teaching, it was not the last. *Many things,* of which only samples are preserved, even by Matthew, and still fewer in the book before us, showing that the writer's aim was not to furnish an exhaustive history, but to illustrate by examples the ministry of Christ. *In parables,* i.e. in the form and in the use of them. Parable is a slight modification of a Greek noun, the verbal root of which has two principal meanings, to propound (throw out or put forth), and to *compare* (throw together or lay side by side.) The sense of the noun derived from the former usage, that of any thing propounded, is too vague to be distinctive, comprehending as it does all kinds of instruction, which, from its very nature, must be put forth or imparted from one mind to another. The more specific sense of comparison, resemblance, is not only sanctioned by the usage of the best Greek writers (such as Plato, Aristotle, and Socrates), but recommended, not to say required, by the employment of a corresponding Hebrew word in precisely the same way. In its widest sense, a *parable* is any illustration from analogy, including the simile and metaphor as rhetorical figures, the allegory, apologue, fable, and some forms of proverbial expression. In a more restricted sense, the word denotes an illustration of moral or religious truth derived from the analogy of human experience. In this respect it differs from the fable, which accomplishes the same end by employing the supposed acts of inferior animals, or even those ascribed to inanimate objects, to illustrate human character and conduct. The only fables found in Scripture, those of Jotham (Judg. 9, 8-15) and Joash (2 Kings 14, 9), are given on human, not divine authority. The parable, in its more restricted sense, as just explained, is not necessarily narrative in form, much less fictitious, although this is commonly assumed in modern definitions of the term. There is good reason to believe that all the parables of Christ are founded in fact, if not entirely composed of real incidents. They are all drawn from familiar forms

of human experience, and with one exception from the present life. This creates a strong presumption that the facts are true, unless there be some positive reason for supposing them fictitious. Now the necessity of fiction to illustrate moral truth arises, not from the deficiency of real facts adapted to the purpose, but from the writer's limited acquaintance with them, and his consequent incapacity to frame the necessary combinaion, without calling in the aid of his imagination. But no such necessity can exist in the case of an inspired, much less of an omniscient teacher. To resort to fiction, therefore, even admitting its lawfulness on moral grounds, when real life affords in such abundance the required analogies, would be a gratuitous preference, if not of the false to the true, at least of the imaginary to the real, which seems unworthy of our Lord, or which, to say the least, we have no right to assume without necessity. In expounding the parables, interpreters have gone to very opposite extremes, but most to that of making everything significant, or giving a specific sense to every minute point of the analogy presented. This error is happily exposed by Augustine, when he says, that the whole plough is needed in the act of ploughing, though the ploughshare alone makes the furrow, and the whole frame of an instrument is useful, though the strings alone produce the music. The other extreme, that of overlooking or denying the significance of some things really significant, is much less common than the first, and for the most part found in writers of severer taste and judgment. The true mean is difficult but not impossible to find, upon the principle now commonly assumed as true, at least in theory, that the main analogy intended, like the center of a circle, must determine the position of all points in the circumference. It may also be observed, that as the same illustration may legitimately mean more to one man than to another, in proportion to the strength of their imaginative faculties, it is highly important that, in attempting to determine the essential meaning of our Saviour's parables, we should not confound what they may possibly be made to mean, with what they must mean to attain their purpose. In addition to these principles, arising from the nature of the parable itself, we have the unspeakable advantage of our Saviour's own example as a self-interpreter. *In his doctrine*, i.e. in the act of teaching, or perhaps the meaning here may be, in this peculiar mode of teaching.

III. THE PARABLE OF THE SOWER, VS. 3-9.

3. *Hearken; Behold, there went out a sower to sow.*

Mark has preserved one introductory ejaculation, not in Luke, and one neither in Luke nor Matthew. *Hear!* implying the power and intention to communicate something particularly worthy of attention. This word, perhaps a part of Peter's vivid recollection, may be said to introduce the whole succession of our Saviour's parables. *Behold!* (Matt. 13:3), lo, see, in one or two specific cases, but intended, no doubt, as a model and a guide in others, both in Hebrew and Hellenistic usage introduces something unexpected and surprising. Some take it even in its primary and strict sense, look! see there! implying that the object indicated was in sight or actually visible; in other words, that Christ was led to use this illustration by the casual appearance of a sower in a neighboring field; and this is often represented as the usual occasion of his parabolic teachings. It seems, however, to regard them as too purely accidental, and too little the result of a deliberate predetermination, such as we cannot but assume in the practice of a divine teacher. A safer form of the same proposition is the one already stated in a different connection (see above, on v. 1), namely, that our Saviour's parables, though not invariably suggested by immediate sights or passing scenes, are all derived from the analogy of human experience, and in most instances of common life. Thus the three here given by Mark are designed not only to exhibit different aspects of the same great subject, the Messiah's kingdom, but to exhibit them by means of images derived from one mode of life or occupation, that of husbandry, with which his auditors were all familiar, and in which, most probably, the greater part of them were constantly engaged. But besides these objections to the general supposition that our Saviour's parables were all suggested casually, such an assumption is forbidden in the case before us by the form of expression used by all these evangelists with striking uniformity. It is not as it naturally would be on the supposition now in question, *See, a sower goes* (or *going*) *out,* but with the article, and in the aorist or past tense, *lo, the sower went out. The sower,* like the *Fox* and the *Lion* in a fable, is generic, meaning the whole class, or an ideal individual who represents it. *Went out,* as we say in colloquial narrative, once upon a time, the precise date being an ideal one because the act is one of constant occurrence. As if he had said, 'a sower went out to sow, as you have often done and seen your neighbor do.' To *sow,* distinguishes his going out for this specific purpose from his going out on other errands. The sower went out as such, as a sower, to perform the function which the name denotes.

4. *And it came to pass as he sowed, some fell by the way-side, and the fowls of the air came and devoured it up.*

It came to pass, or something happened, implying something not indeed uncommon, but yet not belonging as of course to the process of sowin seed. *As he sowed,* literally, *in the* (act of) *sowing,* and therefore in the field, not merely on the way to it. *By the way* must therefore mean *along the path* trodden by the sower himself and hardened by his footsteps, not along the highway leading to his place of labor. This idea is distinctly expressed by Luke (8,5), *and it was trodden down,* i.e. it fell upon the path where he was walking. *Some* is understood by every reader to mean some of the seed which he was sowing, the noun, although not previously mentioned as it is in Luke (8, 4), being necessarily suggested by the kindred verb, *to sow, in sowing.* The principal circumstance in this part of the parable is not the treading of the seed, which Luke only adds to specify the place, but its lying exposed upon the trodden path, and there devoured by the birds. *Fowl,* now confined to certain species of domesticated birds, is co-extensive in Old English with *bird* itself. *Of the air,* literally *of heaven,* a Hebrew idiom, according to which *heaven* (or *heavens,* see above on 1, 10), is applied, not only to the whole material universe, except the earth (Gen. 1, 1) and especially to that part of it regarded as the more immediate residence of God (Gen. 19, 24), but also to the visible expanse or firmament (Gen. 1, 14), and to our atmosphere, or rather to the whole space between us and the heavenly bodies (Gen. 1,20). The version, therefore, is substantially correct, supposing these words to be genuine; but the latest critics have expunged them as a probable assimilation to the text of Luke (8,5): Nothing more is here intended by the phrase than *birds* in general, or *the birds* which his hearers well know were accustomed to commit such depredations. The familiarity of this occurrence and of those which follow, must have brought the illustration home to the business and bosoms of the humblest hearers, and, at the same time, necessarily precludes the idea of a fiction, when real facts were so abundant and accessible. It is idle to object that this particular sower never did go forth, when the opposite assertion can as easily be made, and when the terms employed, as we have seen, may designate the whole class of sowers, including multitudes of individuals, or any of these whom any one of the hearers might select as particularly meant, perhaps himself, perhaps some neighboring husbandman. Such a use of language, when applied to incidents of every-day occurrence, is as far as possible remote from fiction.

5. *And some fell on stony ground, where it had not much earth; and immediately it sprang up, because it had no depth of earth:*

Another (seed, or portion of the seed sown) fell upon the *stony* (or rocky soil), collective singulars equivalent to Matthew's plurals (13, 5.) The reference is not to loose or scattered stones (see below, on 5, 5), but to a thin soil overspreading a stratum or layer of concealed rock. *Immediately,* here used by Matthew also, is emphatic, the rapid germination being a material circumstance, and seemingly ascribed to the shallowness of the soil, allowing the seed no room to strike deep root, but only to spring upwards. The same idea is suggested by the verb itself, a double compound meaning to *spring up and forth.* The cause assigned by Luke

(8, 6), is not that of the speedy germination, but of the premature decay that followed it, as Mark describes more fully in the next verse.

6. *But when the sun was up, it was scorched; and because it had no root, it withered away.*

When the sun was up (or *risen*), is the literal translation of the text adopted by the latest critics, while the common or received text, though the same in meaning, has a different construction, *the sun having risen.* There is a peculiar beauty in the Greek here, which cannot be retained in a translation, arising from the use of the same verb (but in a less emphatic form) to signify the rising of the plant and of the sun, as both are said in English to be *up,* when one is above the surface of the earth and the other above the horizon. *Scorched* (or *burnt*) and withered (or *dried,* see above on 3:1) are different effects ascribed to different causes. The first is the evaporation of the vital sap or vegetable juices by the solar heat; the other their spontaneous failure from the want of a tenacious root. Together they describe, in a manner at once accurate and simple, the natural and necessary fate of a plant without sufficient depth of soil, however quick and even premature its vegetation.

7. *And some fell among thorns, and the thorns grew up, and choked it, and it yielded no fruit.*

Another, as in v. 5. *Into the thorns,* or in the midst of them, as it is more fully expressed by Luke (8, 7). *The thorns,* which happened to be growing there, or which are usually found in such situations. *Came up,* appeared above the surface, an expression constantly employed in English to denote the same thing. *Choked,* stifled, or deprived of life by pressure. This word though strictly applicable only to the suffocation of animal or human subjects (Luke 8:42), is here by a natural and lively figure transferred to the fatal influence on vegetable life of too close contact with a different and especially a ranker growth. Matthew (13: 7) uses a still more emphatic compound of the same verb, corresponding to our own familiar phrase *choked off.* And *fruit did not give,* though implied in all, is expressed only in Mark's account, which throughout this parable exhibits no appearance of abridgment.

8. *And other fell on good ground, and did yield fruit that sprang up, and increased, and brought forth, some thirty, and some sixty, and some an hundred.*

Another, as in vs. 5. 7. It is a minute but striking proof that the evangelists wrote independently of each other, and that their coincidence of language arose not from mutual imitation, but from sameness of original material, that in these three verses Matthew always says *upon,* Mark *into or among. Good ground,* in Greek, *the earth, the good,* earth or soil properly so called in distinction from the beaten, rocky, thorny places before mentioned. *Gave fruit coming up and growing,* the fruit or ripe grain being represented as passing through the changes which are really experienced in the earlier stages of the vegetable process. *Bore,* the same idea that was before expressed by *gave,* the latter having more explicit reference to the use and wants of men, the former to production in itself considered. What the seed bore, whether reaped or not, it *yielded* only on the former supposition. *One,* i.e. one seed, the proportion stated being that of the seed sown to the ripe grain harvested. As the Greek numeral here rendered *one* is distinguished from the preposition *in* by nothing but its accent and its aspiration, which are not given in the oldest copies, one distinguished modern critic substitutes the latter, *in thirty, and in sixty,* i.e. in this ratio or proportion, and another gives as the most ancient text a different preposition, meaning *to* (i.e. to the amount of) *thirty, sixty, and a hundred.* The productiveness ascribed to the nutritious grains in this place is by no means unexampled either in ancient or in modern times. It is indeed a moderate and modest estimate compared with some recorded by Herodotus, in which the rate of increase was double or quadruple even the highest of the three here mentioned, and the recent harvest in our western states affords examples of increase still greater.

9. *And he said unto them, He that hath ears to hear, let him hear.*

This idiomatic and proverbial formula, like many others of perpetual occurrence in our Lord's discourses, is never simply pleonastic or unmeaning, as the repetition often tempts us to imagine. On the contrary, such phrases are invariably solemn and emphatic warnings that the things in question are of the most momentous import, and entitled to most serious attention. They appear to have been framed or adopted by the Saviour, to be used on various occasions and in the pauses of his different discourses. There is something eminently simple and expressive in the one before us, which involves rebuke as well as exhortation. 'Why should you have the sense of hearing, if you do not use it now? To what advantage can you ever listen, if you turn a deaf ear to these admonitions? Now, now, if ever, he who can hear must hear, or incur the penalty of inattention!" But besides the importance of the subject and the juncture, it is here suggested that the very form of the communication calls for close attention, in default of which it can impart no knowledge and confer no benefit. This may be understood as having reference to the parabolic method of instruction which our Saviour now began and afterwards continued to employ so freely." (Alexander)

FACT QUESTIONS 4:1-9

189. What was the pulpit and the auditorium for Jesus' teaching in parables?

190. Did Jesus give these parables in rapid succession? If not, how were they given (Cf. 4:11).
191. If this is the first parable of Jesus what are we to say of 3:23?
192. Show how this parable reveals the method of farming in Jesus' day —There are several intimations—please find them.
193. Does Mark suggest there were three groups of seeds growing by making reference to the 30, 60 and 100 yields? Explain.

B. THE EXPLANATION OF THE PARABLE OF THE SOWER 4:10-20

TEXT 4:10-20

"And when he was alone, they that were about him with the twelve asked of him the parables. And he said unto them, Unto you is given the mystery of the kingdom of God; but unto them that are without, all things are done in parables: that seeing they may see, and not perceive; and hearing they may hear, and not understand; lest haply they should turn again, and it should be forgiven them. And he saith unto them, Know ye not this parable? and how shall ye know all the parables? The sower soweth the word. And these are they by the way side, where the word is sown; and when they have heard, straightway cometh Satan, and taketh away the word which hath been sown in them. And these in like manner are they that are sown upon the rocky places, who, when they have heard the word, straightway receive it with joy; and they have no root in themselves, but endure for a while; then, when tribulation or persecution ariseth because of the word, straightway they stumble. And others are they that are sown among the thorns; these are they that have heard the word, and the cares of the world, and the deceitfulness of riches, and the lusts of other things entering in, choke the word, and it becometh unfruitful. And those are they that were sown upon the good ground; such as hear the word, and accept it, and bear fruit, thirty-fold, and sixty-fold, and a hundred-fold."

THOUGHT QUESTIONS 4:10-20

168. Why wait until there were but twelve before He told the meaning of the parable?
169. What is meant by the expression "mystery of the kingdom"?
170. Please explain in your own words vs. 12.
171. Why the rebuke in vs. 13?
172. Are we to understand that Satan can actually remove the word of God from the heart? How?
173. How can we have "root in ourselves"? Cf. vs. 17.
174. Please notice that those with shallow hearts stumble "because of the word." Please explain.

175. Have the thorns of choking changed? What shall we do with them?
176. Why do some bear only 30 while others yield 100-fold for the Master?

COMMENT 4:10-20

LESSON ANALYSIS

I. SPEAKING IN PARABLES, VS. 10-13.
 1. Disciples Ask an Explanation. Mark 4:10; Matt. 13:10; Luke 8:9.
 2. The Reason for Parables. Mark 4:11, 12; Matt. 13:11-17; Luke 8:10.

II. WAYSIDE AND STONY GROUND, VS. 14-17.
 1. The Good Seed. Mark 4:14; Luke 8:11.
 2. Wayside Hearers. Mark 4:15; Matt. 13:19; Luke 8:12.
 3. Stony Ground Hearers. Mark 4:16, 17; Matt. 13:20; Luke 8:13.

III. THORNS AND GOOD GROUND, VS. 18-20.
 1. The Seed Choked Out. Mark 4:18, 19; Matt. 13:22; Luke 8:14.
 2. Good Seed in Good Ground. Mark 4:20; Matt. 13:23; Luke 8:15.

INTRODUCTION

He privately retired to the margin of the lake, desiring probably to "rest awhile;" but no sooner had he taken his seat beside the cool, still water, than he was again surrounded by the anxious crowd. At once, to escape the pressure and to command the audience better when he should again begin to speak, he stepped into one of the fishing-boats that floated at ease close by the beach, on the margin of that tideless inland sea. From the water's edge, stretching away upward on the natural gallery formed by the sloping bank, the great congregation, with every face fixed in an attitude of eager expectancy, presented to the Preacher's eye the appearance of a plowed field ready to receive the seed. As he opened his lips and cast the word of life freely abroad among them, he saw, he felt, the parallel between the sowing of Nature and the sowing of Grace. Into that word accordingly he threw the lesson of saving truth.—W. Arnot.

OUTLINE OF THE PARABLE OF THE SOWER—It will aid in understanding the lesson to have a clear outline in the mind of the application. This is the first parable the Saviour spoke as far as we have record. He spoke the parable to a vast audience in whose minds the story was lodged and left for reflection without an explanation of its meaning. He had sowed, in this illustrative way, the seed of the kingdom broadcast, and in many a heart it would live until it burst forth, full of meaning, to bear fruit. His apostles, not accustomed to this mode of teaching, come to him privately and ask the meaning. In order to understand the parable we must go with the other disciples and listen to the explanation given in verses 10-20. Christ is the great Sower, and all whom he sends forth to preach are sowers under him. The seed sown is his Word, the Gospel of the Kingdom. The soil where the seed is cast is human hearts. Four kinds of human hearts are described: 1. The *wayside* hearer; the light flippant, indifferent hearer upon whom no impression is produced. 2. The *stony* hearer; the heart that exhibits an evanescent feeling at the appeal of the gospel, but upon whom no permanent impression is made. 3. The *thorny* soil; the heart that takes in the Word, but is so full of worldly cares that these presently gain the mastery. This describes the world-serving hearing. 4. The *good* soil; the good and honest heart; the heart that receives and retains the truth. In such a heart the seed will grow and the new life will be manifest. Three things, then, are needful: 1. A Sower. 2. Good Seed; the pure word of God. 3. A good and honest heart. A dishonest man cannot be converted until he casts out his dishonesty. He who cavils at and deceitfully entreats the word of God will not be profited.

EXPLANATORY NOTES

I. SPEAKING IN PARABLES.—10. *When he was done.* This may have occurred after the public labors of the day were over and the multitude had been dismissed. By comparing with Matthew we learn that the Lord spoke seven parables in succession, and it seems to me more probable that the explanations were given in the quiet when surrounded only by the twelve and "they that were about him with the twelve," a number of his friends and disciples. *Asked of him the parables.* This language shows that the Lord had spoken more than once before the explanation was asked for or given. Though the parable was new to his disciples it was not a new method of instruction. A number occur in the Old Testament, and it was frequently adopted by the Jewish rabbis. It differs from an allegory or fable in that its characters are real and it does not violate possibilities. It is an imaginary illustration of real truth. In this instance the Saviour stated some facts familiar to all the farming population of Palestine and made them the vehicle to carry spiritual truth. Perhaps from where the multitude was gathered a sower on the plain of Gennesaret was visible at work and pointed to by the Lord.

11. *Unto you it is given to know the mystery of the kingdom.* A "mystery" is not something obscure, but something plain to those initiated, but a secret to those without. The Greeks had what were called the "Eleusinian mysteries," unknown to all without, but fully explained to all who were initiated. The Saviour says no more than that there are matters that my disciples shall know that those without can never understand. When one makes Jesus the Master and himself a pupil (disciple), of course he has the vantage ground and will be admitted to spiritual knowledge that he could never obtain had he not entered the school of Christ. The Eng-

lish alphabet is a mystery to tne savage, but is no mystery to even little children who have learned it. *To them that are wihout . . . parables.* The method of instruction by parables was peculiarly adapted to their state. It was interesting, and would excite attention, and many of the similes would be long remembered, and their true meaning would insensibly break forth upon their minds. It would lead them to some correct views before they were aware. At the same time the truths thus delivered were covered by a thin veil, and were not immediately apprehended; thus, while instant rejection might be the result of presenting the naked truth, attention to the truth was secured by the interesting covering under which it was couched. He spake only in parables to these Jewish cavillers, in order to take from them the means of knowing truths which they would merely abuse. He would not cast pearls before swine.

12. *That seeing they may see, and not perceive.* Did he speak in parables because he did not wish them to *know and to enjoy?* Everything shows the reverse. But he was aware, that, in consequence of the inveteracy of their prejudice, they could not, in the first instance, see "the secret of the kingdom" without being repelled in spirit, and confirmed in their dissent and dislike. He wished, therefore, that they should not "see." But, at the same time, he graciously wished that they should "look," and keep "looking," so that they might, if possible, get such a glimpse of the inner glory as might fascinate their interest and attention, and by and by disarm their prejudices, so that they might with safety be permitted to "see".—*Morison.* Though they see the truth intellectually, they shall not appreciate it spiritually; they see it as the horse sees the same prospect with his rider, without appreciation.—*Abbott.* But their position was according to their own choice. Christ forbade none; and the disciples in this case were not merely the twelve chosen by him, but all who would come. Moral inability always is the fruit of moral unwillingness. Those who cannot see, were in the first place unwilling to see. *Lest . . . they should be converted.* His meaning is not, "These things are done in parables, lest they should be converted," but, "Their eyes they closed, etc., lest at any time they should be converted." That is, men willfully close their hearts to the truth, lest they should be led to repentance and reformation. They *will* not, therefore they *cannot.*

13. *Know ye not this parable?* It is not a reproof, but means, "You find you cannot understand this without assistance." The next question, *and how then will ye know all parables?* extends the thought to all parables, but intimates further: "The first parable of the kingdom is the basis of all the rest. If they understand not this, they could not understand any that followed. If they had the explanation of this, they had the key for the understanding of all others." Hence our Lord gives, not rules of inter-

pretation, but examples, one of which is here preserved to be our guide in interpretation.

II. WAYSIDE AND STONY GROUND.—14. *The sower soweth the word.* The great Sower is Christ; the seed sown is the Word of God, the Gospel, whether spoken by Christ, his apostles, preachers, Sunday-school teachers, any disciple, or written in the New Testament, or upon the printed page of the book, tract or newspaper. All spiritual life depends on a divine seed sown in the heart by the divine Sower. The life of the seed depends on, first, receiving it; second, rooting it; third, cultivating it.

15. *These are they by the wayside.* The fields of Palestine were not fenced and lay in the open country while the population lived in hamlets. The roads or paths were through the fields. Thomson, in the *Land and the Book,* says: "There are neither roads, nor thorns, nor stony places in such lots. They go forth into the open country, where the path passes through the cultivated land, where there are no fences, where thorns grow in clumps all around, where rocks peep out in places through the scanty soil, and hard by are patches extremely fertile." Some of the seed fell on the hard-beaten paths where it would lie until picked up by the birds. This, said the Savior, represents the hardened, worldly hearts that never allow the seed of the kingdom to enter at all. These never allow the word to get under the surface of their thoughts. The way is the heart, beaten and dried by the passage of evil thoughts. Sin has so hardened the heart, worldliness has so deadened the feelings, sinful pleasures and desires have so dulled the conscience that God's truth makes no impression, more than a passing dream, or a pleasant song, to be heard and forgotten. *Satan . . . taketh away the word that was sown.* The object of the preaching of the word is to save souls; the aim of Satan is to destroy souls. The word lies there ready for him. It has not pierced the soil of the heart. It has found no entrance. It is all on the surface. It lies quite naked and exposed. The word has been heard, and that is all. It is snatched away at once. Guthrie says: "Wherever there is a preacher in the pulpit, there is a devil among the pews, busy watching the words that fall from the preacher's lips to catch them away." Every preacher is familiar with this class. Upon their hard, flinty hearts the most searching appeals fail to make any impression. They come out of idle curiosity, or to cavil and to scoff and go away as they came.

16. *They which are sown on stony ground.* Under the figure of the stony ground, he depicts that lively but shallow susceptibility of spirit which grasps the truth eagerly, but receives no deep impressions, and yields as quickly to the reaction of worldly temptations as it had yielded to the divine word. Those whose feelings are touched, but not their

conscience or their will. *Immediately.* The seed in such case "springs up"—all the quicker from the shallowness of the soil—"because it has no depth of earth." *Receive it with gladness.* The hearer described has not counted the cost; whatever was fair and beautiful in Christianity, as it first presents itself, had attracted him—its sweet and comfortable promises, the moral loveliness of its doctrines, but not its answer to the deepest needs of the human heart; as neither, when he received the word with gladness, had he contemplated the having to endure hardness in his warfare with sin and Satan and the world.—*Trench.*

17. *Have no root in themselves.* They make profession and begin, but do not hold out, because the good seed has not rooted deeply. These are they who are moved by emotion, not by a deep sense of conviction. *When affliction or persecution.* As the heat scorches the blade which has no deepness of earth, so the troubles and afflictions, which would have strengthened a true faith, cause a faith which was merely temporary to fail. The image has a peculiar fitness and beauty, for as the roots of a tree are out of sight, yet from them it derives its firmness and stability; so upon the hidden life of the Christian his firmness and stability depend.—*Trench.* A sneer from some leading spirit in a literary society, or a laugh raised by some gay circle of pleasure-seekers in a fashionable drawing-room, or the rude jests of scoffing artisans in a workshop, may do as much as the fagot and the stake to make a fair but false disciple deny his Lord.

III. THORNS AND GOOD GROUND.—18. *Sown among thorns.* The seed which takes root, but is stifled by the thorns that shoot up with it, figures the mind in which the elements of worldly desire develop themselves along with the higher life, and at last become strong enough to crush it, so that the received truth it utterly lost. The evil here is neither a hard nor a shallow soil—there is *softness* enough, and *depth* enough; but it is the existence in it of what draws all the moisture and richness of the soil away to itself, and so *starves the plant.*

19. *Cares of this world.* What are these thorns? First, the cares of this world—anxious, unrelaxing attention to the business of his present life; second, the deceitfulness of riches—of those riches which are the fruit of this worldly care; third, the pleasures of this life—the enjoyments, in themselves it may be innocent, in which worldly prosperity enables one to indulge. These "choke" or "smother" the word; drawing off so much of one's attention, absorbing so much of one's interest, and using up so much of one's time, that only the dregs of these remain for spiritual things, and a fagged, hurried and heartless formalism is at length all the religion of such persons.—*J. F. and B.* Our Savior here places riches in the midst

between cares and pleasures; for cares generally precede the gaining of riches, and, when gained, they draw men into pleasures and indulgence.—*Dodd.*

20. *Sown on good ground, etc.* A heart soft and tender, stirred to its depths on the great things of eternity, and jealously guarded from worldly engrossments, such only is the "honest and good heart" (Luke 8:15), which "keeps," i. e., "retains" the seed of the word, and bears fruit just in proportion as it is such a heart. Such "bring forth fruit with patience" (v. 15), or continuance, "enduring to the end;" in contrast with those in whom the word is "choked," and brings no fruit to perfection. The "thirty-fold" is designed to express the lowest degree of fruitfulness; the "hundred-fold," the highest, and the "sixty-fold" the intermediate degrees of fruitfulness. As a "hundred-fold," though not unexampled (Gen. 26:12), is a rare return in the natural husbandry, so the highest degrees ot spiritual fruitfulness are, too, seldom witnessed.—*J.F. and B. Some thirty-fold, some sixty and some a hundred.* Thirty-fold is now a first-rate crop, even for such plains as Esdraelon, just below Nazareth. But in the time of Christ there might be realized, in favorable circumstances, a hundred-fold. Intelligent gentlemen (in the plain of Esdraelon) maintain that they have themselves reaped more than an hundred-fold. Moreover, the different kinds of fertility may be ascribed to different kinds of grain: Barley yields more than wheat; and white maize, sown in the neighborhood, often yields several hundred-fold. An extraordinary number of stalks do actually spring from a single root. Here, on this plain of Sidon, I have seen more than a hundred, and each with a head bowing gracefully beneath the load of well-formed grains. The yield was more than a thousand-fold.—*Land and Book.* Observe the four kinds of seed: The first did not spring up at all; the second sprang up, but soon withered away; the third sprang up and grew, but yielded no fruit; the fourth sprang up, grew, and brought forth fruit. And as there are three causes of unfaithfulness, so there are three *degrees* of fruitfulness, but only one *cause* of fruitfulness.—*Maclear.*

FACT QUESTIONS 4:10-20

194. Show how the parable of the sower was appropriate to the time and place where it was given.
195. Describe briefly the four types of soils.
196. Did Jesus speak more than one parable upon this occasion? How many?
197. Was this a new method of instruction? Show the difference in a parable and an allegory.

198. Explain the expression "mystery of the kingdom."
199. Show how appropriate the use of parables was to "those without."
200. Please explain: "that seeing they may see, and not perceive."—"lest they be converted."
201. What seems to be "the key" to all the parables?
202. In what way can the seed be sown?
203. Where was "the wayside" in the fields of Palestine?
204. Why are wayside hearers so indifferent?
205. Explain how Satan takes away the word or the seed?
206. What causes such a joyful acceptance on the part of some—only to be lost later?
207. Show the difference between emotion and conviction.
208. Discuss carefully the three types of thorns and their interrelation.
209. Show the three causes of unfaithfulness, the three degrees of fruitfulness and the one cause of fruitfulness.

C. THE PARABLE OF THE LAMP 4:21-23

TEXT 4:21-23

"And he said unto them, Is the lamp brought to be put under the bushel, or under the bed, and not to be put on the stand? For there is nothing hid, save that it should be manifested; neither was anything made secret, but that it should come to light. If any man hath ears to hear, let him hear."

THOUGHT QUESTIONS 4:21-23

177. When was this parable given? before or after the explanation of the parable of the sower?
178. Who is represented by the lamp?
179. Isn't there something humorous about the location of the lamp? Why use it?
180. Jesus states a strange purpose for hiding something—explain.
181. What is the main point of this parable?

COMMENT

TIME—Autumn A.D. 28. At the same time as the first parable.

PLACE—In a boat in the Sea of Galilee, the crowd on the shore.

PARALLEL ACCOUNT—Luke 8:16, 17.

OUTLINE—1. The purpose of the lamp, v. 21. 2. Items are hidden for the purpose of later being revealed, vs. 22, a. 3. Secrets are made to be told, vs. 22b. 4. Those who can should understand, vs. 23.

ANALYSIS

I. THE PURPOSE OF THE LAMP. VS. 21.
  1. Not under the bushel.
  2. Not under the bed.
  3. On the stand.

II. ITEMS ARE HIDDEN TO BE REVEALED. 22A.

III. SECRETS ARE MADE TO BE TOLD. 22B.

IV. THOSE WHO CAN SHOULD UNDERSTAND. VS. 23.

EXPLANATORY NOTES

I. THE PURPOSE OF THE LAMP, VS. 21.

21. "*And he said unto them, Is a* (or the) *candle brought to be put under, etc.*

22. *For there is nothing hid which shall not be manifested"* (or, save that it should be manifested).

These verses must be taken together, and their meaning seems to be something of this sort. The Lord had for certain wise, and, we believe, merciful reasons, adopted a new role of teaching, in which He veiled His meaning from the multitude under parables, but this was not because He intended their meaning to be permanently hidden from the world, but because He intended that it might be the better known to the world when the fitting time was come. To his end He made known the interpretation to His Apostles, not for themselves, but for the world. His truth—the truth of the Gospel—was the lamp; this lamp of truth He intended not for a corner of the world, or for a select few, but for all men of all nations, who would turn their faces towards it and receive it, and so He gave it now to the Apostles, who, after Pentecost, were to make it known to all nations for the obedience of faith.

II. ITEMS ARE HIDDEN TO BE REVEALED. 22A.

God does not conceal any mystery, any religious truth, merely for the sake of concealing it. If He conceals any truth it is that He may ultimately make it better known. This very parable is an illustration of this. If any truth ever shone forth upon the lamp-stand of the Church it is that which is taught us by this parable, that the word of the Gospel is efficacious or not, according to the state of heart of the recipients; so that men must in very deed "take heed" as to "how" they hear and "what" they hear. This meaning is still more clearly enforced by the true reading of the first clause of verse 22. There is nothing hidden, save that it should be manifested. So we have this parable given in full in three out of the four Gospels, and we may safely say that, with the exception of that of the returning prodigal, there is none which has been more expounded and enforced by preachers in all ages. The meaning, however, of verse 21, is much obscured by deficiency of translation. We lose much of the significance if we think of the modern candle and candlestick carried about in the hand. On the contrary, it is the lamp of the house put upon the lamp-stand, or candelabrum, which is so elevated that any lamp upon it can lighten up all the interior.

III. SECRETS ARE MADE TO BE TOLD. VS. 22B.

The reader will notice that the Lord uses this aphorism here with quite a different significance to that which He gives to it in Matt. 10:26.

IV. THOSE WHO CAN SHOULD UNDERSTAND. VS. 23

23. If any man have ears to hear, etc. If this was said not in the hearing of the multitude, but to the Apostles, or to those select ones to whom He had just expounded the parable, then it implies that there are still deeper mysteries of grace which require, for their apprehension, a more effectual opening of the soul's ears, and a deeper preparation of heart. Men have ears to hear certain fundamental, or practical truths, who still have not as yet ears to hear certain deep mysteries." (M. F. Sadler).

FACT QUESTIONS 4:21-23

210 Why interpret verses 21 and 22 together?
211. What is "the lamp" of the parable?
212. When was the lamp hidden? Why?
213. When was it put on "the stand"?
214. Show how this parable relates to the parable of the sower.
215. What deficiency in translation has hindered our understanding?
216. If Jesus spoke vs. 23 to the apostles, what does it mean?

D. A WARNING FOR HEARERS. 4:24, 25

TEXT 4:24, 25

"And he said unto them, Take heed what ye hear: with what measure ye mete it shall be measured unto you: and more shall be given unto you. For he that hath, to him shall be given: and he that hath not, from him shall be taken away even that which he hath."

THOUGHT QUESTIONS 4:24, 25

182. Please associate these verses with what has been said—what is "the measure" and " measuring."
183. Who would measure to the apostles?
184. How does this principle apply to today?
185. Isn't it unfair to give to the one who has and take from the one who has not?
186. Please explain in your own words the principle involved.

COMMENT

The four parables of Mark were all given at the same time and place. The parallel accounts are in Matt. 13:18-32 and Luke 8:11-19.

19. This *warning for the hearers* is also found in Luke 8:18.

OUTLINE—1. Measure determines measuring, 24a. 2. He who has, 25a. 3. He who has not, 25b.

ANALYSIS

I. MEASURE DETERMINES MEASURING, VS. 24.
   1. What amount are you giving of what I have given to you?
   2. What you have given determines what you shall receive.

II. HE WHO HAS, VS. 25A.
   1. The one or ones to whom Jesus has given.
   2. If this one gives of what he has received he shall receive more.

III. HE WHO HAS NOT, VS. 25B.
   1. He refuses to give what he has.
   2. What he had is lost.

EXPLANATORY NOTES

I. MEASURE DETERMINES MEASURING, VS. 24.

24, 25. Thus far the duty of using the truth as light has been grounded in the nature of truth and the purpose of the Teacher; now it is grounded in the law of human life itself. The words, *And he saith unto them,* repeated here, probably indicate, not a new beginning with a change of time and place, but rather the narrator's remembrance of the special emphasis with which all this was spoken, very likely after a solemn pause.—*Take heed what ye hear.* Luke, "how ye hear." Not, "Be careful what you listen to," as if he would warn against dangerous teachers, but, "Carefully consider what you are hearing; observe how important it is; remember how necessary that you make the right use of it." It is almost, "Take heed to what you hear." The reason assigned for this caution is that, according to the universal law, what one does will return to him.—The words *that hear* are to be omitted, and the omission considerably changes the structure of the sentence: "With what measure ye mete, it shall be measured to you, and added to you."—This saying, *With what measure ye mete, it shall be measured to you,* proverbial in form, is applied in the Sermon on the Mount (Matt. 7:2) to the retribution that must come upon uncharitableness and self-willed judgment. Here our Lord gives it a quite different application; it is a law of life, and may be applied in many ways. In this case its lesson is, "You will be dealt with, as to truth, as you deal with others. Hide it, and it will be hidden from you; impart it, and it will be imparted to you." How many souls, in dealing with trust as God has given it to them, have found it even so—that concealment was loss, while giving was gain! If the apostles had kept their truth as a private trust, how their souls would have shrivelled!—*Shall more be given* is a promise of a return, which shall be not merely as the gift, but greater. So Luke 6:38. (Compare 2 Cor. 9:8-14).

II. HE WHO HAS, VS. 25A.

Verse 25 contains what was evidently more or less a proverbial saying with our Lord. *He that hath, to him shall be given,* etc. (See Matt. 25:29; Luke 19:26.) Here it fits the connection far otherwise than as in the passages referred to—another illustration of our Lord's various use of single important sayings. Here, by a very striking turn of thought, *he that hath* is identified with him who imparts his trust of truth to others, the free giver, the true apostle, messenger of grace and truth; while *he that hath not* is identified with him who keeps his trust of truth to himself, content to be ever a disciple without becoming an apostle. The giver *hath,* the miser *hath not.* How true a description of men, and how true an interpretation of the law of life!—And now it is declared that for these two classes there shall be retribution. *He that hath, to him shall be given.* So Luke 6:38—a passage that may serve as a link between this and Matt. 7:2: "Give, and it shall be given unto you." (See also Luke 12:48).

III. HE WHO HAS NOT, VS. 25B.

And he that hath not, from him shall be taken even that which he hath. How is this? He "hath not," and yet he "hath," something that he can lose. Yes; the spiritual miser possesses much in his own esteem; much truth has been entrusted to him; but if he is not a giver of truth, and so a possessor, his possession shall become no possession: what he hath shall be worthless to him. Such instruction may well have made the apostles careful what use they made of the parables. Partly to this, perhaps, it is due that they were so faithful in putting the lamp on the lampstand, not only by preaching, but also by making record of his words, especially such words as these." (W. N. Clarke).

FACT QUESTIONS 4:24, 25

217. Read Matt. 7:2 and Luke 6:38 and show the difference in the use of the same principle here.
218. Is this a warning or an encouragement? Discuss.
219. Who is the one to whom much was given?
220. How does the attitude of hearing and heeding the words of Jesus relate to this?

E. THE PARABLE OF SECRET GROWTH. 4:26-29

TEXT 4:26-29

"And he said, So is the kingdom of God, as if a man should cast seed upon the earth; and should sleep and rise night and day, and the seed should spring up and grow, he knoweth not how. The earth beareth fruit of herself; first the blade, then the ear, then the full corn in the ear. But when the fruit is ripe, straightway he putteth forth the sickle, because the harvest is come."

THOUGHT QUESTIONS 4:26-29

187. Please settle in your mind a clear definition of "the kingdom of heaven." We believe it refers in every referenc to the church Jesus establishd—either in the temporal or eternal sense. Do you agree?
188. What is the seed cast upon the earth?
189. Who casts the seed?
190. Who sleeps?
191. Why mention "knoweth not how" in vs. 27b?
192. How can we tell when the grain is ripe? What is the sickle?
193. What is the main point of this parable?

COMMENT

All four parables of Jesus as recorded in Mark were given at the same time and place. Only this parable is not mentioned either by Matthew or Luke.

OUTLINE—*A picture of the kingdom of God.* (1) A man who sows seed, vs. 26. (2) He waits for the growth, vs. 27. (3) The visible growth, vs. 28. (4) The harvest, vs. 29.

ANALYSIS

A Picture Of the Kingdom of God

I. A MAN WHO SOWS THE SEED, VS. 26.
   1. The seed must be broadcast.
   2. The seed must go into the earth.

II. HE WAITS FOR THE GROWTH, VS. 27.
   1. In the ordinary course of living.
   2. The growth occurs he knows not how.

III. THE VISIBLE GROWTH, VS. 28.
   1. First the blade of grass.
   2. Then the ear.
   3. Then the grain in the ear.

IV. THE HARVEST, VS. 29.
   1. When the grain is ripe.
   2. Sickle thrust in for the reaping.

EXPLANATORY NOTES

I. THE MAN WHO SOWS THE SEED, VS. 26.

"26, 27. *he knoweth not how.*—To some extent he knoweth how; it is by the process described in the next verse: "the earth bringeth forth fruit of herself; first the blade, then the ear, after that the full corn in the ear."

II. HE WAITS FOR THE GROWTH, VS. 27.

He may know still further, that it grows by the chemical action of light, warmth, and moisture; but still there is a part of the process that he does not know.

III. THE VISIBLE GROWTH, VS. 28.

28, 29. *But when the fruit.*—Although the sower knows not how the seed grows, and remains not to see its growth, still it grows. From sowing time till harvest the man has nothing to do: no intermediate cultivation is required. This is true of the "corn" (wheat and barley) referred to, though not of our Indian corn.

IV. THE HARVEST, VS. 29.

The kingdom of heaven is like this (verse 26), in that the seed of the kingdom, which is the word of God, when sown in a community, even though the sower go away and neglect it, will spring up of itself and bear fruit, and will be ready at a future day for the harvest. This is often exemplified in the labors of the evangelist. He preaches in a community faithfully, and apparently without success, for a length of time, and then, after a lapse of months or years, returns to the same place, and with comparatively little exertion reaps an abundant harvest. The parable teaches what observation abundantly confirms, that such an adaptation exists between the human soul and the word of God, that when the latter is once implanted a future harvest will usually be the result." (*J. W. McGarvey*).

FACT QUESTIONS 4:26-29

221. Does this parable relate to the fourth type of hearers in the production of fruit?
222. Who is the sower?
223. Why mention the period of time in this parable?
224. Why describe the growth of the grain?
225. Are ministers of the word also reapers? Please discuss.

F. THE PARABLE OF THE MUSTARD SEED. 4:30-32.

TEXT 4:30-32

"An he said, How shall we liken the kingdom of God? or in what parable shall we set it forth? It is like a grain of mustard seed, which, when it is sown upon the earth, though it be less than all the seeds upon the earth, yet when it is sown, groweth up, and becometh greater than all the herbs, and putteth out great branches; so that the birds of the heaven can lodge under the shadow thereof."

THOUGHT QUESTIONS 4:30-32

194. Once again settle in your mind just what is represented by the expression "kingdom of God." Can you see the fulfillment of this expression in the church? We refer to the church described in the book of Acts.

195. Why select the mustard seed for comparison? Is it the smallest seed on the earth?
196. Who are the birds and what are the branches?
197. What is the principle point of this parable?

COMMENT

This is the fourth and last parable here recorded by Mark. Like the previous three it was given in the autumn of A.D. 28 while Jesus sat in a little boat in the Sea of Galilee.

A Picture of the Kingdom

OUTLINE—1. Like a grain of mustard seed, vs. 30, 31. 2. When grown is greater than all the herbs, vs. 32a. 3. A place for the birds of the heaven, vs. 32b.

ANALYSIS

I. A GRAIN OF MUSTARD SEED, VS. 30, 31.
   1. Just like the kingdom of God.
   2. Sown upon the earth.
   3. Less than all the seeds.

II. WHEN IT IS GROWN, 32A.
   1. Greater than all the herbs.
   2. Putteth out branches.

III. A PLACE FOR BIRDS, 32B.
   1. In branches.
   2. Under the shadow.

EXPLANATORY NOTES

I. A GRAIN OF MUSTARD SEED, VS. 30, 31.

Whereunto (or how) *shall we liken the kingdom of God? or with what comparison* (or parable) *shall we compare it?* In using the plural, *we,* our Lord seems to conceive of his disciples as deliberating with him in the choice of a comparison; not that he was in doubt as to how the gospel could be illustrated—comparisons thronged upon him—but because he would have them also watch for comparisons. The world was full of them, and they, the teachers of men in higher things, must learn, as well as their Master, to find them. Yet possibly he may sometimes, like any one of them, have had to feel after an illustration in nature that was suited to his thought.—*A grain of mustard-seed.* There seems to be no good reason for looking elsewhere than to the ordinary mustard of the East. Thomson (*The Land and the Book*) has seen it as high as a horse and rider. (See also the beautiful incident in Dr. Hackett's *Illustrations of Scripture,* p. 124.—A.H.) This is the *Sinapis nigra;* but some have thought that the *Salvadora Persica* was more probably the herb that Jesus had in mind. The former, however, meets all the real requirements of the case, and was the more familiar plant to his hearers. "It (the *Sinapis nigra*) is a small grain producing a large result; the least of the husbandman's seeds, becoming the greatest of the husbandman's herbs. This is the point of the parable, and gives the only sense in which the kingdom of heaven is like a grain of mustard-seed" (*The Bible Educator*, 1. 121).—*Less than* and *greater than* are not to be pressed to the point of minute precision. There may be smaller seeds in existence without giving us reason to stumble at our Saviour's words. The mustard-seed was commonly spoken of as the smallest of seeds, and that is enough.

II. WHEN IT IS GROWN, VS. 32 A.

Becometh greater than all the herbs. Matthew, "is greater than the herbs, and becometh a tree"—i. e., of course, a tree in appearance, not botanically. The *great branches* are such as one would think impossible upon an herb that sprang from so small a seed.—The comparison calls for very little explanation, the lesson—small beginnings and great results—being very plain. Such is the kingdom, begun obscurely, with no human prospect of greatness, no seeming possibility of success. It began among the Jews, a disappointed people chafing under foreign masters; it was the smallest of sects among them; it contradicted their ideas, and was rejected by them; it seemed to be powerless at home, and without opportunities abroad; and its founder died on the cross. Even after the day of Pentecost it seemed but a feeble sect. Yet compare the strong language of Paul in Rom. 16:26; Col. 1:23 as to the wide extension of the gospel within the apostolic times.

III. A PLACE FOR BIRDS, VS. 32 B.

Consider also the power of the name and principles of Jesus in the world today, and the ever-widening circle of Christian influence. The kingdom has grown out of all resemblance to its humble beginning. Such is the kingdom; and the same rule is to be observed in its agencies. They are often obscure and yet mighty. A single act of a quiet person often seems possessed of a germinant power of usefulness that brings most unexpected fruit to the glory of God. Christian history is full of illustrations. Notice that this comparison does not set forth the greatness of the kingdom absolutely, as destined to fill the earth, but only relatively, in contrast with the insignificance of its apparent promise." (W. N. Clarke).

FACT QUESTIONS 4:30-32

226. Who does the planting of the mustard seed? Where?
227. Does it help us in our work for Christ to know the mustard seed is the smallest of all seeds? How?
228. When was the seed of mustard first planted?
229. Show how this parable has been fulfilled—is being fulfilled and can be fulfilled.

G. LAST WORDS ON PARABLES 4:33-34

TEXT 4:33, 34

"And with many such parables spake he the word unto them, as they were able to hear it: and without a parable spake he not unto them: but privately to his own disciples he expounded all things."

THOUGHT QUESTIONS 4:33, 34

198. How many parables did Jesus use? Ans. "The total number of parables is a matter of difference of opinion. Fahling, in his *Harmony,* lists 56: *A. T. Robertson.* 52. *Trench.* 30." (Earle).
199. What is meant by the expression "as they were able to hear"?
200. Is it indeed true that "without a parable He spoke not unto them"? Explain.
201. At this time who were "His own disciples"?

COMMENT

At the conclusion of the record of the parables we have these concluding words of the writer Mark. No outline or analysis is needed here.
PARALLEL ACCOUNTS—Matt. 13:34, 35.

EXPLANATORY NOTES

"33. *And with many such parables spake he the word unto them, as they were able to hear* (it.)

These are mere samples of the parables by which our Lord elucidated or disguised the doctrine of his kingdom to the different classes of his hearers in proportion to their previous knowledge and their present receptivity of such instruction. *As they were able to hear,* i.e. as some understand it, to hear intelligently or with patience. It may however have the stricter and more simple sense, as they had opportunity and leisure to attend on his instructions.

34. *But without a parable spake he not unto them; and when they were alone, he expounded all things to his disciples.*

This cannot mean that he never taught them in any other form, which would be contradicted by the whole course of the history, but only that whatever he did teach in parables he did not also teach in other forms, but, as the last clause more explicitly asserts, reserved the explanation for a private interview with his disciples. This closes Mark's account of our Lord's parables, including, as we have now seen, a full report of one with its author's own interpretation (vs. 1-20), an explanation of his purpose in employing this mode of instruction and direction to his followers how to profit by it (21-25); two additional parables, without a formal explanation (26-32); and a general statement of his practice in relation to this matter (33-34.)" (J. A. Alexander)

FACT QUESTIONS 4:33, 34

230. Please explain: "as they were able to hear."

231. Please explain: "without a parable He spake not unto them."

3. THE FIRST WITHDRAWAL 4:35—5:20

a. The Stilling of the Tempest 4:35-41

TEXT 4:35-41

"And on that day, when even was come, he saith unto them, Let us go over unto the other side. And leaving the multitude, they take him with them, even as he was, in the boat. And other boats were with him. And there ariseth a great storm of wind, and the waves beat into the boat, insomuch that the boat was now filling. And he himself was in the stern, asleep on the cushion: and they awake him, and say unto him, Master, carest thou not that we perish? And he awoke, and rebuked the wind, and said unto the sea, Peace, be still. And the wind ceased, and there was a great calm. And he said unto them, Why are ye fearful? have ye not yet faith? And they feared exceedingly, and said one to another, Who then is this, that even the wind and the sea obey him?"

THOUGHT QUESTIONS 4:35-41

202. On what day (or night) did this incident occur?
203. What is meant by the expression "unto the other side"? Where was it? vs. 35.
204. Explain the expression "even as He was." vs. 36.
205. How far was it "to the other side"?
206. Describe in your own words "the storm."
207. Why was Jesus asleep?
208. What did the disciples imagine Jesus could do about the storm? Did they lack faith?
209. Could this power here exercised by Jesus be compared with the creation of the world? How?
210. There are two uses of the word fear: vs. 40, 41. Explain each.

COMMENT

TIME—Immediately after the telling of the last parable—on the same day—sometime in the autumn of A.D. 28.

PLACE—In the midst of the Sea of Galilee somewhere between Capernaum and Gerasa.

PARALLEL ACCOUNTS—Matt. 8:23-27; Luke 8:22-25.

OUTLINE—1. The day of the miracle, vs. 35. 2. The voyage to the other side, vs. 36. 3. The storm, vs. 37. 4. Jesus asleep, the fear of the disciples, vs. 38. 5. Jesus stills the storm, vs. 39. 6. The calm of Jesus—the reverence of the disciples, vs. 40, 41.

ANALYSIS

I. THE DAY OF THE MIRACLE, VS. 35.

1. The same day as the parables.
2. At eventide.

II. THE VOYAGE TO THE OTHER SIDE, VS. 36.

1. Left multitude.
2. Jesus taken in the little boat from which He taught the parables.

III. THE STORM, VS. 37.

1. The great wind.
2. Waves into the boat.
3. Boat filling up.

IV. JESUS SLEEPS, THE DISCIPLES FEAR, V. 38.

1. Jesus in the stern on a cushion.
2. Awaked and asked for help.

V. JESUS STILLS THE STORM, VS. 39.

1. Rebuked the wind.
2. Stilled the sea.

VI. THE CALM OF JESUS—THE REVERENCE OF THE DISCIPLES, VS. 40, 41.

1. No need of fear when there is faith.
2. What manner of man is this?

EXPLANATORY NOTES

I. THE DAY OF THE MIRACLE, VS. 35.

"These verses describe a storm on the Sea of Galilee, when our Lord and His disciples were crossing it, and a miracle performed by our Lord in calming the storm in a moment. Few miracles recorded in the Gospel were so likely to strike the minds of the disciples as this. Four of them at least were fishermen. Peter, Andrew, James and John, had probably known the Sea of Galilee, and its storms, from their youth. Few events in our Lord's journeyings to and fro upon earth, contain more rich instruction than the one related in this passage.

II. THE VOYAGE TO THE OTHER SIDE, VS. 36.

Let us learn, in the first place, that *Christ's service does not exempt His servants from storms.* Here were the twelve disciples in the path of duty. They were obediently following Jesus, wherever He went. They were daily attending on His ministry, and hearkening to His word. They were daily testifying to the world, that, whatever Scribes and Pharisees might think, they believed on Jesus, loved Jesus, and were not ashamed to give up all for His sake. Yet here we see these men in trouble, tossed up and down by a tempest, and in danger of being drowned.

III. THE STORM, VS. 37.

Let us mark well this lesson. If we are true Christians, we must not expect everything smooth in our journey to heaven. We must count it no strange thing, if we have to endure sicknesses, losses, bereavements, and disappointments, just like other men. Free pardon and full forgiveness, grace by the way, and glory at the end,—all this our Saviour has promised to give. But He has never promised that we shall have no afflictions. He loves us too well to promise that. By affliction He teaches us many precious lessons, which without we should never learn. By affliction He shows us our emptiness and weakness, draws us to the throne of grace, purifies our affections, weans us from the world, makes us long for heaven. In the resurrection morning we shall all say, "It is good for me that I was afflicted." We shall thank God for every storm.

IV. JESUS SLEEPS, THE DISCIPLES FEAR, V. 38.

Let us learn, in the second place, *that our Lord Jesus Christ was really and truly man.* We are told in these verses, that when the storm began, and the waves beat over the ship, he was in the hinder part "asleep." He had a body exactly like our own,—a body that could hunger, and thirst, and feel pain, and be weary, and need rest. No wonder that His body needed repose at this time. He had been diligent in His Father's business all the day. He had been preaching to a great multitude in the open air. No wonder that "when the even was come," and His work finished, He fell "asleep."

Let us mark this lesson also attentively. The Saviour in whom we are bid to trust, is as really man as He is God. He knows the trials of a man, for He has experienced them. He knows the bodily infirmities of a man for He has felt them. He can well understand what we mean, when we cry to Him for help in this world of need. He is just the very Saviour that men and women, with weary frames and aching heads, in a weary world, require for their comfort every morning and night. "We have not an high priest which cannot be touched with the feeling of our infirmities." (Heb. 4:15.)

V. JESUS STILLS THE STORM, VS. 39.

Let us learn, in the third place, *that our Lord Jesus Christ as God, has almighty power.* We see Him in these verses doing that which is proverbially impossible. He speaks to the winds, and they obey Him. He speaks to the waves, and they submit to His command. He turns the raging storm into a calm with a few words,—"Peace, be still." Those words were the words of Him who first created all things. The elements knew the voice of their Master, and like obedient servants, were quiet at once.

Let us mark this lesson also, and lay it up in our minds. With the Lord Jesus Christ nothing is impossible. No stormy passions are so strong but He can tame them. No temper is so rough and violent but He can change it. No conscience is so disquieted, but He can speak peace to it, and make it calm. No man ever need despair, if he will only bow down his pride, and come as a humbled sinner to Christ. Christ can do miracles upon his heart.—No man ever need despair of reaching his journey's end, if he has once committed his soul to Christ's keeping. Christ will carry him through every danger. Christ will make him conqueror over every foe.—What though our relations oppose us? What though our neighbors laugh us to scorn? What though our place be hard? What though our temptations be great? It is all nothing, if Christ is on our side, and we are in the ship with Him. Greater is He that is for us, than all they that are against us.

VI. THE CALM OF JESUS—THE REVERENCE OF THE DISCIPLES, VS. 40, 41.

Finally, we learn from this passage, *that our Lord Jesus Christ is exceedingly patient and pitiful in dealing with His own people.* We see the disciples on this occasion showing great want of faith, and giving way to most unseemly fears. They forgot their Master's miracles and care for them in days gone by. They thought of nothing but their present peril. They awoke our Lord hastily, and cried, "Carest thou not that we perish?" We see our Lord dealing most gently and tenderly with them. He gives them no sharp reproof. He makes no threat of casting them off, because of their unbelief. He simply asks the touching question, "Why are ye so fearful? How is it that ye have no faith?"

Let us mark well this lesson. The Lord Jesus is very pitiful and of tender mercy. "As a father pitieth his children, even so the Lord pitieth them that fear Him." (Psalm 103:13). He does not deal with believers according to their sins, nor reward them according to their iniquities. He sees their weakness. He is aware of their short-comings. He knows all the defects of their faith, and hope, and love, and courage. And yet He will not cast them off. He bears with them continually. He loves them even to the end. He raises them when they fall. He restores them when they err. His patience, like His love, is a patience that passeth knowledge. When he sees a heart right, it is His glory to pass over many a short-coming.

Let us leave these verses with the comfortable recollection that Jesus is not changed. His heart is still the same that it was when He crossed the sea of Galilee and stilled the storm. High in heaven at the right hand of God, Jesus is still sympathizing—still almighty,—still pitiful and patient towards His people.—Let us be more charitable and patient towards our brethren in the faith. They may err in many things, but if

Jesus has received them and can bear with them, surely we may bear with them too.—Let us be more hopeful about ourselves. We may be very weak, and frail, and unstable; but if we can truly say that we do come to Christ and believe on Him, we may take comfort. The question for conscience to answer is not, "Are we like the angels? are we perfect as we shall be in heaven?" The question is, "Are we real and true in our approaches to Christ? Do we truly repent and believe?" (*J. C. Ryle*)

FACT QUESTIONS 4:35-41

232. Who shared in this storm and calm? Cf. 4:36.
233. Try to approximate the activity of Jesus during the day to understand how weary He was at the close of the day.
234. Be specific in the reason for the rebuke of Jesus in vs. 40.
235. Do you believe this storm was planned?
236. What is the greatest lesson in the incident?

SUMMARY
4:1-34

In the parables of this section, especially in those of the sower, the seed and the mustard seed, the prophetic power of Jesus is clearly exhibited. Without superhuman foresight he could not have so accurately traced out the manner in which different classes of men throughout all time would deal with the word of God, as he describes it in the parable of the sower; nor could he have known in advance of experiment, that the seed of the kingdom would grow from its planting until the time for harvest, as described in the next parable; nor that, as declared in the third, the kingdom would ever attain to the prodigious growth which our eyes have witnessed. His divinity is attested by his unfailing foresight into the distant future.—*J. W. McGarvey.*

B. THE FIERCE DEMONIAC. 5:1-20.

TEXT 5:1-20

"And they came to the other side of the sea, into the country of the Gerasenes. And when he was come out of the boat, straightway there met him out of the tombs a man with an unclean spirit, who had his dwelling in the tombs: and no man could any more bind him, no, not with a chain; because that he had been often bound with fetters and chains, and the chains had been rent asunder by him, and the fetters broken in pieces: and no man had strength to tame him. And always, night and day, in the tombs and in the mountains, he was crying out, and cutting himself with stones. And when he saw Jesus from afar, he ran and worshipped him; and crying out with a loud voice, he saith, What have I to do with thee, Jesus, thou Son of the Most High God? I adjure thee by God, torment me not. For he said unto him, Come forth, thou unclean spirit, out of the man. And he asked him, What is thy name? And he saith unto him, My name is Legion; for we are many. And he besought him much that he would not send them away out of the country. Now there was there on the mountain side a great herd of swine feeding. And they besought him, saying, Send us into the swine, that we may enter into them. And he gave them leave. And the unclean spirits came out, and entered into the swine: and the herd rushed down the steep into the sea, in number about two thousand; and they were choked in the sea. And they that fed them fled, and told it in the city, and in the country. And they came to see what it was that had come to pass. And they come to Jesus, and behold him that was possessed with devils sitting, clothed and in his right mind, even him that had the legion: and they were afraid. And they that saw it declared unto them how it befell him that was possesed with devils, and concerning the swine. And they began to beseech him to depart from their borders. And as he was entering into the boat, he that had been possessed with devils besought him that he might be with him. And he suffered him not, but saith unto him, Go to thy house unto thy friends, and tell them how great things the Lord hath done for thee, and how he had mercy on thee. And he went his way, and began to publish in Decapolis how great things Jesus had done for him: and all men did marvel."

THOUGHT QUESTIONS 5:1-20

211. Please locate on a map the "country of Gerasenes."
212. It would seem the demons would run from Jesus—not to Him—explain.
213. What is a demon? Why are they called "unclean."
214. State five facts about the demoniac?
215. What distinction is there in fetters and chains.
216. Was there more than one demon in the man? How many?
217. Why ask his name?
218. What torment did the demon expect from Jesus?
219. Why did not the demon wish to leave the country?
220. Why would demons wish to enter swine?
221. Wasn't it wrong to destroy the property of another?
222. Why ask Jesus to depart?
223. Why did the man who was healed wish to be with Jesus? Why did Jesus refuse?
224. Give two facts added by Matthew and Luke.

COMMENT

TIME—Autumn, A.D. 28. The morning after the stilling of the tempest on the Sea of Galilee, which followed the parables.

PLACE—The country of the Gadarenes, on the southeastern shores of the Sea of Galilee. It was in the country of the Gergesenes (so named from Gergesa, the modern Gersa, directly across the lake from Tiberias), which was a portion of the larger region of the Gadarenes (so named from their capital, Gadara, a large city seven or eight miles southwest of the southern point of the lake). The demoniac may have belonged to Gadara, but have met Jesus in the vicinity of Gergesa. Gadara was one of the ten confederated Gentile cities which, with the district in which they were located, were called Decapolis (The Ten Cities). Though they were located in Palestine, yet in the time of Christ they had a Gentile instead of Jewish population. Matthew speaks in the parallel passage of the Gergesenes. The Gadarenes and Gergesenes were simply two different names for the same people. Gadara and Gergesa were in the same district. Mark and Luke, in this account, speak of the Gadarenes, while Matthew calls the people the Gergesenes. This difference for a long time caused a difficulty to biblical students and caused rationalists to throw a doubt over the whole narrative. Gadara is three hours' journey south of the lake and it is not likely that the miracle was wrought there. The discovery of Gergesa, now called Gersa, on the eastern shore of the lake and on the borders of the district of Gadara, has made all plain. This discovery, made by Dr. Thompson (*Land and Book,* Vol, II, pp. 34, 35), reconciles every difficulty. Two of the writers, writing for Gentiles, mention Gadara, one of the best known Gentile cities of Palestine, in the territories of which it occurred, while Matthew, a tax-gatherer on the shores of the lake and familiar with every locality upon its borders, mentions the obscure village, right on the shores, where it took place. The modern Gersa, or Chersa, is within a few rods of the shore. A mountain rises immediately above it, so near the shore that the swine rushing madly down could not stop, but would be inevitably driven into the sea and drowned; the ruins of ancient tombs are still found on this mountain side, and Capernaum was in full view "over against it" (Luke 8:26) on the other side. See map of Sea of Galilee.

PARALLEL ACCOUNTS—Matt. 8:28-33; Luke 8:26-39.

OUTLINE—1. The Gadarene Demoniac. 2. The Legion and the Swine. 3. Christ and the Gadarenes.

ANALYSIS

I. THE GADARENE DEMONIAC. VS. 1-8.

1. The Lord Crosses to Gergesa. Mark 5:1; Matt. 8:30; Luke 8:26.
2. The Fierce Demoniacs. Mark 5:2-5; Matt. 8:30; Luke 8:27.
3. Runs and Appeals to Christ. Mark 5:6, 7; Matt. 8:29; Luke 8:28.

II. THE LEGION AND THE SWINE. VS. 9-13.
   1. The Name Legion. Mark 5:9; Luke 8:30.
   2. The Appeal of the Demons. Mark 5:10, 11; Matt. 8:31; Luke 8:32.
   3. The Maddened Swine. Mark 5:13; Matt. 8:32; Luke 8:33.

III. CHRIST AND THE GADARENES. VS. 14-20.
   1. The Gadarenes Hear and See. Mark 5:14-16; Matt. 8:33; Luke 8:35.
   2. Desire Christ to Depart. Mark 5:17; Matt. 8:34; Luke 8:37.
   3. A Home Missionary. Mark 5:20; Luke 8:39.

INTRODUCTION

After the discourse in parables, in the evening the Savior with his apostles embarked to the other side of the lake. On the way a great storm arose, which filled the disciples with terror, but was quieted at the voice of the Lord. Crossing over to the southeastern shore of the lake they disembarked in the country of the Gadarenes. On the voyage the Lord quelled the storm of winds and waves; across the sea he quelled a fiercer storm in a human soul. There is something very striking in the connection in which this miracle stands with that other which went immediately before. Our Lord has just shown himself as the pacifier of the tumults and the discords in the outward world. But there is something wilder and more fearful than the winds and the waves in their fiercest moods—even the spirit of man, when it has broken loose from all restraints, and yielded itself to be the organ, not of God, but of him who brings uttermost confusion wheresoever his dominion reaches. And Christ will do here a mightier work than that which he accomplished there: he will speak, and at his potent word this madder strife, this blinder rage, which is in the heart of man, will allay itself; and here also there shall be a great calm.

EXPLANATORY NOTES

I. THE GADARENE DEMONIAC.—1. *In the country of the Gadarenes.* See remarks above on the PLACES. Gadara was a great city which gave name to all the people in the district, while Gergesa was a small village on the shores of the Sea of Galilee.

2. *There met him out of the tombs.* Matthew mentions two demoniacs, while Mark and Luke speak only of one, probably the fiercer of the two. When the Savior and his disciples landed, the demoniac, with his companion, starting from the tombs, which were their ordinary dwelling-place, rushed down to encounter the intruders that had dared to set foot

on their domain. Or it may have been that they were at once drawn to Christ by the secret instinctive feeling that he was their helper, and driven from him by the sense of the awful gulf that divided them from him, the Holy One of God. The tombs were caves formed by nature, or cut in the rocks, with cells at the sides for the reception of the dead. They were ceremonially unclean (Num. 19:11, 16; Matt. 23:27; Luke 11:44), and dwelling in them was of itself a sign of degradation. *With an unclean spirit.* A demon; called unclean because it produced uncleanness of body and of soul; the exact opposite of pure. It is not easy to answer the question, What was this demoniacal possession? But we may gather from the gospel narrative some important ingredients for our description. The demoniac was one whose being was strangely interpenetrated by one or more of those fallen spirits, who are constantly asserted in Scripture (under the name of demons, evil spirits, unclean spirits, their chief being the devil, or Satan) to be the enemies and tempters of the souls of men. He stood in a totally different position from the abandoned, wicked man, who morally is given over to the devil. This latter would be a subject for punishment, but the demoniac for deepest compassion. There appears to have been in him a double will and double consciousness—sometimes the cruel spirit thinking and speaking in him, sometimes his poor crushed self crying out to the Savior of men for mercy; a terrible advantage taken, and a personal realization, by the malignant powers of evil, of the fierce struggle between sense and conscience in the man of morally divided life. It has been not improbably supposed that some of these demoniacs may have arrived at their dreadful state through various progressive degrees of guilt and sensual abandonment. Lavish sin, and especially indulgence in sensual lusts, superinducing, as it would often, a weakness in the nervous system, which is the especial bond between body and soul, may have laid open these unhappy ones to the fearful incursions of the powers of darkness.—*Alford.* To the frequent inquiry, How comes it that similar possessions do not occur at the present day? it may be answered: (1) It cannot be proved that they do not sometimes occur even now. It cannot be said that in many cases of insanity, and in some cases of spiritualism, the malady may not be traced to the direct agency of demons. (2) But, admitting that such possessions are not common, yet there was a reason in our Savior's day for the external manifestation of Satan's power. The crisis of the moral history of the world was at hand. The devil was allowed to exercise unusual power in temptation on the souls and bodies of men, in order that Christ might meet him openly and manifest his power in his victory over him. When God was manifested in the flesh, then demons may have been permitted to manifest themselves specially among men.—*Clark.*

3. *Had his dwelling among the tombs.* This implies habitual residence, and long absence from the homes of the living. Evil or unclean spirits are generally represented as haunting waste, desolate places and tombs. The tombs are not infrequently used in Palestine by certain of the poorer classes as dwelling-places. Their character (caves cut in the rock) makes them a perfect shelter. *No man could bind him.* The better MSS. give, "no man could any longer bind him." The attempt had been so often made and baffled that it had been given up in despair.

4. *Bound with fetters and chains.* The case was probably one of long standing, and repeated efforts had been made to confine him (Luke 8:29). Fetters were for the feet, chains for any other part of the body.—*Schaff.* Luke says (8:29), that "oftentimes it (the unclean spirit) had caught him;" and, after mentioning how they had vainly tried to bind him with chains and fetters, because "he brake the bands," he adds, "and was driven of the devil (or demon) into the wilderness." The dark tyrant-power by which he was held clothed him with superhuman strength, and made him scorn restraint. Matthew (8:28) says he was "exceeding fierce, so that no man might pass by that way." He was the terror of the whole locality.—*J. F. and B. Chains had been plucked asunder.* This is nowise incredible; for there are still some forms of mania in which the sufferer, notwithstanding the constant exhaustion of mind and body, gains a daily increase of muscular strength, and is able to break the strongest bonds and even chains.—*Kitto.*

5. *Night and day . . . in the tombs.* It is a sad story that is told of the unfortunate. He wandered about night and day in the solitudes, like a spectre, but crying aloud like a ravenous beast. *Cutting himself with stones.* There is sometimes a strong propensity in maniacs to wound and even maim themselves. V. Swieten says that he himself "saw a maniac who lacerated all the integuments of his body, and who, during the inclemency of a severe winter, lay naked on straw for weeks, in a place rough with stones."

6. *Ran and worshipped him.* Probably when he saw him land he ran from his lurking place among the tombs on the mountain side. There seems to be a kind of double life in the man; one his own, and the other the overpowering influence of the spirit that possessed him. *Olshausen* refers the act of going to Jesus, and bowing down before him, to the *man* in contradistinction to the *demon.* The man wanted help, and sought it in Jesus; and the will of the demon trying to overpower him made the terrible paroxysms of conflict. *Godet* says: "He felt himself at once attracted and repelled by Jesus; this led to a violent crisis in him, which revealed itself first of all in a cry. Then, like some ferocious beast submitting to the power of his subduer, he runs and kneels, pro-

testing all the time, in the name of the spirit of which he is still the organ, against the power which is exerted over him."

7. *Cried with a loud voice.* It was the man's voice that cried out, but it was the controlling spirit that dictated the words. He had not the control of his own organs, just as I have seen those under hypnotic influence who could not control their words or thoughts. It is no uncommon thing in our time for a person to be absolutely under the influence of another will. *What have I to do with thee?* What have we in common? Why interferest thou with us? Why wilt thou not let us alone? *Son of the most high God.* The spirits, who had possession of the poor man's body, wielded his organism of speech as if it were their own. These demons knew the Lord and confessed him. "The demons believe and tremble." *I adjure thee by God.* To adjure is to entreat solemnly, as if under oath, or the penalty of a curse. This is the language of the demon, not of the man; not a mere blasphemy, but a plausible argument. Nothing is more common than swearing by God, on the part of the ungodly, the infidel, and even the atheistic. *Torment me not.* In Matthew, "Art thou come hither to torment us before the time?" i.e.; we implore thee to deal with us as God himself does; not to precipitate our final doom, but to prolong the respite we now enjoy.—*Alexander.*

8. *Come out of the man.* Leave him; no more control him.

II. THE LEGION AND THE SWINE.—9. *What is thy name?* The Lord asks this question of the afflicted man. For what purpose? There is nothing so suitable as a calm and simple question to bring a madman to himself. There is no more natural way of awakening in a man who is beside himself the consciousness of his own personality than to make him tell his own name. A man's name becomes the expression of his character, and a summary of the history of his life. The first condition of any cure of this afflicted man was a return to the distinct feeling of his own personality. *And he answered.* The man was asked, but the demon answered, showing his entire mastery over him. *My name is Legion,* the unclean spirit answers. The Roman legion consisted of about six thousand. The word had come to signify any large number, with the ideas of order and subordination. It is about equivalent to *host,* and explained by the unclean spirit himself: *For we are many.* One chief, superior one, with inferior ones under him.

10. *He besought him . . . not send them out of the country.* "He" is used in the singular because the man speaks, but he speaks under the influence of the spirits, and pleads for them. The petition of the devils may be regarded as equivalent to, "Send us anywhere, anywhere but to perdition; send us to the most shattered man; send us to the lowest creature, into man or beast, bird or reptile, anywhere but to hell!" The

demons knew well that Christ had come to destroy the power of the devil, and had already (v. 7) implored, "Torment me not."

11. *There was there nigh unto the mountains.* The Revision says: "Now there was there on the mountain side a great herd of swine feeding." The mountain rises a short distance from the lake. *A great herd of swine feeding.* They were the property either of Gentiles, or of Jews engaged in a traffic which was unclean according to the Mosaic law.

12. *The devils besought him . . . Send us,* etc. How could there it is asked, be such a desire on the part of the demons? Why should there not? we would answer. The wish might, on their part, be a mere outburst of wantonness. Or there might be eagerness for anything on which to wreak their evil energy. They might be wishing, as *Richard Baxter* has it, "to play a small game, rather than none." Or there might be cunning malice in their intent—malice toward Christ and toward all the other parties concerned.—*Morison.* They aimed at this, that they might move the owners of the herd, and the rest of the people of the country, to be discontented at our Savior.—*Petter.*

13. *Forthwith Jesus gave them leave.* The fact is stated, but why he should have granted their request is in part conjecture. The following reasons have been suggested: (1) To show the disciples Christ's control over the movements of the spirits. (2) To test the Gergesenes. (3) To make the miracle more notorious, and thus to enhance the effect of the cured demoniac's preaching. (4) The owners, if Jews, drove an illegal trade; if heathens, they insulted the national religion; in either case the permission was just. *Ran violently down a steep place.* Not a cliff, but a steep beach. The declivity at the base of the mountain at Gersa is said to be almost perpendicular. "The bluff behind is so steep, and the shore so narrow, that a herd of swine, rushing frantically down, must certainly have been overwhelmed in the sea before they could recover themselves." *Tristram's Land of Israel. About two thousand.* Immense herds of swine were kept in many provinces of the Roman Empire specially for the provisionment of the Army. A heavy loss was certainly recognized by the people of the city.—*Cook.* Why should they have destroyed the herd of swine, and so deprived themselves, so to speak, of a terrestrial abode? Perhaps the act of the swine was the result of panic, and in spite of the evil spirits. It is the very nature of evil thus to outwit itself.

III. CHRIST AND THE GADARENES.—14. *They that fed the swine.* The herdsmen, fled affrighted, in consternation at the loss and the marvel, to the city, to Gergesa or Gadara.

15. *They come to Jesus.* Matthew says (8:34), "Behold, the whole

city came out to meet Jesus." Note the present *come.* The Evangelist begins to depict the scene as if he and we were present in the midst of it and looking on. *See him that was possessed.* "And (they) behold the demoniac sitting clothed and in sound mind." Note the word *behold.* It is more than *see.* They *gaze* upon the man. *Sitting and clothed.* There is a fine harmony between the statement that the demoniac was now *clothed,* and the statement in Luke that formerly he "ware no clothes" (8:27). The contrast of the man's former condition sets off to advantage the marvel of his present state. *They were afraid.* They felt in the presence of a power which inspired them with awe and alarm. It might, for aught that they could comprehend, be something weird or "uncanny." There was, moreover, the terror of a guilty conscience.

16. *And also concerning the swine.* A notable climax. The people who had witnessed the transaction tell the citizens what had been done for the demoniac and about the swine—*their* swine: that settled their minds. They cared far more for the swine, than for the man who had been healed. They would rather have swine than Christ.

17. *They began to pray him to depart.* Jesus had overcome the rage of the storm that met him when approaching their coast. He had cast out the legion of devils that opposed his entrance into their country. The only thing which could effectually turn away the Savior was the will of man. Christ appears never to have visited the country of the Gadarenes again. He does not abide where he is not wanted.

18. *Prayed . . . that he might be with him.* Was it that he feared, lest in the absence of his deliverer the powers of hell should regain their dominion over him, and only felt safe in immediate nearness to him? or merely that out of the depth of his gratitude he desired henceforth to be a follower of him to whom he owed this mighty benefit?—*Trench.*

19. *Jesus suffered him not.* To be a missionary for Christ, in the region where he was so well known and so long dreaded, was a far nobler calling than to follow him where nobody had ever heard of him, and where other trophies, not less illustrious, could be raised by the same power and grace. *Go home to thy friends.* The first act God requires of a convert is, "Be fruitful." The good man's goodness lies not hidden in himself alone: he is still strengthening his weaker brother. All are not called on to be foreign missionaries. The Lord called upon this man to become a home missionary.

20. *In Decapolis* (ten cities). The region (of ten cities east of the Jordan) of which this immediate district formed a part. The healed man became a preacher, not only where Christ had been rejected, but where he had not gone. His message was his own experience. How much his

preaching effected history does not record, but we know that near forty years later this district of Decapolis became the refuge of the church of Jerusalem when that city was destroyed.

FACT QUESTIONS 5:1-20

237. "Gadara was a great ——— . . . while Gergesa was a small ——— on the shores of the Sea of Galilee."
238. Was there only one demoniac? Explain the reference in Matthew to two.
239. Why dwell in the tombs?
240. Why call a demon an "unclean spirit"?
241. In what sense did a demon possessed man stand in totally different position from the abandoned, wicked man, who morally is given over to the devil?
242. How have some imagined that men became demon possessed?
243. Give two answers to the question, "do we have demon possession today"?
244. What had been done to bind this wild one?
245. Isn't it incredible that this one would have such superhuman strength?
246. Why did he cut himself?
247. Show how the man was both attracted and repelled by Jesus.
248. What is meant by "I adjure thee by God"?
249. Why ask the man his name?
250. What is meant by the name "Legion"?
251. What is the thought of "send us not out of the country"?
252. Why ask to go into the swine?
253. Show three possible answers as to why Jesus gave permission for the demons to enter the swine.
254. Show how the traffic in swine was wrong i.e. the raising and selling swine was wrong for both Gentiles and Jews.
255. Just where did they enter the Sea?
256. What caused the whole city to come out to see Jesus?
257. What was the response of the crowd when they saw the former demon possessed man?
258. What is the only thing that can effectually turn the Savior away?
259. What was the "far nobler calling" of the man who was healed?
260. Where and what was Decapolis?

4. THE RAISING OF JAIRUS' DAUGHTER 5:21-43.

a. The urgent request of Jairus. 5:21-24

TEXT 5:21-24

"And when Jesus had crossed over again in the boat unto the other side, a great multitude was gathered unto him: and he was by the sea. And there cometh one of the rulers of the synagogue, Jairus by name; and seeing him, he falleth at his feet, and beseecheth him much, saying, My little daughter is at the point of death: I pray thee, that thou come and lay thy hands on her, that she may be made whole, and live. And he went with him; and a great multitude followed him, and they thronged him."

THOUGHT QUESTIONS 5:21-24

225. Where did the boat land in which Jesus crossed the Sea? Who was there to meet Him?
226. What is meant by the expression "rulers of the synagogue."
227. Show the humility and sincerity of Jairus.
228. Why call his daughter "My little daughter"?
229. Why was the multitude so interested?

COMMENT

TIME—Autumn, A.D. 28. Probably in the afternoon of the same day He healed the demoniac.

PLACE—Capernaum—at the house of Matthew.

PARALLEL ACCOUNTS—Matt. 9:18, 19; Luke 8:40-42.

OUTLINE—1. Jesus comes back to Capernaum, vs. 21. 2. Jairus—his need—his request, vs. 22, 23. 3. Jesus goes with him, vs. 24.

ANALYSIS

Since this is but the beginning of the incident we will offer an analysis in the later section.

EXPLANATORY NOTES

"21. The miracle on the eastern side of the lake took place in the early morning, and later in the day Jesus and his company were back on the western side, but not in the town of Capernaum. *He was nigh unto the sea,* and there the crowd gathered to him, having been waiting (Luke) for his return. Possibly the change in his mode of teaching and the introduction of parables had for the time quickened the popular curiosity.

22-24. *One of the rulers of the synagogue.* Presumably the synagogue in Capernaum, though nothing positively determines the place.—The name

Jairus is the Greek form of the Hebrew "Jair;" it is the name of one who was a great man at the conquest of Canaan (Deut. 3:14), and later of one of the Judges of Israel (Judges 10:3-5). Of Jairus nothing is known except what is recorded here. If, as is probably the case, he was a ruler of the synagogue in Capernaum, he would naturally be one of those who were sent by the centurion who had "built a synagogue" to intercede for him when his servant was sick (Luke 7:3). In that case he would be no stranger to the healing power of Jesus, and his confidence would be fully explained.—His eagerness appears in his falling down at Jesus' feet and his entreating him *greatly,* "much"—i.e. earnestly and persistently.—*My little daughter lieth at the point of death.* The phrase *eschatos echei,* paraphrased *at the point of death,* is late Greek, and is said to have been condemned by the grammarians as bad Greek. Luke says that "he had an only daughter, about twelve years of age, and she was dying," not "lay a dying." Thus Mark and Luke agree perfectly in their statement; but, in Matthew, Jairus says, "My daughter just now died." The Greek verb is in the aorist, and "is even now dead" is not a good translation of it: that she has died already is distinctly affirmed. But the discrepancy is much less than one might think. Matthew tells the story compendiously; he omits all reference to the subsequent message from the house, in which the tidings of her death are brought; and he groups the two communications in one, making Jairus tell the whole in a single sentence. He gathers into this first request all the information about the case that was brought to Jesus before he reached the house. In Luke the request is only that he will come to the house; in Mark and Matthew the request is added that he will lay his hands upon her, with the full expression of confidence that that will be the means of restoration—according to the story as it is in Mark, of restoration from the verge of death; according to Matthew, of restoration from death itself. A beautiful example of confident resorting to the grace and power of the Saviour. It was not in vain; no refusal awaited such an appeal. The request was brought to the lake-shore, where Jesus arrived in the boat. What he was doing we are not told; perhaps he had not had time to begin; or Jairus may even have been among those who were "waiting for him" when he came.—The crowd heard the request, and *followed,* as *Jesus went with him,* up from the lakeside into the town. He let them follow for a part of the way, not turning them back until his own time had come. He was not helpless in the matter; he did escape from the crowd when he was ready to insist upon it. Both in Mark and in Luke the words that describe the pressure of the throng are very strong words; in Luke, "crowd to suffocation" well represents it. Not much rest for our Saviour after the overpowering weariness of the previous evening—only the sleep on the boat. The healing and the repulse across the lake, a crowd waiting for him on his return, and now a call to go and give life to a dying child! But his compassion never failed, and he never considered himself. We have no reason to imagine that any consideration of himself ever held him back from a deed of love. He was the one perfectly unselfish Being, never false to this divine character. God is the unselfish One, and Christ is the manifestation of God." (*W. N. Clarke*).

FACT QUESTIONS 5:21-24

261. Are we to understand that Jesus came back on the same day He delivered the two demoniacs? Did He use the same boat?
262. Please read Matt. 9:18, 19 and get the connection of the feast of Matthew. Just when did Jairus come to Jesus?
263. Why did Jairus fall at Jesus feet? There could have been at least two reasons; discover them.
264. Why ask Jesus to place His hands upon the girl?
265. If she was "made whole" wouldn't she live? Why the two expressions?
266. Why mention the press of the crowd?

b. THE TIMID WOMAN'S TOUCH 5:25-34

TEXT 5:25-34

"And a woman, which had an issue of blood twelve years, and had suffered many things of many physicians, and had spent all that she had, and was nothing bettered, but rather grew worse, having heard the things concerning Jesus, came in the crowd behind, and touched his garment. For she said, If I touch but his garments, I shall be made whole. And straightway the fountain of her blood was dried up; and she felt in her body that she was healed of her plague. And straightway Jesus, perceiving in himself that the power proceeding from him had gone forth, turned him about in the crowd, and said, Who touched my garments? And his disciples said unto him, Thou seest the multitude thronging thee, and sayest thou, Who touched me? And he looked round about to see her that had done this thing. But the woman fearing and trembling, knowing what had been done to her, came and fell down before him, and told him all the truth. And he said unto her, Daughter thy faith hath made thee whole; go in peace, and be whole of thy plague."

THOUGHT QUESTIONS 5:25-34

230. What is "an issue of blood"?
231. Why mention the fact she had suffered from the physicians?
232. What had it cost this woman to find out she could not be helped?

233. What had she heard about Jesus?
234. Show the determination and faith of this woman.
235. What was it that healed the woman?
236. How can we explain the perception of Jesus in this case?—; was this true everytime He healed someone?
237. Did Jesus know who touched Him before He asked the question?
238. Hadn't others touched Him?; why no effect?
239. Did Jesus see the woman when He looked about the crowd?
240. Why did the woman make the confession she did?
241. Why refer to the woman as "daughter"?
242. How is the word "whole" or "saved" used in this connection?

COMMENT

TIME—Autumn, A. D. 28. Probably in the afternoon of the same day that Christ healed the demoniac of Gadara, or on a day or two after.
PLACE.—Capernaum. At the house of Matthew; on the way to the house of Jairus; at the house of Jairus—all within or near the city. A comparison of the three accounts makes it probable that the Lord was at the house of Matthew, at a feast, when Jairus sent for him to save the life of his daughter, and that the woman was healed while he was on the way.
PARALLEL ACCOUNTS.—Matt. 9:18-26; Luke 8:41-56. See also Matt. 9:10-17, for intervening incidents.
OUTLINE.—1. The Woman's Faith. 2. The Woman Healed. 3. The Woman's Confession.

ANALYSIS

I. THE WOMAN'S FAITH. VS. 25-28.
   1. The Suffering Woman. Mark 5:25, 26; Matt. 9:20; Luke 8:43.
   2. She Touches Christ. Mark 5:27; Matt. 9:20; Luke 8:44.
   3. Moved by Faith. Mark 5:28; Matt. 9:21.

II. THE WOMAN HEALED. VS. 29-31.
   1. Saved by Faith. Mark 5:29; Matt. 9:22; Luke 8:44.
   2. The Secret Made Manifest. Mark 5:30; Luke 8:46.

III. THE WOMAN'S CONFESSION. VS. 32-34.
   1. The Woman at the Feet of Christ. Mark 5:33; Luke 8:47.
   2. The Sympathy of Christ. Mark 5:34; Matt. 9:22; Luke 8:48.

INTERVENING HISTORY.—Having been besought by the Gadarenes to leave their country, Christ passes over the lake again to the western side, to Capernaum, where he was immediately surrounded by the multitude, who had been waiting for him. Being invited by Matthew to a feast at his house, he there held conversation with some Pharisees, and afterwards with some disciples of John (Matt. 9:10-17). While yet speaking with them, Jairus, a ruler of the Capernaum synagogue, came to him, praying him to heal his daughter. While on his way the woman with the issue of blood, timidly pressed through the throng, touched him and was healed.

INTRODUCTION

The following from Farrar's *Life of Christ* gives a bird's eye view of the whole incident and its meaning. Among the throng there was one who had not been attracted by curiosity to witness what would be done for the ruler of the synagogue. It was a woman who had suffered for twelve years from a distressing malady, which unfitted her for all of the relationships of life, and which was peculiarly afflicting, because, in the popular mind it was the direct result of sinful habits. In vain had she wasted her substance, and done fresh injury to her health in the direct effort to procure relief from many different physicians, and now, as a last desperate resource, she would try what could be gained without money and without price from the great Physician. Perhaps, in her ignorance, it was because she no longer had any reward to offer; perhaps because she was ashamed in her feminine modesty to reveal the malady from which she was suffering; but from whatever cause, she determined, as it were, to steal from him, unknown, the blessing for which she longed. And so, with the strength and pertinacity of despair, she struggled in that dense throng until she was near enough to touch him; and then, perhaps all the more violently from her extreme nervousness, she grasped the white fringe of his robe. It was probably the tassel that she touched, and then feeling instantly that she had gained her desire and was healed, she shrank back unnoticed into the throng. Unnoticed by others but not Christ, who stopped and asked, "Who touched me? * * * She perceiving that she erred in trying to filch a blessing that would have been graciously bestowed, came forward fearing and trembling, and, flinging herself at his feet, told him all the truth. All her feminine shame and fear were forgotten in her desire to atone for her fault. Doubtless she dreaded his anger, for the law expressly ordained that the touch of one afflicted as she was, caused ceremonial uncleanness until the evening. But his touch had cleansed her, not hers polluted him.

EXPLANATORY NOTES

I. THE WOMAN'S FAITH.—25. *And a certain woman.* Like many of the New Testament characters this woman appears once and then disappears to be seen no more. Tradition has been busy weaving a fiction to supply the lack of facts. *Eusebius* records a tradition that she was a Gentile, a resident of Cesarea Philippi (or Banias). It is reported that she caused to be erected in front of her residence a bronze monument in commemoration of her cure. It consisted of two statues, one representing herself in the attitude of supplication; the other, her Deliverer. Elsewhere she appears under the name Veronica, who, in the presence of Pilate, proclaimed the innocence of Jesus, and on the way to Golgotha wiped his face with her handkerchief. Dismissing these fables the suggestion of *Dr. W. Thompson* is more to the point: "I think the circumstances of the New Testament narrative render the inference almost certain that this account was meant for the consolation of those multitudes of stricken women in all ages who seem to be afflicted with sorrows in very unequal measure, compared with the stronger, and so generally, also, the more depraved sex." *An issue of blood.* A hemorrhage either from the bowels or the womb, probably the latter. The precise nature of the malady is of no importance. Instead of dwelling upon this point the evangelists direct attention to its long continuance and hopeless state. Perhaps the reason she turned to Jesus was that she had spent all and had nohing left to tempt the cupidity of the quack doctors. Had they not secured all she had, they would still have some way to excite her hopes. It is when our earthly resources are at an end, and human helps are powerless, that we are ready to go to the great Physician with the ailments of the soul. How sad her condition! Impoverished, sick, growing worse, helpless!

27. *When she had heard of Jesus.* She had never met him, did not it is probable live at Capernaum, but she had heard of the wonderful teacher, and of his divine power over disease. She had, it would appear, made herself acquainted with his character and conduct, with the facts of his career, and had thence come to believe that he was full of a divine and gracious energy. *Came in the press behind and touched his garment* (Matthew and Luke give it, "hem or border of his garment"); or rather, "approaching from behind, touched the tassel of his outer robe." The word which we translate by "the hem of the garment" denotes one of the four tassels or tufts of woollen cord attached to the four corners of the outer robe. The ordinary outer Jewish garment was a square or oblong piece of cloth (worn something like an Indian blanket, or with a hole in the center for the neck) with tassels at each corner, and a fringe along the two edges. A conspicuous deep blue thread was required to be in the tassels (Num. 15:38-40. Deut. 22:12). One of the four tassels hung over the shoulder at the back, and this was the one which the woman touched.

28. *For she said.* Matthew says, "within herself;" but it is possible that she may have murmured it again and again as she tried to get through the crowd.—*Schaff. If I may touch but his clothes.* She was timid, not doubtful. It is implied that she wished only to touch some part of his clothes,

no matter which. She may have looked for some magical influence, but twelve years in the hands of physicians in those days would certainly excuse such a thought. *If I but touch his clothes.* This woman's faith was real, notwithstanding many errors. *Trench* says; it would appear as though she imagined a certain magical influence and virtue diffused through his person and round about him, with which if she could put herself in relation, she would obtain that which she desired. And it is probable that she touched the hem of his garment, not merely as the extremest part most easily reached, but attributing to it a peculiar virtue. "The error of her view was overborne, and her weakness of apprehension of truth covered, by the strength of her faith. And this is a most encouraging miracle for us to recollect when we are disposed to think despondingly of the ignorance or superstition of much of the Christian world: that He who accepted this woman for her faith, even in error and weakness, may accept them.—*Alford.*

II. THE WOMAN HEALED.—29. *She felt in her body that she was healed.* Literally, "knew (i.e., by feeling) in the body." The first clause tells of the cessation of the ordinary symptom of her disease: this points to a new sense of health. The cure was effected by an exercise of Jesus' will, which responds to the woman's faith in his miraculous power, not through the mere touching of the garment. The result was instantaneous and complete. Sharing the superstition, and imagining that Christ healed by a sort of magic, this woman touched it in hope of cure. An ordinary teacher would have rebuked her superstition; Christ used it to teach her better, but Christ, full of compassion, overlooking the errors of her ignorance, put forth his power and healed her. She had faith, even if not intelligent and clear. She believed that she was to *receive* something, a real blessing from Christ. This was that in her which was not in the crowd around her. They all traveled on in the highway together, talked about Christ, were interested in him in various ways, discussed his origin and nature, hoped that some good would come of him to the nation. But the woman believed that she should personally receive new life from him.

30. *Knowing . . . that virtue* (healing power) *had gone out of him.* Within that nature there was the inherent power to cure diseases, and a knowledge of all that was going on. He permitted power to go forth for the healing of the woman when her faith was properly exercised.—*George W. Clark.* His healing was an overflow, not an effort—a work so unconscious and so utterly passive that it seems like a miracle spilt over from the fullness of his divine life, rather than a miracle put forth.—*Gordon. Who touched my clothes?* Not because he was ignorant, for his searching glance showed to the woman that she was not hid from him (Luke 8:47), but to draw out her confession of her faith. For illustration

of similar questions, see Gen. 3:9; 4:9; 2 Kings 5:25; Luke: Luke 24:19. —*Abbott.* If she had been allowed to carry away her blessing in secret as she purposed, it would not have been at all the blessing to her, and to her whole after spiritual life, that it now was, when she was obliged by this repeated question of the Lord to own that she had come to seek, and had found health from him.—*Trench.* Christ demands that every soul that is healed should openly confess him. He will not permit that men claim him in secret who refuse to acknowledge him.

31. *And his disciples said.* "Peter and they that were with him" (Luke 8:45). It was much like Peter thus to speak, both for himself and as spokesman for the disciples. But Jesus affirmed that someone had touched him, implying a touch of intention and faith, and not a mere thoughtless and accidental pressing of the multitude.—*George W. Clark.*

III. THE WOMAN'S CONFESSION.—32. *He looked round to see her.* He required no one to point out the one who had pressed upon him the touch of faith, for it cannot be doubted that he was conscious all the time of what was in the woman's heart. His glance, therefore, at once singled her out in the crowd, and fell upon her with a searching glance that showed that all was known.

33. *But the woman fearing and trembling.* The timid woman felt that she had stolen a cure, was amazed at the sudden change wrought within her and knowing little of the tender compassion of Christ was filled with dread of the wonderful being who had wrought her cure. Perhaps, too, she expected to be rebuked for touching him without his permission; perhaps, also, the woman feared Christ's anger and his rebuke for polluting him by her touch; or, possibly, the indignation of others in the crowd, in which she had joined without in any way indicating her uncleanness. *Knowing what was done in her.* A sense of her cure brought her forward to testify to and for Christ. So, always, the sense of pardon and acceptance will lead the trembling believer to full confession and to an open testimony for Christ. It will embolden the timid to speak of the gospel, even before crowds. *Told him all the truth.* This, though it tried the modesty of the believing woman, was just what Christ wanted, her public testimony to the facts of her case—the disease with her abortive efforts at a cure, and the instantaneous and perfect relief which her touching the great Healer had brought her.

34. *And he said unto her, Daughter.* A term of affection, but, no doubt, as employed by our Savior, implying all that was spiritually distinctive in her character had been derived from himself. *Thy faith hath made thee whole.* Literally, *thy faith hath saved thee.* In the higher and in the lower sense, soul and body. Her faith, of course, had not been the efficient cause of her cure. Christ's power had been that. And behind his

power was his person, the real healer. But her faith was the condition on her part, that rendered it fitting on his part to put forth his curative efficiency. Hence it might be represented as having in a certain subordinate respect "made her whole."—*Morison.* The student should observe that hers was not a passive faith, but it led to action. A passive faith is a dead faith. The cure was effected by an exercise of Jesus' will, which responds to the woman's faith in his miraculous power, not through the mere touching of the garment. The result was instantaneous and complete. —*Meyer.*

FACT QUESTIONS 5:25-34

261. What social as well as physical difficulty did this woman suffer because of her illness?
262. Wasn't the woman rather superstitious in her approach to healing? Explain why, and why excusable.
263. What has tradition said about this woman—give three traditional facts.
264. How is she a grand example for us today?
265. Discuss the portion of the robe of Christ touched by the woman.
266. To whom had she said "If I may touch but His clothes . . . "? When?
267. Did Jesus accept the woman's error and weakness?—what did He accept?
268. How did the woman know she was healed—who told her? Was it complete, final and unchangeable? How does this compare with some present day healings?
269. Attempt an explanation of how Jesus could heal almost accidentally through someone else's desire and faith and yet be aware of it?
270. Who answered the question of Jesus?
271. What evidence do we have that Jesus knew what was in the heart of the woman even before she touched Him?
272. What filled the woman with fear and trembling?
273. Did Jesus want a public confession from this woman? Explain.
274. In what sense was the woman a daughter?
275. Please discuss the wonderful "wholeness" of this woman.

c. THE RAISING OF JAIRUS' DAUGHTER 5:35-43

TEXT 5:35-43

"While he yet spake, they come from the ruler of the synagogue's house, saying, Thy daughter is dead: why troublest thou the Master any further? But Jesus, not heeding the word spoken, saith unto the ruler of the synagogue, Fear not, only believe. And he suffered no man to follow him, save Peter, and James, and John the brother of James. And they come to the house of the ruler of the synagogue; and he beholdeth a tumult, and many weeping and wailing greatly. And when he was entered in, he saith unto them, Why make ye a tumult, and weep? the child is not dead, but sleepeth. And they laughed him to scorn. But he, having put them all forth, taketh the father of the child and her mother and them that were with him, and goeth in where the child was. And taking the child by the hand, he saith unto her, Talitha cumi; which is, being interpreted, Damsel, I say unto thee, Arise. And straightway the damsel rose up, and walked; for she was twelve years old. And they were amazed straightway with a great amazement. And he charged them much that no man should know this: and he commanded that something should be given her to eat."

THOUGHT QUESTIONS 5:35-43

243. What was the attitude of Jairus while Jesus stopped to speak to the woman who touched?
244. In what tone of voice do you imagine the message of the death of the daughter was given?
245. In what sense did they feel they were troubling Jesus?
246. What was Jairus to believe? Cf. vs. 36.
247. Why send the crowd away?
248. On what other occasions did Peter, James & John accompany Jesus?
249. What was the point in the demonstration of grief?
250. Did Jesus know some would misunderstand his words about sleeping? Why mention it?
251. In what sense was the girl asleep?
252. Upon what was the laugh of scorn based?
253. Try to understand the feelings of the mother as Jesus spoke to the girl. What were they?
254. Why mention that she was twelve years old?
255. Why ask that she be fed?

COMMENT

TIME—Just a few minutes after the preceding incident of the timid woman.

PLACE—In the home of Jairus—probably in the city of Capernaum.

PARALLEL ACCOUNTS—Matt. 9:23-26; Luke 8:49-56.

OUTLINE—1. The Message of death, vs. 35, 36. 2. To the house of Jairus, vs. 37, 38. 3. The place of death, vs. 39, 40. 4. The resurrection, vs. 41-43.

ANALYSIS

I. THE MESSAGE OF DEATH, VS. 35, 36.
   1. Given while Jesus yet spoke to the woman.
   2. No need to try further, your daughter is dead.
   3. Jesus heard man but believed God—this He wanted Jairus to do.

II. TO THE HOUSE OF JAIRUS, VS. 37, 38.
   1. Just Peter, James and John were to accompany Him.
   2. A great tumult of weeping.

III. THE PLACE OF DEATH, VS. 39, 40.
   1. No need to weep—she sleeps.
   2. Scorn—all are asked to leave except the parents.

IV. THE RESURRECTION, VS. 41-43.
   1. He taketh her by the hand and calls her by name.—"arise"
   2. She immediately arose from the dead.

EXPLANATORY NOTES

"35. *"While he yet spake, there came . . . why troublest thou the Master any further?"* Hitherto He had not shown His power over death, and so there may be an excuse for the message, but surely there might be some consolation in the words of such a Master! His presence need not be out of place in the house of mourning. There is a curtness and abruptness in this message which savors of unbelief.

36. *"As soon as Jesus heard (or not heeding) the word . . . Be not afraid, only believe."* Jesus, perceiving the mischief which the message might work, at once put in a comforting and hope-inspiring word, "Be not afraid, only believe."

Belief is in one sense the only thing needful, because it is the one condition on which we can receive salvation and grace from the Lord. But what does the Lord here mean by "only believe?" Only believe what? Why, evidently, that "I have power after death, that My might reaches beyond the grave." If the man believed that his daughter was dead, and the Lord bid him "fear not," it must mean "fear not, but that I will give her to you again." If He added to this "fear not" the words "only believe," it must mean, "Believe that I am life to the dead. You may not know how, but let not your faith in Me fail, and you shall see."

If it be said that this was too much to require of this ruler, we can only answer that the Lord thought otherwise. The man had known of the healing of the centurion's servant, and of the woman with the issue, most probably also of the casting out of the devils out of the Gergesenes; and we know not how many more mighty works performed in Capernaum, and around the borders of the lake, and now he was asked to go one step further in the same road, i.e., to believe that death was not the termination of the Lord's power.

37. *"And he suffered no man to follow him, save Peter, and James, and John,"* etc. The three who were to be witnesses of His Transfiguration, and of His agony.

38. *"And he cometh to the house . . . wept and wailed greatly."* From the parallel words in St. Matthew, "Saw the minstrels and the people making a noise," there is no doubt that these were hired mourners, such as are described in Jeremiah 9:17, 18: "Consider ye, and call for the mourning women that they may come; and send for cunning women, that they may come, and let them make haste, and take up a wailing for us, that our eyes may run down with tears, and our eyelids gush out with waters."

Dr. Thomson, in *"The Land and the Book"*, says: "Every particular here alluded to is observed on funeral occasions at the present day. There are in every city and community women exceedingly cunning in this business. These are always sent for and kept in readiness. When a fresh company of sympathizers comes in, these women 'make haste' to take up a wailing, that the newly come may the more easily unite their tears with the mourners. They know the domestic history of every person, and immediately strike up an impromptu lamentation, in which they introduce the names of their relations who have recently died, touching some tender chord of every heart, and thus each weeps for his own dead."

39. *"And when he was come in, he saith . . . sleepeth."* There can be little doubt but that the Saviour here employs the same way of speaking as when He says, "Our friend Lazarus sleepeth, but I go that I may awake him out of sleep;" and immediately afterwards He told them plainly, "Lazarus is dead." Some have said that the maiden had fallen into the death-like swoon which often precedes, and then passes into actual death; but those watching her must have been conscious that so far as the help of man was concerned, all was over, or they would not have sent the message to the ruler which they did.

40. *"And they laughed him to scorn."* This ridicule would be stimulated by their interests, for their wages as mourners depended on the death having actually taken place.

"Them that were with him." Only Peter, James and John.

41, 42. *"And he took the damsel by the hand . . . Talitha cumi . . . astonishment."* The very Syriac or Aramaic words which the Lord used are here preserved by the Evangelist, doubtless from the recollection of St. Peter. The words properly translated are, "Girl, arise." *Quesnel's* remarks on this are well worth reproducing: "The sacred Humanity is, as it were, the hand and instrument of the Divinity, to which it is united in the person of the Word. It is from this Humanity that our life proceeds, because it was in this that Christ died and rose again, and completed His Sacrifice. He is man, since He takes the dead person by the hand; He is God since He commands her to live, and to arise, and is immediately obeyed."

43. *"And he charged them straitly . . . given her to eat."* It is to be noticed that in the case of the Gergesene demoniac, after healing He bade him make known what God had done for Him, and He Himself compelled the woman, in the last miracle, to confess her healing before the crowd. How is it that here He forbids the parents to make it known? Very probably He foresees how in some cases the fame of some mighty deed might be an hindrance to, as in other cases it might forward His real work.

Or in each He might have had regard to the spiritual temperament of those whom He charged. *Canon Farrar* has a good remark: "If He added His customary warning, that they should not speak of what had happened, it was not evidently in the intention that the entire fact should remain unknown, for that would have been impossible, when all the circumstances had been witnessed by so many, but because those who had received from God's hand unbounded mercy are more likely to reverence that mercy with adoring gratitude, if it be kept like a hidden treasure in the inmost heart."

"And commanded that something should be given her to eat." There must be some reason why this is specifically mentioned. It may have been to show the completeness of the recovery, in that one, a short time before so utterly prostrated and weak, should be able to take ordinary nourishment. It may be mentioned for a mystical significance, that those to whom God has given spiritual life, require spiritual food for its continuance." (M. F. Sadler)

FACT QUESTIONS 5:35-43

276. Who do you suppose brought the news to Jairus of the death of his daughter?
277. Why ask the question, "Why dost thou trouble the teacher further"?
278. Please read Isa. 42:3 and show how it is fulfilled in the dealing of Jesus with Jairus.
279. Why send the crowd away?
280. Why take the three?

281. What do Matthew and Luke add to the description of the mourning?
282. Why did Jesus say the girl was only asleep?
283. Just what did Jesus say to the little girl?
284. How do we know for certainty the girl was dead?
285. Besides the physical restoration what was the purpose of this miracle? Was it accomplished?

SUMMARY
4:34—5:43

The argument of this section is the same as that of the corresponding section in Matthew. (See Matt. viii. 1-ix. 35.) It proves the divine power of Jesus by showing that he could control by a word the winds and the waves of the sea; could direct and compel the movements of demons; could by his touch remove incurable diseases; and could instantly raise the dead. In other words, it proves the sufficiency of his power to save to the uttermost all who come to him, by proving that all the dangers to which we are exposed, whether from the forces of the physical world, the malice of evil spirits, the power of disease, or the hand of death, may be averted at his command, and that they will be in behalf of all who put themselves under his protection.

A very marked distinction is observable between Mark's treatment of this argument, and that adopted by Matthew. The latter presents an array of ten miracles without much elaboration of any one of them; the former selects four out of the ten, and devotes almost as much space to these as Matthew does to the ten. The one writer depends more on the number of miracles reported, and the other on the character of those selected and on the minuteness with which they are described. Each mode of treatment has its advantages, and the wisdom of God is displayed in giving us both. —*McGarvey.*

5. THE GREAT TEACHER AND THE TWELVE. 6:1-13
TEXT 6:1-13

"And he went out from thence; and he cometh into his own country; and his disciples follow him. And when the sabbath was come, he began to teach in the synagogue: and many hearing him were astonished, saying, Whence hath this man these things? and, What is the wisdom that is given unto this man, and what mean such mighty works wrought by his hands? Is not this the carpenter, the son of Mary, and brother of James, and Joses, and Judas, and Simon? and are not his sisters here with us? And they were offended in him. And Jesus said unto them, A prophet is not without honour, save in his own country, and among his own kin, and in his own house. And he could there do no mighty work, save that he laid his hands upon a few sick folk, and healed them. And he marvelled because of their unbelief. And he went round about the villages teaching. And he called unto him the twelve, and began to send them forth by two and two; and he gave them authority over the unclean spirits; and he charged them that they should take nothing for their journey, save a staff only; no bread, no wallet, no money in their purse; but to go shod with sandals: and, said he, put not on two coats. And he said unto them, Wheresoever ye enter into a house, there abide till ye depart thence. And whatsoever place shall not receive you, and they hear you not, as ye go forth thence, shake off the dust that is under your feet for a testimony unto them. And they went out, and preached that men should repent. And they cast out many devils, and anointed with oil many that were sick, and healed them."

THOUGHT QUESTIONS 6:1-13

256. "He went out from thence;"—from the house of Jairus or the city of Capernaum or the Lake of Galilee or what?

257. How shall we designate or name "His own country"?

258. Why enter the synagogue in Nazareth if He was once rejected? Cf. Luke 4:14-29.

259. Specify just what caused the astonishment of those who heard Jesus.

260. Was Jesus a carpenter or the son of a carpenter?

261. How many children did the mother of Jesus bear?

262. Show how unreasonable was the offence of those in Nazareth.

263. Why did Jesus quote the familiar proverb?

264. Why was Jesus unable to do any mighty works in Nazareth?

265. What caused Jesus to marvel? Why?

266. At what place did Jesus call His apostles and send them out?

267. Why send them out "two by two"?

268. Was the Holy Spirit involved in the authority exercised by the twelve? Prove your answer.

269. Why the instructions concerning the physical needs of the journey?

270. Why the instructions in vs. 10?

271. What was the message of the twelve?

272. Why anoint with oil?

COMMENT

TIME.—Autumn of A.D. 28, and early winter of A.D. 29. This second rejection of Christ at Nazareth (vs. 1-5) was soon after the healing of Jairus' daughter, autumn, A.D. 28. The sending out of the twelve followed very soon, and their labors extended through several weeks of the autumn of 28, and early winter of 29.

PLACES.—From Capernaum the Savior went to "his own country," to Nazareth, where he had been reared, not far from twenty miles to the southwest of Capernaum. Being there rejected a second time, he went into the villages "round about" in the vicinity of Nazareth, teaching. From one of these, what one is unknown, he sent the apostles out on their mission.

PARALLEL ACCOUNTS.—Jesus at Nazareth (vs. 1-5) with Matt. 13:54-58, and Luke 4:16-30. Sending out of the disciples (vs. 6-13) with Matt. 9:35-38; 10:1-42; 11:1; Luke 9:1-6.

LESSON OUTLINE.—1. Christ Rejected again at Nazareth. 2. The Apostles Sent Forth.

ANALYSIS

I. CHRIST REJECTED AGAIN AT NAZARETH. VS. 1-6.
1. Comes to Nazareth. Mark 6:1; Matt. 13:54; Luke 4:16.
2. Teaches on the Sabbath. Mark 6:2; Matt. 13:54; Luke 4:17.
3. The People Offended. Mark 6:3; Matt. 13:57; Luke 4:28.
4. A Prophet Not Honored at Home. Mark 6:4; Matt. 13:57; Luke 4:24.
5. Their Unbelief. Isa. 53.1; Mark 6:5,6; Matt. 13:58.

II. THE APOSTLES SENT FORTH. VS. 7-13.
1. The Twelve Called. Mark 3:14-19; Matt. 10:1-4; Luke 6:13-16.
2. The Twelve Sent Forth. Mark 6:7; Matt. 10:5-15; Luke 9:1-5.
3. The Twelve Charged. Mark 6:8-11; Matt. 10:5-15; Luke 9:1-5.
4. The Twelve on Their Mission. Mark 6:12, 13; Luke 9:6.

INTRODUCTION

After the healing of the woman, the Lord raised from the dead the daughter of Jairus, the account of which is given in Mark 5:35-43. Immediately after this, on his return home (Capernaum) from the house of Jairus, Christ heals two blind men and a dumb possessed, giving the Pharisees new occasion to say that he cast out devils, through Satan. Matthew alone (9:27-34) mentions these incidents. Jesus, then, accompanied by his disciples, goes into Lower Galilee, again visiting Nazareth, where he is the second time rejected, the account given in Luke 4:14-29, being held to describe an earlier incident of the Lord's ministry. If that be correct, the Savior gave them a second opportunity to accept the gospel after his fame as a great Teacher had been established, and when they rejected him a second time he returned no more.

EXPLANATORY NOTES

I. CHRIST REJECTED AGAIN AT NAZARETH.—1. *And he went out from thence.* From Capernaum, where he made his home. *Came to his own country.* To Nazareth, the town where he had been reared from childhood and had lived until he was thirty years of age. Whether his mother still lived in Nazareth is a matter of conjecture. *Cook* says: "The works wrought in the interval (since his first rejection, nine months before, April, A.D. 28), the effects of his personal influence, the progress made in spite of all opposition, might be expected to work upon the minds of the Nazarenes so far as to prepare them for listening to him, notwithstanding their former rejection. Natural sympathy would draw him thither. His sisters, probably married to Nazarenes still dwelt there." *His disciples follow Him.* The twelve apostles are meant. They now constantly attended his footsteps. The presence of the Lord and his companions at Nazareth would, no doubt, produce a strong effect. His fame had extended over all Israel.

2. *When the sabbath day was come.* The seventh day of the week, Saturday, the Jewish Sabbath, always observed by the Savior as a part of the Jewish law which remained in force until he died upon the cross. The language implies that one day or more elapsed between his arrival and his public teaching. It had been the practice of Jesus, from early childhood, to attend all the synagogue services; and he was still suffered to do so, in spite of the opposition he had excited. When Sabbath came, therefore, he went to morning worship. *He began to teach in the synagogue.* The synagogues of the Jews were the town and village churches, where they worshipped in their various quarters for ordinary occasions when they need not go up to Jerusalem. Most probably there would be only one in so small a place. But in all the Jewish synagogues there was a freedom of speech allowed; and there would be no objection, therefore, to one like Jesus, who had already achieved for himself a name as a remarkable rabbi, addressing the assembled congregation. *Many hearing, were astonished.* The usual effect upon those who heard the wonderful Teacher was produced. The sentiments which follow were probably expressed while he was teaching. A Jewish audience was not as decorous as the modern congregation in the United States or Great Britain. Some

uttered one thing and some another. *From whence hath this man these things?* The things, namely, that he was saying. The simple people marvelled at his facility and power of utterance, and at the weighty character of the thoughts that were conveyed by the utterances. *What wisdom is this?* They admitted the existence of great intellectual and rhetorical superiority; but they stood in doubt in reference to the origin of such superiority; was it from above, or from beneath? *Such mighty works.* As the evangelist notes in verse 5, that no mighty work had been done in Nazareth, these must refer to what had been reported there. They do not venture to deny his wisdom or his miracles, but, by wondering at them, really bear witness to them. This admission left them inexcusable, both intellectually and morally, for not receiving Jesus as the true Messiah.

3. *Is not this the carpenter?* This, and the Jewish custom which required every father to teach his son a trade, whatever pursuit in life he might eventually follow, indicate that Christ worked in his earlier years at the carpenter's trade with his father. St. Mark's is the only gospel which gives this name as applied to our Lord himself. In Matt. 13:55, it is said that they called him the "carpenter's son." There is no contradiction; some called him one, some the other name. The word translated *carpenter* here is of wider meaning than our word "carpenter." It includes all workers in wood, our cabinet-maker as well as carpenter. *Son of Mary.* Though neither of the evangelists speak of Joseph's death, yet it may be plainly inferred that Christ was now called "the son of Mary" (Mark 6:3), because of her being a widow. See Luke 8:19; John 2:12, and 19:25-27. *Brother of James, etc., . . . sisters here with us.* These four were either (1) own brothers and sisters of Jesus, children of Joseph and Mary; or (2) children of Joseph by a former marriage; or, (3) cousins (brothers taken in the wider sense of near *relatives*), children of Clopas and Mary, sister of Mary the mother of Jesus (John 19:25, with Mark 15:40). The weight of Protestant authority, on the whole, favors the idea that they were own brothers of Jesus. For a discussion of this subject, see my *Commentary on John,* pp. 48, 49. Of the four brethren here named, James came to have authority hardly, if any, less than that of an apostle, as the leading figure in the church at Jerusalem. He was called by early writers "James the Just," and wrote the Epistle of James. He must not be confounded with the apostle James, who was the brother of John. Of Joses and Simon nothing more is known. Judas was probably the author of the Epistle of Jude. *They were offended.* That is, they stumbled, and fell into error. That Jesus was a carpenter, had grown up in their midst, and that they knew all about his family, proved to them that he could not be the Messiah, whom they expected to be a temporal prince surrounded with earthly splendor. His pure life for thirty years in their

midst, his surpassing wisdom and mighty works counted nothing with them.

4. *A prophet is not without honor.* This was a common proverb that Christ applied to his case, showing that he was rejected on these natural principles, not because they had not evidence in his works, but because they had prejudice against his lowly origin among men. The proverb is founded on human experience. There is a kind of natural jealousy among the companions and neighbors of a man who rises from their level until he is far above them.

5. *And he could there do no mighty work.* His power was not changed. His miracles were not feats of magic, but required two conditions to call them forth—an opportunity, and a sufficient moral purpose. "Unbelief" prevented both. The unbelieving would not come for healing; to heal such would be contrary to his purpose in the miracles, the demonstration of his spiritual power. Hence he "could not." When men do not believe, they do not give him the opportunity to save them, and to save the unbelieving is contrary to his purpose, and impossible.—*Schaff.* He "could not," not from a lack of power, but because the conditions that he always required before he would exercise his power were absent. Those who expect his blessing must come for it in faith.

6. *He marvelled.* Our Lord does not marvel at other human things generally; but he does marvel, on the one hand, at faith, when, as in the case of the centurion, it overcomes in its grandeur all human hindrances, and, on the other, all unbelief, when it can, in the face of numerous divine manifestations, harden itself into a willful rejection on himself. See Matt. 8:10. *And he went.* He now seems to have left Nazareth, never to return to it, or preach in its synagogue, or revisit the home where he had so long toiled as the village carpenter. *Went round about the villages.* On the evening of the day of his rejection at Nazareth, or more probably on the morrow, our Lord appears to have commenced a short circuit in Galilee, in the direction of Capernaum.

II. THE APOSTLES SENT FORTH.—7. *And he called unto him the twelve.* The apostles. After long wanderings and continuous trials, the twelve were now, in their Master's opinion, in a measure prepared to work by themselves in spreading the new kingdom. Matthew gives a touching reason for the mission of the twelve. It was because he pitied the multitude, who were like harassed panting sheep without a shepherd, and like a harvest left unreaped for want of laborers (Matt. 9:36-38). Another reason was that the Master wished to train them for their great work under his direction. *Two by two.* They were sent out in pairs that they might counsel, help and encourage one another, an example that might still be followed with profit. *Gave them power over unclean spirits.* Their work was to cast out unclean spirits in the world and the divine authority was given to cast them out of the men who were possessed of demons. This power was needful that they might be able to demonstrate that they were the Lord's messengers.

8. *Commanded them.* There follows now the charge that he gave them. Matt. 10:5-42, gives this charge at much greater length. *Nothing for their journey.* Make no preparation, such as is ordinarily made on the eve of a journey; set out just as you are. God will provide for all your wants. The open hospitality of the East, so often used as the basis for dissemination of new thoughts, would be ample for their maintenance. *A staff only.* A walkingstick as used in journeys upon foot to support and ease the traveler. Matthew (10:10) gives "neither staves;" i.e., they were to take one only. *Scrip.* A "wallet" or "small bag" (compare 1 Sam. 17:40). It was so called, perhaps, because it was designed to hold scraps, trifling articles, scraped off, as it were, from something larger. It was part of the pilgrim's or traveler's equipage. *Money.* Literally, brass, or rather copper, said to be the first ore that was wrought. Copper having been early used for money, the word has sometimes that meaning.

9. *Be shod with sandals.* Such as they had on at the time, without waiting for shoes especially adapted for the journey. In Matthew, they are directed not to wear *shoes;* here, to be shod with sandals. The shoe of the ancients resembled the modern shoe; the sandal was simply a sole of leather, felt, cloth, or wood, bound upon the feet by thongs. *Not put on two coats.* Literally, tunics. The tunic (Greek) was the inner garment, worn next the skin, usually with sleeves, and reaching to the knees. It answered rather to our shirt than to our coat. The entire oufit shows that they were plain men, to whom there was no extraordinary self-denial in the matter or the mode of their mission. They were going to their brethren (Matt. 10:5), and the best way was to throw themselves on their hospitality. They were accustomed to live in about this way.

10. *In what place soever ye enter into a house.* On their arrival at a city, they were to settle down in the first house to which they obtained access, which, however, was not to exclude prudence and well ascertained information (Matthew); and, once settled in a house, they were to keep to it, and try to make it the center of a divine work in that place. This injunction was meant to exclude fastidious and restless changes.

11. *Shake off the dust . . . testimony against them.* By this symbolical action they vividly shook themselves from all connection with such, and all responsibility for the guilt of rejecting them and their message. Such symbolical actions were common in ancient times, even among others than the Jews. *More tolerable for Sodom and Gomorrah.* See Gen. 13:13; chaps. 18, 19. The cities that stood out in the history of the world, as

most conspicuous for their infamy, were yet less guilty (as sinning less against light and knowledge) than those who rejected the messengers of the King.

12. *They went out, and preached that men should repent.* This is one-half of the brief, unambitious narrative of the first apostolic tour of the apostles. Going out from the Lord's presence, or the place where he delivered these instructions, they proceeded to fulfill them, not at random or confusedly, but on a systematic method, going about or through the country and among the villages, or from town to town. *Men should repent.* The same message which had been already brought by John the Baptist and by Christ himself. The time had come for preaching the cross of Christ.

13. *They cast out many devils.* In this verse we have the other half of the evangelist's report of the first apostolic tour. *Anointed with oil.* To suppose that the oil was used medicinally, is contrary to the whole tenor of the narratives. It was "the vehicle of healing power committed to them" an external sign such as our Lord sometimes used to connect himself and the person cured. It was probably also a symbol of anointing by the Holy Spirit.—*Schaff.* The Jews were in the habit of anointing their faces and hair with oil every day when they went among their fellows. This was omitted when sick or fasting. The apostles anointed a sick man when about to heal him with a word and send him forth. It meant that the patient was able to go out among his fellow-men.

FACT QUESTIONS 6:1-13

286. How far from Capernaum to Nazareth?
287. What other incidents occur after the raising of the daughter of Jairus *before* he arrives at Nazareth? (Cf. Matt. 9:27-34)
288. What of the mother of Jesus—where was she living?—where were his sisters? Were they married?
289. Was Jesus keeping the law by worshipping in the synagogue?
290. How did those of Nazareth express their astonishment?
291. If Jesus did no mighty works in Nazareth which mighty works are meant in vs. 2?
292. What Jewish custom was observed in the fact that Jesus was a carpenter?
293. What is inferred in the expression "Son of Mary"?
294. Give the three opinions as to who were the four of vs. 3.
295. Why is a prophet without honor in his own country?—Please do not give a superficial answer—relate this to our blessed Lord and answer accordingly.
296. What were the two conditions upon which Jesus could perform His mighty works?
297. What are the two things that cause our Lord to marvel?

298. What was the reason for the mission of the twelve? Cf. Matt. 9:36-38.
299. What was the purpose of the mission?
300. Read Matt. 10:10 and Mark 6:8 and explain the apparent contradiction.
301. What was a "scrip"? What kind of "money"? Why "sandals"? What is meant by "two coats"?
302. In what way did Jesus prevent fastidiousness and restless change?
303. Why shake the dust from their feet?
304. Please explain the purpose in anointing with oil.

6. THE DEATH OF JOHN THE BAPTIST 6:14-29

TEXT 6:14-29

"And king Herod heard thereof; for his name had become known: and he said, John the Baptist is risen from the dead, and therefore do these powers work in him. But others said, It is Elijah. And others said, It is a prophet, even as one of the prophets. But Herod, when he heard thereof, said, John, whom I beheaded, he is risen. For Herod himself had sent forth and laid hold upon John, and bound him in prison for the sake of Herodias, his brother Philip's wife: for he had married her. For John said unto Herod, It is not lawful for thee to have thy brother's wife. And Herodias set herself against him, and desired to kill him; and she could not; for Herod feared John, knowing that he was a righteous man and a holy, and kept him safe. And when he heard him, he was much perplexed; and he heard him gladly. And when a convenient day was come, that Herod on his birthday made a supper to his lords, and the high captains, and the chief men of Galilee; and when the daughter of Herodias herself came in and danced, she pleased Herod and them that sat at meat with him; and the king said unto the damsel, Ask of me whatsoever thou wilt, and I will give it thee. And he sware unto her, Whatsoever thou shalt ask of me, I will give it thee, unto the half of my kingdom. And she went out, and said unto her mother, What shall I ask? And she said, The head of John the Baptist. And she came in straightway with haste unto the king, and asked, saying, I will that thou forthwith give me in a charger the head of John the Baptist. And the king was exceeding sorry; but for the sake of his oaths, and of them that sat at meat, he would not reject her. And straightway the king sent forth a soldier of his guard, and commanded to bring his head: and he went and beheaded him in the prison, and brought his head in a charger, and gave it to the damsel; and the damsel gave it to her mother. And when his disciples heard thereof, they came and took up his corpse, and laid it in a tomb."

THOUGHT QUESTIONS 6:14-29

273. Just who was this Herod? i.e. who was his father?—brother?—wife? etc.
274. Why did Herod associate the words of Jesus with John the Baptist?
275. Was Jesus like Elijah or one of the Old Testament prophets? In what way?
276. Why did Herod want to see Jesus?
277. Who was Herod Philip? Who was Herodias?
278. If Herod's sin was so plainly and publicly condemned by John why did Herod want to see him and hear him?
279. Was the fear of the popularity of John a factor in Herod's respect for John? Cf. Matt. 14:5.
280. Who attended the birthday banquet?
281. Why make such a rash offer?—was the dance professional?
282. Was Herodias behind the dance and its purpose? Why?
283. Why the urgency in the request for the head of John?
284. Who beheaded John?
285. Where did this incident take place?
286. What do you imagine Salome and Herodias did with the head after it was brought to them?

COMMENT

TIME—Winter of A.D. 29.

PLACES—At Herod's Palace and capital, *Tiberias* on the Lake of Galilee —or at *Machaerus* the palace-fortress east of the Dead Sea.

PARALLEL ACCOUNTS—Matt. 14:1-12.

OUTLINE—1. The fear of Herod and of others, vs. 14-16. 2. The imprisonment and its reason, vs. 17-18. 3. The hatred of Herodias, vs. 19-20. 4. The dance and the death, vs. 21-29.

ANALYSIS

I. THE FEAR OF HEROD AND OF OTHERS, 14-16.
   1. Fear based on what he heard of the miracles of Jesus.
   2. His conscience said, "this is John risen from the dead."
   3. Others said—"this is Elijah, or a prophet like the prophets of our fathers."

II. THE IMPRISONMENT AND ITS REASON, 17-18.
   1. John in prison because of the hatred of Herodias.
   2. John had rebuked Herod for his marriage to his brother's wife.

III. THE HATRED OF HERODIAS, 19-20.
   1. A continual desire to kill in the heart of Herodias.
   2. Prevented by the respect of her husband for John.

IV. THE DANCE AND THE DEATH, 21-29.
   1. The time of the dance—a birthday supper.

2. The reward of the dance—promised by an oath.
3. The mother of death.
4. A sad departure.
5. The trophy of lust and hate.

EXPLANATORY NOTES 6:14-29

"14. King Herod: "King" by courtesy only, since Herod was but a Tetrarch, that is, a governor of the fourth part of a kingdom or province. Jesus warned His disciples to beware of Herod, saying: *"Take heed and beware of the leaven of the Pharisees and of the leaven of Herod"* (8: 15).

heard: of the fame of Jesus, which the Apostles by their miracles and preaching had helped to spread.

John the Baptist is risen again from the dead. He must have suffered martyrdom during or after the Apostles' first mission, and before the fourth Passover after our Lord's baptism.

is risen again. Evidently Herod was no Sadducee, who said *there is no resurrection, neither angel nor spirit* (Acts 23:8), or his guilty conscience and superstitious fears had obscured his religious belief.

mighty works: miracles. John the Baptist had worked no miracles during his lifetime. *And many resorted to him, and they said: John indeed did no sign* (John 10:41). Herod seems to have imagined that John the Baptist having risen would necessarily do *mighty works.*

14, 15. In these verses three opinions are given concerning our Lord. He is John the Baptist risen from the dead, or Elijah or another prophet.

It is Elijah. According to the prophecy, *Behold I will send you Elijah the prophet, before the coming of the great and dreadful day of the Lord* (Mal. 4:5). Elijah had not died, but had been taken up to heaven while conversing with Elisha. *And as they went on, walking and talking together, behold a fiery chariot, and fiery horses parted them both asunder: and Elijah went up by a whirlwind into heaven* (2 Kings 2:11). There was therefore an expectation among the Jews that Elijah should return to earth as the forerunner of the Messiah. Moses had said, a Prophet should be raised up by God (Deut. 18:15), but this refers to Christ Himself.

16. *John whom I beheaded.* Herod fears to meet his victim again.

17. *Herod . . . had apprehended John,* etc. Mark here refers to a preceding event. Herod had had John the Baptist bound and then imprisoned him, probably in Machaerus (*the Black Fortress*), which Herod the Great had built, and which was situated east of the Dead Sea.

This castle had been in the possession of Aretas, father-in-law to Herod Antipas, and Emir of Arabia Petraea. Probably Herod had seized this castle when his lawful wife, hearing of his approaching marriage with

Herodias, had fled to her father at Petra. Machaerus was both a palace and a prison. At this period Herod was probably living there with an armed retinue, on account of the war with Aretas in which he was engaged. Herod lost the day, and the Jews considered this defeat a punishment for the beheading of John the Baptist.

for the sake of Herodias. Herod's sister-in-law and niece.

he had married her. This was unlawful for four reasons:

(1) Herodias' first husband, Herod Philip I. (not the Tetrarch) was still living.

(2) The daughter of Aretas, Herod's wife was also alive.

(3) Herodias was niece to Herod, being the daughter of Aristobulus, his eldest half-brother.

(4) Herod Antipas was a convert to Judaism, and hence bound to observe the Jewish law. This distinctly forbade marriage with a deceased brother's wife (Lev. 20:21) unless that brother died without issue which was not the case, since Salome was the child of Herodias and Herod Philip I.

18. *to have,*—i.e. to marry.

it is not lawful for thee, etc. John boldly rebuked vice even in the great. As our Lord said, when speaking of him, John was no *reed shaken with the wind;* he was a prophet and *more than a prophet,* and spoke with a prophet's fearlessness. Luke tells us that John also reproved all the evils which Herod had done (Luke 3:19).

19. *Herodias laid snares.* Naturally his boldness in rebuking Herod would arouse her anger and resentment, which was all the keener because she perceived that John had a great influence of Herod, *who feared John.*

20. kept him. Preserved him from Herodias' vengeance, at least for a time.

when he heard him, did many things. Herod was awed by John's virtue. He feared and esteemed him, and did many things to please the Precursor, but not the one thing against which John's rebukes were chiefly directed. Herod would not put away Herodias.

heard him willingly. Herod had his better moments, but he had not the courage to conquer his vices and to amend. It was easier to listen than to yield, and the many things evidently did not cost him so much as the one necessary sacrifice would have done. They were matters of less moment than his sinful marriage. *In like manner, Felix coming with Drusilla* (a daughter of Herodias), *his wife who was a Jew, sent for Paul, and heard of him the faith that is in Christ Jesus* (Acts 24:24).

21. *a convenient day,*—i.e. for the vengeance of Herodias, that she might win by stratagem, where she had failed by direct petition.

made a supper. Probably at the castle of Machaerus.

for his birthday. Herod, like the Roman emperors, made a great banquet on his birthday. The Jews disliked the observance of birthdays, as being connected with idolatry and favouring it, since at these banquets libations and sacrifices were frequently offered to the gods.

princes. High civil or military officials.

tribunes. Doubtless here military tribunes are referred to, of whom there were four or six in each legion. Ten Roman *civil* tribunes were chosen by the people to protect them from the oppression of the senate and nobles. These tribunes would hardly be living in Palestine.

chief men of Galilee. The local authorities, the great landowners.

22. *when the daughter . . . had danced.* Salome here dishonors herself and family by performing the part of a hired scenic dancer. Moreover these oriental dances were generally immodest. It was customary to give some such entertainment at the close of the banquet. Herod and his guests, from their couches, would have a full view of the performers.

Ask me what thou wilt. It would seem as though Salome hesitated as to what request to proffer, since Herod reiterates his offer, and enforces it with oaths, as the original expression indicates.

23. *though it be the half,* etc. Not to be taken literally, but meaning that Herod was willing to bestow great gifts on her. It was a boastful assertion made in presence of his flatterers; possibly he was not sober when he made it. Assuerus had promised Esther the half of his kingdom, but at least it was his to give (Esther 5:3).

24. *What shall I ask?* Herodias does not hesitate as to her reply; she had long since decided what she wished to obtain.

25. *Immediately with haste.* Herodias feared delay, lest she should ultimately meet with a refusal. When Herod was sober, he might again refuse to accede to the request of Salome.

26. *struck sad.* Mark's graphic expression for denoting Herod's consternation. The original Greek word indicates great sorrow and grief. Herod feared to keep his rash oath, yet had not the manliness to break it, by refusing to commit a crime. To keep a rash oath is a sin against the Second Commandment. Herod, by keeping his oath, broke the fifth Commandment also.

27. *an executioner,* literally a *spiculator* which signifies either (1) a scout, (2) a special adjutant, (3) a soldier of the guard. The spiculators formed a special division of the legion, and each emperor had a body of them to guard his person and execute his orders. They were often employed as instruments to execute the emperor's private vengeance. As Herod was at war with Aretas, these spiculators would be in attendance.

28. *the damsel gave it to her mother.*

The crime is now accomplished. Jerome says that Herodias glutted her vengeance by piercing the saint's tongue with needles (as Fulvia did to her enemy Cicero). Nicephorus states that Salome met with a terrible death as a punishment for her share in the sacrilegious crime. When crossing the ice it broke under her, and the fragments drifting together severed her head from her body.

29. *his disciples . . . took his body.* Jerome tells us they buried their master in Sebaste (Samaria). Herod allowed them to perform this act of respect. They buried the headless corpse only. Matthew adds that these disciples *"came and told Jesus."* Possibly some of John's disciples now attached themselves to Christ, while others in outlying districts entered the Church later, through the ministry of the Apostles (see Acts 19:1-7). In this narrative four details are given by Mark alone:

(1) Herodias was John the Baptist's enemy rather than Herod, who esteemed him.
(2) Herod "kept him" for a time at least from her vengeance.
(3) Salome consulted her mother regarding the request.
(4) Herod sent a special executioner to behead John." (*Cecilia*)

FACT QUESTIONS 6:14-29

305. In what sense was the title "king" used for Herod?
306. Was Herod a Sadducee? Discuss.
307. Why associate mighty works with John when John did no mighty works?
308. Show how Mal. 4:5 related to the opinion of some.
309. In what place had Herod imprisoned John? Who was Aretas?
310. Give the four reasons it was unlawful for Herod to marry Herodias.
311. Show how the description of John given by our Lord fit him.
312. John's imprisonment was actually a protection—show how.
313. What respect did Herod show for John the Baptist?
314. Who attended the birthday banquet?
315. Why offer a reward for the dance?
316. Was the dance and the request prepared ahead of time?
317. Why was Herod so sad?—why carry out the rash vow?
318. What does Jerome add to the story?
319. What does Matthew add?
320. State the four details given by Mark not included in the other gospels.

7. THE FEEDING OF THE FIVE THOUSAND 6:30-44.

TEXT 6:30-44

"And the apostles gather themselves together unto Jesus; and they told him all things, whatsoever they had done, and whatsoever they had taught. And he saith unto them, Come ye yourselves apart into a desert place, and rest a while. For there were many coming and going, and they had no leisure so much as to eat. And they went away in the boat to a desert place apart. And the people saw them going, and many knew them, and they ran there together on foot from all the cities, and outwent them. And he came forth and saw a great multitude, and he had compassion on them, because they were as sheep not having a shepherd: and he began to teach them many things. And when the day was now far spent, his disciples came unto him, and said, The place is desert, and the day is now far spent: send them away, that they may go into the country and villages round about, and buy themselves somewhat to eat. But he answered and said unto them, Give ye them to eat. And they say unto him, Shall we go and buy two hundred pennyworth of bread, and give them to eat? And he saith unto them, How many loaves have ye? go and see. And when they knew they say, Five, and two fishes. And he commanded them that all should sit down by companies upon the green grass. And they sat down in ranks, by hundreds, and by fifties. And he took the five loaves and the two fishes, and looking up to heaven, he blessed, and brake the loaves; and he gave to the disciples to set before them; and the two fishes divided he among them all. And they did all eat, and were filled. And they took up broken pieces, twelve basketfuls, and also of the fishes. And they that ate the loaves were five thousand men."

THOUGHT QUESTIONS 6:30-44

287. Where had the apostles been? What had they been doing? Into how many villages and towns do you imagine they went?
288. What reaction would their success have on Herod?
289. There was more than one reason for suggesting they "go apart to a lonely place"—can you discover them?
290. Please attempt to locate the area into which Jesus and His apostles were going.
291. How did the crowds know where they were going?
292. Read John 6:4 and discover why there was such a large crowd.
293. Wasn't Jesus tired?—How is it He was not filled with irritation instead of compassion when He saw the crowd?
294. What two things did Jesus do for the crowds? Does this set some kind of example for medical and preaching work? Discuss.
295. Why ask how many loaves they had?
296. Why were they to sit in companies?
297. At what time of the year was it when this miracle was performed?
298. What particular type of miracle was here performed?
299. How much did the people eat?

COMMENT

TIME.—Spring of A.D. 29.

PLACES.—Capernaum, Bethsaida.

PARALLEL ACCOUNTS—Matt. 14:13-21; Luke 9:12-17; John 6.

OUTLINE—1. The occasion for the miracle, 30-37. 2. The miracle, 38-44.

ANALYSIS

I. THE OCCASION FOR THE MIRACLE, VS. 30-37.
   1. The return and report of the apostles, vs. 30.
   2. The need for retirement, vs. 31.
   3. The unsuccessful attempt to seek solitude, vs. 32-33.
   4. The compassion and teaching of Jesus, vs. 34.
   5. The concern of the disciples and the answer of Jesus, vs. 35-37.

II. THE MIRACLE, VS. 38-44.
   1. Give what you have—five barley loaves and two fish, v. 38.
   2. Sit in ranks of fifty and hundreds on the green grass, v. 39-40.
   3. Blessing and multiplying the bread and fish He distributed to the apostles, v. 41.
   4. They ate their fill, v. 42.
   5. They gathered twelve baskets of fragments, v. 43.
   6. There were 5,000 men who ate, v. 44.

EXPLANATORY NOTES

"30-44. THE APOSTLES HAVING RETURNED, JESUS CROSSES THE LAKE WITH THEM IN SEARCH OF REST, AND THERE FEEDS FIVE THOUSAND. Here, and here alone between the beginning of the Galilean ministry and the week of the Passion, we have four parallel reports. John comes into parallelism with the synoptists at this crossing of the lake, and continues parallel through the record of the return, when Jesus walks on the water, though here we lose our four-fold record by the silence of Luke. John contributes a valuable note of time in the remark that the passover was at hand. The death of the Baptist occurred, therefore, in the spring, and there remained just a year of the ministry of Jesus after the death of the forerunner.

30. The tidings of the death of John would seem to have reached Jesus while he was still alone; but about the same time his company was again gathered around him by the return of the apostles. Of the tone of the report they brought to him nothing is said—whether cheerful or sad—nor is there anywhere any glimpse of them in the work of this mission. *They reported what they had done;* Mark adds, *and what they had taught.* In their teaching he would certainly see defects, but his response to their report would be nothing else than cheering: he was training them, and he would not fail to encourage them.

31, 32. The invitation was addressed to the twelve alone. *Come ye yourselves apart into a desert place, and rest a while*—i.e. a little while. *A while* is by no means an adequate translation of *oligon,* "a little." He did not expect long rest, but he did hope for a little.—The place was probably Capernaum. After the reunion of the company of Jesus the crowd had returned, and those who were *coming and going* gave them *no leisure so much as to eat.* The whole of verse 31 is peculiar to Mark, and both parts of it are intensely characteristic—the representation of our Lord's feeling and the graphic description of the circumstances.—For the invitation two motives appear, one in Mark and one in Matthew. From Mark we should attribute it to tender care of the apostles, weary from their work, and to his desire to be alone with them for a little. This is one of the touching illustrations of his thoughtfulness toward them. In Matthew it is when Jesus heard of the death of the Baptist that he withdrew privately to the desert place. Joined with the other motive was the desire to be in quiet, that he might have leisure for the thoughts that the death of John suggested. The death of such a man must have been a heavy blow to him, more especially since it was such a death. His personal love for John would make him now a mourner; and the event must also have awakened the thought of Matt. 17:12—"Likewise shall also the Son of man suffer of them"—and have brought the certainty of his own death freshly before him. It may also have led him to think of modifying his method thenceforth and giving himself more fully, as he did, to the training of his apostles. Thus the two motives were one in effect, driving him away from the shifting, intruding, exacting crowd to be alone with his own.—They went away, not *by ship, but* "in the boat"—the boat that they were wont to use. They must have gone in the early morning.

33. They succeeded in getting away, but not unobserved. Luke says they went to Bethsaida; John, that Jesus "went up into the mountain;" Matthew and Mark, merely that the place was *desert.*—i.e. uninhabited. The fact seems to be that they went to Bethsaida, which stood at the extreme north of the lake, where the Jordan enters it (see chap. 8:22), and thence proceeded a little to the south-east, to some convenient point in the hills that rise from the shore of the lake, where they might hope to be alone. It may be that at Bethsaida itself they did not touch at all, and that Luke's mention of it is meant only for a general designation of the locality. The distance from Capernaum to the vicinity of Bethsaida would not be more than six or eight miles, and could be traversed on foot about as quickly as by boat; if the boat was in no haste, more quickly. In the journey for rest there would be no haste, and the pursuing crowd arrived first. The people were *out of all cities*—i.e. from many towns in that region, especially from those that must be passed on the way. The crowd

grew in going. John speaks of Jesus already seated in the mountain, lifting up his eyes and seeing the crowd approaching, which may be a reminiscence of the fact that they came, not all at once, but kept streaming in. John also connects the mention of the coming throng with the fact that the passover was at hand. It may be that some part of the multitude was made up of pilgrims to Jerusalem, who turned aside to see the Prophet of Galilee.

34. *He came out.* From the boat. The disciples may have been impatient that the ever-present throng was even here; with the Master, however, it was not impatience, but compassion.—The activity of the day was rich and various. The motive, pity for the spiritual state of the multitude, which seems to have been often affecting him with a sad surprise. The shpherd-impulse was strong in his heart and the sight of sheep unshepherded always drew it forth. So *he began to teach them many things,* or, as in Luke, he "spoke to them of the kingdom of God," into which as a fold he would gather the unshepherded (Luke 15:4-6; 19:10; John 10:16). He also "healed their sick" (Matthew), or, as in Luke, "healed them that had need of healing." Such was the rest that he found, and such the opportunity for quiet meditation. He had had no leisure to eat; but, while he became a shepherd to the shepherdless, no doubt his heart was full of the sentiment of John 4:32-34: "My meat is to do the will of him that sent me, and to finish his work."

35-44. In this paragraph the synoptists are quite closely parallel, save that Matthew condenses a little, as usual, and Mark adds his fresh touches of description. John diverges at the beginning in attributing the inquiry about the possibility of feeding the multitude, not to the amazed disciples when Jesus has proposed that they shall do it, but to Jesus himself, as a question intended to test the faith of Philip. If it were necessary, no doubt the two conversations could be woven in together and harmonized with a tolerable degree of plausibility; but it is more satisfactory to leave them as two independent reports of the same event. Perhaps the independence is worth more to us than an unquestionable harmony would be. (This is true, for the value of several narratives, instead of one, must be due to their independence. Yet harmony is compatible with independence. Nay, if several accounts of the same events are true, they must be in real harmony with one another, though we are sometimes unable to show this. The omission from the narratives of a single connecting act or remark may render it forever impossible for us to see the exact connections or point out the exact sequence of the things reported. But it is desirable to show the harmony of the different narratives wherever this can be done, or at least to show that the several accounts, though independent, need not be supposed to contradict one another at any point. Compare notes on John 6:5).

The suggestion of the apostles (verses 35, 36) seemed not only rational, but the only rational one: the people must not be kept away from the necessary comforts, and the disciples thought that even for Jesus to keep them longer would be no kindness. A startling proposal, *Give ye them to eat.* The words are identical in Matthew, Mark and Luke, showing how sharply the incisive and startling command entered the minds of the hearers. Matthew introduces it with equally astonishing remark, "They need not depart." He proposed that which is impossible to men; but he himself was there. There had been as yet no multiplication of food by his hands, so far as we know, except as the turning of water into wine (John 2:1-11) might be called such. The belief of the apostles in his miraculous power ought by this time to have been perfect; but it is to be remembered that he did not propose himself to feed the multitude: he said, *Give ye them to eat.* After that proposal it was only natural that they should think first of their own resources, and inquire how the thing could be done. It was not altogether unbelief that made them speak of buying bread for the people; he had compelled them to look at the matter from that side. They knew that they had nothing adequate, and were equally sure that it was impracticable to buy.—*Two hundred pennyworth of bread.* The proposal to buy is omitted by Matthew, and the quantity by Luke. This quantity is mentioned in Mark without comment, and in John as insufficient. The denarius ("penny" is a very poor translation, or rather, not a translation at all) was equal actually to about fifteen cents, but relatively to considerably more. In Matt. 20:2 it appears as a suitable return for a day's labor.—In Mark alone are the disciples sent to find how many loaves they have. Their investigation and report are represented in the words *when they knew, they say.* Literally, "knowing, they say." One of Mark's telling brevities. The loaves were thin and brittle; from Luke 11:5, 6 it appears that three would be required for a meal for a single person. The fishes are called in John (not elsewhere) *opsaria,* a word that denotes a condiment, something eaten with bread or other staple food. Hence the idea of "small fishes;" but that idea cannot be insisted on, as the word had come to be used of fish generally. After the report of a hopeless quantity, Matthew adds the reply of Jesus: "Bring them hither to me"—the one hope of making the small supply sufficient. This is the one hopeful thing to do with Christian gifts and resources of every kind—offer them to him in whose hands a handful can feed a multitude.

The proposal thus to feed the people was another suggestion of the Shepherd's heart. Bodily wants were not beneath his notice, and yet this act had predominantly a spiritual purpose. Brief though the record is, that had been a great day of power and teaching, and such a day might well close with a climax of convincing might. The people must sit down in order to secure orderly and impartial distribution. Heavenly things must be handled with earthly wisdom; bread produced by miracle must be distributed in the best human order. The description of the sitting down is peculiar to Mark, and is unlike anything else in the New Testament. *He commanded them to make all sit down by companies—symposia symposia,* company by company"—*upon the green grass. And they sat down prasiai prasiai*—not exactly *in ranks,* but rather in blocks like garden-beds, some in blocks of a hundred and some by fifties. The repetition or doubling of the descriptive words is in the Hebrew style. The change of word from the general *symposia,* "company," to the purely descriptive *prasiai,* "garden-beds," shows how the scene arose pictorially in the memory of the narrator, and he again saw the people arranged in squares and looking, in their vari-colored clothing, like flower-beds on the grass.—The grass is mentioned by Matthew and John. John says that there was "much;" Mark alone calls it green grass—a part, again of the pictorial memory of the scene. The word corresponds, too, to the season, the passover-time, in spring.

He looked up to heaven, and blessed. So Matthew and Mark—i.e. he blessed God, praised God in thanksgiving; Luke, "he blessed them," the loaves and fishes—invoked the blessing of God upon them; John, "he gave thanks." It was simply the grateful prayer before eating, "grace before meat," offered by the host or head of the family. (So Luke 24:30; see notes on Mark 14:22, 23.) Distribution was made by the hands of the disciples; so expressly in all but John. The separate mention of the giving out of the fishes is a slight link between Mark and John.—In Mark's addition to what Matthew and Luke tell, *and the two fishes divided he among them all,* we see distinctly recorded the deep sense of wonder, and yet the keen observation of an observer close at hand. This story, as told in Mark, can be nothing else than the report of an eye-witness; the evidences are of the plainest and most irrestible kind.—As to the process of the miracle, speculations seem to be in vain. Theories of the acceleration of natural processes have been proposed for such occasions, but they were useless, and when closely examined are absurd. If this work was performed at all, it was done by creative power; and that is enough to say of it. It was no insufficient or halfway work: they were all satisfied.—In John the command to gather the fragments is mentioned; in the others, only the gathering. The word for *baskets* here is not the same as in the record of the similar miracle in chap. 8:8. The word here is *cophinus,* the source of our words "coffer" and "coffin." This, apparently, was the wicker provision-basket that was in common use. The collecting of the fragments shows again, like the order in the distribution of the food, the Saviour's purpose that miracles shall never displace prudence. Though divine power can produce a super-abundant supply, still it is right "that nothing be lost."—A fresh sign of the independence of the four narratives is found in the manner of recording the number of the multitude. That "there were about five thousand men" is mentioned by Luke in connection with the hint of the disciples that it was impossible to buy bread for so many; by John, in connection with their sitting down, when their number was ascertained; Mark says at the very end, just after mentioning the great store of fragments that was left, that *they that did eat of the loaves were about five thousand men* (*about,* however, is omitted in the best text); Matthew, at the same point, says that here were "about five thousand men, besides women and children." The women and children would be arranged, according to Jewish custom, separately from the men, and in such a multitude would be less in number. Thus there are three different ways of connecting the number with the story, all natural—a striking proof of independence.

The immediate effect of the great work is reported by John alone (6:14): "Then those men, when they had seen the miracle that Jesus did, said, This is of a truth the prophet that should come into the world." Conviction of his greatness, but conviction of what kind the next section shows." *(W. N. Clarke).*

FACT QUESTIONS 6:30-44

321. Here in vs. 30 is the first use of the term "apostles"—show how appropriate it is just here.
322. What was the possible multiple purpose in withdrawing to a lonely place? Cf. Matt. 14:13.
323. What prevented their eating?
324. Is there any reason to believe there was an excessively large crowd in the district?
325. Did Jesus and His apostles go to the city of Bethsaida? If not why mention it?
326. How far from Capernaum to Bethsaida?
327. Did Jesus have any time for rest or prayer? Was Jesus unhappy about this?
328. In what way is "the independence of two accounts worth more to us than an unquestionable harmony"?
329. Show how the words of Jesus "Give ye them to eat" entered the minds of the hearers.
330. Why mention the amount of "two hundred shillings worth"?

331. What is wonderfully encouraging about the words of Jesus "Bring them hither to me."
332. Show the difference in the use of the two words "symposia" and "prasiai."
333. Why bless the loaves and fish?
334. What are the evidences of an eyewitness in the description?
335. What particular type of miracle was this?
336. Show the striking proof of accurate independent report on the counting of the 5,000.
337. What kind of baskets were used?
338. What was the reaction of the miracle on the multitude?

8. JESUS WALKING ON THE WATER 6:45-52

TEXT 6:45-52

"And straightway he constrained his disciples to enter into the boat, and to go before him unto the other side to Bethsaida, while he himself sendeth the multitude away. And after he had taken leave of them, he departed into the mountain to pray. And when even was come, the boat was in the midst of the sea, and he alone on the land. And seeing them distressed in rowing, for the wind was contrary unto them, about the fourth watch of the night he cometh unto them, walking on the sea; and he would have passed by them: but they, when they saw him walking on the sea, supposed that it was an apparition, and cried out: for they all saw him, and were troubled. But he straightway spake with them, and saith unto them, Be of good cheer: it is I; be not afraid. And he went up unto them into the boat; and the wind ceased: and they were sore amazed in themselves; for they understood not concerning the loaves, but their heart was hardened."

THOUGHT QUESTIONS 6:45-52

300. If they were at Bethsaida when they landed how is it they now came to Bethsaida as recorded in vs. 45?
301. Why the urgency of Jesus in asking His disciples to go over the sea to Bethsaida?
302. Was there some special burden on the heart of Jesus that He wanted to be alone with God in prayer? Cf. John 6:15.
303. Did Jesus know there was to be a storm at sea?
304. How could He see them in the sea if it was at night?
305. What is meant by "distressed in rowing."
306. Why say "and would have passed by them"? (vs. 48b.) What purpose was there in this?
307. Did the disciples believe in ghosts? Why their fear?
308. Show how appropriate were the words of Jesus to them.
309. When and why did the wind cease?

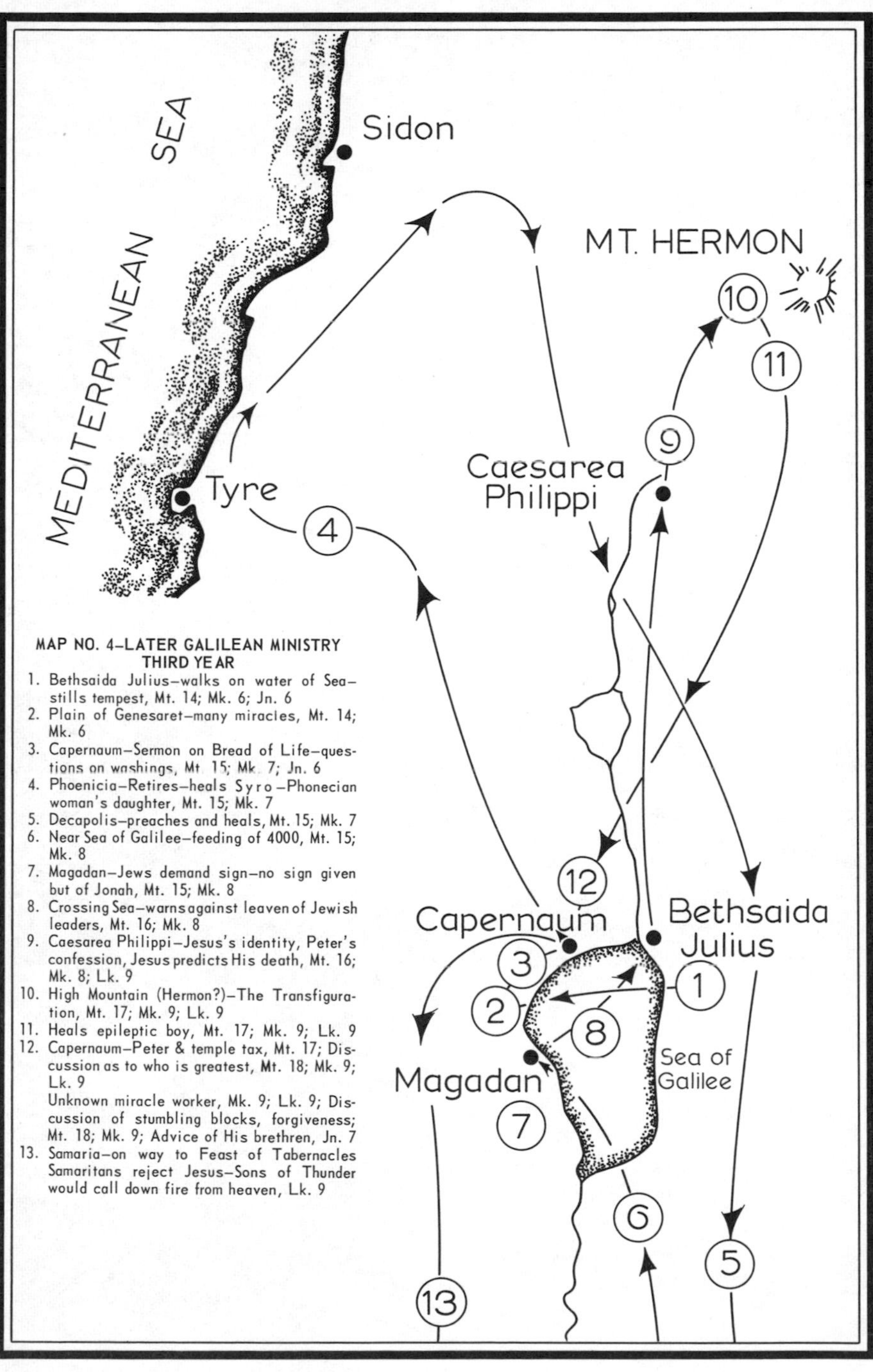
MEDITERRANEAN
SEA
Sidon
MT. HERMON
Tyre
Caesarea
Philippi
Capernaum
Bethsaida
Julius
Magadan
Sea of
Galilee
1
2
3
4
5
6
7
8
9
10
11
12
13
MAP NO. 4–LATER GALILEAN MINISTRY
THIRD YEAR
1. Bethsaida Julius–walks on water of Sea–stills tempest, Mt. 14; Mk. 6; Jn. 6
2. Plain of Genesaret–many miracles, Mt. 14; Mk. 6
3. Capernaum–Sermon on Bread of Life–questions on washings, Mt. 15; Mk. 7; Jn. 6
4. Phoenicia–Retires–heals Syro–Phonecian woman's daughter, Mt. 15; Mk. 7
5. Decapolis–preaches and heals, Mt. 15; Mk. 7
6. Near Sea of Galilee–feeding of 4000, Mt. 15; Mk. 8
7. Magadan–Jews demand sign–no sign given but of Jonah, Mt. 15; Mk. 8
8. Crossing Sea–warns against leaven of Jewish leaders, Mt. 16; Mk. 8
9. Caesarea Philippi–Jesus's identity, Peter's confession, Jesus predicts His death, Mt. 16; Mk. 8; Lk. 9
10. High Mountain (Hermon?)–The Transfiguration, Mt. 17; Mk. 9; Lk. 9
11. Heals epileptic boy, Mt. 17; Mk. 9; Lk. 9
12. Capernaum–Peter & temple tax, Mt. 17; Discussion as to who is greatest, Mt. 18; Mk. 9; Lk. 9
Unknown miracle worker, Mk. 9; Lk. 9; Discussion of stumbling blocks, forgiveness; Mt. 18; Mk. 9; Advice of His brethren, Jn. 7
13. Samaria–on way to Feast of Tabernacles Samaritans reject Jesus–Sons of Thunder would call down fire from heaven, Lk. 9

310. In what manner could it be said "their heart was hardened"? Vs. 52?

COMMENT

TIME—Spring of A.D. 29.

PLACE—The sea of Galilee—near Bethsaida.

PARALLEL ACCOUNTS—Matt. 14:22-36; John 6:15-21.

OUTLINE—1. Jesus urged His disciples to get into the boat and go before Him to Bethsaida, vs. 45. 2. Prayer in the mountain, vs. 46. 3. The boat was in the midst of the sea—The disciples rowing for their life—Jesus came to them walking on the water, vs. 47, 48. 4. They saw Him and were afraid. He calms their fears and the sea, vs. 49-51. 5. They should have understood His powers—but they did not, vs. 52.

ANALYSIS

I. JESUS URGED HIS DISCIPLES TO GET INTO THE BOAT AND GO BEFORE HIM TO BETHSAIDA, VS. 45.
   1. He remained alone.
   2. He sent the multitude away.

II. PRAYER IN THE MOUNTAIN, VS. 46.
   1. Said farewell to disciples.
   2. Alone in prayer.

III. THE DISCIPLES IN THE MIDST OF THE SEA ROWING FOR THEIR LIFE —JESUS CAME TO THEM WALKING ON THE WATER, VS. 47, 48.
   -1. At night.
   2. Came to them three hours before daylight.
   3. Wanted to pass by—(so they could see him).

IV. THEY SAW HIM AND WERE AFRAID—HE CALMS THEIR FEARS AND THE SEA, VS. 49-51.
   1. They cried out in fear because they thought He was a ghost.
   2. He comforts them with "Be not afraid it is I."
   3. When He stepped into the boat, the wind ceased—astonishment.

V. THEY SHOULD HAVE UNDERSTOOD HIS POWER, BUT THEY DID NOT, VS. 52.
   1. The loaves and fishes should have taught them of His power.
   2. Their hearts were dull.

EXPLANATORY NOTES

"The effect of this miracle upon the minds of those present was very great. So mighty and wonderful an exhibition of power, reminding them, perhaps, of the feeding of their fathers in the wilderness by Moses, led them to say, "This is of a truth that prophet that should come into the world." We can scarce doubt from the context that they meant the Messiah, for so great was their enthusiasm that they proposed among themselves to take Him by force and make Him king (John 6:14, 15). It is said by *Pressense*; "The multitudes are ravished, enthusiastic; now, indeed, they believe that they have found the Messiah after their own heart." Thus, the effect of the miracle was to confirm them in their false Messianic hopes, for they interpreted it as a sign and pledge of the highest temporal prosperity under His rule, who could not only heal the sick of all their diseases, but feed five thousand men with five loaves of barley bread. Hence, He must immediately dismiss them. It appears from Matthew and Mark that He sent away the disciples first, perhaps that the excitement of the multitude might not seize upon them. That they were unwilling to leave Him, and that He was obliged to "constrain" them to depart, is not strange, if we remember that they knew no way by which He would rejoin them but by a long walk along the shore; and this in the solitude and darkness of the night, for it was evening when they left the place. (compare Matt. 14:15, 23, where both evenings, the early and late, are distinguished.) Aside from their reluctance to leave Him alone at such an hour, there may also have been fear upon their own part of crossing the lake in the night, remembering their great peril from which He had a little while before delivered them (Matt. 8:24) and perhaps also, seeing signs of an approaching storm.

After His disciples had departed, the Lord proceeded to dismiss the multitude, perhaps now more willing to leave Him that they saw His special attendants had gone. So soon as all had left Him, He went up into the mountain alone to pray—the second instance mentioned of a night so spent; the first being the night prior to the choice of Apostles (Luke 6:12, 13), and both marking important points in His life.

We assume that the place where the people were fed was the southern angle of the plain of Butaiha, where the mountains meet the lake. From this point the Apostles, to reach Capernaum, would pass near Bethsaida at the mouth of the Jordan; and as Jesus proceeding along the shore must necessarily pass through it, we find no difficulty in supposing that they directed their course toward it with the design of stopping there, and taking Him with them into the boat when He should arrive. This is plainly intimated by Mark 6:45, and is wholly consistent with John 6:17. This latter passage is thus translated by *Alford*. "They were making for the other side of the sea in the direction of Capernaum.' He adds: "It would appear as if the disciples were lingering along shore, with the expectation of taking in Jesus; but night had fallen and He had not yet come to them, and the sea began to be stormy." "The great wind that blew" and the tossing waves made all their efforts to reach Bethsaida useless. Nor could they even make Capernaum. In spite of all their endeavors, they were driven out into the middle of the lake and southerly, down opposite the plain of Gennesaret.

Thomson (ii. 32), referring to this night voyage of the disciples, says: "My experience in this region enables me to sympathize with the disciples in their long night's contest with the wind. I spent a night in that Wady Shukaiyif, some three miles up it, to the left of us. The sun had scarcely set, when the wind began to rush down toward the lake, and it continued all night long with constantly increasing violence, so that when we reached the shore next morning, the face of the lake was like a huge boiling caldron. The wind howled down every wady, from the northeast and east, with such fury that no efforts of rowers could have brought a boat to shore at any point along that coast. In a wind like that, the disciples must have been driven quite across to Gennesaret, as we know they were. We subsequently pitched our tents at the shore, and remained for three days and nights exposed to this tremendous wind. No wonder the disciples toiled and rowed hard all night, and how natural their amazement and terror at the sight of Jesus walking on the waves. The whole lake, as we had it, was lashed into fury; the waves repeatedly rolled up to our tent door, tumbling on the ropes with such violence as to carry away the tent pins." The width of the sea opposite the plain of Gennesaret is about six miles, and the disciples, who "had rowed about five and twenty or thirty furlongs" when Jesus met them, were thus something more than half the way over. As this was "about the fourth watch of the night" (Mark 6:48), or from 3-6 A.M., the disciples must have been struggling against the wind and waves some eight or ten hours.

The incident respecting Peter's attempt to walk on the water to meet Jesus is mentioned only by Matthew. That after he had been rescued they entered the ship, is expressly said: "And when they were come into the ship, the wind ceased" (Matt. 14:32). In like manner Mark (6:51): "And He went up unto them into the ship; and the wind ceased." But with this John's narrative has been thought by some to be in contradiction (6:21): "Then they willingly received Him into the ship, and immediately the ship was at the land wither they went" (R.V., "They were willing therefore to receive Him into the boat"). It is said that the disciples willed or desired to take Him into the ship with them, but did not, because the ship immediately came to the shore. *Tholuck,* however, defends the translation of Beza, "they received Him with willingness," which is the same as our English version. "John mentions the will only, assuming that every reader would understand that the will was carried into effect" (M. and M.) Some deny that the ship came to the shore by miracle, but suppose that it came rapidly in comparison with the earlier part of the voyage, the wind having subsided and the sea become smooth. On the other hand, *Luthardt* and most rightly regard it as supernatural." *(Samuel J. Andrews)*

FACT QUESTIONS 6:45-52

339. What false hopes did the multitude obtain from the feeding of the five thousand?
340. How account for the reluctance of the disciples to leave Jesus?
341. Jesus spent a night in prayer once before—when?
342. Read Mark 6:45 and John 6:17 and harmonize them.
343. How does Thomson help us appreciate the plight of the disciples?
344. When Jesus came to them on the water how far and how long had they rowed?
345. Why was the incident of Peter's walking on the water omitted by Mark?
346. Harmonize the following accounts: Matt. 14:32; Mark 6:51; John 6:21.

9. HEALING ON THE PLAIN OF GENNESARET. 6:53-56

TEXT 6:53-56

"And when they had crossed over, they came to the land unto Gennesaret, and moored to the shore. And when they were come out of the boat, straightway the people knew him, and ran round about that whole region, and began to carry about on their beds those that were sick, where they heard he was. And wheresoever he entered, into villages, or into cities, or into the country, they laid the sick in the marketplaces, and besought him that they might touch if it were but the border of his garment: and as many as touched him were made whole."

THOUGHT QUESTIONS 6:53-56

311. Who was with Jesus at this time? Could thirteen men all get into one small boat? Explain.
312. Please locate Gennesaret on the map—how large a district was this?
313. Does the expression "moored to the shore" suggest there was no town here?
314. How did the people know Jesus?
315. Are we to conclude from vs. 55 that many people followed Jesus carrying their sick from place to place? Explain.
316. Why lay the sick in the "market places"? i.e. why select such a place?
317. Wasn't it rather superstitious to desire to touch His garment? Why did Jesus permit it? Why was the touch effective?

COMMENT

TIME—Spring A.D. 29.

PLACE—The plain of Gennesaret and the adjacent villages and cities.

PARALLEL ACCOUNTS—Matt. 14:34-36.

OUTLINE—1. The Landing at the plain of Gennesaret, vs. 53. 2. The gathering of many people, upon recognizing Him, to seek help, vs. 54, 55.

3. The superstitious desire of many people to heal the sick, vs. 56.

ANALYSIS 6:53-56

I. THE LANDING AT THE PLAIN OF GENNESARET, VS. 53.
   1. Occurred just after the feeding of the five thousand.
   2. The boat was moored—or fastened to the shore.

II. THE GATHERING OF MANY PEOPLE FOR HELP, VS. 54-55.
   1. This happened immediately after disembarking.
   2. Prompted by their knowledge of Him.
   3. The whole region turned out to bring their sick wherever they found Him.

III. THE SUPERSTITIOUS DESIRE OF MANY TO HEAL THE SICK, VS. 56.
   1. Occured in villages or cities or in the country.
   2. Sick laid in marketplaces—that they might at least touch His garment.
   3. Those who did touch were healed.

EXPLANATORY NOTES

"53. *And when they had passed over, they came into the land of Gennesaret, and drew to the shore.*

And having crossed (the lake, from east to west) *they came to* (or upon) *the land of Gennesaret,* a small district four miles long and two or three wide, on the west side of the sea of Galilee, or lake of Tiberias, to which it gave one of its names. *Josephus* describes this district as the garden of the whole land and possessing a fertility and loveliness almost unparalleled. Capernaum appears to have been in or very near this delightful region, so that John (6:17) describes this same voyage as a voyage to Capernaum. *Drew to the shore,* or *came to anchor near* it, or retaining the passive form of the original, were brought to anchor (or to land.)

54. *And when they were come out of the ship, straightway they knew him.*

And they going out (or as they went out) *from the ship,* the men of that place (Matt. 14:35), *straightway knowing* (or immediately recognizing) *him,* whom they had often seen before, as they lived so near his home and the centre of his operation. It is an interesting thought, very often incidentally suggested in the gospels, that during the three years of our Saviour's public ministry, his person must have become perfectly familiar to the great mass of the population, at least in Galilee. This, with the certainty that he retains his human body, and is to appear in it hereafter upon earth as he already does in heaven, should preserve us from a tendency to look upon all sensible and bodily associations with the person of our Lord as superstitious and irreverent, an error into which some devout believers are betrayed by their aversion to the opposite extreme of gross familiarity and levity in speaking of his glorified humanity.

55. *And ran through that whole region round about, and began to carry about in beds those that were sick, where they heard he was.*

Running about that whole surrounding country, they began, i.e. at once without delay, and afterwards continued, *upon beds* (or pallets,) *to carry about those having (themselves) ill wherever they heard that he was* (literally, is, the graphic present) *there.* The construction of the last clause is ambiguous, being understood by some as an example of the Hebrew idiom which combines the relative pronoun with the adverb *there,* to express our relative adverb *where;* but this would require a pronoun in the first place. Others refer the first of the two particles to the place where they heard of him, and the last to the place where he actually was. But most interpreters prefer the simpler and more obvious construction which refers both particles to one and the same object, 'of whatever place they heard that he was there.' *The running about and carrying about* may refer to the same act, or the former to the spreading of the news and the latter to the actual bringing of the sick. The meaning is not that each one was carried from place to place in search of him, but that some were carried one way, some another, so as to fall in with him in some part of his circuit.

56. *And withersoever he entered, into villages, or cities, or country, they laid the sick in the streets, and besought him that they might touch if it were but the border of his garment; and as many as touched him were made whole.*

Country, literally, *fields,* as in v. 36 and in such English names as St. Gile's or St. Martin's in the Fields, i.e. outside of old London. *Streets,* or more exactly, *markets* or *marketplaces,* as in every other case where it occurs, but with greater latitude meaning than we now give to the English word. The Greek one according to its etymology and usage, means a place of meeting, especially for business, whether commercial or political, and therefore corresponding both to *forum* and *market.* The *agora* of ancient cities was an open place or square, sometimes immediately within the gates, but usually near the centre of the town. As denoting thoroughfares or public places, *streets* is therefore a substantially correct translation. *The sick,* or more exactly, *the infirm,* a synonymous express with the one in v. 5. If it were but, literally, even, only. This desire was only superstitious so far as it ascribed a magical effect to the mere touch, or regarded contact as essential to the healing power of the Saviour's word. It may have been his purpose to reach greater numbers in a given time without destroying all perceptible connection between the subject and the worker of the miracle. (Compare Acts 5:15; 19:12). This is not a mere repetition of the statement in 1:32-34, but designed to show that throughout the course as well as at the opening of our Saviour's ministry, his miracles were many, those recorded in detail being only a few selected samples, and also that his constant practice was to heal all who needed and desired it." *(J. A. Alexander)*

FACT QUESTIONS 6:53-56

347. In which direction had the crossing been made? How large was the plain?
348. How can we explain the fact that John 6:17 describes this same voyage as going to Capernaum?
349. Why would the people of this district perhaps know Jesus better than some others?
350. What incidental lesson can we learn from the reference to the human appearance or recognition of Jesus?
351. There is no meaning in vs. 55 of "each one carried from place to place in search of Him"—what is the meaning?
352. What is the literal meaning of the word "country"?
353. Show the patience and love of Jesus in healing the sick.

10. CONFLICT WITH PHARISEES 7:1-23.

a. *Conflict over washings* 7:1-8

TEXT 7:1-8

"And there are gathered together unto him the Pharisees, and certain of the scribes, which had come from Jerusalem, and had seen that some of his disciples ate their bread with defiled, that is, unwashen, hands. For the Pharisees, and all the Jews, except they wash their hands diligently, eat not, holding the tradition of the elders: and when they come from the marketplace, except they wash themselves, they eat not: and many other things there be, which they have received to hold, washings of cups, and pots, and brasen vessels. And the Pharisees and the scribes ask him, Why walk not thy disciples according to the tradition of the elders, but eat their bread with defiled hands? And he said unto them, Well did Isaiah prophesy of you hypocrites, as it is written,

> This people honoureth me with their lips,
> But their heart is far from me.
> But in vain do they worship me,
> Teaching as their doctrines the precepts of men.

Ye leave the commandment of God, and hold fast the tradition of men."

THOUGHT QUESTIONS 7:1-8

318. Did these Pharisees and scribes make a special trip from Jerusalem just to criticize Jesus? Discuss.
319. What is meant by "unwashen," or "defiled" hands?

320. Are we to understand from vs. 3 that "all the Jews" observed the tradition of the elders?
321. Who were the elders? What is meant by tradition?
322. Why bathe after going to the marketplace?
323. Is the word baptize here used i.e. in vs. 4 the same as used in reference to baptizing people? If so how could it be applied to couches?
324. In what sense were the hands of the disciples "common"?
325. Wasn't it unkind for Jesus to call these men hypocrites?
326. In what sense had the Pharisees honored God with their lips?
327. Just what is "vain worship"?
328. Please show just how such persons left the command of God.
329. Is Jesus saying such persons prefer the precepts of men to the commandments of God? Why?

COMMENT 7:1-8

TIME—Summer A.D. 29.

PLACE—In or near Capernaum.

PARALLEL ACCOUNTS—Matt. 15:1, 2; 7-9.

OUTLINE—1. Gathering for criticism, vs. 1, 2. 2. The ceremonial carefulness of the Pharisees, vs. 3, 4. 3. Criticism offered and answered, vs. 5-8.

ANALYSIS 7:1-8

I. GATHERING FOR CRITICISM, VS. 1, 2.
   1. Composed of Pharisees and scribes from Jerusalem.
   2. They were there to criticize the lack of ceremonial washing.

II. THE CEREMONIAL CAREFULNESS OF THE PHARISEES, VS. 3, 4.
   1. Never ate until they were ceremonially clean—i. e. according to tradition—no law of God required it.
   2. Never returned from the marketplace or used cups, pots, pans without ceremonial washings.

III. CRITICISM OFFERED AND ANSWERED, VS. 5-8.
   1. Why do your disciples fail to keep the tradition of the elders?
   2. You are fulfilling Isaiah's prophecy of the hypocrites who speak one thing and do another.
   3. Your worship is vain.
   4. You neglect the command of God for the traditions of men.

EXPLANATORY NOTES

"1-4. The place is still Capernaum. *Which came from Jerusalem.* Literally, "having come." The scribes and Pharisees who are mentioned here are probably Galilaeans who had been at Jerusalem and had just returned thence. The definite article is wanting before the participle. Its presence would indicate that they were a delegation from the capital; but probably these were Galilaean religionists, who, returning from

Jerusalem, perhaps after consultation there, made it their first work to "come together to Jesus" and see what he was doing.—*They saw some of his disciples eat bread with defiled*—literally, with common—*hands.* With hands in the ordinary state. Not "with dirty hands"—that was not the point of objection— but with hands *unwashen,* not ceremonially purified according to their ideas of necessity.—*Some of his disciples* were doing thus, not all of them—an indication that he had given them teaching that would render them indifferent to the practice of the Pharisees in this matter, but that only a part of them had yet been freed from their scruples on the subject. —Verses 3, 4 are parenthetical, and the best manuscripts insert an "and" at the beginning of verse 5, which disturbs the grammatical construction and makes a broken sentence. This led copyists to add *they found fault* in verse 2, to complete the structure; but the addition is cancelled by all the chief editors of the text.

The parenthetical passage (verses 3, 4) is wholly peculiar to Mark and is devoted to the explanation, for the benefit of Gentile readers, of the custom of the Pharisees, shared by the Jews in general, about ceremonial cleansings. *The Pharisees, and all the Jews.* A loose popular expression to show that this custom of the Pharisees was widely received; not to be pressed, as if it declared absolute unanimity. Many, of course, had no time for these practices, and the Pharisees despised all who neglected them for that reason or for any other, and thought there was scarcely a hope for them. (See John 7:49 for an utterance of this feeling.)—*Except they wash their hands oft,* or diligently, *pugme.* Literally, "with the fist." Probably descriptive of the washing of one hand by rubbing it with the other. The Sinaitic Manuscript alone has *pukna,* "frequently," which *Tischendorf* alone among editors adopts.—*And when they come from the market,* where in the crowd defilement might most easily be contracted.—*Except they wash, they eat not.* The word is *baptizo, ean me baptisontai.* So in Luke 11:38 the Pharisee wondered that Jesus had not first bathed himself *(ebaptisthe)* before dinner. It is not the baptizing of their hands, but of themselves, or, strictly, the being baptized or bathed, that was thus insisted upon. The word "baptize" is used precisely as in 2 Kings 5:14, where it is said of Naaman, "He dipped himself seven times in Jordan." From the strict literal signification, to "immerse" or "submerge," it comes naturally in certain connections to acquire the sense "to wash by immersing," "to cleanse," of course only in cases where the dipping is into clean water. So *Grimm,* N. T. *Lexicon.*) "Bathe" is an admissible translation in this connection, and any difficulties about giving the word its proper meaning here are purely imaginary. In verse 4 the word for "washings," in *washings of cups,* etc., is from the same root, *baptismous,* a derivative of *baptizo.* But it is not the word that is used to denote the Christian rite, which is a neuter word, *baptisma,* while this is masculine, a form that is found only here and in Heb. 6:2; 9:10. Its signification is properly given by *Liddel* and *Scott* in their *Greek and English Lexicon,* "a dipping in water." It indicates sometimes, in certain connections, a thorough cleansing by water, which would naturally be made, in the case of the objects here mentioned, by dipping, according to the literal signification of the word. The *cups (poteria)* were drinking-cups.—As for the *pots,* the Greek word *xestai* is a corruption of the Latin *sextaurius,* a pot that held about a pint. These were ordinarily wooden vessels.—The *brasen*—or properly bronze—*vessels* were for similar purposes with the wooden. The law provided, at least in certain cases of defilement, that earthen vessels should be broken, and that wooden ones should be rinsed in water (Lev. 15:12).—The word translated *tables (klinon)* cannot possibly mean that; it is "beds" or "couches," and may refer to the platforms on which they reclined around the table, which must often be thoroughly washed for fear of defilement, or to the cushions, which would need washing quite as much, and very likely would be washed oftener. But the words *and of tables* are omitted by some good manuscripts, by *Tishendorf,* and by the revisers.

The greater part of these minute requirements lay outside of the Mosaic law. These things, Mark says, *they have received to hold;* and they do them *holding the tradition of the elders,* the interpretations and supplements of the law, brought down orally from the men of an earlier time. Tradition was the ecclesiastical version of the law—the law as it came out of the hands of the great teachers. It was regarded as equally authoritative with the written law itself, and, by some, more so. It was the very life and mission of the Pharisees to keep the traditional interpretations in full force. (See *Farrar, Life of Christ,* 2. 471.) Whoever reads such descriptions as are given by *Farrar* and *Geikie* of the ingenious wickedness with which this was attempted will not wonder at the denunciations of our Lord or be surprised that the Pharisees were his natural enemies. This was a part of the bondage from which he came to set men free.

5-7. Of course they must call him to account, and not the disciples—the rabbi, not the pupils. He and they were reproved oftener for neglecting the traditions than for departing from the genuine law. His quotation in reply is almost verbally exact from Isa. 29:13 in the LXX., the sole variation—*teaching for doctrines the commandments of men,* instead of "teaching doctrines and commandments of men"—being identical in Matthew and Mark. Traditionalism has met him in its extreme form, and he does not miss his opportunity to scorch it with the fire of his wrath.—Perhaps the tone of indignation is even stronger in Matthew than in Mark. *Well hath Esaias prophesied of you hypocrites*—i.e. concerning such hypocrites as you, in his own age or in any other. He condemned outward worship without heart, the profession of the lips with no inward devotion or obedience.—Isaiah was full of such denunciations (as chap. 1:11-20), and so were all the prophets. Often, as here, they declared that it was *in vain;* it was empty, fruitless work; it went for nothing. Besides the heartlessness, and as another reason for rejecting such worship, God condemns the foisting upon his religion of human traditions and commandments. His worship must be upon the basis of his own requirements, and no human arrangement may take its place beside what he has appointed. The introduction of human tradition was the point in which the passage from Isaiah was directly applicable to the Pharisees.

8. *For* should be omitted at the beginning of this verse, and so should *as the washing of pots and cups: and many other such like things ye do,* at the end. So this strong statement stands alone: *laying aside* (or leaving) *the commandment of God, ye hold the traditions of men.* He charges them, not with addition, but with substitution. They have forsaken command for tradition, God for men. The elders are their chief authority, not Moses or Jehovah; they are not serving God. So, in spirit, Jer. 2:12, 13. The rebuke is there for idolatry; but in the sight of God the sin of the Pharisees was as heinous as that." *(W. N. Clarke)*

FACT QUESTIONS 7:1-8

354. What record does Luke give that is very much like this?
355. Who were these scribes and Pharisees?
356. Why conclude this was not an official delegation?
357. Did the disciples have dirty hands?
358. What has been said earlier about the lack of time for eating?
359. For whose benefit were verses 3 and 4 placed in the text?
360. Read John 7:49 and show how it relates.
361. What is the literal meaning of "wash their hands oft."?
362. Is there some connection with what Naaman the leper did (2 Kings 5:14) and what these Pharisees did? Explain.
363. How is the word "washing" or "baptismous" different than the word used for the action of Christian baptism?
364. Show how immersion is a perfectly natural thought in the "washings" here described.—particularly with "the tables" or "couches."
365. How did the bondage of tradition become a yoke too heavy to bear?
366. Why speak to Jesus and not to His disciples?
367. Do you imagine the Jews who heard the rebuke of Jesus believed it? Did it make them angry? Was it fair? Was it loving?

368. Jesus did not charge them with addition to the law of God but with what? Read Jer. 2:12, 13.

B. CONFLICT OVER PARENTAL CARE. 7:9-13

TEXT 7:9-13

"And he said unto them, Full well do ye reject the commandment of God, that ye may keep your tradition. For Moses said, Honour thy father and thy mother; and, He that speaketh evil of father or mother, let him die the death: but ye say, If a man shall say to his father or his mother, That wherewith thou mightest have been profited by me is Corban, that is to say, Given to God; ye no longer suffer him to do aught for his father or his mother; making void the word of God by your tradition, which ye have delivered: and many such like things ye do."

THOUGHT QUESTIONS 7:9-13

330. What is meant by the expression "full well" as in vs. 9?
331. Did these Jews accept the fact that they had rejected the commandment of God? Does this carry any warning for us today?
332. What were the two areas of respect for parents? i.e. what is involved in the word "honor"—and "speaking evil"?
333. Was there a death penalty for speaking evil of father or mother?
334. Explain in your own words the use of the expression "Corban."
335. What possible advantage was there in the use of Corban?
336. If any belief or practice today makes void or meaningless the word of God can we expect the same rebuke? Cite examples.

COMMENT

TIME—Summer A.D. 29.

PLACE—In or near Capernaum.

PARALLEL ACCOUNTS—Matt. 15:3-6.

OUTLINE—1. Jesus' accusation:—"you reject the commandment of God, vs. 9. 2. The fourth commandment is a specific example, vs. 10-12. 3. The word of God is made void by your tradition, vs. 13.

ANALYSIS

I. JESUS' ACCUSATION:—"YOU REJECT THE COMMANDMENT OF GOD, VS 9.
   1. In a fine, beautiful, admirable sense you reject the commandment of God.
   2. You prefer your tradition to the commandments of God.

II. THE FOURTH COMMANDMENT IS A SPECIFIC EXAMPLE, VS. 10-12.
   1. Moses was very plain (Exodus 20:12; 21:17) about the honor to parents.
   2. You have set aside the law of God by your tradition—what belongs to the parents is supposedly given to the temple (or the priests).

3. Your mother and father can starve while you justify your selfishness and disobedience by tradition.

III. THE WORD OF GOD IS MADE VOID BY YOUR TRADITION. VS. 13.

1. The authority of God's word is set aside by your tradition.
2. There are many other examples that could be cited.

EXPLANATORY NOTES

I. JESUS' ACCUSATION:—"YOU REJECT THE COMMANDMENT OF GOD."

"9. *And he said unto them* probably indicates a break in the discourse; caused, perhaps, by indignant interruptions, or by a call for particulars to illustrate so broad and fearful a charge. So their ancestors asked, "Wherein have we despised thy name?" (Mal. 1:6, 3:8, 13).—Whether called for or not, he was ready with particulars to illustrate the substitution of tradition for command. *Full well*—i. e. finely, beautifully, admirably—*ye reject the commandment of God, that ye may keep your own tradition.* The adverb is the same as in verse 6: "Well hath Isaiah prophesied of you." The repetition is intentional, and the word this time is scathingly ironical: "Admirably do you fulfill the word that Isaiah so admirably spoke concerning you." The holy indignation is thoroughly aroused, and he cares not how heavily he lays on the lash." *(W. N. Clarke)*

II. THE FOURTH COMMANDMENT IS A SPECIFIC EXAMPLE.

"10-12. Yet his first illustration is not the one that called out the question. Instead of beginning with the traditions respecting defilements by contact and the necessary cleansings, he goes at once to the Decalogue, and convicts them of setting aside the fundamental law of God to Israel. *Moses said, Honor thy father and thy mother.* An exact quotation from the LXX. of Ex. 20:12.—He adds a second extract, giving the same law as expounded and applied in the legislation of Moses. *Whoso curseth father or mother, let him die the death.* Emphatic way of saying, "Let him die." Ex. 21:17 quoted almost exactly from the LXX. Both passages are quoted from what *Moses said,* but both are adduced as *the commandment of God* (verse 9) and *the word of God* (verse 13). Thus, Jesus recognizes the Mosaic legislation as the law of his Father; and not merely the milder parts of it, but even the provision for the execution of the disobedient and insulting child. This he brings forward as a part of that law that he has come "not to destroy, but to fulfill" —i.e. to exhibit and establish in the fullness of its spiritual meaning. The principle of honor to parents he recognizes as of perpetual and universal force, and he intends to set up for universal obedience and reverance the truth that was honored by the Mosaic provision of death for the disobedient. Incidentally, his mode of citing the second passage is itself exegetical. Viewed in the light of the context, that passage must mean that the spirit of the prohibition can be violated without a profane or blasphemous word, and that not to bless parents by such care as a child can give is to curse them, according to the true intent of this law. Such, then, is the "commandment of God" respecting parents: they must be treated with honor, and no one is at liberty to withhold from them what blessing he can give.—But now for the *tradition of men* respecting parents which the Pharisees are diligently keeping. Translate verses 11, 12, "But ye say, If a man say to his father or mother, Whatever thou mightest receive in aid from me is Corban, that is, a gift (to God), ye no longer permit him to do anything for his father or mother." *Corban* is a Hebrew word meaning *gift,* but appropriated to use with reference to sacred gifts, acts of devotion to the service of God. The simple uttering of the word *Corban*—"Sacred gift"—over a thing that was supposed to set that thing apart from all ordinary uses and give it the character of a consecrated thing. (See *Ewald, Antiquities of Israel,* p. 81.) Now, Jesus affirms that they apply this mode of consecration to the unholy purpose of escaping duty to parents. If a man utters the magical word "Corban" over his relation to his parents, and so declares that it is devoted to God, he is no longer held under obligation to them. The "Corban" carries no real consecration to God in such a case; it gives no new character to the man's life: it is only a fictitious arrangement for releasing him from a duty that has become irksome. Thus the tradition of men enables them to annul or virtually repeal the commandment of God. The liberty which the tradition gives them is more agreeable to their selfish hearts than the duty to which the commandment binds them; and so they set aside the commandment, in order that they may keep the tradition. To accept such a tradition was to dethrone Jehovah. (See Prov. 28:24.) One is reminded here of Luther's sore conflict as to whether the monastic vow which was urged upon him was consistent with his duty to his aged father, and of innumerable similar cases in the long history of monasticism. True consecration is not the escaping from obligations, but the reacceptance of all genuine duty from the hands of God. Consecration to God never releases from duty to man. He who consents to an obligation to God thereby consents to all obligations that God has placed upon him. To suppose the contrary, as these men did, is to trifle with all obligation."

III. THE WORD OF GOD IS MADE VOID BY YOUR TRADITION.

"13. *Making the word of God of none effect through your tradition.* The word translated *making of none effect (akurountes)* is found in the New Testament only in this discourse and at Gal. 3:17: it means "to deprive of authority or lordship," and so, of a law, "to annul." It implies more than neglect: it tells of actual nullification.—*And many such like things do ye,* which is not genuine in verse 8, is genuine here, and may possibly be the reporter's summary of a further discourse, in which other abuses of a similar kind were treated as sharply as the intrusion of "Corban" to the family. The subsequent discourse seems to imply that something had been said at this very time of the distinction between clean and unclean food. There were abuses enough within reach to justify a long and terrible discourse." *(W. N. Clarke)*

FACT QUESTIONS 7:9-13

369. Do you imagine someone called for specific examples for the general principle laid down in the "fearful charge."?
370. Is Jesus being ironic or sarcastic in the way in which He speaks of Isaiah's prophecy and its fulfillment? Discuss.
371. Jesus does not deal with traditions respecting defilement first—why?
372. Did Jesus recognize the law of Moses as the law of God? Specify.
373. Did Jesus quote from the Greek translation of the Hebrew scriptures? i.e. from the Septuagint?
374. Jesus gives an exegesis of Ex. 21:7 in the manner of citing the passage—what is it?
375. Explain in your own words the tradition invented by the Pharisees called "Corban."
376. What was the problem Luther had with the monastic vow?
377. Can you cite an example in your own experience?
378. What does the expression—"making the word of God of none effect" mean? Cf. Gal. 3:17.
379. Can we make the word of God of none effect by our busy schedule of living?

C. CONFLICT OVER THE SOURCE OF DEFILEMENT. 7:14-23

TEXT 7:14-23

"And he called to him the multitude again, and said unto them, Hear me all of you, and understand: there is nothing from without the man, that going into him can defile him: but the things which proceed out of the man are those that defile the man. And when he was entered into the house from the multitude, his disciples asked of him the parable. And he saith unto them, Are ye so without understanding also? Perceive ye not, that whatsoever from without goeth into the man, it cannot defile him; because it goeth not into his heart, but into his belly, and goeth out into the draught? This he said, making all meats clean. And he said, That which proceedeth out of the man, that defileth the man. For from within, out of the heart of men, evil thoughts proceed, fornications, thefts, murders, adulteries, covetings, wickednesses, deceit, lasciviousness, an evil eye, railing, pride, foolishness: all these evil things proceed from within and defile the man."

THOUGHT QUESTIONS 7:14-23

337. Why now address His words to the multitude?
338. Is Jesus using the same meaning for "defilement" in vs. 15 as used by the Pharisees in vs. 5? Explain.
339. Just what is included in the word "nothing" as in reference to that which goeth into a man? Surely some things would be excluded such as poisons of various kinds—how are we to understand this?
340. There is a change in the figure from food to thought—from physical to mental—why?
341. Give your own understanding of vs. 16.
342. Did Jesus expect the multitude to understand His words?
343. What did the disciples mean by referring to His words as "a parable"?
344. Was Jesus abrogating the law of clean and unclean meats by what He said in verse 18 and 19? Discuss.
345. In what sense is the word "defile" used by Jesus?
346. Define in your own words the twelve things that defile men.

COMMENT

TIME—Summer A.D. 29.

PLACE—In or near Capernaum.

PARALLEL ACCOUNTS—Matt. 15:10-20.

OUTLINE—1. His message to the multitude, vs. 14-16. 2. His message to His disciples, vs. 17-23.

ANALYSIS

I. HIS MESSAGE TO THE MULTITUDE, VS. 14-16.
   1. The multitude called together.
   2. Nothing going into man defiles—only that which cometh out.
   3. Those who will can understand.

II. HIS MESSAGE TO HIS DISCIPLES, 15. 17-23.
   1. Message request by disciples.
   2. They should have understood His message to the multitude.
   3. Man cannot be morally or spiritually defiled by food because it goes to the belly not the heart—what is left is removed by the body.
   4. This He said to indicate all meats are clean.
   5. What proceds from the evil heart out of the mouth defiles man.—such as: fornications, thefts, murders, adulteries, etc.

EXPLANATORY NOTES

I. HIS MESSAGE TO THE MULTITUDE. V. 14-16

"When Jesus had exposed the hyprocrisy of the Pharisees, He took a bold and significant step. Calling the multitude to Him, He publicly announced that no diet can really pollute the soul; only its own actions and desires can do that: not that which entereth into the man can defile him, but the things which proceed out of the man.

He does not as yet proclaim the abolition of the law, but He surely declares that it is only temporary, because it is conventional, not rooted in the eternal distinctions between right and wrong, but artificial. And He shows that its time is short indeed, by charging the multitude to understand how limited is its reach, how poor are its effects.

Such teaching, addressed with marked emphasis to the public, the masses, whom the Pharisees despised as ignorant of the law, and cursed, was a defiance indeed. And the natural consequence was an opposition so fierce that He was driven to betake Himself, for the only time, and like Elijah in his extremity, to a Gentile land. And yet there was abundant evidence in the Old Testament itself that the precepts of the law were not the life of souls. David ate the shewbread. The priests profaned the sabbath. Isaiah spiritualized fasting. Zechariah foretold the consecration of the Philistines. Whenever the spiritual energies of the ancient saints received a fresh access, they were seen to strive against and shake off some of the trammels of a literal and servile legalism. The doctrine of Jesus explained and justified what already was felt by the foremost spirits in Israel."

II. HIS MESSAGE TO HIS DISCIPLES. 15, 17-23

When they were alone, "the disciples asked of Him the parable," that is, in other words, the saying which they felt to be deeper than they understood, and full of far-reaching issues. But Jesus rebuked them for not understanding what uncleanness really meant. For Him, defilement was badness, a condition of the soul. And therefore meats could not defile a man, because they did not reach the heart, but only the bodily organs. In so doing, as Mark plainly adds, He made all meats clean, and thus pronounced the doom of Judaism, and the new dispensation of the Spirit. In truth, Paul did little more than expand this memorable saying. "Nothing that goeth into a man can defile him," here is the germ of all the decision about idol meats—"neither if 'one' eat is he the better, neither if he eat not is he the worse." "The things which proceed out of the man are those which defile the man," here is the germ of all the demonstration that love fulfills the law, and that our true need is to be renewed inwardly, so that we may bring forth fruit unto God.

But the true pollution of the man comes from within; and the life is stained because the heart is impure. For from within, out of the heart of men, evil thoughts proceed, like the uncharitable and bitter judgments of His accusers—and thence come also the sensual indulgences which men ascribe to the flesh, but which depraved imaginations excite, and love of God and their neighbour would restrain—and thence are the sins of violence which men excuse by pleading sudden provocation, whereas the spark led to a conflagration only because the heart was a dry fuel—and thence, plainly enough, come deceit and railing, pride and folly.

It is a hard saying, but our conscience acknowledges the truth of it. We are not the toy of circumstances, but such as we have made ourselves; and our lives would have been pure if the stream had flowed from a pure fountain. However modern sentiment may rejoice in highly coloured pictures of the noble profligate and his pure minded and elegant victim; of the brigand or the border ruffian full of kindness, with a heart as gentle as his hands are red; and however true we may feel it to be that the worst heart may never have betrayed itself by the worst actions, but many that are first shall be last, it still continues to be the fact, and undeniable when we do not sophisticate our judgment, that "all these evil things proceed from within."

It is also true that they "further defile the man." The corruption which already existed in the heart is made worse by passing into action; shame and fear are weakened; the will is confirmed in evil; a gap is opened or widened between the man who commits a new sin, and the virtue on which he has turned his back. Few, alas! are ignorant of the defiling power of a bad action, or even of a sinful thought deliberately harboured, and the harbouring of which is really an action, a decision of the will.

We must remember that it leaves untouched the question, what restrictions may be necessary for men who have depraved and debased their own appetites, until innocent indulgence does reach the heart and pervert it. Hand and foot are innocent, but men there are who cannot enter into life otherwise than halt or maimed. Also it leaves untouched the question, as long as such men exist, how far may I be privileged to share and so to lighten the burden imposed on them by past transgressions? It is surely a noble sign of religious life in our day, that many thousands can say, as the Apostle said, of innocent joys, "Have we not a right? . . . Nevertheless we did not use this right, but we bear all things, that we may cause no hindrance to the gospel of Christ."

Nevertheless the rule is absolute: "Whatsoever from without goeth into the man, it cannot defile him." And the Church of Christ is bound to maintain, uncompromised and absolute, the liberty of Christian souls.

Let us not fail to contrast such teaching as this of Jesus with that of our modern materialism.

"The value of meat and drink is perfectly transcendental," says one. "Man is what he eats," says another. But it is enough to make us tremble, to ask what will issue from such teaching if it ever grasps firmly the mind of a single generation. What will become of honesty, when the value of what may be had by theft is transcendental? How shall armies be persuaded to suffer hardness, and populations to famish within beleaguered walls, when they learn that "man is what he eats," so that his very essence is visibly enfeebled, his personality starved out, as he grows pale and wasted underneath his country's flag? In vain shall such a question strive to keep alive the flame of generous self-devotion. Self-devotion seemed to their fathers to be the noblest attainment; to them it can be only a worn-out form of speech to say that the soul can overcome the flesh. For to them the man is the flesh; he is the resultant of his nourishment; what enters into the mouth makes his character, for it makes him all.

There is that within us all which knows better; which sets against the aphorism, "Man is what he eats;" the text "As a man thinketh in his heart so is he;" which will always spurn the doctrine of the brute, when it is boldly confronted with the doctrine of the Crucified." *(Expositor's Bible, G. A. Chadwick)*

FACT QUESTIONS 7:14-23

380. What was the bold step of Jesus?
381. Did Jesus proclaim the abolition of the law? What did He do?
382. What are some of the evidences that the precepts of the law were not the life of souls?
383. How did Paul use the same principle Jesus laid down?
384. Show how "love fulfills the law."
385. What men attribute to the flesh Jesus attributed to what?
386. How has "modern sentiment" colored the picture of sin?
387. Show how the harbouring of a sinful thought is really an action.
388. There are some who have so debased their own appetites until "innocent indulgence" does reach the heart—what shall be done with them?
389. Contrast the teaching of Jesus here with modern materialism.

SUMMARY
6:1—7:23

The testimony for Jesus furnished by the preceding section, is based chiefly on the opinions which men formed concerning him. The disciples, though slow and hard of heart to realize his true nature, were constrained by the continued demonstration to acknowledge his inherent divine power. The masses of the people who had witnessed his miracles were wild with excitement wherever he went, and they brought to him their sick from every quarter, a practice which could not possibly have been kept up had not his cures been real and unfailing. His enemies, though they differed in opinion as to the source of his miraculous power, with one consent acknowledged its reality, and none of them counted him less than a prophet. The strange conceit that he was John the Baptist, or that he was one of the old prophets raised to life again, attests the struggle of unbelieving minds in trying to solve the problem of his power and of his being. Even the Nazarenes, who, of all his enemies, knew him most intimately and rejected him most scornfully, were constrained to wonder whence he obtained his wisdom and his mighty works. There was only one solution of the problem which was satisfying to the mind, and those alone were satisfied with their own conclusion and rested in it, who believed him to be the Christ and the Son of God. And to this day the men who have rejected this conclusion and have tried to account for the career of Jesus in some other way, have been driven to conceits as baseless and as unreasonable as any of those adopted by the Jews.—*McGarvey.*

C. THE THIRD PERIOD 7:24-9:50

1. THE SYROPHOENICIAN WOMAN. 7:24-30

TEXT 7:24-30

"And from thence he arose, and went away into the borders of Tyre and Sidon. And he entered into a house, and would have no man know it: and he could not be hid. But straightway a woman, whose little daughter had an unclean spirit, having heard of him, came and fell down at his feet. Now the woman was a Greek, a Syrophoenician by race. And she besought him that he would cast forth the devil out of her daughter. And he said unto her, Let the children first be filled: for it is not meet to take the children's bread and cast it to the dogs. But she answered and saith unto him, Yea, Lord: even the dogs under the table eat of the children's crumbs. And he said unto her, For this saying go thy way; the devil is gone out of thy daughter. And she went away unto her house, and found the child laid upon the bed, and the devil gone out."

THOUGHT QUESTIONS 7:24-30

347. From where was Jesus going to Tyre and Sidon?
348. Why did Jesus want to be unknown?
349. Give three facts about the woman who came to Jesus at this time.
350. Who are "the children" in vs. 27—who are "the dogs"?
351. Explain the eating the crumbs under the table.
352. What admirable qualities are seen in this woman?
353. What other miracle did Jesus perform at a distance? Cf. Matt. 8:5-13.

COMMENT

TIME—Summer A.D. 29.

PLACE—In the district of Tyre and Sidon.

PARALLEL ACCOUNTS—Matt. 15:21-28.

OUTLINE—1. Jesus and His disciples seeks seclusion, vs. 24. 2. A distraught woman seeks help, vs. 25-26. 3. Jesus tests her faith, vs. 27. 4. She answers in faith and humility, vs. 28. 5. Her request is granted, vs. 29, 30.

ANALYSIS

I. JESUS AND HIS DISCIPLES SEEKS SECLUSION, VS. 24.
   1. Leaves Capernaum or near area.
   2. Into the district of Tyre and Sidon.
   3. Into a house to hide from the multitudes.

II. A DISTRAUGHT WOMAN SEEKS, HELP, VS. 25, 26.
   1. Came immediately upon their entrance into the house.
   2. Came seeking help for her demon-possessed daughter.
   3. Fell at his feet with continual requests.
   4. She was a Greek, a Syrophoenician by race.

III. JESUS TESTS HER FAITH, VS. 27.
   1. The children (Jews) must first be fed.
   2. It is not right to give the children's bread to dogs. (Gentiles)

IV. SHE ANSWERS IN FAITH AND HUMILITY, VS. 28.
   1. I agree—you are right.
   2. But even dogs eat crumbs from the children's table.

V. HER REQUEST IS GRANTED, VS. 29, 30.
   1. Because of your faith and humility your request is granted—your daughter is free.
   2. She went home to find it as He had said.

EXPLANATORY NOTES

I. JESUS AND HIS DISCIPLES SEEK SECLUSION. VS. 24

"*Thence,* i.e. from the place where the foregoing words were uttered. But where was this? The last particular place mentioned was Gennesaret (6,53), but followed by a notice of his visiting "that whole surrounding country" (55), and entering into "villages, cities, and fields" (56.) This may seem to cut off the connection and prevent our ascertaining the locality referred to here. But as *thence* implies a definite place previously mentioned, and as the general statement in 6, 53-56 is incidentally and parenthetically introduced, and relates not so much to what occurred at any one time as to the general and constant practice, as appears from the use of the imperfect tense, it is still most probable that the reference is here to the land (or district) of Gennesaret, or to the neighboring city of Capernaum. *Arising*, standing up, an idiomatic phrase of frequent occurrence in the Greek of the New Testament, and often denoting nothing more than what we mean by starting, setting out, putting one's self in motion, especially though not exclusively in reference to journeys. *Went*, or more exactly *went away,* i.e. withdrew, retreated (Matt. 15, 21), from the malice of his enemies, as some suppose, or as others, from the crowd and bustle even of his friends and followers. It is probable, however, that a higher and more important motive led to this retreat, to wit, the purpose to evince by one act of his public life that, though his personal ministry was to the Jews (see below, on v. 27, and compare Matt. 15:24. Rom. 15, 8), his saving benefits were also for the Gentiles. It is important to remember that these movements were not made at random or fortuitously brought about, as infidel interpreters delight to represent, and some of their believing admirers do not venture to deny, but deliberately ordered in accordance with a definite design, the reality of which is not affected by our being able or unable everywhere to trace it in the history. *Into* (not merely *to* or *towards*, which would be otherwise expressed) *the borders*, a compounded form of the word used twice in v. 31 below, and not applied like it to all contained within the bounds, but to the bounds themselves, in which specific sense it is employed by Xenophon, Thucydides, and Plato, who speaks of the bounds (or limits) of the philosopher and politician. The Greek word is properly an adjective, and means bordering or frontier parts (Matt. 15, 21.) *Tyre and Sidon*, the two great seaports of Phenicia, put for the whole country, which apart from them had no importance. The whole phrase does not mean the region between Tyre and Sidon, but the boundary or frontier between Galilee and Phenicia. *Would* and *could*, as in so many other cases, are not mere auxiliary tenses, but distinct and independent verbs; *he wished* and *he was able.* The construction *he was willing to know no one* (i. e. to make no acquaintance or receive no visit), though grammatically possible, is not so natural or obvious as the common one, *he wished no one to know* (him), or *to know* (it), i.e. his arrival or his presence. To *be hid,* or lie concealed, the Greek verb being active in its form."

II. A DISTRAUGHT WOMAN SEEKS HELP. VS. 25, 26

"The reason that he could not be concealed is now recorded. *For a woman, having heard of him,* i.e. of his arrival now, or of his miracles before; but even in the latter case, the other fact must be supplied. *Whose little daughter* (an affectionate diminutive, used also in 5, 23) *had an unclean spirit,* in the sense repeatedly explained already. It appears from this case, that these demoniacal possessions were not confined to Jews, or to any age or sex. *Coming* (into the house where he was) *and falling at his feet,* the full phrase which occurs in a contracted form above, the act denoting not religious adoration but importunate entreaty.

26. The remarkable circumstance in this case, which in part accounts for its insertion in the history, is that the woman here described was a Gentile, not only by residence but by extraction. A Greek, not in the strict sense, but in the wider one arising from the Macedonian conquests, which diffused the Greek civilization through the whole of western Asia, so that in the later Jewish dialect, Greek was substantially synonymous

with Gentile, even where the language was not actually spoken, as it may have been in this case. A *Syrophenician*, so called either in distinction from the Libyophenicians in Africa, or because Phenicia, as well as Palestine, belonged to the great Roman province of Syria. Both countries also had been peopled by the sons of Canaan, so that this woman was at once a Greek, a Syrophenician, and a Canaanite (Matt. 15:22.) By *nation,* race, extraction, birth. (Compare Acts 4, 36. 13, 26. 18. 2 24. Phil. 3, 5.) *Asked,* in the secondary sense of *begged,* and therefore followed by *that,* and not by *whether.* (Compare Luke 4, 38.) *Cast forth the devil*, or *expel the demon."* (*J. A. Alexander*)

III. JESUS TESTS HER FAITH. VS. 27

"Another singularity of this case, which suggests a further reason for its being so minutely stated, is our Lord's refusal to perform the miracle, of which this is the first and only instance upon record. Even here, however, it was not an absolute and permanent refusal, but a relative and temporary one, designed to answer an important purpose, both in its occurrence and in the historical account of it. *Let*, or more emphatically, *let alone* (implying an untimely interference), suffer or permit, the same verb which we have already had in different applications. *Filled*, sated, satisfied, the same verb as in 6, 42, and there explained. *Meet*, i.e. suitable, becoming, handsome, which approaches nearest to the strict sense of the Greek word, namely, *fair* or *beautiful*, though commonly applied in Scripture to excellence or beauty of a moral kind. *To take*, not pleonastic, as it often is in vulgar English, but *to take away* from them and bestow it upon others. *The children's bread*, the bread intended and provided for them, and when actually given belonging to them. *Dogs*, a diminutive supposed by some to be contemptuous, like *whelps*, or *puppies*, but by others an expression of affectionate familiarity, like *little* daughter (A Greek word of the same form) in vs. 25. This question is connected with another, as to the sense in which dogs are mentioned here at all, whether simply in allusion to the wild gregarious oriental dog, regarded as an impure and ferocious beast, or to the classical and modern European notion of the dog as a domesticated animal, the humble companion and faithful friend of man. The objection to the former explanation is not only its revolting harshness and the ease with which the same idea might have been expressed in a less unusual manner, but the obvious relation here supposed between the children and the dogs, as at and under the same table, and belonging as it were to the same household. John, it is true, uses dogs in the offensive sense first mentioned; but his language is "without are dogs" (Rev. 22, 15), apparently referring to the homeless dogs which prowl through the streets of eastern cities (compare Ps. 22, 20. 59, 6. Matt. 7, 6. Phil. 3, 2); but here the dogs are represented as within, and fed beneath their master's table. The beauty of our Saviour's figure would be therefore marred by understanding what he says of savage animals, without relation or attachment to mankind. *Cast*, throw away, a term implying waste of the material as well as some contempt of the recipient. Like most of our Lord's parables or illustrations from analogy, this exquisite similitude is drawn from the most familiar habits of domestic life, and still comes home to the experience of thousands."

IV. SHE ANSWERS IN FAITH AND HUMILITY. VS. 28

"28. There is no dispute as to the meaning of this admirable answer, which might almost be applauded for its wit, if Christ himself had not ascribed to it a higher merit, as an evidence of signal faith, combined with a humility no less remarkable. There is, however, some dispute as to its form, particularly that of the first clause, which some explain as a denial of what he had said, and others more correctly as a partial affirmation or assent, but followed by a partial contradition, as in our translation. The best philological interpreters are now agreed that *yet* is not a correct version of the Greek phrase, which can only mean agreeably to usage, *for* or *for even.* The meaning of the answer then will be, 'Yes, Lord (or Sir), it is true that it would not be becoming to deprive the children of their food, in order to supply the dogs; for these are not to eat the children's bread, but the crumbs (or fragments) falling from the table.' The whole is therefore an assent to what our Lord had said, including his description of the Gentiles (Matt. 15, 24) as the dogs beneath the table, and a thankful consent to occupy that place and to partake of that inferior provision. *Of* (literally *from*) *the crumbs* is not here a partitive expression, as it sometimes is, but simply indicates the source from which the nourishment is drawn. The idea suggested by an ancient and adopted by a modern writer, that the word translated *crumbs* here means the pieces of bread which the ancients used as napkins, is not only a gratuitous refinement, but a needless variation from the usage of the word, which is a regular diminutive of one itself denoting a crumb, bit, or morsel, especially of bread. *Children* is also a diminutive, the same with that in 5, 39-41, and entirely distinct in form, though not in meaning, from the one here used in the preceding verse."

V. HER REQUEST IS GRANTED. VS. 29, 30

"29. *For* (the sake of, on account of) *this word* (saying, speech, or answer), *go thy way* (i.e. in modern English, *go away*, depart), perhaps to be taken as an abbreviation of the full phrase, *go in peace* (or into peace) employed above in 5, 34, and there explained. The merit of her answer was its faith (Matt. 15, 28), to which her whole request was granted instantaneously, the demon having actually left her child when these gracious words were uttered. Now as this faith was the gift of Christ himself, there could neither be surprise on his part, nor legal merit upon hers, but only a benignant recognition of his own work in her heart, which his discouraging reception of her prayer at first had served both to strengthen and illustrate, and was therefore no more unkind than the similar processes continually going on in true believers, though of course unknown to the experience of those skeptical interpreters, who either sneer at this as cruel treatment of a distressed mother, or assume a real change of purpose wrought in Christ by her persistent importunity.

30. This is merely a distinct historical statement of the fact that she found the Saviour's declaration verified on reaching home, *the demon* (actually) *gone out and the daughter laid upon the bed,* or rather *thrown* there (as the Greek word strictly means) by the fiend at his departure, so that her mother found her just as he had left her. This removes all appearance of departure from the general rule previously laid down, and derived by induction from the history at large, that in cases of miraculous restoration there was no protracted convalescence, but an instantaneous return to ordinary occupations. Had this been a case of mere corporeal healing or resuscitation, the effect would probably have been the same as in the cases just referred to. But the miracle was here one of dispossession, and this was no doubt sudden and complete; for the bodily exhaustion which ensued was not a remnant of the previous disease, or even a transition from an abnormal to a normal state, but rather a decisive indication that the latter had been reinstated as the preternatural excitement which accompanied possession, and was usually symptomatic of it (see above, on 5, 5), would not have allowed her to lie quietly upon her bed, the sight of which recumbent posture must have satisfied the mother instantly, not that her daughter was recovering, but that she was recovered, from her fearful preternatural disorder. In recording this most interesting miracle, Mark treats it as an instance of extraordinary faith, without making prominent its bearing on our Lord's relation to the Jews and Gentiles, which belongs therefore rather to the exposition of the parallel account in Matthew (15, 21-28.)" *(J. A. Alexander)*

FACT QUESTIONS 7:24-30

390. "From thence" refers to what place?
391. How were the movements of the Saviour decided?
392. What is meant by the word "borders" of Tyre and Sidon?
393. What was the probable purpose in Jesus' desire to be hid?
394. Just what did the woman do when she came into the house where Jesus was staying?
395. In what sense was this woman a "Greek"? In what sense a "Canaanite"?

396. How is the word "take" used in reference to the children's bread?
397. In what sense was the word "dogs" used by our Lord?
398. Did the woman agree with Jesus in the evaluation of children and dogs? What were the crumbs?
399. When did the demon leave the daughter?
400. Did Jesus change His purpose with the woman because of her begging?
401. Was the child laid out on the bed by friends or the demon—explain.
402. Was there ever any period of convalescence in the healings of Jesus?

2. HEALING A DEAF MUTE 7:31-37

TEXT 7:31-37

"And again he went out from the borders of Tyre, and came through Sidon unto the sea of Galilee, through the midst of the borders of Decapolis. And they bring unto him one that was deaf, and had an impediment in his speech; and they beseech him to lay his hand upon him. And he took him aside from the multitude privately, and put his fingers into his ears, and he spat, and touched his tongue; and looking up to heaven, he sighed, and saith unto him, Ephphatha, that is, Be opened. And his ears were opened, and the bond of his tongue was loosed, and he spake plain. And he charged them that they should tell no man: but the more he charged them, so much the more a great deal they published it. And they were beyond measure astonished, saying, He hath done all things well: he maketh even the deaf to hear, and the dumb to speak."

THOUGHT QUESTIONS 7:31-37

354. Please trace on the map the route of Jesus on this occasion.
355. What is the meaning of the word "Decapolis"? How used here?
356. Who brought the deaf mute to Jesus?
357. Why did Jesus take him away from the multitude—please attempt an answer.
358. How would this deaf-mute feel as Jesus took Him to Himself?
359. Into whose ears does Jesus place His fingers?—into His own or into the deaf-mute? Why do this? Was this sign language?
360. Please notice the actions of Jesus and remember they were given for the benefit of the deaf-mute—the deaf-mute was intently watching the actions and expressions of Jesus—each action spoke to him—what did they say?
361. Did the deaf-mute hear the word—"Ephphatha"?
362. Why charge them that they should tell no man?
363. Who gave voice to the thought "He hath done all things well"?

COMMENT

TIME—Summer A.D. 29.

PLACE—Tyre—Sidon—Decapolis.

PARALLEL ACCOUNTS—Only Mark records this incident.

OUTLINE—1. The place of the healing, vs. 31. 2. The man to be healed, vs. 32. 3. Preparations for healing, vs. 33, 34a. 4. The healing and results, 34b-37.

ANALYSIS

I. THE PLACE OF HEALING, VS. 31.
   1. Journeyed from the borders of Tyre and Sidon.
   2. Through Sidon to the shore of Galilee.
   3. Into the midst of the district of Decapolis.

II. THE MAN TO BE HEALED, VS. 32.
   1. Brought by his friends.
   2. Deaf with a serious speech impediment.
   3. Begged Jesus to lay His hands upon him.

III. PREPARATIONS FOR HEALING, 33-34a.
   1. Jesus took him aside from the multitude unto himself.
   2. Jesus placed His fingers in the ears of the man.
   3. Spat on the ground and touched the man's tongue.
   4. Looked up to heaven and sighed.

IV. THE HEALING AND RESULTS, 34b-37.
   1. He was healed when Jesus said "Ephphatha" or "Be opened."
   2. Ears were opened—tongue was loosened—he spoke plainly.
   3. Jesus strongly urged them to tell no man about this—the more He urged them the more they did publish it.
   4. They were beyond measure astonished and said, "He hath done all things well."

EXPLANATORY NOTES

I. THE PLACE OF HEALING.

"31. According to the text adopted by the revisers, the course of the journey is here quite definitely marked out: "And again he went out from the borders" (region) "of Tyre, and came through Sidon unto the sea of Galilee, through the midst of the borders" (region) "of Decapolis." That he visited the city of Tyre itself is not affirmed, but from the course of the journey it seems probable. He did pass through Sidon, which lay, like Tyre, on the shore of the Mediterranean. From Capernaum to Tyre may have been thirty English miles, and from Tyre to Sidon twenty more. Between the two cities were Zarephath (called Sarepta in Luke 4:26), where Elijah was preserved alive in famine and restored the widow's son to life (1 Kings 17). His alluding to the event in the synagogue at Nazareth is enough to assure us that our Lord did not pass the spot without remembering again how it was a Gentile widow to whom the prophet was sent. From Sidon he turned south-eastward, and crossed the upper Jordan, and came down on the eastern side. But he did not merely make the journey downward along the river; he appears to have extended his tour still eastward—we cannot tell how far—through some part of the region known as Decapolis, probably visiting some of the cities from which that region took its name. The reasons that determined the route, of course, cannot be ascertained. Thus he made his way down to the Sea of Galilee, reaching it somewhere on the eastern side. The limits of Decapolis are somewhat uncertain, but its extent was such that his journey may have taken him farther south than his destination; so that it is impossible to tell from what direction he approached the lake or what point of its shore he probably first touched. Of course the length of the journey cannot be measured; but it can scarcely have been, from Capernaum back to the lake, less than one hundred and fifty English miles, and it may have been more. On the east as well as on the north this was a tour into heathen territory, but in no part, so far as we can judge, was it a tour of missionary activity. It was rather an episode in his ministry when he was alone with his disciples. By comparison with Matthew it appears that this miracle was wrought, most probably, on some "mountain" near the lake, where many were gathered about him."

II. THE MAN TO BE HEALED.

"32. *They bring unto him one that was deaf.* The adjective literally means "stricken," or "smitten" (*kophos*, from the verb *kopto*, "to strike"); the thought is that the person has been smitten in some of the organs of sensation, so as to be deprived of power. Sometimes it is the organs of speech that are thus conceived of as smitten, and the word then means "dumb;' sometimes it is the organs of hearing, and it then means "deaf," as here. The other descriptive word (*mogilalos*) means "speaking with difficulty;" not "speechless" (*alalos*), as in verse 37. It is used here alone in the New Testament. It cannot be smoothly rendered without paraphrase, and *had an impediment in his speech* represents it well. Yet the word is used broadly for "dumb' in the LXX. (Isa. 35:6).—The great healer was asked to put his hand on the man; so Matt. 9:18: "But come and lay thy hand upon her, and she shall live." But now, as then, the great Healer had a way of his own."

III. PREPARATIONS FOR HEALING.

"33, 34. Three peculiarities appear in this act of healing—the privacy of the transaction, the use of signs and physical media, and the unusual vocal utterances of the Healer. These peculiarities all appear again in the other miracle in chap. 8:22-26, already alluded to. In studying them in this case it is to be remembered that this is the only detailed report that we possess of the healing of a deaf man; and, although we may not be justified in inferring that all healings of the deaf resembled this, we may find in the peculiar method now adopted a special significance in connection with the nature of the affliction that was to be removed. In healing the blind, Jesus, so far as we know, always made some appeal to the senses and powers of which the afflicted ones were possessed, drawing out their faith by word or touch or by requiring the performance of some act. (See Matt. 9:29; Mark 8:23; 10:49; John 9:6). So, usually, in healing the lame and helpless. (See John 5:6-8; Mark 3:3; Luke 17:14.) In the case of a deaf man words would be of no avail; and if any such appeal was to be made, it must be done by signs. In the present case Jesus probably saw in the man himself some reason for judging it best that the cure should be private. The withdrawal from the crowd would impress him, though he could not hear its tumult, with a sense of solemnity. Perhaps Jesus saw in him a vanity that would render anything like a public act of healing hurtful to him. In any case, it was a solemn and touching experience to be alone, or almost alone, with Jesus to be healed.—As for the signs and the physical media, they were such as he could well understand. Jesus *put his fingers into his ears.* Not a mere touch, but an insertion—a sign of the impartation or transference of something from one person to the other, with reference now to the powerless organs of hearing. This was the laying on of his hand that had been asked for, made definite, appropriate, and instructive by his wisdom. Then *he spit, and touched his tongue*—i.e. touched the man's tongue with a finger perhaps moistened with his own saliva—another sign of the transference of something from himself to the afflicted man, this time with reference to his injured organs of speech. Then he stood *looking up to heaven,* to indicate that this was an act that depended upon a heavenly power—an act, indeed, of Heaven upon the earth. Of course there had been no opportunity, because no possibility, of preaching to the man, and in his ignorance he may easily have supposed that this was some influence of a magical kind. He may not have known to what power he was submitting himself, and the reverent heavenward look of Jesus may have been intended silently to lift his heart and faith to God. How better could he show a deaf man that he was receiving a gift from above? Then *he sighed*, or rather, "groaned." The word is not used elsewhere of him, but it is found in Rom. 8:23 and 2 Cor. 5:2, where evidently no less a word than "groan" is needed to represent its meaning. This was no artificial utterance intended for effect: it was a spontaneous utterance of genuine sorrow in sympathy with human suffering. It came from the same source as the tears at the grave of Lazarus. Although the man could not hear the groan, he might be aware of it, for doubtless his eyes were busy in observing what his Benefactor was doing; and if he was aware of it, he must have felt, however dimly, that there was a deep and genuine sympathy in the Healer's heart. This could be no magician's performance to him: this was a deed of love. And then at last he spoke; and, though the man might not hear the word he may have known, as before, that it was spoken."

IV. THE HEALING AND RESULTS.

"34b. *Ephphatha, that is, Be opened.* Here, as in chap. 5:41, Mark has preserved the very word in the Aramaic tongue that fell from the lips of Jesus. No other evangelist has done this, except in the case of the utterance on the cross, "Eli, Eli, lama sabachthani." In the other case (chap. 5:41) the Aramaic words that Mark preserves were spoken when of the disciples only Peter, James, and John were present; and it is not unlikely that the same special three were the only auditors at this time also. Whether others were present or not, this must certainly have come down to us from one who heard it. The *Ephphatha, Be opened,* was addressed to the man with reference to his organs of sense, which are conceived of as closed.

35. It would seem that the moment of the *Ephphatha* was the moment of the change. Of course we know that the preceding parts of the transaction were in no sense necessary to the cure, and were introduced for the sake of the man himself; and we may judge that he received no new power of speech or hearing until the symbolic or pictorial part was finished and the word was spoken.—The cure itself is detailed in Mark's peculiar way. The revisers omit *straightway,* and thus represent the result: "And his ears were opened, and the bond of his tongue was loosed, and he spake plain," or rightly, normally.—*The string of his tongue* is an unfortunate phrase, from which a reader might suppose that the man was in some way tongue-tied. But the reference is merely to the bond or restraint that was upon his powers of speech, and there is no indication as to the nature of that restraint.—But now the organs of sense were *opened*, and henceforth all was done (orthos) in the natural or normal way.

It is worth while to look back at this act and observe how beautifully our Lord brought to light all that was essential in a work of healing. Perhaps the symbolic action was all the more beautiful, because it must be made to do the whole work of words. Two signs of the transferring of power from himself to the afflicted—the upward look to heaven, to indicate the source of power; the deep sigh or groan of genuine sympathy with the suffering that is to be removed—and the word of power by which the deed is done, and the bond is broken. A beautiful story for deaf-mutes.

36, 37. He charged them. Not merely the man himself, but the people who were around. Of course they would quickly know what had been done, and must be included in his prohibition. Often did he thus plead for silence about his works (as in chap. 3:12 and 5:43), and now, while

MAP NO. 5—THIRD YEAR, LATER JUDEAN MINISTRY (about 3 months)

1. Temple; Feast of Tabernacles; Sermons on Light of World; Freedom; Abraham's Children; Man born blind healed; Good Shepherd; 70 sent out to evangelize, Jn. 7-8-9-10 & Lk. 10
2. Bethany; Jesus, Mary & Martha, Lk. 10
3. Place of Prayer; Discourse on Prayer, Lk. 11
4. Place unknown; charged with being in league with Satan, Lk. 11
5. Dining in Pharisee's home; denounces Pharisaism, Lk. 11
6. Before multitudes of 1000's Great evangelistic appeals on Hypocrisy, Anxiety, Covetousness, Lk. 12-13
7. In a Synagogue; heals woman bowed double; controversy over healing on the Sabbath, Lk. 13
8. Feast of Dedication (December); Jews seek to kill Jesus, Jn. 10

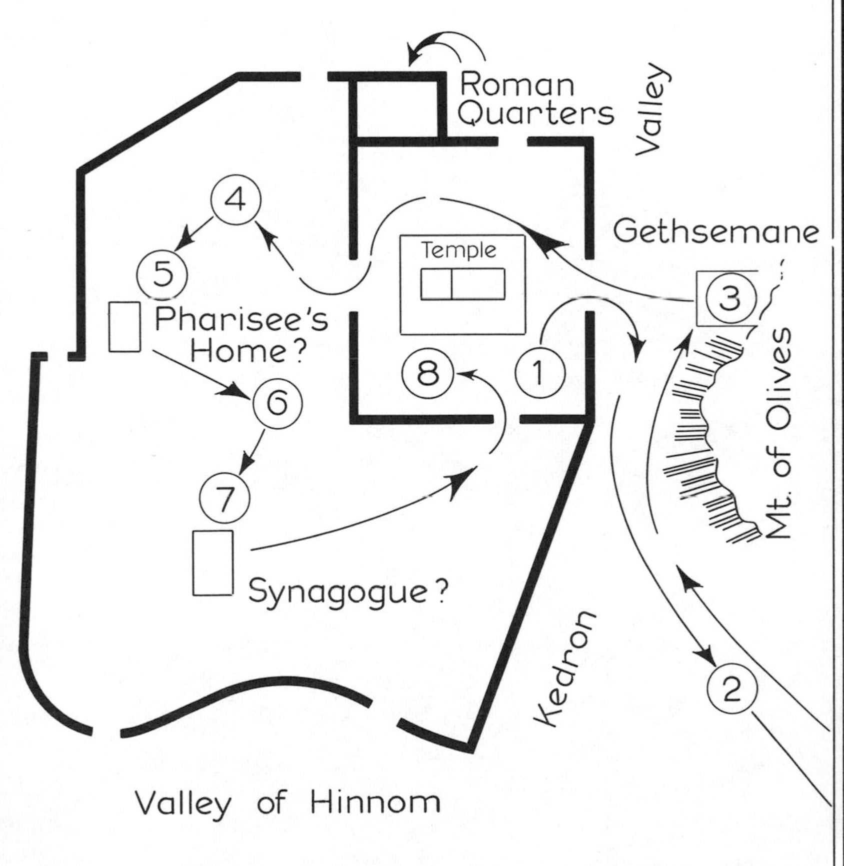

he was in search of retirement and quietness, the request was especially to be expected. But, as usual, it was all in vain: the gratitude of the healed and the wonder of the spectators were too strong, and the story must be told. It seems probable that this miracle was the means of bringing on the great period of thronging that is described in Matt. 15:30, 31. Mark's expressions in description of the abundant proclamation and the excessive amazement are of the very strongest character.—The final testimony of praise seems to have been called out by the many healings that took place, though first suggested by the one. *He hath done all things well* (perfect tense)—he has been gracious everywhere and successful in everything—*he maketh* (present tense) *both the deaf to hear, and the dumb to speak.* —*The dumb.* A stronger word than in verse 32." (*W. N. Clarke*)

FACT QUESTIONS 7:31-37

403. Read Matt. 15:29-31 and relate it to this record in Mark.
404. Show how Mark 8:22-26 compares with this incident.
405. How far from Capernaum to Tyre?; from Tyre to Sidon? What place was between the two cities?
406. What was the total distance traveled from Capernaum to the place of the healing?
407. They bring to him one that was "stricken"—explain the word "stricken" as here used.
408. The man to be healed could speak—but how?
409. Jesus never healed without a genuine personal concern for the one to be healed (if they were present)—show how he adapted His words and actions to the one to be healed—with the blind; the lame; the deaf.
410. What did the deaf-mute think when Jesus looked to heaven?
411. What is a better word than "sigh" in reference to Jesus? Why?
412. Why preserve the very word Jesus spoke?
413. The man was in no way "tongue-tied"—how do we know?
414. This is a beautiful story for deaf-mutes—show how.
415. Why would His request for quietness about His work be especially expected at this time and place?
416. Read Matt. 15:30, 31 and show the relation to this incident.

3. FEEDING THE FOUR THOUSAND. 8:1-10

TEXT 8:1-10

"In those days, when there was again a great multitude, and they had nothing to eat, he called unto him his disciples, and saith unto them, I have compassion on the multitude, because they continue with me now three days, and have nothing to eat: and if I send them away fasting to their home, they will faint in the way; and some of them are come from far. And his disciples answered him, Whence shall one be able to fill these men with bread here in a desert place? And he asked them, How many loaves have ye? and they said, Seven, And he commandeth the multitude to sit down on the ground: and he took the seven loaves, and having given thanks, he brake, and gave to his disciples, to set before them; and they set them before the multitude. And they had a few small fishes: and having blessed them, he commanded to set these also before them. And they did eat, and were filled: and they took up of broken pieces that remained over, seven baskets. And they were about four thousand: and he sent them away. And straightway he entered into the boat with his disciples, and came into the parts of Dalmanutha."

THOUGHT QUESTIONS 8:1-10

364. Where did the feeding of the four thousand take place?
365. For how many days had some in the multitude been without food? What does this indicate as to interest in what Jesus was teaching?
366. Please read the record of the feeding of the five thousand and show at least three contrasts in the comparison of the two incidents.
367. Note the use of the term fasting in vs. 3. Why worry about them?
368. Why refer to the district of Decapolis as a "desert place."
369. Does the reply of the disciples in vs. 4 indicate any knowledge of a previous multiplying of loaves? Please read the context carefully.
370. Did the apostles know what Jesus was going to do before He did it? i.e. with the loaves and the people?
371. Just what type of bread did they have?
372. What order did Jesus give to the multitude?
373. Was it the prayer of thanks for the loaves and fish that resulted in the multiplying of them in the hands of Jesus?
374. Just how many small flat loaves would it take to feed 4,000? How many small fish?—please estimate.
375. Consider the fact that all ate until they were "filled" not just a little, but until they were filled. What does this mean to you?
376. Why gather up the fragments?
377. Were there actually more than 4,000 fed? Explain.
378. Had Jesus arrived in a boat? Where was the miracle performed? Cf. 7:31; Matt. 15:32-38.

COMMENT

TIME—Summer A.D. 29.

PLACE—In Decapolis.

PARALLEL ACCOUNTS—Matt. 15:32-38.

OUTLINE—1. The occasion for the miracle, vs. 1. 2. The need for the miracle, vs. 2, 3. 3. The disciples and the miracle, vs. 4, 5. 4. Preparation for the miracle, vs. 6a. 5. The miracle, vs. 6b, 7. 6. The results of the miracle, vs. 8-10.

ANALYSIS

I. THE OCCASION FOR THE MIRACLE, VS. 1.
  1. In the days of Jesus' time in Decapolis.
  2. A great multitude had gathered.
  3. They had nothing to eat.

II. THE NEED FOR THE MIRACLE, VS. 2, 3.
  1. Three days without food.
  2. If sent home they would faint on the way.

III. THE DISCIPLES AND THE MIRACLE, VS. 4, 5.
  1. How shall such a multitude be filled?
  2. We have seven loaves.

IV. PREPARATION FOR THE MIRACLE, VS. 6a.
  1. Sit down in anticipation of eating.
  2. Gave thanks for the loaves.

V. THE MIRACLE, 6b, 7.
  1. By power of His own will he created enough loaves for the multitude.
  2. The apostles were the waiters.
  3. Also blessed and created fish for the multitude.

VI. THE RESULTS OF THE MIRACLE, VS. 8-10.
  1. They ate and were filled.
  2. Seven large baskets of fragments gathered.
  3. They were dismissed.
  4. Jesus and His disciples departed in a boat for Dalmanutha.

EXPLANATORY NOTES

I. THE OCCASION FOR THE MIRACLE.

"1. "In those days the multitude being very great," etc. We now come to whát is called "The Second Miracle of the loaves." From the fact that we have two miracles performed almost under the same circumstances, and in the same manner, and the accompanying details very much resembling one another in both cases, we cannot but gather that we have here a peculiar phase of Christ's love and power presented to us, and by its repetition commended very urgently to our notice, so that we should be very anxious to realize all that is taught us in these two accounts. It would seem at first sight impossible to do more than repeat what has been before remarked on the two miracles, as related in St. Matthew, and on the first one which has already been fully described in Mark, but it is not so. We have yet many fragments to gather up if nothing is to be lost. In the first place, then, the Lord here takes the initiative."

II. THE NEED FOR THE MIRACLE.

"2, 3. 'I have compassion on the multitude, because they have now been with me three days,' etc. In the former miracle He felt equal compassion for the multitude, but did not express it. The disciples urge upon Him to send them away, and then He, as it were, invites them to suggest some exercise of the mighty power which they had so repeatedly seen put forth by Him. But they can suggest nothing except what is natural, that they should be dismissed to take care of themselves. Now the Lord Himself begins: "I have compassion on the multitude, they have been with me three days. If I send them to their own houses, they will faint by the way," etc. Here was the hint given that they should ask Him to do as He had done just before, but apparently not a thought of the former mighty work presented itself. They seem to have altogether forgotten it."

III. THE DISCIPLES AND THE MIRACLE.

"4. 'And his disciples answered him, From whence,' etc. We marvel at (must not the word be said?) this stupidity, but is it not natural? This surprise arises out of our ignorance of man's heart, of our own hearts, and of the deep root of unbelief therein. "It is ever more thus in times of difficulty and distress. All former deliverances are in danger of being forgotten, the mighty interpositions of God's hand in former passages of men's lives fall out of their memories. Each new difficulty appears insurmountable, as one from which there is no extrication; at each recurring necessity it seems as though the wonders of God's grace are exhausted, and have come to an end. God may have diverted the Red Sea for Israel, yet no sooner are they on the other side than, because there are no waters to drink, they murmur against Moses, and count that they must perish through thirst (Exod. xvii. 1-7), crying 'Is the Lord amongst us or not?' Or, to adduce a still nearer parallel, once already the Lord had covered the camp with quails (Exod. xvi. 13), yet for all this, even Moses himself cannot believe that He will provide flesh for all that multitude." (*Trench*)

But the backwardness of the Apostles to believe in Christ's readiness to feed the multitudes miraculously, is in strong contrast with their readiness to believe in His powers of healing. They had but a short time before urged the Lord to grant the request of the Syrophenician woman, when He seemed unwilling. May it not, in part, have arisen from the infrequency of this sort of miracle? As *Theophylact* says, "He did not always work miracles for the feeding of the multitude, lest they should follow Him for the sake of food."

And may there not be also something typical, something prophetical, about it? Do not many true disciples of the Lord in these days, who thankfully acknowledge the Lord's power to cleanse and heal, seem to have their eyes closed to the supernatural or eucharistic feeding, of which this miracle is so remarkable an adumbration?

Again, do we not learn from this miracle how Christ will exercise acts of special providence to help and succour those who are following

Him? Is there any life of a poor humble Christian which does not contain some account of interpositions almost supernatural in favour of those who have given up all to follow Him? *Dean Hook,* in a lecture on this very miracle, gives a striking one: "There was an individual who gave up a profitable employment, acting under advice, and not from the mere caprice of his own judgment, because he thought, taking his temptations into account, he could not follow it without peril to his soul. And after many reverses he was reduced to such a state of distress, that the last morsel in the house had been consumed, and he had not bread to give his children. His faith did not, however, forsake him; and when his distress was at the height, he received a visit from one who called to pay him a debt he had never hoped to recover, but the payment of which enabled him to support his family until he again obtained employment." And he adds, "Many a similar tale can our poorer brethren tell."

5. 'And he asked them, How many loaves have ye?' etc. This question was not for information. He knew well how many they had, but he asked it that there should be no mistake about the miraculous nature of the feeding. There were two more loaves and a somewhat smaller multitude than on the former occasion, but this does not, in the smallest degree, affect the character of the mighty work."

IV. PREPARATION FOR THE MIRACLE.

"6. 'And he commanded the people to sit down on the ground,' etc. From the fact that it is expressly mentioned in the account of the former miracle, that there was much grass in the place, and that they sat by companies on the green grass, it has been argued with much probability that this second miracle took place at a much later time in the year, when the grass had been dried up by the scorching rays of the sun.

'And gave thanks.' We have before noticed the symbolical character of this "giving thanks" as foreshadowing the Eucharistic Benediction; but we learn also from it a more homely lesson, how that for all food, whenever received, thanks should be rendered, and we also learn how we ought to be thankful for all means and opportunities of doing good. The thanks of the Lord would be tendered to His father not only in anticipation of the actual food soon to be so marvellously provided, but for the opportunity of showing forth the Divine glory and power, and also of relieving the wants of so many who were following Him for a good purpose.

'And gave thanks, and brake, and gave to his disciples,' etc. From the circumstantiality with which these details are given in each of the four accounts, it is clear that there is some particular lesson which the Lord and His Spirit would have us draw from this. That lesson seems to be that the true feeding in the Church of Christ is not that each man should take for himself, but that all that can be called food is to be given through ministerial intervention."

V. THE MIRACLE.

"7. And they had a few small fishes . . . seven baskets . . . sent them away. From the mention of a few small fishes, it seems evident that the disciples gave all their provisions of every kind for the sustenation of the multitude; but notwithstanding this they were not in want, for a much larger quantity of fragments or broken pieces was taken up than in the case of the miracle of the feeding of the five thousand: the word here used signifying hampers or panniers, rather than baskets. The same word is used to denote the basket in which St. Paul was let down from the walls of Damascus (2 Cor. 11:33)."

VI. THE RESULTS OF THE MIRACLE.

"10. 'And straightway he entered into a ship . . . parts of Dalmanutha.' *Dr. Thomson,* in "The Land and the Book," thinks that he can identify this place with a certain Dalhamia, about half-way down on the western side of the Lake. It is about two miles south of El Medjet, which has been supposed to be the site of the ancient Magdala (or Magadan) (Matt. 15:39)." (*M. F. Sadler*)

FACT QUESTIONS 8:1-10

417. What difference would it make if we did feel the two accounts of feeding the multitudes were actually two versions of the same event?
418. Please show at least three distinct differences in the two records.
419. Why did the disciples ask the question of vs. 4? Please attempt an answer.
420. Jesus did not ask the disciples to give them to eat, (as he did before)—What does this mean?
421. At what point in the events did the miracle occur?
422. Which baskets were the largest—the ones here or the ones in the feeding of the 5,000?
423. What type of miracle occurred here?
424. Locate Dalmanutha on the map.

4. THE DEMAND FOR A SIGN 8:11-13

TEXT 8:11-13

"And the Pharisees came forth, and began to question with him, seeking of him a sign from heaven, tempting him. And he sighed deeply in his spirit, and saith, Why doth this generation seek a sign? verily I say unto you, There shall no sign be given unto this generation. And he left them, and again entering into the boat departed to the other side."

THOUGHT QUESTIONS 8:11-13

379. What type of sign did the Pharisees want?

380. What test or trial was this to Jesus?
381. What emotion filled the Saviour's heart as He "sighed deeply"?
382. Read Matt. 16:1-4 for a little more complete account of this.
383. Show how unreasonable was this request for a sign.
384. Was Jesus disappointed as He turned to get in the boat to go across the lake? Discuss.

COMMENT

TIME—Summer A.D. 29.

PLACE—Capernaum.

PARALLEL ACCOUNTS—Matt. 15:39—16:4.

OUTLINE—1. The dispute and question, vs. 11. 2. The disappointment and refusal, vs. 12. 3. The departure, vs. 13.

ANALYSIS

I. THE DISPUTE AND QUESTION, VS. 11.
   1. The Pharisees sought Him out.
   2. Disputed and sought a sign from heaven.
   3. This was only to justify themselves.

II. THE DISAPPOINTMENT AND REFUSAL, VS. 12.
   1. Sighed deeply from the bottom of His heart.
   2. Why seek a sign when it is here.
   3. No sign such as you seek will be given.

III. THE DEPARTURE, VS. 13.
   1. Left them.
   2. Once again sought seclusion to instruct His apostles.
   3. Sailed from Capernaum eastward.

EXPLANATORY NOTES

I. THE DISPUTE AND QUESTION.

"11. *The Pharisees came forth, and began to question with him.*—i.e. came out from their homes when they heard that he was there. By some it is assumed that he went beyond Dalmanutha to Capernaum, and that this interview took place there; but the intenion of both evangelists apparently was to tell what happened almost as he had landed. Hence these were in all probability Pharisees of Dalmanutha. Matthew associates Sadducees with them.—*Seeking of him a sign from heaven.* See similar requests in John 2:18; Matt. 12:38; John 6:30, all previous to this. What they asked for was something like the manna (so, expressly, in John 6:31), or thunder from a clear sky (1 Sam. 12:18), or fire from heaven, such as came to Elijah (1 Kings 18), or the signs of Joel 2:30, 31. There was a popular impression that, although miracles upon the earth might be spurious and deceptive, signs from heaven could not be counterfeited. It was expected that they would accompany the coming of the Messiah, and therefore Jesus was repeatedly asked to fulfill this expectation. If he was the Christ, they thought he would certainly be able and willing, and even anxious, to give this proof of his claim.—But they were *tempting him*, nevertheless—i.e., as in Matt. 19:3 and Mark 12:13, they were trying to entangle him, to his own injury with the people. They knew well enough that he would not give them a sign from heaven; all the Pharisees in Galilee must have known the great refusal recorded in Matt. 12:39 and the more recent one of John 6. He would not give them the sign, but by repeatedly calling for it they might discredit his claims with the people, who expected it of the Messiah. Since they themselves hated him, they must take all measures to prevent Israel from supposing its hopes to be fulfilled in him; so they would play upon false hopes and studiously repress all spiritual expectations. This was his welcome when he landed again on the soil of Galilee. He had been absent long enough to allow calm thought about him, and had now returned after a few days of gracious working just across the lake. This was his reception—the old wearisome demand of spiritual blindness: *Give us a sign from heaven.*"

II. THE DISAPPOINTMENT AND REFUSAL.

"12. At human misery he sighed (chap. 7:34); at human sin amounting to criminal inability to discern the truth he *sighed deeply in his spirit.*—a touch of personal remembrance peculiar to Mark. This deep sigh, or groan, was the sign of the chafing of his spirit against spiritual barriers. To the physically deaf he could say "Ephphatha," but not to these spiritually hardened and self-imprisoned Pharisees. What voice could reach them? When the rich young man departed sorrowful, he pointed his disciples to the brighter side, saying, "With God all things are possible." But in the case of these proud and hardened men he could only sigh, for the gates of spiritual possibility seemed closed.—*Why doth this generation seek after a sign? This generation,* the men of his time, who had the opportunity to know him—why should they ask for a sign? If there was no spiritual recognition of him, the case was hopeless; signs would teach them nothing. He himself was the true Sign from heaven, the living Witness to the present God. If they did not see that he was in the Father and the Father in him, their blindness must remain. Therefore he told them, with his emphatic *verily I say unto you,* that no sign should be given them.—In Matthew three additions are placed here, all exceedingly significant: (1) He contrasts their quickness in detecting signs of coming changes of weather with their slowness in discerning spiritual signs. (2) He traces their lack of perception of a present God to spiritual adultery. The prophets represent Israel as the wife of Jehovah, and often as the unfaithful and adulterous wife. This generation, says Jesus, is thus adulterous; it has broken faith with God, and has become carnal and unloving. Therefore it has lost all spiritual sense and consciousness of him, and, instead of discerning his holy presence in him whom he hath sent, must be asking for visible signs and portents to certify his nearness. But for the spiritual adultery there would be felt no need of signs. (3) "There shall be no sign given but the sign of the prophet Jonah," of which he had before spoken (Matt. 12:39,40), and which he seems to have wished to keep in their sight as a suggestive lesson, which might possibly awaken some right questionings in their hearts."

III. THE DEPARTURE.

"13. Disheartened and repelled by this reception in "his own country," he abruptly turned back, without going on, as it appears, to Capernaum, and re-embarked to return to the eastern shore. It is little to say that he must have gone in sadness. "He was despised and rejected of men, a man of sorrows, and acquainted with grief." We should greatly misread his life if we interpreted such language almost entirely in the light of his latest sufferings. He felt the grief of rejection, not merely as a personal wrong, but more as the rejection of God and goodness and of saving love. Bringing the message of infinite mercy, he must have longed to be accepted; and it could not be other than a constant grief to him that "he came to his own, and his own received him not."

Not more than a few hours at the most does he appear to have remained on the western shore, and now he is again afloat on the lake with his disciples, setting out on another journey alone with them, not to return until they have visited the region of Caesarea Philippi." (*W. N. Clarke*)

FACT QUESTIONS 8:11-13

425. From where did the Pharisees (and Saducees) come?—how soon did they come?
426. Explain just what kind of sign these Pharisees wanted.
427. Did they actually expect a sign? Why ask?
428. How was their spiritual blindness indicated?
429. What two things caused Jesus to sigh?
430. Show how the rich young ruler had more promise than these men.
431. What was the true sign they failed to recognize?
432. What three additional facts are given by Matthew?
433. Show how this incident fulfills John 1:10.

SUMMARY
7:24—8:13

This section contains an account of three more remarkable miracles—the expulsion of a demon from the Gentile woman's daughter; the restoration of speech and hearing to the deaf stammerer; and the feeding of four thousand men with seven barley loaves and a few small fishes. By these the divine power of Jesus is once more exhibited. The section also exhibits the tenderness of his compassion in his dealing with the Gentile woman and the hungry multitude, and his judicial indignation against hypocrisy in his conversation with the Pharisees. These are attributes of character which, though they do not prove their possessor to have been superhuman, are necessary to that perfection of character which must be found in the Son of God.—*McGarvey.*

5. WARNING AGAINST THE LEAVEN OF THE PHARISEES. 8:14-21

TEXT 8:14-21

"And they forgot to take bread; and they had not in the boat with them more than one loaf. And he charged them, saying, Take heed, beware of the leaven of the Pharisees and the leaven of Herod. And they reasoned one with another, saying, We have no bread. And Jesus perceiving it saith unto them, Why reason ye, because ye have no bread? do you not perceive, neither understand? have ye your heart hardened? Having eyes, see ye not? and having ears, hear ye not? and do ye not remember? When I brake the five loaves among the five thousand, how many baskets full of broken pieces took ye up? They say unto him, Twelve. And when the seven among the four thousand, how many basketfuls of broken pieces took ye up? And they say unto him, Seven. And he said unto them, Do ye not yet understand?"

THOUGHT QUESTIONS 8:14-21

358. Why does Mark mention the fact that they had forgotten to take bread?
386. Why mention at this time "the leaven of the Pharisees"?
387. Define in your own words: The leaven of the Pharisees—the leaven of Herod.
388. Why connect the word leaven with the subject of bread?
389. How did Jesus know of the reasoning of their hearts?
390. Note please the three questions of Jesus in vs. 17—discuss each one as they relate to the apostles—as they relate to us today.
391. Distinguish between the use of the eyes—ears—memory in the process of understanding.
392. Why refer to the feeding of the 5,000 and the 4,000?
393. Do you believe the apostles did understand after Jesus rebuked them?

COMMENT

TIME—Summer A.D. 29.

PLACE—On the lake of Galilee.

PARALLEL ACCOUNT—Matt. 16:5-12.

OUTLINE—1. Forgot to take bread on their trip, vs. 14. 2. Jesus said:

"beware of the leaven of the Pharisees and Herod," vs. 15. 3. The disciples thought He referred to their supply of bread, vs. 16. 4. Jesus rebuked them for their lack of spiritual perception, vs. 17, 18. 5. "Why worry about physical bread when I fed 5,000 & 4,000 with a few loaves"? vs. 19, 20. 6. Do you now see *I* refer to something more important than physical bread?, vs. 21.

ANALYSIS

I. FORGOT TO TAKE BREAD ON THEIR TRIP, VS. 14.
   1. Left in haste.
   2. Had with them in the boat only one loaf.

II. JESUS SAID: "BEWARE OF THE LEAVEN OF THE PHARISEES AND HEROD," VS. 15.
   1. This was given as an order.
   2. This was given as a warning.

III. THE DISCIPLES THOUGHT HE REFERRED TO THEIR SUPPLY OF BREAD, VS. 16.
   1. They reasoned or conversed among themselves as to what He meant.
   2. They agreed He must have reference to buying bread from their enemies.
   3. But then this is no danger because we have no bread.

IV. JESUS REBUKED THEM FOR THEIR LACK OF SPIRITUAL PERCEPTION, VS. 17, 18.
   1. He read their minds.
   2. Why are you worried about your bread supply?; what I have said does not refer to your bread.
   3. Are you still void of depth?
   4. Are you yet without understanding?
   5. Is your heart stone?
   6. What has happened to the eyes, ears, and memory of your heart?

V. WHY WORRY ABOUT PHYSICAL BREAD WHEN I FED 5,000 AND 4,000 WITH A FEW LOAVES? VS. 19, 20.
   1. When I fed the 5,000 how many baskets were left over?—12.
   2. And how many for the 4,000?—7.

VI. DO YOU NOW SEE I REFER TO SOMETHING MORE IMPORTANT THAN PHYSICAL BREAD? VS. 21.

EXPANATORY NOTES

I. FORGOT TO TAKE BREAD ON THEIR TRIP.

"14. The neglect to take a supply of bread was doubtless the result of their haste in again setting out; and, in that view of the matter, Jesus himself was responsible for it, since he had hurried them away."

II. JESUS SAID: "BEWARE OF THE LEAVEN OF THE PHARISEES AND HEROD."

"15. It is Mark alone who mentions the *one loaf* that they had with them in the boat; plainly a touch of definite remembrance from one who was present.—*And he charged them.* The emphatic word is peculiar to Mark.—*Take heed, beware of the leaven of the Pharisees, and of the leaven of Herod.* In Matthew, "of the Pharisees and Saducees." From this grouping it has sometimes been inferred that Herod was a Sadducee; but that seems too definite a conclusion to draw from such premises. Undoubtedly, Herod's position was such as to give him more in common with the Sadducees than with the Pharisees, and the Sadducees may have been the Herodians of Galilee; but Herod Antipas was probably too much of an indifferentist to hold very strongly the doctrines of any Jewish sect. —The *leaven* is expressly, according to Matthew, the "doctrine" of the Pharisees and Sadducees, or of the Pharisees and Herod. But "doctrine" (didache) is an active word rather than a passive, and refers rather to the teaching than to the substance of what was taught; and when used of Herod it must be substantially equivalent to "influence."—The warning must be understood in the light of what had just occurred, for it must certainly have been suggested by the demand for *a sign from heaven.* To the corrupting influence of Pharisaism and Sadduceeism or of political Herodianism—i.e. to the spirit that was manifested in these forms—it was due that Israel had departed from God, and had so lost all spiritual sense of him as to be clamoring for signs from heaven. So the warning means, "Beware of the unspiritual, irreligious, godless teaching through which it has come to pass that God is no longer recognized." Reflecting on the conversation that had sent him, disheartened, back from Galilee, he thought of his own disciples, who were but too prone to a similar unbelief; and he said to himself, "They must not be possessed by the ungodly blindness that cannot perceive a spiritual meaning and is dependent upon signs to show them God and truth. Yet the land is full of it under the influence of this unholy teaching, and it cannot fail to be working as a leaven in their minds." Therefore he spoke in warning."

III. THE DISCIPLES THOUGHT HE REFERRED TO THEIR SUPPLY OF BREAD.

"16. According to the most probable reading, adopted by the revisers, we may translate, *And they reasoned,* or considered, together, "saying, We have no bread." The common English version, *It is because we have no bread,* represents the spirit of their utterance perfectly, though not a good translation. They dimly supposed he must mean that food received from the hands of his enemies was to be rejected, because of the unworthiness of those who might offer it: if Pharisees and Herodians were so defiled, they were not fit persons for them to obtain food from. "There is a childish *naivete* in their self-questioning which testifies to the absolute originality and truthfulness of the record, and so to the genuineness of the question that follows—a question that assumes the reality of the two previous miracles" (*Plumptre*). They tried to understand him, but this low and uncharacteristic meaning was all that they could find, as if he had said, "You will have bread to buy, and you must be careful from whom you buy it," and had forbidden them to eat the bread of his enemies."

IV. JESUS REBUKED THEM FOR THEIR LACK OF SPIRITUAL PERCEPTION.

"17, 18. Mark's report here is much more full than Matthew's. The last two questions of verse 17 are peculiar to Mark, and so is the whole of verse 18, with the exception of the last word; so are the responses of the disciples in verses 19 and 20, and so is verse 21. The translation of verses 18, 19, according to *Tischendorf's* text, is, "Having eyes do ye not see, and having ears do ye not hear, and do ye not remember when I broke the five loaves unto the five thousand, and how many baskets full of fragments ye took up?" The readings of verse 21 vary, but, according to the most probable, the question is simply, "Do ye not yet understand?" These questions of Jesus are sharp and cutting, full of surprise and indignation. So far as the record goes, they are the sharpest words that he ever spoke to the twelve. We can scarcely wonder at his indignation, for he saw already in them *the leaven of the Pharisees,* the same blindness that had just disheartened him, in their inability to perceive a spiritual meaning. They were like the generation that was described in chap. 4:12, which, having eyes, saw not, and having ears heard not."

V. WHY WORRY ABOUT PHYSICAL BREAD WHEN I FED 5,000 AND 4,000 WITH A FEW LOAVES?

"19, 20. Whatever meaning they might have found in his warning, the one that they did find was one that their experience with him ought to have rendered impossible. They had been with him twice when he fed thousands from a handful, yet they were talking perplexedly among themselves, as if he could possibly be thinking of where the food was to come from. His rebuke means, "When you are with me, and I am responsible for your want of food, you need have no anxiety, and you may know that whatever I may say refers to something else than the way in which food is obtained." They ought, moreover, to have known that he who had plainly abolished distinctions of food (chap. 7:15) would not now set up a new distinction of a personal or sectarian kind, and teach them that they would be defiled by food bought from ungodly men. Surely it would seem to be asking but very little to ask that they should understand him well enough to escape such an idea. Here was indeed the unspiritual heart, upon which the spiritual thought seemed almost wasted. More than in the case of his townsmen at Nazareth, he "marvelled because of their unbelief." If Christian teachers find even their brethren slow of perception in spiritual things, they may hear their Master saying to them, in the spirit of John 15:18, "Ye know that they misunderstood me before they misunderstood you."

VI. DO YOU NOW SEE I REFER TO SOMETHING MORE IMPORTANT THAN PHYSICAL BREAD?

"21. In Matthew the final question, "Do ye not yet understand?" is expanded into a direct intimation that the warning did not refer to bread. Matthew adds also that they did at last perceive that he was warning them against the teaching or the principles of the Pharisees and Sadducees. But it is quite certain that they did not take in his full meaning, and that when the subject was dropped he knew that his utterance had not reached its aim. He had had to expend the energy that might have been given to the work of enforcing an idea in the vain effort to get it apprehended, and then to withdraw baffled by the unreceptiveness of his hearers. It was not his method to urge truth upon them faster than they were able to receive it. John 16:12 illustrates his real method: "I have yet many things to say unto you, but ye cannot bear them now."—Observe, again, the distinct reference in these questions to the two separate miracles of feeding—a reference which cannot possibly be removed from the passage without utterly destroying one of the most vivid and self-witnessing scenes in the whole Gospel narrative. Observe, again, too, that in referring here to the first miracle Jesus employs the word *cophinus* in mentioning the baskets, and in referring to the second the word *spuris,* preserving the very distinction that has been made in the two narratives of Mark." (*W. N. Clarke*)

FACT QUESTIONS 8:14-21

434. Who was responsible for the lack of food?
435. What definite indications of an eye-witness do we have in this section?
436. Are we to conclude that Herod was a Sadducee from Matthew's reference to the leaven of the Pharisees and Sadducees? What are we to conclude?
437. Please explain the distinctive influence of each of these groups; (1) Pharisees (2) Sadducees (3) Herodians.
438. How does the request for a sign from heaven relate to this warning of Jesus?
439. As they reasoned among themselves what conclusion did they form?

440. What is it that testifies to the "absolute originality and truthfulness of the record"?
441. Why was Jesus so sharp with the disciples?
442. What particular attitude in the hearts of the disciples disappointed Jesus the most?
443. When the subject was dropped was Jesus satisfied that His teaching was understood? Discuss.
444. How is the use of the two words for "baskets" as used in this record an indication of two incidents of feeding the multitudes?

6. HEALING THE BLIND MAN OF BETHSAIDA 8:22-26

TEXT 8:22-26

"And they come unto Bethsaida. And they bring to him a blind man, and beseech him to touch him. And they took hold of the blind man by the hand, and brought him out of the village; and when he had spit on his eyes, and laid his hands upon him, he asked him, Seest thou aught? And he looked up, and said, I see men; for I behold them as trees, walking. Then again he laid his hands upon his eyes; and he looked stedfastly, and was restored, and saw all things clearly. And he sent him away to his home, saying, Do not even enter into the village."

THOUGHT QUESTIONS 8:22-26

394. Please locate Bethsaida on the map.
395. Who brought the blind man to Jesus?
396. What is meant by the word "beseech"?
397. Why lead the blind man out of the village?
398. Did Jesus actually spit upon the eyes of the blind man? for what purpose?
399. Is this an example of a progressive healing? Discuss.
400. There must have been some purpose in the two stages of the healing —what was it?
401. Did the blind man have faith in order to be healed?
402. Why send the man who was healed away?

COMMENT

TIME—Summer A.D. 29.

PLACE—Bethsaida Julias, on the east bank of the Jordan River where it flows into the Lake of Galilee.

PARALLEL ACCOUNTS—only in Mark.

OUTLINE—1. A blind man brought to Jesus, vs. 22. 2. The blind man led out of the city for healing, vs. 23a. 3. Two stages of healing, 23b-25. 4. Sent home, vs. 26.

ANALYSIS

I. A BLIND MAN BROUGHT TO JESUS, VS. 22.
   1. They were in Bethsaida Julias.

2. An urgent request made for healing.

II. THE BLIND MAN LED OUT OF THE CITY FOR HEALING, VS. 23A.

1. Jesus led him by the hand.
2. Away from the multitude so the healing would teach the lesson intended.

III. TWO STAGES OF HEALING, 23B-25.

1. Spat on his eyes and laid his hands upon him.
2. Asked: "Do you see anything"?
3. He looked up and saw the disciples in an indistinct manner.
4. Jesus laid his hands upon his eyes—he looked intently and saw clearly.

IV. SENT HOME, VS. 26.

1. He was not from Bethsaida.
2. He was refused permission to return to Bethsaida—sent directly home.

EXPANATORY NOTES

I. A BLIND MAN BROUGHT TO JESUS.

"22. Mark here records a miracle not given in the other gospels, one of the very few passages entirely peculiar to him. His reason for inserting it cannot be merely that it followed the dialogue above recorded (vs. 14-21); for he often omits multitudes of miracles in writing of the periods to which they belong. So far as his design can be conjectured, it was probably to illustrate and exemplify still further our Lord's variety of method in the working of his cures, by stating a case (perhaps the only one) in which the cure was gradual. *He cometh,* or, according to the older manuscripts, *they come, i.e.* Jesus and his company, the twelve apostles and perhaps some others who attended him from place to place. *To* (or into) *Bethsaida,* or, as a few copies have it, *Bethany,* an obvious error of transcription, probably occasioned by the resemblance of the names, both which are compounded with the Hebrew *beth* (a house or place.) *Bethsaida* is supposed by some to be the town so called in Galilee, the birthplace of Andrew and Peter (John 1, 44); but the best interpreters and highest geographical authorities understand it of Bethsaida in Perea, on the north-east shore of the lake in a solitude near which (or belonging to it) the five thousand were fed. This Bethsaida was distinguished from the other by its Greek or Roman name, *Julias,* which it bore in honour of a daughter of Augustus. *They,* indefinitely, some men, certain persons, otherwise unknown; or more specifically, the man's relatives, friends, neighbours. A *blind (man),* not one born blind (as in John 9:1), for he knew the shape of trees (see below, on v. 24), but blinded by disease or accident. *Besought,* in Greek *beseech,* the graphic or descriptive present being still continued. *To touch him,* literally, *that he would* (or still more closely, so that, in order that, he might) *touch him.* These words in the original rather state the motive than the substance of the prayer, a nicety of form without effect upon the meaning yet entitled to attention as an illustration of the difference of idiom. This specific prayer is not a sign of strong but rather of deficient or contracted faith, assuming contact to be necessary to the cure, an error which our Saviour did not think it necessary in the present instance either to reprove or correct."

II. THE BLIND MAN LED OUT OF THE CITY FOR HEALING.

"23b. *And taking,* laying hold upon, *the hand of the blind (man),* which in the order of the words in the original, although the construction in the version is grammatical and justified by usage; the sense of course remains the same in either case. *He led him forth out* (or *outside*) *of the village,* a term applied with considerable latitude to towns of every size. Out is twice expressed in Greek, once by the compound verb, and once by the adverbial preposition. The reason of this movement has been variously conjectured; some supposing an intention to express displeasure towards the people of the town for reasons now unknown; others a desire to be uninterrupted in the process which was more than commonly protracted. But these and other explanations, which need not be stated, assume that Mark intended to describe this and the following proceedings on our Lord's part as having a distinct significance, whereas he rather means to show how far he was from following a fixed routine, or countenancing the idea that a certain outward form was necessary to the curative effect. Against this error he provided by sometimes doing more, sometimes less, sometimes nothing, in the way of gesture or manipulation, and of all these methods we have instances recorded in the book before us."

III. TWO STAGES OF HEALING.

"23b-25. *Having spit on* (or rather *into*) *his eyes,* which some regard as a medicinal appliance, healing virtue being ascribed to the human saliva by *Tacitus, Suetonius, Pliny,* and in various dicta of the Talmud. Others find a symbolical meaning in the transfer of something from the person of the healer to the person of the healed. But the necessity of these conjectures is precluded by the view of the matter just suggested. *And putting* (laying or imposing) *hands upon him,* as had been requested by his friends (vs. 22). *Asked;* interrogated, questioned. *If he saw* (literally, *sees,* another instance of the graphic present) *ought,* an old word, not yet wholly obsolete, for anything. This pause, as it were, in the midst of the cure, to ask him as to its effect, is so unlike the usual immediate restoration, that it may be confidently reckoned as at least one reason for Mark's giving a detailed account of this case.

And looking up, raising his eyes, trying to use them. The particle with which the Greek verb is compounded sometimes denotes upward motion, sometimes repetition. Hence the verb itself may either mean to *look up* or to *see again,* but the latter, though preferred by some interpreters, is a less natural anticipation of what follows in the next verse. The sensations of the blind man, on his first attempt to see again, are strangely but expressively described in his own language, the peculiarity of which, however, is exaggerated to the English reader by an equivocal construction, quite unknown to the original, and only partially removed by careful punctuation in the version. It is probably one of the most common and inveterate misapprehensions of a scriptural expression, that the participle *walking* here agrees with trees, and that the blind man intended to describe his partially restored sight by saying that the men around him were like walking trees. But in Greek there is and can be no such ambiguity, the concord being there determined, not by the position of the words, which is far more free and discretionary than with us, but by their form or termination, which distinguishes their gender and requires *walking* to agree with *men,* and *trees* to be taken by itself without any qualifying epithet. The word *men* also has the article which shows it to mean not men in general, but *the men* who were passing or at hand, perhaps the twelve apostles; for although he led him out of town, it is not said that they were unaccompanied, or that the place to which he brought him was a solitude. This meaning therefore of the clause, according to the common or received text, is, *I see the men walking about as trees,* i.e. undefined in form and figure. Except by their motions, which were those of men, he could not distinguish them from trees. It is remarkable however that the oldest manuscripts almost without exception have another reading, which appears to give the patient's words more fully. *I behold men because as trees I see (them) walking.* This is an awkward sentence, it is true, but not on that account less likely to have been pronounced on this occasion, while its very awkwardness may possibly have led to its abbreviation in the later copies. The weight of manuscript authority in favour of this reading is confirmed by its internal fitness, as a broken expression of surprise and joy, beginning with a sudden exclamation, *I see the men!* then qualifying or explaining it by adding, *because* (that is, at least), *as trees I see (them) walking.*

Then, afterwards, or in the next place, a Greek particle often employed to separate the items in an enumeration, and intended here to mark distinctly the successive stages of the healing process, an effect secured still further by the word *again,* which is the next in the original though not in the translation. As if he had said, having gone thus far and partially restored the man's sight, he proceeded in the next place to impose his hands upon the eyes themselves, as he had previously done upon some other part, perhaps the head. It is possible indeed that even in the former instance he had laid his hands upon his eyes, but this is a less natural construction of the language, *spitting in his eyes and laying his hands on him,* where the mention of the eyes in one clause and of the person in the other, favours, though it may not peremptorily require, the former explanation. *Made him,* caused him, i.e. in this case both required and enabled him. *Look up, or see again,* the same two sense of the verb that are admissible in the verse preceeding. If the latter be adopted here, the meaning of the phrase is, that he *caused him to receive his sight;* if the former, that he *caused him to look up,* or try to see, on which he found his sight restored completely. The only objection to the first construction is that the restoration of his sight is then distinctly stated three times, whereas on the other supposition, it is only stated once, the other two expressions being then descriptive of the effort or experiment by which the patient was assured first of partial then of total restoration. He looked up once and saw men like trees; he looked up again and saw them clearly. *Was restored* to (reinstated in') his sound or normal state, another term implying that he was not born blind. *Every (man)* or *all (things),* as the Greek may be either masculine and singular, or neuter and plural. Another reading, found in some editions, removes the ambiguity by making it both masculine and plural, *(all men),* which may then be understood to mean specifically all those whom he saw before *as trees* (but) *walking.* Clearly, an expressive Greek word which originally means *farsightedly,* in opposition to near (or short) sight, although here, as in the classics it may have the wider secondary sense expressed in the translation and opposed to the dimness of his sight when only partially recovered."

IV. SENT HOME.

"26. *And he sent him away into his house* (or *to his house*), which was not in the town or village, as appears from the ensuing prohibition. The modern philologists deny that the Greek particle repeated here ever corresponds to *neither . . . nor* in English, as expressing an alternative originally present to the speaker's mind; and one of them explains the first to mean *not even,* and the last *nor even.* 'Do not even go into the village, nor so much as speak to any (person) in the village.' The supposed inconsistency of these two precepts, or at least the superfluousness of the last, as he could not tell it in the town unless he went there, has produced no less than ten variations in the text of this clause, all intended to remove the incongruity, and therefore all to be rejected as mere glosses. This may serve to show by a remarkable example the extraordinary principle, on which the ancient copyists frequently proceeded, of deciding what the writer should have said, instead of simply telling what he did say. To this single error may be traced a large proportion of existing variations in the text of the New Testament, most of which happily have never become current, but are found exclusively in certain copies or at most in certain families or classes of manuscripts. This erroneous principle or practice is the more to be condemned as the necessity of emendation is in almost every case imaginary. In the one before us, for example, the supposed incongruity arises from the strict fidelity with which the very words of Christ (or their equivalents) are here reported just as he pronounced them, not in a rhetorical or rounded period, but in short successive clauses, the natural form of a peremptory order. The man having just been brought out of the town, though not residing there, would naturally think of going back to tell and show what had been done to him. But this our Lord, for reasons which have often been explained before, is determined to prevent by pointed positive directions, which, without a change of meaning, may be paraphrased as follows: 'Go home—go directly home—no, not into the town, but home —not even for an hour or a moment—do not go into the town at all—not even to tell what I have done—do not so much as speak to any person in the town—but go directly home'." (*J. A. Alexander*)

FACT QUESTIONS 8:22-26

445. Since Mark is the only gospel writer to record this miracle what is his purpose in giving it?
446. There is some question as to which Bethsaida is involved here—why?
447. Who brought the blind man?
448. Do you believe the blind man had partial sight before Jesus touched him? Discuss.
449. What conclusion do you have for the reason of leading the blind man out of the city?
450. Why spit into the eyes of the blind man?
451. Why did Jesus ask the blind man if he could see?
452. Just what did the blind man say?—what did he see?
453. After Jesus place His hands upon the blind man the second time did He make him look up or did the blind man do this of his own will?
454. Verse 26 is a remarkable example of the mistake of copyist—explain.

7. JESUS THE MESSIAH 8:27—9:1

TEXT 8:27—9:1

"And Jesus went forth, and his disciples, into the villages of Caesarea Philippi: and in the way he asked his disciples, saying unto them, Whom do men say that I am? And they told him, saying, John the Baptist: and others, Elijah; but others, One of the prophets. And he asked them, But whom say ye that I am? Peter answereth and saith unto him, Thou art the Christ. And he charged them that they should tell no man of him. And he began to teach them, that the Son of man must suffer many things, and be rejected by the elders, and the chief priests, and the scribes, and be killed, and after three days rise again. And he spake the saying openly. And Peter took him, and began to rebuke him. But he turning about, and seeing his disciples, rebuked Peter, and saith, Get thee behind me Satan: for thou mindest not the things of God, but the things of men. And he called unto him the multitude with his disciples, and said unto them, If any man would come after me, let him deny himself, and take up his cross, and follow me. For whosoever would save his life shall lose it; and whosoever shall lose his life for my sake and the gospel's shall save it. For what doth it profit a man, to gain the whole world, and forfeit his life? For what should a man give in exchange for his life? For whosoever shall be ashamed of me and of my words in this adulterous and sinful generation, the Son of man also shall be ashamed of him, when he cometh in the glory of his Father with the holy angels. And he said unto them, Verily I say unto you, There be some here of them that stand by, which shall in no wise taste of death, till they see the kingdom of God come with power."

THOUGHT QUESTIONS 8:27—9:1

403. How far from Bethsaida to Caesarea Philippi? Please locate on the map.
404. Why ask the disciples of the opinion of others? What meaning is there in the name Jesus applied to Himself? Cf. Matt. 16:13, 14?
405. How would Jesus meet the designations given concerning Him—i.e. in what way was He like John the Baptist?; like Elijah?; like one of the prophets?
406. Who thought Jesus was John the Baptist risen from the dead?
407. Show how appropriate this question was at this particular time in the life of Jesus.
408. What did Peter mean in his use of the name "Christ"?
409. Why doesn't Mark record the blessing pronounced by Christ upon Peter?
410. Define each of the three classes of persons referred to in vs. 31.
411. What is meant by the expression "He spake the saying openly"?
412. Please attempt an explanation of the attitude of Peter when he rebuked the Lord.
413. Why look at all the disciples and rebuke Peter? In what sense was Jesus *not* speaking to Peter?
414. Show the connection of denying self with the rebuke of Peter.
415. Define in your own words what it means to "take up his cross and follow . . ."

416. How do we attempt to save our life and in the process lose it?
417. Specifically how can we lose our life for His sake? Please be personal and practical.
418. How is the word "soul" or "life" used in vs. 36?
419. Is Jesus saying a man has no real life or is not really living unless he is giving himself to His service?
420. How does being ashamed of Jesus fit into this context?

COMMENT

TIME—Summer of A.D. 29. From six to eight months before the Lord's Crucifixion.

PLACE—In the neighborhood of Caesarea Philippi, about thirty miles northeast of Capernaum and the Sea of Galilee. It was upon the upper sources of the Jordan, the largest of the three streams that unite to form the river springing from a fountain near Caesarea Philippi. *Professor McGarvey* says: The city of Caesarea Philippi stood at the northeastern curve of the upper Jordan valley, and about twenty-six miles north of the lake of Galilee. Mountains 2,000 feet high rise abruptly from the eastern side of it, while the snow covered summit of Mt. Hermon, 9,000 feet high, swells heavenward but a few miles north of it. Its earliest name known to us was Paneas, so called in honor of the god Pan, and on or near its side Herod the Great erected a temple in honor of Augustus Caesar. Afterward Philip the Tetrarch, to whom Herod gave the district at his death, rebuilt the old town, and called it Caesarea Philippi in honor of himself and Tiberius Caesar. The city is now in ruins, but the wall can be traced on every side, and in some points on the east and south sides it is standing at almost its original height. Just outside the northeastern angle of the wall is the famous spring which is one of the three principal sources of the Jordan.

PARALLEL ACCOUNTS—Matt. 16:13-28; Luke 9:18-27.

LESSON OUTLINE—1. The Good Confession. 2. The Cross of Christ. 3. Losing and Finding Life.

ANALYSIS

I. THE GOOD CONFESSION, VS. 27-30.
   1. Christ at Caesarea Philippi. Mark 8:27; Matt. 16:13; Luke 9:18.
   2. Opinions of Christ. Mark 8:28; Matt. 16:14; Luke 9:19: John 6:69.
   3. Peter's Confession. Mark 8:29; Matt. 16:16.

II. THE CROSS OF CHRIST, VS. 31-34.
   1. The Prophecy of the Cross. Mark 8:31; Matt. 16:21; 17:22: Luke 9:22.
   2. Peter Rebuked. Mark 8:32, 33; Matt. 16:22, 23.
   3. Bearing the Cross. Mark 8:24; Matt. 16:24; Luke 9:23.

III. LOSING AND FINDING LIFE, VS. 35 TO 9:1.

1. The Way to Save Life. Mark 8:35; Matt. 16:25; Luke 9:24.
2. Gain or Loss. Mark 8:36, 37; Matt. 16:26; Luke 9:25.
3. Ashamed of the Cross. Mark 8:38; Luke 9:26; Rom. 1:16.
4. Coming in the Kingdom. Mark 9:1; Matt. 16:28; Luke 9:27.

INTRODUCTION

It was after our Lord had closed his public ministry in Galilee, and while he was seeking retirement in order to communicate special instruction in the principles of his kingdom to the apostles, who were to succeed in his work, that he gave the great lesson concerning the foundation on which he would found his church, and the lesson on consecration and self-denial that its extension in the world requires. Here begins the second great division of the Savior's ministry, a period that leads directly to his sufferings and death. The first period culminated in the confession of Peter; the second in the cross and resurrection.

EXPANATORY NOTES

I. THE GOOD CONFESSION.—27. *Jesus went out, and his disciples. Went out* is the word regularly used in this gospel when a departure from one scene of work to another is notified. In this case, our Lord, leaving the district in which he had hitherto been chiefly working, proceeded in a northeasterly direction along the valley of the Upper Jordan. *And his disciples.* Their presence is here mentioned expressly, calling attention to the object of a journey through a district to a great extent heathen, and lately traversed, viz., their special instruction (Mark 9:31). *Into the towns.* Away from the populous cities The solitude of the beautiful district, wither the Savior now journeyed, is illustrated by the fact that it is the only district in Palestine where a recent traveller found the pelican of the wilderness (Ps. 102:6). *Caesarea Philippi.* A city at the northeast extremity of Palestine and at the foot of Mount Lebanon, anciently called Paneas, and now Banias. It has now about fifty houses, many ruins of columns, towers, temples, a bridge, and a remarkable castle. *And by the way.* His conversation by the way: (1) The turn it often took when the disciples were left to themselves—disputes concerning greatness, etc. (2) The turn Christ gave to it—inquirings concerning his mission and person. Learn: (1), Avoid foolish and worldly talk; (2), Improve passing opportunities; (3), Let your talk be often about the Savior.—*Biblical Museum. Whom do men say that I am?* The following conversation refers to three points: (1) The Christ. (2) The suffering Christ. (3) The disciples of the suffering Christ. The object of this first question is evidently to prepare the way for the next. The inquiry was not concerning the opinions of the Scribes and Rabbis, but concerning the opinions of the people.

28. *And they answered.* As Jesus had not openly declared that he was the Messiah, but had allowed men to hear his surpassing wisdom and see his life and works and draw their own conclusions, there would naturally be various opinions. *John the Baptist.* Who had been killed by Herod a few months before, now restored to life. That was one popular notion regarding him, circulating, no doubt, chiefly among those who had never seen him. Herod Antipas entertained it (chap. 6:16). *Elias.* The great ideal of a prophet and spiritual reformer. It was very generally expected that he was to return to the earth in connection with the Messiah's advent (Mal. 4, 5).—*Morison. One of the prophets.* The Jews believed that at the coming of the Messiah the prophets were to rise again. They did not declare their belief in him as the Messiah himself, doubtless for this reason, that the whole ministry of Christ appeared to them to stand in contradiction to their Messianic expectations.

29. *Whom say ye that I am?* He had never openly spoken of his Messiahship. It was his will that the revelation should dawn gradually on the minds of his children; that it should spring more from the truths he spake, and the life he lived, than from the wonders which he wrought. It was *in the Son of man* that they were to recognize *the Son of God.* —*Farrar.* The time was come when it was of the greatest moment that they should have a settled conception of his real character and mission. *And Peter answereth.* With that honest readiness and impulsiveness which were so characteristic of his nature, and which fitted him for being a leader of the little circle.—*Morison. Thou art the Christ;* Matthew adds, *the Son of the living God.* This confession not only sees in Jesus the promised Messiah, but in the Messiah recognizes the divine nature. —*Cambridge Bible.* The confession of Peter is the first fundamental Christian confession of faith, and the germ of the Apostles' Creed.—*Lange.* It was a decisive answer, and given as out of a higher inspiration. The Lord himself, as we learn from Matt. 16:17, traced the thought to its divine source. And yet it was, no doubt, founded on evidence which the disciple had diligently studied, and logically construed to his own inner satisfaction. The Lord in the passage in Matthew declares that the grand truth confessed by Peter is the rock on which his church shall be built. By faith in this truth men become disciples of Christ and members of his church.

30. *Charged them that they should tell no man.* The time had not yet come to proclaim that he was the Christ. To do so prematurely would result in harm rather than good. He must first demonstrate his Messiahship by his resurrection.

II. THE CROSS OF CHRIST.—31. *He began to teach them . . . must suffer many things.* The great lesson of our two years of his ministry was that he was the Christ; after this had been learned by his apostles they were ready to be taught he must die a violent death. So from this time onward we find him speaking more and more plainly of the "decease which he must accomplish." The supreme purpose of his advent was not to teach truth, nor to work miracles, nor to illustrate the perfection of manly character, but to die, to die for sinners, to bear their sins in his own body on the tree. *Rejected of the elders, chief priests and scribes.* The three constituents of the Sanhedrim. The elders (leading men) would be chosen because of their material and political influence; the high priests, because of their elevated ecclesiastical position; the scribes, because of their literary and rabbinical qualifications. Now, for the first time, the disciples received full and clear information of the sufferings and death of Christ.

32. *And he spake that saying openly.* Without reserve, publicly. The previous statements respecting this subject, made by our Lord, were expressed in figurative language.—*Godwin. And Peter began to rebuke him.* The same Peter who but just now had made so noble and spiritual a confession, and received so high a blessing, now shows the weak and carnal side of his character. This world has many Peters, who wish to be wiser than Christ, and to prescribe to him what it is needful to do.

33. *Turned about and looked on his disciples.* A sudden movement is indicated. Looking at all, he singles out Peter for special warning. *Rebuked Peter, saying Get thee behind me, Satan.* Christ saw, with the lightning glance of his spirit, in the words of Peter a suggestion not so much of his as of Satan's. This is the very temptation that fell from the lips of Satan in the wilderness when he offered to surrender the kingdoms of this world to Jesus without his suffering on the cross. The Lord when he says, with sudden vehemence, "Get thee behind me Satan!" was not speaking directly to Peter but to the prince of darkness, who had for a moment taken possession of Peter's mind and lips. Peter had been greatly elated over the Messiahship of Jesus, but still expected an earthly king Messiah after the type of David, in whose kingdom he would have a great place. To hear the Lord talk of the cross was a cruel disappointment to his ambitious hopes.

III. LOSING AND FINDING LIFE.—34. *When he had called the people unto him.* The great lesson of his Christhood and death on the cross had been given to the apostles alone. Now the throng and his disciples are united and the Lord teaches a grand truth that springs directly from what had occurred just before. *Will come after me.* Will become my disciple. There was an eagerness among many of the people to "come after him." The wistfulness of a considerable proportion of the northern population had been awakened. They were ruminating anxiously on Old Testament predictions, and filled with vague expectancy. *Let him deny himself.* The word is strong in the original—"let him deny himself off, let him entirely renounce himself." Let him be prepared to say "no" to many of the strongest cravings of his nature, in the direction more particularly of earthly ease, comfort, dignity and glory. Our common thoughts of "self-denial," i.e., the denial to ourselves of some pleasure or profit, fall far short of the meaning of the Greek. The man is to deny his whole self, all his natural motives and impulses, so far as they come into conflict with the claims of Christ. *And take up his cross.* Even as the Lord would take up his cross at Jerusalem. So every disciple must "crucify the old man," his selfish nature (Rom. 6:6), give up his old life, and become dead to it. The cross is the pain of the self-denial required in the preceding words. The cross is the "symbol of doing our duty, even at the cost of the most painful death." Christ obeyed God, and carried out his work for the salvation of men, though it required him to die upon the cross in order to do it. And ever since, the cross has stood as the emblem, not of suffering, but of suffering for the sake of Christ and his gospel as the highest ideal of obedience to God at any and every cost. *Follow me.* Obey and imitate Christ.

35. *Whosoever will save his life.* Whoever makes this the end will lose life. A great principle is stated. All self-seeking is self-losing. Even in spiritual things, he who is perpetually studying how to secure joy and peace for himself loses it. A certain measure of self-forgetfulness is the condition of the highest success, even in Christian grace. *But whosoever shall lose his life.* In the sphere of the present. *For my sake, and the gospel's.* It is only loss for the sake of Christ that has this promise. Multitudes of people lose their lives for gain, for pleasure, for fashion. Each of these has more martyrs than the cross ever required; but the loss was without compensation or hope. But whosoever loses for the love of Christ, for the sake of preaching and advancing the gospel *shall save it*—shall have a blessedness and glory which will a thousand times compensate for every loss.

36. *What shall it profit a man?* This is one of the searching questions that the Scriptures are wont to throw out to arouse reflection. Let each student try to conscientiously answer this question and the one which follows.

37. *What shall a man give in exchange for his soul?* What would a man not give? If he had the whole world, would he not willingly give it, provided he really knew, believed, or felt, that otherwise he would be utterly lost? The Saviour has gone forward in thought, and taken his standpoint in eternity. It is from that standpoint that he puts the question.

38. *Shall be ashamed of me and of my words.* As many would be

prone to be. The temptation to *shame,* in reference to the Savior and the Savior's sayings or doctrines, continues to the present day, and is pervading society to the core, even in countries called Christian. It is one of the severest temptations which young converts have to encounter. The anticipation of it is one of the mightiest motives to keep men away from conversion, and on the other side of Christian faith and fealty. *This adulterous and sinful generation.* Adulterous here, as in the Old Testament, means "unfaithful to God." *When he cometh,* etc. The glorious coming to judge the world when all nations shall appear before him.

9:1 *Some of them that stand here, etc.* The allusion to the final coming of the kingdom of Christ in power which took place on the day of Pentecost. The day of Pentecost, when the descent of the Spirit took place, marks the beginning of "the dispensation of the Spirit," "the new economy," or the kingdom of righteousness. Its consummation will be seen when all souls shall be converted to righteousness and Jesus shall come.

FACT QUESTIONS 8:27—9:1

455. Give three facts about Caesarea Philippi.
456. The verses before us begin what great division in our Lord's ministry?
457. What area of public ministry concludes with the eighth chapter?
458. What was the purpose of our Lord in going into the district of Caesarea Philippi?
459. Give three lessons we can learn in the example of our Lord.
460. Did Jesus want the opinions of the scribes and rabbis? Why not?
461. Show how Mal. 4:5 helped form the opinion of some.
462. Show how "the whole ministry of Christ appeared to them to stand in contradiction to their Messianic expectation?
463. "It was in the Son of man that they were to recognize the ——— of ———."
464. The confession of Peter sees in Jesus the Messiah but even more—what was it?
465. The confession of Peter had both a human and divine origin—explain.
466. How was Jesus going to demonstrate His Messiahship?
467. It took two years to teach one great truth—what was it? What was the second great truth to be taught in the next few months?
468. What was the supreme purpose of His advent?
469. Why choose the three classes mentioned in vs. 31? Do we have their counterpart today? Discuss.
470. What hurt Peter the most—the words that Jesus would be killed or being called Satan? Discuss.

471. Satan repeated his temptation to Jesus through the words of Peter —explain.
472. Were there many who wanted to follow Him? Who? Why? How?
473. Explain the strong meaning of "deny himself."
474. Discuss in your own words the meaning of "the cross" as here ascribed to every disciple.
475. Even in spiritual matters "he who would save his life shall lose it" —please apply.
476. Multitudes lose their lives—discuss two or three areas where this loss takes place—with no gain—only loss!
477. In what way do we save our life?
478. Isn't the use of the word "soul" in vs. 37 an unfortunate one?— it has a wider use than the eternal nature of man—Discuss.
479. How is the temptation to be ashamed overcome?
480. What is the fundamental error in being ashamed?

9. THE TRANSFIGURATION 9:2-8

TEXT 9:2-8

"And after six days Jesus taketh with him Peter, and James, and John, and bringeth them up into a high mountain apart by themselves: and he was transfigured before them: and his garments became glistening, exceeding white; so as no fuller on earth can whiten them. And there appeared unto them Elijah with Moses: and they were talking with Jesus. And Peter answereth and saith to Jesus, Rabbi, it is good for us to be here: and let us make three tabernacles; one for thee, and one for Moses, and one for Elijah. For he wist not what to answer; for they became sore afraid. And there came a cloud overshadowing them: and there came a voice out of the cloud. This is my beloved Son: hear ye him. And suddenly looking round about, they saw no one any more, save Jesus only with themselves."

THOUGHT QUESTIONS 9:2-8

421. Six days after what?
422. Was there some particular reason for taking three men? For taking these particular three?
423. What mountain? Please locate the previous events on the map.
424. Please attempt a definition of the word "transfiguration."
425. What caused his garments to become so bright?
426. In what form did Moses and Elijah appear? How did Peter, James and John know Moses and Elijah?
427. Read Matt. 17:1-8; Luke 9:28-36 and tell of the topic of their conversation.
428. What was the immediate reaction on Peter, James & John, to the appearance of Moses and Elijah? Why?

429. Why did Peter make the suggestion of building booths? Please notice that Mark gives the reason.
430. When did the cloud overshadow them? What type of a cloud was it? (Read the parallel accounts)
431. Who spoke out of the cloud? Cf. II Peter 1:16.
432. Why was this declaration concerning the Son made at this particular time? What did it mean to those who heard it?
433. Where were Peter, James & John when Moses and Elijah disappeared i.e. where were they physically? Cf. parallel accounts.
434. What prompted Peter, James and John to look around? Cf. Parallel accounts.

COMMENT

TIME—Summer A.D. 29.

PLACE—Uncertain in the vicinity of Caesarea Philippi or Mt. Tabor—some think Mt. Hermon.

PARALLEL ACCOUNTS—Matt. 17:1-8; Luke 9:28-36.

OUTLINE—1. The time and the participants, vs. 2. 2. The event, vs. 3. 3. The appearance of Moses and Elijah, vs. 4. 4. Peter's unthinking suggestion, vs. 5, 6. 5. The voice of God, vs. 7. 6. They saw no one save Jesus, vs. 8.

ANALYSIS

I. THE TIME AND THE PARTICIPANTS, VS. 2.
   1. Six days after the events in Caesarea Philippi.
   2. Peter, James and John by themselves.
   3. Into a high mountain.

II. THE EVENT, VS. 3.
   1. His garments became exceedingly white and glistering.
   2. This is called a transfiguration or a "metamorphosis" (vs. 25)

III. THE APPEARANCE OF MOSES AND ELIJAH, VS. 4.
   1. Sudden, unexpected appearance.
   2. Moses and Elijah recognized.
   3. Talked with Jesus (about his coming death).

IV. PETER'S UNTHINKING SUGGESTION, VS. 5, 6.
   1. Peter was greatly impressed.
   2. Let us build three memorials.
   3. He was so filled with awe he did not know what to say.

V. THE VOICE OF GOD, VS. 7.
   1. A bright cloud covered them.
   2. The voice spoke out of the cloud—"This is my beloved Son: hear ye him."

VI. THEY SAW NO ONE SAVE JESUS, VS. 8.
   1. The disappearance was sudden.

2. Jesus touched them as they were prostrate only then did they know Moses and Elijah had disappeared.

EXPANATORY NOTES

I. THE TIME AND THE PARTICIPANTS.

"2. *after six days.*) In the note on Matt. 17:1, it has been observed that these days were probably passed in the neighborhood of Caesarea Philippi. To the reasons there given, it may be added (1) There is no indication of a change of place: but Mark never omits to notice our Lord's arrival at, or departure from, any place; he has a regular formula for both "He came to," "He went forth," cf. chh. 1:14, 21, 35; 2:1, 13; 3:7; 4:35; 5:1; 6:1, 32, 53; 7:24, 31; 8:10, 13, 22, 27. The beginning of the journey to this district is distinctly marked in ch. 8:27, the termination in ch. 9:30. (2) The space of six days for the sojourn is not more than might be expected, considering the special object of our Lord's journey and the novelty and paramount importance of the truths which He there prepared the minds of His disciples to receive.

There is, therefore, little room for doubt as to the scene of the Transfiguration: Tabor being out of the question, it must have been some considerable height in the immediate vicinity. Not, however, as Dr. Thomson supposes, Mount Panium, a lower spur of the chain of heights, of which the summit would be within sight of the followers of Jesus. We read, *"He leadeth them up* (words which denote a steep and difficult ascent, such as Dr. Tristram describes in his visit to Lake Phiala) *to a high mountain."* Which height cannot, of course, be determined; but, considering the special relation of Mount Hermon to Palestine, commanding a prospect over its whole extent, visible in its snowy splendour from every district, and bearing in mind the last view of Moses from a corresponding height over the promised land, we can scarcely resist the conclusion, to which late travellers and critics have been led, that the supernatural transaction took place on one of its loftiest peaks.

transfigured.) Literally, "He was changed in form." This may be illustrated by Phil. 2:6, "being in the form of God;" for the radiant form of the Transfiguration was an effulgence of the Divine glory."

II. THE EVENT

"3. *exceeding, white.*) St. Matthew, more forcibly, "as the light;" the pure, essential light of the Godhead.

as snow). Possibly, as *Dean Stanley* suggests, a reference to the snow of Hermon; but the words are not found in the oldest MSS, and are properly omitted in late critical editions.

no fuller on earth). The comparison may seem to modern ears somewhat strange; but it is just one which would have been used by Dante, who, like Mark, always endeavours to make his readers vividly realize objective facts. Mark, however, has a still higher aim; he would mark the difference between earthly and heavenly brightness. The "fuller on earth" restores material clothing to its natural whiteness: the heavenly Fuller gives perfect purity. Cf. Mal. 3:2."

III. THE APPEARANCE OF MOSES AND ELIJAH.

IV. PETER'S UNTHINKING SUGGESTION.

"6. *For he wist not.*) Luke has, "not knowing what he said." Our Evangelist adds the explanation; the words were spoken in bewilderment and great terror. Critics, therefore, are not justified in imputing to the apostle a weak or superstitious feeling, as though he held it fortunate that he and the other apostles were there to prepare tabernacles for the heavenly visitants, or that he expressed a desire to remain there, devoting his life to monastic contemplation, much less, as some have suggested, as though he were shrinking from the Cross. We have, at the most, a touch of nature: Peter then, as usual, seeking to give expression to his feelings in hasty outward action."

V. THE VOICE OF GOD.

"7. *that overshadowed.*) The cloud, as Matthew remarks, was bright; but brightness is the Divine veil. "His brightness was as the light; there was the hiding of His power."

my beloved Son.) Matthew adds, "in whom I am well pleased." So also Peter, in his second Epistle, ch. 1:17. It is not easy to account for the omission here."

VI. THEY SAW NO ONE SAVE JESUS.

"8. Here Mark omits to notice the coming and touch of Jesus, recorded by Matthew; but he has characteristic and graphic expressions, which may suggest both. *Suddenly,* as though startled by the touch of Jesus, *they looked round about*—a word almost peculiar to Mark, implying searching or curious look; and at the end of the verse Mark adds the touching words, "with themselves:" a preparation for His great promise, "I am with you always"—not, as then, for a season only, but to the end of time." *(F. C. Cook)*

FACT QUESTIONS 9:2-8

481. Give two reasons for concluding the six days were spent in the district or neighborhood of Caesarea Philippi.

482. Why does Mr. Cook seem to favor Mt. Hermon as the place of the transfiguration?

483. In what sense are we to understand Jesus was changed in form? Cf. Phil. 2:6.

484. Why the detailed and repeated reference to the appearance of His clothes?

485. Why do some critics feel Peter was weak or superstitious? Explain.

486. Why mention the brightness of the cloud?

487. Isn't the pleasure of the Father inferred even though not stated? i.e. in the omission of the words "In whom I am well pleased"?

488. What does the word used by Mark—translated "looked round about" suggest?

10. THE DISCIPLES ASK ABOUT ELIJAH. 9:9-13.

TEXT 9:9-13

"And as they were coming down from the mountain, he charged them that they should tell no man what things they had seen, save when the Son of man should have risen again from the dead. And they kept the saying, questioning among themselves what the rising again from the dead should mean. And they asked him, saying, The scribes say that Elijah must first come. And he said unto them, Elijah indeed cometh first, and restoreth all things: and how is it written of the Son of man, that he should suffer many things and be set at nought? But I say unto you, that Elijah is come, and they have also done unto him whatsoever they would, even as it is written of him."

THOUGHT QUESTIONS 9:9-13

435. Why would the transfiguration mean more after the resurrection?

436. Had the three disciples heard of the approaching death of Jesus? —had any word of His resurrection been given?

437. Why inquire at this particular time about Elijah? Cf. Mal. 4:5, 6.

438. Who were the scribes mentioned in vs. 11?

439. In what sense had Elijah already come?

440. What was to be restored by Elijah?

441. In what way did Jesus associate His death with the coming of Elijah?

442. To whom did Jesus refer when He said Elijah had come?

443. Where was it written concerning the death of John the Baptist— Cf. 1 Kings 19:2, 10.

COMMENT

TIME—Summer A.D. 29 immediately after the transfiguration.

PLACE—Coming down from the mount of transfiguration.

PARALLEL ACCOUNTS—Matt. 17:9-13.

OUTLINE—1. The command for silence, vs. 9. 2. The thought of resurrection was strange to the disciples, vs. 10. 3. They ask about the coming of Elijah, vs. 11. 4. Jesus answers, vs. 12, 13.

ANALYSIS

I. THE COMMAND FOR SILENCE, VS. 9.
1. As they came down from the mount.
2. Tell no man what you have seen.
3. Wait to tell until I have been raised from the dead.

II. THE THOUGHT OF THE RESURRECTION WAS STRANGE TO THE DISCIPLES, VS. 10.
1. They thought on what Jesus said.
2. They asked among themselves what He might mean by "rising from the dead."

III. THEY ASKED ABOUT THE COMING OF ELIJAH, VS. 11.
1. If you are the Messiah (as we believe you are);
2. In light of your prediction of death and resurrection how is it said Elijah must come first?

IV. JESUS ANSWERS, VS. 12, 13.
1. It is true—Elijah must come first and restore all things.
2. It is also true that the Son of man must suffer and be rejected.
3. Elijah in the person of John the Baptist has come and they have treated him as predicted.

EXPLANATORY NOTES

THE DESCENT FROM THE MOUNT

"In what state of mind did the apostles return from beholding the glory of the Lord, and His ministers from another world? They seem to have been excited, demonstrative, ready to blaze abroad the wonderful event which ought to put an end to all men's doubts.

They would have been bitterly disappointed, if they had prematurely exposed their experience to ridicule, cross-examination, conjectural theories and all the controversy which reduces facts to logical form, but strips them of their freshness and vitality. In the first age as in the nineteenth, it was possible to be witnesses for the Lord without exposing to coarse and irreverent handling all the delicate and secret experiences of the soul with Christ.

Therefore Jesus charged them that they should tell no man. Silence would force back the impression upon the depths of their own spirits, and spread its roots under the surface there.

Nor was it right to make such a startling demand upon the faith of others before public evidence had been given, enough to make scepticism blameworthy. His resurrection from the dead would suffice to unseal their lips. And the experience of all the Church has justified that decision. The resurrection is, in fact, the centre of all the miraculous narratives, the sun which keeps them in their orbit. Some of them, as isolated events, might have failed to challenge credence. But authority and sanction are given to all the rest by this great and publicly attested marvel, which has modified history, and the denial of which makes history at once untrustworthy and incoherent. When Jesus rose from the dead, the whole significance of His life and its events was deepened.

This mention of the resurrection called them away from pleasant day-dreams, by reminding them that their Master was to die. For Him there was no illusion. Coming back from the light and voices of heaven, the cross before Him was as visible as ever to His undazzled eyes, and He was still the sober and vigilant friend to warn them against false hopes. They however found means of explaining the unwelcome truth away. Various theories were discussed among them, what the rising from the dead should mean, what should be in fact the limit to their silence. This very perplexity, and the chill upon their hopes, aided them to keep the matter close.

One hope was too strong not to be at least hinted to Jesus. They had just seen Elias. Surely they were right in expecting his interference, as the scribes had taught. Instead of a lonely road pursued by the Messiah to a painful death, should not that great prophet come as a forerunner and restore all things? How then was murderous opposition possible?

And Jesus answered that one day this should come to pass. The herald should indeed reconcile all hearts, before the great and notable day of the Lord come. But for the present time there was another question. That promise to which they clung, was it their only light upon futurity? Was not the assertion quite as plain that the Son of Man should suffer many things and be set at nought? So far was Jesus from that state of mind in which men buoy themselves up with false hope. No apparent prophecy, no splendid vision, deceived His unerring insight. And yet no despair arrested His energies for one hour.

But, He added, Elias had already been offered to this generation in vain; they had done to him as they listed. They had re-enacted what history recorded of his life on earth.

Then a veil dropped from the disciples' eyes. They recognized the dweller in lonely places, the man of hairy garment and ascetic life, persecuted by a feeble tyrant who cowered before his rebuke, and by the deadlier hatred of an adulterous queen. They saw how the very name of Elias raised a probability that the second prophet should be treated "as it is written of" the first.

If then they had so strangely misjudged the preparation of His way, what might they not apprehend of the issue? So should also the Son of man suffer of them.

Do we wonder that they had not hitherto recognized the prophet? Perhaps, when all is made clear at last, we shall wonder more at our own refusals of reverence, our blindness to the meaning of noble lives, our moderate and qualified respect for men of whom the world is not worthy.

How much solid greatness would some of us overlook, if it went with an unpolished and unattractive exterior? Now the Baptist was a rude and abrupt person, of little culture, unwelcome in king's houses. Yet no greater had been born of woman." *(G. A. Chadwick)*

FACT QUESTIONED 9:9-13

489. In what state of mind did the apostles return from beholding the glory of the Lord, and His ministers from another world?
490. What would have happened if they had told prematurely the events of the mount?
491. How would silence help the disciples?
492. Show how all other miracles relate to the resurrection.
493. Why was it that Jesus was thinking about His death upon coming down from the mount?
494. What Malachi 4:5, 6 said—what the scribes had said did not agree with what Jesus said—at least in the minds of the disciples—explain.
495. Are we to yet expect the return of Elijah? i.e. before the second coming of Christ?
496. When did the veil drop from the eyes of the disciples?
497. In what sense are we in danger of doing the same thing the three apostles did?

11. HEALING THE EPILEPTIC BOY 9:14-29

TEXT 9:14-29

"And when they came to the disciples, they saw a great multitude about them, and scribes questioning with them. And straight-way all the multitude, when they saw him, were greatly amazed, and running to him saluted him. And he asked them, What question ye with them? And one of the multitude answered him, Master, I brought unto thee my son, which hath a dumb spirit; and wheresoever it taketh him, it dasheth him down: and he foameth, and grindeth his teeth, and pineth away: and I spake to thy disciples that they should cast it out: and they were not able. And he answereth them and saith, O faithless generation, how long shall I be with you? how long shall I bear with you? bring him unto me. And they brought him unto him: and when he saw him, straight-way the spirit tare him grievously; and he fell on the ground, and wallowed foaming. And he asked his father, How long time is it since this hath come unto him? And he said, From a child. And oft-times it hath cast him both into the fire and into the waters, to destroy him: but if thou canst do anything, have compassion on us, and help us. And Jesus said unto him, if thou canst! All things are possible to him that believeth. Straightway the father of the child cried out, and said, I believe; help thou mine unbelief. And when Jesus saw that a multitude came running together, he rebuked the unclean spirit, saying unto him, Thou dumb and deaf spirit, I command thee, come out of him and enter no more into him. And having cried out and torn him much, he came out: and the child became as one dead: insomuch that the more part said, He is dead, But Jesus took him by the hand and raised him up; and he arose, And when he was come into the house his disciples asked him privately saying. We could not cast it out. And he said unto them This kind can come out by nothing, save by prayer."

THOUGHT QUESTIONS 9:14-29

444. Where had Jesus and the three apostles left the other apostles?
445. What was it that caused the excitement and amazement when the people saw Jesus?
446. For what purpose had the scribes followed the disciples? About what were thcy disputing? Show the futility of such a dispute.
447. To whom is the question of vs. 16 addressed?
448. What is meant by the words of the father who said his son: "had a dumb Spirit"?

449. How do we know this boy was suffering from epilepsy? Cf. Matt. 17:15—Are we to conclude that epilepsy is caused by demon possession? Explain.
450. What is meant by the expression "pineth away"?
451. Discuss the inability of the disciples as related to casting out this demon.
452. Who was the "faithless generation" of vs. 19?
453. Why the reaction of the evil spirit upon seeing Jesus?
454. Did Jesus know all about the boy? Why ask the father the question of vs. 21?
455. Did the father have some doubt as to whether Jesus could help him?
456. Jesus picked up the words of the father and made a special appeal —what was it?
457. How did the father interpret the words of Jesus? In what sense did he believe? In what sense didn't he believe?
458. Jesus hastened to perform the miracle—why?
459. Note how Jesus addressed the demon—what significance is there as to the power—nature and work of demons?
460. If the boy was dumb how could he cry out?
461. What is meant by the phrase "torn him"?
462. Was the boy dead when Jesus raised him?
463. What rebuke and lesson for the disciples were in the words of Jesus in vs. 29?

COMMENT

TIME—Summer A.D. 29.

PLACE—At the foot of the mount of transfiguration—in the district of Caesarea Philippi.

PARALLEL ACCOUNTS—Matt. 17:14-20; Luke 9:37-43.

OUTLINE—1. The place and the people of the healing, vs. 14, 15. 2. The occasion of the healing, vs. 16-18. 3. The healing, vs. 19-27. 4. The question of the disciples, vs. 28,29.

ANALYSIS

I. THE PLACE AND THE PEOPLE OF THE HEALING, VS. 14, 15.
   1. The nine disciples at the base of the mount questioning with the scribes; a great multitude gathered.
   2. Many were shocked to see Jesus—ran to him and greeted him.

II. THE OCCASION OF THE HEALING, VS. 16-18.
   1. Jesus asked about the point of the discussion.
   2. The father with his possessed son said he had asked for help from the disciples but could not get it.

III. THE HEALING, VS. 19-27.

1. The grief of Jesus because of their unbelief, vs. 19.
2. The son brought to Jesus—the demon convulsed him, vs. 20.
3. The sympathy of Jesus—the desperation of the father, vs. 21, 22.
4. All things are possible to him who believes–do you believe?—"Yea Lord, I believe—help thou my unbelief." vs. 23, 24.
5. Because the multitude was about to make a scene Jesus delayed no longer in the healing, vs. 25.
6. The final attempt of the demon to destroy the boy, vs. 26.

IV. THE QUESTION OF THE DISCIPLES, VS. 28, 29.

1. In someone's house the disciples asked—"why couldn't we do it"?
2. Jesus said, "you lacked the proper attitude to exercise healing power."

EXPLANATORY NOTES. 9:14-29.

I. THE PLACE AND THE PEOPLE OF THE HEALING.

"14-15. The time was the day after the Transfiguration (Luke), and the place was the foot of the mountain. Early in the day, probably, Jesus and the three came down, the three burdened and uplifted by their glorious secret; thinking, perhaps how Moses with shining face, and Joshua, came down Mount Sinai. It is to Peter, who was one of them, that we owe the mention of what *he saw* in coming down. (Instead of *he,* the revisers, on manuscript authority, read "they.") It was an excited throng listening eagerly to the discussion of "scribes" (not *the scribes*) with the nine apostles and any other disciples who may have been present. How vivid is the picture of the effect of Jesus' approach!—the excitement, the amazement, the instantaneous turning away from the one object of interest to him.—*Greatly amazed,* or awestruck; not, so far as we can judge, from any peculiarity in his appearance, as if some light of the glory were still shining in his face, as when Moses drew near to Israel at the foot of the mountain (Ex. 34:29-35), for, if that had been the case, we should certainly have heard of it; and such a shining, too, would have defeated the purpose of concealment. Rather was it because he was the person of whom they were talking, and they were at once delighted and impressed by a certain sense of solemnity by the appearing of him who had never failed in a work of miraculous healing.—The eager interest with which they all turned from futile discussion and failure to the Mighty One appears in their running to meet him."

II. THE OCCASION OF THE HEALING.

"16-18. But he cared for his own and came down like a father to his children in trouble, asking the crowd, and especially the scribes, what they were discussing with his friends. He knew their weakness, and saw that they were perplexed and defeated. They were saluting him with welcome after his absence—not the nine only, but the multitude—when he broke in with his question.

The answer came from the most interested, and the one who had the best right to tell the story. *One of the multitude.* Matthew says that he "came kneeling," and Luke that he "cried out" with his request.—*I have brought unto thee my son, which hath a dumb spirit*— i.e. a spirit that makes its victim dumb; so in Matt. 9:32, and 12:22. When Jesus addressed the spirit (verse 25), he spoke to it as *dumb and deaf,* perhaps because of what he had observed in addition to what the father told him. —The additional symptoms described in verse 18 are those of violent convulsions, and plainly they are those of epilepsy, which in this case was complicated with insanity. Luke uses the word *sparassein,* "to convulse," and Mark, at verse 20, the stronger compound word *susparassein.* Matthew says that the child was "lunatic," or epileptic; but he adds that the lunacy was the work of a demon. More particularly, when the demon seized the boy he tore or convulsed him, or, as some explain it, threw him to the ground; and then he foamed and gnashed his teeth, and the consequence was that he pined away or was steadily wasting. These are the symptoms of epilepsy, which was well known among the ancients, and was regarded by the Greeks and Romans as a sacred disease, brought on directly by supernatural power and of evil omen. The word "lunatic," or "moonstruck," is applied to the victim in this case, as often, probably because the attacks were associated with the recurrence of the full moon. The questions, both physiological and psychological, that are connected with the subject of demoniacal possession are full of difficulty; but nothing is more certain than that our Lord on many occasions, and most emphatically on this, recognized the presence of a personality distinct from that of the victim and commanded it away.

The man said, I have brought unto thee my son.—i.e. to the place where he supposed that Jesus was, because his company was there; brought him, apparently, half in hope and half in despair; this was the last resort, and he came to it without much faith.—But Jesus was not there; probably the man came in the cool of the morning, when Jesus and the three were about coming down from the mountain. *And I spake to thy disciples, that they should cast him out; and they could not.* In Luke, "I entreated thy disciples." Their inability is often explained by the fact that Jesus was not with them, but they had cast out many demons in his absence when he sent them forth for such work (chap. 6:13). Then, however, they were sent; and perhaps the lack of the consciousness of mission now embarrassed them. The three leading apostles, too, were absent, and perhaps the company at the foot of the mountain felt itself to be really the less, though actually the larger. No doubt, also, the severity of the case gave them pause. Their confidence was not strong enough to bear the sense of publicity and of being tested that came with the challenge; for the scribes at once followed up their failure, plying them with questions that must have made them most uncomfortable. The penalty of unbelieving fear is confusion. (See Jer. 1:17.) Nor was there much to help them in the faith of the father."

III. THE HEALING.

"19. *He answereth him, and saith.* The revisers' text, more correctly, "He answereth them and saith." Not to the afflicted father, but to the inefficient disciples.—*O faithless generation!* Not now "of little faith;" in Matthew and Luke, "Faithless and perverse generation." Here expressly, as in chap. 8:18 implicitly, he ranks his own disciples with the generation to which they belong, since he finds in them the ordinary unbelief. They ought, he implies, to have been able to cast out the evil spirit. Perception of the sadness of the case probably repressed their faith; but it ought to have aroused their compassion, and their compassion ought to have increased their sense of the possibility of healing through the grace of Christ. Our Saviour is exacting in the expectation that his friends will be in possession of the spiritual gifts and graces that he offers them. His almost impatient question means, "How long shall this generation, whose unbelief I am learning so thoroughly, vex me so? How long must I live among the faithless?"—But he ends with *Bring him unto me.* The Mighty One now takes hold where the weak have failed.

20. The sufferer was brought, but the sight of the great Healer maddened the malign spirit; so that the boy went into a violent convulsion and *wallowed foaming* on the ground. Was it the dumbness of the victim that prevented such confession as that of chap. 1:34; 3:11; 5:7? There was no confession, and no vocal objection or entreaty on the part of the spirit.

21, 22. The sad sight arrested even the Healer's mind in the midst of his act of mercy. Compassion was prompting the act, and one would think compassion would urge him on to finish it. But nowhere does the true human thoughtfulness of Jesus appear more plainly; he looked on pityingly while the boy suffered, and compassion even stopped him for a moment while he tenderly inquired how long the infliction had been upon him.—The naturalness of this pause is inimitable; and not less so is the father's answer. We can hear in it the tones of anxiety and despair, and of eagerness for the utmost that can be done. *Of*—or from—*a child.* Then, apparently, the boy had passed beyond early childhood, though in verse 24 he is called by the diminutive name *paidion,* "a young or little child."—*And ofttimes it hath cast him into the fire, and into the waters to destroy him.* But it has been baffled thus far. This demoniac had more watchful friends than the one at Gergesa (chap. 5:3), who had no home but in the tombs. It was but too common in ancient times so to turn maniacs loose, and this boy was fortunate above many in having care and protection.—For healing at the hand of Jesus the father had strong desire, but very little faith. *If thou canst do any thing, have compassion on us, and help us,* counting himself in with the child as calling for the gift, but looking upon this as a kind of forlorn hope, concerning which he had as much despair as confidence. The disciples had failed; it was supposed that the Master had more power, but who could tell? *If thou canst do any thing* was much as he could say. Was not this one of the faithless generation? But there was more excuse for him than for the disciples, who had seen so much.

23. As by the revisers, the word *believe* should be omitted. It was doubtless added by copyists, though very early, to complete an imperfect construction and explain a sentence which without some help they could not understand. With the word omitted, Jesus took up the father's words, "If thou canst do any thing for us," or rather, merely, *If thou canst,* indicates, moreover, that the quoted words form grammatically a part of his sentence. We have not an indignant exclamation, as if he had said in amazement, "If thou canst!" and we have not a question, as if he had asked, "Do you say, If thou canst?" rather did he mean, "As for that if thou canst of thine, that *ei dune,* all things are possible (*dunata*) to him that believeth." The play upon the words (*dune, dunata*) cannot be reproduced in English, except very imperfectly, but it is something like, "As for that if thou canst of thine, all things can be to him that believeth." By this he means, "You have inquired about ability and whether any help is possible, but you have misplaced the question. The question of ability is in you, not in me. Faith is the secret of ability and of possibility. The power is sufficient on my part; is it on yours? I can give, but can you receive?" Yet the thought is expressed, not so much reprovingly as cheeringly; for the conclusion is not a severe one, but rather the hopeful announcement of the boundless breadth of the possibilities

of faith. This is another way of saying, "Believest thou that I am able to do this?" but with a gracious hint that the man will do well to believe. So does the great Object of faith love to encourage faith. He loves to be trusted.

24. The father's answer was a cry strong and eager, but the words *with tears* are of doubtful manuscript authority. *Lord* should quite certainly be omitted, and the insertion of *thou,* which in the Greek is unexpressed, misrepresents the rapidity of the man's utterance in the eagerness of his impassioned prayer. "I believe, help my unbelief." The saying is commonly, perhaps, taken to mean, "I believe, but I desire to believe more worthily; increase my faith." This makes help to mean "remove" or "abolish"—a sense for which no good support can be found. If the man had meant to ask that his faith might be rendered equal to the occasion, one would not expect him to ask it in this ambiguous way; and especially is it certain that he would not use the same word, *help*, that he had just employed in quite another sense.—This word is repeated from the former prayer, *have compassion on us, and help us,* and naturally means, as there, "heal my son." So the thought is, "I believe, and yet my faith is scarcely worthy of the name; I hardly dare to call it faith or to plead by it as a believing man. Yet do not wait for something better, but grant my prayer, even to this faith which is no faith. I do believe; but if my belief is no better than unbelief, still heal my son. Do not sternly judge my faith, but help me as I am." There is no contradiction here, and scarcely even paradox, but only deep sincerity in the beginnings of faith, joined with the eagerness of strong desire for a special gift. This is an early "Just as I am," and a very rich and suggestive one. If the man had paused to study his own faith and to make it sufficient, and withheld his prayer till he could make it satisfactory, would he more have injured himself or grieved the Master? He was pleasing Jesus best when he ventured wholly on him, trusting all the defects of his faith to the mercy from which he was imploring help. "Just as I am" is the word most acceptable to him.

25-27. The excitement was rising, and it was time that the scene should be brought to an end, more especially as the father was now ready in heart to receive the gift for which he prayed. The form of exorcism employed in this case was the most elaborate and solemn of all that are recorded in the Gospels. *Thou dumb and deaf spirit.* So addressed with reference to its work upon the child, the effects of its agency.—*I charge thee. I* is emphatic in the Greek—"I, thou knowest who," as the spirit knew at chap. 1:24. The emphasis upon the pronoun is our Lord's solemn self-assertion in the spiritual realm.—*Come out of him.* The customary command; but the addition, *and enter no more into him,* is found here alone. It is pleasant to think that this exceptional command sprang from our Lord's perception of the exceptional severity of the case, and the more than usual interest that he seems to have taken in it.—The rage of a hostile will when compelled to yield vented itself in the final cry and convulsion; for here also the word is "convulsed." rather than *rent.*—How intensely vivid is the narrative in verses 26, 27—the prostration of the child, the whisperings of the spectators, the kindness of the Healer! *He took him by the hand, and lifted him up; and he arose.* Luke, and he alone, notes the amazement of the beholders at the mighty power or majesty of God. The same word is used in 2 Pet. 1:16 of the glory or majesty which the three disciples had seen in Jesus on the very night before this healing.—This is one of the many cases in which we would be thankful to see what has been hidden, and know the subsequent relations of this father and child to Jesus. Did the child appreciate the Healer and grow up into a holy Christian manhood? Were all the demons exorcised in his soul? Did the father grow in faith, as one ought after such a beginning?"

IV. THE QUESTION OF THE DISCIPLES.

"28, 29. This final reference to the failure of the disciples is omitted by Luke and given more fully by Matthew who adds here a saying about the power of faith similar to that which followed the blighting of the fruitless tree (Mark 11:23). *When he was come into the house,* or "home," to the temporary home that the company had in that region.—*Why could not we cast him*—rather, "it"—*out*? The question had already been answered by the exclamation, *O faithless generation!* in verse 19, but they were not quick to take reproof, and this inquiry was one of the many illustrations of their slowness, with which he had to be patient. Yet perhaps unbelief never fully understands its own failures, but supposes there must be some reason for them to be sought.—*This kind* (of demons) *can come forth by nothing but by prayer and fasting* (some manuscripts omit *and fasting*)—i.e. This is an extreme case, one that can be made to yield only to faith nourished by the earnest use of all the means of strength. Prayer is recognized as the first great spiritual agency; and if the reference to fasting is genuine, our Lord associates with prayer self-denial, regarded, evidently, as the fitting means of attaining a holy self-command. Fasting in itself, considered as an end, would certainly command his instantaneous and unutterable contempt, as did the many performances of a similar kind that came under his notice; and fasting in general received from him such comments as showed that he esteemed it not very highly. But prayer and self-control go harmoniously together as the means by which an efficient faith may best be sought." (W. N. Clarke).

FACT QUESTIONS 9:14-29

498. What is the peculiar value of Mark's narrative of the healing of this demoniac?
499. How is the genuineness of this record observed? Why is this important?
500. How would any shining or glow on the face of Jesus have defeated the purpose of concealment?
501. Why were the people so eager and happy about the appearance of Jesus?
502. Who was best qualified to answer the question of Jesus as of vs. 16?
503. Specifically describe the illness of the boy.
504. In what sense was the boy "moonstruck"?
505. Describe the characteristics of epilepsy.
506. Our Lord on many occasions, and most emphatically recognized one fact about demon possession—what was it?
507. In what sense had the father brought his boy to Jesus? Hadn't the disciples cast out demons before? (6:13) Why not here?
508. Jesus classified His apostles with others in calling them a "faithless generation." Why? Cf. 8:18.
509. Why didn't the evil spirit confess the diety of Jesus? Cf. 1:34; 3:11; 5:7.
510. What caused Jesus to pause in the midst of healing the boy to ask a question of the father?
511. If the demon cast the boy into water how is it he did not drown?
512. Show how there was more excuse for the faithlessness of the father than for the disciples.
513. Explain just how Jesus used the words of the father—: "If thou canst."
514. The answer of the father is commonly understood to mean—: "I believe, but I desire to believe more worthily; increase my faith."—but this is not the true or whole meaning—what is the meaning?
515. Show how the expression "Just as I am" fits the father.
516. What word was emphasized in the charge of Jesus to the evil spirit? Why?
517. Why did Jesus use the words—"and enter no more into him."?
518. Show how intensely vivid the narrative is in vs. 26, 27.
519. What was the reaction of the healing—i.e. on the beholders?

520. Why did the apostles ask about their inability—? didn't they already know it was because of unbelief?
521. What are the efficient means by which faith may best be exercised?

12. THE RETURN TO GALILEE, AND THE RENEWED PREDICTION OF THE DEATH AND RESURRECTION 9:30-32

TEXT 9:30-32

"And they went forth from thence, and passed through Galilee; and he would not that any man should know it. For he taught his disciples, and said unto them, The Son of man is delivered up into the hands of men, and they shall kill him; and when he is killed, after three days he shall rise again. But they understood not the saying, and were afraid to ask him."

THOUGHT QUESTIONS 9:30-32

464. Please trace on the map the movement of the Lord.
465. What did Jesus want no man to know? i.e. in vs. 30.
466. In what sense was Jesus already being delivered up into the hands of men?
467. Why didn't the apostles understand the very plain words of Jesus about His death and resurrection? Show an example where we have been just as dull of hearing.
468. Why were they afraid to ask Him?

COMMENT

TIME—Autumn of 29 A.D.

PLACE—Turning southward from the district of Caesarea Philippi and Mount Hermon Jesus and His company return to their old home in Capernaum.

PARALLEL ACCOUNTS—Matt. 17:22, 23; Luke 9:43-45.

OUTLINE—1. Jesus departs the area—travels as secretly as possible, vs. 30. 2. He wants to have as much time as possible to teach His apostles of His coming passion, vs. 31. 3. Even when He plainly told them they did not understand, vs. 32.

ANALYSIS

I. JESUS DEPARTS THE AREA—TRAVELS AS SECRETLY AS POSSIBLE, VS. 30.
   1. The twelve apostles and Jesus leave the district of the transfiguration and healing.
   2. They travel through the province of Galilee (—upper and lower Galilee).
   3. Their movements were unannounced and sudden so as to enable Jesus to be alone with His apostles.

II. HE WANTED TO HAVE AS MUCH TIME AS POSSIBLE TO TEACH HIS APOSTLES OF HIS COMING PASSION, VS. 31.

1. He taught them personally.
2. He said, "The Son of Man is being delivered into the hands of men, and they shall kill Him; after His death He will rise from the dead on the third day."

III. EVEN WHEN HE HAD PLAINLY TOLD THEM THEY DID NOT UNDERSTAND HIM, VS. 32.

1. They heard but did not understand.
2. They were ashamed of their ignorance and therefore did not ask Him for an explanation.

EXPLANATORY NOTES

I. JESUS DEPARTS THE AREA—TRAVELS AS SECRETLY AS POSSIBLE.

"30. *and passed through Galilee.*) Or, "and were passing along through Galilee." The meaning is, that our Lord, with His disciples, then left the district of Caesarea Philippi, and on their journey passed through Upper Galilee. They probably crossed the Upper Jordan by the bridge or ford called Binat Jacob, below Lake Huleh, and thence followed the route to Capernaum.

and he would not.) The reason is given in the next verse. Our Lord would prevent a concourse of people—not, as some hold, because He was now in the territory of Herod Antipas, but because the disciples needed further instruction, specially concerning His death. St. Matthew's account is less full, but agrees with this. He says, "while they abode in Galilee," i.e. were no longer in the district of Caesarea Philippi."

II. HE WANTED TO HAVE AS MUCH TIME AS POSSIBLE TO TEACH HIS APOSTLES OF HIS COMING PASSION.

III. EVEN WHEN HE HAD PLAINLY TOLD THEM THEY DID NOT UNDERSTAND HIM.

"32. This verse gives additional information. St. Matthew notices the deep sorrow of the disciples; St. Mark says that they still failed to understand the saying. He uses the imperfect tense throughout denoting the continued or repeated result of His teaching. If the disciples understood what was meant by suffering and death, they could not reconcile it with what they knew of His Person, and were probably at an utter loss as to the sense in which He was to rise again: whether it implied entrance into a higher state, or restoration to common life. The narrator evidently feels that the fear to inquire, through natural and evincing reverence, was detrimental to them, showing an imperfect appreciation of His character and of their duty." (F. C. Cook)

FACT QUESTIONS 9:30-32

522. Trace the route of our Lord from Caesarea Philippi to Capernaum.
523. Why do some hold that since Jesus was in the territory of Herod Antipas He wanted to remain in secret?
524. Why were His Words concerning His death hard to reconcile to what they knew of His life?

13. THE CHILDLIKE SPIRIT 9:33-43

TEXT 9:33-43

"And they came to Capernaum: and when he was in the house he asked them, What were ye reasoning in the way? But they held their peace: for they had disputed one with another in the way, who was the greatest. And he sat down, and called the twelve; and he saith unto them, If any man would be first, he shall be last of all, and minister of all. And he took a little child, and set him in the midst of them: and taking him in his arms, he said unto them, Whosoever shall receive one of such little children in my name, receiveth me: and whosover receiveth me, receiveth not me, but him that sent me.

John said unto him, Master, we saw one casting out devils in thy name: and we forbade him, because he followed not us. But Jesus said, Forbid him not: for there is no man which shall do a mighty work in my name, and be able quickly to speak evil of me. For he that is not against us is for us. For whosoever shall give you a cup of water to drink, because ye are Christ's, verily I say unto you, he shall in no wise lose his reward. And whosoever shall cause one of these little ones that believe on me to stumble, it were better for him if a great millstone were hanged about his neck, and he were cast into the sea. And if thy hand cause thee to stumble, cut it off: it is good for thee to enter into life maimed, rather than having thy two hands to go into hell, into the unquenchable fire."

THOUGHT QUESTIONS 9:33-43

469. Didn't Jesus know of what they reasoned on the way? Why ask them?
470. Had anything happened in the experience of the apostles which would suggest the topic of greatness in the kingdom? Discuss.
471. What confession was made by the silence of the apostles?
472. Why call the twelve to come close to Him?
473. Show how the very nature of the desire to be first would place such a person last in the kingdom of Christ?
474. What principle is at work in the one who wants to serve all that makes him first of all?
475. Name two qualities of a child to be much desired by the citizen of Christ's kingdom.

476. Please explain how receiving a child relates to receiving Christ?
477. Discuss the meaning of the word "receive" as here used.
478. What possible connection do the words of John in vs. 38 have to do with what Jesus said in vs. 37?
479. These disciples fell into the terrible sin of sectarianism—show how.
480. When and where had the apostles seen such a man?
481. How was such a one enabled to cast out demons?
482. Was it wrong for this unknown disciple to cast out demons? Why did John think it was wrong?
483. What principle is involved in the words of Jesus in vs. 39-41 which is applicable to us today?
484. "For he that is not against us is for us." is this always absolutely true? Discuss.
485. Why the illustration of the cup of cold water?
486. Is there any connection between offending the little ones and forbidding one to cast out demons or giving a cup of water in the name of Christ? Please *think* on this question.
487. Who are the "little ones" of vs. 42?
488. What is the meaning of "stumble" as here used?
489. Show how mention of sinking into the water of the sea fits the place where it was said.
490. In what sense could the hand be the cause of sin? What basic lesson is taught here?
491. Isn't Jesus suggesting rather drastic action to avoid sinning? Is it practiced today? Discuss.
492. What is the meaning of "life" and "hell" as used in vs. 43-47.
493. Give your own meaning of vs. 48, 49.
494. Show how vs. 50 relates to what has preceded.

COMMENT

TIME.—The autumn of A.D. 29; probably five or six weeks after the last insident.

PLACE—The place of this event is Capernaum, "the Lord's own city," on thc northwest shore of the Sea of Galilee, to which he had now returned from the neighborhood of Caesarea Philippi, on the head waters of the Jordan.

PARALLEL ACCOUNTS.—Matt. 18:1-14; Luke 9:46-50.

LESSON OUTLINE—1. Who shall be Greatest? 2. Bigotry in the Kingdom. 3. Christ's Care of the Little Ones.

ANALYSIS

I. WHO SHALL BE GREATEST? VS. 33-37.
 1. Disputing about Pre-eminence. Mark 9:1, 2; Matt. 18:1; Luke 9:46; 22:24.
 2. The Path to True Greatness. Mark 9:35; 10:35-40; Matt. 20:26-27.
 3. The Child as a Text. Mark 9:36, 37; 10:13-16; Matt. 18:2.

II. BIGOTRY IN THE KINGDOM. VS. 38-41.
 1. A confession of Bigotry. Mark 9:38; Luke 9:49, 50; Num. 11:26-29.
 2. Bigotry Rebuked. Mark 9:39, 40; 1 Cor. 12:3; Num. 11:29.
 3. No Good Deed Lost. Mark 9:41; Matt. 10:42.

III. CHRIST'S CARE OF THE LITTLE ONES. VS. 42, 43, 44-50.
 1. Offending the Little Ones. Mark 9:42; Matt. 18:6; Luke 17:1.
 2. Cutting off Offenses. Mark 9:43; Matt. 5:29; 18:8; Deut. 13:6.
 3. Punishment for offenders. 44-50.

INTRODUCTION

The great revelations of Caesarea Philippi, considered last were followed by the manifestation of the glory of the Savior on the Mount of Transfiguration, related in Mark 9:2-13, and parallel passages, and this wonderful event was evidently succeeded by a few weeks of partial retirement, during which the Lord sought to impress upon his apostles the great truths that had been so recently revealed. Shortly after the Transfiguration he healed a lunatic child (Mark 9:14-32), somewhere among the foot-hills of Mt. Hermon; and then, probably crossing the Jordan near its sources, he would enter the northern parts of Galilee, and thus journey towards Capernaum. Matthew's language (Matt. 17:22), "And they abode in Galilee," implies that some time was spent there instructing the disciples in the truths he had just opened to them. During these journeyings, and probably just before their arrival at Capernaum the dispute referred to in the lesson had arisen among the disciples.

EXPLANATORY NOTES.

I. WHO SHALL BE GREATEST?

33. *And he came to Capernaum.* On his return from his journey to Northern Galilee, from the neighborhood of Caesarea Philippi and the Mount of Transfiguration. During his absence he had been confessed and had acknowledged himself as the Christ. Though this was followed by his declaration that he must be crucified, yet his disciples had so little conception of the true nature of his kingdom that they expected a speedy establishment of a royal Messianic throne on the earth with the various accompaniments of earthly royalty. Not free from earthly ambition, a strife

had arisen among them as to which of them should be the great ministers of the Messianic King. This had occurred on the way back to Capernaum. The Lord had taken no part in it; they no doubt sought to conceal their dispute from him, but after their return and they had entered into the house where he was abiding he suddenly startled them by demanding the cause of their dispute. He asked, not for information, but as an introduction to the lesson he sought to impress.

34. *But they held their peace.* Deep shame kept them silent, and that silence was the most eloquent confession of their sinful ambitions. *Who should be the greatest.* Who should occupy the chief position under the King—the position of prime minister, as it were, in the kingdom that they thought he was about to inaugurate.—*Morison.* What seductive dreams lay for Galilean fishermen in their being commissioned by the Messiah, as his confidential friends, and the first dignitaries of his kingdom! They had as yet no other notion of the kingdom that was shortly to appear than that it would be a temporal one; that their Master was to become a powerful prince, with places, honors, wealth, at his command.

35. *And he sat down.* As teachers did while teaching. The lesson, which touched the fundamental principle of the Christian life, was impressed formally and with all solemnity. *And called the twelve.* To come close to him. He wanted all of them to hear him. *If any man desire to be first, the same shall be last of all.* Simply because the desire to be first, self-seeking, is exactly opposite to the spirit which is the law of Christ's kingdom, the spirit of love, of self-denial, of helpfulness of others, of humility. Therefore the more any one has of the desire to be first, the less he has of Christ's kingdom. So that the very desire to be first makes him last by the very nature of things. *And servant of all.* Despotism, self-seeking, ambition, ever make a man a slave. No one is so much a slave as he who desires to be first of all. He is a slave to his ambition, to the whims and opinions of other people, to circumstances. But voluntary service in the kingdom of love, and under the impulse of humility and self-denial, makes a man a spiritual power, gives him an unconscious and blessed greatness. To be truly great one must (1) forget himself in his work, (2) be humble instead of conceited, and (3) be a helper of his race, or the servant of all. Paul, Luther, Washington and Lincoln were the servants of humanity.

36. *And he took a child.* Matthew's account indicates that the disciples asked him a question concerning who should be greatest, or the grounds of greatness in his kingdom. The Lord answers by an object lesson. He called a child (Matthew) and first placed the child in the midst, and then took it in his arms, possibly drawing a lesson for his disciples from its

ready submission and trustfulness. *Set him in the midst.* As an illustration; as a living parable. Matthew says that he went on to say, "Except ye be converted and become as little children, ye shall not enter into the kingdom of heaven." They not only should not be *first,* but they should not enter at all, if they indulged their present spirit. Chrysostom says: "For such a little child is free from pride, and the mad desire of glory, and envy, and contentiousness, and all such passions, and having many virtues—simplicity, humility, unworldliness—prides itself on none of them; having a two-fold severity of goodness—to have these things and not to be puffed up about them."

37. *Whosoever shall receive one of such children in my name, receiveth me.* There is scarcely a better test of a Christian's character than his bearing toward children and the childlike. Our Lord sets a little child in the midst of his disciples everywhere—in the family, in the Sunday-school, in the congregation, in the community; that child is our Lord's representative, and the object of his watchful care. Just in proportion as there would be a readiness to receive our Lord as he is, if he were visibly present in person, is that child welcomed in heartiness and cared for tenderly. How does that father treat his children, and his neighbor's children? How does that pastor minister to the children of his flock? How does that church provide for the children of its congregation and membership? How are those Christian citizens looking after the children of their community? These are questions which we may suppose our Lord to be asking as he searches the fidelity of his professed followers.—*Trumbull. In my name.* Receiving in my name is serving with Christian love, and as belonging to Christ. Influenced by regard to my name. We should lay emphasis on this expression. *Receiveth me.* Observe that the true way to receive Christ is to receive into our hearts, for Christ's sake, those who need the hospitality of our sympathies, as the way to serve Christ is by serving the needy and suffering (Matt. 25:40).—*Abbott. Receiveth . . . him that sent me.* When we love or receive him who was one with the Father, we enter into fellowship with him who is the Supreme and Eternal Love. Compare John 14:10, 23.

II. BIGOTRY IN THE KINGDOM

38. *And John answered him.* The words were so far an "answer" to what our Lord had said, that they were suggested by it. The disciple desired to show, as in self-vindication, that he not only "received" his Master, but that he was unwilling to "receive" any who did not openly follow him as a disciple.—*Ellicott.* The expression, "in my name," seems to have suggested to John a sudden question. They had

seen, he said, a man who was casting out devils in Christ's name; but since the man was not one of them, they had forbidden him. Had they done right?—*Farrar. We saw one.* The disciples had shortly before returned to Christ from their first missionary tour, in which they were empowered to cast out devils (Matt. 10:8). The man here referred to they probably met during this tour. He must have been a disciple of Christ, who was enabled by his faith, yet without a commission, to cure the possessed.—*Abbott. Casting out devils in thy name.* Really, and not in a wrong spirit, as did the Jewish exorcists (Acts 19:13, 14); for it was done *in thy name.* Such workers as this man believed in him, or they would not have used his name. *And he followeth not us.* What perplexed John was, that one not belonging to the apostolic band should have wrought precisely the miracle which stood foremost among the signs of apostleship; that which the disciples themselves had so lately attempted, but failed to work. See Mark 9:18, 23. Nor are we able to explain the case because we know nothing more of the man or circumstances than is here stated. *And we forbade him.* Hindered him, so far as blaming him, and insisted on the abandonment of the exercise of his gift.

39. *Forbid him not.* He neither praises nor blames him for following an independent course, and not working with his disciples. He simply declares that he must not be forbidden, and that those who work the same kind of work that we do should be regarded not as enemies, but allies. Thousands, in every period of church history, have spent their lives in copying John's mistake. They have labored to stop every man who will not work for Christ in their way from working for Christ at all. —*Ryle. No man which shall do a miracle in my name.* He who does a mighty work in the name of Christ cannot be an enemy of the Lord. The principle inculcated forbids discouraging any work, by whomsoever undertaken, minister or layman, man or woman, which is really accomplishing spiritual results.—*Abbott.* If we see any one really accomplishing results that are for Christ it is wrong to hinder his work.

40. *For he that is not against us is on our part.* Note the social *us.* The Savior graciously associates the disciples with himself. On another occasion (Matt. 12:30) he said, "He that is not with me is against me." There is no belt or border-land between right and wrong. He who is not good is bad; he who is not bad is good. In the highest sphere Christianity and goodness are identical. Christ is impersonated goodness.—*Morison.*

III. CHRIST'S CARE FOR HIS LITTLE ONES.

41. *For whosoever shall give.* The idea is, that, if so small a service as is here referred to goes not unrewarded, much more will the ejection of a demon in his name be approved and rewarded of him. *A cup of water.* Here mentioned as the cheapest of all bodily refreshments, and therefore suitable to represent the smallest act of kindness done by man to man. *In my name.* With this motive, because he belongs to Christ; with the desire to serve Christ, and honor him, and express his love to him. *He shall not lose his reward.* He shall be treated as if it were done to Christ himself. It will be accepted as an expression of love and honor to his Master.

42. *Whosoever shall offend* (cause to stumble) *one of these little ones that believe in me.* The weakest and feeblest of God's flock, not merely the children, but the little ones, in intellectual and spiritual power and in ecclesiastical position and earthly honor. The child yet nestling in his arms, and furnishing the text for his remarks, he warned them of the awful guilt and peril of offending, of tempting, of misleading, of seducing from the paths of innocence and righteousness, of teaching any wicked thing, or suggesting any wicked thought to one of those little ones. *Better that a millstone were hanged about his neck.* We are taken, in imagination, into the presence of a certain dreadful scene. We see a millstone attached to a man's neck. The fastening, passing through the central perforation of the stone is made secure. It is a sad sight. Yet, turning from another scene, we say, "This is better." It is better than that the same man should act the part of a seducer, and entrap a childlike follower of Jesus. *And were cast into the sea.* Which was within sight. Death is a less evil than sinning—much less than causing others to sin; for one kills the body, the other the soul. No language or figures could more powerfully portray the deep interest of the Master in the little children. How terrible to lead them astray!

43. *If thy hand offend.* Cause you to sin or stumble; ensnare you into evil. Are we to understand these passages literally? No, certainly not. The meaning is, if an object dear as the right eye, and useful as the right hand, stand between you and your progress to heaven, and your complete surrender to Christ, that object, however dear, you are to part with.—*Cumming. Hand.* The temptation to do what is wrong—forgery, stealing, murder. *Eye.* Lusting, coveting. *Foot.* Going into forbidden ways. He goes on to warn them that no sacrifice could be too great if it enabled them to escape any possible temptations to put such stumbling-blocks in the way of their own souls or the souls of others.—*Farrar. Into life maimed.* The meaning is, not that any man is in such a case that he hath

no better way to avoid sin and hell; but, if he had no better, he should choose this. Nor doth it mean that maimed persons are maimed in heaven; but, if it were so, it were a less evil.—*Richard Baxter. Into hell.* Not *Hades* but *Gehenna,* the place of eternal punishment. The name was derived from the valley of Hinnom near Jerusalem where refuse was burned.

"48. *where their worm dieth not.* Yet another strong figure, again in terms of Isa. 66:24, and expressing a future penalty that does not exhaust itself.

49. *every one shall be salted with fire.* Once more the connection hangs on a phrase, here 'fire'; but in this case the continuity of thought between 48 and 49 is deep and strong, far more so than in the next case, that of the 'salting' in 49 and the 'salt' in 50. The clause added by the A. V., 'and every sacrifice shall be salted with salt' (cf. Lev. 2:13), is no part of the original . . . The addition was originally an interpretation of the genuine text (which falls out in some early MSS.): then it was added to it. The genuine saying, a very striking one, seems connected with the preceding mention of a fire that is not quenched, thus: 'Yes, the fire, I say, is not quenched; for with fire—of one sort or another—all must, sooner or later, be salted.'

The key to its meaning is found probably in the Levitical regulation which provided that with all oblations salt was to be offered (Lev. 2:13), as the glossing addition rightly suggests. Salt was used in connection with the making of covenants (Lev. 2:13; Num. 18:19; 2 Chron. 13:5); and the sacrificial salt of the Levitical offerings was the symbol of the covenant-relation between God and Israel. It was interpreted by this time, at least, with reference to the properties of salt as a preservative against corruption in things apt to putrify, a preservative, however, with a stinging, painful effect on sentient life. In this respect it is like 'fire,' which also causes pain, yet it may be, wholesome and purifying pain; hence the combination of the two metaphors in the one idea 'salted with (purifying) fire.' To this discipline of suffering in one form or another, Jesus says, all men must submit, whether freely or by constraint. The form he here sets before his disciples, for their good, is that of discipline; voluntarily accepted for the sake of the true life, to be safeguarded thereby from corruption; and illustrations of this positive or cleansing function of moral fire have just been given in 43-47. But these are only special cases of the general principle of suffering as integral to the path of his disciples, as of their Master, which Jesus had set himself to bring home to them ever since he had hinted, while near Caesarea Philippi, at the Cross looming before him (see 9:31 f).

The best commentary on the whole saying is another equally striking, in Luke 12:49: 'I came to cast fire (of testing) upon the earth: and what will I, if it is already kindled?' There he adds that he has himslf to be 'baptized' with this kind of searching 'baptism' (cf. Matt. 3:11, for the metaphor, 'He shall baptize you with holy spirit and fire'), and is sore pressed or 'straitened' in spirit 'til it be fulfilled.' The context which precedes this in Luke (12:47 f.) makes the parallel most illuminative, teaching as it does that 'stripes' for servants will be 'few' or 'many,' according as their unreadiness for the Lord's arrival is accompanied by knowledge or ignorance of his declared purpose to return ere long, so that they should be ready for Him. The broad moral for all ('every one') is the necessity for practice of the sacrifice of self, that 'life' may be gained and loss escaped.

50. *Salt is good. lost its saltness.* The sweeping out of salt that has lost its virtue, and become useless or hurtful, is still, travellers tell us, a common sight in Palestine.

wherewith will ye season it? Salt once spoilt can never have its saltness restored. So if the qualities which make up the 'saltness' of the true disciple—fidelity at all costs of pain, self-abnegation, and the like—are turned to faithlessness and selfishness, what becomes of the discipleship which should save others from the corruption of worldliness and selfhood? There is no human source of 'saltness' capable of renewing it.

Have salt in yourselves. Keep the purifying sacrificial fire alive in your souls, and in particular let it burn up the egoism that destroys unity.

and be at peace one with another. Let the saving salt of fidelity to your Divine calling fulfill itself in brotherly relations with one another. So the words seem to bring us back to the disputing of the disciples (9:33) with which the conversation started. Selfish claims for the chief places destroy peace among men, and are not of the spirit of Jesus' disciples." (J. Vernon Bartlet).

FACT QUESTIONS 9:33-50

525. State two very important things that had happened during Jesus' absence from Capernaum.
526. What was the basic misconception of the disciples as it related to the Messianic kingdom?
527. What did the disciples mean by the use of the term "greatest"? Greatest what?
528. Was there any significance in the fact that He sat down?
529. The more one has a desire to be first the less he has of what?
530. State the two things the truly great one must do.
531. A little child is free from what undesirable qualities?

532. Why is it true that there is scarcely a better test of a Christian's character than his bearing toward children or the childlike?
533. In what sense was John in his comment of vs. 38 showing his self-vindication?
534. How was it possible to cast out demons without being one of the twelve or one of the seventy?
535. What does the principle laid down by Christ in vs. 39 inculcate?
536. In what sense is Christ "impersonated goodness"?
537. How does giving a cup of cold water relate to forbidding the casting out of a demon?
538. Relate the offending or stumbling of the little ones to the context.
539. Is death better than sin? Is this literally true?
540. If we are not to understand the passages of vs. 43, 44 literally how are we to understand them?
541. Explain the "hell" or "Gehenna" here mentioned by Christ.
542. In what sense does "the worm die not" in the place of eternal punishment?
543. Give your exegesis of vs. 49.
544. There seems to be two or three uses of the word "salt" in vs. 49, 50—discuss them.

SUMMARY 8:14-9:50

The two miracles recorded in the preceding section—the cure of the blind man at Bethsaida (viii. 22-26), and the casting out of the obstinate demon (ix. 14-29)—are additional demonstrations of the divine power of Jesus. They are not mere repetitions of former proofs, but they possess peculiar force in that the blind man was cured by progressive steps, each one of which was a miracle in itself, and in that the demon in question was one of peculiar power and obstinacy.

The foreknowledge of Jesus is again displayed in his two predictions concerning his own death (viii. 31-33; ix. 30-32), and with his foreknowledge, his predetermined purpose to submit to death at the hands of his enemies.

But the crowning argument of the section is contained in the account of the transfiguration. If the testimony of those who witnessed his scene is not false testimony, his divine majesty and his God-given right to be heard in all that he chooses to speak, are established beyond all possibility of a mistake.

End of Part First.

We have now reached the close of the first general division of Mark's narrative. Hitherto, after a few introductory statements in the first chapter (i. 1-13), all the incidents which he records occurred in Galilee, or in the regions immediately adjoining. Now the writer leaves Galilee, and returns to it no more. (*McGarvey*)

III. THE PEREAN MINISTRY 10:1-52

Jesus Leaves Galilee. 10:1 (on His way to Jerusalem)

TEXT 10:1

"And he arose from thence, and cometh into the borders of Judea and beyond Jordan: and multitudes come together unto him again; and, as he was wont, he taught them again."

THOUGHT QUESTIONS 10:1

495. Please note the expression: "he arose from thence" has more meaning than just a move from one place to another. What significance is there here?
496. Please locate this move on the map—just what is involved in "the borders of Judea"? Where is "beyond the Jordan"?
497. Refer to the parallel pasage in Luke. Explain the harmony—or lack of it.
498. What was the purpose in the gathering of the multitude?
499. Do the gospel writers indicate that teaching was the major work of Christ? Discuss.

EXPLANATORY NOTES

"1. *And he arose from thence, and cometh into the coasts of Judea by the farther,*" etc. It will be necessary to say a word or two respecting the sequence of events. Gresswell, with whose "Harmony" most commentators substantially agree, having inserted as the continuation of this discourse, as given in Matt. 18:10-35, the dealing with an offending brother, and St. Peter's question respecting how often he ought to forgive, and the parable of the Unmerciful Servant, then puts down the events from Jesus' going up to Jerusalem at the Feast of the Tabernacles in John 7:2, to the departure of the Lord, after His discourse respecting the Good Shepherd, to Bethany, beyond Jordan, where John first baptized (John 10:40). Either during this stay at Jerusalem, or at its conclusion, the Lord enters into a certain village, no doubt Bethany, near Jerusalem, where He is entertained by the sisters Martha and Mary (Luke 10:38). After this when in Bethany, beyond Jordan, he hears of the sickness of Lazarus, and returns to Jerusalem and raises him from the dead, then He again retires, but now into the "city called Ephraim" (John 11:54). Between this retirement and the final entry into Jerusalem occur most of the events recorded between Luke 10:1 and Luke 18:14, and at the account of the Lord's taking up and blessing the little children the three Synoptics again coincide (Matt. 19:13; Mark 10:13; Luke 18:15) and substantially continue to do so to the end.

We cannot then understand the word "thence" as referring to the place where the Lord had been speaking of the salt losing its savour, and was urging the Apostles to "have salt in themselves." It is quite necessary to understand it, so far as we are concerned, indeterminedly as referring to some place in Galilee not mentioned.

"Cometh into the coast of Judea by the farther side of Jordan," i.e., by Peraea. This was the second residence in Peraea, and so the Evangelist intimates, by twice making use of the word "again."

"And the people resort unto him *again;* and as he was wont he taught them *again.*"

A. JESUS IS QUESTIONED ABOUT MARRIAGE 10:2-12

TEXT 10:2-12

"And there came unto him Pharisees, and asked him, Is it lawful for a man to put away his wife? tempting him. And he answered and said unto them, What did Moses command you? And they said, Moses suffered to write a bill of divorcement and to put her away. But Jesus said unto them, For your hardness of heart he wrote you this commandment. But from the beginning of the creation, Male and female made he them. For this cause shall a man leave his father and mother, and shall cleave to his wife; and the twain shall become one flesh: so that they are no more twain, but one flesh. What therefore God hath joined together, let not man put asunder. And in the house the disciples asked him again of this matter. And he saith unto them, Whosoever shall put away his wife, and marry another, committeth adultery against her: and if she herself shall put away her husband, and marry another, she committeth adultery."

THOUGHT QUESTIONS 10:2-12

500. Where was Jesus when the Pharisees approached Him?
501. Read the parallel account in Matthew to understand the question was not only a matter of divorce but of the cause for divorce.
502. In what sense was this a trial question?
503. Read Deut. 24:1—Tell what relation this text has to the question.
504. Both Jesus and the Pharisees referred to Moses but with very different results—show why.
505. What is meant in vs. 5 by the statement "hardness of heart"?
506. Wasn't Moses compromising the law of God by writing the commandment of Deut. 24:1?
507. Why refer back to the conditions existing at the time of creation?
508. For what cause will a man leave his father and mother?
509. What is the meaning of the word "cleave" as here used?
510. Just how is the relationship of "one flesh" effected? In what sense are the two one?

511. When, where and how does God join the husband and wife together?
512. Is Jesus forbidding all divorce?
513. Discuss the force of the expression "put asunder."
514. Why did the disciples continue the question of the Pharisees?
515. Please show how completely and finally the words of Jesus answered the question.
516. Can marriage ever become adultery? When?
517. Are there any innocent persons in these acts of adultery? Discuss.

COMMENT 10:2-12

TIME—A.D. 30—Probably the month of March.

PLACE—On the farther side of the Jordan, near the borders of Judea.

PARALLEL ACCOUNTS—Matt. 19:3-12.

OUTLINE—1. The trial question, vs. 2. 2. The answer of Jesus, vs. 3-9. 3. The disciples ask further questions, vs. 10-12.

ANALYSIS

I. THE TRIAL QUESTION, VS. 2.
  1. Posed by Pharisees.
  2. Asked as a snare.
  3. Can a man divorce his wife? (for every cause)

II. THE ANSWER OF JESUS, VS. 3-9.
  1. What did Moses command you?
  2. Moses was very lenient as recorded in Deut. 24:1.
  3. This commandment was a concession for your weakness—and hardness of heart.
  4. From the beginning God created two to become one.
  5. What God has joined together man can not and should not divide.

III. THE DISCIPLES ASK FURTHER QUESTIONS, VS. 10-12.
  1. This occurred in a house.
  2. The reason a man should not divorce his wife (except for fornication) is because when he marries again he commits adultery against his wife.
  3. The same principle applies to the wife in regard to her husband.

EXPLANATORY NOTES

I. THE TRIAL QUESTION.

"2. The questioners are *the Pharisees*—omnipresent tempters!—and the old practice of trying to catch him by questions still survives.—*Is it lawful.* Perhaps not asked in the narrowest technical sense, as if calling for an interpretation of the Mosaic law, but more generally, asking the judgment of the Rabbi: "May a man put away his wife?" The law of divorce in Deut. 24:1 was not entirely plain in the statement of the admissible grounds of complaint against a wife, and the ambiguity had occasioned endless discussion. The schools of Shammai, the stricter, and Hillel, the more lax, contended about it, and the people were divided. Therefore, however Jesus might reply, his answer could be trusted to make him enemies. Moreover, he was in the territory of Herod, under whom the Baptist had suffered for his boldness in the matter of an adulterous marriage. Matthew's addition, "for every cause," was as nearly as possible the translation of the current phrase justified by the lax school of Hillel; and so the question meant, "Is the lax school right?"

II. THE ANSWER OF JESUS.

"3,4. His answer drove them back to their own authorities. The law under which all their discussions were, and ought to be, conducted was the law of Moses, and what he said must be first considered. *What did Moses command you?* was the first legitimate question. But their answer was evasive. They stated the permission as if it were unlimited, omitting all references to the occasions of divorce which the law recognized.

5-9. Yet he accepted their report of the law, imperfect as it was, without criticism. They had omitted the crucial point, the determination of occasions for divorce, and so would he. They had spoken of permission; of permission he would speak. Divorce was a permitted thing, and the permission was so vague that there might be difficulty in defining its limits. It was permitted, but why? *For the hardness of your heart he wrote you this precept.* The preposition means "on account of," or "out of regard for." The noun means "hard-heartedness;" "spiritual dullness and incapacity;" "unresponsiveness to God," amounting to inability to accept high motives. Moses wrote you this precept, said Jesus (in Matthew, "he suffered you to put away your wives"), because you were not up to the level of a better precept. He said that Moses wrote the precept; but, according to their view of the matter and according to his (see Mark 7:13), the legislation of Moses expressed the appointment of God. It was Jehovah himself who permitted them to put away their wives.—But this precept was not given because there was not a better one at hand. A better was provided in the constitution of man. *From the beginning of the creation*—from the very origin of things—*God,* the Creator, *made them male and female.* An exact quotation from Gen. 1:27, Septuagint. Verse 7 and half of verse 8 are exactly quoted from Gen. 2:24, Septuagint, though in Mark some manuscripts (and Tischendorf) omit *and cleave to his wife.*

This passage from the narrative of the Creation was cited to show that the distinction of sexes was originally constituted the ground of marriage. By this law marriage is the union of a male and a female of the human race; and it is such a union as shall form a new centre of life to both. For this cause—i.e. because he created them male and female—a man shall leave the parents, into natural unity with whom he was born, and find the centre for a new unity in his union with a fellow-being of the opposite sex. Thus the distinction of the sexes was given as the foundation of the family.—Now, the duration for which God intended this union may be inferred from his own testimony as to its closeness and completeness. This testimony Jesus now quotes—*and they twain shall be one flesh*—and then he adds his own emphatic restatement of the fact: *so then they are no more twain, but one flesh*—that is, the union that is founded on the relation of the sexes makes the two to be one flesh, makes each to be, physically, part and property of the other. Marriage has wrought an actual unity which is not to be broken. It is the union of one man and one woman, and the blending of life in sexual union establishes between that one man and that one woman a real unity. By establishing such a relation the Creator showed his intention that a union thus formed should be irrevocable and inviolable, to be legitimately terminated only by death."

In verse 9 is given the better precept that springs from this original order. The verb is in the aorist, not in the perfect; and the reference is not to special cases in which God *hath joined together* two given individuals, but to the original constitution of the race, in establishing which he *joined together* in permanent unity every pair who should ever come together in the union of sex with sex.—*What therefore God hath joined together, let no man put asunder.* That one flesh or one body (see 1 Cor. 6:16, where Paul expressly recognizes the truth that physical union establishes true and permanent unity) which has been formed in accordance with God's appointment in the creation of man, let not man put asunder.—Note the contrast between God and man: man may not break what God has made. Man may break this unity, either by personal unfaithfulness to the obligation of marriage or by contradictory enactments permitting dissolutions that God does not permit. Of the possible dissolution, for one cause, he speaks below.

This law of exclusive and permanent union was the original law of marriage; and this law Jesus reaffirms. But a lower law was given in that legislation which Jesus distinctly recognized as the work of God. Now, Jesus declares that that law was given because of the incapacity of men for this. He thus announces the imperfection of the Mosaic law—not only its incompleteness, but its imperfection—and asserts also its educational purpose. It was meant to train men for a better life than they could then accept. Accordingly, there was in the law a certain amount of what is called accommodation. "God often speaks and gives law, not as he himself is able to do, but as we are able to hear" (*Chrysostom,* on Ps. 95)—a sound principle, but always to be accompanied by this: "When God thus speaks and gives law, it is in order that he may make us able to hear all that he is able to say to us." We need have no difficulty in admitting that God has dealt in rudimentary instruction, and, so far, in inferior instruction, if only we keep steadily in view his purpose of moral education for men."

III. THE DISCIPLES ASK FURTHER QUESTIONS.

10-12. Mark alone tells of the later inquiry of the disciples. In Matthew the address to the Pharisees is continued, with the solemn assertion that he who puts away his wife, except for fornication, and marries another commits adultery. In Mark "except for fornication" is omitted; but it is sufficiently implied. The statement in both Gospels is that a man is charged with adultery when he enters into a new sexual union while the first is still unbroken— i.e. when he breaks the exclusive unity of flesh with his wife by an act of union with another. Of course an equal union of sexes can be broken by either member; and so the "except for fornication" is implied clearly enough in principle in Mark. Verse 12, indeed, distinctly enforces the principle of equal responsibility. The custom to which it alludes, of the wife putting away the husband, was a custom, not of Jews, but of Romans and of other Gentiles. Possibly Jesus saw that there was danger, under Roman influence, of its coming in among the Jews.—Here, in verses 11, 12, is our Lord's own answer to the original question, whether a man might put away his wife. It is, "No, unless she has already broken her unity with him." Sexual unfaithfulness forfeits the bond, but nothing else does.

The teaching of this passage is strong and conclusive for all who acknowledge the authority of Jesus Christ. The inviolability of marriage is grounded, not in any principles of expediency or advantage, right as these might be, but in its correspondence to the constitution of man as male and female. The sexual element in marriage makes of the two one flesh—i.e. it was meant that sexual union should be inseparable from permanent personal unity—and only by sexual unfaithfulness can the unity, once established, be broken. This is not to affirm that sexual unfaithfulness is necessarily more guilty than any other sin—a life-long course of drunkenness and abuse may be as guilty—but the sexual relation is the groundwork of the family, and its purity is absolutely essential to the physical and moral welfare of mankind. With good reason, therefore, God has made faithfulness in this relation the determining element in the perpetuity of marriage. To this divine appointment human laws should be made to correspond. Separations for other causes than adultery there may be, but dissolution of marriage, never. If it is said that such a law works hardship in many cases, the answer is that all laws that are for the general good sometimes work hardship while sin continues. But the purity and the permanency of the family are worth so much to mankind that individuals may well afford to suffer hardship rather than contribute to the overthrow of so precious an institution.

FACT QUESTIONS 10:2-12

545. Is the attitude of the Pharisees the same throughout the ministry of our Lord? Why?
546. Who was Shammai and Hillel—what school of thoughts did they represent? What reference in the Old Testament was of particular concern on the matter of divorce?
547. How was the question of the Pharisees framed in such a way to put Jesus in an undefendable position?
548. Why raise the question about Moses? Who raised it—see Matt. 19:7.
549. What is meant by "hardness of heart"?
550. What was originally constituted the ground for marriage?
551. Why mention the thought of the two becoming one? When does this occur?
552. How is the imperfection and incompleteness of the Mosaic law shown?
553. What is meant by saying that in the law of God "a certain amount of accommodation is found?"
554. How can it be said that the exception of divorce for fornication is inferred by Mark? Explain.
555. Does Jesus say a person guilty of sexual unfaithfulness is necessarily more guilty than any other sinner? Discuss.
556. Does Jesus add anything to the Mosaic law by saying a wife could put away her husband?
557. Why is the home the most precious institution in the world?

B. CHRIST'S LOVE TO THE YOUNG. 10:13-22

TEXT 10:13-22

"And they brought unto him little children, that he should touch them: and the disciples rebuked them. But when Jesus saw it, he was moved with indignation, and said unto them, Suffer the little children to come unto me; forbid them not: for of such is the kingdom of God. Verily I say unto you, Whosoever shall not receive the kingdom of God as a little child, he shall in no wise enter therein. And he took them in his arms, and blessed them, laying his hands upon them.

And as he was going forth into the way, there ran one to him, and kneeled to him, and asked him. Good Master, what shall I do that I may inheret eternal life? And Jesus said unto him, Why callest thou me good? none is good save one, even God. Thou knowest the commandments, Do not kill, Do not commit adultery, Do not steal, Do not bear false witness, Do not defraud, Honour thy father and mother. And he said unto him, Master, all these things have I observed from my youth. And Jesus looking upon him loved him, and said unto him, One thing thou lackest: go, sell whatsoever thou hast, and give to the poor, and thou shalt have treasure in heaven: and come, follow me. But his countenance fell at the saying, and he went away sorrowful: for he was one that had great possessions."

THOUGHT QUESTIONS 10:13-22

518. Had little children been brought to Jesus before this time? Why? Who brought them?
519. Was Jesus baptizing the children? Where was Jesus when this incident occurred?; please be as specific as possible.
520. Notice the tense in the verb "rebuked"—it denotes continuing action —what would this suggest?
521. Why wasn't Jesus patient with His disciples instead of being "moved" with indignation?
522. Does the expression "to come unto me" suggest anything about the age of the children?
523. Was Jesus saying the children were already in the kingdom of God? Discuss.
524. Specify three ways in which we should be like little children.
525. What is the meaning of "the kingdom of God" as here used? Does this refer to the church? Discuss.
526. What is the meaning of the word "blessed" as used in vs. 16?
527. In approximately what place did Jesus meet the rich young ruler?
528. Designate the urgency and eagerness of this young man.
529. Mark the humility and trust of this one.
530. What did the ruler mean by the words "Good Teacher"?
531. Was the ruler asking for the way to go to heaven or was there something more in the question?
532. Why did Jesus pick up the words "good teacher" and make a point out of them?

533. In what sense is God the only one who is "good"?
534. Did Jesus tell the rich young man that he could find eternal life in keeping the commandments? Discuss.
535. Why mention the particular six commandments He did?
536. Was the young man bragging or lying when he said he had kept the commandments since his youth?
537. Why does Mark say "Jesus looking upon him loved him"?
538. Just what did the young man lack?
539. Mention six things he did not lack.
540. This one was to trade one treasure for another—please explain how this transaction was to be made.
541. Show the connection of heavenly treasure and following Jesus.
542. As carefully as you can, tell what you believe the young man expected Jesus to say in answer to his question.
543. Was the young ruler lost? Discuss.

COMMENT 10:13-22

TIME.—A.D. 30. This conversation probably occurred in the month of March, on Christ's last journey to Jerusalem, only a few weeks before his crucifixion.

PLACE.—On the farther side of the Jordan, near the borders of Judea. (See Mark 10:1). After the raising of Lazarus, the Lord retired to escape the storm of persecution to "Ephraim, a city of Judea," and after a short interval of rest crossed the Jordan into Perea, where he was still at this date, en route to Jerusalem. If the student will locate a point in the the Jordan valley, east of the river, not far from Jericho it will be near where the little children were brought to the Lord. This region east of the Jordan was called Perea (beyond) because it was *beyond* the river. It included the districts of Bashan and Gilead and in the time of the Savior was fertile and populous, with a mixed population, partly Jewish and partly Gentile.

PARALLEL ACCOUNTS.—The blessing of the little children (vs. 13-16), in Matt. 19:13-15, and Luke 18:15-17. For the lesson to the rich young man, see Matt. 19:16-30; 20:16 and Luke 18:18-30.

INTERVENING HISTORY.—Many events occurred, the chief of which were: 1. The visit of our Lord to Jerusalem at the Feast of Tabernacles, October, A.D. 29 (John 7:8-10), which was marked by (1) solemn discourses during the feast, and an attempt of the Sanhedrim to apprehend him (John 7:11-51, 8:12-59); (2) the opening of the eyes of one born blind (John 9:1-41), the revelation of himself as the Good Shepherd (John 10:1-18). 2. Return to Galilee (October). 3. Final departure from Galilee (November), (Luke 9:51; Mark 10:1). 4. Ministrations in Judea, and mission of the seventy (Luke 10-13: 17). 5. Visit to Jerusalem at the Feast of Dedication (John 10:22-39), (December). 6. Tour in Perea (Luke 13:22-17; 10). 7. The raising of Lazarus (John 11:10-46). 8. Resolve of the Sanhedrim to put him to death, and his retirement to Ephraim (John 11:47-54), (January, A.D. 30). 9. Goes to the borders of Samaria and Galilee; heals ten lepers (January, February). 10. Starts towards Jerusalem down on the east side of the Jordan (March). 11. Discourse on marriage and divorce on the way.

OUTLINE—1. Christ and the Children. 2. The Rich Young Seeker. 3. The One Great Lack.

ANALYSIS

I. CHRIST AND THE CHILDREN, VS. 13-16.
1. Children Brought to the Lord. Mark 10:13; Matt. 19:13; Luke 18:15.
2. The Disciples Rebuked. Mark 10:14; Matt. 19:14; Luke 18:16.
3. Of Such is the Kingdom of God. Mark 10:14; Matt. 19:14; Luke 18:16.
4. Christ Blessing the Children. Mark 10:16.

II. THE RICH YOUNG SEEKER, VS. 17-20.
1. The Great Question. Mark 10:18; Matt. 19:16; Luke 18:18.
2. None Good but One. Mark 10:19; Matt. 19:17; Luke 18:19.
3. What Doest Thou? Mark 10:20; Matt. 19:18, 19; Luke 18:20.
4. A Self-Righteous Spirit. Mark 10:21; Matt. 19:20; Luke 18:21.

III. THE ONE GREAT LACK, VS. 21, 22.
1. One thing Thou Lackest. Mark 10:21; Matt. 19:21; Luke 18:22.
2. Christ Rejected. Mark 10:22; Matt. 19:22; Luke 18:23.

EXPLANATORY NOTES

I. CHRIST AND THE CHILDREN.

In this incident the very heart of Christ is published to poor sinners; and we may clearly perceive the freeness and fullness of the mighty grace of the Redeemer, who is willing to receive the youngest child as well as the oldest man.—*Spurgeon.*

13. *And they brought young children.* Of varying ages, for according to Luke, Christ called them to him. There were parents in those days wise enough to know that it was not well to wait until children were old enough to become hardened in sin before seeking for them the blessing of a Savior. We bring children to Christ (1) by daily, constant, earnest

prayer on their behalf; (2) by teaching them the truth; (3) by consecrating them to God for this life and the life to come; (4) by training them up for Christ. "Set before your child life and death, hell, and heaven, judgment and mercy, his own sin, and Christ's most precious blood, labor with him, persuade him with tears and weeping to turn unto the Lord."—*Spurgeon. That he should touch them.* An act expressive of imparting a blessing, and showing that the nearer we are to Jesus the greater the blessing which comes to us from him. Blessings come to those who are near, which cannot come to those that are afar off. This is true of physical healing, and of moral and intellectual influences. We must draw near to Christ in order to receive his blessing. *His disciples rebuked those that brought them.* "The erroneous apostles," as Richard Baxter calls them, thought that the Great Rabbi would be annoyed, and his attention diverted from matters of greater importance than anything connected with little children. They think it is to abuse the goodness and misuse the time of their Master, Dr. Tyng says: "It seems to me that the Devil would never ask anything more of a minister than to have him look upon his mission as chiefly to the grown up members of his congregation, while somebody else was to look after the children."

14. *When Jesus saw it he was much displeased.* The language of the original is much stronger: so it is expressed in the Revised Version, "moved with indignation." The disciples had already been cautioned about their treatment of children (Matt. 18:10-14). Some sign of displeasure was probably on his countenance. How careful we should be not to call forth his displeasure by keeping children from him! Peloubet assigns five reasons for the Lord's indignation. (1) Because they were keeping away from him those who wanted to come to him, and for whom he died. (2) They were taking away those who were the very hope of the church, the kingdom they were appointed to build up. (3) Because the children are the type of all who shall enter his kingdom. (4) Because he loved little children, and rejoiced in their love. (5) Because they were hindering the best workers in his kingdom, the mothers. *Suffer the little children to come unto me.* To refuse children access to his grace was to misrepresent his spirit, his mission, and his kingdom. In bringing the children at that moment the mothers interrupted him in an important doctrinal discourse: yet Jesus suspended his teaching, and pronounced a blessing. It signified that there was a place in his thought, in his heart, in his mission, in his church, for children. *For of such is the kingdom of God.* Such as have the childlike disposition toward God. God wants little children in his kingdom. People are most likely to come into the kingdom when children, since all must become like little children in order

to enter the kingdom. *Children in the kingdom of God in heaven.* Such as die before they have wandered out of God's kingdom into the kingdom of Satan are certainly saved, since they are "of the kingdom of heaven."—*Abbott.* Then, beyond a doubt, in that kingdom shall all the little ones be found. For it is not as children of Christians, it is not as baptized, but it is as *children,* that of such is that kingdom.—*Alford. Children in the kingdom of God on earth.* Perhaps it is as well for us to learn the lesson at once, so that we might accept the statement which the words of the Savior would teach; namely, that little children are the true wards of the church, and ought to be welcomed, cherished, and valued highly.—*Sunday School Times.*

15. *Whosoever shall not receive,* etc. Christ now holds up the children as an example to his disciples. He had the ideal childlike spirit, and delighted to see in little ones his own image. Purity, truthfulness, simplicity, docility, and loving dependence made them his favorite types for his followers. The apostles needed the lessons their characteristics impressed. —*Geikie.*

16. *Took them up in his arms.* He ever giveth more than men ask or think. He had been asked only to touch the children. He takes them into his arms, and lays his hands upon them, and blesses them.—*Cambridge Bible for Schools.* As I look at Christ in this, the most stirring period of his history, with the dark events of his last agonies thickening on his horizon, condescending to take little children in his arms and bless them, I feel deeper chords in my nature touched than when I see him hush the furious tempest, or raise the buried dead.—*Thomas.* It is well to note (1) that these children were not babes. The Lord called them to him. (2) They were not brought to be baptized, but that the Lord might touch them. (3) He did not baptize them, but laid hands on them and blessed them. (4) All parents and all mothers especially should bring their children to Christ for his blessing, should teach them of him, his demand for their hearts, and that they should obey him.

II. THE RICH YOUNG SEEKER.

17. *When he was gone forth on the way.* Had continued his slow journey towards Jerusalem. As his aim was to teach the people, his daily journeys were very short and he often paused for days together where an open door was presented. *There came one running.* This incident is described in Matt. 19:16-23, and Luke 18:18-23. The three accounts should be carefully compared by the student. This case presents some remarkable points. (1) The man was of irreproachable moral character; and this amidst all the temptations of youth—for he was a "young man" (Matt. 19:22)—and wealth, for "he was very rich," (v. 22). But (2)

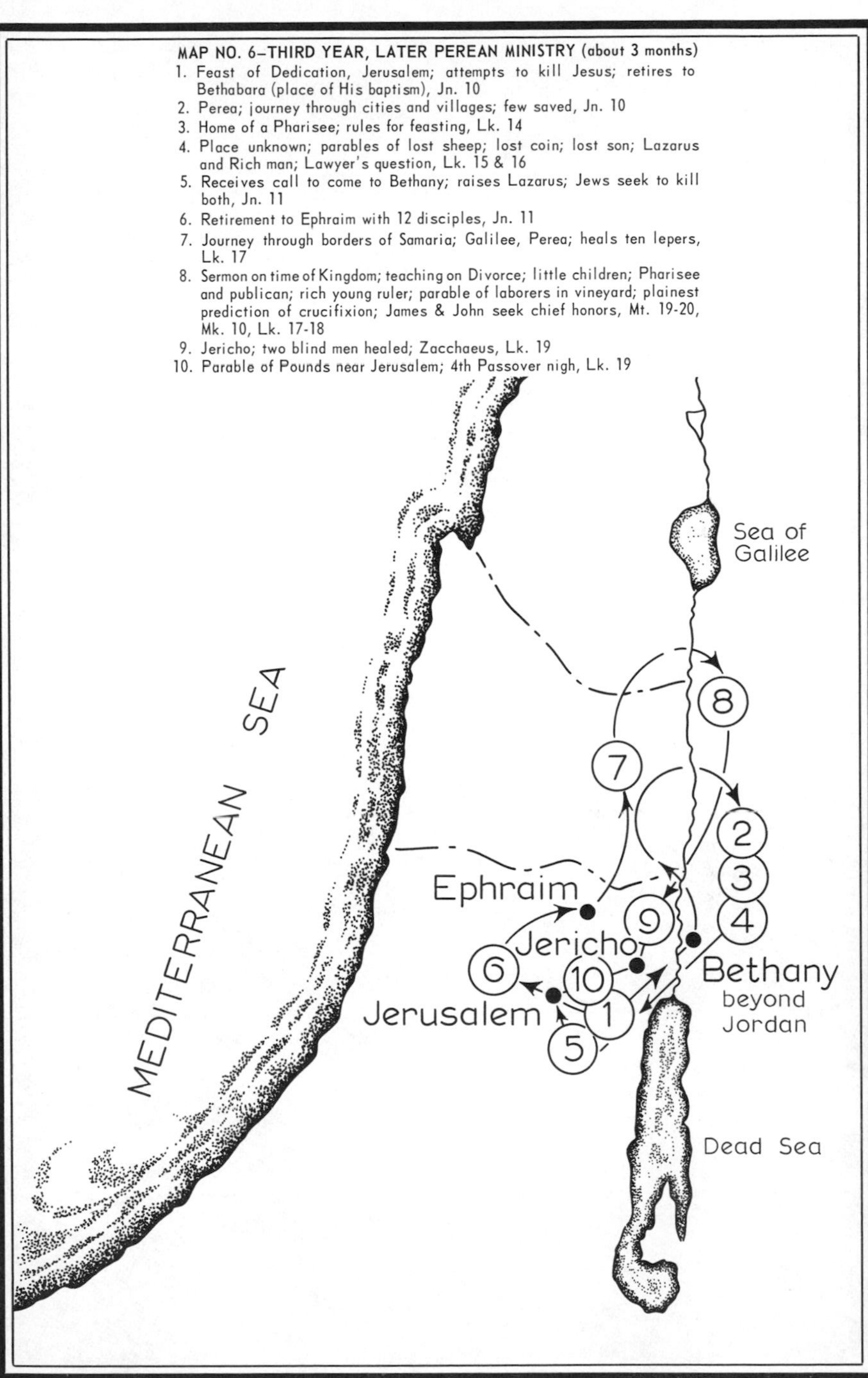
MAP NO. 6–THIRD YEAR, LATER PEREAN MINISTRY (about 3 months)
1. Feast of Dedication, Jerusalem; attempts to kill Jesus; retires to Bethabara (place of His baptism), Jn. 10
2. Perea; journey through cities and villages; few saved, Jn. 10
3. Home of a Pharisee; rules for feasting, Lk. 14
4. Place unknown; parables of lost sheep; lost coin; lost son; Lazarus and Rich man; Lawyer's question, Lk. 15 & 16
5. Receives call to come to Bethany; raises Lazarus; Jews seek to kill both, Jn. 11
6. Retirement to Ephraim with 12 disciples, Jn. 11
7. Journey through borders of Samaria; Galilee, Perea; heals ten lepers, Lk. 17
8. Sermon on time of Kingdom; teaching on Divorce; little children; Pharisee and publican; rich young ruler; parable of laborers in vineyard; plainest prediction of crucifixion; James & John seek chief honors, Mt. 19-20, Mk. 10, Lk. 17-18
9. Jericho; two blind men healed; Zacchaeus, Lk. 19
10. Parable of Pounds near Jerusalem; 4th Passover nigh, Lk. 19
Sea of Galilee
MEDITERRANEAN SEA
8
7
2
3
4
Ephraim
9
Jericho
Bethany beyond Jordan
6
10
Jerusalem
1
5
Dead Sea

restless, notwithstanding, his heart craves eternal life. (3) He so far believed in Jesus as to be persuaded he could authoritatively direct him on this vital point. (4) So earnest is he, that he comes "running" and even "kneeling before him," and that when he was gone forth "into the way" (v. 17)—the high road—by this time crowded with travelers to the passover.—*J. F. and B. Running.* They that will have eternal life must run for it; because the Devil, the law, sin, death, and hell follow them.—*Bunyan. Good Master, what shall I do?* He sincerely desired salvation; and he imagined that some generous action, some great sacrifice, would secure this highest good.—*Godet. What shall I do?* (In Matthew, What good thing shall I do?) He had not yet learned that he needed first to be good, to have a pure and holy heart, before he could have eternal life. *To inherit eternal life?* That I may be among those that are true children, and, as such, lawful inheritors of the kingdom.—*Cook.*

18. *Why callest thou me good?* Christ does not rebuke the young man for employing what was nothing more than the language of respect by any pupil to a teacher.—*Abbott.* But he asks him whether he looks upon him merely as any other teacher; or does he recognize him as a divine teacher—the only one who is truly good; the "good master" who knows all things, and whose teaching is eternally true.—*P. There is none good but one, that is God.* He does not deny that he is good; for he is the one who is good, even God (1 John 3:5). Some have mistakenly found in these words an affirmation that Christ is not divine. To whom Stier relies; "Either there is none good but God; Christ is good; therefore Christ is God: or, there is none good but God, Christ is not God; therefore Christ is not good." There is no answer to these syllogisms but to deny the sinlessness of Christ.

19. *Thou knowest the commandments.* After uttering his mild rebuke, our Lord proceeds to answer the young man's question by exhibiting the moral character requisite as "meetness" for the enjoyment of everlasting life.—*Morrison.* St. Matthew says that our Lord first answered, "Keep the commandments;" and when the young man asked, "What kind of commandments?" he seems purposely to have mentioned only the plainest commandments of the second table, to show the young man that he had fallen short, even of these in their true interpretation, much more of that love to God which is the epitome of the first table. Thus does Christ "send the proud to the law, and invite the humble to the gospel." —*Farrar. Defraud not.* It seems as if intended to be a special application of the tenth commandment. One who had great possessions, gathered in the usual ways by which men gain wealth, needed to examine himself

specially by that text. Were there no ill-gotten gains in his treasure?—*Ellicott.* Our Lord gives this enumeration of the commandments to bring out the self-righteous spirit of the young man, which he before saw.

20. *All these have I observed.* There was, no doubt, great ignorance in this reply. He knew but little of any one of these precepts in the strictness, spirituality, and extent of its requirements, who could venture on any such assertion. Yet there was sincerity in the answer, and it pointed to a bygone life of singular external propriety.—*Hanna.*

III. THE ONE GREAT LACK.

21. *Jesus beholding him loved him.* Jesus read his heart in a moment, and was won by the evident worth of his character. As he looked at him, so earnest, so humble, so admirable in his life and spirit, he loved him. Could he only stand the testing demand that must now be made, he would pass into the citizenship of the kingdom of God.—*Geikie.* Jesus loves all men, but his sympathies are called forth specially in behalf of those seeking for eternal life. It is out of his sympathy and love that he makes a demand on him that will reveal to the young man his own heart. *One thing thou lackest.* He thus proposed to him one short crucial test of his real condition, and way to clear self-knowledge. He had fancied himself willing to do whatever could be required; he could now see if he were really so. *Go thy way.* He now gives him proof of what he lacked. Far from arresting on their way those who believe in their own strength, he encourages them to prosecute it faithfully to the very end, knowing well that if they are sincere they shall by the law die to the law (Gal. 2:19). *Sell whatsoever thou hast.* The Lord loved him so well that he invited him to the highest honors, even to become a member of his immediate attendants, like the apostles. These had all given up everything in order to follow Christ, and the same test and opportunity was offered to this young man. It was the crisis of his life. Had he accepted the opportunity perhaps his would have been one of the great names in the early history of the church; but the world gained the victory, he loved it better than Christ, he rejected the offer and thus he disappears from sight forever. *Follow me.* All these things are parts of one whole, the Christian life. He must have all, would he enter eternal life. Note his possible future as a disciple, compared with his obscure future as a nameless rich man.

22. *And he was sad.* He had been touched where weakest, but this was exactly what his repeated request demanded.—*Geikie. And went away grieved.* He shrank from the one test that would really have led him to the heights of glory at which he aimed. *Great possessions.* It was too much. He preferred the comforts of earth to the treasures of heaven;

he would not purchase the things of eternity by abandoning those of time; he made, as Dante calls it, "the great refusal." And so he vanishes from the gospel history; nor do the evangelists know anything of him further.—*Farrar.* Which would have been better for this young man—to leave his goods to become the companion in labor of the St. Peters and St. Johns, or to keep possessions so soon to be laid waste by the Roman legions?—*Godet.*

FACT QUESTIONS 10:13-22

558. How is Mark 10:13-22 to be associated with the raising of Lazarus?
559. Why is this district called "beyond the Jordan"? What territory was included in it?
560. Name five events that occurred between the feast of the Tabernacles and the healing of the ten lepers.
561. How is the "mighty grace of the Redeemer" seen in His attitude toward the little children?
562. Name three ways children are brought to Christ today.
563. What lesson can be gained from the fact that Jesus touched the children?
564. What error was made by the apostles in rebuking the children?
565. Name three reasons for the Lord's indignation.
566. Are all children who die going to heaven? Discuss.
567. In what sense are children today in the kingdom of God on earth?
568. Is it true that Jesus saw in children His own image, and therefore held them up to his disciples as examples?
569. Show how the time and circumstance of blessing the children shows something of the beautiful character of Jesus.
570. Johnson says it is well to note four facts about this incident—mention three of them.
571. Why were some of the days' journeys of Jesus very short?
572. Note three remarkable things about the one who came running to Jesus.
573. Just what was the young man seeking?
574. "Either there is none good but ————; Christ is good; therefore Christ is ————; or, there is none good but God; Christ is not God; therefore Christ is not ————."
575. In what way does Christ "send the proud to the law, and invite the humble to the gospel"?
576. How did "defraud not" apply to the young man?

577. Show how there was both ignorance and sincerity in the answer of the young ruler.
578. Why did Jesus love the young man?
579. What is meant by the phrase "go thy way"?
580. What wonderful opportunity did Jesus offer the young man?
581. Why couldn't the young man follow Christ and keep his money?
582. What is "the great refusal"?

C. THE RICH MAN AND HEAVEN 10:23-27

TEXT 10:23-27

"And Jesus looked round about, and saith unto his disciples, How hardly shall they that have riches enter into the kingdom of God! And the disciples were amazed at his words. But Jesus answereth again, and saith unto them, Children, how hard is it for them that trust in riches to enter into the kingdom of God! It is easier for a camel to go through a needle's eye, than for a rich man to enter into the kingdom of God. And they were astonished exceedingly, saying unto him, Then who can be saved? Jesus looking upon them saith, With men it is impossible, but not with God: for all things are possible with God."

THOUGHT QUESTIONS 10:23-27

544. Why mention the appearance or looks of Jesus?
545. Show how appropriate this question was.
546. What is "the kingdom of God" as used here?
547. Why were the disciples so amazed?
548. Show how the exaggerated illustration of the camel and the needle's eye fit the circumstance.
549. Did the disciples believe there was some connection between being rich and God's approval? Discuss.
550. Did the disciples think—"if a rich man cannot be saved no one can be saved"? Why?
551. What was impossible and possible in the salvation of a rich man?

COMMENT

TIME.—March—A.D. 30. Shortly after the conversation with the rich young ruler.

PLACE.—In Perea—the east side of the Jordan, near the borders of Judea.

PARALLEL ACCOUNTS.—Matt. 19:23-26; Luke 18:24-27.

OUTLINE.—1. Jesus states the rich man's poor chances for heaven, vs. 23. 2. The disciples are very surprised, vs. 24a. 3. Jesus repeats with emphasis and illustration His first assertion, vs. 24b-25. 4. "Who can be saved?"—God can make it possible, vs. 26, 27.

ANALYSIS

I. JESUS STATES THE RICH MAN'S POOR CHANCES FOR HEAVEN, VS. 23.
   1. This was said as Jesus looked intently into the faces of His disciples.
   2. It is almost impossible for a rich man to be saved.

II. THE DISCIPLES ARE VERY SURPRISED, VS. 24a.
   1. This surprise was because of their thought that a man was rich because God had blessed him.
   2. Jesus had flatly contradicted their concept.

III. JESUS REPEATS WITH EMPHASIS AND ILLUSTRATION HIS FIRST ASSERTION, VS. 24b-25.
   1. Jesus calls His disciples "children" (in understanding) as He repeats His statement.
   2. The possibility is like that of a camel going through the eye of a needle.

IV. WHO THEN CAN BE SAVED?—GOD CAN MAKE IT POSSIBLE, VS. 26, 27.
   1. The increased amazement of the disciples.
   2. Jesus again looked searchingly at them—"what man cannot do, God can do."

EXPLANATORY NOTES

I. JESUS STATES THE RICH MAN'S POOR CHANCES FOR HEAVEN.

"23. Now again the deliberate look of Jesus round the whole circle of his disciples, gazing into each face, impressed itself on the memory of Mark's informant. His saying, *How hardly*—i.e. with what difficulty—*shall they that have riches enter into the kingdom of God*! is amply confirmed by experience. Christian men often become rich, but rich men rarely become Christians. The reason is not far to seek: the process of gaining wealth encourages self-seeking, and the possession of it encourages self-importance; but the spirit that can enter the kingdom is the spirit of a little child."

II. THE DISCIPLES ARE VERY SURPRISED.

"24a. This remarkable verse is peculiar to Mark. The astonishment of the disciples was natural, with their ideas of the kingdom. "Hard for rich men! What can he mean?" All the splendid imagery of the prophets (as in Isa. 60) might rise in their minds to contradict him; and the idea of delivering Israel from oppression by a kingdom that rich men could scarcely enter must have seemed to them absurd."

III. JESUS REPEATS WITH EMPHASIS AND ILLUSTRATION HIS FIRST ASSERTION.

"24b-25. Jesus solemnly repeated his hard saying; yet his mood was tender, as his word *Children* shows, here alone addressed to them. ("Little children," in John 13:33.)—According to the common reading, the repetition of the saying explains and softens it by the modification. *How hard is it for them that trust in riches to enter.* But there seems sufficient reason to accept the reading of ancient manuscripts by which the words *for them that trust in riches* are omitted. In that case the repetition of the saying removes it from the special case of rich men and applies the sentiment more widely: *Children, how hard it is to enter into the kingdom of God*! Plainly, such a remark was a natural outcome of the incident, for it was not chiefly his riches, but his heart, that sent the man away sorrowful, and a like heart is in all men. To all men, therefore, rich or poor, it is by nature *hard to enter into the kingdom of God*—hard in itself, since sin is what it is.—Let us not be afraid that such a text will prove too discouraging. It is better to know things as they are; and perhaps the doctrine of free grace has been so used as to lead to an untrue idea of the easiness of salvation.

25. *It is easier for a camel to go through the eye of a needle.* This comparison may have been proverbial, as the Talmud contains, at a later date, a closely similar saying. The Koran exactly reproduces it from the New Testament. As for the popular explanation—that the small gate in the city wall, too narrow for a camel to pass through, was called the needle's eye—there is no sufficient evidence of the antiquity of such a use of the name. The comparison needs no special explanation; it is a strong way of representing impossibility: "It is so hard for sinful men, rich or poor, to enter the kingdom, that for a rich man—one who is especially involved in the unchildlike habits of the world—to enter is harder than for a camel to go through a needle's eye." This is no contradiction of any gracious and winning Scripture. It is the Saviour's emphatic statement of a fact, parallel to Luke 13:24 and 14:26-33, and to many other of his words."

IV. WHO THEN CAN BE SAVED?—GOD CAN MAKE IT POSSIBLE.

"26, 27. *Astonished* before; *astonished out of measure* now.—The inquiry was *among themselves,* a whispering of amazement. *Who then can be saved*? With such a standard, how would the kingdom receive any one? For was not the love of money everywhere? and how could the kingdom live, with a law so strict?—*Jesus looking upon them.* Again

Peter remembered his look. The word, both here and in verse 21, is the same as in Luke 22:61: "The Lord turned and looked on Peter."—*With men it is impossible.* Not now difficult, but more. On human principles or by any power of man it cannot be done; the proud man cannot be brought into the kingdom of the humble, or the worldly-minded rich man into the kingdom of the poor in spirit. So in John 3:3: "Except a man be born again, he cannot see the kingdom of God."—*But not with God: for with God all things are possible.* He can make new creatures of men; he can impart the spirit of the kingdom. He has command, too, of all means, earthly and heavenly. So he can bring into his kingdom men who are spiritually incompatible with it. (See 1 Tim. 1:12-17; 1 Cor. 15:9, 10.) The implication is that, even though this case looks so hopeless, God can yet find means of bringing the unwilling rich man to a better mind. In his hands are even life and death." (W. N. Clarke)

FACT QUESTIONS 10:23-27

583. Why is it that Christian men often become rich, but rich men rarely become Christians?
584. What could arise in the mind of the disciples to contradict the words of Jesus?
585. Is the thought of difficulty in entering the kingdom general or specific? i.e. does this principle apply to all—explain.
586. Is there any truth in the thought of a needle's gate in the city wall of Jerusalem? Why was this explanation offered in the first place?
587. Why were the disciples particularly amazed at this time?
588. How will God make the impossible possible? Discuss.

C. PETER'S HASTY WORDS. 10:28-31

TEXT 10:28-31

"Peter began to say unto him, Lo, we have left all, and have followed thee. Jesus said, Verily I say unto you, There is no man that hath left house, or brethren, or sisters, or mother, or father, or children, or lands, for my sake, and for the gospel's sake, but he shall receive a hundredfold now in this time, houses, and brethren, and sisters, and mothers, and children, and lands, with persecutions; and in the world to come eternal life. But many that are first shall be last; and the last first."

THOUGHT QUESTION 10:28-31

552. Why did Peter ask this question?
553. Show the low spiritual tone in the question asked by Peter.
554. Did Peter feel he and the other apostles had done what Jesus asked the rich young ruler to do?

555. Had Jesus said anything about the advantages in following Him? (Cf. His words to the rich young ruler.)

556. Is Peter saying that he and the other apostles actually left all to follow Jesus with the thought of getting more than they left?

557. Please notice that Jesus did not direct His answer to Peter— what does this imply? There are to be rewards—but for whom? How?

558. Please be specific in your understanding of just how we can receive a hundred fold of houses, brethren, sisters, mothers, children, lands—with persecutions. If you can not give a specific answer—(one with personal meaning) think and pray and study until you can.

559. Why add the warning of vs. 31? What does it mean?

COMMENT 10:28-31

TIME.—March, A.D. 30.

PLACE.—In Perea—at the same time and place as the incident with the rich young ruler.

PARALLEL ACCOUNTS.—Matt. 19:27-30; Luke 18:28-30.

OUTLINE.—1. "Look at us: we have left all to follow you." vs. 28. 2. No one has left all to follow me who will not be rewarded a hundred fold along with persecutions and in the age to come eternal life, vs. 29, 30. 3. Warning—the first may be last—The last may be first, vs. 31.

ANALYSIS

I. LOOK AT US: WE HAVE LEFT ALL TO FOLLOW YOU, VS. 28.
   1. Right after Jesus' words to the disciples about riches and the kingdom Peter responds.
   2. We are examples of those who have left all to follow. (What shall we receive in return?)

II. NO ONE HAS LEFT ALL TO FOLLOW ME WHO WILL NOT BE REWARDED A HUNDRED-FOLD—ALONG WITH PERSECUTIONS—IN THE AGE TO COME ETERNAL LIFE, VS. 29, 30.
   1. Jesus replied emphatically—"truly"—
   2. This principle applies to all—anyone who leaves all to follow Me will be rewarded a hundred-fold and at the end—eternal life.
   3. Such reward will be accompanied with persecution.

III. WARNING—THE FIRST MAY BE LAST—THE LAST MAY BE FIRST, VS. 31.
   1. Some—like you, Peter—start poorly but finish well.
   2. Some—like the rich young ruler—start well but do not finish.

EXPLANATORY NOTES

I. LOOK AT US: WE HAVE LEFT ALL TO FOLLOW YOU.

"28. Peter, as usual, speaks for them all, saying, in substance, "We have done what this man would not: we have accepted the kingdom on the right terms at personal sacrifice." The question, "What shall we have, therefore?" added in Matthew, is plainly implied here and in Luke. Here is a frank statement of self-seeking, even in self-renunciation; self-denial in the hope of direct returns. The apostles were still hoping that their special honors in the kingdom would make amends for everything. Yet in the words of Peter now there may be a tone of despair, in view of the depression of their prospects implied in the words just spoken: "What shall we have, what amends, if the kingdom is to be of this exacting and unambitious kind?" No concealment anywhere of the low spiritual tone of the disciples."

II. NO ONE HAS LEFT ALL TO FOLLOW ME WHO WILL NOT BE REWARDED A HUNDRED-FOLD—ALONG WITH PERSECUTIONS—IN THE AGE TO COME ETERNAL LIFE.

"29, 30. How tender and wise the answer! There is no distinct rebuke, but there is a silent one in the fact that the promise is made, not to the apostles only, but to all who make such sacrifices as they speak of. Apostles have no exclusive claim, nor even an assurance of pre-eminence in this respect. The rewards of the kingdom are for all the faithful, all who, *for my sake, and the gospel's*, have forsaken what they held dear. Note the true suggestion—that the forsaking must be for a person and for a principle. Jesus wishes not to be regarded apart from the gospel, nor can the gospel be regarded as a true object of sacrifice apart from Jesus. So in chap. 8:38. The promise seems to mean (for of course the promise of multiplication of goods cannot be taken literally) that all good that is given up for Christ shall be immeasurably more precious to the soul for the surrender. It shall be given back to the soul, if not to the hands, enhanced a hundred-fold in value. It may be given back to the hands—i.e. sacrifices may be required in spirit that are not called for in the course of divine providence—and in that case the hundred-fold of new preciousness is always found. But to the soul all that is given up for Christ shall be returned, and thus graciously multiplied. (The possible thoughts of the lad who gave up his loaves and fishes, John 6:9). The principle of self-sacrifice sweetens life instead of embittering it, and the experience of self-denial surprises the soul with unthought-of wealth. So much at present; and in the age that is coming, with its full spiritual rewards, eternal life. So 1 Tim. 4:8.—But the warning lies in the solemn reservation, preserved by Mark alone. *With persecutions.* No easy way leads to these honors and rewards (2 Tim. 3:12; 2 Cor. 11:23-27; 6:4-10). Even when outward persecution is not, still the principle is the same: it is no easy way.—The *hundred-fold* will not prevent the persecutions; but neither will the persecutions interfere with the coming of the hundred-fold."

III. WARNING—THE FIRST MAY BE LAST—THE LAST MAY BE FIRST.

"31. A wise caution. "The judgment of God is according to truth," and rank will finally be determined by true judgment and not according to present appearances. Let no man boast; even the rich young man who has gone away sorrowful may possibly yet outrank the apostles. Here, according to Matthew, our Lord adds the parable of the Laborers (Matt. 20:1-16) to illustrate the solemn warning, *many that are first shall be last; and the last first,* to which, at the end of the parable, he returns.—The rich young man we see no more, unless under his proper name. Those who think that he may have been Lazarus suggest that his sickness, death, and resurrection, or some part of that great experience, may have been used by God, to whom all things are possible, in bringing him to the spirit of the kingdom. Whoever he may have been, we cannot suppress the hope that he who is said to have loved him did not leave him to himself." (W. N. Clarke)

FACT QUESTIONS 10:28-31

589. Is there in the words of Peter a tone of despair? Why?
590. Show how there is not a distinct rebuke to Peter but a very real silent one.
591. What was said about a person and a principle?
592. What sweetens life? What surprise is in store for the soul who exercises self-denial?
593. Why say "with persecutions"—Show how this principle is reflected in other references.
594. Read Matt. 20:1-16 and show the connection with Mark 10:31.
595. Why do some say the rich young man was Lazarus? or Saul of Tarsus?

C. JESUS FORETELLS HIS DEATH AND RESURRECTION 10:32-34

TEXT 10:32-34

"And they were in the way, going up to Jerusalem; and Jesus was going before them: and they were amazed; and they that followed were afraid. And he took again the twelve, and began to tell them the things that were to happen unto him, saying, Behold, we go up to Jerusalem; and the Son of man shall be delivered unto the chief priests and the scribes; and they shall condemn him to death, and shall deliver him unto the Gentiles: and they shall mock him, and shall spit upon him, and shall scourge him, and shall kill him; and after three days he shall rise again."

THOUGHT QUESTIONS 10:32-34

560. What was the reason for the amazement of the disciples? Please remember the purpose of going to Jerusalem.
561. Who were "those who followed" mentioned in vs. 32?
562. When and where had Jesus before mentioned His death and resurrection?
563. List the eight particulars in the prophecy made by Jesus.
564. Who were "the Gentiles" to whom the priests and scribes were to deliver our Lord?

COMMENT

TIME.—March, A.D. 30.

PLACE.—In Perea—at the same place and time as the previous incident.

PARALLEL ACCOUNTS.—Matt. 20:17-19; Luke 18:31-34.

OUTLINE.—1. On the way to Jerusalem the disciples were filled with fear as they anticipated what would happen to them in the city. Jesus confirmed their fears, vs. 32. 2. Jesus details in prophecy what would happen to Him at Jerusalem, vs. 33, 34.

ANALYSIS

I. ON THE WAY TO JERUSALEM THE DISCIPLES WERE FILLED WITH FEAR AS THEY ANTICIPATED WHAT WOULD HAPPEN TO THEM IN THE CITY. JESUS CONFIRMED THEIR FEARS, VS. 32.
   1. Going up to Jerusalem—Jesus led the way.
   2. He spoke privately to the twelve of His coming passion.

II. JESUS DETAILS IN PROPHECY WHAT WILL HAPPEN TO HIM AT JERUSALEM, VS. 33, 34.

The Son of man will be: (1) delivered to the chief priests and scribes. (2) condemned to death. (3) delivered to the Gentiles. (4) Mocked. (5) Spit upon. (6) Scourged. (7) Killed. (8) After three days raised from the dead.

EXPLANATORY NOTES

I. ON THE WAY TO JERUSALEM THE DISCIPLES WERE FILLED WITH FEAR AS THEY ANTICIPATED WHAT WOULD HAPPEN TO THEM IN THE CITY. JESUS CONFIRMED THEIR FEARS.

"32. *And they were in the way* (or on the road) *ascending to Jerusalem*, i.e. they were still upon their journey when the following discourse was uttered. This is another intimation that we have before us a connected narrative. *And Jesus was going before them* (or leading them forward), which seems to imply some unusual activity or energy of movement, as if he was outstripping them, in token of his eagerness to reach the scene of suffering. This may throw some light upon the next clause, *and they were amazed,* or struck with awe, the same verb that is used in v. 24, here denoting probably some dark foreboding of the scenes which were before them in Jerusalem, a feeling which would naturally make them slow to follow in that dangerous direction, and dispose them to wonder at his own alacrity in rushing, as it were, upon destruction (John 11:8). *And following they feared* (or were alarmed), i.e. although they followed him, it was not willingly, but with a painful apprehension of danger both to him and to themselves. There is something very striking in the picture here presented of the Saviour hastening to death, and the apostles scarcely venturing to follow him. This backwardness would not be diminished by his *taking again the twelve*, i.e. taking them aside from the others who accompanied him on his journey. *He began* (anew what he had done more than once before) *to tell them the (things) about to happen to him.* This is commonly reckoned our Lord's third prediction of his passion to the twelve apostles; but including the less formal intimation in 9:12 it may be counted as the fourth."

II. JESUS DETAILS IN PROPHECY WHAT WILL HAPPEN TO HIM AT JERUSALEM.

"33, 34. *Behold* invites attention and prepares them for something strange and surprising, as the intimation of his death still was to them, although so frequently repeated. *We are ascending to Jerusalem*, the form of expression always used in speaking of the Holy City, on account both of its physical and moral elevation. (Compare Luke 2:42. John 2:13; 5:1; 7:8. 10. 14. 11:55. Acts 11:2; 15:2; 18:22; 21:4. 12. 15. 24:11; 25:1. 9. Gal. 2:1. 2.) The prediction is the same as in the former cases, but with a more distinct intimation that he was to suffer by judicial process, or by form of law. *They* (the Sanhedrim, the national council or representatives) *shall condemn him unto death, and deliver him to the Gentiles* (literally, nations, meaning all nations but the Jews) for the execution of the sentence, all which was literally fulfilled, as we shall see below.

This verse describes the part to be taken by the Gentiles in the sufferings of Christ, every particular of which has its corresponding facts in the subsequent narrative; the mocking; the scourging; the spitting; the killing; and the rising. Here again the terms of the prediction may appear to us too plain to be mistaken; but, as we have seen already, the correct understanding does not depend upon the plainness of the language, but upon the principle of interpretation. If they attached a mystical or figurative meaning to the terms, it mattered not how plain they might be in themselves or in their literal acceptation, which they probably supposed to be precluded by the certainty that he was to reign and to possess a kingdom." (J. A. Alexander)

FACT QUESTIONS 10:32-34

596. What intimation do we have in these verses of a connected narrative?
597. What is striking in the picture in these verses?
598. Do we have here the third or fourth prediction by Jesus of His death? (Cf. 8:31; 9:31; 9:12)
599. Why always speak of "going up to Jerusalem"?
600. Why say "behold" before the comment Jesus made?
601. What was added in this prediction not found in the former ones?
602. How was it possible for Jesus to be so plain in His words of His coming death and still be misunderstood by His disciples?

D. SELFISH AMBITION REPROVED. 10:35-45

TEXT 10:35-45

"And there came near unto him James and John, the sons of Zebedee, saying unto him, Master, we would that thou shouldest do for us whatsoever we shall ask of thee. And he said unto them, What would ye that I should do for you? And they said unto him, Grant unto us that we may sit, one on thy right hand, and one on thy left hand, in thy glory. But Jesus said unto them, Ye know not what ye ask. Are ye able to drink the cup that I drink? or to be baptized with the baptism that I am baptized with? And they said unto him, We are able. And Jesus said unto them, The cup that I drink ye shall drink; and with the baptism that I am baptized withal shall ye be baptized: but to sit on my right hand or on my left hand is not mine to give: but it is for them for whom it hath been prepared. And when the ten heard it, they began to be moved with indignation concerning James and John. And Jesus called them to him, and saith unto them, Ye know that they which are accounted to rule over the Gentiles lord it over them: and their great ones exercise authority over them. But it is not so among you: but whosoever would become great among you, shall be your minister: and whosoever would be first among you, shall be servant of all. For verily the Son of man came not to be ministered unto, but to minister, and to give his life a ransom for many."

THOUGHT QUESTIONS 10:35-45

565. Your understanding of this section is not going to be at all complete unless you also read Matt. 20:20-28. Please read it!
566. Who actually voiced the petition?
567. Isn't it strange such a thought even entered the heart of those who made it? Discuss.
568. In what manner did these three look upon Jesus?
569. James and John wanted to sit at His right and left in His "glory" —what type of "glory" did they contemplate?
570. What was "the cup" and "baptism" of vs. 38?
571. Why did Jesus ask the question about the cup and baptism? Did they understand the question?
572. When did James and John drink the cup and experience the baptism?
573. For whom was the right and left of Jesus' throne prepared?
574. Why were the ten indignant? Be specific.
575. Why wasn't Jesus angry with the sad lack of understanding evidenced by the apostles?
576. Why not refer to the Jews in their exercising of power? Who were "the Gentiles" of vs. 42?
577. What a revolutionary thought Jesus proposed in vs. 43, 44—! What type of greatness did Jesus envision?
578. Why refer to Himself as "the Son of man"?
579. Show how Jesus fulfilled His purpose.
580. In what sense was Jesus' life "a ransom for many"?

COMMENT

TIME.—March A.D. 30.

PLACE—Perea—across from Jericho.

PARALLEL ACCOUNTS—Matt. 20:20-28.

OUTLINE—1. The selfish request, vs. 35-37. 2. Jesus' answer and rebuke, vs. 38-45.

ANALYSIS

I. THE SELFISH REQUEST, 35-37.
   1. Made by James and John the sons of Zebedee (through their mother).
   2. Asked as to a great potentate who had all power (—as well as favorites).
   3. A bold, blantant request for special favor.

II. JESUS' ANSWER AND REBUKE, VS. 38-45.

1. You ask out of ignorance.
2. You want to share my glory. Are you ready to also share my suffering?
3. Without understanding the apostles answer "yes." Jesus confirms that they will indeed share His suffering.
4. He could not grant preference.
5. The ten were angry with James and John for making such a request.
6. Jesus explained by comparison the place of true greatness.
7. The Son of man is come to serve not to be served—indeed His life is given as a ransom for all.

EXPLANATORY NOTES

I. THE SELFISH REQUEST.

"35. *James and John, the sons of Zebedee.* They were among the earliest disciples, John having been, with Andrew, one of the first who followed Jesus (John 1:36-40), and James having probably been brought by John to Jesus on that same day (John 1:41, where the form of expression in the Greek implies that, though Andrew was the first to find his brother, Simon, and bring him to Jesus, John also quickly found his brother, James, and brought him too). James and John were two of the three nearest to Jesus. In Matthew the request at this time comes from their mother, whose name was Salome (compare Matt. 27:56 with Mark 15:40), and who was probably the sister of Mary, the mother of Jesus. The request was probably suggested by the words just spoken, and recorded only by Matthew (19:28): "When the Son of man shall sit in the throne of his glory, ye also shall sit upon twelve thrones, judging the twelve tribes of Israel." Of course they took this literally, or nearly so; and now the two disciples, or their mother for them, came asking for the two thrones nearest the King himself. Their personal nearness to him in the apostleship and the early date of their following may have emboldened them to this; and if they were first-cousins to him, as seems probable, this would be another reason for expecting a favorable answer. —Yet, as if they feared failure, they would try, with a genuine human impulse, to pledge the answer in advance. *We would that thou shouldest do for us whatsoever we shall desire*, or, rather, "ask." He gave no pledge but asked for their request; when, behold, in spite of all that he had said, now of death, and before (chap. 9:35) of humility, it was the most ambitious request that could be made—a request for the two chief thrones."

II. JESUS' ANSWER AND REBUKE.

"38. Personal loyalty was at the bottom of the desire: they had cast in their lot with him and with him they desired to have their portion. Yet it was a childish desire, an ambition for the end in profound ignorance of the way.—*Ye know not what ye ask.* It is like the reply of a father to foolish children. When addressed to men—ambitious men—how humiliating! yet in this case how searchingly appropriate! It is not less appropriate with reference to many of our requests to our Heavenly Father; for often do we pray for the end in ignorance of the way, and often when the way be by no means acceptable to us.—The principle of his rejoinder is that of Matt. 10:24: "The disciple is not above his master." There is but one way to all the thrones, the way the King has taken.—*Can ye drink* (not "drink of") *the cup that I drink*—i.e. which I have to drink, and in spirit am already drinking, the cup of utter self-sacrifice, even unto martyrdom. He drinks the cup, he does not merely drink of it; and he proposes the same to them.—*And be baptized with the baptism that I am baptized with*? "that I am already in spirit enduring?" Another simile for the coming death, omitted by Matthew. The baptism is the overwhelming in pain and death; the woe is to come like the rushing of the water over the body of one whom John plunged in the Jordan. Perhaps he could not have found, within the range of their common thoughts, a stronger simile for his purpose; but he seems to have chosen it partly, also, because it was a sacred simile, the sanctity of baptism having given to the form a suggestive character that made it especially suitable for his use. When it comes to this symbolic use of the word, no one doubts that the act which forms the basis of the symbolism is a complete immersion.—The two questions mean the same, and the thought is, "You ask for thrones: can you die, and in spirit suffer death before death, as I do? Can you take up the cross and come after me, and go to the throne by the way that I take?"

39. Their unqualified *We can* contained both good and evil. They knew that they were attached to Jesus, and it was their loyal hearts that spoke. But they knew not themselves, and spoke in ignorant assurance. The third of the special three put himself similarly on record (Luke 22:33); so that Peter, James and John are the men to whom we owe the most remarkable utterances of the confidence that is easy to an ignorant heart. Yet the *We can* of James and John and the profession of Peter came true in later times, when they had learned the secret of their Master more deeply. Their claims of victory were premature, but their hearts already had the secret of future victory.

The kindness of the answer is something wonderful. There is no tone or spirit of rebuke in it, although there was so much room for reproof. On the surface it is a denial of the request—at least, it would put an end to all exclusive expectations. Yet the prediction *Ye shall indeed drink the cup that I drink* is really a promise of all that is precious in what they asked for. If he could truthfully say, "Ye shall suffer in my spirit," the thrones were assured, though no promise was given of the special ones that were ambitiously chosen. "To him that overcometh will I grant to sit with me in my throne" (Rev. 3:21). This prediction scarcely amounts to an announcement of martyrdom for each of the two brothers; it might be fulfilled by life in the martyr's spirit. But James drank that cup (Acts 12:2) and John suffered, if he did not die (Rev. 1:9). Both attained to high seats at the Master's side, but thrones how unlike all that they were thinking of! and by a way how different from all that they expected! In both aspects was the answer true, that they knew not what they asked. The real thrones were more glorious than they thought, and the way was such as they knew not.

"40. The remainder of the answer surprises us; for, instead of giving them some reason why they must beware of looking too high or expecting too much, he disclaims the power to grant their request. *To sit on my right hand and on my left hand is not mine to give*: "but it is for them for whom it hath been prepared." So, correctly, in the Revision. Matthew adds "by my Father."—*But* (alla) is not equivalent to "except;" as if he had said, "It is not mine to give, except to those for whom it hath been prepared." Such a translation, though sometimes proposed, is inadmissible. Two statements are here—that the assignment of the highest rank is the prerogative of the Father, which reminds one of the language of Mark 13:32, and that the highest rank shall be assigned by him to those for whom it has been prepared. But who are they for whom the highest rank has been prepared by the Father? (See verses 42-44). They are the disciples who are most like the Master. The nearest thrones are prepared for the truest followers, just as the crown is prepared for the successful contestant (1 Cor. 9:24). Here, again, the last may be the first, and even the chief apostles cannot be sure that some servant of humbler name may not at the end be above them.

41. *The ten*—the remainder of the apostolic band—*began to be much displeased with James and John.* Began, but were soon interrupted and brought to account by the Master.—*Displeased.* The same word as in verse 14. Why displeased? Had they not all been questioning who should be greatest (chap. 9:34)? and would they not all have been glad of the places James and John had chosen? It was human nature: they thought it very wrong when two petitioned for what all would gladly have claimed.

42. *Jesus called them*—not necessarily the ten—apart from James and John; this word was for all.—First he states the worldly principle of greatness—a principle with which he says they are familiar. *Ye know that they which are accounted to rule over the Gentiles*, or "the nations" i.e. the recognized and accepted rulers of the world—*exercise lordship*, or "lord it," *over them*—that is, over the Gentiles, or nations, their subjects—*and their great ones exercise authority upon them.* This is the ordinary human conception of greatness. Recognized greatness among the nations of the world implies the exercise of domination over men; the great ones lord it. This is the ideal of greatness and a kingdom which Jesus rejected in the wilderness, and again when the Jews became his tempters (John 6:15).

43, 44. *But so shall it not be*—or, on manuscript authority, "it is not so"—*among you.* Your principle is not the principle of the world, and you have your own type of greatness and your own way of becoming great. Accordingly, he proceeds to tell of the Christian way of becoming great. The verbs in the future tense may best be rendered by "will" instead of *shall*, for Jesus is telling not what he requires, but what a man will do who intelligently seeks the Christian greatness in the Christian way. Also, instead of *whosoever will be great,* read "whosoever wishes to become great," and, in verse 44, "whosoever wishes to become chiefest," or "first."—What, now, is the Christian principle of greatness and the way by which a wise Christian will seek high rank? The Christian greatness consists in humble service; and a Christian who wishes to be great will seek it, if he seeks as a Christian, only through humble service.—The desire for greatness is here represented in two degrees, "whosoever wishs to become great among you" telling of the general desire for eminence, and "whosoever of you wishes to become first" expressing the still higher desire for pre-eminence. It is not "the first," as if a Christian could distinctly set his ambition on that it is "first"—that is, a person of first rank, one of the highest.—Observe particularly that our Lord does not forbid or discourage such desires; he does not say that there are no honors in his kingdom or bid us look for a dead-level of spiritual equality; and he does not hint that it is wrong to desire to have a place among the "first." But he proceeds to tell how a Christian, if he intelligently adopts the Christian principle, will act on such a desire. Does he wish to become great? he will be *your minister* (diakonos), attendant, or assistant—i.e. he will make himself a helper to his brethren. Does his ambition reach higher, so that he wishes to become a man of first rank? he will bow still lower, and be *the servant of all,* a slave (doulous) for the service of all to whom he can be useful. There is a threefold climax. "First" is higher than "great," indicating a higher ambition in the aspiring soul.

Slave (doulous) is lower than minister, attendant (diakonos), indicating a deeper humility as the means of reaching the higher honor. *Of all* is broader than "of you," in *your minister*, indicating that the deeper humility will seek and find opportunities of wider as well as greater usefulness. The higher one wishes to rise, the lower will he bend in brotherly service, and the more freely will he give himself to many.—It may be asked whether our Lord's teaching is not self-contradictory here; whether, in practice, we can conceive of seeking first rank by means of humility and service; whether the two motives are not incompatible. Certainly they are incompatible, so long as we hold the worldly conception of thrones and rewards. But the idea of greatness through any elevation that would gratify vanity he has just expressly ruled out, and has placed the honors of the kingdom in something else. The honor in this kingdom consists in being like the King, and the first rank in being most like the King. Whoever seeks this intelligently will seek it exactly as Jesus said, by humble and loving service to many. In this veiw of the matter it is evident that the honors are not altogether in the future. Whoever is doing the service in the Master's spirit is already of high rank, already on the throne. But the aristocracy in the kingdom is unconscious. They who belong to it are the last to suspect the fact, and any who may suppose themselves to belong to it are wrong (Matt. 25:37-39).

45. The great illustration and example is the Christ himself, in whose glory the ambitious disciples were hoping to share. He came to illustrate, not the human idea of greatness by being served, but the divine idea by serving. The great God himself is greatest in his helpfulness of love, and when he came nearest to men to show them his glory he came thus, in the self-sacrificing Son of man.—*Not to be ministered unto.* Not to "lord it" or "exercise authority" over men, after the manner of the Gentiles, *but to minister*, "serve," *and to give his life a ransom for many.* The extreme act of service. Compare the similar teaching at another time, in Luke 22:24-27, culminating in the words, "I am among you as he that serveth," and the matchless object-lesson in John 13:1-17; also Rom. 15:1-3; Phil. 2:5-11. In all these passages, and in many more (as Gal. 6:2; 2 Cor. 8:1-9; 1 Peter 5:1-4), the footsteps of the Master are shown to the disciples that they may follow. The act of God in providing the propitiation for our sins, and the act of Christ in laying down his life for us, are given as the supreme examples for us in 1 John 4:10, 11; 3:16. This was our Saviour's way to glory: the chief throne was prepared for the chief servant, and it will be found that the king is he who has done the most for his brethren. This is the only way by which any throne in his kingdom can be reached. (See John 12:26, spoken when only death remained to him.)—*To give his life a ransom for many.* A

ransom is the price paid for the release of prisoners or captives. The word *for,* in the sense of "instead of" ("a ransom for many"), is entirely appropriate, since a ransom is naturally conceived of as taking the place of the persons who are delivered by it, or serving instead of them. An idea of vicariousness, or action in the place of others, resides in this word, as well as in the word *ransom* itself. The phrase falls in with the other language of Scripture which represents the giving up of his life as the indispensable means for the deliverance of men from sin; and of this he was thinking when he spoke of the supreme act of service, the giving of his life a ransom for many. In order to *minister* thus to men he came into the world.—We often think of his way to the cross as rich in example for us; but here the cross itself is made the chief example. So Eph. 5:2. Here we are called to the spiritual "fellowship of his sufferings." (W. N. Clarke)

FACT QUESTIONS 10:35-45

603. Of what is this section a living illustration?
604. Give three facts concerning the former association of James and John.
605. Who was the mother of James and John?
606. Can we catch anything in the words of Jesus to indicate why James and John made the request they did?
607. Did James and John have any special nearness to Jesus that would encourage such a request? Discuss.
608. Did James and John actually believe Jesus would grant the request even before He knew what it was?
609. What was the basic motive in making the request?
610. Show how humiliating were the words of Jesus "Ye know not what ye ask."
611. Please explain the symbolism of the two figures of "the cup"—"the baptism."
612. Show how the immediate answer of "we can" contains both good and evil.
613. Show how James and John indeed were given "high seats at the Master's side."
614. Who are they for whom the highest rank has been prepared by the Father?
615. Show how the Father gives such positions and not the Son.
616. Show the inconsistency of the disapproval of the ten.

617. What is the worldly principle of greatness? When and where had Jesus rejected this principle?
618. What is the Christian principle of greatness?
619. Does Jesus discourage ambition by His words of rebuke for a certain type of greatness? Discuss.
620. Show the "threefold climax" in the words of Jesus.
621. What will be found by the "deeper humility"?
622. Aren't the two concepts of humility and greatness contradictory? Discuss.
623. What of the "aristocracy" of the kingdom?
624. Show how Jesus was the greatest and grandest illustration of what He taught.
625. How does the example of God also illustrate the principle of true greatness?
626. In what sense is the word "ransom" here used?
627. In what manner can we share in the "fellowship of his sufferings"?

F. BLIND BARTIMEUS 10:46-52

TEXT 10:46-52

"And they come to Jericho: and as he went out from Jericho, with his disciples and a great multitude, the son of Timeus, Bartimeus, a blind beggar, was sitting by the way side. And when he heard that it was Jesus of Nazareth, he began to cry out, and say, Jesus, thou son of David, have mercy on me. And many rebuked him, that he should hold his peace: but he cried out the more a great deal, Thou son of David, have mercy on me. And Jesus stood still, and said, Call ye him. And they call the blind man, saying unto him, Be of good cheer; rise, he calleth thee. And he, casting away his garments, sprang up, and came to Jesus. And Jesus answered him, and said, What wilt thou that I should do unto thee? And the blind man said unto him, Rabonni, that I may receive my sight. And Jesus said unto him, Go thy way; thy faith hath made thee whole. And straightway he received his sight, and followed him in the way."

THOUGHT QUESTIONS 10:46-52

581. Read Luke 18:35-43 and note the difference in the location of the healing—please attempt an explanation.
582. Why was there a great multitude with the disciples?
583. Why mention the father of Bartimeus?
584. Why were there more beggars in the days of our Lord?

585. How did Bartimeus come to have faith in Jesus?
586. Why call Jesus "son of David"?
587. What is the meaning of "mercy" as here used?
588. Give two possible reasons for the attempt of the disciples to silence this beggar.
589. How account for the change in attitude of the disciples from vs. 48 to vs. 49?
590. Why ask him what he wanted? (as in vs. 51)
591. What is the meaning of the expression: "Go thy way"?

COMMENT

TIME.—A.D. 30; the latter part of March.

PLACE.—Jericho, the "city of Palm Trees," situated fifteen to twenty miles northeast of Jerusalem, in the valley of Jordan, at the foot of the pass that led up from the Jordan valley to the central highlands and to Jerusalem. It was about six or seven miles north of the Dead Sea and about five miles from the Jordan at the base of the mountain rampart. After Jerusalem, it was at this date the most important city of Judea. It was 900 feet below the Mediterranean, and about 3,400 feet lower than Jerusalem. See the section of Palestine from east to west. The district was a blooming oasis in the midst of an extended sandy plain, watered and fruitful, rich in palms, roses and balsams; hence the name, "the fragrant city." Built by the Canaanites, and destroyed by Joshua, it was rebuilt and fortified at a later day, and became a seat of a school of the prophets. Herod the Great beautified it, and it was the most luxuriant spot in Palestine. In the twelfth century scarcely a vestige of the place remained. There is now on the site a wretched village with about 200 inhabitants. Sloping gently upwards from the level of the Dead Sea, 900 feet under the Mediterranean, it had the climate of lower Egypt and displayed the vegetation of the tropics. While snow is falling at Jerusalem, thin clothing is comfortable in Jericho.

PARALLEL ACCOUNTS.—Matt. 20:29-34; Luke 18:35-43; 19:1.

LESSON OUTLINE.—1. The Blind Beggar's Petition. 2. The Lord's Call. 3. The Blind Beggar Healed.

ANALYSIS

I. THE BLIND BEGGAR'S PETITION, VS. 46-48.
   1. The Beggar by the Wayside. Mark 10:46; Matt. 20:30; Luke 18:35.
   2. Appeal to the Son of David. Mark 10:47; Matt. 20:31; Luke 18:38.
   3. The Beggar Rebuked. Mark 10:48; Matt. 20:32; Luke 18:39.

II. THE LORD'S CALL, VS. 49, 50.

1. The Lord Hears the Cry for Mercy. Mark 10:49; Matt. 20:32; Luke 18:40.
2. The Beggar Comes to Jesus. Mark 10:50; Matt. 20:32; Luke 18:40.

III. THE BLIND BEGGAR HEALED, VS. 51, 52.

1. The Prayer for Sight. Mark 10:51; Matt. 20:33; Luke 18:41.
2. Saved by Faith. Mark 10:52; Luke 18:42.
3. Following Jesus. Mark 10:52; Matt. 20:34; Luke 18:43.

EXPLANATORY NOTES

I. THE BLIND BEGGAR'S PETITION.

46. *They came to Jericho.* The Lord and his disciples, on their way to Jerusalem. The exact position of the ancient Jericho is not known, but it was not far from the site of the present village, and was from five to seven miles from the Jordan on the great highway from the Trans-Jordanic county to Jerusalem. It was several hundred feet above the Jordan level, but still many hundred feet below the level of the sea, and there was a continual ascent from thence to the highlands on which stood Jerusalem. *His disciples and a great number of people.* At this season Jericho would be full of people who were going up to attend the Passover. The number would be greatly increased by those coming from Galilee by the way of Perea, to avoid passing through Samaria. These, added to the Trans-Jordanic pilgrims, would, within a week or two of the Passover, crowd the great highway at Jericho with travelers. Besides, curiosity and expectation caused the crowds to travel in the company of Jesus. *Blind.* Ophthalmia is fearfully prevalent, especially among children, in the East, and goes on unchecked, in many or most instances, to its worst results. It would be no exaggeration to say, that one adult out of every five has his eyes more or less damaged by the consequences of the disease.—W. G. Palgrave. *Bartimeus, the son of Timeus.* His being mentioned by name implies that he was well known. His father, too, would appear to have been noted for some reason or other. Perhaps they both became ultimately attached to the cause of the Savior and the fellowship of the disciples. *Bar* is the Aramaic word for *son,* Timeus being the name of the father. Matthew mentions two beggars. He was present. Mark and Luke who wrote upon the testimony of others only mention the more prominent one whose name had been preserved. Dean Howson says: "These difficulties we may dismiss. The particular spot is of no consequence; and, if there were two blind men, there certainly was one. Our attention is to be fixed on this one, Bartimeus." *Sat by the wayside begging.* Both

beggary and blindness are much more common in the East than with us—the former owing to unjust taxation, uneven distribution of wealth, and the total absence of public and systematized charities; the latter owing to lack of cleanliness, and to exposure to an almost tropical sun, and to burning sands.—*Abbott.*

47. *When he heard that it was Jesus of Nazareth.* A designation never used by the evangelist, save in recording the words of others. He was familiarly, and also contemptuously, known as the *Nazarene*—inhabitant of Nazareth. He had heard of him before—heard of healings wrought by him, of blind eyes opened, of dead men raised. It had never crossed his thoughts that he and this Jesus should meet, when now they tell him that he is near at hand. He can do that for him which none but he can do. It is his one and only chance. *He began.* Immediately, as soon as he heard this, and continued so to do until he gained his end. *To cry out.* For God loves to be entreated, he loves to be compelled, he loves to be even vanquished by our persevering importunity.—*St. Gregory. Jesus, thou son of David.* He therefore believed that Jesus of Nazareth was the son of David, i.e., the expected Messiah. The cry of the blind man was a recognition of Christ's dignity as the Messiah; for this name, "son of David," was the popular designation of the Messiah. There was, therefore, upon his part, a confession of faith. *Have mercy on me.* The emphasis naturally falls on the word "me"; for Bartimeus, hearing that it was Jesus, and knowing his own disadvantage from his blindness in the crowd, fears he may be overlooked.

48. *Many charged him that he should hold his peace.* Not because he called Jesus the son of David, but (1) because he presumed to intrude a private grief upon the King of Israel, when, as they supposed, he was going in triumph to Jerusalem to assume his throne and deliver the nation. This spirit of rebuke is exactly the same as that of Matthew (19:13). (2) Perhaps from selfishness, not wishing to have the Lord's attention called away from their instruction. (3) From indifference to other's needs. (4) They thought they were pleasing the Master in defending him from a beggar. *Cried the more a great deal.* They were not to be silenced, and the litanies of Christendom for centuries have been modeled on the *Kyrie Eleison* (Lord have mercy on us) which came from their lips.—*Plumptre.* Methinks we hear his shout. There would be the very strength and might and blood and sinew of that man's life cast into it; he would be like Jacob wrestling with the angel, and every word would be a hand to grasp him that he might not go. The gate of heaven is to be opened only in one way, by the very earnest use of the knocker of prayer.—*Spurgeon. Thou son of David.* He suffers himself now to be

publicly appealed to as the Messiah in the presence of all the people, which he had never done before. The time for his acceptance of, and sympathy with, the Messianic hope of his people had now arrived.—*Lange.* It was a great act of faith in this blind man to call him the son of David, whom the people pointed out as being Jesus of Nazareth.—*Bengel. Have mercy on me.* This is prayer. There is no preamble, no vague utterance, no redundancy of expression in real prayer. Much of what is called prayer in these modern times is nothing but a weak and windy string of sentences.—*Thomas.* Jesus was passing by—would soon be past—might never pass that way again. It was a short opportunity; it seemed likely it would be the only one.—*Tyng.* The preaching of the gospel is a perpetual announcement that Jesus is near.—*Luther.*

II. THE LORD'S CALL.

49. *Jesus stood still.* The multitude had rebuked the blind Bartimeus for his intercession, but the Lord stopped at his cry. He is kinder than men. He is no respecter of persons. The blind beggar is to him as the rich ruler. He came to die for both. *And commanded.* This is a reproof of the reprovers. *To be called.* Making those help who had hindered. *They call the blind man.* Nothing could be more natural than the sudden change which is effected in the conduct of the multitude, as soon as they observe the favorable disposition of Jesus. *He calleth thee.* The call of Christ is always full of cheer—always, too, a call to do something as a token of trust in him.—*Abbott.* His call is always a call for an act of faith. He bids Bartimeus come.

50. *Casting away his garment;* i.e., his outer garment. This was his cloak, or mantle, which is often used by the poor at night for a covering, and which the law of Moses gave them a special claim to, that it should not be kept from them over night when it was given as a pledge. The outside garment hindered his speed, could be spared, and is therefore thrown aside. In dead earnest is he, and can brook no delay. *Rose.* The Revised Version says Bartimeus threw off his "garments," so sinners should throw away everything that hinders their going to him —everything that obstructs their progress—and cast themselves at his feet. No man will be saved while sitting still. The command is, "Strive to enter in;" and the promise is made to those only who "ask" and "seek" and "knock." *Came to Jesus.* The blind man runs to Jesus without seeing him. So must we hasten to him in faith, though we see him not. He does not need to be told a second time; he does not wait for any guiding hands to lead him to the center of the path. A few eager footsteps, he stands in the presence of the Lord!

III. THE BLIND BEGGAR HEALED.

51. *What wilt thou that I should do?* With a majesty truly royal, Jesus seems to open up to the beggar the treasure of divine power, and to give him, if we may so speak, *carte blanche.—Godet.* Jesus asks, not for information, but to draw from them an expression of their desire. The gift is of more value when given in answer to prayer. *Lord.* Better, *Rabboni,* as in the Revised, the word being the same as in John 20:16, and occurring in these two passages only. The word was an augumentative form of Rabbi, and as such expressed greater reverence. The gradations of honor were Rab, Rabbi, Rabban, Rabboni. *That I might receive my sight.* Not *how* or *why*, but the *desire*, which he believes the Lord can grant in the best way. The man, whose cry has been hitherto a vague, indeterminate cry for mercy, now singles out the blessing which he craves, designates the channel in which he desires that his mercy should run.

52. *Go thy way.* Matthew states that he touched his eyes. Other blind men had called him the son of David, but he had straitly charged them not to make him known. No such charge is given to Bartimeus. He is permitted to follow him, and glorify God as loudly, as amply as he can (Luke 18:43). As the time draws near, all the reasons for that reserve which Jesus had previously studied are removed.—*Hanna. Thy faith hath made thee whole.* It was the confidence which the blind man cherished in the ability and benevolence of Jesus that induced him to seek aid from Jesus, and that induced him to persevere while the crowd sought to restrain him. Such confidence Jesus delighted to acknowledge and to honor. The faith of this man was great; because, being blind, he could not see the miracles which Jesus did. Faith came to him by hearing. He believed on the testimony and report of others; and so he inherited, in a manner, the promise of the Lord his Savior, "Blessed are they who have not seen and yet have believed" (John 20:20). Christ was always ready to heal. No one was ever refused who asked him. It rested with the man; the healing could not have its way and enter in, save the man would open his door. Hence the question, and the praise of the patient's faith. *Made thee whole.* Complete, sound, nothing wanting. A sinner is never whole; never a complete, perfect man. Christ makes us whole. *And followed Jesus.* Glorifying God, as Luke adds (18:43), and joining the festal company of His Healer, who all likewise gave praise unto God for the miracle which they had witnessed. Compare Acts 3:8-10. Thus, as our Lord journeyed toward Jerusalem, he gathered in his train fresh monuments of his power. The march of earthly conquerors is tracked with blood; smoking villages and mangled corpses

mark the way which they had trodden, while weeping captives are chained to their triumphal chariots. But the Savior left joy behind him wherever he went, and collected new trophies of his mercy.—*Tyng.*

APPLICATION.—This miracle is in one sense a parable. It teaches most forcibly the doctrine and methods of salvation by faith. It has been so represented by commentators of all ages. The blind man represents one, without faith, who is blind to the unseen interests of his soul. In his darkness, "the passing of the Saviour," in his gospel preached, may stir him to a sense of his needs. He then calls for mercy upon Jesus, confessing his faith in him as the Messiah King and Healer. Men may try to hinder him coming to Jesus. The Lord calls him, but he has first called unto the Lord. The Lord gives him the election who has elected the Lord. The sinner is required to arise and go to Christ in obedience, is then healed of his sins and blindness and follows the Master.

FACT QUESTIONS 10:46-52

628. Give five facts about Jericho.
629. Why would the great number of persons already in Jericho be greatly increased at the time Jesus and His disciples came into it?
630. What type of blindness did Bartimeus have?
631. What is implied by mentioning Bartimeus by name?
632. Why does Matthew mention *two* beggars? How reconcile these accounts?
633. What designation concerning our Lord is never used by the evangelist Mark except in recording the words of others? Why?
634. How did Bartimeus know Jesus?
635. What example for us is in the cry of the beggar?
636. What did the designation "Son of David" indicate?
637. Give three possible reasons for asking Bartimeus to hold his peace.
638. How was the response of Jesus to the acknowledging Him as the Messiah by Bartimeus different than others?
639. How did Jesus reprove the reprovers?
640. What is always included in the call of Christ?
641. Why did the beggar cast aside his garment? In what manner did he arise?
642. How could he so eagerly come to Jesus if he could not see Him?
643. Why did Jesus ask the question: "What wilt thou that I should do"?
644. What was the meaning of the word "Rabboni"?
645. What was included in the expression "Go thy way"?
646. Show how great was the faith of the blind man.
647. What is added by Luke 18:43?

SUMMARY 10:1-52

In this section Jesus is exhibited as a teacher, a prophet, and a worker of miracles. His instruction on the subject of divorce (1-12), displays a knowledge of the primary intention of God concerning the relation of the sexes, and an insight into the design of the Mosaic statute on the subject, which not only rose high above the Jewish learning of his own age, but laid claim to a knowledge of the unrevealed counsel of God. None but the Son of God, or one specially commissioned to speak the mind of God, could blamelessly speak as he speaks on this subject. He sets aside, for the future, the statute of Moses, stating the reason which governed the mind of God in giving it, and restores as the law of his kingdom the original law of wedded life prescribed in the garden of Eden.

His teaching, in the same section, on the spiritual relations of infants; on the duties and dangers connected with riches; on the rewards of self-sacrifice for his sake; and on the true exercise of ambition, are alike suited to his character as the Son of God, and to the highest happiness of mankind. It is inconceivable that they can be the teachings of an ignorant or a wicked pretender.

While his superhuman wisdom is thus displayed in his teaching, his ability to look with divine foreknowledge into all the details of future events is demonstrated by minute description of the sufferings which awaited him.

The account of blind Bartimeus, while it proves again his power to heal, reflects additional credibility on the account of his previous miracles. This man, being blind, could have known of the previous miracles only by hearsay; he could not have seen them for himself. That he did, then, believe in the power of Jesus to heal, shows the abundance and sufficiency of the testimony; and the very existence of this testimony in regard to a matter about which men could not be mistaken, is proof that real miracles had been wrought. (*McGarvey*)

IV. THE LAST WEEK 11:1-15:47

A. SUNDAY: THE TRIUMPHAL ENTRY 11:1-11

TEXT 11:1-11

"And when they draw night unto Jerusalem, unto Bethphage and Bethany, at the mount of Olives, he sendeth two of his disciples, and saith unto them, Go your way into the village that is over against you: and straightway as ye enter into it, ye shall find a colt tied, whereon no man ever yet sat; loose him, and bring him. And if any one say unto you, Why do ye this? say ye, The Lord hath need of him; and straightway he will send him back hither. And they went away, and found a colt tied at the door without in the open street; and they loose him. And certain of them that stood there said unto them, What do ye, loosing the colt? And they said unto them even as Jesus had said: and they let them go. And they bring the colt unto Jesus, and cast on him their garments; and he sat upon him. And many spread their garments upon the way; and others branches, which had been cut from the fields. And they that went before, and they that followed, cried, Hosanna; Blessed is he that cometh in the name of the Lord: Blessed is the kingdom that cometh, the kingdom of our father David: Hosanna in the highest. And he entered into Jerusalem into the temple; and when he had looked round about upon all things, it being now eventide, he went out unto Bethany with the twelve."

THOUGHT QUESTIONS 11:1-11

592. Please attempt to locate the place described in vs. 1 as "nigh unto Jerusalem, unto Bethphage and Bethany."
593. Who were the two disciples of vs. 2?
594. Into which village did the disciples go?
595. Why was it important to mention the colt had never carried a man? Cf. Zech. 9:9.
596. Was this not a rather presumptuous request on the part of Jesus? Explain.
597. Why would the owner of the animal be so willing to comply with the request?
598. Why promise immediate return of the colt?
599. At what particular place was the colt tied?
600. Did they bring one or two animals. Cf. Matt. 21:2.
601. Were the people and the disciples aware of the prophetic import of their actions?
602. Why cast garments upon the colt?
603. Why was symbolized or typified in casting the garments and leaves in the way?

604. Why did Jesus permit this public demonstration?
605. What is the meaning of the word "Hosanna"?
606. How is the word "blessed" used here?
607. In what sense did Jesus restore the kingdom of David?

COMMENT

TIME.—A.D. 30. Sunday, 2d April, 10th Nisan (Palm Sunday), the fifth day before the great Jewish Passover. It was the first of their secular days after the Jewish Sabbath had ended.

PLACES.—(1) Bethany. (2) The main road from Bethany to Jerusalem. (3) Jerusalem. The places connected with this lesson are among those hallowed by the most tender associations of our Lord. He slept the night preceding the entry into Jerusalem at Bethany, the home of Lazarus, Martha and Mary, where he had raised Lazarus from the dead, to which sweet place of rest and sympathy the Lord often retired when at Jerusalem. It stood about two miles east of the city on the eastern slope of the Mount of Olives, which lay between it and Jerusalem. Through it led the highway from the Jordan to the Holy City. A small village with a similar name still stands upon its ancient site. From Bethany the road led through Bethphage, a small village of the time of our Lord, nearer Jerusalem, that has not even left a trace by which its position can be certainly known. Over the *Mount of Olives* there were three paths, one on the north between two peaks of the hill, a second over the summit of the southern peak, and a third on the south around the slope, between the Mount of Olives and the Hill of Offence. This was the best and most frequented road and was the one taken by the Savior. The Mount of Olives lay just east of Jerusalem, with the vale of the Kedron, or valley of Jehoshaphat, as it was called, between. The summit was about a mile from the city and overlooked it. It took its name from the olive trees that grew upon its sides until they were cut down by the Roman general, Titus, for use in the siege of Jerusalem. It was a kind of "park," or pleasant resort for the inhabitants. It rises 2,724 feet above the sea level and 300 feet higher than the Temple hill.

INTERVENING HISTORY.—Many interesting events occurred between the healing of Bartimeus and our present event; the following is their probable order: (1) Our Lord, after giving sight to Bartimeus, converts Zaccheus, and is entertained by him in Jericho (Luke 19:1-10), where he remains during the night. (2) In the morning he speaks to the people the parable of the pounds (Luke 19:11-28). (3) He leaves Jericho, and apparently reached Bethany on the evening of Friday, March 31, Nisan 8. There (4) in quiet retirement he spent his last earthly Sabbath (our

Saturday, April 1); and (5) in the evening, the Sabbath being over at Sunset, he sat down to a festal meal provided by the sisters of Lazarus at the house of one Simon, who had been a leper. (Matt. 26:6; John 12:2). (6) At this feast he was anointed by Mary (John 12:3); and (7) during the night a council of the Jews was convened to consider the propriety of putting, not him only, but Lazarus also, to death (John 12:10).—*Maclear.*

PARALLEL ACCOUNTS.—Matt. 21:1-11; Luke 19:29-44; John 12:12-19.

LESSON OUTLINE.—1. The Lord's Charge. 2. The Charge Obeyed. 3. The King Proclaimed.

ANALYSIS

THE LORD'S CHARGE, VS. 1-3.

1. The Two Disciples Sent. Mark 11:1; Matt. 21:1; Luke 19:29.
2. The Charge to the Disciples. Mark 11:2; Matt. 21:2; Luke 19:30.
3. The Lord Hath Need. Mark 11:3; Matt. 21:3; Luke 19:31.

II. THE CHARGE OBEYED, VS. 4-7.

1. The Disciples on their Mission. Mark 11:4; Matt. 21:6; Luke 19:32.
2. The King's Demand. Mark 11:6; Luke 19:34.
3. The King Obeyed. Mark 11:7; Matt. 21:7; Luke 19:35.

III. THE KING PROCLAIMED, VS. 8-11.

1. Homage to the King. Mark 11:8; Matt. 21:8; Luke 19:36.
2. Hosanna to the King. Mark 11:9, 10; Matt. 21:9; Luke 19:38; John 12:13.
3. The King in Jerusalem. Mark 11:11; Matt. 21:10; Luke 19:41; John 12:19.

INTRODUCTION

We may suppose that as our Savior crossed the Jordan, and came across the desert tract between the Jordan and Jericho, he walks at the head of his train of twelve disciples. As he departs from Jericho, his fame, and the idea that he is on his way to Jerusalem, attract the multitude to follow him. From Jericho he mounts the ascending hills of bleak limestone rocks, celebrated at that time as a route of danger from robber hordes, and characterized from that time to this as a scene of desert dreariness. It was the scene of the parable of the good Samaritan. By the same route that the men went down from Jerusalem to Jericho, and fell among thieves, did our Lord go up from Jericho to Jerusalem. Some miles he walks, when Bethany appears in a distant view, a little widespread village, perched upon a shelf of the eastern side of the Mount of Olives, about two miles from Jerusalem. He arrived at Bethany, according to John 12:1, six days before his last passover; the six days of what has been called in the church, with true propriety, the *Passion Week*. The significance of this entry into Jerusalem has been too little considered. It was Christ's nature to shun crowds; his custom to avoid them. He forbade his disciples from disclosing to others that he was the Messiah, and this prohibition was repeatedly given. Matt. 16:20; 17:9; Mark 3:12; 5:43; 6:36, etc. This exceptional assumption of dignity and acceptance of homage is for this reason the more remarkable and significant. I believe it to be an emphasis of the truth that he was a King and came as King; that it throws forth into prominence a truth respecting him often forgotten, namely, that he is Lord and Master, as well as Savior, crowned with authority as well as with humility and love.—*Abbott.*

EXPLANATORY NOTES

I. THE LORD'S CHARGE.

1. *When they came nigh to Jerusalem.* Luke says, "ascended up to Jerusalem," because Jericho is 3,000 feet lower than Jerusalem. A journey of about eighteen miles up the rugged ravine that leads from Jericho to Jerusalem. As the passover, with its sacrifices, was just at hand, companies of pilgrims, driving sheep for the altar, would be seen in the highways, all gathering up from the four quarters to the center of the nation's faith. Among them goes the Lamb of God—the one sacrifice—final, perfect, and sufficient, whom these typical altars of thousands of years had heralded with their banners of smoke and flame. *To Bethphage and Bethany.* Two suburban villages east of Jerusalem on the east slope of the Mount of Olives. Mark omits all mention of the stay at Bethany, which is narrated in John 12:1-11. The Lord reached Bethany Friday evening, remained over the Sabbath at that quiet hamlet, and on Sunday made his entry into Jerusalem. *Sendeth forth two of his disciples.* The sending of the two disciples proves the deliberate intention of Jesus to give a certain solemnity to the scene. Till then he had withdrawn from popular expressions of homage; but once, at least, he wished to show himself as King Messiah of his people. It was a last call addressed by him to the population of Jerusalem. This course, besides, could no longer compromise his work. He knew that in any case death awaited him in the capital.—*Godet.* He would have a public testimony to the fact that it was their King the Jews crucified. It is not merely the Messiah that saves, nor the crucified One that saves, but the Messiah crucified (1 Cor. 1:23). An analogous commission to prepare the passover was given to Peter and John (Luke 22:8). They may have been the two sent forth.—*Abbott.*

2. *Into the village over against you.* Leaving Bethany on foot, attended by his disciples and others, he comes to the place where the neighboring

village of Bethphage is in view, over against them, perhaps separated from them by a valley. To this village he probably sent his disciples. *Ye shall find a colt tied.* It was the colt of an ass, an animal in disfavor in the West, but highly esteemed in the East. Geikie says: "Statelier, livelier, swifter than with us, it vies with the horse in favor. In contrast to the horse, which had been introduced by Solomon from Egypt, and was used especially for war, it was the symbol of peace. To the Jew it was peculiarly national. For had not Moses led his wife, seated on an ass, to Egypt? had not the Judges ridden on white asses? Every Jew, moreover, expected, from the words of one of the prophets (Zech. 9:9), that the Messiah would enter Jerusalem riding on an ass. No act could be more perfectly in keeping with the conception of a king of Israel." Matthew speaks of the "she-ass and the colt" together, to show that it was a colt which yet went with its mother—so fulfilling the Scripture, that it was one "upon which never man sat." *Whereon never man sat.* The fact is mentioned by Mark and Luke only (19:30). It was probably, in their eyes, significant, as showing that he who used the colt did so in his own right, and not as filling a place which others had filled before him. This was not, we think, as Hengstenberg maintains, to indicate humility, but sacredness. See Luke 23:53. Our Lord was "laid in a sepulcher that was hewn in stone, wherein never man was laid before." And so our Lord was born of a pure virgin. His birth, His triumph, His tomb, were thus alike. His appearance, His history, and his departure are thus indicated to be above the level of ordinary humanity. *Loose him, and bring him.* The demand was kingly. On this day the Lord's acts are all those of a King. The owner of the colt either was impressed by the authority of the expected Messiah King, or was a disciple.

3. *The Lord hath need of him.* It was enough for the loyal subject of an eastern king to know that his Lord made the demand and it was instantly obeyed. Hence, on this occasion, the only explanation to be offered was that the King had need. All Israel should be made to know that he who had come to Jerusalem to die was their King.

II. THE CHARGE OBEYED.

4. *And found the colt tied by the door without.* Trusting their Master, the two disciples obeyed, and found all as the Lord declared. The colt was tied, without the door, in front, "in the open street," as the Revision translates, rather than at a street corner, as the Common Version implies. It is not likely that Bethphage had any cross streets, but was built on each side of the road leading to Jerusalem. It was a small village.

5. *What do ye, loosing the colt?* This was spoken by the owner, or members of his household. The reply given was that which the Lord

directed, and had the expected effect. The disciples were simply to obey orders, and all the rest would follow.

6. *And they let them go.* All this was in accordance with a plan predicted 600 years ago. The prophet Zechariah had declared (Zech. 9:9) that thus the King would make his entry.

7. *They brought the colt to Jesus.* It was not the mother, but the colt, upon which no man had ever sat, that Jesus chose for his purpose. *Cast their garments on him.* Combining the four accounts, we get the following features: Some took off their outer garments, the burnoose, and bound it on the colt as a kind of saddle; others cast their garments in the way, a mark of honor to a king (2 Kings 9:13); others climbed the trees, cut down the branches, and strewed them in the way (Matt. 21:8); others gathered leaves and twigs and rushes (Mark 11:8). This procession was made up largely of Galileans, but the reputation of Christ, increased by the resurrection of Lazarus, had preceded him, and many came out from the city to swell the acclamations and increase the enthusiasm (John 12:13). Matthew adds that all this was in fulfillment of prophecy (Matt. 21:4, 5). Compare Zech. 9:9. *He sat upon him.* Our Lord sat on the foal (Mark, Luke), and the mother accompanied, apparently after the manner of a sumpter, as prophets so riding would be usually accompanied (but not, of course, doing the work of a sumpter). He who in all his journeys travelled like a poor man on foot, without noise and without train, now he goes up to Jerusalem to die for sinners; he rides, to show his great forwardness to lay down his life for us. Every Jew, moreover, expected, from the words of one of the prophets, that the Messiah would enter Jerusalem, poor and riding on an ass. No act could be more perfectly in keeping with the conception of a king of Israel, and no words could express more plainly that the King proclaimed himself the Messiah.

8. *Spread their garments.* The custom is still sometimes seen in the East. Dr Robinson relates that shortly after a rebellion which had taken place among the people of Bethlehem, "when some of the inhabitants were already imprisoned, and all were in deep distress, Mr. Farran, the English consul at Dasmascus, was on a visit to Jerusalem, and had rode out with Mr. Nicolayson to Solomon's pools. On their return, as they rose the ascent to enter Bethlehem, hundreds of the people, male and female, met them, imploring the consul to interfere in their behalf, and afford them his protection, and all at once, by a sort of simultaneous movement, "they spread their garments in the way" before the horses." It has not been uncommon to carpet the way for a king. *Cut down branches.* John says of palm trees. The wide, spreading leaf of the palm would be well adapted to the purpose of making a carpet for his way. The "branches

of palm trees" are not strictly branches at all, but the enormous leaves, twelve to sixteen feet long, which spring from the top of the tall, straight trunk. A few palm trees are still to be seen in Jerusalem.

III. THE KING PROCLAIMED.

9. *That went before and . . . that followed.* Two vast streams of people met on that day. The one poured out from the city; and, as they came through the gardens whose clusters of palm rose on the southeastern corner of Olivet, they cut down the long branches, as was their wont at the Feast of Tabernacles, and moved upward toward Bethany with shouts of welcome. From Bethany streamed forth the crowds who had assembled there the previous night. The two streams met midway. Half of the vast mass, turning round, preceded: the other half followed. Gradually the long procession swept up and over the ridge where first begins "the descent of the Mount of Olives" towards Jerusalem. At this point the first view is caught of the southeastern corner of the city. The temple and the northern portions are hid by the slope of Olivet on the right: what is seen is only Mount Zion. It was at this point, "as he drew near, at the descent of Mount Olives," that the shout of triumph burst forth from the multitude.—*Stanley. Hosanna.* A Greek modification of the Hebrew words, "Save now, I beseech thee," in Psalm 118:25, the next verse of which formed part of their song, "Blessed," etc. It is used as an expression of praise, like hallelujah. The faith of the holy Jews under the law, and of the holy Gentiles under the gospel, was one and the same. They that went before Christ in the one, and they that followed Christ in the other, did both cry, "Hosanna to the Son of David!" did both obtain salvation by the same Savior, and by the same way (Eph. 2:18).—*Lightfoot. That cometh in the name of the Lord.* The words are taken in part from Psalms 118:25, 26, a hymn which belonged to the great hallelujah chanted at the end of the Paschal Supper and the Feast of Tabernacles. The people were accustomed to apply it to the Messiah.—*Godet.*

10. *Blessed be the kingdom of our father David, that cometh.* (Better as in the Revised.) This recognizes clearly that Christ's kingdom is the continuation of the old kingdom of God's people, whose future glories are prophesied so often in the Old Testament. *Hosanna in the highest.* In the highest degree, in the highest strains, in the highest heavens.

11. *Entered into Jerusalem.* It was hereafter never possible to say that he had never declared himself in a wholly unequivocal manner. When Jerusalem afterwards was accused of the murder of the Messiah, she could not say that he had omitted to give an intelligible sign to all alike.—*Lange. Into the temple.* Jesus, the true Paschal Lamb, thus pre-

sented himself, as required by the law, that the victim to be offered should be set apart four days before the great day of atonement.—*Mimpriss.* He went to the temple that the prophecy might be fulfilled (Mal. 3:1-3).—*M. Henry. And had looked round about.* It was an act by which he took possession as it were, of his Father's house, and claimed dominion over it—an attitude maintained by him throughout this final visit to the holy city. *And now the eventide was come.* The word "eventide" is somewhat indefinite; but it included the two or three hours before sunset, as well as after. The procession, if it started in the morning, had probably been delayed by frequent halts; and its movements through such a dense crowd must have been but slow.—*Plumptre. He went out.* The day's work is completed with the Messianic entry itself; and only a visit to the Temple, and a significant look round about it, form the close, What the Messiah has still further to do (the cleansing of the temple, etc.) follows on the morrow.—*Meyer. To Bethany.* Where he spent the nights of this eventful week.

FACT QUESTIONS 11:1-11

648. Give the day, month and year for Palm Sunday. Why call it *Palm* Sunday?
649. What "tender associations" were maintained by our Lord at Bethany?
650. Where was Bethphage?
651 Locate the mount of Olives as related to Jerusalem.
652. Name at least three events between the healing of Bartimeus and entering Jerusalem.
653. What route did Jesus take from Jericho to Bethany? Why wasn't it dangerous for Jesus?
654. Show how Jesus' actions in this entrance into Jerusalem was especially significant.
655. Describe the procession from Jericho to Jerusalem; how far was it?
656. What occurred in John 12:1-11 omitted by Mark?
657. How did Jesus give expression to His "deliberate intention"?
658. Show just who it is that saves.
659. How does Luke 22:8 relate to sending out the two for the colt?
660. In what village were they to find the colt?
661. In what historical connection was the colt in contrast with the horse?
662. Show how use of the ass was peculiarly national.
663. Show how our Lord's birth, triumph and tomb were all alike.
664. Was the colt tied at a street corner? Explain the K.J.V. vs. 4b.
665. Show how the whole plan of the entrance into Jerusalem was 600 years old.

666. Refer to II Kings 9:13 and show how it compares here.
667. What particular people made up the procession who hailed Jesus as King?
668. What is a "sumpter" and "the work of a sumpter"?
669. What great forwardness is shown by our Lord?
670. Show how the experience of Dr. Robinson confirms the event of the scripture.
671. How would palm branches be especially appropriate for this occasion?
672. What two vast crowds met midway?
673. Show the relation of Psa. 118:25, 26 to this event.
674. Lightfoot makes a beautiful comparison of the two crowds—what is it?
675. What had Jesus declared in a very unequivocal manner?
676. In what way was Jesus keeping the law for the Paschal lamb?
677. What prophecy was fulfilled in Jesus' going into the temple? Cf. Mal. 3:1-3.
678. Why look about in the temple?
679. What hours are included in the word "eventide"?
680. When did Jesus weep over Jerusalem?

B. MONDAY:

1. THE BARREN FIG TREE. 11:12-14.

TEXT 11:12-14

"And on the morrow, when they were come out from Bethany, he hungered. And seeing a fig tree afar off having leaves, he came, if haply he might find anything thereon: and when he came to it, he found nothing but leaves; for it was not the season of figs. And he answered and said unto it, No man eat fruit from thee henceforward for ever. And his disciples heard it."

THOUGHT QUESTIONS 11:12-14

608. If Jesus stayed in the home of Mary and Martha why was He hungry?
609. Where was the fig tree? Cf. Matt. 21:18, 19.
610. In what way are leaves an indication of figs?
611. Didn't Jesus know before He came to the tree that there were no figs? For whose benefit did He search among the leaves?
612. It it was not the season for figs why expect them?
613. Wasn't there something terribly symbolic about this whole action? What was it?

614. Did the disciples understand the prophetic judgment against the Hebrew nation in the cursing of the fig tree? If not why do it?

COMMENT

TIME.—A.D. 30, Monday, 3rd April, 11th Nisan (Monday) the fourth day before the great Jewish Passover.

PLACES.—On the road from Bethany to Jerusalem—Jerusalem—the Temple—Bethany—the home of Mary, Martha and Lazarus.

PARALLEL ACCOUNT.—Matt. 21:18, 19.

OUTLINE.—1. The time, place and cause for judgment, vs. 12. 2. The object of judgment, vs. 13. 3. Judgment pronounced, vs. 14.

ANALYSIS

I. THE TIME, PLACE AND CAUSE FOR JUDGMENT, VS. 12.
   1. "on the morrow" probably Monday morning.
   2. Just outside Bethany was the place.
   3. Jesus was hungry.

II. THE OBJECT OF JUDGMENT, VS. 13.
   1. A fig tree in full view.
   2. Full of leaves.
   3. A hypocrite—no figs.

III. JUDGMENT PRONOUNCED, VS. 14.
   1. Addressed directly by word.
   2. Its mission removed forever.
   3. Those for whom the lesson was given heard and saw.

EXPLANATORY NOTES

I. THE TIME, PLACE AND CAUSE FOR JUDGMENT.

"We see, in the beginning of this passage, one of the many proofs that our Lord Jesus Christ was really man. We read that "He was hungry." He had a nature and bodily constitution like our own in all things, sin only excepted. He could weep and rejoice and suffer pain. He could be weary and need rest. He could be thirsty and need drink. He could be hungry and need food.

Expressions like this should teach us the condescension of Christ. How wonderful they are when we reflect upon them! He who is the eternal God,—He who made the world and all that it contains,—He from whose hand the fruits of the earth, the fish of the sea, the fowls of the air, the beasts of the field, all had their beginning,—He, even He was pleased to suffer hunger, when He came into the world to save sinners. This is a great mystery. Kindness and love like this pass man's understanding. No wonder that St. Paul speaks of the "unsearchable riches of Christ." (Eph. 3:8).

Expressions like this should teach us Christ's power to sympathize with His believing people on earth. He knows their sorrows by experience. He can be touched with the feeling of their infirmities. He has had experience of a body and its daily wants. He has suffered Himself the severe sufferings that the body of man is liable to. He has tasted pain, and weakness, and weariness, and hunger, and thirst. When we tell Him of these things in our prayers, He knows what we mean, and is no stranger to our troubles. Surely this is just the Saviour and Friend that poor aching, groaning, human nature requires!"

II. THE OBJECT OF JUDGMENT.

"We learn, in the second place, from these verses, the great danger of unfruitfulness and formality in religion. This is a lesson which our Lord teaches in a remarkable typical action. We are told that coming to a fig tree in search of fruit, and finding on it "nothing but leaves," He pronounced on it the solemn sentence, "No man eat fruit of thee hereafter for ever." And we are told that the next day the fig tree was found "dried up from the roots." We cannot doubt for a moment that this whole transaction was an emblem of spiritual things. It was a parable in deeds, as full of meaning as any of our Lord's parables in words."

III. JUDGMENT PRONOUNCED.

"But who were they to whom this withered fig tree was intended to speak? It was a sermon of three-fold application, a sermon that ought to speak loudly to the consciences of all professing Christians. Though withered and dried up, that fig tree yet speaks. There was a voice in it for the Jewish Church. Rich in the leaves of a formal religion, but barren of all fruits of the Spirit, that Church was in fearful danger at the very time when this withering took place. Well would it have been for the Jewish Church if it had had eyes to see its peril! There was a voice in the fig tree for all the branches of Christ's visible Church, in every age and every part of the world. There was a warning against an empty profession of Christianity unaccompanied by sound doctrine and holy living, which some of those branches would have done well to lay to heart.—But above all there was a voice in that withered fig tree for all carnal, hypocritical, and false-hearted Christians. Well would it be for all who are content with a name to live while in reality they are dead, if they would only see their own faces in the glass of this passage.

Let us take care that we each individually learn the lesson that this fig tree conveys. Let us always remember that baptism, and church-membership, and reception of the Lord's supper, and a diligent use of the outward forms of Christianity, are not sufficient to save our souls. They are leaves, nothing but leaves, and without fruit will add to our condemnation. Like the fig leaves of which Adam and Eve made themselves garments, they will not hide the nakedness of our souls from the eye of an all-seeing God, or give us boldness when we stand before Him at the last day. No: we must bear fruit, or be lost for ever! There must be fruit in our hearts and fruit in our lives—the fruit of repentance toward God, and faith toward our Lord Jesus Christ,—and true holiness in our conversation. Without such fruits as these a profession of Christianity will only sink us lower into hell." (*J. C. Ryle*)

FACT QUESTIONS 11:12-14

681. How is the humanness of Jesus shown in this passage?
682. What does the humanness of Jesus teach us?
683. What great encouragement is found in His human qualities?
684. How do these verses become a "parable in deeds"?
685. Discuss and answer in your own words the two difficulties in this incident.
686. What does the withered fig tree say to the Jewish nation?
687. What does it say to the church of today?
688. Above all the withered fig tree speaks to whom?
689. In what sense are baptism, the Lord's supper and church-membership nothing but leaves?

2. THE CLEANSING OF THE TEMPLE 11:15-19

TEXT 11:15-19

"And they come to Jerusalem: and he entered into the temple, and began to cast out them that sold and them that bought in the temple, and overthrew the tables of the money-changers, and the seats of them that sold the doves; and he would not suffer that any man should carry a vessel through the temple. And he taught, and said unto them, Is it not written, My house shall be called a house of prayer for all the nations? but ye have made it a den of robbers. And the chief priests and the scribes heard it, and sought how they might destroy him: for they feared him, for all the multitude was astonished at his teaching. And every evening he went forth out of the city."

THOUGHT QUESTIONS 11:15-19

615. Is this the same cleansing as recorded in John 2:13-22? Discuss.
616. In what particular part of the temple does this incident occur?
617. Was it altogether wrong to buy and sell in the temple?
618. Why overthrow the tables and seats?
619. Explain vs. 16.
620. From what two references did Jesus quote?

621. How could the Jewish temple be a "house of prayer for all nations."
622. Why would the words and actions of Jesus especially anger the chief priests?
623. Give two or three possible reasons for the hatred of the leaders.
624. How is the word "astonished" used in vs. 18b?
625. Why mention the fact that He left the city every evening?

COMMENT

TIME.—A.D. 30—Monday, 3rd April, 11th Nisan, the fourth day before the great Jewish Passover.

PLACES.—The Temple—in the court of the Gentiles—Bethany.

PARALLEL ACCOUNTS.—Matt. 21:11-13; Luke 19:45-48.

OUTLINE.—1. What He did, vs. 15, 16. 2. What He taught, vs. 17. 3. The results, vs. 18, 19.

ANALYSIS

I. WHAT HE DID, VS. 15, 16.
   1. Entered the temple and cast out those who bought and sold.
   2. Overturned the tables of the money changers and the seats of those who sold doves.
   3. Would not permit the traffic of those carrying various burdens.

II. WHAT HE TAUGHT, VS. 17.
   1. It is written—"My house shall be called a house of prayer for all nations."
   2. Ye have made it a den of robbers.

III. THE RESULTS, VS. 18, 19.
   1. His words and actions were known by the chief priests and scribes.
   2. They sought a way to kill Him because of jealousy.
   3. He could not stay overnight in Jerusalem.

EXPLANATORY NOTES

I. WHAT HE DID.

"15. *'And they come to Jerusalem: and Jesus went into the temple, and began to cast out,' etc.* It seems, at first sight, almost incredible that men who professed such reverence for the temple, and were so scrupulous about the slightest ceremonial defilement (John 18:28), should actually let out, as they did, a portion of the sacred precincts, the court of the Gentiles, or a part of it, to dealers in cattle and sheep and doves, and to money-changers, but unscrupulous men will do anything for the sake of gain. It would be a great convenience to a Jew from a distance to buy his Passover Lamb close to the spot where it had to be killed; and the

Sadducean priests, taking advantage of this, were themselves the real desecrators of the most sacred building of which they were the guardians, by encouraging the unholy traffic. But the Lord, Who ever regarded the temple as His Father's house, and looked upon the very building as imparting its sanctity to all in it, resented this as He had done on a former occasion, alone and unaided, for this occurred on the day after His arrival, and the enthusiastic crowds were dispersed. He drove out all the traffickers, overthrew the tables of the moneychangers, and the seats of those who sold doves to those who were too poor to bring a more costly offering, and according to our Evangelist, even went further, by forbidding the temple to be made a thoroughfare, so that vessels should be carried through it.

Now we must ask first, "Was this an ordinary exercise of power?" and then, "What was its significance?"

It would have been a natural, though, of course, a remarkable exercise of power if it had been, as is asserted, through the personal greatness and intensity of will that showed itself in our Lord's look and word and tone. But if this personal greatness means a very commanding presence, so that all enemies should be at once overawed, why did not this save Him from the insults and outrages which were heaped upon Him during this very week? We have no reason to believe from anything in the gospel that the Lord had a presence which greatly overawed men, and He must have had a very commanding personal presence indeed, to disperse without apparently the faintest opposition a crowd of cattle-dealers and money-changers. It seems to me that the faculty of transfiguring Himself at will, so as on one day to put on an appearance which overawed the roughest of men, and on the next day so to disguise His majesty as that the very slaves should spit on Him and strike Him, is as much a supernatural endowment as the power of healing the sick or casting out devils."

Why do men treat the exercise of the Lord's Divine power as if it were something immoral, something to be ashamed of, something that we must get rid of even at the expense of common sense, unless we are compelled to acknowledge it? It may interest the reader to contrast with the modern view, that of a Father of the Church, St. Jerome: "To me it appears that amid all the signs of our Lord, this was the most wonderful; that one single man, at a time too when He was an object of scorn, and accounted so vile as soon after to have been crucified, while the Scribes and Pharisees (chief priests?) moreover were furiously raging against Him, on account of the loss through Him of their worldy gain, should nevertheless have succeeded with a whip of small cords (John 2:15), in driving out of the temple so vast a multitude, overthrowing the tables and the seats, and doing other like things, which scarcely a troop of soldiers could have accomplished."

The second question is, "What is the significance of the act? Did its significance cease when the fame whose sanctity Christ thus marvelously vindicated, was forever desecrated and cast to the ground, or has it any reference to the new state of things in the kingdom of God? To this we answer, it asserts an universal principle, that whatsoever is consecrated to the true God, be it building, or society, or body, cannot be profaned without bringing on those who desecrate it the severe anger of God. God has nowhere, in so many words, commanded that the buildings devoted to the prayers and Lord's Supper of the New Covenant should be dedicated with a special service. He has left such a thing to be inferred from his Word, and a certain Divine instinct has led Christians everywhere solemnly to set apart their material churches to the exclusive service of God; but when they do so God holds them to their word. They have set apart these buildings to Him, He has accepted the offering, and inasmuch as He has not ceased to be a jealous God, He will certainly regard any desecration of them as profanity and impiety. If it be asserted that the Jewish temple was of greater sanctity than a Christian Church, because so much is said in Scripture about its dedication, we answer, No. A building, however humble, set apart for the offering up of prayer in the Name of Jesus, must be greater than a temple, however magnificent, in which His Name was never invoked—a building set apart for the celebration of the Lord's Supper must be holier than a building set apart for the offering of bullocks and calves. It also is defiled by heresy and false doctrine, and traffic in holy offices; and Christ will assuredly look upon this with more anger than He looked upon the profanation of the temple, inasmuch as a temple of living stones, built into a spiritual house, is a greater thing than a building even of marble and gold. And so with the bodies of Christians, which together with their souls, are so made the temple of God in Holy Baptism, that an inspired Apostle could ask, "Know ye not that your body is the temple of the Holy Ghost which is in you?" and so he says, "If any man defile the temple of God, him will God destroy." Let us then cleanse our souls by prayer and thoughts about the holiest things, or Christ may suddenly visit us and cast us out of the true house of God.

With respect to our Lord's not suffering anyone to carry a vessel through the temple, *Dr. South* has a good remark: "We must know that the least degree of contempt weakens religion; because it is absolutely contrary to the nature of it; religion properly consisting of reverential esteem for things sacred." (Quoted in *Ford*).

II. WHAT HE TAUGHT.

"17. *'And he taught, saying unto them, My house shall be called,'* etc. If, as is probable, the marginal translation ("a house of prayer for all nations") is the true one, then there may be here a tacit reference to the fact that the court of the Gentiles, as being the least sacred part of the temple, had been employed, in part at least, for the infamous traffic; in which case the Lord's words would mean, 'My house shall be called the house of prayer for all the Gentiles, but ye have driven them out and polluted their share, and made it a den of thieves.'

It has been asked, Were not the future houses of God to be houses of preaching—was not, that is, preaching to be their characteristic? No, we answer, and for this reason: preaching may be and ought to be, everywhere; wherever people can be congregated to hear it: Whereas the celebration of the Lord's supper and also united Church prayer ought, if possible, to be in places set apart from the world, its associations, its businesses, and pleasures; and ought to be in places, the architecture and arrangement and associations of which tend to raise the worshipper above the world. The restriction on the part of the authorities of the English Church, for nearly two centuries, of preaching to the interior of churches, has been most disastrous. It has been the real reason why she has lost so many of the working classes. Our missionaries, in India preach to the heathen in thoroughfares, in bazaars, at times even in the temples, and the heathen of England require to be met in the same way."

III. THE RESULTS.

"18. *'And the scribes and chief priests heard it, and sought how they might,'* etc. This is the first instance in the Synoptics of the "chief priests" taking serious measures to destroy Him, and the reader will notice how closely it follows upon the cleansing of the temple.

'They sought how they might destroy him.' Their fears made them think that it would be no easy thing to destroy Him. They did not count upon the fleeting nature of all popularity. Three days after this the people who were astonished at His doctrine made no effort to save Him." (*M. F. Sadler*)

FACT QUESTIONS 11:15-19

690. For one thing unscrupulous men will do anything—What is the "one thing"?

691. Who encouraged this unholy traffic? Why?
692. Why would carrying items through the temple defile it?
693. Just how did Jesus accomplish what scarcely a troop of soldiers could have done? Discuss.
694. How does Sadler relate this incident to the transfiguration? Do you agree?
695. What universal principle is given in the cleansing of the temple?
696. How can it be thought that church buildings today are in any way sacred unto God?
697. In what sense is the most humble building today holier than the temple?
698. In what way is Christ attempting to cleanse the church of today?
699. What about cleansing the temple of our body? Mention scriptural support.
700. Are not the meeting houses of today to be houses of preaching? Discuss as related to prayer.
701. Specify and discuss how our Lord is at work cleansing His temple today.

C. TUESDAY:

1. THE LESSON OF THE WITHERED FIG TREE. 11:20-26

TEXT 11:20-26

"And as they passed by in the morning, they saw the fig tree withered away from the roots. And Peter calling to remembrance saith unto him, Rabbi, behold, the fig tree which thou cursedst is withered away. And Jesus answering saith unto them, Have faith in God. Verily I say unto you, Whosoever shall say unto this mountain, Be thou taken up and cast into the sea; and shall not doubt in his heart, but shall believe that what he saith cometh to pass; he shall have it. Therefore I say unto you, All things whatsoever ye pray and ask for, believe that ye have received them, and ye shall have them. And whensoever ye stand praying forgive, if ye have aught against any one; that your Father also which is in heaven may forgive you your tresspasses."

THOUGHT QUESTIONS 11:20-26

626. Is there any significance in the amount of time involved in the withering of the fig tree?
627. What is indicated in the withering from the roots up?
628. Of what was Peter reminded when he saw the withered tree?
629. Was there a question implicit in the statement of Peter in vs. 21? What was it?
630. Show the connection of the words of Peter in vs. 21 and those of our Lord in vs. 22.

631. Was there a special need for faith at this time? Why?
632. Did Jesus have reference to a literal mountain?
633. Please associate this faith with the supernatural powers exercised by the apostles throughout their ministry.
634. Discuss the context of vs. 25, 26 i.e. show how they relate to what has preceded.

COMMENT

TIME.—A.D. 30—Tuesday, 4th April, 12th of Nisan, the third day before the great Jewish Passover.

PLACES.—On the road from Bethany to Jerusalem.

PARALLEL ACCOUNTS.—Matt. 21:19-22.

OUTLINE.—1. The withered fig tree—how did it happen?, vs. 20, 21. 2. By faith in God—you could do even greater, vs. 22-24. 3. But not if you do not forgive, vs. 25, 26.

ANALYSIS

I. THE WITHERED FIG TREE—HOW DID IT HAPPEN?, VS. 20, 21.
   1. This question raised in the morning as Jesus and the apostles passed the withered fig tree.
   2. Peter asked the question.

II. BY FAITH IN GOD—YOU COULD DO EVEN GREATER, VS. 22-24.
   1. Faith in God essential.
   2. Real faith can remove mountains.
   3. No request is denied those with genuine faith.

III. BUT NOT IF YOU DO NOT FORGIVE, VS. 25, 26.
   1. When you pray forgive that you might be forgiven.
   2. If you do not forgive you can not be forgiven.

EXPLANATORY NOTES

I. THE WITHERED FIG TREE—HOW DID IT HAPPEN?

"Here begins the record of Tuesday, which extends (if we include with the day the evening, according to our way of reckoning) to the end of chap. 13. The other records of the day are Luke, chaps. 20, 21, and Matthew, 21:20-25, 46. This was the last day of his public ministry. Of no other day have we so full a record, and none that we know of was more significant in his personal history. Now came the great decisive conflict, in which his enemies were openly worsted, one after another, and driven to the desperation of hatred.—But first, on the way to the city, they observed the blighted tree. *Dried up from the roots.* It was no mere injury or weakening, no withering of the foliage; the tree was destroyed and already ruined.—*And Peter, calling to remembrance.* Peculiar to Mark, and doubtless a personal reminiscence of Peter.—Yet here, as elsewhere, he uttered the general thought. *Which thou cursedst.*—i.e. which thou didst devote to evil. Beware of associating with the word in the least degree the idea of profanity. The ordinary name for this act, "the cursing of the fig tree," is an unfortunate one. To modern ears it suggests strong language, even profane language, and improper feeling; whereas the language was moderate and feeling was right. "Blighting," or "destruction," is far better."

II. BY FAITH IN GOD—YOU COULD DO EVEN GREATER.

"22. *Have faith in God.* Literally, "faith of God," God being conceived of as the object of faith. A very unexpected turn of discourse, the purpose of his act upôn the tree being entirely ignored. Why did he not explain the symbolic meaning of the act? And why did he content himself with giving an object-lesson in faith? It was on the principle of John 16:12: "I have yet many things to say unto you, but ye cannot bear them now." He preferred to leave the sad symbolic meaning to be perceived at a later time, when they could better understand it. Before the day was over they might begin to understand it for themselves by observing how Jerusalem treated their Master. If not so, his discourse at evening might begin to open their eyes. For that discourse this act was a kind of text. It did not now need unfolding; it would be opened soon enough. But of a lesson in faith they were in need; and so, instead of telling them why this had been done, he told them how works of faith still greater might be performed.

23. *Whosoever shall say unto this mountain, Be thou removed, etc.* A similar saying had been given the disciples after their failure to heal the lunatic child (Matt. 17:20). Such language cannot possibly have been understood by them or meant by him in any sense but that of hyperbole. (See an allusion to this saying in 1 Cor. 13:2). The thought is that works as impossible to human strength as the moving of the Mount of Olives to the sea shall be possible to faith and shall actually be wrought. "With God all things are possible." For an illustration of Jesus bringing divine possibilities near to human faith, see his words to Martha (John 11:23-27).—Undoubting confidence is the secret of such power; but confidence in what? The belief that *those things which he saith shall come to pass* must have some foundation; what is the true foundation? Plainly, the confidence that is here encouraged is the confidence that the proposed act is accordant with the will of God, and that the will of God can and will be done. Such confidence, if it is to be of any value, cannot be blind. It must have its rational and spiritual supports. No man can expect, under this promise, that a mountain will be removed until he is convinced by good reasons that God wishes it to be removed. If he is sure

of that, and sure that what God wishes can and will be done, he will believe that the mountain is to be removed. The promise is made to undoubting confidence; but if there is room for question whether the confidence is not irrational, how can it continue undoubting? So this promise gives no encouragement to random, enthusiastic prayers or to selfish petitions. Prevailing prayer is reasonable.

24. *Therefore*—i.e. because faith is so mighty—*I say unto you*—a sign of special emphasis—*What things soever ye desire when ye pray.* This is given correctly by the revisers: "all things whatsoever ye pray and ask for." *Desire* is a mistranslation for "ask."—"Believe that ye received (them), and they shall be to you." So literally. The verb "received" is in the aorist. The best commentary on this saying is found in Rom. 8:26, 27, where the acceptable petitions which are destined to be granted are said to have been given to the suppliant by the Holy Spirit, and by him made so strong in the soul as to be unutterable groanings of desire. Thus our Lord says, "Believe that you received these things from the Spirit of God as the materials of prayer; believe that these longings were awakened in you from above; and your requests shall be granted." But this faith, again, cannot be blind, if it is to inherit such a promise. It must have its reasons—so good that the whole man shall be satisfied with them. The reading of the will of God must be rational, as well as the pleading of it. The promise is, in meaning, "When you have reason to believe, and do believe that your prayer came to your heart from the Spirit of God, you may be sure that an answer to your prayer will also come from God." Compare the profound yet simple testimony concerning prayer in 1 John 5: 14, 15. There, as here, the crucial point is the knowing that we are asking according to his will. But thanks be to God that there is a Spirit who maketh intercession for the saints according to the will of God, working in them that which is well-pleasing in his sight!"

III. BUT NOT IF YOU DO NOT FORGIVE.

"25, 26. *Forgive, if ye have aught against any: that your father also which is in heaven may forgive you.* This saying is very similar to Matt. 6:14, 15 and 18:35. Verse 26 is properly omitted by the revisers as having been added here by free quotation from Matt. 6:15. The solemn words concerning forgiveness were added, perhaps, partly to prevent misunderstanding of his act upon the fig tree and false inferences from it. Prayer is a tremendous power, but it cannot be used for the gratification of personal resentments. So far from that, the cherishing of such resentments is fatal to prayer itself, being fatal to that full acceptance with God upon which, as a basis, prevailing prayer proceeds. An unforgiving prayer against an enemy would be null and fruitless by its own nature according to this law. Still further, the unforgiving spirit would vitiate all prayer. In this searching law, expressed in verse 26, there is nothing retaliatory or narrow on the part of God. The reason for the law lies in the nature of things. The unforgiving spirit is not the penitent and humble spirit to which forgiveness is promised. Rather is it the hard and self-asserting temper to which the remission of sins cannot be granted. To harbor resentment while pleading for pardon is to cherish the "guile" of Ps. 32:2. This law, limiting the availability of prayer, makes power contingent upon love: the true Christian relation.—For other illustrations of what things are contingent upon love, study the First Epistle of John. Do not shrink from the Epistle, either. No part of Scripture is more searching or more fundamental." (*W. N. Clarke*).

FACT QUESTIONS 11:20-26

702. What is especially significant about the day on which this incident occurred?
703. In what sense are we to understand the use of the word "cursed" as in vs. 21? What would be a better word? Why?
704. Why didn't Jesus explain the symbolic meaning of destroying the fig tree? Cf. John 16:12.
705. Show the similarity of Mark 11:23 and Matt. 17:20.
706. What is the essential thought in vs. 23?
707. What is the true foundation for removing a mountain to the sea?
708. Show how Rom. 8:26, 27 and 1 John 5:14, 15 illustrate the meaning of vs. 24.
709. Why were the words on forgiveness added to those on faith?
710. What was said about Psa. 32:2 and the first letter of John?

2. JESUS' AUTHORITY CHALLENGED. 11:27-33.

TEXT 11:27-33

"And they come again to Jerusalem: and as he was walking in the temple, there come to him the chief priests, and the scribes, and the elders; and they said unto him, By what authority doest thou these things? or who gave thee this authority to do these things? And Jesus said unto them, I will ask of you one question, and answer me, and I will tell you by what authority I do these things. The baptism of John, was it from heaven, or from men? answer me. And they reasoned with themselves, saying, If we shall say, From heaven; he will say, Why then did ye not believe him? But should we say, From men—they feared the people: for all verily held John to be a prophet. And they answered Jesus and say, We know not. And Jesus saith unto them Neither tell I you by what authority I do these things."

THOUGHT QUESTIONS 11:27-33

635. How many times had Jesus been to Jerusalem since He was found in its precincts by His mother?
636. Why were Jesus and His apostles in the temple?
637. Who did these three groups represent?
638. What "things" were of particular interest to those asking the question?
639. Why did Jesus ask the question about John the Baptist?
640. Did these men know the correct answer to Jesus' question?
641. Why fear the multitude?
642. Why did Jesus refuse to answer the question of His authority?—or did He refuse? Discuss.

COMMENT

TIME.—A.D. 30—Tuesday, 4th April, 12th of Nisan, the third day before the great Jewish Passover.

PLACES.—In the temple courts.

PARALLEL ACCOUNTS.—Matt. 21:23-27; Luke 20:1-8.

OUTLINE.—1. The place and people of the question, vs. 27. 2. The question, vs. 28. 3. The answer, vs. 29-33.

ANALYSIS

I. THE PLACE AND PEOPLE OF THE QUESTION, VS. 27.
   1. In the temple in Jerusalem.
   2. Representatives of the Sanhedrin: chief priests, scribes and elders.

II. THE QUESTION, VS. 28.
   1. By what power do you do what you do?
   2. Who gave you permission to do what you do?

III. THE ANSWER, VS. 29-33.
   1. You answer my question and I will answer yours.
   2. Was John the Baptist a prophet or a pretender?
   3. This forced an admission they were unwilling to voice.
   4. They lied and said, "we do not know."
   5. Jesus kept His word.

EXPLANATORY NOTES

I. THE PLACE AND PEOPLE OF THE QUESTION.

"And they come again to Jerusalem: and as he was walking in the temple," etc. This was, no doubt, on the Tuesday.

As He was walking in the temple, very probably employed in works of mercy, according as St. Matthew says, "The lame and the blind came to him in the temple, and he healed them." St. Luke also adds, "As he preached the gospel."

"There come to him the chief priests," etc. This was the one public intimation which He received from these very dignified persons that His pretensions were known to them. Hitherto they had simply ignored Him as a body, though individual priests or rulers may have remonstrated with Him."

II. THE QUESTION.

"28. *"By what authority doest thou these things?"* What is meant by "these things?" If it was the healing of the lame and the blind, such power of doing good, especially in the very temple of God, must have come from the Author of all good; and they ought to have been the very first to confess it. If they alluded to His preaching and teaching, there seems to have been among the Jews a very great liberty for preaching—the rulers of the synagogues frequently sending to strangers to ask them if they had any word of exhortation. But if, as no doubt was the case, it was because He had interfered in the management of the temple, then, as rulers of the temple, they had a perfect right to ask the question, only they must come with clean hands, which they were not doing, as their hands were defiled with the ill-gotten gains of sacrilege. They must also ask the question in sincerity, which they were not doing: for they had prejudged Him, and were watching for their opportunity to destroy Him."

III. THE ANSWER.

"But the question arises, seeing that they were the religious rulers and leaders of the Jewish nation,—how was it that they were so late in inquiring personally into His claims? They had sent a deputation to the Baptist on the banks of the Jordan to inquire who he was: how was it, then, that they allowed the Lord to teach and preach and perform miracles in the most open way, all over the Holy Land, for three years, and did not solemnly, and as the God-appointed leaders of Israel, require publicly and personally of Him to give account of Himself? It was surely their duty to do so. It was clearly the most cowardly dereliction of their highest functions, as judges in matters of religion, to ignore such claims. They knew well all that He had done. They knew well the resurrection of Lazarus, which had taken place but a very short time before. They had had their solemn conclave, and an animated discussion about it (John 11:47); but all conducted with the determination of condemning Him, no matter what the signs of His Messiahship. Such was the spirit in which they approached the Lord—insincere, hypocritical, crafty, bloodthirsty. And the Lord met them—met not their words only, but the secret machinations of their hearts, and at once and effectually silenced them, not only by a simple question, but by one which, above all men, He had a right to ask. They had sent to John to ask who he was, and John had told them that he was but a forerunner—a voice to call men's minds to the One Who should come after. They must have known, their emissaries must have told them, that the One Whom John pointed to was Jesus; and the Lord fulfilled in His own person all that John had foretold: for He had filled the Holy Land, and the neighbouring territories, even Jerusalem itself, with the fame of His mighty deeds. John baptized, but it was not into the belief of himself, but of One that should come after him. What was the significance of John's baptism—His baptism, of course, including his whole mission—was it earthly or heavenly?

30. *"The baptism of John, was it from heaven, or of men?"* And, apparently, they were confounded by the question; and, after pausing for an answer, He, no doubt, looked them in the face, and said, "Answer me."

31.*"And they reasoned with themselves, saying, If we shall say," etc. "Why then did ye not believe him?"* Of course, here means, Why did ye not believe him when he testified of Me? John's mission and baptism had no meaning, except as preparing for Another's. He founded no Church, no institution, no sect. He was a herald, and, so far as office was concerned, nothing more; and yet he had so stirred the religious heart of the whole people that they were persuaded that he was a prophet indeed. And the chief priests and scribes dare not shipwreck their whole influence with the people by denying this. And so they were in a dilemma. The Lord in His wisdom conducted them, with their eyes wide open, into the snare. And they were forced to say, "We cannot tell." We, the judges of the faith and worship of Israel, cannot tell whether the greatest teacher who has appeared amongst us for many centuries is from God or not.

To have to make such a confession was to seal their own condemnation as the leaders of the people of God.

And so the Lord answered them: "Neither do I tell you by what authority I do these things." If they had possessed the smallest residue of the spirit of their great and holy predecessors, Phinehas, Abiathar, Zadok, Jehoiada, Joshua, the Lord would not have answered them thus." (*M. F. Sadler*)

FACT QUESTIONS 11:27-33

711. What was Jesus doing in the temple besides walking?
712. To what three areas could "these things" of vs. 28 be applied?

713. Show proof that the spirit of these who asked the question was insincere, hypocritical, crafty and bloodthirsty.
714. Indicate the very valid right Jesus had to ask the question He did.
715. What was the mission of John?
716. Show how their answer sealed their influence as leaders of the people.

3. THE REJECTED SON 12:1-12

TEXT 12:1-12

"And he began to speak unto them in parables. A man planted a vineyard, and set a hedge about it, and digged a pit for the winepress, and built a tower, and let it out to husbandmen, and went into another country. And at the season he sent to the husbandmen a servant, that he might receive from the husbandmen of the fruits of the vineyard. And they took him, and beat him, and sent him away empty. And again he sent unto them another servant; and him they wounded in the head, and handled shamefully. And he sent another; and him they killed, and many others; beating some, and killing some. He had yet one, a beloved son: he sent him last unto them, saying, They will reverence my son. But those husbandmen said among themselves, This is the heir; come, let us kill him, and the inheritance shall be ours. And they took him, and killed him, and cast him forth out of the vineyard. What therefore will the lord of the vineyard do? he will come and destroy the husbandmen, and will give the vineyard unto others. Have ye not read even this scripture; The stone which the builders rejected, The same was made the head of the corner: This was from the Lord, And it is marvellous in our eyes? And they sought to lay hold on him; and they feared the multitude; for they perceived that he spake the parable against them: and they left him, and went away."

THOUGHT QUESTIONS 12:1-12

643. Show how especially appropriate the parable was by way of time and persons.
644. Who was the owner of the vineyard? i.e. who was represented by the owner?
645. Why use parables at this time?
646. Who was represented by the vine-growers?
647. Who were the servants?
648. Why was the owner of the vineyard so exceedingly patient?
649. Did anyone understand the obvious prophetic words about the son?
650. Who were "the others" to whom the vineyard was to be given?
651. What was the import of the "chief corner stone"?
652. If they wanted to seize and kill Him why didn't they do it?

COMMENT

TIME.—Tuesday, April 4, A.D. 30, two days after the entry into Jerusalem.
PLACE.—The words here were uttered in the temple, probably in the court of the Gentiles, where the Lord often taught the people. We shall later give a description of the temple and its courts.
INTERVENING HISTORY.—On Sunday April 2, the Lord made his official entrance into Jerusalem, looked through the temple and then retired to Bethany for the night. On Monday, April 3, he returned and taught in the temple. This teaching continued over Tuesday, and embraces a number of parables and discourses, either referring to his own rejection, the end of the Jewish state, or the end of the world, either on Monday or Tuesday, probably the latter.
PARALLEL ACCOUNTS.—Matt. 21:33-46; Luke 20:9-19.
LESSON OUTLINE.—1. The Wicked Husbandmen. 2. The Son Rejected and Slain. 3. Judgment Inflicted.

ANALYSIS

I. THE WICKED HUSBANDMEN, VS. 1-5.
   1. The Vineyard Planted. Mark 12:1; Matt. 21:33; Luke 20:9.
   2. Fruits Demanded. Mark 12:2; Matt. 21:24; Luke 20:10.
   3. The Lord's Servants Persecuted. Mark 12:3-5; Matt. 21:35, 36; Luke 20:5.

II. THE SON REJECTED, VS. 6-8.
   1. The Son Chosen. Mark 12:6; Matt. 21:37; Luke 20:6.
   2. Evil Counsel. Mark 12:7; Matt. 21:38; Luke 20:7.
   3. The Son Slain. Mark 12:8; Matt. 21:39; Luke 20:8.

III. JUDGMENT INFLICTED, VS. 9-12.
   1. The Wicked Husbandmen Destroyed. Mark 12:9; Matt. 21:16; Luke 20:9.
   2. The Rejected Stone. Mark 12:10; Matt. 21:42; 44; Luke 21:10.

INTRODUCTION

The enemies of Christ had already determined on his death. Their only ground of hesitation was his popularity with the throngs who now crowded Jerusalem. This day was one of constant conflict. The chief ecclesiastical authorities had come to him to demand his authority for driving the money changers out of the temple but had been silenced by a question that he had hurled upon them. After Jesus had put to silence the chief priests and scribes, he spoke to them three parables. The Two Sons, recorded only by Matthew; the Wicked Husbandmen, and The Marriage of the King's Son, given only by Matthew. It was as if in a glass held up before them they might see themselves. Yet even these parables, wearing as they do so severe and threatening an aspect, are not words of defiance, but of earnest, tenderest love—spoken, if it were yet possible to turn them from their purpose to save them the fearful sin they were about to commit, to win them also for the kingdom of God.

EXPLANATORY NOTES

I. THE WICKED HUSBANDMEN.

1. *He began to speak to them.* To the chief priests and scribes whom he had just silenced, as related in the last chapter. The people were present but his words and their rebuke are for their rulers whom he directly addressed in parables of which they could see the application. *A certain man.* The man who planted the vineyard represents the Heavenly Father who had planted the Jewish nation. *A vineyard.* Our Lord draws, as was his wont, his illustration from common life and familiar objects. Palestine was emphatically a vine-growing country, and fitted, in consequence of its peculiar configuration and climate, for rearing the very finest grapes. The image of the kingdom of God as a vinestock or as a vineyard is not peculiar to this parable, but runs through the whole Old Testament (Deut, 32:32; Ps. 80:8-16; Isa. 5:1-7; 27:1-7; Jer. 2:21; Ezek. 15:1-6; 19:10); and has this especial fitness, that no property was considered to yield so large a return (Cant. 8:11, 12). None was therefore of such price and esteem. It no doubt belongs to the fitness of the image, that a vineyard does, if it is to bring forth richly, require the most diligent and never ceasing care; that there is no season in the year in which much has not to be done in it. *Set an hedge about it.* Probably a hedge of thorns; possibly a wall. Enclosures of loose stone, everywhere catch the eye on the bare slopes of Hebron, of Bethlehem, and of Olivet. The hedge around them is the law, separating them from the Gentiles. By their circumscription through the law (Eph. 5:14) the Jews became a people dwelling alone, and not reckoned among the nations; that law being at once a hedge of separation and defense—a wall of fire, which, preserving them distinct from the idolatrous nations round them and from their abominations, gave them the pledge and assurance of the continued protection of God. *Digged a place* (or pit) *for the wine-fat* (or wine-press). The wine-press (Matt. 21:33) consisted of two parts—(1) the press, or trough, above, in which the grapes were placed, and there trodden by the feet of several persons amidst singing and other expressions of joy (Judg. 9:27; Isa. 16:10; Jer. 25:30); (2) a smaller trough (yekeb), into which the expressed juice flowed through a hole or spout (Neh. 13:15; Isa. 63:2; Lam. 1:15). Here the smaller trough, which was often hollowed (digged) out of the earth or native rock and then lined with masonry, is put for the whole apparatus, and is called a wine-fat.—*Cambridge Bible. Built a tower.* Towers were erected in vine-

yards, of a very considerable height, and were intended for accommodation of keepers, who defended the vineyards from thieves and from troublesome animals. *Let it out to husbandmen.* Representing the rulers of the Jews (Matt. 21:45); but the people as a whole, a nation or a church, are included (Matt. 21:43). It is customary in the East, for the owner to let out his estate to husbandmen; i.e., to tenants, who pay him an annual rent, either in money or, as apparently in this case, in kind. *Went into a far country.* "For a long while" (for time), adds Luke. At Sinai, the Lord may be said to have openly manifested himself to Israel, but then to have withdrawn himself again for a while, not speaking to the people again face to face (Deut. 34:10-12), but waiting in patience to see what the law would effect, and what manner of works the people, under the teaching of their spiritual guides, would bring forth.

2. *At the season.* By the Mosaic law the fruit of the trees was not to be eaten for five years after planting. This reasonable provision, though based on religious grounds, gave the tree opportunity of maturing before use. Lev. 19:23-25. In the vineyard of our probation all the time of our responsible years is harvest time, in which we are expected to bring forth fruit to Him who hath planted and let to us the vineyard. But as applied to Israel it refers to the period of her history when, Canaan being fully possessed, God sent his prophets to remind his people of their duty. *Sent . . . a servant*—The different sendings must not be pressed; they probably imply the fullness and sufficiency of warnings given and set forth the long suffering of the householder, and the increasing rebellion of the husbandmen is shown by their increasing ill-treatment of the messengers.—*Alford.* These servants, like Elijah, Isaiah and Jeremiah, were sent to demand that a nation for whom God had done so much should yield fitting fruit to God.

3. *They caught him.* The gradual growth of the outrage is clearly traced: (1) The first servant they "caught, beat, and sent away empty;" (2) at the second they "cast stones, and wounded him in the head, and sent him away shamefully handled;" (3) the third "they killed." *Empty.* Empty-handed; i.e., without that which he came for. According to the obvious design of the whole parable, this is a lively figure for the undutiful and violent reception often given to the prophets or other divine messengers, and the refusal to obey their message. (See Matt. 23:29-31, 34, 37; Luke 11; 47-50; 13:33, 34. Compare 1 Thess. 2:15; Rev. 16:6; 18:24).

4. *Another servant.* God sent many prophets to the Jews, as he sends many influences to us. *Shamefully handled,* or dishonored. It is the

generic summing up of all that the imagination naturally suggests when we think of what must have been done to the man in the affray in which his head was seriously wounded.—*Morison.*

5. *Him they killed.* Some of the prophets were not merely maltreated, but actually put to death. Thus, if we may trust Jewish tradition, Jeremiah was stoned by the exiles in Egypt, Isaiah sawn asunder by Manasseh; and, for an ample historical justification of this description, see Jer. 27:38; 1 Kings 18:13; 22:24-27; 2 Kings 6:31; 21: 16; 2 Chron. 24:19-22; 36:16; and also Acts 7:52; and the whole passage finds parallel in the words of the apostle (Heb. 11:36). The patience of the householder under these extraordinary provocations is wonderful.

II. THE SON REJECTED.

6. *Having yet therefore one son.* This was the last and crowning effort of divine mercy; after which, on the one side, all the resources even of heavenly love are exhausted; on the other the measure of sins is perfectly filled up. Undoubtedly they who were our Lord's actual hearers quite understood what he meant, and the honor which in these words he claimed as his own; though they were unable to turn his words against himself, and to accuse him, on the strength of them, of making himself, as indeed he did then affirm himself, the Son of God.—*Trench. One son, his well beloved, he sent him.* This saying, put at that time by Jesus in the mouth of God, has a peculiar solemnity. There is his answer to the question, "By what authority doest thou these things?" See Mark 11:28. *They will reverence my son.* That is, they will respect and treat with due esteem such a messenger (John 3:16, 17).—*Jacobus.* The expression of the hope that the husbandmen will reverence the son implies, of course, no ignorance, but the sincere will of God that all should be saved.

7. *This is the heir.* He for whom the inheritance is meant, and to whom it will in due course rightfully arrive—not, as in earthly relations, by the death, but by the free appointment of the actual possessor. Christ is "heir of all things" (Heb. 1:2). *Come, let us kill him.* The very words of Genesis (37:20), where Joseph's brethren express a similar resolution. This resolution had actually been taken (John 11:53). It is the *heart* which speaks in God's hearing. The thought of men's hearts is their true speech, and therefore given as though it were the words of their lips. *And the inheritance shall be ours.* They were so connected with a system which must pass away with Christ, with wrong ideas and principles and customs which Christ was doing away, that, if Christ prevailed, they must fall. But they imagined that, if they could destroy Christ, they could continue in possession of the inheritance, be rulers

over Israel, teachers and leaders of the people, the possessors of the nation. See, also, John 11:48.

8. *And killed him.* As the Jews did Jesus. They killed that they might possess; and because they killed they lost. *Cast him out of the vineyard.* This may involve an allusion to Christ suffering "without the gate" (Heb. 13:12, 13; John 19:17).

III. JUDGMENT INFLICTED.

9. *What shall therefore the lord of the vineyard do?* In Matthew 21:41, the people answer this question. It may be that the Pharisees, to whom he addressed himself, and who gave the answer reported, had as yet missed the scope of the parable, answering as they did, and so, before they were aware, pronounced sentence against themselves. *He will come.* The coming of the Lord in this place is to be interpreted of the destruction of Jerusalem. *And destroy the husbandmen.* The polity of the Jews was destroyed, their temple razed to the ground, their capital laid waste by the Romans, about forty years after this. *Give the vineyard unto others.* Expressed by the apostle when he said, "Lo, we turn to the Gentiles" (Acts 13:46). The others were the Christian Church which Christ ordained for his kingdom.

10. *Have ye not read this scripture.* Referring them to Psalm 118:22, 23—a psalm which the Jews applied to the Messiah. Peter twice applied it to him (Acts 4:11; 1 Pet. 2:7). In the primary meaning of the psalm the illustration seems to have been drawn from one of the stones, quarried, hewn, and marked, away from the site of the temple, which the builders, ignorant of the head architect's plans, or finding on it no mark (such as recent explorations in Jerusalem have shown to have been placed on the stones of Solomon's temple in the place where they were quarried, to indicate their position in the future structure of the fabric), had put on one side as having no place in the building, but which was found afterwards to be that on which the completeness of the structure depended—on which, as the chief corner-stone, the two walls met and were bonded together.—*Plumptre. The stone.* The "stone" is the whole kingdom and power of the Messiah summed up in himself.—*Alford. The builders rejected.* The builders answer to the husbandman; they were appointed of God to carry up the spiritual building, as these to cultivate the spiritual vineyard. The rejection of the chief corner-stone answers exactly to the denying and murdering the heir.—*Trench. Become the head of the corner.* The most important foundation-stone, joining two walls. A reference to the union of Jews and Gentiles in Christ, as in Eph. 2:19-22, may be included (see *Alford*); but the main thought is that the Messiah, even

if rejected by the "builders," should become the corner-stone of the real temple of God (his new spiritual kingdom).—*Schaff.*

11. *This was the Lord's doing.* The making the Rejected Stone the head of the corner. It is still marvelous and incredible to many that one rejected, despised, and put to death as a malefactor, should be exalted as the Lord of life and glory.

12. *And they sought to lay hold on him.* The three accounts supplement each other here. The purpose to seize him is plainly stated in all. Mark shows that it was a continued effort (literally, "they were seeking"), while Luke tells that they would have done so on the spot, had they not been afraid of the people. *For they knew, etc.* Matthew gives the more general reason for this fear: "Because they held him as a prophet." Their desire to seize him was increased by this parable; but their fear of the people was also increased, since they (i.e. the rulers) perceived *that he spake the parable against them,* and in the presence of the people (Luke 20:9), so that they felt themselves convicted before the people. Conscience made them cowards.—*Schaff.*

FACT QUESTIONS 12:1-12

717. At what particular place or area in the temple was this parable told?
718. What was "the only ground of hesitation" in the plan to kill our Lord?
719. Name the three parables Jesus gave on this Tuesday.
720. What was the ultimate purpose in these parables?
721. To whom was this parable addressed?
722. Who was the "certain man"—what was represented by the "vineyard"?
723. Give two examples of Israel represented as a vineyard.
724. What did the wall represent?
725. What were the two parts to the wine-press?
726. For what purpose were the towers?
727. Read Matt. 21:45 and state who in the parable is here indicated.
728. When did the Lord in a sense withdraw Himself for awhile?
729. What is represented by "the season"?
730. Elijah, Isaiah and Jeremiah are represented by whom?
731. Show how the gradual growth of outrage is indicated.
732. Who was sent "empty away"?
733. Which of the prophets did they actually put to death?
734. In what one act are all the resources of heaven's love exhausted and all the measure of man's sin filled up?
735. Show how the words of Gen. 37:20 relate to the parable. Cf. John 11:53.

736. How did the rulers and teachers of Israel imagine they would obtain the inheritance?
737. How did the Pharisees pronounce sentence against themselves?
738. When did the Lord of the vineyard come and destroy the husbandman? To whom was the vineyard given?
739. How would the builders know which stone was the cornerstone?
740. Show the importance of the cornerstone.
741. To what incident in the parable does the rejection of the cornerstone compare?
742. What was marvelous and incredible?
743. What does Mark add about the effort to seize Him that is not included in Matthew or Luke?

4. THE QUESTION OF PAYING TAXES 12:13-17

TEXT 12:13-17

"And they send unto him certain of the Pharisees and of the Herodians, that they might catch him in talk. And when they were come, they say unto him, Master, we know that thou art true, and carest not for any one: for thou regardest not the person of men, but of a truth teachest the way of God: Is it lawful to give tribute unto Caesar, or not? Shall we give, or shall we not give? But he, knowing their hypocrisy, said unto them, Why tempt ye me? bring me a penny, that I may see it. And they brought it. And he saith unto them, Whose is this image and superscription? And they said unto him, Caesar's. And Jesus said unto them, Render unto Caesar the things that are Caesar's and unto God the things that are God's. And they marvelled greatly at him."

THOUGHT QUESTIONS 12:13-17

653. Who sent the Pharisees and Herodians?
654. Who were the Herodians? Were they friends of the Pharisees? Discuss.
655. Why desire to catch Jesus in His speech?
656. What is meant by the use of the word "true" as in vs. 14?
657. In what sense didn't Jesus "care for anyone"?
658. Did these enemies of Jesus believe what they said to Him about Him?
659. Whose law was involved in paying tribute to Caesar? Discuss.
660. In what sense were these inquirers hypocrites?
661. Why ask about the inscription on the coin?
662. Did Jesus recommend paying taxes?
663. What things belong to God—are they the same things that belong to Caesar? Discuss.

COMMENT

TIME.—Tuesday, April 4, A.D. 30, two days after entry into Jerusalem.
PLACE.—In the temple, probably in the court of the Gentiles.
PARALLEL ACCOUNTS.—Matt. 22:15-22; Luke 20:20-26.
OUTLINE.—1. The trap setters, vs. 13. 2. The trap set, vs. 14, 15a. 3. Caught in their own trap, vs. 15b-17.

ANALYSIS

I. THE TRAPPERS, VS. 13.
   1. They were official—i.e. sent by others.
   2. Made up of two opposing forces, who now joined together to oppose Jesus.

II. THE TRAP, VS. 14, 15a.
   1. Flattery used as a camouflage.
   2. The trap is a question; shall we pay taxes to usurpers?

III. THE TRAPPED, VS. 15b-17.
   1. He knew their purpose.
   2. He sprang the trap on them.

EXPLANATORY NOTES

I. THE TRAPPERS.

"13. Although thus foiled in their direct attempt to silence him, they lose no time in aiming at the same end by a more insidious method, all the parties hostile to him coalescing for a moment in a joint and several effort to destroy his popularity and influence, by setting him at variance either with the Roman government or Jewish people. The means employed for this end was a series of entangling questions upon difficult and controverted points, both doctrinal and practical, to which it seemed impossible for him to return any answer that would not commit him in the eyes of some important party. This design is apparent from the coalition of two adverse sects or parties in the first attack, the Pharisees, or bigoted opponents of all heathenish and foreign domination, and the Herodians, or followers of Herod, who sustained him as the instrument and vassal of the Romans. This unnatural alliance between parties diametrically opposite in principle was caused by their common hostility to Christ, whose growing influence was far more dangerous to both than either could be to the other. By combining, too, they seemed to render his escape impossible, as any answer which would satisfy the one side must of course afford a ground of opposition to the other. Of this crafty and unprincipled contrivance, on the part of men whose only bond of union was their hatred of our Lord and their desire to destroy him, it might well be said that their design was *to catch him,* as a bird is caught in fowling, *by a word,* i.e. by a perplexing question, or, as some explain it, by an unguarded answer."

II. THE TRAP.

"*And they coming say to him,* their first words being not a peremptory challenge, as in the preceding case (11, 27), but a flattering address intended to allay suspicion and conceal their real purpose, so as to throw him off his guard and make it easier to entrap him. *Master*, i.e. Teacher, *we know*, not necessarily a false profession, since the character here ascribed to Christ was not only true but universally acknowledged. *True,* i.e. honest, candid, truthful, one who spoke the truth without regard to consequences. Carest for no man, in the Greek a double negative, as usual enforcing the negation. *It does not concern thee about no man.* The impersonal verb is that employed in 4, 38, and there explained. What they here ascribe to him is not indifference or unconcern as to the welfare of others, but independence of their influence and authority, as motives for suppressing an unwelcome truth. The flattery here lies, not in the falsehood or extravagance of the description, but in the honesty with which they seem to comprehend themselves among those for whom he did not care in the sense above explained. As if they had said, we come to you not only as a wise and famous teacher, but because we know that you will tell us to our faces what you think, without considering how it will affect us. *Regardest not the person,* literally *dost not look into the face* (or at the outward appearance) *of men*, i.e. art not influenced by any difference of rank, position, wealth, or power, a regard to which in the administration of justice was forbidden in the law of Moses as *respect of persons* or judicial partiality. (See Lev. 19, 15. Deut. 1, 17. 16, 19, and compare Prov. 24, 23. 28, 21.) The same thing is here denied of Christ, not as a judge, but as a teacher. *In truth or of a truth*, i.e. truly, really, sincerely, without any such reserves or personal regards as those just mentioned. Such adulation has blinded the eyes and warped the judgment of its thousands and its tens of thousands among human sages, and especially of those who glory in their insusceptibility of flattery. It is not surprising, therefore, that these crafty casuists and politicians, who regarded Jesus as a mere man, though an eminently wise and good one, should have hoped to find him as susceptible of flattery as others. Having thus prepared the way for their ensuing question, they at length propound it, in a very categorical and simple form. *Is it lawful*, is it right, not in itself or in the abstract, but for us as members of the chosen people, subjects of a theocracy, *to give tribute*, literally *census*, one of the Latin words embedded in the Greek of Mark, strictly meaning an enrollment of the people and assessment of their property with a view to taxation (compare Luke 2, 1-5), but also used in the secondary sense of the tax itself, here distinguished as a Roman not a Jewish impost by the Latin word applied to it and by the express mention of the taxing power. *Cesar,* a surname of the Julian family at Rome, inherited from Julius Caesar by his grand nephew and adopted son, Octavius or Augustus, the first emperor of Rome, was afterwards transmitted through the line of his successors, not only those who were connected with his family, but those exalted by a popular or military nomination. It is here applied abstractly to the office, or rather to the actual incumbent, Tiberius, the stepson and successor of Augustus, who reigned from the 14th to the 37th year of the Christian era. It is not however in his personal capacity, but as the representative of Roman power, that he is here mentioned. *Or not?* an artful presentation of the question as requiring a direct and categorical solution, without qualifications or distinctions, but as we say in English, "Yea or nay?"

15a. May we give, or may we not give? the form of the Greek verb being not future but subjunctive and indefinite. It is therefore really another form of the preceding question, not a second one consequent upon it, as the English version seems to intimate. 1. Is it lawful? 2. Shall we do it? for a thing may be lawful and yet not expedient or binding. (Compare 1 Cor. 6, 12. 10, 23). But in Greek no such distinction is expressed or suggested, but a simple repetition of the same inquiry in a different and more laconic form, thus rendering it still more categorical and peremptory, as admitting of no answer but a simple affirmation or negation. While the preamble to the question, therefore, was adapted to conciliate and prepossess an ordinary wise man, the question itself was so framed as almost to extort a categorical and therefore compromising answer. But he with whom they had to deal saw not only through their question but themselves, and shaped his course accordingly, so as at one stroke to solve the difficulty and defeat their malice."

III. THE TRAPPED.

"15b. *Knowing* (or according to some copies, *seeing*) *their hypocrisy,* the part which they were acting, but here from the connection necessarily suggesting the idea of dissimulation, false pretenses, which we commonly attach to the derivative in English. *Why tempt ye me?* not why entice me into sin, which is the ordinary sense of tempting (see 1, 13), but why do you try me, prove me, put me to the test, which is its primary and proper import. (See 8, 11. 10, 2.) Then, instead of answering *in thesi,* as they evidently wished and expected, he gives a striking popularity and vividness to what he is about to say, by addressing it not only to the ears but to the eyes of those about him. *Bring me a penny, a denarius*, another of Mark's Latin words, denoting a silver coin in common circulation since the Roman conquest, worth from fifteen to seventeen cents of our money, but here mentioned not with any reference whatever to its value, but as the tribute money (*coin of the census or taxation*) as it is expressed in Matthew (22, 19.) *That I may see* (it), is almost sarcastic, for though he did desire and intend to see it, yet the words, if seriously understood, seem to imply that he had never done so, and expected to derive some information from an inspection of the coin itself. But this was no doubt understood by all about him as a sort of grave rebuking irony, intended to disclose his knowledge of their secret motives, and his scorn of their hypocrisy, in raising such an abstract question on a point decided by their every-day transactions in the way of business. As if he had said, 'What! Are you required to pay taxes to the Romans? And in what coin? Let me see one'—thus attracting the attention of all present to the question, and preparing them to understand his memorable answer.

16. *And they* (either those who put the question or some others present) *brought* (it). We may now conceive of him as holding the denarius in his hand, or displaying it to those around, as if it had been something new, thus still more exciting curiosity and gradually opening the way for the solution of the difficulty which had been suggested. *Whose is this image and inscription?* referring to the well-known head and title of the emperor by which the money was authenticated as a legal tender. As if he had continued in the same tone as before. 'See this money has a man's head and a man's name stamped upon it; what does this mean? who is this, here represented both in words and figures?' The inevitable answer, Cesar's, may to some have suggested, at least vaguely and obscurely, the solution just about to be expressed in words, while others, perhaps most, still continued in suspense, until the words were uttered.

17. The first words of this verse are not to be slurred over as mere expletives or words of course, but read with great deliberation and strong emphasis. *And Jesus* (having thus directed attention to the captious and unreasonable nature of the question, not evading it, but) *answering* (at last) *said unto them,* i.e. directly to his tempters, as a solution of their abstract question, but at the same time through them and as it were over their heads to the surrounding masses, as a practical direction or a rule of duty. *Render* (return, pay back) *the (things) of Cesar to Cesar, and the (things) of God to God,* a collocation more emphatic (though identical in meaning) than the one in the translation, as it places last in either clause, not the thing to be paid but the person to receive it. Some attach to the Greek verb the diluted sense of simply giving out or

paying, but the strong sense of paying back, restoring, correctly though not clearly enough given in our version, is not only permitted by the etymology and favoured by the usage of the word (compare Matt. 5, 26. 33. 6, 4. 18, 25. 20, 8. Luke 4, 20. 9, 42. 19, 8. Rom. 12, 17. 13, 7. 1 Th. 5, 15. 1 Pet. 3, 9), but required by the whole connection and essential to the full force of our Saviour's answer. Of the numerous specific senses put upon that answer there are probably but two exegetically possible and yet essentially unlike. The first of these supposes Christ to represent the two things as entirely distinct and independent of each other, belonging to excentric incommensurable spheres, and therefore not to be reduced to any common principle or rule. As if he had said, Pay your taxes and perform your religious duties, but do not mix the two together or attempt to bring them either into conflict or agreement; for they really belong to different worlds or systems, and have nothing common or alike by which they can even be compared. This paradoxical interpretation would deserve no notice had it not been gravely urged by one of the most celebrated modern German writers. The other exegetical hypothesis supposes Christ to say precisely the opposite of this, to wit, that the two duties are in perfect harmony and rest on one and the same principle. Within this general hypothesis, however, there are several gradations or distinct forms of opinion as to the principle here laid down. Without enumerating all these, it will be sufficient to state two, the lowest and the highest, which can be reduced to this class. The former understands our Lord as rather distinguishing the two obligations, but affirming their consistency and equal obligation, when they are not in collision. The latter understands him as identifying both as parts of one and the same system, as if he had said, your civil duties are but parts of your religious duties. By rendering to Cesar what is his you render unto God what is his. But the question still remains, what doctrine did he teach as to the Roman domination and the duty of the Jews while under it? The most approved and prevalent opinion is that in accordance with the maxim of Maimonides and other rabbis, he regards the circulation of the coin of any sovereign as a practical proof that his sovereignty not only exists but is submitted to. So long as the Jews submitted to the Romans and enjoyed their protection they were not only authorized but bound to pay for the advantage. Others make the prominent idea that of penal visitation, or subjection to the Romans as a punishment of sin. The other precept, render unto God, etc., is understood according to these different hypotheses as meaning either, give your souls or yourselves (which bear his image) back to him by faithful service or by true repentance, as you give back to the emperor in tribute the coin which he circulates among you. All these constructions seem to me too artificial, and the only satisfactory one that which understands our Lord as first suggesting by the very aspect of the coin that they were under obligations to the civil power, and then reminding them that till these came in conflict with religious obligations they were no less binding. As if he had said, 'Yes, if you are actually under Roman domination, yet allowed to serve God in the way of his appointment, and indeed protected in that service, you are bound to pay back what you thus receive, but no such obligations can destroy those which you owe to God himself, or suspend them when they come in competition. In a word, repay to Cesar what he gives you, and to God the infinitely greater gifts which you receive from him'." (*J. A. Alexander*)

FACT QUESTIONS 12:13-17

744. What was meant by the expression "It does not concern thee about no man"?
745. In what sense did our Lord "look into the face of man?"
746. What immediate advantage was hoped for in the use of flattery?
747. Just what was meant by the word "tribute"? How is the word "Caesar" used?
748. Are there two questions—one in vs. 14 and another in vs. 15? Explain.
749. What kind of an answer did these men want? Why?
750. Just what was the point of hypocrisy, i.e. in what were they being hypocritical?
751. Why ask to see the coin? Why ask about the superscription?
752. To whom did Jesus address His answer? Why?
753. Where is the emphasis? On the thing to be paid, or the person to receive it?
754. State the two possible interpretations of this expression i.e. general ones.
755. Which of the gradations of the above two views is to be preferred? Why?
756. What did Jesus teach about the duty of the Jews to Roman domination?; to God?

5. THE QUESTION ABOUT THE RESURRECTION 12:18-27

TEXT 12:18-27

"And there come unto him Sadducees, which say there is no resurrection; and they asked him, saying, Master, Moses wrote unto us, If a man's brother die, and leave a wife behind him, and leave no child, that his brother should take his wife, and raise up seed unto his brother. There were seven brethren: and the first took a wife, and dying left no seed; and the second took her, and died, leaving no seed behind him;

MAP NO. 7—LAST WEEK

1. Bethany—Feast, Mary anoints Jesus, Mt. 26:6-13; Mk. 13:3-9; Jn. 12
2. Jerusalem—Triumphal entry (Sunday) Mt. 21; Mk. 11; Lk. 19; Jn. 12
3. Temple, enters, looks around, says nothing, leaves, Mk. 11:11
4. Curses fig tree (Monday), Mt. 21; Mk. 11
5. Temple—cleanses 2nd time (Monday), Mt. 21; Mk. 11; Lk. 19
6. Temple courts?—Great day of discussions (Tuesday)—Mt. 21-22-23-24-25; Mk. 11-12-13-14; Lk. 20-21-22
7. Retirement to Rest?—(Wednesday), Judas plots to betray Jesus, Mt. 26; Mk. 14; Lk. 22
8. Upper Room—(Thursday), 4th Passover, Lord's Supper, Mt. 26; Mk. 14; Lk. 22; Jn. 13-14
9. Gethsemane—(Thursday night), Parting discourses, agony, betrayal and arrest, Jn. 15-16-17; Mt. 26; Mk. 14; Lk. 22
10. Trial before Annas and Caiaphas, Mt. 26-27; Mk. 14-15; Lk. 22-23
11. Trial before Sanhedrin, Jn. 18
12. Trial before Pilate
13. Trial before Herod
14. Trial before Pilate (2nd)
15. Golgotha—(Friday), Crucifixion, Mt. 27; Mk. 15; Lk. 23; Jn. 19
16. Garden—(Sunday), Resurrection, appears to Mary, other women, Mt. 28; Mk. 16; Lk. 24; Jn. 20

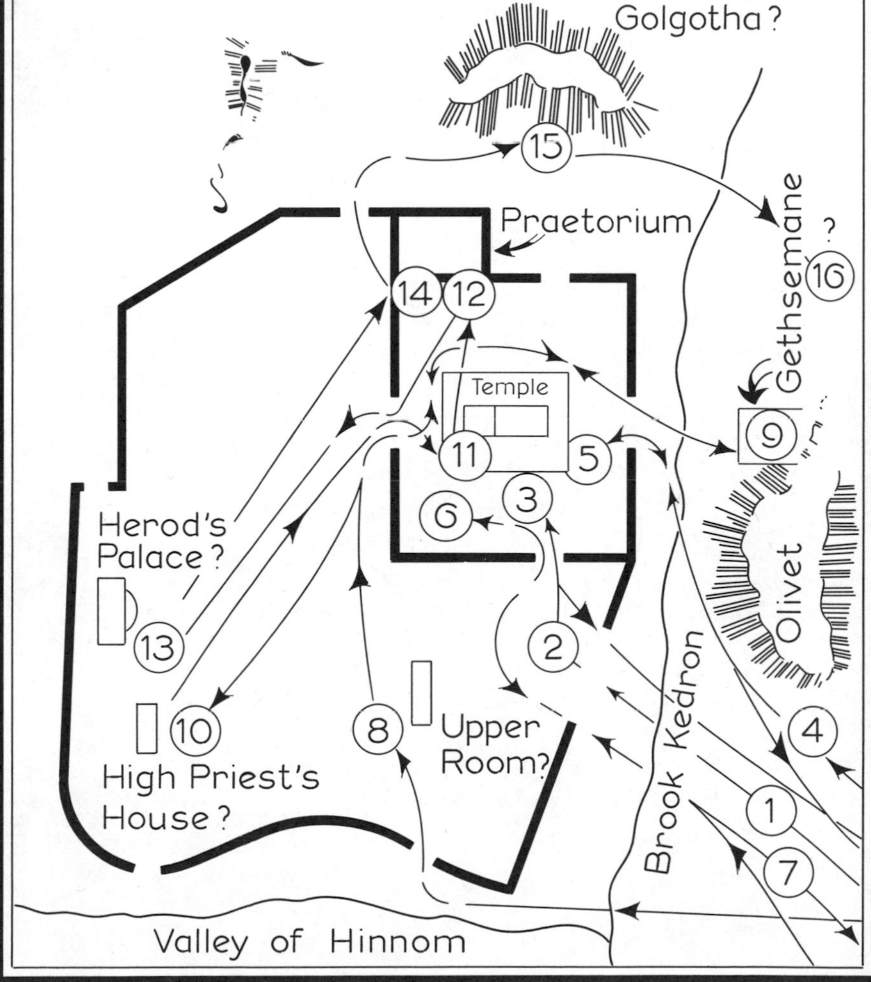

and the third likewise: and the seven left no seed. Last of all the woman also died. In the resurrection whose wife shall she be of them? for the seven had her to wife. Jesus said unto them, Is it not for this cause that ye err, that ye know not the scriptures, nor the power of God? For when they shall rise from the dead, they neither marry, nor are given in marriage; but are as angels in heaven. But as touching the dead, that they are raised; have ye not read in the book of Moses, in the place concerning the Bush, how God spake unto him, saying, I am the God of Abraham, and the God of Isaac, and the God of Jacob? He is not the God of the dead, but of the living: ye do greatly err."

THOUGHT QUESTIONS 12:18-27

664. Why this concerted effort to ensnare our Lord in His speech?
665. Give three facts about the Sadducees.
666. Since they did not believe in a resurrection why ask a question involving it?
667. Was this a real case or only a hypothetical one? What does a discussion of the sex relationship of marriage reveal about the hearts of the men who ask it?
668. There are two things absolutely essential in escaping religious error —Jesus states them in vs. 24—what are they?
669. Why not marry in heaven? Are we to understand we will lose our identity as husband and wife? Discuss.
670. Are angels distinguishable—i.e. are they recognized as separate beings?
671. Why add the comment on the resurrection?
672. Show how the reference to Abraham, Isaac, and Jacob proves the natural immortality of man. Discuss.
673. In what did the Sadducees err?

COMMENT

TIME.—Tuesday, April 4, A.D. 30, two days after entry into Jerusalem.
PLACE.—In the temple, probably in the court of the Gentiles.
PARALLEL ACCOUNTS.—Matt. 22:23-33; Luke 20:27-38.
OUTLINE.—1. The Sadducees ask an ignorant question, vs. 18-23. 2. Jesus answers their question and spiritual need, vs. 24-27.

ANALYSIS

I. THE SADDUCEES ASK AN IGNORANT QUESTION, VS. 18-23.
   1. Asked by those who did not believe in a resurrection.
   2. Their question was based on the law of Moses.
   3. Whose wife will the much married woman be in the resurrection?

II. JESUS ANSWERS THEIR QUESTION AND THIER SPIRITUAL NEED, VS. 24-27.

1. You do not know because you do not know the scriptures or the power of God.
2. There is no marriage relationship in the world to come.
3. Read again about the burning bush—Abraham, Isaac and Jacob are still alive for God said He was their God. There can be and will be a resurrection.

EXPLANATORY NOTES

I. THE SADDUCEES ASK AN IGNORANT QUESTION.

"18. The Pharisees and Herodians having been silenced, it was the turn of *the Sadducees* to come forward. Their question is as insincere as the preceding; it was a puzzle upon a doctrine in which they were total unbelievers. It proves, however, that the doctrine of the resurrection was everywhere recognized as a doctrine of Jesus.

19-23. This is the so-called Levirate marriage (from Latin *levir,* "a brother-in-law"). (See Deut. 25:5-10.) This provision corresponded to the universal desire in Israel for the perpetuation of name and family. So strong was the desire that this provision was made for a putative offspring in default of actual. The custom was older than the law, however (Gen. 38:8), and exists in many Eastern nations. But the obscure expression in Deut. 25:5, "If brethren dwell together, and one of them die," leaves us uncertain in exactly what circumstances the law was applicable. There is no case recorded in the Old Testament, though there is an illusion to the custom in Ruth 1:11-13. The transaction of Ruth 4:1-8 is of another kind. These questioners stated the law fairly, but their illustration was an extreme one, meant for a *reductio ad absurdum.* The language of verse 19 is awkward, but there is no difficulty about the sense.—*There were seven brethren.* In Matthew, "There were with us," as if the case were fresh from the life. Verse 22 should be, simply, *and the seven left no seed: last of all the woman died also.* Childless by all the marriages, the woman was not linked to any one of the husbands more than to the others.—*In the resurrection, therefore, when they* (the woman and the seven brothers) *shall rise, whose wife shall she be of them?* It is assumed that she be someone's wife, and how will Jesus judge between the rival claims of the seven?"

II. JESUS ANSWERS THEIR QUESTION AND THIER SPIRITUAL NEED.

"24. There is something wonderful in the gentleness of the answer, considering the insincerity of the question. He quietly assumed that there was an error, and proceeded to account for it; he did not even distinctly assert it. *Do ye not therefore* (from this cause) *err*—is it not for this cause that ye err—*because ye know not the scriptures, neither the power of God?* Is not ignorance the secret of your error? Ignorance (1) as to the Scriptures. He did not mean, of course, that the resurrection was mentioned in the Old Testament plainly, as it was mentioned by him. He meant that if they had understood the Old Testament rightly, they would have found the resurrection implied in its teaching, or at least would have been prepared to receive the doctrine. Not unfamiliarity with the Scriptures, but ignorance of their true meaning, kept them from believing in the resurrection. Moreover, a true knowledge of the Scriptures would have prevented their ideas from being so grossly carnal. (2) As to the power of God. All their conceptions of a resurrection were of a low and carnal kind that underestimated the power of God as shown therein. They thought only of re-establishment of the present fleshly life. No conception had they of the power of God to make life altogether new in the resurrection-state, but this is what he will do. Now follows the truth on these two points: (1) The Power of God; (2) The Scriptures.

THE POWER OF GOD.—25. He tells them that they have not understood the resurrection: it is something far nobler than they have supposed, and it will work changes such as they never thought of. *When they shall rise from the dead.* General, and equal to "in the resurrection" of Matthew. —*They neither marry*—contract marriage as husbands—*nor are given in marriage,* by the act of their parents, as wives. In the resurrection-state there will be no marriage. The reason, as expressly given in Luke, is that they "cannot die any more." Marriage, especially as suggested by the Levirate institution, exists for the sake of offspring. But birth and death are correlatives; they belong in the same world: if one ceases, the other must cease. In that world there is no death; hence no birth, hence no marriage. The power of God will have brought into being that which Paul calls the spiritual body, in which sexual relations will not continue. Notice that this is not a denial of the perpetuity of those mental characteristics which distinguish the sexes in this world. It is not affirmed that they are excluded from the resurrection-state. It is not said that the holy spiritual relations and personal affinities that may have accompanied marriage will not continue, or that husband and wife will be nothing to each other in the future life. The questioners thought of that life as a continuation of this, with its relations unchanged; and he simply told them that marriage, in that world, would be out of place. Upon the relations of soul with soul in that world he did not touch.—*But are as the angels which are in heaven.* Not "are angels," but "are as angels." The most that we know of angels is drawn from such allusions as this. What is here implied concerning them is that they are immortal, and hence among them the marriage relation does not exist.

Thus far, Jesus expounded the doctrine of the resurrection. The Sadducees rejected it, but they knew it only in a gross form. Very beautiful is his kindness in thus commending a rejected doctrine by presenting it in a nobler form; as much as to say, "Would not even you have believed it, if you had known it thus?" An example to all preachers and teachers. State your doctrine at its noblest; perhaps those who reject it have never understood it.

THE SCRIPTURES.—26, 27. Now he turns to prove the doctrine that he has been expounding—i.e. to find it in the Holy Writings. He quoted from the book of the law (the Pentateuch), because from it the question had been drawn; possibly, also, because the Sadducees prized it above the other Scriptures. The relation of this extract to the doctrine in discussion is somewhat peculiar. The expectation of a life beyond the present was expressed with greater or less clearness here and there in the Old Testament. Many of the writers had shown that they cherished such a hope, though not with clearness of the gospel. But it was not the hope or expectation that Jesus now wished to bring out: it was the fact. Hence an expression of human desire or aspiration would not suit his purpose, even though it were made under the guidance of the Divine Spirit. He must find a direct utterance of God. This passage, therefore, may be expected to be of unusual importance respecting a future life. To this peculiarity of the case well corresponds Luke's word: "That the dead are raised, Moses also revealed"—brought to light—"at the bush."—Translate, in verse 26, "have ye not read, in the book of Moses, at the bush, how God spake unto him"—i.e. in the section or paragraph where "the bush" is the subject of discourse. (Compare 2 Sam. 1:18.)—*I am the God of Abraham, and the God of Isaac, and the God of Jacob.* The citation here is from Ex. 3:6, the words of Jehovah to Moses.—The words might be found in many other places of Scripture: no language was more characteristic of the old covenant or more familiar to Jewish ears. He took no recondite passage, but one of the great words of the old dispensation.—In verse 27, *therefore* is to be omitted. The reading is, *He is not the God of the dead, but the God of the living: ye do greatly err.*—i.e. ye greatly err in interpreting the text as if he called himself the God of men who do not now exist. If he is any man's God, you may know that that man exists.

How did he draw such an inference? By a fresh and rich principle of interpretation, arguing from the nature of God, and of God's relations to man. The Sadducees took the passage to mean, "I am the God in whom Abraham, Isaac, and Jacob put their trust during their brief existence, which is now forever ended." But Jesus reasoned thus: "A God who did for the patriarchs what he did would not speak so of himself. He was gloriously their God—so gloriously that he could not call himself their God in such a sense, if their being had been but transient. If men were destined to become extinct, he could not be so gloriously a God to them. That such a God is or can be their God is proof that they are more than mortal." The argument is that the relations in which God enters, or proposes to enter, with men imply their immortality. The richness of man's relation to God is the fact from which Jesus infers his continued existence. See what a God becomes man's God, and it will be plain that he is no creature of a day. Notice that he does not present this as a fact that lies upon the face of Scripture, so that no one can miss it. The Sadducees missed it, and others may; but Jesus teaches us that they who explore the Scriptures by the light of God's nature will find it.—As if in order to ensure that this should not be taken as an argument for conditional immortality—i.e. immortality for Abraham, Isaac, and Jacob as chosen ones—Luke adds that "all live unto him"—i.e. in such sense that he is "God of the living" to them, all are alive. A distinct statement of the continued existence of all human beings. The relation to God from which the argument is derived is naturally possible to all, if not actual; and so the conclusion, of immortality, is true of all.—Notice that he draws no distinction here between continued existence and resurrection. The assertion of the former he regards as sufficient to establish the latter. If persons continue to exist, it is proper to speak of their resurrection. Compare John 5:29, where resurrection is predicted for the two classes that include all men.

Luke adds that after this answer some of the scribes responded, "Rabbi, thou hast well said," being, perhaps, as Farrar says, "pleased by the spiritual refutation of a scepticism which their reasonings had been unable to remove."—The fresh method that he thus introduced, of interpreting Scripture in the light of the nature of God and of his relations to men, is a method of boundless suggestiveness. This one specimen of exegesis is enough to prove the freshness and originality of the Christian light upon the word of God." *(W. N. Clarke)*

FACT QUESTIONS 12:18-27

757. How can we know the question of the Sadducees was as insincere as that of the Pharisees?
758. To ask the question in the manner they did was to admit the doctrine of Jesus—what was it?

759. What was a Levirate marriage? Why was it practiced?
760. What was wonderful about the manner in which Jesus answered the question?
761. Did Jesus mean to say that the resurrection was taught in the Old Testament? Explain.
762. Not unfamiliarity with the Scriptures but something else kept them from believing in the resurrection, what was it?
763. How was their understanding of the power of God limited?
764. Why no marriages in the resurrection-state?
765. Are there to be no sexes in heaven? Discuss.
766. What beautiful example in teaching is given here for preachers and teachers of today?
767. Why quote from the Pentateuch?
768. Jesus wasn't concerned with merely the hope or the expectation of life beyond but with the ———— of it.
769. Just how did Moses reveal that the dead are raised?
770. Please explain how Jesus drew the inference He did concerning man's immortality?
771. Are all men inherently immortal?
772. Notice that Jesus draws no distinction between continued existence and resurrection—what does this prove?
773. How does John 5:29 relate to this section?
774. Were some of the questioners helped by His answer?
775. The method here introduced by Jesus of interpreting scriptures is one of "boundless suggestiveness."—what is it?

6. THE TWO GREAT COMMANDMENTS 12:28-34

TEXT 12:28-34

"And one of the scribes came, and heard them questioning together, and knowing that he had answered them well, asked him, What commandment is the first of all? Jesus answered, The first is, Hear, O Israel; The Lord our God, the Lord is one: and thou shalt love the Lord thy God with all thy heart, and with all thy soul, and with all thy mind, and with all thy strength. The second is this, Thou shalt love thy neighbour as thyself. There is none other commandment greater than these. And the scribe said unto him, Of a truth, Master, thou hast well said that he is one; and there is none other but he: and to love him with all the heart, and with all the understanding, and with all the strength, and to love his neighbour as himself, is much more than all whole burnt offerings and sacrifices. And when Jesus saw that he answered discreetly, he said unto him, Thou art not far from the kingdom of God. And no man after that durst ask him any question."

THOUGHT QUESTIONS 12:28-34

668. What were the circumstances of the questioning of vs. 28?
667. What was the motive of the scribe in asking this question?
668. Why preface the greatest commandment with an expression concerning the nature of God? Cf. Deut. 6:4ff. and Lev. 19: 18.
669. What is involved in loving God with all your heart? i.e. what is the heart?
670. What is involved in loving God with all your soul?—your mind?—your strength?
671. Specify areas of love involved in loving our neighbor as ourselves?
672. In the answer of Jesus what was the first thing that appealed to the scribe? Why?
673. Why mention "whole burnt offerings and sacrifices?"
674. What is the meaning of the word "discreetly" as here used by Jesus?
675. What "kingdom" was involved?
676. Had Jesus set up His kingdom? Discuss.

COMMENT

TIME.—A.D. 30; Tuesday, April 4, same day as the last event.

PLACE.—The temple in Jerusalem.

PARALLEL ACCOUNTS.—Matt. 22:15-33; Luke 20:20-40.

OUTLINE.—1. Love the Lord thy God. 2. Love Thy Neighbor. 3. Not Far from the Kingdom.

ANALYSIS

I. LOVE THE LORD THY GOD, vs. 28-30.
   1. The Scribe's Question. Mark 12:28; Matt. 22:35.
   2. The Lord One Lord. Mark 12:29; Deut. 6:4.
   3. The First Commandment. Mark 12:30; Matt. 22:37; Luke 10:27; Deut. 6:4.

II. LOVE THY NEIGHBOR, v. 31.

III. NOT FAR FROM KINGDOM, vs. 32-34.
   1. None Other God. Mark 12:32; Deut. 4:39; Isa. 45:6, 14.
   2. More than Burnt Offerings. Mark 12:33; 1 Sam. 15:22; Hosea 6:6.
   3. Near the Kingdom. Mark 12:34.
   4. Christ's Enemies Silenced. Mark 12:34; Matt. 22:46.

INTRODUCTION

This was one of the busiest days of the Lord's ministry, a day of bitter conflict with his enemies right in the citadel of their power. After the parable of the wicked husbandmen, Jesus utters one more parable, that of the king's son (Matt. 22:1-14). There was but one of two courses before them. They will see their sins and repent; or, being thus accused, and refusing to repent, they will be still more enraged against him. They refused to repent, and, filled with a desire for vengeance, they take counsel with the Herodians how they may compel him to say something that will refute his claims as the Messiah, or give ground for an accusation against him before the government. The Herodians first asked a question that they hoped would be so answered that they could accuse him of sedition; then the Sadducees attempted to involve him in confusion; then the Pharisees put forward a scribe to ask another, still in the hope that he would betray some weakness that would destroy confidence in his wisdom.

EXPLANATORY NOTES

I. LOVE THE LORD THY GOD.

28. *One of the scribes came.* Matthew in the Parrallel Account says he was a Pharisee and a lawyer, which was another designation for a scribe. The scribes were learned men who preserved, copied and expounded the Jewish law. They were called by Jewish writers, "the schoolmasters of the nation." Many of them were Pharisees and members of the Sanhedrim. *Having heard them reasoning together.* The question of the Sadducees concerning the resurrection and the Lord's remarkable reply. See Mark 12:18-26. *Asked.* Matthew (22:35) adds, "tempting him." Not, perhaps, maliciously, but in the sense of testing on another question the wisdom of one who answered so admirably. I judge that he was neither a caviller, nor a disciple, but one curious to see what reply Christ would make to one of the puzzling theological problems of the day. *Which is the first commandment of all?* First in importance: the primary, leading commandment, the most fundamental one. This was a question which, with some others, divided the Jewish teachers into rival schools, and was a constant bone of contention—one of those "strivings about the law" against which Paul warns Titus (Tit. 3:9). The Jews divided the commandments of their law into greater and lesser; but they were not agreed in the particulars. Some contended for the law of circumcision; others, for that of sacrifice; others, for that of phylacteries; others, for that concerning ablutions. The Jewish Talmud reckons the positive laws of Moses at 248, and the negative at 365, the sum being 613. To keep so many laws, said the Jews, is an angel's work, and so they had much question which was the great commandment, so that they might keep that in lieu of keeping the whole.

29. *Hear, O Israel; the Lord our God is one Lord.* Our Lord begins with the creed of Israel. This passage (Deut. 6:4-9) was one of the

four places of Scripture inscribed on the phylacteries.—*Cook.* It was called the Shema. To say the Shema, was a passport into paradise for any child of Abraham.—*Ellicott.* This every devout Jew recited twice every day; and they do it to this day, thus keeping up the great ancient national protest against the polytheisms and pantheisms of the heathen world, the great utterance of the national faith in one living and personal God. This mighty text contains far more than a mere declaration that God is one. It asserts that the Lord God of Israel is absolutely God, and none other.

30. *Thou shalt love.* We have here the language of law, expressive of God's claims. What, then, are we here bound down to do? One word is made to express it. And what a word—LOVE! Had the essence of the divine law consisted in deeds, it could not possibly have been expressed in a single word; for no one deed is comprehensive of all others embraced in the law. But, as it consists in an affection of the soul, one word suffices to express it—but only one. But love is an all-inclusive affection, embracing not only every other affection proper to its object, but all that is proper to be *done* to its object; for, as love spontaneously seeks to please its object, so, in the case of men to God, it is the native well-spring of a voluntary obedience. It is, besides, the most personal of all affections. One may fear an event, one may hope for an event, one may rejoice in an event, but one can love only a *person.* It is the tenderest, the most unselfish, the most divine, of all affections. Such, then, is the affection in which the essence of the divine law is declared to consist.—*Brown. Heart, soul, mind, strength.* We may understand this four-fold enumeration as a command to devote all the faculties to the love of God.—*Cook.* "Heart" denotes in general terms the affection and will; affectionate choice, "the love of conscious resolve, expressed with will, which must at once become a second nature." "Soul" is the individual existence, the person himself, the seat of the will, disposition, desires, character. The two words are united to teach that the entire, undivided person must share in that which it has to perform with the heart.—*Cremer's Biblico-Theol. Lexicon. With all thy mind.* This commands our intellectual nature: "Thou shalt put intelligence into thine affection"—in opposition to a blind devotion, or mere devoteeism. *With all thy strength.* Enjoins the full and entire devotion of all these powers. Such is the "first" of the commandments, in the order of importance. Taking these four things together, the command of the law is, "Thou shalt love the Lord thy God with all thy powers—with a sincere, a fervid, an intelligent, an energetic love." This subordinates the whole life to the love of God and brings the whole being into willing obedience. *This is*

the first commandment. A precept so narrow as to measure the smallest thought of the smallest man; so broad, as to compass the mightiest outgoings of the largest angel; so perfect, as to bind all moral beings to the throne of God, and produce eternal and universal harmony and happiness and progress.

II. LOVE THY NEIGHBOR.

31. *The second is like.* To complete the lesson, and to leave no room for perverse distinctions between duties to God and man, our Lord makes the second commandment the necessary result and complement of the first. The first is the sun, so to speak, of the spiritual life; this the *lesser* light, which reflects the shining of that other. It is like to it inasmuch as both are laws of love; both deduced from the great and highest love; both dependent on "I am the Lord thy God." Supreme love to God is to manifest itself in love to men. Alike binding, the two are correspondent, not contradictory. He who loves God must love those who are in the image of God. *Thy neighbor.* On "Who is my neighbor?" see Luke 10:25-37, and Jas. 1:27. The words were found, strangely enough, in the book which is for the most part ceremonial (Lev. 19:18). *As thyself.* (1) Not as he *does* love himself, but as he *ought* to love himself. (2) After the same manner; i.e., freely and readily, sincerely and unfeignedly, tenderly and compassionately, constantly and preservingly. Cases arise where a man ought to love his neighbor more than his life—physical life—and has done so, sacrificing it for his fellows, his country, and the church, an imitation of the example of Christ and the martyrs.—*Schaff. None other commandment greater.* The unity of the moral law prevents any discrimination between its precepts; it is one law of love, the hinge of the whole Old Testament revelation. There can be none greater. No one can love God without loving his fellowmen, and no one can truly love man without loving God. The former is the source of the latter. Hence the first table (the first five commandments) enjoins love to God; the second table (the last five commandments), love to our neighbors.—*Schaff.* All duty springs from the single principle of love.

He only wanted (but the want was indeed a serious one) repentance and faith to be within it. The Lord shows us here, that even outside his flock those who can answer discreetly, who have knowledge of the spirit of the great command of law and gospel, are nearer to being of his flock than the formalists; but then, as Bengel adds, "If thou are not far off, enter; otherwise, it were better that thou wert far off."—*Alford.* This scribe saw that an outward, formal obedience would not satisfy God, but had yet perhaps failed to see that a heart wholly surrendered to God would require an implicit obedience, not only in the heart, but outwardly to the Divine will. "If a man love me," says Christ, "he will keep my words." The demonstration of love is a loving and faithful obedience. Whether this scribe finally decided to follow the Lord and entered into the kingdom, upon the borders of which he stood, we are not told. It may be that we are left in suspense concerning his fate in order to teach us how important it is that those near the kingdom should enter in.

III. NOT FAR FROM THE KINGDOM.

32. *The scribe said unto him.* Mark alone records the effect of our Lord's answer upon the scribe. It came home to his heart with convincing power. Doubtless he never before saw so plainly the deep spiritual truths of these commands. Entering into our Lord's reply, he cannot but express his approval, and even admiration.

33. *Burnt offerings and sacrifices.* The scribe gathers up in his reply some of the great utterances of the prophets, which prove the superiority of Love to God and man over all mere ceremonial observances. See 1 Sam. 15:22; Psalm 51; Hosea 6:6; Mic. 6:6-8. The reply shows that he had either read the prophets with much greater discernment than most of his fellow scribes, or that his understanding had been enlightened by the teachings of the Lord. To say that love was greater than burnt offerings and sacrifices was a daring utterance, directly opposed to the rigid ceremonial ideas of the Jewish leaders.

34. *Discreetly.* With knowledge and understanding. *Thou art not far from the kingdom of God.* This man had hold of that principle in which law and gospel are one. He stood, as it were, at the door of the kingdom of God.

FACT QUESTIONS 12:28-34

776. What two courses did Jesus place before the religious leaders of His day? Which one did they take? Why?
777. Compare Matthew's account of this incident—was this man a lawyer or a scribe? What is meant by such a designation?
778. In what sense was this man "tempting" our Lord? (Cf. Matt. 22:35).
779. How was the word "first" used in the question about the "first" commandment?
780. What choices had some made as to which commandment was first?
781. How many positive, and how many negative laws given by Moses? Why worry over which one was the greatest?
782. What was the "Shema"? How and why was it used?

783. Show how love encompasses all that God wants us to be and to do.
784. Attempt a definition and illustration of the use of the four words: heart, soul, mind, strength as related to love.
785. Why does our Lord make the second commandment the necessary result and complement of the first?
786. Why would it be impossible to keep the first commandment without keeping the second?
787. How was the question of "who is my neighbor" answered? Cf. Luke 10:25-37 and James 1:27.
788. Give three characteristics of the love we ought to have for our neighbor.
789. How were the tables of the law divided in content?
790. Read 1 Sam. 15:22; Psa. 51; Hosea 6:6; Mic. 6:6-8 and show how the scribe arrived at his conclusion as expressed in vs. 33.
791. What did the scribe need to admit him to the kingdom?
792. What had the scribe yet failed to see?
793. Why are we left without a knowledge of what the scribe did?

7. JESUS' QUESTION ABOUT THE SON OF DAVID 12:35-37

TEXT 12:35-37

"And Jesus answered and said, as he taught in the temple, How say the scribes that the Christ is the son of David? David himself said in the Holy Spirit, The Lord said unto my Lord, Sit thou on my right hand, Till I make thine enemies the footstool of thy feet. David himself calleth him Lord; and whence is he his son? And the common people heard him gladly."

THOUGHT QUESTIONS 12:35-37

677. Why did Jesus raise this question? i.e. at this particular time and place.
678. What would be a synonym for "the Christ" of vs. 35?
679. Why was it important that the Christ should be of the lineage of David?
680. Is Jesus saying the Psalms were divinely inspired? Of what importance is this?
681. Who are the two "Lords" of vs. 36?
682. How does the promise of vs. 36 relate to the Jewish nation?
683. In what sense was the Messiah to be both the son of David and the Lord of David? i.e. how was this possible?
684. Why were the people so responsive to the teaching of Jesus?—was it the subject?—was it the place?—was it the people?

COMMENT

TIME.—A.D. 30. Tuesday, April 4.

PLACE.—The temple area, probably the court of the Gentiles.

PARALLEL ACCOUNTS—Matt. 22:41-46; Luke 20:41-44.

OUTLINE.—1. The scribes say the Messiah is David's Son, vs. 35. 2. David said the Messiah was his Lord, vs. 36. 3. How do these views find agreement? vs. 37.

ANALYSIS

I. THE SCRIBES SAY THE MESSIAH IS DAVID'S SON, vs. 35.
1. This question was asked in connection with what had just preceded.
2. This question was asked amid His teaching while in the Temple court.

II. DAVID SAID THE MESSIAH WAS HIS LORD, vs. 36.
1. He said this under the impulse of the Holy Spirit.
2. God addressed this word to the Messiah.
3. It included a promise of Lordship over all the world.

III. HOW DO THESE VIEWS FIND AGREEMENT, vs. 37.
1. If the Messiah is David's Son, in what sense can He also be his Lord?
2. The people heard His teaching with genuine relish.

EXPLANATORY NOTES

I. THE SCRIBES SAY THE MESSIAH IS DAVID'S SON.

"35. Thus far our Lord's position had been wholly a defensive one; but now he turns the tables and asks a question in his turn, not merely for the purpose of silencing his enemies, but also with a view to the assertion of his own claims as the Messiah. *Answering,* retorting their interrogations. While he *taught,* literally, *teaching,* not in private conversation, but in the course of his public and official instructions. *In the temple,* i.e. in its area or enclosure. *How,* in what sense, upon what ground, or by what ground, or by what authority. *Say,* i.e. officially, or *ex cathedra,* here equivalent to teach. *The scribes,* as the expounders of the law and the religious teachers of the people. *The Christ,* the *Messiah,* Greek and Hebrew synonyms, both meaning *Anointed,* and applied to the Prophet, Priest and King of Israel, predicted by the prophets, and expected by the people. *Is,* in the doctrine of the scriptures, or *is to be,* in point of fact. Son, descendant, heir, *of David,* as the first and greatest theocratical sovereign."

II. DAVID SAID THE MESSIAH WAS HIS LORD.

"36. *For* assigns the reason of the question or the ground of the objection which it states; but the latest critics have expurged the particle.

In the Holy Spirit, i.e. in intimate union with and under the controlling influence of that divine person. *My Lord,* i.e. David's, as our Saviour explicitly declares in the passages already cited; yet not of David merely as a private person, nor even as an individual king, but as representing his own royal race and the house of Israel over which it reigned. The person thus described as the superior and sovereign of David and his house and of all Israel, could not possibly be David himself, nor any of his sons and successors except one who, by virtue of his twofold nature, was at once his sovereign and his son. See Rom. 1, 3. 4. That the Lord here meant was universally identified with the Messiah by the ancient Jews, is clear, not only from their own traditions, but from Christ's assuming this interpretation as the basis of his argument to prove the Messiah's superhuman nature, and from the fact that his opponents, far from questioning this fact, were unable to answer him a word, and afraid to interrogate him further (Matt. 22, 46.) The original form of expression, in the phrase *Sit at my right hand,* is the same as in Ps. 109, 31. A seat at the right hand of a king is mentioned in the Scriptures as a place of honour, not arbitrarily, but as implying a participation in his power, of which the right hand is a constant symbol. See Ps. 45, 10, and compare Matt. 19, 28. The sitting posture is appropriate to kings, who are frequently described as sitting on their thrones. (Compare Ps. 29, 10). In this case, however, the posture is of less moment than the position. Hence Stephen sees Christ *standing* at the right hand of God (Acts 7, 55. 56), and Paul simply says he is there (Rom. 8, 34). The participation in the divine power, thus ascribed to the Messiah, is a special and extraordinary one, having reference to the total subjugation of his enemies. This idea is expressed by the figure of their being made his footstool, perhaps with allusion to the ancient practice spoken of in Josh. 10, 24. This figure itself, however, presupposes the act of sitting on a throne. It does not imply inactivity, as some suppose, or mean that Jehovah would conquer his foes for him, without any intervention of his own. The idea running through the whole psalm is, that it is in and through him that Jehovah acts for the destruction of his enemies, and that for this very end he is invested with almighty power, as denoted by his session at the right hand of God. This session is to last until the total subjugation of his enemies, that is to say, this special and extraordinary power of the Messiah is then to terminate, a representation which agrees exactly with that of Paul in 1 Cor. 15, 24-28, where the verse before us is distinctly referred to, although not expressly quoted. It is therefore needless, though grammatical, to give the *until* an inclusive meaning, namely, until then and afterwards, as in Ps. 112, 8, etc. This verse, it has been said, is more frequently quoted or referred to, in the New Testament, than any other in the Hebrew Bible. Besides the passages already cited, it lies at the foundation of all those which represent Christ as sitting at the right hand of the Father. See Matt. 26,64. 1 Cor. 15,25. Eph. 1, 20-22. Phil. 2,9-11. Heb. 1,3. 14. 8,1. 10, 12. 13. 1 Pet. 3, 22, and compare Rev. 3,21."

III. HOW DO THESE VIEWS FIND AGREEMENT?

"37. *Therefore,* or *so then, David calls him Lord,* i.e. his own superior or rather sovereign. *Whence,* from what source, or by what means? How is he at once his superior and inferior, his son and sovereign? The only key to this enigma is the twofold nature of the Messiah as taught even in the Old Testament, and applied to the solution of this very question in the beginning of the epistle to the Romans (1, 3.4.) But this doctrine had been lost among the Jews, and more especially among the scribes or spiritual leaders, so that to them the question was unanswerable. They still held fast however to the doctrine, that he was to be the Son of David, which indeed became a reason for their giving up the doctrine of his higher nature, as being incompatible with what the scripture taught so clearly as to his descent and lineage. It is an instructive instance of perverted ingenuity, that one of the most eminent of modern German critics and interpreters maintains that Jesus, far from admitting that the scribes were right in making Christ the Son of David, teaches here that he was not! The effect of this unanswerable question upon those to whom it was addressed, or at whom it was aimed, is said by Matthew (22, 46) to have been that no one could answer him a word, nor did any one dare from that day any more to question him. There is of course no inconsistency between this statement and the one in v. 34, above, as both occurrences took place upon the same day; and as it has been well said, while Mark exhibits him as silencing their questions. Matthew goes further and describes him as silencing their very answers. On the other hand, Mark here describes the impression which his teaching made upon the masses. *And the common people* (literally, the *much* or *great crowd) heard him gladly,* sweetly, pleasantly, with pleasure." *(J. A. Alexander)*

FACT QUESTIONS 12:35-37

794. In what way did our Lord "turn the tables" on His opponents?
795. What purpose did He have?
796. Who were the scribes, i.e. in official capacity?
797. Who was David's Lord?
798. What is implied in the request to sit at His right hand?

799. Sitting does not imply inactivity—what does it imply?
800. Show how 1 Cor. 15:24-28 relates to Mark 12:35-37.
801. Mention at least three more places where this reference is referred to in the New Testament.
802. Show how Romans 1:3, 4 answers the question of Jesus.
803. Give two results to this question of Jesus.

8. JESUS WARNS AGAINST THE SCRIBES 12:38-40

TEXT 12:38-40

"And in his teaching he said, Beware of the scribes, which desire to walk in long robes, and to have salutations in the market-places, and chief seats in the synagogues, and chief places at feasts: they which devour widows' houses, and for a pretence make long prayers; these shall receive greater condemnation."

THOUGHT QUESTIONS 12:38-40

685. Were some of "the scribes" present to hear this warning? Wasn't this unfair to the honest scribes? Discuss.
686. What is inferred in the reference to the "long robes"?
687. Why desire the salutations in the market-places?
688. What advantage was there in the chief seats?
689. How would scribes be especially prepared or able to "devour widows' houses"?
690. How was it possible to rob and pray in the same day?
691. Why would long prayers be needed by these scribes?
692. Is Jesus teaching measures of punishment in hell?

COMMENT

TIME.—A.D. 30—Tuesday, April 4.

PLACE.—The temple area, probably the court of the Gentiles.

PARALLEL ACCOUNTS.—Matt. 23:1-39; Luke 20:45-47.

OUTLINE.—1. Beware of certain scribes, vs. 38, 39. 2. They devour widow's houses, vs. 40.

ANALYSIS

I. BEWARE OF CERTAIN SCRIBES, vs. 38, 39.
   1. Those who love to walk in long robes.
   2. Those who love to be greeted in the market-places.
   3. Those who want the chief seats in the synagogue and at feasts.

II. THEY DEVOUR WIDOWS' HOUSES, vs. 40.
   1. To cover up their crime they pray long prayers (in public).
   2. They should receive heavier judgment.

EXPLANATORY NOTES

I. BEWARE OF CERTAIN SCRIBES.

"How much of Matthew's twenty-third chapter is parallel, as having been now uttered, it is perhaps impossible to say. A large part of that chapter has a close parallel in Luke 11:37-52, and Luke 13:34, 35 is identical with the conclusion of the discourse in Matthew. According to Luke 11, the chief part of this discourse was spoken in a Pharisee's house, somewhere in Perea. It seems most probable that Matthew, not having recorded the Perean ministry, here combined several discourses of denunciation, which were actually delivered at various times. At the same time, the brief report in Mark and Luke may be only a fragment of what was said on this occasion. This appears to have been his last word with his enemies, as the discourse of John 14-16 was his last word with friends.

Beware of the scribes, which love—correctly, desire—*to go in long clothing, and* (desire) *salutations in the market-places.* Luke inserts "love" before "salutations", but Mark carries the verb "desire" through the sentence.—*In long clothing.* Liddell and Scott render "in full dress"—i.e. in whatever official robes they were entitled to wear; not, as Jesus, in the clothing of common life.—*Salutations,* formal and prolix, forbidden by Jesus to his disciples on their journeys for work (Luke 10:4).—*Chief seats in the synagogues.* The seats nearest to where the sacred rolls of the law were kept.—*Uppermost rooms*—chief places, or couches—*at feasts.* The places of honor at the table. "Uppermost rooms" was once intelligible, but is strangely misleading now. "Room" meant "place," not apartment, when the translators used it thus. (For explanation of the allusion, see Luke 14:7-11.)

II. THEY DEVOUR WIDOWS' HOUSES.

"Devour widows' houses. As if this were what they fed upon in their first places at the feasts. Covetous designs that we cannot further specify are meant. "Insinuating themselves with defenceless women, as if they would truly be their defenders" (Theophylact).—*These shall receive greater*—or more abundant—*damnation,* or "condemnation." Greater, because they had misused their spiritual privileges, betrayed the trust of the simple, and brought reproach upon the name of God.—Our Lord's denunciations of the representatives of Judaism in his day seem terribly severe and almost cruel; but what is known of the absurd and heartless refinements of the Pharisaism of that age fully supports the strong language that he used. What must have been the indignation of such a soul as his at such perversion of the religion of his Father!" *(W. N. Clarke)*

FACT QUESTIONS 12:38-40

804. How much of Matt. 23:1-39 is parallel to this account? Discuss.
805. How do Mark and Luke relate to the longer discourse of Matt.?
806. What did the love of "full dress" indicate?
807. Is there something wrong in greeting one another? Cf. Luke 10:4—Discuss.
808. Where were the chief seats?
809. What is meant by "rooms" in K.J.V.?
810. Wasn't our Lord terribly severe with the religious leaders of His day?
811. Discuss the deadly danger of pretence in prayer. i.e. today?

9. THE POOR WIDOW AND HER OFFERING 12:41-44

TEXT 12:41-44

"And he sat down over against the treasury, and beheld how the multitude cast money into the treasury: and many that were rich cast in much. And there came a poor widow, and she cast in two mites, which make a farthing. And he called unto him his disciples, and said unto them, Verily I say unto you, This poor widow cast in more than all they which are casting into the treasury: for they all did cast in of their superfluity; but she of her want did cast in all that she had, even all her living."

THOUGHT QUESTIONS 12:41-44

693. Identify a diagram of the temple—locate the treasury.
694. What was of particular interest to our Lord as He watched the worshippers at the Treasury?
695. Why was the multitude giving?
696. For what was the money used?
697. Is there some connection in thought with this widow and the ones mentioned in vs. 40?
698. How much did the widow give?
699. If she had two coins why didn't she keep one? Wasn't she foolhardy in her generosity?
700. Why call the disciples to Him—where were they? Cf. 13:1.
701. According to Jesus what is a truly liberal gift?

COMMENT

TIME.—A.D. 30—Tuesday, April 4

PLACE.—The temple area, probably the court of the Gentiles.

PARALLEL ACCOUNTS.—Luke 21:1-4.

OUTLINE.—1. Jesus by the treasury, vs. 41. 2. He sees a poor widow, vs. 42. 3. He points out true generosity, vs. 43,44.

ANALYSIS

I. JESUS BY THE TREASURY, VS. 41.
   1. He was seated near for careful observation.
   2. He noticed the manner of giving as well as the amount.
   3. The rich were especially conspicuous.

II. HE SEES A POOR WIDOW, VS. 42.
   1. Of her own choice she came.
   2. She put in two copper coins amounting to less than a cent.

III. HE POINTS OUT TRUE GENEROSITY, VS. 43. 44.
   1. He called His disciples to Him.
   2. Attention was called to the widow as giving more than anyone else.
   3. Her heart was given with her gift—she gave her life—her living in the gift.

EXPLANATORY NOTES

I. JESUS BY THE TREASURY.

"*And Jesus sat over against the treasury. —The treasury test:*—The lesson thaught by this narrative is—man's treatment of God's treasury the true touchstone of piety. I. GOD HAS A TREASURY IN HIS CHURCH. God has conferred on man various kinds of material possessions and property for uses and enjoyment. Among these, money has become the portable representative and circulating medium of all. Far above these possessions is the privilege of sacred worship. This would be an urgent necessity and a lofty privilege even if man were holy. How much more now that he is a sinner! As all material arrangements are costful, so also is worship. If man could not meet this cost, God would. As man can, Why should he not? Is he not honoured in being allowed to do it? Does not this test his character?"

II. HE SEES A POOR WIDOW.

"II. MEN CONTRIBUTE TO GOD'S TREASURY IN VARIOUS MEASURES AND FROM VARIOUS MOTIVES. The Divine rule has ever been according to one's power. This principle is definitely stated in an instance for universal guidance (Lev. v. 7, 11.): "As God hath prospered." "According to that a man hath." In the temple scene before us, we behold the devotion of every coin, from the golden mineh, of three guineas value, to the mite of brass, three-quarters of a farthing. Motives also differ, often as much as coins. Some give from necessity. Some give from a sense of honesty; if they did not give, debt and dishonour must ensue. Some give with pride and self-righteousness even before God. Some give from habit acquired from youth. Some give with holy love and joy, as a blessed privilege and rich delight: thus did the widow; so also have many done till now. III. THE SAVIOUR OBSERVES HOW MEN TREAT HIS TREASURY, AND BY THIS TESTS THEIR LOVE TO HIMSELF. As worship is man's highest act, its gifts should be rich and substantial. Jesus beheld men at the treasury. He still directs His eye thither; not that He needs man's gifts; but deeds and gifts test man's love; also they elevate and refresh man's heart. Men test others' love by deeds and gifts. Jesus challenges us to test the love of God thus."

III. HE POINTS OUT TRUE GENEROSITY.

"IV. JESUS ESTIMATES GIFTS CHIEFLY BY WHAT IS RETAINED. This principle alone accounts for the higher worth of the widow's gift. 1. This estimate of gifts according to what is retained agrees with reason. Man's gauge of the moral value of a deed is the power of the doer. The child is not expected to put forth the strength of a man. Less force is looked for from the feeble than the strong man. A small gift from a narrow income is esteemed as much as a large gift from a vast income. 2. This treasury test accords with general life. This principle is acknowledged in all departments of life. Men readily meet the cost of their chosen pursuits and pleasures, in the measure of their means. True patriots willingly pay national charges, according to their ability. Faithful husbands provide for their wives, in the measure of their power. Loving parents nourish their children, as their resources allow. Should not Christians thus provide for the service and glory of Christ? Notice God's rebuke of Israel's neglect of this principle (Isa. 43:22-24; Jer. 7:18). 3. This treasury test accords with universal Scripture demands. God tested man's confidence and honesty by the forbidden fruit. We know the sad issues. Jesus tests our obedience, love, and devotion by a treasury. Besides the large dedication of their property to the national religious service, Israel was commanded to open a treasury to the Lord, to build a tabernacle (Exod. 35, 36); David to build a temple (1 Chron. 29); Joash to meet the expenses of worship (2 Kings 12:1, 9). This woman would give her all to His worship. Who doubts her love? But did she act prudently? She acted according to the rule. She acted for the hour and the occasion. She would not make herself an exception to the rule. She gave her all to God. She left the future to Him. Does any one think she starved by this? Behold what a grandeur the smallest service acquires, when it is done for God! Observe what magnificent interest and enduring renown accrue from the devotion of a creature's all to God. Jesus did not disparage the other gifts; He simply indicated their true relative value, and attached to the widow's His highest commendation. Application:—1. God has a treasury for human hearts, His own heart. He would have your heart centre in love, safety, and joy in His own heart. He wants you there, as a creature who can love, serve, and delight in Him. He claims and demands you for His. Christ has died to redeem and win you back to Him. Will you give yourself to Him now just as you are, that He may make you all that He can delight in, that you may find in Him all that your soul can desire? 2. Christ gathers the funds of His kingdom in His Church. 3. All worshipers are required to give as a duty. 4. To give cheerfully is to elevate a duty into a privilege. 5. Jesus thus tests His friends and foes, the obedient and the disobedient. 6. Jesus waits at the treasury for your gift, to receive it at your hands, to bless it, and to teach you how to use it. If Christ is Lord of your mind, and heart and life, let Him be also of your silver and gold. *(John Ross.)*"

FACT QUESTIONS 12:41-44

812. What is the touchstone of true piety?
813. What is the "portable representative and circulating medium" of all material possessions?
814. State two measures and two motives men use in contributing to God's treasury.
815. Just how does the Saviour test our love to Him?
816. How does Jesus chiefly estimate man's gifts? Show how this principle agrees with reason.
817. Illustrate the above principle from a life situation.
818. By three examples show how the treasury test accords with all of the scripture.
819. What is God's treasury for human hearts?
820. Where does God gather His funds for His kingdom?
821. Are we required to give? Discuss.
822. If we do not give our gold and silver to Christ can we in honesty say we have given anything else to Him?
823. Please remember the two things that God said He saw and remembered about that good man Cornelius? Cf. Acts 10:4.

SUMMARY
11:1-12:44

In this section the historian has presented only one miracle, that of withering the barren fig-tree. The section is chiefly taken up with conversations and speeches, in which some of the peculiar teachings of Jesus are set forth, and in which his superhuman wisdom is conspicuously exhibited. In the conversations about his own authority, the tribute to Caesar, the resurrection of the dead, the great commandment, and the Lordship of the Christ, he not only silenced his enemies, so that no man dared to ask him any more questions, but he displayed a wisdom which has never ceased to command the admiration of wise and good men. All men, in the presence of his utterances on these subjects, feel themselves in contact with a mind which towers above their own as the heavens are above the earth. They contain a subtile but irresistible proof, that he who spoke to them was filled with a wisdom which came down from heaven; and such must be the ever deepening conviction of all who dwell on them thoughtfully. (*J. W. McGarvey*)

10. THE DESTRUCTION OF THE TEMPLE FORETOLD. 13:1-13.

TEXT 13:1-13

"And as he went forth out of the temple, one of his disciples saith unto him, Master, behold, what manner of stones and what manner of buildings! And Jesus said unto him, Seest thou these great buildings? There shall not be left here one stone upon another, which shall not be thrown down. And as he sat on the Mount of Olives over against the temple, Peter and James and John and Andrew asked him privately, Tell us, when shall these things be? and what shall be the sign when these things are all about to be accomplished? And Jesus began to say unto them, Take heed that no man lead you astray. Many shall come in my name, saying, I am he; and shall lead many astray. And when ye shall hear of wars and rumours of wars, be not troubled: these things must needs come to pass: but the end is not yet. For nation shall rise against nation, and kingdom against kingdom: there shall be earthquakes in divers places; there shall be famines: these things are the beginning of travail. But take ye heed to yourselves: for they shall deliver you up to councils; and in synagogues shall ye be beaten; and before governors and kings shall ye stand for my sake, for a testimony unto them. And the gospel must first be preached unto all the nations. And when they lead you to judgment, and deliver you up, be not anxious before hand what ye shall speak: but whatsoever shall be given you in that hour, that speak ye: for it is not ye that speak, but the Holy Spirit. And brother shall deliver up brother to death, and the father his child; and children shall rise up against parents, and cause them to be put to death. And ye shall be hated of all men for my name's sake: but he that endureth to the end, the same shall be saved."

THOUGHT QUESTIONS 13:1-13

702. What was the motive of the disciple of Jesus in calling attention to the stones and buildings?
703. What size stones were involved in the prediction of Jesus?
704. In what year was the prediction of destruction made?—when was it fulfilled?

705. At about what time of the day was the question about the temple asked and answered? What side of the city and temple was in view?
706. Is there any significance in who asked the questions?
707. How many questions were asked? (Compare the parallel accounts in Matt. 24:1-22 and Luke 21:5-24).
708. Why associate the destruction of Jerusalem and the second coming of Christ?
709. In what particular area of misleading did Jesus speak in vs. 5?
710. Was Jesus saying certain persons would appear as the Messiah?—in His first or second advent?
711. What "end" is discussed in vs. 7? The end of the world?; The end of Jerusalem?; The end of the Jewish nation?
712. When was vs. 8 fulfilled? or is it to be fulfilled?
713. One translation says "the beginning of birth pangs" in verse 8b. What does this mean?
714. Were the four disciples who heard the words of vs. 9 treated in the manner described? was this a fulfillment of the prediction?
715. Was the gospel ever preached to "all the nations"? Cf. Col. 1:23. Why *must* the gospel first be preached to all nations?
716. Verses eleven and twelve seems to indicate a promise to be fulfilled in the lifetime of the apostles—was it? How does it fit the context of the world—or the destruction of Jerusalem?
717. In what sense "saved" as in vs. 13?

COMMENT

TIME.—A.D. 30; Tuesday, April 4; the same day after our Lord's farewell to and final departure from the temple.

PLACES.—The lesson begins in the temple, as the Lord departs from it, and ends upon the Mount of Olives, over against and over-looking Jerusalem and the temple, from the east.

INTERESTING HISTORY.—After the incidents of the widow's mite (Mark 12:41-43). Certain Greeks desire to see Jesus (John 12:20-27); a voice from heaven (John 12:28-36); reflections on the unbelief of the Jews (John 12:37-50); the scathing rebuke to the Pharisees, scribes and lawyers (Matt. 23:1-36) and the farewell to the temple (Matt. 23:37-39).

PARALLEL ACCOUNTS.—Matt. 24:1-22. Luke 21:5-24.

LESSON OUTLINE.—1. The Temple Doomed. 2. False Christs and Trouble. 3. The Era of Persecution.

ANALYSIS

I. THE TEMPLE DOOMED, VS. 1-4.
   1. The Lord Forsakes the Temple. Mark 13:1; Matt. 24.1; Luke 21:5.
   2. The Temple's Fate. Mark 13:2; Matt. 24.2; Luke 21:6.

3. Christ on the Mount of Olives. Mark 13:3; Matt. 24.3.
4. When shall these things be? Mark 13:4; Matt. 24:3; Luke 21:7.

II. FALSE CHRISTS AND TROUBLE, vs. 5-8.

1. Beware of Deceivers. Mark 13:5; Matt. 24:4; Luke 21:8.
2. False Christs. Mark 13:6; Matt. 24:5; Luke 21:8.
3. Wars and Rumors of Wars. Mark 13:7; Matt. 24:6; Luke 21:9.
4. Universal Commotion. Mark 13:8; Matt. 24:7; Luke 21:10, 11.

III. THE ERA OF PERSECUTION, vs. 9-13.

1. The Suffering Church. Mark 13:9; Matt. 24:8-13; Luke 21:12-19.
2. The Gospel Among all Nations. Mark 13:10; Matt. 24:14.
3. The Divine Helper. Mark 13:11; Luke 21:15.
4. Saved by Endurance. Mark 13:13; Matt. 24:13.

INTRODUCTION

In order to fully understand the student must have pictured before him the circumstances. On Sunday the Lord had proclaimed probably, for the first time, by his entry into Jerusalem that he was the Messiah King. On Monday and Tuesday, in the temple, before the leaders of the nation, he had for the last time offered them the divine message. When it was rejected he warned them in parables and then, passing from the parable, he delivered the withering denunciations recorded in the twenty-third chapter of Matthew. This discourse has never been surpassed in indignant rebuke, withering denunciation, and tearful sorrow over the coming fate of confirmed sinners who would not be saved. It contains Christ's last words to the Jewish nation. The contest had been growing fiercer, the opposition of his enemies was more bitter, their plots against his life were working, their utter perverseness was fully manifested, the time for tender appeal had passed by, and the Lord turns upon the "Whited Sepulchers," the "generation of vipers," the hypocritical pretenders, in a philippic that we believe has never been equalled. But even in the midst of it, like a rift of blue sky in the fearful storm cloud, his love and pity shine forth with wonderful beauty in the pathetic exclamation of verse thirty-seven. In his parting words, "Behold, your house is left unto you desolate," he seemed to see the awful picture of a ruined temple and city smoking among the starved and mangled carcasses of the people of Israel; the fearful doom of many that listened to his voice. When this farewell was spoken he turned to depart from a temple that had rejected God and which he never more would enter. As he passed through its courts, his disciples apparently to make an appeal in behalf of so splendid a structure, pointed to the massive stones used in its construction. Then he replied, "Not one stone shall be left upon another."

EXPLANATORY NOTES

I. THE TEMPLE DOOMED.

1. *As he went out of the temple.* After the solemn and pathetic farewell recorded in the latter part of the twenty-third chapter of Matthew. Those words closed his public ministry to the Jewish nation, and he left the temple never to return. He left it "desolate." He probably passed from the exclusively Jewish part to the court of the Gentiles and then the reference was made to the stones of the structure by one of the disciples which drew forth his prediction. *What manner of stones and what manner of buildings?* Josephus, the Jewish historian, who was present when Jerusalem was destroyed by the Romans nearly forty years after the Lord's prediction speaks of the immense stones used in the structure. He, in his *Antiquities* (xv. 11, 3), speaks of the stones of a certain part of the edifice, as being "each, in length, 25 cubits (37 to 44 feet); in height, 8 (12 to 14 feet); in breadth, about 12 (18 to 21 feet)." In his *Wars* (5:5,6), he speaks of "some of the stones as 45 cubits in length, 5 in height, and 6 in breadth." Few buildings, in ancient or modern times, have equalled in magnificence Herod's Temple. With its out-buildings it covered an area of over 19 acres, was built of white marble, was 46 years in building (John 2:20), and employed in its construction 10,000 skilled workmen. Josephus also speaks of the great strength of the structure and tells that "the strongest of the batterings was worked against the wall without effect, for five days in succession; the size and joining of the stones were too strong for it, and for all the others." The descriptions vie with each other in describing the splendor of the temple as rebuilt by Herod the Great. Says Farrar: "The disciples eagerly pointed to goodly stones and splendid offerings; to the nine gates overlaid with gold and silver, and to the one of Corinthian brass, yet more precious; those graceful and towering porches; those double cloisters and stately pillars; that lavish adornment of sculpture and arabesque; those alternate blocks of red and white marble, recalling the crest and the hollow of sea waves.

2. *There shall not be one stone left upon another.* At the time this was spoken no event was more improbable than this. The temple was vast, rich, splendid. It was the pride of the nation, and the nation was at peace. Yet in the short space of forty years all this was exactly accomplished. Jerusalem was taken by the Roman armies, under the command of Titus, A.D. 70. The account of the siege and destruction of the city is left us by Josephus. *That shall not be thrown down.* The fortifications of Jerusalem and its natural advantages rendered it so apparently impregnable, that, after its fall, Titus, the captor, is reported by Josephus *(Wars*

of the Jews, 6:9,1) to have said, "It was no other than God who ejected the Jews out of these fortifications." Titus ordered the whole city and the temple to be dug up, leaving only two or three of the chief towers, so that those who visited it could hardly believe that it had ever been inhabited *(Wars,* vii I). Of the temple proper not a vestige remains. It was built, however, upon an immense platform, partly composed of natural masonry. This platform is still standing. The remains which recent explorations have disinterred belong, all of them, to the substructure of the temple—its drains, foundations, underground passages, and the like.

3. *And as he sat.* The words fell on the ears of the disciples, and awed them into silence. It was not till they had crossed to the Mount of Olives that even the foremost and most favored ventured to break it. Jesus paused before passing the ridge of Olivet, and sat down with his disciples to look back upon Jerusalem. The sun was setting, and the whole city, with the surrounding valleys and hillsides alive with the camps of pilgrims, lay beneath him in the evening light. The history of a thousand years, the divine oracles speaking by a thousand voices, the monuments of prophets, patriarchs, and kings, the visitations of angels, miraculous inter-positions in judgment and in blessing, from the offering of Isaac and the building of the temple, were present to him, as he looked upon Moriah and Zion, and heard the murmur and the evening songs of a million people gathered within and around the walls of the holy city. Nowhere on earth was it possible to find another scene of such commanding interest as that which lay before the eyes of Jesus when he turned to look upon Jerusalem for the last time *(—March.) Over against the temple.* On leaving the temple Jesus would descend into the valley of the Kedron, and ascend the opposite slope of the Mount of Olives. Then full in view the temple would rise with its colonnades of dazzling white marble, surmounted with golden roof and pinnacles. At a distance the whole temple looked literally like a mount of snow, fretted with golden pinnacles. *Peter, James, John, Andrew.* The four fishermen first called, and first named in the lists, the confidential disciples. *Asked him privately.* Either apart from the multitude, but in the presence of the other disciples, or apart from the other disciples, in a private conference.

4. *When shall these things be?* The things of which they had heard him speak. The question is given more fully by Matthew (24:3). It embraced three points: (1) the time of the destruction of the temple; (2) the sign of his coming; and (3) of the end of the world.—*Maclear. What shall be the sign?* By what signs shall we know when these things shall be accomplished? They wanted some insight into his plans, so that

they might know when and how he was to come, and all the events he had foretold should take place, and his kingdom be established.

II. FALSE CHRISTS AND TROUBLE.

5. *Jesus answering them began.* Our Lord's answer to these questions was framed to afford all the information needful to them, or useful for their guidance, but little to gratify a vague curiosity. Neither did he answer their questions categorically, but so intermingled his replies that it required after knowledge and experience to discriminate more than was actually needful for their safety and warning to know. We can now distinguish that he spoke of his coming, not personally, but by the fulfillment of his predictions concerning Jerusalem, and for the final uprooting of that theocracy which had become obstructive to the progress of the gospel; and again of his final coming to judge the world, of which, also, they inquired. Much that our Lord said might be applicable to both these great events—both these "comings," being, in fact, comings to judgment; but toward the close his language grew more distinctly applicable to his final coming to judge the world *(—J. Kitto.) Lest any man deceive you.* The Lord does not answer *when,* but by admonitions not to be deceived. It is not given to us to know the times and the seasons. The Lord's purpose in this first part of his discourse is not to tell what are, but what are not, the premonitions of the great catastrophe to which he here refers.

6. *For.* Introducing the ground or reason of this unexpected warning *(—Alexander.) Many shall come.* Five tokens are here given, to which the Lord direct the attention of his disciples: (1) The rise of false prophets; (2) wars and rumors of wars; (3) the rising of nation against nation; (4) earthquakes; (5) famines *(—Cambridge Bible.) In my name.* Pretending to be the Messiah. As the destruction of their holy city drew near, and the Messianic hopes of the Jews were at fever-heat, many enthusiasts arose, and awakened false expectations, and drew large numbers after them (Acts 5:36, 37; 1 John 2:18). Josephus says that in the reign of Claudius (who died A.D. 54), the land was overwhelmed with deceivers who pretended to be the Christ. The names and abortive efforts of several of these deceivers are given by Josephus and other historians.

7. *Ye shall hear of wars and rumours of wars.* A seeming anti-climax, but a real climax. The rumors of an expected invasion are often more dreadful than the invasion itself.—*Abbott.* Wars and rumors of wars there certainly were during this period; but the prophecy must be interpreted rather than those of which the Hebrew Christians would be most

likely to hear as a cause of terror. Such, undoubtedly, were the three threats of war against the Jews by Caligula, Claudius, and Nero; of the first which Josephus says, "that it would have brought extermination to the Jewish nation had it not been for Caligula's death."—*Alford. Be ye not troubled.* (1) As if everything were going to ruin. Be not troubled; for *you* will be safe, both at the judgment and at the destruction of Jerusalem. Every Christian escaped from that destruction. (2) These things do not prove that the great catastrophe and final consummation is at hand. *The end not yet.* Neither that destruction of Jerusalem, nor the end of the world. These are not the certain signs of the end, for they occur at other times as well as then.

8. *Nation shall rise against nation.* Bear in mind the massacres of Caesarea, between Syrians and Jews, in which 20,000 of the latter fell, while in Syria almost every city was divided into two armies, which stood opposed to one another as deadly enemies; the quick succession of the five emperors in Rome within a few years, Nero, Galba, Otho, Vitellius, Vespasian, and the tumults connected therewith in wider and narrower circles. The war-fiend ran riot in Palestine, Syria, Egypt, and throughout the whole Roman empire. The ten years ending with the destruction of Jerusalem was such a period of civil commotion as the world has seldom witnessed. *Earthquakes.* The principal earthquakes occurring between this prophecy and the destruction of Jerusalem were, (1) a great earthquake in Crete, A.D. 46 or 47; (2) one at Rome on the day when Nero assumed the manly toga, A.D. 51; (3) one at Apamaea in Phrygia, mentioned by Tacitus, A.D. 53; (4) one at Laodicea in Phrygia, A.D. 60; (5) one in Campania.—*Alford. Famines and troubles.* These would naturally follow the devastating civil wars. These woes all precede the awful end of Jerusalem and the Jewish nation.

III. THE ERA OF PERSECUTION.

9. *Take heed to yourselves.* Not as a means of escaping from persecution, but as a means of preparing for it, as Christ bade Peter take heed against temptation (Matt. 26:41). *For.* "Before all these things" (Luke 21:12); i.e., before these public calamities come, *they shall deliver you up to councils; and in the synagogues ye shall be beaten.* These refer to ecclesiastical proceedings against them. *And ye shall be brought before rulers and kings.* Before civil tribunals next. *For my sake, for a testimony against them.* Rather, "unto them"; to give you an opportunity of bearing testimony to me before them. In the Acts of the Apostles we have the best commentary on this announcement (Matt. 10:17, 18). The martyrdoms and persecutions have ever called attention to the religion of Christ, and opened ways for its promulgation.

10. *The gospel must first be published.* Preached, proclaimed, which is the proper conception of preaching. *Among all nations.* The gospel had been published through the Roman world as then known, and every nation had received its testimony before the destruction of Jerusalem. See Col. 1:6, 23; 2 Tim. 4:17. But further, the gospel has yet to be preached universally for a testimony. And the universal diffusion of it by modern Christian missions is now a leading sign of the end.

11. *Take no thought beforehand.* "Be not anxious," as in the New Version. The idea is: You need not distress yourselves by anxiously considering beforehand how you ought to speak before such high and august personages. "Let all your thoughts beforehand be concerned about the publishing. Let your words and thoughts be aggressive; I will take care for the defense. Delivered from care of the future, be occupied with present duty." This verse is best interpreted by such practical illustrations as are afforded by Acts 4:19, 20; 5:20-32; 22:3-21. Observe that this direction affords no countenance whatever to preaching the truth without previous preparation. It is simply a warning against allowing the mind to be divided in time of danger between the desire of personal safety and the desire to be faithful to the truth.

12. *Brother shall betray the brother to death, and the father the son.* As there is nothing that excites such love as the gospel when intelligently received, so there is nothing that occasions such hate as this same gospel when passionately rejected. In that reception or rejection the heart of the heart is concerned.—*Morison.* In missionary lands this is literally fulfilled today, as we all know.

13. *Hated of all men.* The Roman historian, Tacitus, speaks of the early Christians as a hated race. It is difficult for us in these days to understand how literally this was fulfilled. The most shameful practices were attributed to Christians; and partly in consequence of these falsehoods, partly from hatred of good, they were treated as the offscouring of the earth. *Endure unto the end, the same shall be saved.* The primary meaning of this seems to be that whosoever remained faithful till the destruction of Jerusalem should be preserved from it. No Christian, that we know of, perished in the siege or after it. But it has ulterior meanings, according to which *the end* will signify, to an individual, the day of his death (Rev. 2:10), his martyrdom, as in the case of some of those here addressed; to the church, endurance in the faith to the end of all things.—*Alford.*

FACT QUESTIONS 13:1-13

824. State the five points or events occurring between the close of Mark

chapter twelve and the opening of the thirteenth chapter. Cf. John 12:20-27; 28-36; 37-50; Matt. 23:1-36; 23:37-39.

825. What occurred when for the last time our Lord offered His divine message and it was rejected?
826. What is meant by the expression "your house is left unto you desolate"?
827. Where were Jesus and His disciples when the disciples made the comment they did about the stones.
828. Give the length, height and breadth of some of the stones according to Josephus.
829. What was the area covered by the temple?
830. How many years was the temple in being built? How many skilled workmen were employed in building the temple?
831. Give three facts stated in Farrar's description.
832. Who said, "It was no other than God who ejected the Jews out of these fortifications"? Why?
833. How did Titus accomplish the prediction of Jesus?
834. There was a long pause between the words of Jesus and the answer of His disciples—what happened during the pause?
835. How was it possible for the temple to appear as "a mount of snow, fretted with golden pinnacles"?
836. What three points were involved in the question: "When shall these things be?"
837. What was "the sign" of vs. 4?
838. How was the answer of Jesus both adequate and yet disappointing?
839. What two "comings" were involved in His answer?
840. What five tokens are mentioned to which the Lord directs the attention of the disciples?
841. What caused the Messianic hopes of the Jews to rise to a fever-heat?
842. What were the three wars and rumors of war especially significant to the Hebrew Christians?
843. What two reasons are given for not being troubled?
844. When in particular did "nation rise against nation"?
845. Name the five earthquakes in the period between the time of our Lord and 70 A.D.
846. Specify where and when and to whom the prediction of vs. 9 found fulfillment.
847. Prove scripturally that "every nation had received its (the gospel's) testimony before the destruction of Jerusalem. Cf. Col. 1:6; 23; II Tim. 4:17.
848. Show how Acts 4:19, 20; 5:20-32; 22:3-21 fulfill the 11th verse.
849. Does verse eleven give some encouragement to the thought of

preaching the gospel without preparation? Discuss.

850. Under what conditions would verses 12 and 13 be fulfilled?
851. What two or three "ends" are possible as of vs. 13b?

11. THE ABOMINATION OF DESOLATION 13:14-23

TEXT 13:14-23

"But when ye see the abomination of desolation standing where he ought not (let him that readeth understand), then let them that are in Judea flee unto the mountains: and let him that is on the housetop not go down, nor enter in, to take anything out of his house, and let him that is in the field not return back to take his cloke. But woe unto them that are with child and to them that give suck in those days! And pray ye that it be not in the winter. For those days shall be tribulation, such as there hath not been the like from the beginning of the creation which God created until now, and never shall be. And except the Lord had shortened the days, no flesh would have been saved: but for the elect's sake, whom he chose, he shortened the days. And then if any man shall say unto you, Lo, here is the Christ; or, Lo, there; believe it not: for there shall arise false Christs and false prophets, and shall shew signs and wonders, that they may lead astray, if possible, the elect. But take ye heed: behold, I have told you all things beforehand."

THOUGHT QUESTIONS 13:14-23

718. Read Daniel 9:27; 11:37; 12:11 and Matt. 24:15 for help in the meaning of the strange phrase "abomination of desolation." Does this refer to an incident at the destruction of Jerusalem or at the end of the world?
719. Who said "let him that readeth understand"—Jesus or Mark?
720. How could we possibly refer "the abomination of desolation" to the end of the world when those involved are instructed to flee from Judea to the Mountains?
721. Why the urgency as suggested in vs. 15 through 18.
722. Are we to believe the destruction of Jerusalem was worse than dropping an atomic bomb on a city? Cf. vs. 19.
723. Who are "the elect" of vs. 20? (This is perhaps one of the most difficult questions to answer—but attempt one—make it thoughtful.)
724. During what period of time were the false Christs to appear?
725. The words of Jesus seem to have a direct reference to His apostles is this true? Discuss.

COMMENT

TIME—Late Tuesday afternoon, April 4, A.D. 30.

PLACE—The Mount of Olives. After the final departure of Jesus from the temple.

PARALLEL ACCOUNTS—Matt. 24:15-28; Luke 21:20-24.

OUTLINE—1. What to do when you see the abomination of desolation, vs. 14-18. 2. The tribulation of those days, vs. 19, 20. 3. A warning against false Christs, vs. 21-23.

ANALYSIS

I. WHAT TO DO WHEN YOU SEE THE ABOMINATION OF DESOLATION, VS. 14-18.

1. Those in Judea are to flee to the mountains.
2. He that is on the housetop should not enter the house for possessions.
3. He that is in the field should not come to the house for his cloak.
4. It will be very difficult for those in pregnancy or with young children.
5. Pray it may not happen in the winter.

II. THE TRIBULATION OF THESE DAYS, VS. 19-20.

1. More severe than any before or after.
2. Without the providential help of God the whole Jewish Nation would have been lost.
3. The severity and time of the tribulation was shortened because of "the elect."

III. A WARNING AGAINST FALSE CHRISTS, VS. 21-23.

1. There shall be many claims to Messiahship—do not accept them.
2. False Christs and prophets will perform signs and wonders—do not believe them.
3. These prophetic warnings and careful details should forearm you against that day.

EXPLANATORY NOTES

I. WHAT TO DO WHEN YOU SEE THE ABOMINATION OF DESOLATION.

"14. But when ye see the abomination of desolation standing where he ought not. In the Authorized Version, after the word "desolation," the words "spoken of by Daniel the prophet," are introduced, but without sufficient authority. They were probably interpolated from Matthew, where there is abundant authority for them; and thus their omission by Mark does not affect the argument drawn from them in favour of the genuineness of the Book of Daniel, against those, whether in earlier or in later times, who reject this book, or ascribe it to some more recent authorship. The "abomination of desolation" is a Hebrew idiom, meaning "the abomination, that maketh desolate." Luke (21:20) does not use the expression; it would have sounded strange to his Gentile readers. He says, "When ye see Jerusalem compassed with armies, then know that her desolation is at hand." This reference to the Roman armies by Luke has led some commentators to suppose that the "abomination of desolation" meant the Roman eagles. But this was a sign from without; whereas "the abomination of desolation" was a sign from within, connected with the ceasing of the daily sacrifice of the temple. It is alluded to by the Prophet Daniel in three places, namely, Dan. 9:27; 11:31; 12:11. We must seek for its explanation in something within the temple, "standing in the holy place" (Matt. 24:15)—some profanation of the temple, on account of which God's judgments would fall on Jerusalem. Now, Daniel's prophecy had already received one fulfillment (B.C. 168), when we read (1 Macc. i. 54) that they set up "the abomination of desolation upon the altar." This was when Antiochus Ephiphanes set up the statue of Jupiter on the great altar of burnt sacrifice. But that "abomination of desolation" was the forerunner of another and a worse profanation yet to come, which our Lord, no doubt, had in his mind when he called the attention of his disciples to these predictions by Daniel. There is a remarkable passage in Josephus *("Wars of the Jews,"* iv.6,) in which he refers to an ancient saying then current, that "Jerusalem would be taken, and the temple be destroyed, when it had been defiled by the hands of the Jews themselves." Now, this literally took place. For while the Roman armies were invading Jerusalem, the Jews within the city were in fierce conflict amongst themselves. And it would seem most probable that our Lord had in his mind, in connection with Daniel's prophecy, more especially that at 9:27, the eruption of the army of Zealots and Assassins into the temple, filling the holy place with the dead bodies of their own fellow-citizens. The Jews had invited these marauders to defend them against the army of the Romans; and they, by their outrages against God, were the special cause of the desolation of Jerusalem. Thus, while Luke points to the sign from without, namely, the Roman forces surrounding the city, Matthew and Mark refer to the more terrible sign from within, the "abomination of desolation"—the abomination that would fill up the measure of their iniquities and cause the avenging power of Rome to come down upon them and crush them. It was after these two signs—the sign from within and the sign from without—that Jerusalem was laid prostrate. Therefore our Lord proceeds to warn both Jews and Christians alike, that when they saw these signs they should flee unto the mountains—not to the mountains of Judea, for those were already occupied by the Roman army *(Josephus, lib. iii. cap.* xii.), but those further off, beyond Judea. We know from Eusebius (iii.15) that the Christians fled to Pella, on the other side of the Jordan. The Jews, on the other hand, as they saw the Roman army approaching nearer, betook themselves to Jerusalem, as to an asylum, thinking that there they would be under the special protection of Jehovah; but there, alas, they were imprisoned and slain.

15. Let him that is on the housetop not go down, nor enter in, to take anything out of his house. The roofs of the houses were flat, with frequently a little "dome" in the centre. The people lived very much upon them; and the stairs were outside, so that a person wishing to enter the house must first descend by these outer stairs. The words, therefore, mean that he must flee suddenly, if he would save his life, even though he might lose his goods. He must escape, perhaps by crossing over the parapet of his own housetop, and so from housetop to housetop, until he could find a convenient point for flight into the hill country.

16.—And let him that is in the field not return back to take his cloke. This was the outer garment or pallium. They who worked in the field were accustomed to leave their cloak and their tunic at home; so that, half-stripped, they might be more free in labour. Thereafter our Lord warns them that in this impending destruction, so suddenly would it come, they must be ready to fly just as they were. It was the direction given to Lot, "Escape for thy life; look not behind thee."

17. But woe unto them that are with child and to them that give suck in those days! Women in this condition would be specially objects of pity, for they would be more exposed to danger. The words, "Woe to them!" are an exclamation of pity, as though it was said, "Alas! for them." Josephus (vii. 8) mentions that some mothers constrained by hunger during the siege, devoured their own infants!

18. And pray ye that it be not in the winter. According to the best authorities, "your flight" is omitted, but the meaning remains very much the same. Matthew (xxiv. 20) adds, "neither on a sabbath." But this would be comparatively of little interest to those to whom Mark was writing. Our Lord thus specifies the winter, because at that season, on account of the cold and snow, flight would be attended with special difficulty and hardship, and would be almost impossible for the aged and infirm."

II. THE TRIBULATION OF THOSE DAYS.

"19. For those days shall be tribulation, such as there hath not been the like from the beginning of the creation. These expressions are very remarkable. To begin with, the tribulation would be so unexampled and so severe that the days themselves would be called "tribulation." They would be known ever after as "the tribulation." There never had been anything like them, and there never would be again. Neither the Deluge, nor the destruction of cities of the plain, nor the drowning of Pharaoh and his host in the Red Sea, nor the slaughter of the Canaanites, nor the destruction of Nineveh, or of Babylon, or of other great cities and nations, would be so violent and dreadful as the overthrow of Jerusalem by Titus. All this is confirmed by Josephus, who says, speaking of this overthrow, "I do not think that any state ever suffered such things, or any nation within the memory of man." St. Chrysostom assigns the cause of all this to the base and cruel treatment of the Son of God by the Jews. The destruction of their city and their temple, and their continued desolation afterwards, were the lessons by which the Jews were taught that the Christ had indeed come, and that this was the Christ whom they had crucified and slain.

20. And except the Lord had shortened the days, no flesh would have been saved: but for the elect's sake, whom he chose, he shortened the days. St. Matthew's record (xxiv. 22) differs from that of St. Mark in the omission of the words "the Lord," and the clause "whom he chose." If the time of the siege of Jerusalem had lasted much longer, not one of the nation could have survived; all would have perished by war, or famine, or pestilence. The Romans raged against the Jews as an obstinate and rebellious nation, and would have exterminated them. But "the Lord" shortened the time of this frightful catastrophe, for the elect's sake, that is, partly for the sake of the Christians who could not escape from Jerusalem, and partly for that of the Jews, who subdued by this awful visitation, were converted to Christ or would hereafter be converted to him. We learn from hence how great is the love of God towards his elect, and his care for them. For their sakes he spared many Jews. For their sakes he created and preserves the whole world. Yea, for their sakes, Christ the eternal Son was made man, and became obedient unto death. "All things are yours, and ye are Christ's, and Christ is God's." It may be added that a number of providential circumstances combined to shorten these days of terror. Titus was himself disposed to clemency, and friendly towards Josephus. Moreover, he was attached to Bernice, a Jewess, the sister of Agrippa. All these and other circumstances conspired in the providence of God to "shorten the days."

III. A WARNING AGAINST FALSE CHRISTS.

"21, 22. And then if any man shall say unto you, Lo, here is Christ; or, Lo, there, believe it not; for there shall arise false Christs and false prophets. Josephus mentions one Simon of Gerasa, who, pretending to be a deliverer of the people from the Romans, gathered around him a crowd of followers, and gained admission into Jerusalem, and harassed the Jews. In like manner, Eleazar and John, leaders of the

Zealots, gained admission into the holy place, under the pretence of defending the city, but really that they might plunder it. But it seems as though our Lord here looked beyond the siege of Jerusalem to the end of the world; and he warns us that as the time of his second advent approaches, deceivers will arise, to seduce, if it were possible, even the elect. The word "to seduce" is more properly rendered, as in the Revised Version, to lead astray. Every age has produced its crop of such deceivers; and it may be expected that, as the time of the end draws nearer and nearer, their number will increase. Sometimes those idiosyncrases in them which show themselves in lying wonders, are the result of self-delusion; but still oftener they are deliberate attempts made for the purpose of imposing on the unwary. Sometimes they are a combination of both. In the cases to which our Lord refers there is evidently an intention to lead astray, although it may have had its origin in self-deceit. In our day there is a sad tendency to lead men astray with regard to the great fundamental verities of Christianity. And the words of St. Jerome may well be remembered here: "If any would persuade you that Christ is to be found in the wilderness of unbelief or sceptical philosophy, or in the secret chambers of heresy, believe them not."

23. But take ye heed. The "ye" is here emphatic. The disciples were around him, hanging upon his lips. But his admonition is meant for Christians everywhere, even to the end of the world." *(Bickersteth)*

FACT QUESTIONS 13:14-24

852. How do some critics use Mark (13:14) against the early date of the book of Daniel? How answered?
853. How does Luke 21:20 help (us Gentiles) in understanding the meaning of the expression "abomination of desolation"?
854. Why is it wrong to conclude that the "abomination" was the Roman eagles?
855. Show how Daniel's prophecy had already received one fulfillment.
856. How does Josephus help us in our understanding of "the abomination of desolation"?
857. Why were there so many Jews in Jerusalem when Titus attacked? Why no Christians?
858. If the occupant was not to come down from the housetop where was he to go? How would this help?
859. Why return for "the cloke"?
860. What words of Josephus help us to appreciate the words of Jesus "woe unto them that are with child etc."?

861. Who would be hindered in a winter flight?
862. Mention three or four other violent events which are of less violent a character than the overthrow of Jerusalem.
863. Who confirmed the words of Jesus as in vs. 19? Discuss.
864. Who were "the elect" of vs. 20—what great lesson is here for our learning?
865. Mention one or two of the providential circumstances combined to shorten the days.
866. Who was "Simon of Gerasa"?
867. Who were "Eleazar and John"?
868. Show how pertinent the words of Jerome are for our day.
869. To whom is vs. 23 directed?

12. THE COMMAND TO WATCH 13:24-37

TEXT 13:24-37

"But in those days, after that tribulation, the sun shall be darkened, and the moon shall not give her light, and the stars shall be falling from heaven, and the powers that are in the heavens shall be shaken. And then shall they see the Son of man coming in clouds with great power and glory. And then shall he send forth the angels, and shall gather together his elect from the four winds, from the uttermost part of the earth to the uttermost part of heaven.

Now from the fig tree learn her parable: when her branch is now become tender, and putteth forth its leaves, ye know that the summer is nigh; even so ye also, when ye see these things coming to pass, know ye that he is nigh, even at the doors. Verily I say unto you, This generation shall not pass away, until all these things be accomplished. Heaven and earth shall pass away: but my words shall not pass away. But of that day or that hour knoweth no one, not even the angels in heaven, neither the Son, but the Father. Take ye heed, watch and pray: for ye know not when the time is. It is as when a man, sojourning in another country, having left his house, and given authority to his servants, to each one his work, commanded also the porter to watch. Watch therefore: for ye know not when the lord of the house cometh, whether at even, or at midnight, or at cockcrowing, or in the morning; lest coming suddenly he find you sleeping. And what I say unto you I say unto all, Watch."

THOUGHT QUESTIONS 13:24-37

726. Just what "days" are contemplated in vs. 24?
727. Is this prediction of literal events or is this symbolic language? i.e. "sun"—"the moon" etc.

728. Who will see the Son of man when He comes? Why refer to "the sun"—"the moon" etc.
729. Who are "the elect"?
731. Who would be in the "uttermost part of the heaven"?
730. What is the meaning of "the four winds"?
732. Have we learned from the fig tree her parable?
733. Please specify some of the signs of His coming.
734. What "generation" is meant in vs. 30?
735. Why the emphatic statement of vs. 31?
736. Why was it important to say that no one knew the day or the hour?
737. For what are we to watch and pray? (Please be specific)
738. Who is the man sojourning in another country?
739. Has the Lord given to each of us a work to do? List ten separate areas of work for our Lord.
740. What was the one sin against which our Lord warned us?

COMMENT

TIME.—Late Tuesday afternoon, April 4, A.D. 30.

PLACE.—The Mount of Olives. After the final departure of Jesus from the temple.

PARALLEL ACCOUNTS.—Matt. 24:23-42; Luke 21:25-36.

OUTLINE.—1. The Coming of the Son of Man. 2. The Lesson from the Fig Tree. 3. Be Ye Always Ready.

ANALYSIS

I. THE COMING OF THE SON OF MAN, vs. 24-27.
   1. The Sun and Moon Darkened. Mark 13:24; Matt. 24:29; Luke 21:25.
   2. The Heavenly Powers Shaken. Mark 13:25; Matt. 24:29.
   3. The Sign of the Son of Man. Mark 13:26; Matt. 24:30; Luke 25:27.
   4. The Saints Gathered. Mark 13:27; Matt. 24:31.

II. THE LESSON FROM THE FIG TREE, vs. 28-31.
   1. The Sign that it is near. Mark 13:28, 29; Matt. 24:32, 33; Luke 25:29.
   2. This Generation shall not pass. Mark 13:30; Matt. 24:34; Luke 25:32.
   3. Christ's word sure. Mark 13:31; Matt. 24:35; Luke 25:33.

III. BE YE ALWAYS READY, vs. 32-37.
   1. The Time Known only to the Father. Mark 13:32; Matt. 24:36.
   2. Therefore be Watchful. Mark 13:33; Mark 24:42; Luke 25:36.
   3. Watchfulness Enforced by Parable. Mark 13:34-37; Matt. 24:43-51.

INTRODUCTION

This is a part of the same prophecy as just considered, foretelling so much of the future as was necessary for the comfort and courage and watchfulness of the disciples then and for all time. The developments of Divine Providence filled up the outline of the divine word, and no man with the word of God in one hand, and the history of the Jews in the other, can fail to see a most minute and perfect correspondence between the two. And so long as the world reads the words of Jesus, and beholds those words fulfilled in Jerusalem, still trodden down of the Gentiles, and in the Jews still scattered and homeless among the nations, it has an argument for the infallibility of the Founder of Christianity, and for the truth of the religion proceeding forth from him and his teaching, which nothing can gainsay or resist. Out of the dust and ashes of the holy city for nineteen hundred years has risen a voice in attestation of the Messiahship of him who was crucified without her walls; and the people who denied the Holy One and the Just in all their dispersion have, for an equal period, been proclaiming him their true though rejected Lord.—*H. S. Kelsey.*

EXPLANATORY NOTES

I. THE COMING OF THE SON OF MAN.

24. *In those days, after that tribulation.* In the period of history that lies after the final overthrow of Jerusalem, which is meant by "that tribulation." It will help the reader to compare the 24th chapter of Matthew, which is fuller. The following from my *Lesson Commentary* for 1887 will suggest some hints towards the understanding of these prophecies: "As the Lord and his disciples passed out of the temple, after his farewell and prediction of its desolation, in the close of chapter 23, his disciples pointed out the solidity and splendor of the structure, as though in doubt whether such massive walls could be destroyed. The answer was that not one stone should be left on another. When they had reached the Mount of Olives and from its summit looked down on the city and temple, as upon a map, the disciples, still thinking of what he had uttered, asked three questions: 1. When shall these things be? That is, when shall the temple and city be destroyed? 2. What shall be the sign of thy coming? 3. What shall be the sign of the end of the world? The interpreter, in order to understand the Savior's answer, must keep in mind that not one, but three questions are answered. The answer to the first extends to verse 28. Immediately after follows the answer to the second with various warnings and exhortations, while in the 25th chapter we have given an account of the end of the world and a picture of the judgment day." The present study comes in the answer to the

second question and is an exhortation to be ready for Christ's coming. *The sun shall be darkened.* Some interpret all that is said of sun, moon and stars literally, as great natural phenomena that shall precede the coming of the Lord. Others suppose that these are symbols of great disturbances in the history of mankind. I believe that a correct interpretation only requires that these words be given their usual symbolic meaning. This is prophecy and prophecy always chooses symbols. While we can never be certain of the *exact* meaning of unfulfilled prophecy, I believe that this prediction has been a great part fulfilled. The sun is the usual symbol of Christ, "the Light of the world," "the Sun of Righteousness;" the moon, which only shines with the reflected splendor of the sun, is the church, which only shines in the light of Christ. The stars are apostles and other great lights of the church. Without consuming space, I will say that this is the usual meaning of these symbols in New Testament prophecy. As to the application, the Lord is outlining history to the end of the world. When the apostasy began to develop, about three centuries after these words were spoken, the rays of light that came from Christ's teaching were obscured by the traditions of men, the church therefore ceased to shed her light on mankind, and the apostles were no longer recognized as the great authorities of religious life. They fell from their high place, or from heaven. The Bible was taken from men and what history has pleased to call significantly "The Dark Ages" came upon the world. Certainly this interpretation is in precise harmony with history. Still, at this time, two-thirds of Christendom are destitute of the Bible and wrapped in the darkness of human tradition. The "Sun" is still darkened, the "moon" does not yet give her light, and the "stars" are not restored to their places in the heavens.

25. *The powers that are in heaven shall be shaken.* For the interpretation, see comment on verse 24. These powers refer to the spiritual forces that should control mankind.

26. *And then shall they see the Son of man.* After this spiritual darkening. Therefore, still in the future. As the spiritual darkness seems to be slowly lifting we have in this a cheering omen that the coming draws nearer. I understand this to be a literal coming. "They shall see him." See, also, Acts 1:9-11. As the apostles saw the Lord ascend, "in like manner" shall he return. Certain facts may be noted: (1) The Lord shall come as the Son of man. They that pierced him shall look upon him. (2) His coming shall be seen by all mortals. "Every eye shall see him." (3) It will be glorious. He shall ride upon the clouds of heaven and shall have "all his holy angels with him."

27. *Then shall he send his angels.* "With a great sound of a trumpet"

(Matt. 24:31). *And shall gather together his elect, etc.* As the tribes of Israel were anciently gathered together by sound of trumpet (Exod. 19:13, 16, 19; Lev. 23:24; Ps. 81:3-5), so any mighty gathering of God's people, by divine command, is represented as collected by sound of trumpet (Isa. 27:13; Rev. 11:15); and the ministry of angels, employed in all the great operations of Providence, is here held forth as the agency by which the present assembling of the elect is to be accomplished. *The four winds.* Used to denote the quarters of the earth's surface; i.e., from all parts of the earth. *The uttermost part of the earth to the uttermost part of heaven.* Probably an allusion to the apparent junction of earth and sky at the visible horizon, but in any case it refers to the whole world.

II. THE LESSON FROM THE FIG TREE.

28. *Learn a parable of the fig tree.* More literally, Learn *the* parable *from* the fig tree. The fig is a native product of the East, and grows in spontaneous plenty in Palestine. In a warm climate fruit forms a very large proportion of customary food, and hence the fruit tree is a favorite source for illustration. Our Lord spoke this upon the Mount of Olives where fig trees were growing all around him. He was near to Bethphage (or Fig-ville), so-called, probably, from the abundance of this product. It was now about the last of March, and though "the time of figs was not yet," the trees were doubtless beginning to verify the words by opening signs of the season. As the sprouting leaf was a sign of the approach of summer, so the events just named foreshadowed the coming of the Son of man.

29. *So ye, in like manner, when ye shall see these things come to pass.* Rather, "coming to pass." *Is nigh, even at the doors.* That is, the full manifestation of it; for till then it admitted of no full development. In Luke (21:28) the following words precede these: "And when these things begin to come to pass, then look up, and lift up your heads: for your redemption draweth nigh." Their redemption, in the instance certainly, from Jewish oppression (1 Thess. 2:14-16; Luke 11:52), but in the highest sense of these words, redemption from all the oppressions and miseries of the present state at the second appearing of the Lord Jesus.

30. *This generation shall not pass* (away) *till all these things be done.* Accomplished. There are two explanations: (1) Generation is taken in its ordinary sense of the persons then living. And the prophecy had one exact fulfillment within that generation. (2) The word translated generation has sometimes the meaning of race or nation; having, it is true, a more pregnant meaning, implying that the character of one generation stamps itself upon the race, as here in this verse also.—*Alford.* The last

meaning is, no doubt, correct. The word in the Greek (genea) also means "nation." Dean Alford in his Critical Greek Testament says: "It may be well to show that the original (genea) has in Hellenistic Greek the meaning of a *race or family of people,* for this purpose see Jer. 8:3 (where *genea* occurs in the Septuagint Greek); compare Matt. 23:36 with verse 35, and observe that the living generation did not slay Zacharias, so that the *whole* people were addressed. See also Matt. 12:45 where the sense absolutely requires that the meaning of *nation* should be attached to the word. See also Matt. 17:17 . . . In all these passages *generation* is equivalent to nation." Mark 13:30 should therefore read "This race shall not pass away until all these things be done"; a prediction of the marvelous and miraculous preservation of the Jewish race, despite the awful overthrow of the nation, its dispersion to the ends of the earth, the constant persecution and oft-repeated massacres, such calamities as no other race ever endured, to the end of time as a living witness to the truth of Christ's testimony. Without a country or a temple, scattered among all nations, persecuted as no other people, the Jews have been preserved through 1900 years separate, distinct, and virtually unchanged; a case without parallel in history.

III. BE YE ALWAYS READY.

32. *Of that day and that hour.* Of Christ's coming. *Knoweth no man.* "The signs of the times" are left to us; the times themselves are in the hands of God. *Not the angels . . . neither the Son.* The practical lesson of the verse is well put by Dr. Schaff: "His voluntarily not knowing the day of judgment, during the days of his flesh, is a warning against chronological curiosity and mathematical calculations in the exposition of Scripture prophecy. It is not likely that any theologian, however learned, should know more or ought to know more on this point than Christ himself, who will judge the quick and the dead, chose to know in the state of his humiliation."

33. *Watch and pray.* To watch, denotes (1) to be sleepless; (2) to be vigilant.—*Maclear.* In view of the suddenness and unexpectedness of this coming, "watch and pray"; not be always expecting what will come unexpectedly, nor be seeking to know what cannot be known, but be always in a state of readiness, because, of the uncertainty.

34. *For the Son of man.* Better, "It is as when a man." The whole matter of watching is as in the following parable. *Taking a far journey.* Sojourning in another country. *Gave authority;* power to conduct his household, and to manage his affairs while absent. *To every man his work.* The authority being joined with duty. Even so our Lord left his Church,

gave authority to his servants the apostles, and to those who should come after them, and to every man his work, and is now waiting for the consummation of all things. *Commanded the porter to watch.* After he had given all the orders concerning the internal affairs, he gives finally, at the door, to the porter, the additional command to watch: this is the point of the parable. I do not suppose that the Lord designs any particular official in the church by the porter, rather to enforce the duty of watchfulness.

35. *Watch.* It is the fundamental law of watchfulness, to be always watching. *Ye know not when the master of the house cometh.* But with all the obscurity thus intentionally thrown around the day and the hour of Christ's coming, let us not forget that no obscurity, no uncertainty, hangs around the great event itself. In all that future which lies before us, these are the only two events of which we are absolutely certain: our own approaching death, our Lord's approaching advent.—*Hanna. At even, or at midnight, or at the cockcrowing, or in the morning.* The four regular watches, from eventide to daybreak, representing, either periods in the world's history, or epochs in human life.

36. *Lest coming suddenly he find you sleeping.* During the night the captain of the temple made his rounds. On his approach the guards had to rise, and salute him in a particular manner. Any guard found asleep when on duty was beaten, or his garments were set on fire—a punishment, as we know, actually awarded.—*Edersheim.*

37. *What I say unto you I say unto all.* Though the apostles and the ministry are watchmen and porters, yet all believers are to be incessantly watchful, and for the same reasons.—*Schaff. Watch.* Observe in this chapter the emphasis given to Christ's exhortation, "Watch!" Matthew tells us how the Lord sought to impress these lessons of watchfulness and faithfulness still more deeply by the parables of the "Ten Virgins" (Matt. 25:1-13), and the "Talents" (Matt. 25:14-30), and closed all with a picture of the awful day when the Son of man should separate all nations one from another as the shepherd divideth his sheep from the goats (Matt. 25:31-46).

FACT QUESTIONS 13:24-37

870. "No man with the word of God in one hand and the history of the Jews in the other, can fail to see ______________" what?
871. How does Jerusalem and the scattering of the Jews become a grand witness for the infallibility of the Founder of Christianity?
872. State the three questions of the disciples—which question is being answered in vs. 24?

873. Why does Johnson choose to use a symbolic meaning for the sun, moon, and stars of vs. 24?
874. Who is represented by "the sun," "the moon"—"the stars"?
875. What do "the Dark Ages" have to do with this prophecy?
876. What are "the powers that are in heaven"? How shaken?
877. Could we believe Christ could come at any time and still believe Johnson's interpretation of the signs of His coming? Discuss.
878. Are we nearer to His coming today according to this symbolic interpretation of the signs than when Johnson wrote it seventy-six years ago? Discuss.
879. What three facts are to be noted in His coming "in like manner"?
880. Why was a trumpet used in gathering together His elect? Cf. Matthew 24:31.
881. What is represented in the expression "uttermost part of heaven"?
882. Show how appropriate in time and place was the use of the fig tree for an illustration.
883. If we were to wait for the literal sun, moon, and stars to be affected, couldn't we become negligent in our waiting? Discuss.
884. Read Luke 21:28 and state what "redemption" is involved.
885. How could it be possible that the prophecy of Jesus was fulfilled during the generation of the apostles?
886. Read Jer. 8:3 and Matt. 23:36 and 35 and Matt. 12:45; 17:17—what is taught in these verses about the meaning of the word "generation"?
887. What case is without parallel in history?
888. What warning does Christ give to certain theological prophets?
889. What is involved in the expression "watch and pray"?
890. What one subject is developed in the parable?
891. What are we to do while we watch and wait?
892. Who is represented by "the porter" in the parable?
893. Of what two events are we absolutely certain?
894. What is represented by the four watches mentioned?
895. What did Edersheim say about sleeping on duty?
896. What does Matthew add to this exhortation to watchfulness? Cf. Matt. 25:1-13; 14-30.

SUMMARY

13:1-37

In this section Mark sets forth his Master as a prophet. At the time that his narrative was composed, some of the predictions recorded in the section had already been fulfilled, but the chief part was yet in the future. He staked the validity of his argument, and the reputation of Jesus as a prophet, partly on the former, but chiefly on the predictions which were yet to be fulfilled, and fulfilled before the eyes of the then living generation. The discourse, as he wrote it out, contained in itself a challenge to that generation of Jews to watch the course of events in their own national history, and to say whether its predictions proved true or false. No generation has lived that was so competent to expose a failure had it occurred, or that would have done so more eagerly. But the events, as they transpired, turned the prophecy into history, and demonstrated the foreknowledge of Jesus. But if Jesus possessed this foreknowledge, his claim to be the Christ the Son of God was miraculously attested thereby; and even his admission that he knew not the day or the hour of his own second coming, detracts nothing from the argument; for foreknowledge is still displayed, notwithstanding this limitation of it, and the limitation itself is known only by his own voluntary admission — an admission which is a singular and conclusive proof of his perfect honesty and candor. (*J. W. McGarvey*)

13. THE ANOINTING AT BETHANY 14:1-9

TEXT 14:1-9

"Now after two days was the feast of the passover and the unleavened bread: and the chief priests and the scribes sought how they might take him with subtlety, and kill him: for they said, Not during the feast, lest haply there shall be a tumult of the people. And while he was in Bethany in the house of Simon the leper, as he sat at meat there came a woman having an alabaster cruse of ointment of spikenard very costly; and she brake the cruse, and poured it over his head. But there were some that had indignation among themselves, saying, To what purpose hath this waste of the ointment been made? For this ointment might have been sold for above three hundred pence, and given to the poor. And they murmured against her. But Jesus said, Let her alone; why trouble ye her? She hath wrought a good work on me. For ye have the poor always with you, and whensoever ye will ye can do them good: but me ye have not always. She hath done what she could: she hath anointed my body beforehand for the burying. And verily I say unto you, Wheresoever the gospel shall be preached throughout the whole world, that also which this woman hath done shall be spoken of for a memorial of her."

THOUGHT QUESTIONS 14:1-9

741. If the feast of the Passover was held on Thursday (as traditionally represented) then this plot was made on Tuesday or Wednesday—do you agree with this thought? Discuss.
742. Why did they want to kill Him?

743. When did the feast of unleavened bread begin? How long did it last?
744. Please read John 12:2-8. When did this anointing take place? Isn't there a break in the chronology? Discuss.
745. Read Luke 7:36-50—please notice the differences in the two anointings.
746. Read Matt. 26:6-13—note the additions Matthew makes to Mark's account.
747. Why refer to Simon as a "leper"; was he a leper at the time of the anointing?
748. We know by reading John's account who the woman was—who was it?
749. Was this a common meal? A celebration? What is meant by "as he sat at meat"?
750. Why was the ointment in an alabaster container?
751. What is "pure nard"?
752. How could she pour it if she broke the container?
753. Wasn't it "messy" to thus be covered with this ointment?
754. Was the complaint of waste a justifiable one? Discuss.
755. In what sense were they to "let her alone"?
756. Jesus accepted the anointing in spite of criticism—does this offer some encouragement to us?
757. Jesus says something about good intentions vs. good works, in His words of vs. 7—what is it?
758. Why say "she has done what she could"?
759. Did Mary intend a pre-burial anointing by her actions?
760. How have the words of Jesus in vs. 9 been fulfilled?

COMMENT

TIME—Mark has placed the account of the anointing out of its chronological order. The preceding incident was dated Tuesday, April 4, A.D. 30. This event, instead of following, occurred on Saturday, April 1st, three days before, the day before the Lord's entry into Jerusalem. It was during the Lord's stay at Bethany on his way to the Holy City. The consultation of the priests referred to in verses 1, 2, was on Tuesday evening, April 4, the same day as Jesus' predictions.

PLACES—The consultation of the priests and scribes took place in Jerusalem, probably in the palace of Caiaphas. The anointing and feast were at Bethany, the home of Lazarus and his sisters, the beloved retreat of the Saviour two miles east of Jerusalem, on the eastern slope of the Mount of Olives, on the highway that led to Jericho and the country east of the Jordan.

PARALLEL ACCOUNTS—The plotting against Jesus (vs. 1, 2, 10, 11) is recorded also, Matt. 26:1-5, 14-16; Luke 22:1-6. The supper (3-9) in Matt. 26:6-13; John 12:2-8.

LESSON OUTLINE—1. The Conspiracy of the Rulers. 2. The Lord Anointed. 3. The Lord's Commendation.

ANALYSIS

I. THE CONSPIRACY OF THE RULERS, VS. 1, 2.

1. The Chief Priests Hold Counsel. Mark 14:1; Matt. 26-2; Luke 22:1; John 11:55.
2. Fear of the People. Mark 14:2; Matt. 26:5; Luke 22:2.

II. THE LORD ANOINTED, VS. 3-5.

1. The Ointment Poured on His Head. Mark 14:3; Matt. 26:6; John 12:1, 3.
2. The Indignation of Disciples. Mark 14:4; Matt. 26:8; John 12:4.
3. The Charge of Waste. Mark 14:5; Matt. 26:9; John 12:5.

III. THE LORD'S COMMENDATION, VS. 6-9.

1. A Good Work. Mark 14:6; Matt. 26:10.
2. Have the Poor Always. Mark 14:7; Matt. 26:11; John 12:8.
3. The Lord Anointed for Burial. Mark 14:8; Matt. 26:12.
4. The Woman's Deed Praised in All the World. Mark 14:9; Matt. 26:13.

INTRODUCTION

We have before us here a simple-hearted, loving woman, who has had no subtle questions of criticism about matter of duty and right, but only loves her Lord's person with a love that is probably a kind of mystery to herself, which love she wants somehow to express. She comes, therefore, with her box of ointment, having sold we know not what article or portion of her property to buy it, for it was very costly, and pours it on the Saviour's head—just here to encounter, for the first time, scruples, questions, and rebuffs of argument.—*Bushnell.* John says that this was six days before the Passover. From the order in which Matthew and Mark mention it, it would have been supposed that it was but two days before the Passover, and after the cleansing of the temple. But it is to be observed, (1) That Matthew and Mark often neglect the exact order of the event that they record; (2) That they do not affirm at what time this was. They leave it indefinite, saying that while Jesus was in Bethany he was anointed by Mary; (3) That Mark introduced it here for the purpose of giving a connected account of the conduct of Judas. Judas murmured at the waste of the ointment (John 12:4), and one of the effects of his indignation, it seems, was to betray his Lord.—*Barnes.*

I. THE CONSPIRACY OF THE RULERS.

1. *After two days was the feast of the passover.* It was Tuesday evening with us, but after Wednesday began with the Jews a new day began at sunset. Two days after would bring Friday, the day the Passover was slain. This date locates the time of the meeting of the rulers, not of the feast at the house of Simon the leper. *Of unleavened bread.* The Passover meal was the beginning of the feast of unleavened bread, which lasted for seven days. The whole paschal week was termed the feast of unleavened bread; the Passover was, strictly speaking, the 15th of Nisan, "the great day of the feast." *The chief priests and the scribes* (members of the Sanhedrim). The meeting of the chief priests and the scribes for consultation was at the palace of Caiaphas, the high priest (Matt. 26:3), (which tradition places on the "Hill of Evil Counsel"). From the fact that the council met at the palace of Caiaphas, and also that its session was in the evening, we may infer that it was an extraordinary meeting, held for secret consultation. This plotting was begun at least three months before, after the raising of Lazarus; and more recently the triumphal entry, the driving out the money-changers from the temple, the parables spoken against the Jewish leaders, seem to have enraged them, so that they felt that something must be done immediately to put a stop to his career. No doubt there was long debate. Some certainly opposed the putting him to death, as Joseph of Arimathea (Luke 23:51), and Nicodemus (John 7:50, 51), who were members of the Sanhedrim. For an instance of the debate in a like meeting for the same purpose, see John 11:46-51. —P. The first step in putting Christ to death was taken by the religious teachers of the Jewish nation. The very men who ought to have welcomed the Messiah were the men who conspired to kill him. *By craft.* With subtlety. That is, by some secret plan that would secure possession of him without exciting the opposition of the people.

2. *Not on the feast day*—As it was a time when vast multitudes were present from all parts of the land, and the Jews of Galilee and Perea being more friendly to Jesus than those of the capital, might make a disturbance if he were publicly arrested. Josephus computes that three million persons attended the Passover which is not incredible, seeing that the nation was expected to assemble at this greatest of the festivals. The acclamations on the Sunday before, as the Lord entered Jerusalem, demonstrated the favor he enjoyed with the people.

II. THE LORD ANOINTED.

This anointing is not to be confounded with the anointing mentioned in Luke 7:36-50. There is nothing in common between them, except the name of the householder, Simon; and this was a very common name in Palestine. The occasion, the time, the parties, and the spiritual significance are all different. The repetition of the incident is not at all strange. "An act of this kind, which had been once commended by our Lord (as in Luke), was very likely to have been repeated."—*Abbott.*

3. *Being in Bethany.* See *Time.* Jesus arrived in Bethany Friday; and the supper was Saturday evening, just after the close of the Jewish sabbath, and, as John expressly states (12:1), the evening before the triumphal entry into Jerusalem. *Bethany.* A village about two miles east of Jerusalem (John 11:18), being on the other side of the Mount of Olives. It was the home of Mary and Martha, where Christ was wont to visit when in Jerusalem (Luke 10:38-41; Matt. 21:17; Mark 11:11, 12). It was the scene of the resurrection of Lazarus (John, chap. 11), and of Christ's own ascension (Luke 24:50). It is not mentioned in the Old Testament.—*Abbott. Simon the Leper.* Perhaps he had been healed of his leprosy by Jesus. He dwelt in Bethany. It is natural to suppose that he had made Jesus a feast in gratitude. According to a tradition, he was the father of Lazarus; according to others, he was the husband of Martha, or Martha was his widow. Very likely he was in some way related to the family of Lazarus. Mary and Martha served (John 12:2). *There came a woman.* Mary, the sister of Martha and Lazarus (John 12:3), not the woman in Luke 7, "who was a sinner." The latter person is generally, but without reason, identified with Mary Magdalene, and the three women confounded.—*Schaff. Having an alabaster box,* or flask, called an alabaster; as we say, "a glass." These *alabastra,* or unguent flasks, were usually made of the Oriental or onyx alabaster, with long narrow necks, which let the oil escape drop by drop, and could easily be broken. *Ointment of spikenard.* The American portion of the Revision Committee would render this "pure nard" (with marginal reading, or liquid nard). Spikenard, from which the ointment was made, was an aromatic herb of the valerian family. It was imported from an early age from Arabia, India, and the Far East. The ointment of nard was highly esteemed, and was a costly luxury. *Very precious.* It was the costliest anointing oil of antiquity, and was sold throughout the Roman Empire, where it fetched a price that put it beyond any but the wealthy. Mary had bought a vase or flask of it containing twelve ounces (John 12:3).—*Cambridge Bible.* The three hundred pence given as its selling value (verse 5) would make it worth about $300 in our money. The value of the ointment only expressed the depth of her love. *She brake the box;* i.e., she broke the narrow neck of the small flask,

and poured the perfume, first on the head and then on the feet of Jesus (John 12:3), the Oriental custom of reclining at table made the latter easier than the former. *Poured it on his head.* Anointing with oil was a primitive custom of consecration (Gen. 18:18). It was then used for the ritual of consecration of priests; occasionally, also, of prophets. The anointing of the head was also a distinction which was conferred upon the guest of honor (Luke 7:46)—not only among the Jews, but generally in the East, and among the ancients. Mary may have intended only to show this honor; but this action symbolized Christ's Messiahship, and had a deeper significance, as our Lord points out in vs. 8.

4. *Some that had indignation.* Matthew (26:8) states that "the disciples" had indignation; Mark reports that "some" had indignation; John (12:4), as knowing who had whispered the first word of blame, fixes the uncharitable judgment on "Judas Iscariot, Simon's son." The narrow, covetous soul of the traitor could see nothing in the lavish gift but a "waste." His indignation, partly real, partly affected, was perhaps honestly shared by some of his fellow-disciples. *Why was this waste?* Worldly men would of course agree with the idea of Judas, that money laid out in the cherishing or expression of mere devotional sentiment is "waste." There is no waste in anything that helps the soul.

5. *Might have been sold for more than three hundred pence.* A penny here is the *denarius,* a Roman coin worth from fifteen to seventeen cents, or as the values of silver and gold were much greater then than now, about one dollar at the present time. The three hundred pence would make about forty-five dollars in silver, or at present, would amount to about $300. *And have been given to the poor.* The true friends of the poor, who give most and do most for them, will always be found among those who do most for Christ. It is the successors of Mary of Bethany, and not of Judas Iscariot, who really "care for the poor."—*Ryle. Murmured against her.* Scolded her.—*De Wette.* Addressed her harshly.

III. THE LORD'S COMMENDATION.

6. *Jesus said, Let her alone.* "Let her alone," is the language of sharp rebuke. Christ was indignant at the hypocrisy which made a pretended consideration of the poor an excuse for attacking and condemning an act of love toward himself. The answer of Jesus indicates the woman's cordial, unstudied sacrifice. *Why trouble ye her?* This indicates that Mary was herself abashed and downcast by the criticism of the twelve. Perhaps, as Maurice says, "She could not herself have answered Judas Iscariot's complaining question."—*Abbott. She hath wrought a good work on me.* Christ measured the moral quality of the act by the motive, the disciples by its seeming utility.

7. *Ye have the poor with you always.* You will have plenty of opportunities to aid them; and the more they did for their Master, the more they would do for the poor, for the poor are left in his stead, and through them will be expressed the increased love of the Master.

8. *She hath done what she could.* This praise is more precious than the ointment, coming from such a one as Christ. It is like that which he passed upon the poor widow: "She hath cast in all that she had." Blessed are they of whom the Master will say, "They have done what they could." *Come aforehand to anoint my body to the burying.* She had anticipated the hour of my decease; anointing my body before death, and thus preparing it for burial. It is worthy of note that this was all the anointing which our Lord's body received from the hand of Mary or her female friends, inasmuch as he had risen before they reached the sepulchre with their spices.

9. *Wheresoever this gospel.* The tidings of salvation, with special reference to Christ's death, just alluded to.—*Schaff. Preached throughout the whole world.* A prediction of the world-wide preaching of his death. *This also that she hath done . . . a memorial.* Fulfilled to the letter. It is right to record and remember the good deeds of those who love Christ; but when the desire to be put on record enters, the ointment is spoiled. This is the only case where such a promise is made; therefore the incident has a weighty lesson, and holds up a noble example.—*Schaff.*

FACT QUESTIONS 14:1-9

897. Is it true that Mark placed the anointing out of its chronological order? When did the anointing occur?
898. When and where did the consultation of the priests take place?
899. How did Mary obtain this costly ointment?
900. What possible purpose did Mark have in introducing the incident of the anointing at the time he did?
901. Who did the most murmuring? Why?
902. On what day of the week was the Passover slain? What day and month of the Jewish calendar?
903. When was the feast of unleavened bread observed?
904. How does Matt. 26:3 help us in our understanding of the plot of the chief priests and scribes?
905. What prompted the thought that something must be done immediately to stop Jesus?
906. Who would oppose putting Him to death?
907. What is meant in the word "craft" or "subtlety"?
908. What group of Jews were especially friendly toward Jesus? How

many Jews in Jerusalem for the Passover?

909. How could the commending given by our Lord as related in Luke 7:36-50 relate to this incident?
910. At what precise time was the feast held? Cf. John 12:1.
911. Three facts about Bethany:
912. Who was Simon the leper? Why the feast?
913. The woman (Mary) really never had a "box" at all—what was it?
914. From what plant was the ointment made? From where was it imported?
915. How many ounces in the flask of Mary?
916. B. W. Johnson states the ointment was worth $300 in 1889—what would be the value today?
917. In what way did she break the jar?
918. What special honor was associated with anointing the head?
919. Who was involved in the "indignation"?
920. There was no waste—explain why.
921. Who really cares for the poor?
922. What sharp rebuke was delivered by our Lord? Why?
923. Was Mary affected by the criticism of the twelve? In what way? What answer did she have to Judas' question?
924. How did Jesus measure the moral quality of the act? How did the disciples measure it?
925. What is meant by the expression "ye have the poor with you always"?
926. What praise is more precious than the ointment?
927. Did Mary really anticipate our Lord's death and come to "aforehand" anoint his body?
928. What prediction is made of the world-wide preaching of the death of Christ?
929. When is "the ointment spoiled"?

14. THE TREACHERY OF JUDAS 14:10, 11

TEXT 14:10, 11

"And Judas Iscariot, he that was one of the twelve, went away unto the chief priests, that he might deliver him unto them. And they, when they heard it, were glad, and promised to give him money. And he sought how he might conveniently deliver him unto them."

THOUGHT QUESTIONS 14:10, 11

761. Was the betrayal of Judas at all related to the incident which just preceded it? Discuss. Cf. Matt. 26:14.
762. What possible motive or motives did Judas have in the betrayal? Suggest at least two.

763. Just what agreement did Judas make with the chief priests?
764. Did the priests pay him at the time of his agreement with them?
765. How could these religious men act in such an irreligious manner—discuss the chief contributing cause to such a condition.
766. Did the betrayal of Judas include delivering Jesus into their hands?

COMMENT

TIME—Late Saturday evening, April 1, A.D. 30.
PLACES—Temple—the house of Caiaphas.
PARALLEL ACCOUNTS—Matt. 26:14-16; Luke 22:3-6.
OUTLINE—1. The man of the betrayal, vs. 10a. 2. Those who paid, vs. 10b-11a. 3. Waiting and watching, vs. 11b.

ANALYSIS

I. THE MAN OF THE BETRAYAL, VS. 10a.
  1. Judas Iscariot.
  2. One of the Twelve.

II. THOSE WHO PAID, VS. 10b-11a.
  1. Chief priests.
  2. They were pleased.
  3. Money promised.

III. WAITING AND WATCHING, VS. 11b.
  1. Waiting as a supposed friend.
  2. Watching as a traitor for the best time to deliver Him up.

EXPLANATORY NOTES

I. THE MAN OF THE BETRAYAL, VS. 11b.

"Verses 10, 11—*Volunteering to betray.* The "and" connects this with the preceding paragraph, not only historically but psychologically. His present action was (immediately) determined by the gift of Mary and the mild rebuke of the Master.

To deliver up Christ to his enemies. Whether he fully realized how much was involved as a result of this step is uncertain. He might imagine that not death, but the checking of his Master upon the career he had marked out, would ensue. But there is recklessness as to any consequences, provided he himself should be no loser. In robbing the alms from the bag, he was guilty of a breach of trust; in this new development of his master passion the unfaithfulness culminated. It is manifest that the spiritual side of Christ's ministry had for him no value. It was only the earthly rewards that might attend on discipleship that made it attractive to him. Was it to force the hand of the ideal, unpractical Christ that he sought to deliver him up? A miracle of deliverance might then result in a realization greater than his most brilliant hopes could depict, and thus his (passing) act of villainy be condoned. Or was it in sheer disgust and desperation respecting the course affairs seemed to be taking that he conceived of his deed? We cannot tell. In a mind like that of Judas there are depths beyond depths.

II. THOSE WHO PAID, VS. 10b-11a.

That selfishness was at the root we may be sure. *Avarice* is the direction it took. He proposed money, and asked how much (Matt. 26:15). Thirty pieces of silver a small sum? Yes, but he might be at that moment in real or fancied need, or the amount might be looked upon as a mere instalment of further reward, when he might have made himself useful, perhaps necessary, to the rulers. *Fear of consequences,* if he followed Christ further in the direction in which he was moving, may also have influenced his mind. And there can be no question as to the immediate impulse of *wounded feeling,* through baffled dishonesty and the sense that Christ saw through him. Falling short of the higher illumination and power of the Spirit, he was at the mercy of his own base, earthly nature.

III. WAITING AND WATCHING, VS. 11b.

The background to all this mental and spiritual movement on the part of Judas is the attitude of the chief priests and scribes, "seeking how they might take" Christ. But for opportunity afforded the treachery of Judas might have remained an aimless mood or a latent disposition, instead of becoming a definite purpose. In this consists the danger of unspiritual states of mind: they subject those in whom they are indulged to the tyranny of passing influences and circumstances.—M." (*Bickersteth*)

FACT QUESTIONS 14:10, 11

930. Show the psychological connection of this act to the gift of Mary and the rebuke of Jesus.
931. Does one sin lead to another in the life of Judas? Discuss.
932. What had no attraction—what had great attraction in the life of Judas?
933. How could it be said by some that Judas was attempting to "force the hand of an unpractical Christ"?
934. Show how selfishness turned to avarice.
935. Show how fear of consequences in following Christ and wounded feelings could have contributed to the motive for betrayal.
936. Except for something "the treachery of Judas might have remained an aimless mood or a latent disposition"—what was it? Please note the vast import of this for us.

D. THURSDAY: THE LORD'S SUPPER

TEXT 14:12-26

"And on the first day of unleavened bread, when they sacrificed the passover, his disciples say unto him, Where wilt thou that we go and make ready that thou mayest eat the passover? And he sendeth two of his disciples, and saith unto them, Go into the city, and there shall meet you a man bearing a pitcher of water: follow him; and wheresoever he shall enter in, say to the good man of the house, The Master saith, Where is my guestchamber, where I shall eat the passover with my disciples? And he will himself shew you a large upper room furnished and ready: and there make ready for us. And the disciples went forth, and came into the city, and found as he had said unto them: and they made ready the passover.

And when it was evening he cometh with the twelve. And as they sat and were eating, Jesus said, Verily I say unto you, One of you shall betray me, even he that eateth with me. They began to be sorrowful, and began to say unto him one by one, Is it I? And he said unto them, It is one of the twelve, he that dippeth with me in the dish. For the Son of man goeth, even as it is written of him: but woe unto that man through whom the Son of man is betrayed! good were it for that man if he had not been born.

And as they were eating, he took bread, and when he had blessed, he brake it, and gave to them, and said, Take ye: this is my body. And he took a cup, and when he had given thanks, he gave to them: and they all drank of it. And he said unto them, This is my blood of the covenant, which is shed for many. Verily I say unto you, I will no more drink of the fruit of the vine, until that day when I drink it new in the kingdom of God.

And when they had sung a hymn, they went out unto the mount of Olives."

THOUGHT QUESTIONS 14:12-26

767. Just when was the first day of unleavened bread? i.e., according to our time—and according to Jewish time?
768. Who was responsible for sacrificing the passover lamb?
769. Had Jesus eaten the passover with His disciples before this occasion?
770. Why did the disciples feel responsible for preparation of the passover? How elaborate was the preparation?
771. Where were Jesus and His disciples when He gave the instructions for the Passover preparation?

772. Who were the two disciples?
773. Was there anything strange about a man carrying a pitcher of water?
774. What was the purpose of these rather strange instructions?
775. Why was the householder so willing to offer his large upper room? (There is a good deal of traditional information as to who owned the upper room—read some of it.)
776. What was the reaction of the disciples when they saw the words of Jesus fulfilled?
777. At what time was the Passover eaten?
778. Why did Jesus predict His own betrayal? Be specific.
779. Did any of the disciples feel they were capable of betraying Him?
780. How specific was Jesus in pointing out His betrayer?
781. What is meant by the expression "dipping bread in the same dish with me."?
782. If Jesus was betrayed in fulfillment of prophecy why blame the one who did it?
783. How could a man be better off if he was never born?
784. What is involved in "blessing bread"?
785. What type of bread was broken? What had it symbolicly represented before Jesus used it to represent His body?
786. By reading all the accounts of the Lord's Supper attempt to reconstruct the order of service in the passover feast.
787. If there was just *one* cup in the institution of the Lord's Supper how is it we use more than one?
788. Some can believe the bread underwent a change when Jesus said "This is my body"—the fruit of the vine did the same when He said "this is my blood." How can such a thought be gathered from the text?
789. Did Jesus drink fermented grape juice?
790. Did the apostles have any idea what "covenant" was meant when Jesus referred to "the blood of the covenant"?
791. When were the words of promise in vs. 25 fulfilled?
792. Why sing a hymn?
793. What thoughts filled their hearts as they departed?

COMMENT

TIME.—Thursday evening, April 6 (14th Nisan), A.D. 30. With the Jews the 15th Nisan had begun.

PLACE.—Jerusalem, in an upper room with the disciples.

PARALLEL ACCOUNTS.—Matt. 26:17-25; Luke 22:7-18, 21-23; John 13: 21-26.

INTERVENING HISTORY.—Christ spent Tuesday eve, all day Wednesday,

and part of Thursday in retirement at Bethany, it is supposed. The historians, however, do not indicate how or where Wednesday was spent, but on Thursday the Lord came in from Bethany to eat the passover.
OUTLINE.—The Passover Made Ready. 2. The Last Passover Feast. 3. The First Lord's Supper.

ANALYSIS

I. THE PASSOVER MADE READY, vs. 12-16.
   1. The First Day of Unleavened Bread. Mark 14:12; Matt. 26:17; Luke 22:7.
   2. The Two Disciples Sent. Mark 14:13; Matt. 26:18; Luke 22:8.
   3. The Guest Chamber Prepared. Mark 14:16; Matt. 26:19; Luke 22:13.

II. THE LAST PASSOVER FEAST, vs. 17-21.
   1. The Lord Cometh with the Twelve. Mark 14:17; Matt. 26:20; Luke 22:14.
   2. The Traitor Pointed Out. Mark 14:18; Matt. 26:21; Luke 22:20; John 13:26.
   3. The Traitor's Fate Predicted. Mark 14:21; Matt. 26:24; Luke 22:22.

III. THE FIRST LORD'S SUPPER, VS. 22-26.
   1. The Emblem of the Lord's Body. Mark 14:22; Matt. 26:26; Luke 22:19.
   2. The Emblem of the Blood. Mark 14:23; Matt. 26:27; Luke 22:20.
   3. The Blood of the New Covenant. Mark 14:24; Matt. 26:28; Luke 22:20.
   4. Departure to Gethsemane. Mark 14:26; Matt. 26:30.

INTRODUCTION

The most probable hypothesis combines these accounts as follows: Christ gives two of his disciples directions as to the preparation of the passover supper for himself and the twelve (Mark 14:12-16; Luke 22:7-13); when the even is come he goes with the twelve to the place prepared for them, where an unseemly strife occurs as to which shall be greatest (Luke 22:24-30); this Christ rebukes by washing the feet of the disciples (John 14:1-20); all then take their places at the table (Matt. 26:20); Christ prophesies his betrayal (Matt. 26:21-25; Mark 14:18-21; Luke 22:21-23; John 13:21-26); Judas, learning that his treachery is known, goes out to complete it (John 13:27-30). The supper, which has been interrupted by this incident, now goes on and ends with the institution of the Lord's supper at the close of passover feast (Matt. 26:26-29; Mark 14:22-25; Luke 22:19, 20; 1 Cor. 11:23-25). After or during this meal Christ gives his disciples the instructions and utters for them the prayer recorded in John, chapters 14-17 inclusive.—*Abbott.* At the close of the discourse recorded in John, chapters 14-16, and the prayer of chapter 17, the Lord and his disciples left the upper chamber, went out into the darkness of the night, passed out of the city gates and across the Kedron to the ascent of the Mount of Olives, where he retired within the garden of Gethsemane.

EXPLANATORY NOTES

I. THE PASSOVER MADE READY.

12. *And the first day of unleavened bread.* Strictly speaking, the 15th of Nisan (part of our March and April), after the Paschal lamb was killed, but here the 14th day (Thursday). See Exodus 12: 16. This suggests one of the most difficult questions of Scripture chronology, whether the Lord ate the passover one day before the regular Jewish passover, or at the same time. *Pressnse, Millman, Ellicott, Townsend, Alford, Neander, Farrar,* and many other great authorities, hold that he ate it the day preceding, and died on the day and about the time the Jewish passover lambs were slain. This view I have accepted and shown the reason why in the *Commentary on John,* pp. 208, 209. *The statements of John that the supper was eaten, the Lord betrayed and condemned before the passover, seem positive. For a fuller discussion we must refer to the *Commentary of John. When they killed the passover.* Or at which the passover was sacrificed, as in the Revised Version. The word "passover" signifies a *passing,* and commemorates the manner in which the Israelites were spared in Egypt when the Almighty "passed over" their houses, sprinkled with the blood of the lamb, without slaying their first-born. This name, which originally denoted the lamb, was applied later to the supper itself, then to the entire feast (Exodus 12). The passover was the feast of spring, after the death of winter; the national birthday feast; the springtime of grace, pointing to the birth of the true Israel. The rabbis claimed that, (1) all were to be present; (2) they must offer thanksgiving offerings; (3) it was a feast of joyousness, looking forward to their complete deliverance. *Where wilt thou that we go and prepare . . . the passover?* According to the directions given in Deut. 16:1-5, the passover must be eaten in the place where the Lord's name was recorded, or where the tabernacle or temple was located. Jesus was at Bethany at this time. As that place was within a Sabbath day's journey of Jerusalem, the passover could be eaten there according to the rabbis, and the disciples might have supposed that this would be the Lord's decision. The preparation involved the selection of a guest chamber (Mark 14:15), the selection, sacrifice and cooking of the lamb, the procurement of unleavened bread, and the bitter herbs. *That we go and prepare.* The lamb had, we

*B. W. Johnson's commentary on John.

may believe, already been bought on the 10th of Nisan, according to the rule of the law, the very day of which He, the true Paschal Lamb, entered Jerusalem in meek triumph.—*Cambridge Bible. That thou mayest eat.* Note the reverential feeling that dominated the disciples. They did not say, "in order that *we* may eat the passover." They hid themselves behind their Lord.

13. *Two of his disciples.* Luke gives their names—Peter and John. *Saith unto them.* There can be no question that this direction was given them in superhuman foresight. *The city.* Jerusalem. *A man bearing a pitcher of water.* A very unusual sight in the East, where the water is drawn by women. He must probably have been the servant of one who was an open or secret disciple, unless we have here a reference to the Jewish custom of the master of a house himself drawing the water with which the unleavened bread was kneaded on Nisan 13th. On the evening of the 13th, before the stars appeared in the heavens, every father, according to Jewish custom, had to repair to the fountain to draw pure water with which to knead the unleavened bread.

14. *To the goodman of the house;* or, "master of the house." The expression, "goodman," as used by *Tyndale,* and preserved in our Authorized Version, is a relic of an olden time, when the heads of a household establishment expressed to one another, in their habitual intercourse, their mutual esteem. In some parts of the country the custom still lingers, and husbands and wives address each other as "goodman," "goodwife."—*Morison. The guest chamber.* The Revision says, correctly, "my guest chamber." The correct reading, "my," is suggestive. Our Lord lays claim to it. During the passover week, hospitality was recognized as a universal duty in Jerusalem; pilgrims and strangers were received, and rooms were alloted to them for the celebration of the feast. But it is not probable that a room would have been given to entire strangers without previous arrangement; and the language which the disciples are instructed to use, "The Master saith unto theee," seems to me clearly to indicate that the goodman of the house recognized Jesus as Master; in other words, was in some sense at least a disciple.—*Abbott. Where is the guestchamber, where I shall eat the passover?* The Master saith. It is a personal question, a proposal to the inner life of all. It is an offer of the one infinite divine blessing; for, in receiving the Master, Christ, the Son of Mary and the Son of God, we receive all the real good there is in earth and heaven.—*F. D. Huntington.*

15. *He will shew you a large upper room furnished and prepared.* A room on the second floor. Some think it was the "Alijah," or the room on the housetop. *Furnished;* i.e., with tables and couches. *Prepared.*

Already swept, and clean, and in order for the feast. Even at the present day, the very humblest Jewish family generally has at the passover time the walls of the house white-washed, the floor scrubbed, the furniture cleaned, and all things made to put on a new appearance. *Make ready.* The further preparations necessary for the passover. There are evidently two preparations for the passover mentioned in this sentence; that of the room, already made by the proprietor, and that of the lamb, with its accompaniments, bread and wine and bitter herbs, which was now to be made by the two disciples, and which they did make, as recorded in verse 16, where we learn no new fact but the simple execution of the Savior's orders.

16. *They made ready.* That is, they procured a "paschal lamb," multitudes of which were kept for sale in the temple; they procured it to be killed and flayed by the priests, and the blood to be poured at the altar; they roasted the lamb, and prepared the bitter herbs, the sauce, and the unleavened bread.—*Barnes.* As the new day opened, at sunset, the carcass was trussed for roasting, with two skewers of pomegranate wood, so that they formed a cross in the lamb. It was then put in an earthen oven of a special kind, resting, without bottom, on the ground, and was roasted in the earth. The feast could begin immediately after the setting of the sun and the appearing of the stars, on the opening of the 15th of Nisan, which was proclaimed by new trumpet-blasts from the temple.—*Geikie.*

II. THE LAST PASSOVER FEAST.

17. *In the evening he cometh with the twelve.* It was probably while the sun was beginning to decline in the horizon that Jesus and the disciples descended once more over the Mount of Olives into the Holy City. Before them lay Jerusalem in her festive attire. White tents dotted the sward, gay with the bright flowers of early spring, or peered out from the gardens and the darker foliage of the olive plantations. From the gorgeous temple buildings, dazzling in their snow-white marble and gold, on which the slanting rays of the sun were reflected, rose the smoke of the altar of burnt-offerings. The streets must have been thronged with strangers, and the flat roofs covered with eager gazers, who either feasted their eyes with a first sight of the sacred city, for which they had so often longed, or else once more rejoiced in view of the well-remembered localities. It was the last day-view which the Lord had of the Holy City—till his resurrection—*Edersheim's "The Temple and its Services."*

18. *As they sat and did eat.* Or, rather, "reclined at table." The passover was originally eaten standing; but this was altered by the Jews when they came to the land of promise and rest. *One of you which eateth with me shall betray me.* This indefinite announcement would give

Judas an opportunity of repentance; but it produced no effect. The announcement by Jesus of his knowledge of the traitor was needed to show the apostles that the manner of his arrest was no surprise to him. The words would seem to have been intentionally vague, as if to rouse some of those who heard them to self-questioning.

19. *They began to be sorrowful.* The very thought of treason was to their honest and faithful hearts insupportable, and excited great surprise and deepest sorrow. John (13:33) describes their perplexed and questioning glances at each other, the whisper of Peter to John, the answer of our Lord to the beloved disciple, announcing the sign by which the traitor was to be indicated. *Unto him.* They both inquired among themselves (Luke 22:23), and of Christ. *Is it I?* Their language expresses in the original a much stronger negation than in our version—*Surely not I, Lord?*

20. *One . . . that dippeth with me.* This answer, apparently given only to John (John 13:25, 26), does not designate the betrayer to the disciples. According to the Jewish ritual, the administrator in the course of the supper dipped the bitter herbs in a prepared sauce, and passed the dish to the rest. This Christ now did. His reply to the question of John was simply an emphatic reiteration of his previous declaration (John 13:28), "He that eateth bread with me hath lifted up his heel against me." That it did not designate the traitor to any of the disciples is clear from John 13:28. Judas alone perceived that his treachery was known to Christ.—*Abbott.*

21. *The Son of man indeed goeth.* He marches with unfaltering step in the way to the scene of death, as marked out by the divine prophecies. Yet that does not exculpate the authors of his betrayal and murder. *Good were it for that man, etc.* A proverbial expression of the most terrible destiny, forbidding the thought of any deliverance, however remote.—*Schaff.* Observe incidental confirmation of the doctrine elsewhere taught, that for the finally lost soul there is no redemption.—*Abbott.*

III. THE FIRST LORD'S SUPPER.

22. *As they did eat.* While they were still at the passover table. One memorial institution had now ended its mission; as it departed another was ordained. *Jesus took bread.* The bread that was broken was a round cake or cracker of unleavened bread. Throughout the entire passover week no leavened bread was allowed in the house. Exodus 12:8, 15. The administration of the Lord's Supper was subsequently termed the "breaking of bread." The bread, then, is (1) a symbolic reminder that Christ is God's unspeakable gift to us, (John 3:16; 2 Cor. 9:15;) (2) that the gift is perfected only in that he is broken for us, (John

3:14; 10:15; 12:32;) (3) that it is efficacious only as we partake of him, i.e., receive him into ourselves, so that he becomes one with us as he is one with the Father, (John 17:23,) as the bread when eaten becomes part of our nature, and so the sustainer of our life. *This is my body.* His language here closely conforms to that of the Jewish ritual. When the lamb was passed the master was asked by one of the children, "What is this?" and the father replied, "This the body of the lamb which our fathers ate in Egypt." Christ uses, but modifies, the same formula. Does any one suppose the lamb slain in Egypt was miraculously multiplied through all the subsequent ages?—*Abbott.* The word for *is* denotes only *likeness* in all metaphors and in the explanation of all symbols. "The seven good kine are seven years;" "These bones are the house of Israel;" "The seed is the Word of God;" "This is he who hears the Word;" "The field is the world;" "The rock was Christ;" 'The women are two covenants;" "The seven lamps are seven churches." Resemblance and representation are certainly implied in these and similar statements, but nothing more.—*Biblical Museum.* In view of this usage how illogical are those who insist, contrary to their senses, that the bread is literally the flesh of Christ.

23. *He took the cup.* The cup was provided for the celebration of the paschal feast and was at hand as well as the bread. As before he gave thanks, and then commanded: *Drink ye all of it.* Observe that he simply said of the bread, Take, eat; but of the wine, *Drink ye all,* as if he intended to uproot the Catholic innovation of denying the cup to the laity.

24. *This is my blood.* A sign or emblem of my blood. This formula occurs again from the forms of the passover feast. "The blood is the life" (Lev. 17:14). He laid down his life. It pleased the Lord to bruise him (Isa. 53).—*Jacobus.* Up to this time the blood of bulls and goats had represented Christ's blood: henceforth the simple wine of this memorial supper should represent it (Heb. 9:13, 14). *New testament;* or, convenant. Convenant is the preferable sense here, as in most passages where the word occurs in the New Testament: the new covenant is contrasted with "the covenant which God made with our fathers" (Acts 3:25). It need hardly be remarked that the title of the New Testament is derived from this passage. The new covenant was, that God would renew and save all who believed in Jesus. In ancient times the ratification of important covenants was made by a sacrificial feast. *Shed for many.* Shed, in one sense, for all, for the benefits of the blood are offered to all; but "many" accept it and are saved.

25. *I will drink no more of the fruit of the vine.* He is done with

earthly rites, and at this sad moment points them to a future re-union at the marriage supper of the Lamb. The ordinance now receives its prophetic meaning (Cf. 1 Cor. 11:26, "till he come") directing believers to the perfect vision and fruition of that time, through the foretaste which this sacrament is designed to give.—*Schaff. Drink it new.* At the marriage supper of the Lamb. Rev. 19:9.

26. *When they had sung an hymn.* It was customary to conclude the passover by singing the Psalms from 115th to 118th. *To the Mount of Olives.* To the garden of Gethsemane which was on the slope of that mount.

FACT QUESTIONS 14:12-26

937. On what day of the week did Jesus eat the Passover? What Jewish month?—what day of the month? To which of our months does this correspond?
938. Please mark carefully the order of progression of the nine or ten incidents beginning with the preparation for the passover and ending with retirement in the garden.
939. When and where did the prayers and promises of John 14-17 occur?
940. What is meant by the expression "the first day of unleavened bread"?
941. What problem of chronology is found in vs. 13? What was the conclusion of B. W. Johnson? Do you agree? Discuss.
942. Show the progressive use of the term "passover". How did it become a "birthday feast"?
943. What does Deut. 16:1-15 say about the place of the eating of the the passover?
944. What was involved in preparing the passover? How could it have been lawful to eat the passover in Bethany?
945. When was the lamb for the passover purchased?—how related to the activities of Jesus?
946. How did the disciples show respect for Jesus in their question about the passover?
947. Who was the man with the pitcher of water?—show the possible significance.
948. Why use the word "goodman"?
949. How did Jesus refer to the guest chamber or the upper room? Why?
950. What is "an offer of the one infinite divine blessing"?
951. What preparation in the room had the householder made?—what preparations were the disciples to make?
952. Where was the lamb purchased?—in what preparation did the priest engage?
953. Besides the roasted lamb what was on the paschal table?

954. In what particular manner was the lamb roasted?—is there any possible symbolism here?
955. Silver trumpets were blown in the night—when and why?
956. Please read and re-read the beautiful description of Edersheim on vs. 17. Pause—close your eyes—conjure up the scene in your mind's eye.
957. When was the posture at the table changed?
958. Why the indefiniteness of the announcement of the betrayal of Judas?—it had a dual purpose—what was it?
959. Why were the apostles so surprised?—how did they express their surprise?
960. What strong expression did the apostles use in inquiring about their betrayal?
961. The answer of vs. 20 was not given to all—to whom? Why? How did Judas know?
962. Was the passover meal finished before Jesus instituted His Supper?—Discuss.
963. What type of loaf was used? Why?
964. Show how very appropriate is the expression "breaking of bread" when referring to the Lord's Supper. Specify three ways.
965. Show how closely the words "this is my body" conform to the Jewish ritual.
966. Show how illogical those are (Roman Catholics) who insist the bread was literally the flesh of Jesus.
967. What Catholic innovation is uprooted in vs. 23?
968. Before Jesus said of the fruit of the vine—"this is my blood" what had represented Christ's blood?
969. Why is "covenant" a better word than "testament"? What was the covenant?
970. Was the blood shed for "many" or for "all"? Explain.
971. When was—or will—the promise of vs. 25 fulfilled? Will we drink grape juice in heaven?
972. What hymn was sung? Why? Read the hymn for an answer.

4. PETER'S BOAST 14:27-31

TEXT 14:27-31

I will smite the shepherd, and the sheep shall be scattered abroad. Howbeit, after I am raised up, I will go before you into Galilee. But Peter said unto Him, Although all shall be offended, yet will not I. And Jesus saith unto him, Verily I say unto thee, that thou today, even this night, before the cock crow twice, shalt deny me thrice. But he spake exceeding vehemently, If I must die with thee, I will not deny thee. And in like manner said they all."

THOUGHT QUESTIONS 14:27-31

794. Where was Jesus when He spoke of the defection of the disciples?
795. In what sense were the apostles to stumble?—how did prophecy relate to the stumbling of the disciples?
796. What appreciation did the apostles have of the resurrection of Jesus?
797. Why mention His visit to Galilee?
798. What prompted Peter's pledge of loyalty? Please note that pride was not the only element.
799. Read Matt. 26:34 and John 13:38—harmonize these two accounts with Mark 14:30.
800. Why did Jesus predict the multiple denial of Peter?
801. Didn't Peter believe Jesus knew all things? Why did he continue to contradict the words of Jesus?
802. Just what did all the disciples say? Where they just as guilty as Peter? Discuss.

COMMENT

TIME.—Thursday evening, April 6th (14th Nisan), A.D. 30. With the Jews the 15th of Nisan had begun.

PLACE.—Jerusalem, in an upper room with the disciples.

PARALLEL ACCOUNTS.—Matt. 26:31-35; Luke 22:31-38.

OUTLINE.—1. The prediction and promise of Jesus, vs. 27, 28. 2. The poor pride of Peter, vs. 29. 3. Pointing up the prediction, vs. 30. 4. personal and public pride, vs. 31.

ANALYSIS

I. THE PREDICTION AND PROMISE OF JESUS, VS. 27, 28.
   1. The prediction: All ye shall be offended: for it is written, I will smite the shepherd, and the sheep shall be scattered abroad.
   2. The promise: after I am raised up, I will go before you into Galilee.

II. THE POOR PRIDE OF PETER, VS. 29.
   1. He took exception with Jesus.
   2. He promised the highest of loyalty.

III. POINTING UP THE PREDICTION, VS. 30.
   1. It shall happen this very night.
   2. Before the cock crows twice you shall deny me thrice.

IV. THE PERSONAL AND PUBLIC PRIDE, VS. 31.
   1. Personal pride of Peter: ". . . he spake exceeding vehemently, If I must die with thee, I will not deny thee."
   2. Public pride of the rest of the apostles: "And in like manner also said they all."

EXPLANATORY NOTES

I. THE PREDICTION AND PROMISE OF JESUS.

"27. *You will all be scandalized in my regard.* Our Lord means that when the disciples witnessed His humiliations and sufferings, it would be a sore trial to their faith, and would lead them to doubt that He was the Messiah. That this actually occurred we see from Luke 24:21. *But we hoped that it was he that should have redeemed Israel; and now besides all this,* etc. Evidently these disciples no longer hoped, and all were incredulous at first as regards the resurrection of Christ.

I will strike the shepherd, etc. The prophecy is not literally quoted; it runs thus, *Awake, O sword, against my shepherd, and against the man that cleaveth to me, saith the Lord of hosts: strike the shepherd and the sheep shall be scattered, and I will turn my hand to the little ones* (Zech. 13:7). Jesus refers the prophecy to Himself as *the good shepherd* (John 10:11).

In quoting this prophecy the Evangelist represents God as saying I will strike, etc., and in truth the death of the Son was willed by the Father, that thus the Redemption of man might be effected, but He allowed human agents to accomplish His designs. God could not will man's sin, but he can make it serve His designs, and thus bring good out of evil.

the sheep shall be dispersed. Primarily the prophecy referred to the Jewish priests and to the Israelites, but there is a secondary reference to Christ the Messiah and to the disciples, the sheep of His flock. These words were fulfilled when in Gethsemane *his disciples leaving him, all fled away* (14:50). They were also accomplished in the dispersion of the Jews.

28. *But after I shall be risen,* etc. Christ now turns His hand to *His little ones.* In spite of their weak faith and of their cowardice, He promises to see them again, and foretells once more His resurrection.

I will go before you into Galilee. The angel of the Resurrection used these very words, and reminded the disciples of Christ's promise, *Remember how he spoke unto you, when he was yet in Galilee, saying, The Son of man must . . . the third day rise again* (Luke 24:6, 7). *And going quickly, tell ye his disciples that he is risen: and behold he will go before you into Galilee; there you shall see him. Lo, I have foretold it to you* (Matt. 27:7). In spite of the disciples' predicted defection, Jesus consoles them—

(1) by the assurance that He will rise again.

(2) by promising to meet them in Galilee.

The prediction itself after its accomplishment, would strengthen their faith, since knowing that they would forsake Him, Christ had promised to see them in Galilee. There is perhaps in these words an allusion to the shepherd preceding his flock.

II. THE POOR PRIDE OF PETER.

29. *Peter saith to him: Although all, etc.* Peter, always impulsive and generous, cannot believe such desertion possible.

In his reply we notice—

1. Peter rejects the very idea as an impossibility, and bluntly contradicts our Lord. He evidently regarded our Lord's words as a mark of distrust of the disciples rather than as a prediction and solemn warning.
2. Peter asserts his strength of character to be greater than that of the other disciples.
3. He trusts to his own strength, though the remembrance of how his faith failed when he was sinking in the Lake of Galilee, should have presented this presumption.

III. POINTING UP THE PREDICTION.

"30. *Truly I say to thee.* Our Lord uses His solemn asseveration to check Peter's assumption and enforce the warning.

today, even in this night, etc. Notice the gradation "to-day" (the day had begun at sunset), "even this night," hence before tomorrow's dawn, before the second cock-crowing. The cock crew at midnight, and again about three o'clock in the morning.

In this chapter (verses 68-72) we find the fulfillment of this prediction. It has been objected that it was forbidden to have cocks and hens in Jerusalem, but this prohibition (if observed, which is very doubtful) could not affect the Romans, who would certainly have kept fowls in the Castle of Antonia, and whence Jews could hear the cock crowing distinctly. The Romans used these birds, and even carried them with them when on the march, since they required chickens for the *auspices.* It is mentioned by one of the rabbinical writers that a cock, which had killed a little child in Jerusalem, was slain.

deny me thrice: not merely once, but thrice. Mark alone gives the details—

(a) that the cock should crow twice.

(b) Peter's vehement, second declaration of fidelity."

IV. THE PERSONAL AND PUBLIC PRIDE.

"31. *spoke the more vehemently.* He denied the bare possibility of such a denial, with increased energy. Peter, from whom Mark received his gospel, reveals his own weakness with profound humility.

Some writers affirm that Peter never lost faith in our Lord, since Christ had prayed that his faith *fail not,* but that he sinned against charity in lacking the courage to profess his faith openly.

Although I should die, etc. Peter was sincere in his protestations of fidelity, but he had yet to learn how weak human nature is in the face of temptation and suffering. Luke and John give Peter's protestation more fully. *I will lay down my life for thee* (John 13:37.) *Lord, I am ready to go with thee both into prison and to death* (Luke 22:33). Thomas likewise had made a protestation of fidelity in the name of his companions. *Let us also go, that we may die with him* (John 11:16).

in like manner also said they all (i.e. all the Eleven). Judas was not present. We may be sure that they were sincere in their offer, but their inexperience led them to underestimate the force of the trial that awaited them." *(Cecilia)*

FACT QUESTIONS 14:27-31

973. Show when and where the words of our Lord, "you will all be scandalized in my regard" found fulfillment.
974. Who struck the shepherd? Why?
975. "God could not will man's ———, but He can make it serve His designs, and thus bring ——— out of ———."
976. Show at least two places and times when the words "the sheep shall be dispersed" were fulfilled.
977. In spite of the disciples predicted defection, Jesus consoles them in two thoughts—what are they?
978. Peter misunderstood the purpose of the words of Jesus—what purpose did he find in the prediction of defection?
979. Peter had reason to doubt the strength of his faith—what was it?
980. How is it that the expression "today", and "this night" mean the same period of time? At what two times did the cock crow?
981. Where was the cock when it crowed?
982. How could some writers affirm that Peter never lost his faith in his denial?
983. Show how Thomas and Peter were alike.
984. What caused the disciples to underestimate the force of the trial that awaited them?

E. FRIDAY

1. STRONG CRYING AND TEARS 14:32-42

TEXT: 14:32-42

"And they come unto a place which was named Gethsemane: and he saith unto his disciples, Sit ye here, while I pray. And he taketh with him Peter and James and John, and began to be greatly amazed, and sore troubled. And he saith unto them, My soul is exceeding sorrowful even unto death: abide ye here, and watch. And he went forward a little, and fell on the ground, and prayed that, if it were possible, the hour might pass away from him. And he said, Abba, Father, all things are possible unto thee; remove this cup from me: howbeit not what I will but what thou wilt. And he cometh, and findeth them sleeping, and saith unto Peter, Simon, sleepest thou? couldest thou not watch one hour? Watch and pray, that ye enter not into temptation: the spirit indeed is willing, but the flesh is weak. And again he went away and prayed, saying the same words. And again he came, and found them sleeping, for their eyes were very heavy; and they wist not what to answer him. And he cometh the third time, and saith unto them, Sleep on now, and take your rest: it is enough; the hour is come; behold, the Son of man is betrayed into the hands of sinners. Arise, let us be going: behold, he that betrayeth me is at hand."

THOUGHT QUESTIONS 14:32-42

803. Why did Jesus go to Gethsemane? Did this visit fill a need in His heart? Show what significance this place had in the life of our Lord.
804. What did Jesus want Peter, James and John to do while He was praying? Cf. vs. 37.
805. How would you explain the words "greatly amazed, and sore troubled?"
806. How is the word "soul" used in vs. 34?
807. Was there any possibility of Jesus dying in the garden? Could this possibility be "the cup" which He asked might "pass away"?
808. Is "the hour" of vs. 35 the same as "the cup" of vs. 36? Discuss.
809. What is the meaning of the expression "Abba" as in 36a?
810. Didn't Jesus know the will of the Father?—why then make the request He did?
811. Wasn't the will of our Lord constantly the will of God?—how shall we reconcile this fact with the request which includes "my will" and "your will"?
812. What did Jesus want the three apostles to do that they did not do?—what is included in the expression "watch"?
813. Notice how Jesus addressed Peter, i.e. in name—why?

814. About what were the three to pray?
815. What temptation was here present?
816. Explain the little phrase "the spirit indeed is willing but the flesh is weak"—*do it in its context.*
817. Why repeat the prayer as in vs. 39?
818. What question did Jesus ask the disciples as in vs. 40? Why no answer?
819. In what attitude were the words, "sleep on now, and take your rest" spoken? Was Jesus ironic? critical? sympathetic? sad? explain.
820. What was "enough" as in vs. 41b?
821. Who were the "sinners" into whose hands the Son of man was betrayed?

COMMENT

TIME.—Thursday evening, April 6th (14th Nisan), A.D. 30. With the Jews the 15th of Nisan had begun.

PLACE.—Jerusalem—the Garden of Gethsemane.

PARALLEL ACCOUNTS.—Matt. 26:36-46; Luke 22:40-46.

OUTLINE.—1. The place and persons of the Saviour's agony, vs. 32-34. 2. Surrender in prayer, vs. 35, 36. 3. Disappointing disciples, vs. 37, 38. 4. He prayed and wept alone, vs. 39, 40. 5. The Saviour's hour and the disciples failure, vs. 41, 42.

ANALYSIS

I. THE PLACE AND PERSONS OF THE SAVIOUR'S AGONY, VS. 32-34.
1. The place:—Gethsemane.
2. The persons:—disciples—and the three.
3. His agony:—greatly amazed—sore troubled—exceeding sorrowful.

II. SURRENDER IN PRAYER, VS. 35, 36.
1. The place of surrender:—"he went forward a little, and fell on the ground,"
2. The struggle of the surrender—"if it were possible, the hour might pass away from him."—"remove this cup from me."
3. The victory in surrender—"howbeit not what I will, but what thou wilt."

III. DISAPPOINTING DISCIPLES, VS. 37, 38.
1. He came for comfort and found them asleep.
2. He called Peter by his old name of "Simon"—"is one hour too long to watch for me?"
3. He helped them (when they should have helped Him) with a warning—watch (be spiritually vigilent) and pray—in this way you (like me) will escape temptation. You have assented to my

will but you can never carry it out without being spiritually awake and in prayer—your flesh is too weak for such action.

IV. HE PRAYED AND WEPT ALONE, VS. 39, 40.
1. Away from the apostles—alone with God—the same need—the same answer.
2. Still asleep—yielded to the flesh—no human answer to spiritual need.

V. THE SAVIOUR'S HOUR AND THE DISCIPLES FAILURE, VS. 41, 42.
1. "Are you still sleeping and taking your rest?" (Ralph Earle)
2. "You have slept long enough" (Thayer).
3. "The great hour of the world's redemption has come." (Ralph Earle)
4. "Let us go to meet the betrayer."

EXPLANATORY NOTES

I. THE PLACE AND PERSONS OF THE SAVIOUR'S AGONY.

"32. *And they come.* We are taken back, and look on. *To a place which was named Gethsemane.* The word means *oil-press.* And, no doubt, originally there would be, in the spot, an olive-oil press. The real locality cannot now be precisely determined; neither is it necessary. There is an enclosed spot, lying at the base of the western slope of the mount of Olives, which is called Gethsemane (El-Jesmaniye). It is kept by the Latin Christians, and contains eight extremely aged olive trees. "If," says Dr. Wilson, "the "Gethsemane of the Bible be not here, and we can see no reason for disturbing thc tradition regarding it, it cannot certainly be far distant, as must be apparent from the incidental notices of the evangelists." (*Lands of the Bible,* vol. 1, p. 481.)

And He saith to His disciples, Sit here, until I shall pray. Until My prayer shall be past. The great crisis was at hand; and it was casting its dark shadow before on the spirit of our Lord. He felt that He must get into comparative retirement, in order that He might, without distraction, grapple with the appalling difficulties of the trial, and open up His heart, in the time of extremity, to His Father.

Vers. 33. *And He taketh with Him Peter and James and John.* The elite of his elect, who had been witnesses of the counterpart scene, the transfiguration (chap. ix. 2). They were admitted by their own brethren to be a representative triumvirate, and *primi inter pares.* For, even among those who are good and true, some are better fitted than others for posts of eminence, and for intimacy of intercourse.

And began to be dismayed. Stunned, as it were. That is the radical idea of the word. (See G. Curtis, *Grundzuge,* p. 206.) He was *astonished.* Probably never before, within the limitations of His finite experience, had the sphere of our Lord's vision, in reference to sins, and their desert and effects, been so vast. Probably never before had the corresponding sphere of His emotions, in relation to these sins, been so profoundly agitated and heaved. This state of things now 'began.' And, as it 'began,' it caused an *amazement,* that culminated in consternation. Wycliffe translates the verb to *drede* (to dread); Coverdale, to *waxe fearefull.*

And greatly distressed. Comp. Phil. 2:26. Tyndale's version is borrowed from Luke, *to be in an agony.*

Vers. 34. *And He saith to them.* Namely after the terrible experience had 'begun' to roll in on His spirit.

My soul is exceeding sorrowful. The idea is, *My soul is* sorrowful all round and round. It was a kind of moral midnight within the periphery of His soul. At no point in the circumference was a single gleam of light.

Unto death. Not a mere rhetorical addition. The weight of woe was literally crushing out the Saviour's life. In bearing it He was making more literal sacrifice of Himself than ever had been made on literal altar. The sacrifice would have been complete, then and there, had it not been that it appeared to Him and to His Father that certain momentous purposes of publicity, in reference to the conclusion of the tragedy, would be better subserved by shifting the scene.

Remain here and watch. He had wished His chosen three to be near Him in His woe; and yet, as it advanced, He felt that He must retire even from them, and be alone with Himself and His Father. 'Of the people' none could be 'with Him' in the agony, none on the altar. Still He wished that His chosen ones should not be at a great distance, and hence He said, *Remain here.* He desired to be the object of their active sympathy, and hence He said, *and watch.*

II. SURRENDER IN PRAYER.

"Vers. 35. *And He went forward a little.* Still farther from the spot where the eight disciples had been asked to halt (vs. 32).

And fell on the ground. Gradually. The verb is in the imperfect. He would kneel first of all (Luke 22:41).

And prayed. He continued in prayer. The verb is in the imperfect. He *kept addressing* His heavenly Father. His aim in thus addressing His Father is brought out in the next clause.

That. In order that.

If it were possible. Very literally, if it is possible. We are taken back to the very time when the Saviour's prayers were uttered, and to the spot whence they were uttered, and we hear the very words which He used. *Possible:* the reference is not so much to *absolute* as to *relative possibility,* possibility in consistency with the great objects contemplated in the mission of the Saviour.

The hour might pass from Him. The *hour* that was imminent, and that embraced within its compass His betrayal, His arrestment, and the desertion of His disciples. He did not pray that the hour of the atoning sacrifice might pass by. It was the incidental woes, inflicted so superflously and wantonly by men, and to no small extent by His own chosen disciples, it was these apparentlv these more particularly at least, to which the cry of His spirit referred.

Vers. 36. *And He said, Abba Father.* The filial element in His spirit rose up and overshadowed all the other elements of relationship. Mark alone records the 'bilingual' appellation, Aramaic and Greek. No doubt it would be genuine; and most likely it would be current in certain bilingual' home circles, more especially at moments of earnest address on the part of children. At such moments there is often a tendency to emphatic redundancy or repetitiousness of expression. Comp. Rom. viii. 15, and Gal. iv. 6. As employed by our Lord, the dual form of the appellation is delightfully fitted to suggest that, in His great work, He personated in His single self not Jews only, but Gentiles also.

All things are possible to Thee. Literally true. *A thing* is a *think;* and all things thinkable are possible to almightiness. To imagine that there are actual limits to God's power is merely to bewilder oneself in *unthinkabilities.* In the preceding verse the reference is to conditional possibility: hence the 'if.' In this the reference is to absolute possibility: hence the 'all.'

Remove this cup from Me. The Reheims translation is, *transferre this chalice from Me.* Not that our Saviour rued His enterprise, or desired to 'back out of it.' Infinitely far from that. The cup, which He felt it so dreadful to drink, had in it ingredients which were never mingled by the hand of His Father, such as the treachery of Judas, the desertion of His disciples, denial on the part of Peter, the trial in the Sanhedrim, the trial before Pilate, the scourging, the mockery of the soldiery, the crucifixion, etc., etc. All these incidental and unessential ingredients were put into the cup by men, wilfully and wantonly. Hence the petition, *Remove from Me this cup,* this cup as it is. Without these superadded ingredients the potion would have been unquestionably bitter enough; and it need not be doubted that, in consideration of that bitterness, the exquisite sensibility of our Lord would be conscious of a feeling of shrinking and instinctive recoil. But still He had come for the very purpose of 'tasting death for every man,' and was no doubt willing and wishful to die.

But not what I will, but what Thou wilt. But the question is not, What will I? but What wilt Thou? The reference in the word will, in so far as it is applied by the Saviour to Himself, is to that which Peter calls the *sensitive* will, and the schoolmen *voluntas sensualitatis.* The more literal translation however of the verb is *wish* rather than *will.* The question with the Savior was not, *What do I wish? but What does My Father wish?* There was infinite submissiveness to the wish and will of His Father. If the Father deemed it best that the cup, just as it was, should be drained, the Son was absolutely acquiescent. It is easy to conceive of the greatest possible diversity in the circumstantial incidents of the atoning sacrifice. The Saviour would have wished them to have been different from what they were. Who would not? But on almost everything that is done in the world, or that has to be endured, the foul fingers of sin are laid."

III. DISAPPOINTING DISCIPLES.

"37. *And He cometh.* To His disciples, viz. at some intermission in the agony of His spirit, when He had got strength through prayer. See Luke xxii. 43.

And findeth them sleeping. So far were they from profoundly realizing the solemnities that were imminent.

And saith to Peter. Peter is no doubt singled out, partly because he was the leader of the three, and partly because he had singled himself out but a little before. See ver. 29, 31.

Simon, sleepest thou? Although thou sawest that I was in such distress, and although I expressly desired thee to keep awake and watch?

Couldst thou not watch one hour? Hadst thou not strength for that? Surely thou wilt not say so. Why then not use thy strength to watch, when I desired it, that I might have the consolation of thy sympathy? Note the expression *one hour.* It seems to indicate that our Savior had suffered an entire hour of agony. How long that period! when we remember that every moment would be stretched to its utmost.

Ver. 38. *Watch ye.* The three disciples, we may suppose, had waked up when Peter was addressed. What our Lord said to one, He meant for all; and here He expressly addresses all.

And pray, that ye may not enter into temptation. They were in danger of losing confidence in Him as the Messiah. There was therefore much need for faithful watching and earnest praying.

The spirit indeed is willing, but the flesh is weak. The Saviour's gracious apology for the languor of His disciples. Even while He spoke to them, they had but imperfectly waked up. He saw them struggling with the oppressive languor, but ineffectively. And yet, true, as well as gracious, though His apology was, *the spirit was nevertheless to be somewhat blamed.* If it had been sympathetic to the quick, it would have roused the *flesh.* Some have supposed that the words, *the spirit is willing, but the flesh is weak,* are the Saviour's explanation of His own distress. Unnatural. The supposition proceeds on the false assumption that the Saviour's horror was a weakness, and that it would have been more magnanimous and glorious to have had no experience of shrinking from the ingredients of the dreadful cup."

IV. HE PRAYED AND WEPT ALONE.

"Vers. 39. *And again He went away.* His agony returned on Him. Perhaps the very lethargy of His disciples might call up before His view the whole appalling succession of incidental and unessential woes that were about to overtake Him.

And prayed, saying the same words. More literally, as the Rheims, has it, *saying the selfsame word.* The term word is used collectively, as when we speak of *the word of God.*

Ver. 40. *And when He returned, He found them asleep again, for their eyes were heavy.* Were, so to speak, 'weighted', or, according to the better reading, *weighed down.* The *for* introduces, not a reason for, but an illustration of, their sleepiness. It would appear that they had not deliberately surrendered themselves to sleep. They did not lie down, for instance. They sat, and, to a certain extent, sought to keep themselves awake. But ever and anon, and prevailingly, their eyelids closed.

And they wist not what to answer Him. They knew not what they could say to Him in reply. They had no excuse which they could honestly plead. *Wist,* or *wissed* as it were, that is *knew,* is now obsolete, but is connected with an interesting group of words, *wise, wisdom, wizard,* and the German *wissen* 'to know.' On another line it is connected with the Anglo-Saxon *witan,* the Dutch *weten,* and the Gothic *vitan,* 'to know,' around which we have another group of words, *wit, wits, witty, witless, witch, outwit, to-wit.*"

V. THE SAVIOUR'S HOUR AND THE DISCIPLES' FAILURE.

"Ver. 41. *And He cometh the third time.* After a third retirement for a solitary endurance of His overwhelming agony.

And saith to them, Sleep on now. A rather unhappy translation, almost suggesting irritation and irony on the part of our Lord. Petter actually thinks that our Lord spoke 'in a taunting manner.' But the verb rendered *sleep on,* a translation got from Coverdale, is simply *sleep,* the translation of Tyndale, the Geneva and the Rheims; and the expression rendered *now* means literally *the remainder,* that is, *the remainder of the time that is available.* Tyndale and the Geneva render it *henceforth. Sleep the remaining interval!* It was in compassion that our Lord thus spoke. His own struggle was meanwhile past. He did not feel the same need of the intense active sympathy of His disciples which, in the crisis of His agony, He had so fervently desired. He saw too that they were still overpowered with drowsiness, notwithstanding the persevering efforts they were making to wake up. He hence spoke to them soothingly; and, as Cardinal Cajetan expresses it, 'indulgently,' that they might get the refreshment they so much required, *Sleep for the interval that remains. I can now calmly wait and watch alone.*

And take your rest. Or, as the Rheims has it, and *take rest. Rest yourselves,* that is, *refresh yourselves.* The word is so rendered in 1 Cor. 16:18; 2 Cor. 7:13; Philem. 7, 20.

It is enough. An expression that has given almost infinite trouble to critics. It fairly puzzled the Syriac translator. He renders it, *the end is at hand.* Our English translation is just a reproduction of the Vulgate version (sufficit), which must, one should suppose, have been dashed off in a fit of despair. But howsoever dashed off, or otherwise introduced, there it stands; and Luther, in his version, simply accepted it, without any attempt at an independent judgement; as did Erasmus also, and Tyndale, and Coverdale. Henry Stephens, the lexicographer, was much perplexed with the word, and in particular with its Vulgate translation; but at length he found a solitary passage, in one of the apocryphal *Odes of Anacreon* (xxviii. 33), in which the term would seem to bear no other interpretation. It afforded him great relief. Beza too found in the same ode a corresponding relief, and speaks indeed of the passage 'occurring to him,' in the midst of his doubts, as if it had been he, and not Henry Stephens, who had first alighted on it. He makes no reference at all to Stephens. The translation of the Vulgate, thus fortified out of *Anacreon,* was thenceforward regarded as confirmed. It was accepted by Castellio, the Geneva, Piscator, Erasmus Schmid, Sebastian Schmidt. It is found in all the Dutch versions, the earlier, the later, the latest. So too in Diodati, Zinzendorf, Rilliet; and in many other versions. Accepting the translation (and Wetstein hunted up another passage from *Cyril* on Hag. ii.9), the great body of expositors have interpreted the expression as a repetition 'in earnest' of the ironical expression that precedes, as if our Lord were now saying plainly, *ye have had enough of sleep.* See Diodati, Petter, and Schleusner. But Wolf supposes that the Saviour refers to His own sufferings, *I have suffered enough for the present, and it only remains that I endure the sufferings that are to come!* Neither phase of thought seems satisfactory. Grotius felt this, and imagined that the phrase must have an idiomatic import, corresponding to the technical expression employed in the Roman amphitheatre, when a gladiator was wounded, 'Habet,' *He has it, he has got it, he has got the fatal wound.* The Saviour, according to Grotius, as it were says, *It is all over with Me now. The time is past for any benefit to Me from your sympathy.* An unlikely interpretation, both on philological and on moral grounds, but accepted nevertheless by Principal Campbell, who renders the phrase *All is over.* Bengel's translation corresponds to a degree, only he gives it a turn in the direction of the disciples, not of the Saviour, *It is over,* viz. *with your rest.* So Felbinger. Kypke's interpretation is, *The time is up.* Heumann again, and Wahl, and Godwin, would render the phrase, *it is past,* or *It is away,* that is, *My agony is past.* Le Clerc, *The thing is past, My resolution to go on is taken.* There are other modifications of idea suggested by other expositors. But the great objection to all such interpretations is that the verb does not mean, *to be away, to be past,* or *to be over,* or *to be all over.* It means, when used intransitively, *to have off, to hold off, to be distant.* Such is its meaning in all the other passages of the New Testament in which it occurs with its intransitive signification. So Matt. 15:8 and Mark 7:6, 'their heart is *far* from Me,' 'is *distant* from Me.' So Luke 7:6, 'when He *was* now not far *distant* from the house.' So Luke 15:20, 'when he *was* yet a great way *off*,' that is, 'when he *was* yet a long way *distant*.' And Luke 24:13, 'A village called Emmaus, which was from Jerusalem about threescore furlongs,' that is, 'which *was distant* from Jerusalem.' We see no reason for departing, in the passage before us, from this, the word's accredited and ordinary signification. But the question arises, to what, or to whom, does the Saviour refer, when He says 'is distant'? He refers, as we apprehend, not to a thing, but to a person, of whom He was thinking much, as is evident at once from the last clause of this verse, and from the next verse. But, though thinking much of him, He did not feel inclined expressly to name him. The reference we take to be to Judas, *He is distant, He is at a distance.* The expression is thus not the unmasking of a previous sarcasm. It is the gracious utterance, partly to His own mind, and partly to the minds of His lethargic disciples, of a reason for indulging them in a few minutes more of rest. We shall lose much of the true significance of the whole scene, and of the grandeur of the Saviour's demeanor, if we imagine that there was anything like hot haste and semi-irritation on the part of our Lord. There is not the slightest need for supposing that all the words, recorded by the evangelist, were spoken in rapid succession. It was, we believe, far otherwise. After our Saviour had got relief from the overwhelming pressure of His agony, and had graciously approached His disciples, and sympathised with them in their feelings of oppression, He would most probably seat Himself beside them, and say soothingly, *Sleep for the remainder of the little time that we still have, and refresh yourselves.* Then He would add, as a reason for this indulgence, the word before us, a word which did not demand, on the part of the disciples, any mental determination regarding the subject of the proposition. It was enough that they knew that, whether a person or a thing were referred to, *distance* was affirmed. They might indeed have waked up, and inquired, 'who is distant?' what is? who is? But this was not necessary, if they understood that the reason for making a final effort to shake off their drowsiness was yet *at a distance.* After the Lord had said (He) *is at a distance,* we may suppose that He paused, and turning His eyes in the direction of Jerusalem, wrapped Himself up in His own meditations. At length, when the moving lights of the band around Judas became visible, the Lord broke silence, and spoke as follows.

The hour has come. The *hour,* the crisis time, the beginning of the end.

Lo, the Son of Man is delivered up. Is in the act of being delivered up, viz. by Judas. The verb is in the present tense. The event was now so imminent that the Saviour speaks of it as transpiring.

Into the hands of sinners. Literally, *of the sinners.* The word is used, as often elsewhere, in its emphatic acceptation, and hence Godwin's translation does justice to its spirit, of *the wicked.* Such was the character of the white-washed men who bore sway in the Sanhedrim, and of the others who would co-operate with them in their eagerness to get rid of all who might disturb them in their hypocritical repose.

Ver. 42. *Rise up. Rouse yourselves up.* There was no longer time for repose.

Let us be going. Let us voluntarily lead ourselves on, viz. that we may confront the traitor and his band. How sublimely does the heroism of our Lord reveal itself!

Lo, he who delivereth Me up is at hand. Instead of naming Judas, the Lord described him, and, in the description, verified His own former predictions regarding Himself." (*James Morison*)

FACT QUESTIONS 14:32-42

985. What is the meaning of the word "Gethsemane"? What do we know of its location?
986. Why did Jesus separate Himself from His disciples?
987. In what sense were the three apostles "the elite of the elect"?
988. What is the meaning of the word "dismayed" as in vs. 33?
989. Why use the word "began" in connection with amazed?
990. How else could we say "greatly distressed"?
991. What thought or idea is behind the expression "my soul is exceeding sorrowful"?
992. Was there literal danger of death in the garden? Explain.
993. Discuss: "none could be with Him in the agony, none on the altar."
994. Show the meaning of the imperfect verbs of "fell" and "prayed."
995. "Jesus did not pray that the hour of the atoning sacrifice would pass away"—what then is included in the expression "the hour might pass from Him"?
996. What element in the spirit of Jesus arose to overshadow all other elements—show how touchingly and beautifully fitting is the bilingual use of the term "Father."
997. Explain—"all things are possible to thee".
998. Jesus did not request that the cup the Father gave Him to drink would be removed—what cup then is referred to in vs. 36?
999. Show how the expression "Not what do I wish, but what does my Father wish"—gives a better meaning to "not what I will, but what thou wilt."
1000. Why single Simon out of the group?
1001. What temptation was imminent when He said "that ye enter not into temptation"?
1002. What was "the Saviour's gracious apology for the languor of His disciples"?
1003. Why go again to pray the same words?
1004. What is meant by the expression "and they wist not what to answer Him."?
1005. How or in what manner did Jesus say "sleep on now"? What did He mean?
1006. Give at least three meanings to the little expression "it is enough".
1007. Do you agree with Morison's preference? Discuss.
1008. Who were "the sinners" of vs. 41?
1009. How does the sublime heroism of our Lord show itself?

2. JESUS BETRAYED, 14:43-54

TEXT: 14:43-54

"And straightway, while he yet spake, cometh Judas, one of the twelve, and with him a multitude with swords and staves, from the chief priests and the scribes and the elders. Now he that betrayed him had given them a token, saying, Whomsoever I shall kiss, that is he; take him, and lead him away safely. And when he was come, straightway he came to him, and saith, Rabbi; and kissed him. And they laid hands on him, and took him. But a certain one of them that stood by drew his sword, and smote the servant of the high priest, and struck off his ear. And Jesus answered and said unto them are ye come out, as against a robber, with swords and staves to seize me? I was daily with you in the temple teaching and ye took me not; but this is done that the scriptures might be fulfilled. And they all left him and fled.

And a certain young man followed with him, having a linen cloth cast about him, over his naked body: and they lay hold on him; but he left the linen cloth, and fled naked.

And they led Jesus away to the high priest: and there come together with him all the chief priests and the elders and the scribes. And Peter had followed him afar off, even within, into the court of the high priest; and he was sitting with the officers, and warming himself in the light of the fire."

THOUGHT QUESTIONS 14:43-54

822. Please attempt a location of Jesus and His apostles when he said, "Behold, he that betrayeth me is at hand."
823. At what time was the betrayal made? How many were with Judas?
824. Show how each of the three groups mentioned were involved in the betrayal—i.e.: (1) "the chief priests, (2) the scribes, (3) the elders".
825. Did Judas hate Jesus? Why betray Him?
826. Why the need for "a token". Why use a kiss as a sign? Notice the footnote on the word "kiss"—this was not just a casual kiss.
827. Is there any thought that some feared Jesus would escape?
828. Show how Jesus willingly gave Himself up to His betrayer.
829. What is the meaning of "Rabbi"? Why use this greeting?
830. What was involved in "laid hands on Him."
831. What was right and wrong with Peter's defense of Jesus?
832. What did Peter imagine Jesus would do when he began his attack?
833. Why strike the servant of the high-priest?;—was he the nearest one or was there some other reason?

834. What particular rebuke was in the words of Jesus in vs. 48 & 49? i.e. what reflection on their power?
835. What scripture was fulfilled in the betrayal and capture of Jesus?
836. Why the incident of the young man as in verses 51, 52?
837. Why was this young man following Jesus?
838. Why take Jesus to the high-priest for trial?

COMMENT

TIME.—After the midnight of Thursday, April 6, A.D. 30. Probably between one and three o'clock on the morning of Friday, April 7th.
PLACE.—The betrayal took place at Gethsemane, near the base of the western slope of the Mount of Olives, where the Lord had passed the agony. Gethsemane was at the western foot of the Mount of Olives, beyond the Kedron ("black brook"), so called from its dark waters, which was still more darkened by the blood from the foot of the altar in the temple. The spot now pointed out as Gethsemane lies on the right of the path to the Mount of Olives. The wall has been restored. Eight olive trees remain, all of them very old, but scarcely of the time of our Lord, since Titus, during the seige of Jerusalem, had all the trees of the district cut down.—*Schaff*.

PARALLEL ACCOUNTS.—Matt. 26:47-58; Luke 22:47-55; John 18:2-18.

LESSON OUTLINE.—1. The Traitor's Kiss. 2. The Flight of the Disciples. 3. The Lord Delivered to the Priests.

ANALYSIS

I. THE TRAITOR'S KISS, vs. 43-46.
   1. Enemies Guided by Judas. Mark 14:43; Matt. 26:47; Luke 22:47; John 18:3.
   2. The Traitor's Sign. Mark 14:44; Matt. 26:48.
   3. Betrayed by a Kiss. Mark 14:45; Matt. 26:49; Luke 22:48.
   4. The Lord Laid Hands Upon. Mark 14:46; Matt. 26:50.

II. THE LIGHT OF THE DISCIPLE:, vs. 47-50.
   1. Peter Draws the Sword. Mark 14:47; Matt. 26:51; Luke 22:50; John 18:10.
   2. The Lord's Demand of His Enemies. Mark 14:47, 48; Matt. 26:55, 56; Luke 22:52, 53.
   3. The Apostles Panic-stricken. Mark 14:50; Matt. 26:56.

III. THE LORD DELIVERED TO THE PRIESTS, vs. 51-54.
   1. Mark Following at a Distance. Mark 14:51,52.

2. Jesus Led to the Sanhedrim. Mark 14:53; Matt. 26:57; Luke 22:54; John 18:13.
3. Peter in the Palace of Caiaphas. Mark 14:54; Matt. 26:58; Luke 22:54; John 18:18.

INTRODUCTION

After his prayer (recorded in John 17) was ended, Jesus went with his disciples over the brook Kedron to the garden of Gethsemane, where he would await the coming of Judas. The apostate, after leaving the supper-room, had gone to the priests, and with them made arrangement for the immediate arrest of the Lord. Coming to the garden, Jesus takes with him Peter and James and John, and retires with them to a secluded spot. Here he begins to be heavy with sorrow, and, leaving the three, goes alone to pray. Returning, he finds them asleep. Leaving them, he again prays, and, in his agony, sweats a bloody sweat, but is strengthened by an angel. Again returning to the three disciples, he finds them asleep; he goes a third time and prays, and returning bids them sleep on, but soon announces the approach of Judas.—*Andrews.* The order of events, as indicated by a comparison of the four accounts, I think it to have been substantially as follows: Christ's prayer is broken in upon by the tramp of the approaching guards, and the gleaming of their lights as they issue from the gate of the city; their approach, observed across the intervening brook Kedron, he interprets as God' final answer to his prayer—it is the divine will that he should drink the bitter cup. He proceeds to the entrance of the garden and arouses his disciples (v. 46); Judas, who leads the band, draws near to kiss Jesus according to the pre-arranged signal; is abashed by the Lord's reproachful question, "Betrayest thou the Son of man with a kiss?" and makes no reply (vs. 49, 50; Luke 22: 48); the band shares his confusion, and, under the influence of the superhuman majesty of our Lord, falls backward (John 18:4-6); the disciples, emboldened, ask permission to resist (Luke 22:49), and Peter, more impetuous than the rest, does not wait for an answer, but initiates the attack (v. 51; John 18:10); Christ rebukes him (vs. 52-54), heals the wounded servant (Luke 22:51), and demands of the officers that they let the disciples go their way (John 18:8); the disciples, forbidden to resist, interpret this as a hint to escape, and flee (v. 56); at the same time the officers, who have recovered from their momentary awe, proceed to bind Jesus (John 18:12), disregarding his dignified remonstrance against being treated as a thief (v. 55). For a full understanding of all the elements in this midnight scene, all the accounts should be carefully compared, but especially Matthew and John. —*Abbott.*

EXPLANATORY NOTES

I. THE TRAITOR'S KISS.

43. *Cometh Judas.* Between one and two o'clock Friday morning. The movements of Judas, after the last supper, we may readily picture to ourselves in their outline. Going immediately to Caiaphas, or to some other leading member of the Sanhedrim, he informs him where Jesus is, and announces that he is ready to fulfill his compact, and at once to make the arrest. It was not the intention to arrest Christ during the feast, lest there be a popular tumult (Matt. 26:5); but, now that an opportunity offered of seizing him secretly at dead of night, when all were asleep or engaged at the paschal meal, his enemies could not hesitate.—*Andrews.* Judas knew the place, for it was a frequent resort of Jesus with his disciples (John 18:2). *A great multitude.* This consisted, (1) of "the band" (John 18:3, 12), or Roman cohort, which, consisting of 300 to 600 men, quartered in the tower of Antonia, overlooking the temple, and ever ready to put down any tumult or arrest any disturber. Probably so much of the band as could be spared was present. (2) There were "the captains of the temple" (Luke 22:52), with their men, who guarded the temple and kept order. (3) Some of the "chief priests and elders" (Luke 22:52). (4) And, finally, their servants, such as Malchus (John 18:10), and others, who had been commissioned by the Jewish authorities. —*Clark. Swords and staves.* The soldiers were armed with swords, the officers of the priests with staves. They also had torches, though the moon was at the full, probably to search under the shadows of the trees and the rocks.

44. *He that betrayed . . . a token.* Judas had given them the sign previously. It was necessary, inasmuch as (the Roman soldiers did not personally know Christ, and) in the darkness he might be confounded, by the officers, with the disciples. The whole account indicates anxiety lest he should escape as he had done before (John 7:45, 46; 8:59; 10:39). —*Abbott. Shall kiss.* The kiss, among the ancients, was a sign of affectionate and cordial intimacy, and particularly a token of fidelity. Nothing could be baser than to come in enmity with the signs of deepest affection. Thus Joab betrayed and murdered Abner; a treacherous deed that David could not forget when he was dying.

45. *Master, master; and kissed him.* The salutation was hypocritical reverence. Master is the same as Rabbi, or teacher. *Kissed him.* An emphatic compound of the verb in the preceding verse, without exact equivalent in English, but denoting that he kissed him in an affectionate and earnest manner, adding to the guilt of the betrayal by the manner of committing it.

46. *Laid their hands on him.* This is an epitome of the following verses describing the capture. *And took him.* But only because Christ offers himself to be taken. He could have had twelve legions of angels to defend and rescue him, had he desired (Matt. 26:53). It was to be emphatically set forth before the eyes of all—Judas as well—that no man had power to bind this Jesus, or to lead him away to death, unless "he himself should lay down his life."

II. THE FLIGHT OF THE DISCIPLES.

47. *One of them . . . drew a sword.* The "one of them" was Peter (John 18:10). Why he was not mentioned is idle to inquire; one supposition only must be avoided, that there is any *purpose* in the omission. It is absurd to suppose that the mention of his name in a book current only among Christians, many years after the fact, could lead to his apprehension, which did not take place at the time, although he was recognized as the striker in the palace of the high priest (John 18:26). The real reason of the non-apprehension was that the servant was *healed* by the Lord.—*Alford. And smote a servant of the high priest.* His name was Malchus (John 18:10). The impetuosity of the attack was just like Peter. He asked, Shall we fight? and waited not for the answer, but struck at once. It is likely that Malchus was one of those who had seized the Lord. Peter's blow was one of his mistakes. Carnal weapons cannot defend the cause of the Lord. Besides, the Lord needed no defenders. The death of Christ was a voluntary surrendering of himself for the redemption of the world. Knowing the designs of the Pharisees against him, he could have eluded them by remaining beyond Jordan. Knowing the purpose of Judas to betray him, he could have withdrawn to some place of safety. But now that his mission of teaching, of healing, of guiding, was accomplished, the hour of sacrifice had come; and he was prepared to meet it. At the last, he could have summoned legions of angels to his help; but *he gave himself for us.*

48. *Are ye come out, as against a thief?* The word is the same as that used in John 18:40, of Barabbas, and points to the brigand chieftain of a lawless band, as distinct from the petty thief of towns or villages.—*Plumptre.* Judas had cautioned the guard to lead Jesus away securely (Mark 14:44), and when they finally arrested him they bound him (John 18:12). This indignity, it appears to me, probably called forth the remonstrance of this verse. Compare the language of Luke 22:52, 53—*Abbott.* Throughout his prolonged sufferings he complained of no other injury done to him than this; namely, that they came to apprehend him as a criminal.

49. *I was daily with you in the temple teaching.* This was not like a brigand. Why did they not arrest him then? *Took me not.* The offense with which he was charged was one of teaching, not of robbery or violence; it was open, public, unconcealed, and the time to arrest him was the time of his teaching; he had neither hid himself, nor surrounded himself with his followers for self-protection; the indignity of this midnight arrest was, therefore, gratuitous.—*Abbott. The Scriptures must be fulfilled.* As, for instance, relative to Judas (Ps. 41:9), relative to Christ being treated as a transgressor (Isa. 53:12), relative to the desertion of the disciples (Zech. 13:7). According to the counsel of God, for the salvation of a sinful world, as declared in the Scriptures, the Messiah must suffer; that suffering must be thus brought about. Our Lord's death could not be incidental or accidental. This declaration also contained consolation for his terrified disciples.

50. *They all forsook him and fled.* All had said they would never forsake him, but as soon as he submitted to his captors they were all panic-stricken and fled like sheep. They had never taken up the idea that it would be consistent with the ends contemplated in the mission of the Messiah that he should be ignominiously arrested. "This statement of the desertion of Jesus by 'all the disciples' is one of the most remarkable instances of that honesty which led the evangelists to record facts, though to their own dishonor."—*Mimpriss.*

III. THE LORD DELIVERED TO THE PRIESTS.

51. *A certain young man.* The incident of this young man occurs very briefly, and is narrated apparently for no purpose whatever. The only solution, certainly the best, is the supposition that it was no other than Mark himself. Mark was at this time a young man, living probably in Jerusalem with his mother, and was more or less a follower of Jesus, and very likely to be present, from his interest in our Lord, during these awful transactions. That he should not name himself is very naturally explained, on the same principle of personal delicacy as induced the evangelist John to allude to himself in the third person. Such are the views of Schaff, Ellicott, Godet, and others. The minuteness of Mark's details of these events points to one who writes from personal knowledge. *A linen cloth.* A wrapper thrown over his undressed body. Doubtless this was the *aba,* an outer cloth thrown over the dress, and used even in sleep to enwrap the body. Dr. Thomson (vol. 1, p. 500) speaks of the very poor who sleep in their *aba,* or outer garment, and have no other "raiment for their skin." But the word rendered here "naked" often signifies undressed, that is, clad in the under-garments alone. Mark had, probably, been roused from sleep, or just preparing to retire to rest

in a house somewhere in the valley of Kedron, and he had nothing to cover him except the upper garment; but, in spite of this, he ventured, in his excitement, to press on amongst the crowd. This upper garment was worn much like a scottish plaid.

52. *And he left the linen cloth.* In attempting to lay hold on him, they grasped only the loose folds of the linen cloth. Letting this remain with them, he fled away and escaped, either not being pursued, or taking advantage of his knowledge of the place, in the darkness of the night, to elude his pursuers.

53. *Led Jesus away.* Jesus was now absolutely alone in the power of his enemies. At the command of the tribune his hands were tied behind his back, and, forming a close array around him, the Roman soldiers, followed and surrounded by the Jewish servants, led him once more through the night, over the Kedron, and up the steep city slope beyond it, to the palace of the high priest.—*Farrar. To the high priest.* We learn from John (18:13-15) that Jesus was first taken to the house of Annas, and, after a brief delay here, to the palace of Caiaphas, the high priest.—*Andrews.* It was the duty of Annas to examine the sacrifices, whether they were "without blemish;" there was significancy in it that Christ, the great Sacrifice, was presented to him, and sent away bound as approved and ready for the altar.—*Lightfoot.* The actual high priest at the time was Caiaphas; but this Annas had been high priest, and as such enjoyed the title by courtesy. Being also a man of great wealth and influence, and of active habits, he took upon him much of the business of that office, as a sort of assessor to, or substitute for, Caiaphas, who was his son-in-law. Hence the evangelist describes them both as "high priests" (Luke 3:2), as they were in fact. *Were assembled all the chief priests and the elders and the scribes.* It was against the rules of Jewish law to hold a session of the Sanhedrim or council for the trial of capital offenses by night. Such an assembly on the night of the paschal supper must have been still more at variance with usage. The present gathering was therefore an informal one—probably a packed meeting of those who were parties to the plot; Nicodemus and Joseph of Arimathaea, and probably not a few others, like the young "ruler" of Luke 18:18, not being summoned.—*Ellicott.*

54. *Peter followed him afar off.* After their flight in the garden, at least two of the apostles, Peter and John, turned about and followed from a distance the band that led the Savior. Peter followed secretly to see what the result would be. *Into the place of the high priest.* John, who was acquainted there, as we learn from his account, secured admission for Peter and himself. *And warmed himself at the fire.* The spring nights at Jerusalem, 2,600 feet above the sea, are often cold. The fire was built

in an open court in the interior of the building, open to the sky, around which the palace was constructed.

SUMMARY
14:1-52

This section exhibits, on the one hand, the evil purpose and wicked plottings of the enemies of Jesus, and on the other, the self-sacrifice with which he prepared himself for the fate which he foresaw, and to which he voluntarily submitted. It shows, by the counsel of the scribes and priests (1, 2), by the agreement with Judas (10, 11), by the remark concerning Judas at the supper-table (17-21), and by the manner of the arrest (44, 48, 49), that his death was sought for through malice and corruption. It shows, on the other hand, by the remarks of Jesus at the supper in Bethany (3-9), by his statement when instituting the Supper (22-25), and by his prayer in the garden (36), that he submitted voluntarily, though at the cost of unspeakable mental suffering, to a sacrificial death for the sins of the world. This last fact shows that he was impelled by a purpose which could originate in no human soul, and which no human being could under such circumstances maintain: for what mere human being, acquainted with the true God, could suppose that his own death would be an atonement for the sins of the world, and, having formed a purpose to die for this object, could maintain that purpose through such sufferings as Jesus endured? Here is an unmistakable mark of the divinity which dwelt in Jesus, giving direction to both his life and his death. (*J. W. McGarvey*)

FACT QUESTIONS 14:43-54

1010. At what time did the betrayal occur? Why?
1011. Describe the location of the garden of Gethsemane.
1012. What shall we say of the olive trees shown to tourists as the very ones under which our Lord knelt?
1013. Was it necessary to go over the Brook Kedron to reach Gethsemane? —Trace the route.
1014. At what juncture in His agony was our Lord strengthened by an angel?
1015. Why did Jesus return to His disciples three times?—was there any excuse for the sleep of the disciples?
1016. What does Christ interpret as God's final answer to His prayer?
1017. What very unusual event occurs to Judas and those who have come to arrest Jesus? Why?
1018. What two rebukes are given by Jesus during this betrayal scene?
1019. What was the circumstance that prompted the enemies of Christ not to hesitate in the arrest?

1020. Describe briefly the four groups in "a great multitude" who came to arrest Jesus.
1021. Read John 7:45, 46; 8:59; 10:39 and show the reason for the anxiety of those who came to take Jesus.
1022. How did Judas add to the guilt of his betrayal?
1023. How did Jesus plainly show to all that no man could have taken Him without Jesus' consent?
1024. What purpose was there in not mentioning the name of Peter as one who struck Malchus?
1025. Show three ways Jesus could have used to prevent His capture.
1026. In what way did Jesus link himself with Barabbas? Cf. John 18:40.
1027. For what was Jesus arrested? Show how appropriate are the words of vs. 49a.
1028. Read Ps. 41:9; Isa. 53:12; Zech. 13:7 and show how these were all fulfilled.
1029. Show how vs. 50 contains a remarkable instance of honesty on the part of the writer Mark.
1030. Why record the incident of "a certain young man"? Who was this young man?
1031. Why was the young man undressed?
1032. Did the soldiers arrest the apostles? Why attempt to arrest the unnamed young man?
1033. Describe the manner in which Christ was led away.
1034. To whom was Jesus first led? Why—What special significance is there in this action?
1035. How could it be that there were two high-priests? Who were they?
1036. What type of assembly gathered to judge Jesus? Who was and who wasn't there?
1037. Who followed with Peter? Why?—Where?

3. JESUS BEFORE THE COUNCIL 14:55-65

TEXT 14:55-65

"Now the chief priests and the whole council sought witness against Jesus to put him to death; and found it not. For many bare false witness against him, and their witness agreed not together. And there stood up certain, and bare false witness against him, saying, We heard him say, I will destroy this temple that is made with hands, and in three days I will build another made without hands. And not even so did their witness agree together. And the high priest stood up in the midst, and asked Jesus, saying, Answerest thou nothing? what is it which these witness against thee? But he held his peace, and answered nothing. Again the high priest asked him, and saith unto him, Art thou the Christ, the Son of the Blessed? And Jesus said, I am; and ye shall see the Son of man sitting at the right hand of power, and coming with the clouds of heaven. And the high priest rent his clothes, and saith, What further need have we of witnesses? Ye have heard the blasphemy: what think ye? And they all condemned him to be worthy of death. And some began to spit on him, and to cover his face, and to buffet him, and to say unto him, Prophesy: and the officers received him with blows of their hands."

THOUGHT QUESTIONS 14:55-65

839. Why were the chief priests and the whole council so determined to put Jesus to death?
840. Just what was involved in the testimony of witnesses? Why were they unable to find witnesses?
841. What was "unequal" about the testimony of the witnesses?
842. Why were the authorities so opposed to Jesus? Please attempt to be specific.
843. Read John 2:19 and show how the words of Jesus were twisted to say what Jesus did not say. Cf. 13:2.
844. Why the personal attempt on the part of the high priest to provoke a response from Jesus?
845. Why did Jesus answer the second question but not the first one?
846. What was the purpose of our Lord in speaking of "the Son of man sitting at the right hand of power"?
847. What is suggested in the action of the high priest in tearing his clothes?
848. Just what was the specific charge of the blasphemy?
849. Are we to understand the members of the Sanhedrim spit upon Jesus?
849. Are we to understand the members of the Sanhedrim spat upon Jesus? What was the cause of such intense hatred?

COMMENT

TIME.—Early Friday morning, April 7, A.D. 30, between one and six o'clock. This meeting took place before the dawn of day on Friday morning.

PLACE.—The palace of Caiaphas, the high priest in Jerusalem. The exact location of the palace of Caiaphas is unknown, but it was probably not far from the temple.

PARALLEL ACCOUNTS.—Matt. 26:59-75. The trial (vs. 55-65) is found in Luke 22:63-71 and John 18:19-24.

ORDER OF EVENTS.—After the arrest, and its incidents: (1) Jesus was taken first to the house of Annas, ex-high priest (John 18:13). (2) Next to the palace of Caiaphas, Peter and John following (John 18:15). (3)

Here was a preliminary examination before Caiaphas (John 18:19-24. (4) The trial before the council, illegal because held at night—before three o'clock the cock-crowing (Matt. 26:59-65. Mark 14:55-64). (5) Peter's three denials during the trial (Matt. 26:69-75. Mark 14:66-72). (6) After the Sanhedrim had pronounced him guilty, it suspends its session till break of day. (7) During this interval Jesus is exposed to the insults of his enemies (Matt. 26:67, 68. Mark 14:65. Luke 22:63-65). (8) At the dawn of day the Sanhedrim reassembles (Matt. 27:1. Mark 15:1. Luke 22:66). (9) After hearing Christ's confession again, he is formally condemned to death for blasphemy (Luke 22:66-71.) (10) He is bound, and sent to Pilate (Mark 15:1).

OUTLINE.—1. False Witness Against Christ. 2. The Lord bears Witness. 3. The Lord Condemned to Die.

ANALYSIS

I. FALSE WITNESS AGAINST CHRIST, VS. 55-59.

1. False Testimony Sought. Mark 14:15; Matt. 26:59.
2. The False Witnesses fail to Agree. Mark 14:56; Matt. 26:50; 1 Pet. 3:16.
3. The False Witness Concerning the Temple. Mark 14:57-59; Matt. 26:51.

II. THE LORD BEARS WITNESS, VS. 60-62.

1. The High Priest Examines Christ. Mark 14:60; Matt. 26:52.
2. The Silence of Christ. Mark 14:61; Matt. 26:63; Issiah 53:7.
3. The Great and Good Confession. Mark 14:62; Matt. 26:64.

III. THE LORD CONDEMNED TO DIE, VS. 63-65.

1. The High Priest Pronounces Judgement. Mark 14:63; Matt. 26:65.
2. The Sanhedrim Votes the Death of Christ. Mark 14:64; Matt. 26:66.
3. The Lord Abused and Insulted. Mark 14:65; Matt. 22:67.

INTRODUCTION

I. THE COURT. The court convened to try Jesus Christ was the Sanhedrim, or Sanhedrin. It consisted of chief priests, that is, the heads of the twenty-four priestly classes; scribes, that is, rabbis learned in the literature of the church; and elders, who were chosen from amongst the most influential of the laity. Jewish tradition puts the number of members at seventy-one. The high priest usually presided: the vice-president sat at his right hand. The other councillors were ranged in front of these two in the form of a semicircle. Two scribes or clerks attended, who on criminal trials registered the votes, one for acquittal, the other for condemnation.—*Abbott.* The priests were there, whose greed and selfishness he had exposed; and, worse than all, the worldly, sceptical Sadducees, the most cruel and dangerous of opponents, whose empty sapience he had confuted. —*Farrar.* The Sanhedrin had power to try those charged with capital offences, but it had no power to execute the sentence of death (John 18:31).

II. THE TRIAL. The whole criminal procedure in the Pentateuch rests upon three principles: (1) publicity of the trial, (2) entire liberty of defence allowed to the accused, and (3) a guaranty against the dangers of testimony: "one witness is no witness." There must be at least two or three who know the facts.—*M. Dupin.* Throughout the whole course of the trial, the rules of Jewish law of procedure were grossly violated, and the accused was deprived of rights belonging even to the meanest citizen. He was arrested in the night, bound as a malefactor, beaten before his arraignment, and struck in open court during the trial. He was tried on a feast-day, and before sunrise. He was compelled to criminate himself, and this under an oath of solemn judicial adjuration; and he was sentenced on the same day of the conviction. In all these particulars the law was wholly disregarded.—*Prof. Greenleaf's Trial of Jesus, in the Testimony of the Evangelists.*

III. THE ACCUSATION. The crime for which Jesus was condemned before the Sanhedrin was his alleged blasphemy; i.e., an assumption of power and authority which belonged to Jehovah alone (Matt. 26:65). But when he was brought before Pilate they changed the accusation to one of treason against the Roman government, as the only one of which Pilate would take cognizance (Luke 23:2).

EXPLANATORY NOTES

I. FALSE WITNESS AGAINST CHRIST.

55. *The chief priests,* Annas and Caiaphas, the ex-high priest and the acting high priest, and the heads of the twenty-four courses. *All the council.* The priests just named and certain scribes and elders to the number of seventy-one (see *Introduction*) constituted the Sanhedrim, or council. Geikie says: "In imitation of the traditional usages of the Sanhedrin, while it existed, the judges before whom Jesus was led sat, turbaned, on cushions or pillows, in Oriental fashion, with crossed legs, and unshod feet, in a half circle; Caiaphas, as high priest, in the center, and the chief or oldest, according to precedence, on each side. The prisoner was placed, standing before Caiaphas; at each end of the semicircle sat a scribe, to write out the sentence of acquittal or condemnation; some bailiffs, with cords and thongs, guarded the accused, while a few others stood behind, to call witnesses, and, at the close, to

carry out the decision of the judges." *Sought for witness.* Not to ascertain the truth, but to destroy one whom they considered a personal enemy, was this trial conducted. *Found one.* It was necessary to find two who had been present at the same or a precisely similar offense, whatever it might be. The difficulty, then, was not that they found none, as the English Bible renders it, but, as the Greek words literally mean, they did not find (what they were seeking,) i.e., probably, two witnesses to one and the same act. It would have been strange indeed if no one could be found to testify at all; but it was not strange that they found it hard to obtain two concurrent witnesses to one and the same thing.—*Alexander.*

56. *Many bare false witness.* The charge against Jesus of declaring himself the Son of the God and so making himself equal with God (John 10:33), was one which it was impossible to substantiate by any witnesses outside the immediate circle of Christ's disciples, for his ministry had been one of singularly commingled boldness and caution—boldness in the truths he uttered, caution in the methods of his utterance. He never publicly proclaimed himself the Messiah. He forbade the evil spirits from announcing his character. Mark 1: 34. He received the confession of his disciples, but refused to permit them to repeat it to others. Matt. 16:20. Interrogated by the Jews whether he was the Christ, he had refused a direct reply, and had referred them to his works. John 10:24, 25. He had given the same response to the public questioning of John's disciples. In most of his later ministry he had veiled his meaning in parables. Hence the witnesses were contradictory and failed to meet the demands of the law.

57. *There arose certain.* At least two were found who were willing to give a distorted version of something Christ had said over two years before.

58. *We heard him say, I will destroy this temple.* The false witness consisted in giving that sense to his words which it appears by Matt. 27:63 they knew they did not bear. There is perhaps a trace, in the different reports of Matthew and Mark, of the discrepancy between the witnesses. There is considerable difference between the words attributed to him here, and there. These witnesses falsely reported his words, and failed also to understand what he did say but gave a new version according to their understanding.

59. *Neither so did their witness agree.* Their statements varied so much that there was not sufficient testimony on any one point to convict. Therefore this first plan failed.

II. THE LORD BEARS WITNESS.

60. *The high priest stood up.* Thus far, during all the wicked attempts to torture testimony against him the Lord had maintained unbroken silence. This was galling to the pride of Caiaphas, who saw that nothing remained but to force him, if possible, to criminate himself. *In the midst.* The high priest, leaving his official seat, came forward into the middle of the semi-circle, in which the members of the Sanhedrim were seated. The accused stood facing them, so that the high priest was then immediately side by side with our Lord. *Answerest thou nothing?* The question implies a long-continued silence, while witness after witness were uttering clumsy falsehoods. In the silence itself we may perhaps trace a deliberate fulfilment of Isa. 53:7. *What is it which these witness?* The first object of Caiphas was to draw out an answer to the allegations, which, as he well knew, would not suffice, as they then stood, for condemnation.

61. *But he held his peace.* It was no part of his duty, as a defendant, to unravel the contradictions of his unprincipled accusers. Our Lord was silent; for in answering he must have opened to them the meaning of his words, which was not the work of this hour, nor fitting for that audience. Truth is never mute for want of arguments of defence, but sometimes silent, out of holy wisdom. *Said unto him.* "I adjure thee" (Matt. 26:63). This was the regular legal formula for administering oaths, and was binding on witnesses without their answering (Lev. 5:1). *Art thou the Christ?* Caiaphas became desperate, and adopted a resource which our own rules of evidence would declare most infamous, and which was also wholly adverse to the first principles of Mosaic jurisprudence, and the like of which occurs in no circumstance of Hebrew history. It was that of putting the prisoner upon his oath to answer questions framed for his own crimination.—*Kitto.*

62. *And Jesus said, I am.* His declaration of his divine Sonship constitutes Christ's solemn testimony to himself, uttered at the momentous crisis of his life, under the solemn sanction of an oath, in the course of judicial proceedings, in the presence of the highest council of the realm, in the far more sacred presence of God and his recording angels, at the peril of his life, and with a clear comprehension of the meaning which not only priests and people would attach to it, but with which it would be forever invested by humanity. If it had not been true it would have been blasphemy.—*Abbott. Ye shall see.* The "shall ye see" is to the council, the representatives of the chosen people, so soon to be judged by him to whom all judgment is committed—the power in contrast to his present

weakness—sitting, even as they now sat, to judge him; and the *coming in the clouds of heaven* (see Dan. 7:13) looks onward to the awful time of the end, when every eye shall see him.—*Alford.* Let it be noted that this is the Lord's first formal, public declaration of his divinity. He now offered up his life in attestation of his Messiahship and divine character.

III. THE LORD CONDEMNED TO DIE.

63. *The high priest rent his clothes.* The act was almost as much a formal sign of condemnation as the putting on of the black cap by an English judge.—*Plumptre.* The practice of rending the clothes on occasions of supposed blasphemy was based on 2 Kings 18:37. Originally it was a natural outburst of intense grief, and was involuntary; but at a later period it became a mere form regulated by special rules. The rent made in the garment was from the neck downward, and about a span in length. The body dress and outer garment were left untouched.—*Lange. What need we any further witnesses?* They had called but one true witness; his testimony they rejected; and yet on the strength of his testimony they were about to condemn him!

64. *Ye have heard the blasphemy.* Blasphemy here denotes "reproachful, irreverent, or insulting language concerning God, or any of his names or attributes." Such would be the making God to be only like a man. Hence, had Jesus not been the Messiah, what he said *would* have been blasphemy. *What think ye?* A formal putting of the question. *And they all.* It may therefore be inferred that none had been summoned who were known or suspected to favor our Lord, though they may have been called to the more formal council at daybreak. *Condemned him.* This formal condemnation was, as they imagined, according to the law (Lev. 24:16). Compare Deut. 18:20. The Sanhedrim was forbidden to investigate any capital crime during the night, and according to the Roman law a sentence pronounced before dawn was not valid. This test vote, however, they considered as settling the question.—*Schaff.* The council now adjourned, to meet at daybreak, when they could legally pronounce the sentence. In the mean time occurred the maltreatment by his lawless enemies described in the next verse. The daybreak meeting, at which the sentence already pronounced was formally ratified, is described in Luke 22:66-71. John only relates the examination before Annas; Matthew and Mark give the account of the packed and illegal meeting of the Sanhedrim before day, presided over by Caiaphas. Luke only gives the account of the ratification meeting of the Sanhedrim at the dawn of day. All the accounts must be studied in order to get the full account of the Jewish condemnation of the Lord.

65. *Began to spit on him.* One under sentence of death was always, in these rough ages, the sport of mockery of his guards, and those in charge of Jesus, made worse than common by the example of the judges, vented their cruelty on him with the coarsest brutality. Their passions, indeed, intensified their bitterness, for they were fierce Jewish bigots.—*Geikie.* *To say unto him, Prophesy.* He who claims to be chief of the prophets should now give us a specimen of his prophetic powers. He was blindfolded, so that they were putting his prophetic powers to a mock test. Compare these insults before the Jews, which alluded to his claims of Messiahship with the insults by the Romans, which alluded to his political claims.

FACT QUESTIONS 14:55-65

1038. Please retrace carefully the three incidents leading to the trial of Jesus and the seven following.
1039. How many chief priests in the council? From whence did they come?
1040. Who were the scribes? the elders?
1041. Who presided? How was the condemnation or acquital recorded?
1042. Show why each class in the Sanhedrim were adverse in their opinion of Jesus.
1043. "The whole criminal procedure in the Pentateuch rests upon three principles"—what were they?
1044. Show at least four particulars in which throughout the course of his trial the rules of Jewish law were grossly violated.
1045. What were the two accusations brought against Jesus?
1046. Why did the council seek a witness?
1047. The problem was not that they could not find witnesses but rather in the quality of the ones they found—explain.
1048. Why would it be almost impossible to substantiate the charge of Jesus declaring Himself to be the Son of God?
1049. When had anyone heard Him say "I will destroy this temple?" Cf. Matt. 27:63.
1050. The testimony of the witnesses was rejected—why?
1051. Why did Caiaphas stand up in the midst of the council?
1052. Show how Isa. 53:7 was fulfilled in the trial.
1053. What did Caiaphas hope to do in any testimony Jesus would give?
1054. "Truth is never mute for want of arguments of defense, but sometimes silent out of____________ ____________."
1055. In what manner did Caiaphas attempt to cause Christ to criminate Himself?
1056. Please read Abbott's beautiful comment under vs. 62. "And Jesus

said, I am"—give three or four of the momentous circumstances attending this confession.

1057. To whom did Jesus address the words "Ye shall see"? Why did He make such a stupendous prediction? Cf. Dan. 7:13.

1058. What significance was there in the rent clothes of the high priest? How did the practice originate?

1059. The claim of Jesus would have been indeed blasphemy except for one fact—what was it?

1060. Who was called to this Council meeting? When was it held?

1061. Read Lev. 24:16; Deut. 18:20 and show how the Council felt they had acted according to law—Show two particulars where they had not.

1062. In what sense was a "test vote" taken?

1063. Between the early morning meeting and daybreak what happened in the treatment of Jesus?

1064. Who spit on Jesus?

1065. Read Luke 22:66-71 for the daybreak meeting.

1066. When was Jesus tried before Annas?

1067. How can we imagine the dignified religious elders of the supreme court spitting on anyone?

1068. The Jews mocked Jesus for one claim, the Romans for another—what were the claims? Were they true?

4. PETER'S DENIALS 14:66-72

TEXT 14:66-72

"And as Peter was beneath in the court, there cometh one of the maids of the high priest; and seeing Peter warming himself, she looked upon him and saith, Thou also wast with the Nazarene, even Jesus. But he denied, saying, I neither know, nor understand what thou sayest: and he went out into the porch; and the cock crew. And the maid saw him and began again to say to them that stood by, This is one of them. But he again denied it. And after a little while again they that stood by said to Peter, Of a truth thou art one of them; for thou art a Galilean. But he began to curse, and to swear, I know not this man of whom ye speak. And straightway the second time the cock crew. And Peter called to mind the word, how that Jesus said unto him, Before the cock crow twice, thou shalt deny me thrice. And when he thought thereon, he wept."

THOUGHT QUESTIONS 14:66-72

850. Please attempt a picture in mind of the Court of Caiaphas—what is meant by the expression "beneath the court" or "below in the courtyard"?

851. Why had Peter followed Jesus? What were his feelings about Jesus at this time?
852. Since it was dark (in the early morning hour) how could the maid recognize Peter?
853. Read John 18:16—could we identify this maid with the one mentioned by John?
854. What tasks were performed by these "maids of the high priest"?
855. Why was Peter so quick in his denial? Wouldn't it have been easier to ignore the accusation? Discuss.
856. Of what did Peter have to be ashamed in his association with Jesus?
857. What was "the porch" or "vestibule" into which Peter went? Where was the cock? Why go into the vestibule?
858. Read Matt. 26:29-75; Luke 22:55-62 and discuss who the second maid was in the second denial by Peter.
859. Who accused Peter in his third denial? Why? Cf. Luke 22:59.
860. What caused the by-standers to join in the verbal attack? Cf. Matt. 26:73.
861. Please attempt a careful explanation as to what is involved in "curse and to swear"—it is *not* profanity.
862. Read Luke 22:61 for a reason for the weeping of Peter.
863. What is meant by the word "having thought thereon"? i.e. in what manner did Peter think thereon?
864. Why was Peter willing to defend his Lord in Gethsemane—"face a mob armed with swords and clubs" and yet wilt before a maid who pointed her finger at him?
865. Attempt an explanation of the depth of repentance in the weeping of Peter.

COMMENT

Time.—Early Friday morning, April 7, A.D. 30, between one and six o'clock.

Place.—The palace of Caiaphas, the high priest in Jerusalem. The exact location of the palace of Caiaphas is unknown, but it was probably not far from the temple.

Parallel Accounts.—Matt. 26:69-75; Luke 22:55-62; John 18:15-18; 25-27.

Outline.—1. The first denial, vs. 66-68. 2. The second denial, vs. 69, 70a. 3. The third denial, vs. 70b-71. 4. Peter's repentance, vs. 72.

ANALYSIS

I. THE FIRST DENIAL, vs. 66-68.

1. The place of the denial—"beneath in the courtyard."
2. The accuser in the denial—"there cometh one of the maids of the high priest."
3. The light for the denial—the fire of the enemies of Jesus—"seeing Peter warming himself."—"she looked upon him."
4. The accusation of the denial—"Thou also wast with the Nazarene, even Jesus."
5. The hasty, embarrassed denial—"I neither know, nor understand what thou sayest."
6. Peter's retreat—"he went out into the porch."
7. The sermon of the cock—"and the cock crew."

II. THE SECOND DENIAL, vs. 69, 70a.

1. Either the same maid or another one again accused Him. Cf. Matt. 26:71; Luke 22:58.
2. "He again denied it."

III. THE THIRD DENIAL, vs. 70b-71.

1. Made by those who stood by—perhaps aroused by the words of the maid.
2. Peter bound himself under an oath that he did not know Jesus.

IV. PETER'S REPENTANCE, vs. 72.

1. The second crowing of the cock immediately after the third denial.
2. The promise of Jesus called to mind.
3. The meaning of what he had done broke his heart.

EXPLANATORY NOTES

I. THE FIRST DENIAL.

"66. *beneath in the palace.*) Or below in the court. Matthew, *without in the hall.* The chamber in which the Sanhedrim met was an upper room.

68. *neither understand I.*) Mark is careful to give every word; even this slight addition aggravates Peter's sin.

And he went out into the porch.) The exact place designated was a small forecourt in the open air. There the crowing of the cock might be heard more easily than in the inner court; this crowning was about one or two o'clock,—see note on v. 30—some three or four hours before the second crowing, giving therefore some intimation as to the length of the proceedings. According to the late Jewish tradition cocks were not kept in Jerusalem, being considered unclean; but there are distinct proofs to the contrary in the Talmud.

And the cock crew.) This is omitted by B, but is found in MSS of the highest authority, and in most ancient versions. It should certainly be retained."

II. THE SECOND DENIAL.

"69. *And a maid.*) This might give an impression that the same maid is meant; but Peter was then near the gate or outer door, and the person who would naturally see him was the portress. We know from John, chapter 18:16, that a female kept the door. She could speak positively to his identity. Then came the second denial. There was an interval, it might be of two hours, between this and the preceeding denial: another interval of about an hour (Luke v. 59) passes and the bystanders, who had been present at the arrest, one recognizing him as the smiter of Malchus, unanimously charged him."

III. THE THIRD DENIAL.

"71. *curse and to swear.* Matthew has the same strong, expression, which Luke, the *Pauline Evangelist,* omits. But Mark adds a few sharp painful words, *this* (contemptuous), and the expression, *"whom ye speak"* of, as though he knew Him only from their statement.

The oldest MSS have *immediately* before the second time, which one omits."

IV. PETER'S REPENTANCE.

"72. *the second time.* This was about an hour before dawn. The trial was then just over: our Lord was now in the court passing towards the porch, bound and in the hands of the attendants, and turned, as Luke alone tells, to cast a look on the denier. That look Peter could not forget, but he could hardly bear to speak of it; it told too of unbroken affection, and that in relating his own great sin he might scarcely dare to record. What he does relate is the sudden reaction at the second cock-crowing, "and when he thought thereon he wept"—he will not even dwell on the *bitterness* of his anguish, which the other Synoptists record with natural sympathy. He omits also the words, "he went out." He will say nothing of himself save what concerned the greatness of his fall, and the simple fact of his grief (a long weeping,) on the awakening of conscience. The rendering "when he thought thereon," is correct; the Greek word implies exactly that when he turned his thought and recalled those words, he began to weep, and continued weeping. Other explanations are doubtful and unsatisfactory. N. B. Grimm (Lex. s.v.) gives good authority for this (Antonin. 10, 30; Plut. Plac. Phil. 4, 1), and adds, "absol. sc. quum perpendisset effatum Christi." Rather, "quum animum advertisset ad effatum Jesu."

Thus terminates the preliminary inquiry. The sentence of death is not pronounced in a formal and legal way, but the decision that death was the proper penalty has been given; the only question that remains is how it is to be executed. On the illegality of the whole proceeding, see note on Matt. xxvii. I." (*F. C. Cook*)

FACT QUESTIONS 14.66-72

1069. What slight addition in the report by Mark aggravates Peter's sin?
1070. What intimation do we get of the length of the proceedings?
1071. What was the total time involved in the three denials?
1072. How is the word "this" used in vs. 71?
1073. How do we learn of the unbroken affection between Jesus and Peter?
1074. On what did Peter think that made him weep?

5. JESUS BEFORE PILATE 15:1-20

TEXT 15:1-20

"And straightway in the morning the chief priests with the elders and scribes, and the whole council, held a consultation, and bound Jesus, and carried him away, and delivered him up to Pilate. And Pilate asked him, Art thou the King of the Jews? And he answering saith unto him, Thou sayest. And the chief priests accused him of many things. And Pilate asked him, saying, Answerest thou nothing? behold how many things they accuse thee of. But Jesus no more answered anything; insomuch that Pilate marvelled.

Now at the feast he used to release unto them one prisoner, whom they asked of him. And there was one called Barabbas, lying bound with them that had made insurrection, men who in the insurrection had committed murder. And the multitude went up and began to ask him to do as he was wont to do unto them. And Pilate answered them, saying, Will ye that I release unto you the King of the Jews? For he perceived that for envy the chief priests had delivered him up. But the chief priests stirred up the multitude, that he should rather release Barabbas unto them. And Pilate again answered and said unto them, What then shall I do unto him whom ye call the King of the Jews? And they cried out again, Crucify him. And Pilate said unto them, Why, what evil hath he done? But they cried out exceedingly, Crucify him. And Pilate, wishing to content the multitude, released unto them Barabbas, and delivered Jesus, when he had scourged him, to be crucified.

And thc soldiers led him away within the court, which is the Praetorium; and they called together the whole band. And they clothe him with purple, and plaiting a crown of thorns, they put it on him; and they began to salute him, Hail, King of the Jews! And they smote his head with a reed, and did spit upon him, and bowing their knees worshipped him. And when they had mocked him, they took off from him the purple, and put on him his garments. And they led him out to crucify him."

THOUGHT QUESTIONS 15:1-20

866. Why were the Jews so anxious to bring Jesus before Pilate?
867. If they had already condemned Jesus why hold another consultation?
868. Are we to understand from the little expression "the whole council" in vs. 1 that the whole council was not present at the first meeting?
869. Why ask about the Lordship of Jesus?
870. What did the answer of Jesus mean to Pilate?
871. Of what did the chief-priests accuse Jesus? (Please remember Jesus is before Pilate not Caiaphas)
872. Why didn't Jesus give answer to the accusations of the chief priests?
873. The marvelling of Pilate—was it an ordinary thing for this governor of Judea? Why did he marvel?
874. What feast was about to be held? Cf. vs. 6.
875. What purpose was served in releasing a prisoner during the feast?
876. Please mark how completely Barabbas was guilty of everything of which Jesus was accused.
877. What interest did the multitude have in the release of a prisoner?
878. Did Pilate believe Jesus was the actual "King of the Jews"?
879. Pilate knew the real motive for the arrest of Jesus—what is meant by the expression "for envy the chief priests had delivered Him up"?
880. What do you imagine the chief-priests would say to the multitude to stir them up?
881. Cf. Matt. 27:1, 2; 11-26. Luke 23:1-25; John 18:28-40; 19:1 to get a complete record of all the events. Pilate put forth a real effort to save Jesus—indicate three attempts.
882. What was the great sin of Pilate?
883. Why scourge Jesus? What was involved?
884. Where was the trial before Pilate held?
885. Why call together "the band" or "cohort"?
886. Was it customary to mock prisoners? Who did the mocking?
887. Discuss the details of His suffering—show how appropriate the method of mockery was as related to His suffering for us as the King of glory.

COMMENT

Time.—Friday morning, April 7, A.D. 30, between five and nine o'clock.

Place.—The last and formal condemnation of the Sanhedrim, described in Luke 22:66-71, was probably in their usual council chamber, called *Gazith,* at the southeast corner of one of the courts of the temple; or else in a hall near the gate Shusan, close by the temple. The trial before Pilate was either in the tower of Antonia, near the temple, or at Herod's palace, on the northern brow of Mount Zion.

Parallel Accounts.—Matt. 27:1, 2, 11-26; Luke 23: 1-25; John 18:28-40; 19:1.

ORDER OF EVENTS AT CHRIST'S TRIAL BEFORE PILATE:

1. Second session of the Sanhedrim (Matt. 27:1; Mark 15:1).
2. First application to Pilate (John 18:28-32).
3. Formal accusation before Pilate (Matt. 27:11; Mark 15:1,2).
4. First colloquy between Christ and Pilate (John 18:33-38; Mark 15:2.)
5. Acquittal; further charges; Christ's silence (Matt. 27: 12-14; Mark 15:3-5; Luke 23:4, 5).
6. Case sent to Herod (Luke 23:6-12).
7. Before Pilate again. Formal acquittal (Luke 23:13-16).
8. Jesus or Barabbas (Matt. 27:15-18; Mark 15:6-10).
9. Message of warning from Pilate's wife (while people are deciding) (Matt. 27:19).
10. Barabbas chosen. Cries to "Crucify him!" (Matt. 27:20-22; Mark 15:11-13).
11. Efforts of Pilate to save Jesus (Matt. 27:23; Mark 15:12-14).
12. Pilate washes his hands (Matt. 27:24, 25).
13. Sentence of crucifixion (Mark 15:15; Luke 23:24, 25).
14. Scourging and mockery (Matt. 27:26-30; Mark 15:16-19; John 19:1-3).
15. Further efforts to save Jesus (John 19:4-16).
16. Led away to be crucified (Matt. 27:31; Mark 15:20).

Outline.—1. The Lord Sent to Pilate. 2. Barabbas or Christ. 3. The Lord Delivered to be Crucified.

ANALYSIS

I. THE LORD SENT TO PILATE, VS. 1-5.

1. The Sanhedrim Delivers Jesus. Mark 15:1; Matt. 27:1; Luke 23:1; John 18:28.
2. The King of the Jews. Mark 15:2; Matt. 27:11.
3. As a Lamb before his Shearers. Mark 15:3-5; Matt. 27:11; John 19:9; Isa. 53:7.

II. BARABBAS OR CHRIST, VS. 6-11.

1. The Custom of the Feast. Mark 15:6; Matt. 27:15; Luke 23: 17; John 18:39.

2. Barabbas the Murderer. Mark 15:7.
3. Pilate's Offer to Release Christ. Mark 15:9; Matt. 27:15; Luke 23:17; John 18:39.
4. Barabbas Chosen. Mark 15:11; Matt. 27:20; Acts 3:14.

III. THE LORD DELIVERED TO BE CRUCIFIED, vs. 12-20.

1. Pilate Importuned to Crucify Christ. Mark 15:12-24.
2. Jesus Scourged. Mark 15:15; Matt. 27:26; John 19:1.
3. Jesus Mocked. Mark 15:16-20; Matt. 27:27-32; Luke 23:26.

INTRODUCTION

Though the Sanhedrim had condemned Jesus to death on the charge of blasphemy, they had no power to carry out the sentence and were compelled to carry their prisoner to Pilate, the Roman governor, to secure his sanction. There they charge him with being a malefactor, and Pilate directs them to take him and judge him themselves. As they cannot inflict a capital punishment they bring the charge of sedition; and Pilate, re-entering the judgment hall, and calling Jesus, examines him as to his Messianic claims. Satisfied that he is innocent, Pilate goes out and affirms that he finds no fault in him. The Jews renewing their accusations, to which Jesus makes no reply, and mentioning Galilee, Pilate sends him to Herod, who was then at Jerusalem; but Jesus refuses to answer his questions, and is sent back to Pilate. The latter now resorts to another expedient. He seats himself upon the judgment-seat, and calling the chief priests and elders, declares to them that neither himself nor Herod had found any fault in him. According to custom, he would release him. But the multitude, beginning to cry that he should release Barabbas, not Jesus, he leaves it to their choice. During the interval, while the people were making their choice, his wife sends a message to him of warning. The people, persuaded by the priests and elders, reject Jesus and choose Barabbas, and Pilate makes several efforts to change their decision. At last he gives orders that Jesus be scourged previous to crucifixion. This was done by the soldiers with mockery and abuse, and Pilate, going forth, again takes Jesus and presents him to the people. The Jews continue to demand his death, but upon the ground that he made himself the Son of God. Terrified at this new charge, Pilate again takes Jesus into the hall to ask him, but receives no answer. Pilate strives earnestly to save him, but is met by the cry that he is Caesar's enemy. Yielding to fear, he ascends the tribunal, and, calling for water, washes his hands in token of his innocence, and then gives directions that he be taken away and crucified.

EXPLANATORY NOTES

1. THE LORD SENT TO PILATE.

1. *In the morning the chief priests held a consultation.* This was the meeting of the Sanhedrim described by Luke as held at the dawn, to ratify formally what had been done before with haste and informality. The circumstances under which its members had been convened at the palace of Caiaphas sufficiently show that the legal forms, which they were so scrupulous in observing, had not been complied with. The law forbidding capital trials in the night had been broken; the place of session was unusual, if not illegal; perhaps the attendance, so early after midnight, had not been full. On these accounts it was expedient that a more regular and legal sitting should be held as early in the morning as was possible. For a full account of this meeting see Luke 22:65-71. *Carried him away.* While the Sanhedrim had power to try those charged with capital offenses, it had no power to execute the sentence of death. It is generally agreed that from the time Judea became a Roman province the authority to punish capitally had been taken away from the Jewish tribunals. Shortly after the death of Herod the Great, Judea was annexed to the great Roman province of Syria, and governed by deputies called Procurators, the fourth of whom was Valerius Gratus, and the fifth Pontius Pilate, appointed in the thirteenth year of Tiberius. Like his predecessors and successors in that office, he resided commonly at Caesarea, but attended at Jerusalem during the great festivals, in order to preserve the peace.

2. *Pilate asked him.* The Jews, carefully suppressing the religious grounds on which they had condemned our Lord, had advanced against him a triple accusation of, (1) seditious agitation; (2) prohibition of the payment of the tribute money; and (3) the assumption of the suspicious title of "King of the Jews" (Luke 23:2). This last accusation amounted to a charge of treason—the greatest crime known to Roman law. Of the three points of accusation, (2) was utterly false; (1) and (3), though in a sense true, were not true in the sense intended. *Art thou the King of the Jews?* The question is asked because the Jews charged that he made such claims. Pilate may well have been perplexed. Christ had claimed to be King; promulgated laws; organized in the heart of Caesar's province the germ of an imperishable kingdom; entered Jerusalem in triumph, hailed by the throng as King of the Jews; and his arrest had been forcibly resisted by one of his followers. These facts a wily priesthood could easily pervert and exaggerate so as to give color to their accusation. *Thou sayest.* This is not to be taken as a doubtful answer, but as a strong

affirmation. The answer of defense of Jesus (John 18:34-38) is that he is King, but that his "kingdom is not of this world," therefore (it is inferred) the "perversion of the people" was not a rebellion that threatened the Roman government. The defense was complete, as Pilate admits: "I find no fault in him" (Luke 23:4). This is Pilate's first emphatic and unhesitating acquittal (John 18:38).

3. *Chief priests accused him.* Pilate's public decided acquittal only kindled the fury of his enemies into yet fiercer flame. After all that they had hazarded, was their purpose to be foiled by the intervention of the very Gentiles on whom they had relied for its bitter consummation?—*Farrar. Of many things.* Some are given in Luke 23:2-5 (see under v. 2). *Answered nothing.* He had already explained to Pilate the nature of his kingdom, and satisfied him that he is innocent of sedition; after that he keeps silence. He will answer honest perplexity, but not willful slander.

5. *Pilate marvelled.* Convinced as Pilate was of the innocence of Christ, he was all the more at a loss to understand the forbearance with which he maintained such sublime silence.—*Meyer.*

II. BARABBAS OR CHRIST.

6. *At that feast he released unto them one prisoner.* It was a Greek and Roman custom to release prisoners on birthdays of rulers and festive occasions, a custom still followed by rulers. On the jubilee of her coronation, Queen Victoria ordered the prisons of India to be opened. This custom had been introduced into the subject provinces of the Roman Empire and at the passover a prisoner was released in Jerusalem.

7. *There was one named Barabbas.* Matthew says he was a notable prisoner. Barabbas was plainly a ringleader in one of those fierce and fanatic outbreaks against the Roman domination, which fast succeeded one another in the latter days of the Jewish commonwealth. *Committed murder.* In this particular insurrection blood had been shed, and apparently some Roman soldiers had been killed. Note particularly the Revised Version here. It is remarkable that this man Barabbas was confessedly guilty of the very crime with which the priests and rulers had falsely charged Jesus—that of sedition; and no plainer proof of their hypocrisy could be given to the watchful Pilate than their efforts to release the former and condemn the latter.

8. *The multitude . . . began to desire him.* Note the wording in the New Version. The mob of the city, pouring from street and alley in the excited Oriental fashion, came streaming up the avenue to the front of

the palace, shouting for this annual gift. The cry was for once welcome to Pilate, for he saw in it a loophole of escape from his disagreeable position.—*Stalker.*

9. *Will ye that I release unto you the King of the Jews?* The events may be thus arranged: Pilate presents to the people the two—Jesus and Barabbas—between whom they were to choose. A little interval followed, during which he received his wife's message. He now formally asks the people whom they wished to have released (Matt. 27:21; Mark 15:9; Luke 23;16-18). They answer, "Barabbas," Pilate, hoping that by changing the form of the question he could obtain an answer more in accordance with his wishes, says "What shall I do, then, with Jesus, which is called Chsist?" (Matt. 27:22; Mark 15:12). To this they reply, "Let him be crucified." His use of the term, "the King of the Jews," was probably an attempt to enlist the patriotic feeling of the multitude on the side of the prisoner.

11. *Chief priests moved the people.* They dared not openly apprehend him, for fear of the people; but, taking him secretely and surrendering him with all the appendages of a culprit guilty of something, the people are induced to consider him as a deceiver and blasphemer and traitor. Doubtless the friends of Jesus were mostly absent, frightened away by this fearful revolution, or ignorant of what was in progress, since not more than six hours had passed since Jesus was seized, and those hours of darkness.

III. THE LORD DELIVERED TO BE CRUCIFIED.

12. *What .. . then that I shall do unto him.* That he did not permanently protect him, rose partly from his character, and partly from his past history as procurator. Morally enervated and lawless, the petty tyrant was incapable of a strong impression of righteous firmness, and besides, he dreaded complaints at Rome from the Jewish authorities, and insurrections of the masses in his local government.—*Geikie. Do unto him.* This is remarkable; since it shows that Pilate made, so to speak, a second offer. He was called upon by the people to release one prisoner only at the festival; but his question implies, that, even after their declared preference of Barabbas, he was willing to leave the fate of the man to their decision —*Cook.*

13. *Cried out again.* There had been various outcries of the people; and with this fresh outburst of fury there was the demand for death.

14. *Then Pilate said unto them, Why what evil hath he done?* The question attested the judge's conviction of the innocence of the accused,

but it attested also the cowardice of the judge. We find from Luke 23:22, that he had recourse to the desperate expedient of suggesting a milder punishment, chastising, i.e., scourging; but the suggestion itself showed his weakness. Pilate sought to satisfy all; the people, by releasing him; the priests and elders, by chastising him; and himself, by delivering him from death. But he satisfied none.

15. *Willing to content the people.* Observe the pitiful vacillation of a man, devoid of all principle or conscience of duty. Pilate is willing to release Jesus (Luke 23:20), and Pilate is also willing to content the people. Heaven and hell strive in his bosom for the mastery and the latter gains the victory.

SUMMARY
14:53—15:15

If Jesus had been arrested on some charge of criminal conduct, and if his trial and sentence had been marked by the due forms of justice, these facts would have detracted somewhat from the force of the evidence of his innocence. But the proceedings connected with his arrest and condemnation by the Sanhedrim, and those by which the sentence of death was procured from Pilate, furnish evidence in favor of his claims. It is only when justice is to be perverted, and the innocent condemned, that men resort to practices so corrupt. Though false witnesses were purposely employed in his trial before the Sanhedrim, and though their testimony when presented was contradictory, still the high priest pretended that it contained evidence of guilt (xiv. 57-60). Not willing, however, to rest the case on this testimony, Jesus was then called on to testify in his own case, and though his answer was merely a repetition of what he had claimed for himself from the beginning, on this he was pronounced worthy of death (xiv. 61-64). After thus condemning him on a false charge of blasphemy, they went before Pilate with an entirely different charge, that of disloyalty to Caesar, a charge of which they had special reasons to know that he was not guilty (xv. 1, 2; comp. xii. 13-17). Pilate was now subjected to the alternative of either vindicating the cause of justice, or giving success to the iniquitous prosecution of Jesus. He knew that the chief priests had accused him through envy (xv. 10), and he openly proclaimed that he could find no evil in his conduct (xv. 14); yet, "to content the people, he released Barabbas unto them, and delivered Jesus to be crucified" (xv. 15). Thus the condemnation and the sentence of Jesus, viewed merely in the light of Mark's account, contain unmistakable proofs that they were brought about by the employment of such measures, and such only, as are employed in the condemnation and death of innocent persons. (*J. W. McGarvey*)

16. *Led him into the hall called Praetorium.* The Praetorium, translated "hall of judgment," was the headquarters of the Roman military governor, wherever he happened to be. *The whole band.* The "whole band," or cohort, which was gathered to join in the mockery, was the tenth part of a legion, embracing from there three to six hundred men.

17. *Clothed him in Purple.* A kind of round cloak, which was confined on the right shoulder by a clasp, so as to cover the left side of the body, worn by military officers, and called *paludamentum.* Those of the emperors were purple. This cloak or robe, called by Matthew scarlet, is by Mark called purple. The two colors blend into each other, and the words are interchangeable. *Platted a crown of thorns.* Made of a plant similar to the cactus. What crown could have been imagined for our King Jesus which should have so exactly suited him as this crown of thorns? He who came to obtain for us the blessing bears what the curse-laden earth brings forth, being made a curse for us.

18. *Hail, king of the Jews.* "The king of the Jews," the title which he had assumed, and which these soldiers, like their commander, thought supremely ridiculous, as borne by such a person. It has been well observed that, as the Jews especially derided his prophetic claims, so the Romans mocked at his regal pretensions.

19. *Smote him on the head.* The blow of the reed would have been too light to inflict much pain upon any other part than the head, and there it would aggravate the pain of the thorns. *Spit upon him.* As their excitement increased, they spat upon him, following the example of the chief priests (Mark 14:65). It is remarkable that during the whole of this treatment Christ offered no resistance, and uttered no word—he who with a glance of his eye could have scathed them into ashes.

20. *Put his own clothes on him.* He was thus mocked, not in his own clothes, but in another's, to signify that he suffered not for his own sin. *Led him out.* That is, from the city; the place of execution was without the city walls (Heb. 13:12). Quesnel says: He suffered "without the gate," in order to show us that we are not to expect sanctification by the sacrifices offered within that city; and that he died, not for the Jews only, but for all mankind. Heb: 13:11-14. After the mocking, and before the royal robes were taken off, we have to insert the account which John gives (19:4, 5) of Pilate's last attempt to rescue the "just Man" whom he had unjustly condemned. He showed the silent Sufferer in the mock insignia of royalty, as if asking them, Is not this enough? The cries of "Crucify him!" were but redoubled; and once again the cowardly judge took his place in the official chair, and passed the final sentence.

FACT QUESTIONS 15:1-20

1075. Please read again the order of events at Christ's trial before Pilate.
1076. What was Pilat's first reaction to the charge of the Jews that Jesus was a malefactor?
1077. Why send Jesus to Herod?
1078. When did Pilate's wife send him a message? What did it say?
1079. What was terrifying in the charge that Jesus made Himself the Son of God?
1080. What was the cry that caused Pilate to deliver Jesus to be crucified?
1081. What laws (name two) were broken in the first meeting of the council?
1082. When did Pilate begin his rule?
1083. What was the triple accusation against our Lord? Show how they were false.
1084. How had the "wily priesthood" perverted the facts so as to perplex Pilate?
1085. What was the defense of Jesus that satisfied Pilate that he was innocent? Cf. John 18:34-38.
1086. "Pilate's public decided acquittal only kindled the fury of his enemies"—why?
1087. Some things Jesus would answer—some things he would not—what were they?
1088. Where had the custom of releasing prisoners originated?
1089. Give three facts about Barabbas.
1090. What cry of the multitude was far more welcome to Pilate? Why?
1091. Why ask the second question—"what shall I do, then, with Jesus who is called Christ"?
1092. Where were the friends of Jesus? Why were they absent?
1093. Why didn't Pilate permanently protect Jesus if He was innocent?
1094. What statement of Pilate shows his cowardice?
1095. Read Luke 23:22 and tell what desperate expedient Pilate attempted to use.
1096. Show how heaven and hell strove in the bosom of Pilate—which won? Why?
1097. What is the meaning of "Praetorium"—where was it?—how many men joined in the mockery of Jesus?
1098. What is meant by "clothed Him in Purple"?—was the robe purple or scarlet?
1099. Show how very appropriate it was for Jesus to wear "the crown of thorns."
1100. What was the estimation of Pilate and the soldiers of the title "King of the Jews"? Why?

1101. Why didn't Jesus offer resistance to the ridicule?
1102. Is there some significance in that Jesus suffered in someone else's clothes?
1103. What was the final attempt of Pilate to release Him? Describe it in your own words.

6. JESUS CRUCIFIED 15:21-39

TEXT 5:21-39

"And they compel one passing by, Simon of Cyrene, coming from the country, the father of Alexander and Rufus, to go with them, that he might bear his cross. And they bring him unto the place Golgotha, which is, being interpreted, The place of a skull. And they offered him wine mingled with myrrh: but he received it not. And they crucify him, and part his garments among them, casting lots upon them, what each should take. And it was the third hour, and they crucified him. And the superscription of his accusation was written over, THE KING OF THE JEWS. And with him they crucify two robbers: one on his right hand, and one on his left. And they that passed by railed on him, wagging their heads, and saying, Ha! thou that destroyest the temple, and buildest it in three days, save thyself, and come down from the cross. In like manner also the chief priests mocking him among themselves with the scribes said, He saved others; himself he cannot save. Let the Christ, the King of Israel, now come down from the cross, that we may see and believe. And they that were crucified with him reproached him.

And when the sixth hour was come, there was darkness over the whole land until the ninth hour. And at the ninth hour Jesus cried with a loud voice, Eloi, Eloi, lama sabachthani? which is, being interpreted, My God, my God, why hast thou forsaken me? And some of them that stood by, when they heard it, said, Behold, he calleth Elijah. And one ran, filling a sponge full of vinegar, put it on a reed, and gave him to drink, saying, Let be; let us see whether Elijah cometh to take him down. And Jesus uttered a loud voice, and gave up the ghost. And the veil of the temple was rent in twain from the top to the bottom. And when the centurion, which stood over against him, saw that he so gave up the ghost, he said, Truly this man was the Son of God."

THOUGHT QUESTIONS 15:21-39

888. Who compelled Simon of Cyrene to carry the cross?
889. Cf. Luke 23:26—some feel Simon carried the cross *with* Jesus—what do you think?
890. Are we to conclude Simon was a negro?

891. Why mention that Simon was the father of Alexander and Rufus?
892. Why was Simon of Cyrene coming to Jerusalem?
893. How far was the cross carried?—a mile? less than a mile? More than a mile?
894. Why call the place of crucifixion—"Golgotha"?
895. What was the purpose of offering the wine and myrrh? Who offered it to Him? (Please read the parallel accounts.) Matt. 27:34.
896. Why didn't Jesus drink the potion offered?
897. Are we to understand that since four garments and the robe were taken from our Lord that He was crucified without any covering? Cf. Matt. 27:35; John 19:23; Luke 23:34.
898. Did they cast lots for all the garments?
899. Please read the four versions of the superscription (1) Matt. 27:35 (2) Mark 15:26 (3) Luke 23:38 (4) John 19:16—how shall we account for this difference? (—please remember in how many languages it was written).
900. The two robbers could have been partners in crime with whom?
901. Who were the persons who railed on Him? What incited such persons to do this?
902. Why mention especially the destruction of the temple?
903. Why couldn't Jesus answer their taunts and save Himself?
904. Note vs. 31—it contains the greatest truth in the universe—and yet a terrible lie. Designate each.
905. If Jesus had delivered Himself from the cross what would have been the reaction of those who mocked Him?—the immediate reaction and the lasting reaction.
906. Did both thieves deride Jesus?—Discuss.
907. What particular type of darkness was present?—i.e. an eclipse—a storm? or What? Name the hours (our time).
908. How extensive was the darkness?—how intense?
909. What happened during the three hours from 12 to 3?
910. Was Jesus quoting scripture intentionally or was this a spontaneous expression of His own deep need? Did God forsake Him? Discuss.
911. Why did some think He called for Elijah?
912. What was the purpose of offering wine at this time? What is the difference between a reed and hyssop? Cf. John 19:29.
913. When Jesus cried with a loud voice what did He Say? Cf. John 19:30 and Luke 23:46.
914. Is there some significance in the fact that He cried with a *loud* voice? i.e. as the manner of His death.
915. What meaning is there in the fact that the temple veil was torn?

916. The centurion at the cross seems to admit two things in his statement—what were they?

COMMENT

Time.—Friday, April 7, A.D. 30, between the hours of 9 A.M. and 3 P.M.

Place.—The Lord was taken by the soldiers without the city to a place called Calvary (the place of a skull), or Golgotha, to be crucified. The site is uncertain, and travelers have differed much concerning its location. Dr. Barclay thinks it was on the east side of the city, just south ot St. Stephen's gate, on the Goath of Jeremiah 31:39, a tongue or spur of land projecting southeasterly into the Kedron valley toward Gethsemane. Others place it on the northwest of the city. It was, (1) apparently a well-known spot; (2) outside the gate (compare Heb. 13:12); but (3) near the city (John 19:20); (4) on a thoroughfare leading into the country (Luke 23:26); and (5) contained a "garden" or "orchard" (John 19:41). Tradition has for sixteen centuries pointed out the site of the present Church of the Holy Sepulchre as the actual spot; but it is highly probable that this spot was inside the city wall at that time. The question is of little practical importance; for the apostles and evangelists barely allude to the place of Christ's birth, death, and resurrection. They fixed their eyes on the great facts themselves, and worshipped the exalted Savior in heaven where he forever lives.

Parallel Accounts.—Matt. 27:27-37; Luke 23:26-38; John 19:1-24.

Outline.—1. The Lord Nailed to the Cross. 2. The Lord Numbered with Transgressors. 3. The Earth Draped in Mourning.

ANALYSIS

I. THE LORD NAILED TO THE CROSS, VS. 21-26.
   1. The Lord Led to Golgotha. Mark 15:22; Matt. 27:33; Luke 23:33; John 19:17.
   2. The Stupefying Cup Refused. Mark 15:23; Matt. 27:34.
   3. His Garments Parted by Lot. Mark 15:24; Matt. 27:35; John 19:23; Luke 23:34.
   4. The Superscription on the Cross. Mark 15:26; Matt. 27:37; John 19:19.

II. THE LORD NUMBERED WITH TRANSGRESSORS, VS. 27-32.
   1. The Lord Between Thieves. Mark 15:27; Matt. 27:38; Luke 23:32; Isaiah 53:12.
   2. The Railing of the Multitude. Mark 15:29; Matt. 27:40; Luke 23:35.
   3. The Rulers Mock Him. Mark 15:31; Matt. 27:41; Luke 23.35.

III. THE EARTH DRAPED IN MOURNING, VS. 33-39.
1. The Land Darkened. Mark 15:33; Matt. 27:45; Luke 23:45.
2. The Cry Upon the Cross. Mark 15:34; Matt. 27:46.
3. It is Finished. Mark 15:37; Matt. 27:50; Luke 23:46; John 19:30.
4. The Veil of the Temple was Rent. Mark 15:38; Matt. 27:51.
5. The Centurion's Confession. Mark 15:39; Luke 23:47.

INTRODUCTION

Crucifixion.—Nothing demonstrates more forcibly the malignity of the Jews than their persistent and boisterous demand that Jesus should be crucified. Other forms of execution were common; stoning, as in the case of Stephen; killing with the sword, as in the case of James; beheading, as in the case of John the Baptist, and, among the Romans, strangling. Crucifixion had never been adopted by the Jews. Even to hang a corpse upon a tree was accounted among them a great indignity (Deut. 21:22, 23). It was inflicted on Jewish malefactors by the Romans because it was regarded with such horror. Cicero called it a punishment most inhuman and shocking, and wrote of it that it should be removed from the eyes and ears and every thought of man. The Romans reserved it for slaves and foreigners whom they despised. Yet it was this most shameful and terrible of all deaths which the Jews call on Pilate to inflict upon a prisoner whom he had pronounced innocent. The terrible details of such a death should be noted in order to comprehend what our Savior suffered for us, and I have condensed from Farrar and Geikie the following description of a death on the cross: He was stripped naked of all his clothes. He was laid down upon the implement of torture. His arms were stretched along the cross-beams, and at the center of the open palms the point of a huge iron nail was placed, which, by the blow of a mallet, was driven home into the wood. Then through either foot separately, or possibly through both together, as they were placed one over the other, another huge nail tore its way through the quivering flesh. To prevent the hands and feet being torn away by the weight of the body, which could not "rest upon nothing but four great wounds," there was, about the center of the cross, a wooden projection strong enough to support, at least in part, a human body, which soon became a weight of agony. And then the accursed tree, with its living human burden hanging upon it in helpless agony, and suffering fresh tortures as every movement irritated the fresh rents in hands and feet, was slowly heaved up by strong arms and the end of it fixed firmly in a hole dug deep in the ground for that purpose. The body was terribly wrenched when the cross was raised and dropped into its place; the concussion often dislocated the limbs. Inflammation of the wounds in both hands and feet speedily set in, and ere long rose also in other places where the circulation was checked by the tension of the parts; intolerable thirst and ever-increasing pain resulted; the blood, which could no longer reach the extremities, rose to the head, swelling the veins and arteries in it unnaturally, and causing the most agonizing tortures in the brain; besides, it could no longer move freely from the lungs; the heart grew more and more oppressed, and all the veins were distended. Had the wounds bled freely it would have been a great relief, but there was very little lost. The weight of the body itself, resting on the wooden pin of the upright beam, the burning heat of the sun, scorching the veins, and the hot winds which dried up the moisture of the body, made each moment more terrible than that before. The numbness and stiffness of the more distant muscles brought on painful convulsions; and this numbness, slowly extending, sometimes through two or three days, at last reached the vital parts, and released the sufferer by death.

EXPLANATORY NOTES

I. THE LORD NAILED TO THE CROSS.

21. *They compel one Simon a Cyrenian.* The Roman officer had official authority to press into the military service, for a special purpose, either horses or men. See Matt. 5:41. *A Cyrenian.* There were many Simons, or Simeons, among the early Christians; but this one was distinguished from all the rest as Simon of Cyrene, a great and flourishing city of North Africa. It lay between Alexandria on the east and Carthage on the west. This ancient city is now a heap of ruins. *Coming out of the country.* Going up to Jerusalem to attend the feast of the passover. *Alexander and Rufus.* It is taken for granted that they were well known at the time when the gospel was written, and hence, doubtless, they were Christians of some note in the church. *Bear his cross.* Jesus at first bore his own cross (John 19:17), as was customary. Tradition says that our Lord sunk to the ground beneath the load; but the more exact expression of Luke 23:26 shows that the after-part of the cross alone, which usually dragged upon the ground, was put upon Simon.—*Schaff.* Here, as always, the Savior bears the heaviest part of the burden.

22. *Golgotha.* A Hebrew word, meaning a skull. From its Latin equivalent, *calvaria,* comes our English word Calvary, which occurs in the English New Testament only in Luke 23:33, where it should be translated "a skull." The significance of the name is uncertain. Some suppose it was the common place of execution, and that the skulls of those who were executed lay about; others that it was a bare rounded knoll, in form like a skull. For further remarks on the locality see *Place.*

23. *They gave him to drink wine mingled with myrrh.* This was a stupefying drink to deaden the pain. It was composed of vinegar or sour wine, in which were mingled certain bitter drugs. It was customary for compassionate people to give a stupefying drink to criminals on their way to execution. It is stated in the Talmud that there was an association of women in Jerusalem who sought to alleviate the sufferings of the crucified in this way. Luke 23:27 may refer to the women who provided the drink. The effect of the draught was to dull the nerves, to cloud the intellect, to provide an anaesthetic against some part, at least, of the lingering agonies of that dreadful death. *He received it not.* The "tasting" (Matt. 27:34) implied a recognition of the kindly purpose of the act, but a recognition only. In the refusal to do more than this we see the resolute purpose to drink the cup which his Father had given him to the last drop, and not to dull, either the sense of suffering or the clearness of his communion with his Father with the slumbrous potion.

24. *When they had crucified him.* Nailed him to the cross. For details see "Crucifixion" in the *Introduction.* There were three forms of crosses; the first in the shape of the letter X, called the crux decussato, or, later, St. Andrews' cross; one in the form of the letter T, called the crux commissa, or, later, St. Anthony's cross; and third, the Latin cross, or crux immissa, like the preceding one, except that the upright beam projects above the horizontal one. That the Latin cross was the one on which Jesus was crucified, is indicated by uniform tradition. *They parted his garments, casting lots.* The garments were perquisites of the executioners. As there were four soldiers there would be four shares. The inner robe, however, like the robes of the priests, was of one piece, woven from the top, without any seam or stitching and would be destroyed by rending. The dice were ready in their pocket, and one of their brazen helmets would serve to throw them; it would be better to cast lots for this, and let him who won the highest number keep it for himself; and so it was done. No wonder that both Matthew and John, looking back on the scene, were struck by the fact that it had been written, ages before, in the twenty-second Psalm, which the Jews of that day, as well as Christians, rightly believed to refer to the Messiah, "They parted my garments among them, and for my vesture they cast lots."—*Geikie.*

25. *The third hour,* according to the Jewish reckoning, that is, from sunrise, about nine o'clock of our time. But, according to John (19:14), it was already the sixth hour when Pilate made his last attempt to rescue him. A solution is, that John, writing primarily for the churches of Asia Minor, uses the Roman mode of reckoning, that is, from midnight.

26. *The superscription of his accusation.* It was the Roman custom to place on the cross over the criminal's head, a *titulus,* or placard, stating the crime for which he suffered. Luke (23:38) says that the title was written in Greek, Latin, and Hebrew, the chief languages then spoken, and all spectators would be able to read it. The superscription is given differently by each evangelist: "This is Jesus the King of the Jews" (Matt. 27:37). "The King of the Jews" (Mark 15:26). "This is the King of the Jews (Luke 23:38). "Jesus of Nazareth the King of the Jews" (John 19:16). Although no serious and sensible writer would dream of talking about a "discrepancy" here, it is very probable that the differences arise from the different forms assumed by the title in the three languages. *King of the Jews.* The inscription stated the offense of which Jesus had been found guilty. Pilate intended that the inscription should have a sting in it for the chief priests and elders and scribes.

II. THE LORD NUMBERED WITH TRANSGRESSORS.

27. *With him they crucify two thieves.* Rather, robbers; in all probability partners in the crime of Barabbas. The mountain robbers, or banditti, were always ready to take part in such desperate risings against the Roman power. Thus he touched life at its lowest point, plunged into the stream of humanity where it was blackest.

28. This verse is omitted in the Revised Version, not being found in the oldest manuscripts.

29. *They that passed by railed at him.* The people going in and out of the city, on the thoroughfare near the place of crucifixion. *Wagging their heads.* Derisively and insultingly. Compare 2 Kings 19:21; Job 16:4; Psalm 109:25. *Thou that destroyest the temple.* It is evident that the Lord's saying (John 2:19-21), or rather this perversion of it (for he claimed not to destroy but to rebuild the temple destroyed by them), had greatly exasperated the feelings which the priests and Pharisees had contrived to excite against him.

30. *Save thyself.* This may be ironical, or it is a recognition of his miracles of mercy, to taunt him with a supposed loss of power just when he needed it most for himself. His very mercy is used in mockery.—*Schaff.* If Christ had saved himself he could not have saved others.

31. *The chief priests.* The chief priests, and scribes, and elders, less awestruck, less compassionate, than the mass of the people, were not ashamed to add their heartless reproaches to those of the evil few.

32. *Descend now from the cross, that we may see and believe.* A true index to their religious ideas. If they saw Him with their bodily eyes

by a miracle come down from the cross, they would believe. Their religion rested on their five senses. The invisible spiritual power, in which Jesus taught, did his work, and founded his kingdom, had no existence for them. The only authority for their faith was what they could grasp with their hands, or see with their eyes.—*Geikie. They that were crucified with him reviled him.* It is not certain whether both of the malefactors reviled him, or but one; Matthew and Mark speak of both; Luke of but one. Most, after Augustine, suppose that Matthew and Mark speak in general terms of them as a class of persons that joined in deriding Jesus, but without meaning to say that both actually derided him.

III. THE EARTH DRAPED IN MOURNING.

33. *The sixth hour . . . there was darkness.* This was no eclipse of the sun, for it was full moon at the time—nor any partial obscuration of the sun such as sometimes takes place before an earthquake—for it is clear that no earthquake in the ordinary sense of the word is here intended. Those whose belief leads them to reflect Who was then suffering, will have no difficulty in accounting for these signs of sympathy in nature nor in seeing their applicability. The consent, in the same words, of all three evangelists, must silence all question as to the universal belief of this darkness as a fact; and the early Fathers appeal to the testimony of profane authors for its truth.—*Alford. Over the whole land.* The darkness began at the sixth hour, or twelve A.M., and continued till the ninth, or three P.M. The forms of expression, "over all the land," (Matthew), "over the whole land," (Mark and Luke), do not determine how far the darkness extended. Many would confine it to the land of Judea as our version does.

34. *At the ninth hour.* Three o'clock; so far as appears, during the three hours of gloom the Lord was silent, and, doubtless, all were silent around him. *My God, my God.* The Savior here applies the holy psalm (Psalm 22) to himself as prophetic. The particular words are expressive of the divine abandonment, of the departure of the divine presence, as part of his atonement endurance. They are uttered by him to show that he is enduring an intolerable agony, deeper than any external infliction. "The finest thing in all this dear history of Immanuel on the earth is exhibited just here. When he began his suffering on the cross, he said, "Father"; and when he reached its end he also said "Father"; but in the deep midnight of woe between them, he said "My God, My God!" Reasons for the forsaking: one is, God rejects sin, and sin was then laid on Jesus. Again, perhaps the almighty Father meant that Jesus should now fight the battle single-handed, in order that the glory of the final victory to be gained might be his own."—*Robinson.*

35. *He calleth for Elias.* The resemblance between the word "Eli" and the name Elijah is very close in the original. There is here an allusion to the belief that Elijah would come before the Messiah, and hence a sarcastic denial of his Messiahship. The words may have been imperfectly understood.

36. *Sponge full of vinegar.* The vinegar is the *posca,* sour wine, or vinegar and water, the ordinary drink of the Roman soldiers. *Put it on a reed.* The "reed" is described by John as the *hyssop.*

37. *Cried with a loud voice.* Emitting a great voice, not a mere cry, but an articulate, intelligible utterance, the words of which have been preserved by John (19:30), and Luke (23:46). *Gave up the Ghost.* A better translation is "yielded up his spirit."

38. *The veil of the temple was rent.* The great work of salvation was now, at last, completed; prophecy fulfilled; the ancient covenant at an end, the new inaugurated. Judaism was forever obsolete, and the holy of holies had ceased to be the peculiar presence chamber of Jehovah among men. Nor was a sign wanting that it was so, for the great veil of purple and gold—sixty feet long and thirty broad—before the inner sanctuary of the temple, suddenly rent itself in two from the top to the bottom at the moment of Christ's death, as if he who had hitherto dwelt there had gone forth to lead up his eternal Son to his own right hand. —*Geikie.*

39. *The centurion.* An officer of the Roman answering to the captain in our own organization. He commanded a century, answering to our "company," originally a hundred men, subsequently from fifty to a hundred. *This man was the Son of God.* Observe that he says not *is* but *was* a Son of God; evidently in his thought the death of Christ was the end. It is worth noticing that the cross had greater effect on the centurion, who had been before simply ignorant of and indifferent to Christ, than on the Pharisees.

FACT QUESTIONS 15:21-39

1104. What two places are identified as the location of Calvary?
1105. Give three Scriptural facts about Calvary.
1106. Why do we reject the location chosen by the Roman Catholics?
1107. Mention three other forms of capital punishment than crucifixion.
1108. What was the Jewish opinion of crucifixion?
1109. What did Cicero say about crucifixion?
1110. It would help in our appreciation of what our Savior suffered for us if we were to attempt to rewrite in our own words what Johnson has given us from Farrar and Geikie. Try it.

1111. How does Matt. 5:41 relate to Simon of Cyrene?
1112. Where is Cyrene?
1113. Do you agree with Johnson and Schaff that Jesus and Simon carried the cross?
1114. The English word "Calvary" (Cf. Luke 23:33) should not appear at all—why not?
1115. Why called "the place of a skull"?
1116. The Talmud says there was a certain association of women in Jerusalem—what was their work?
1117. The refusal to drink the wine and myrrh indicated a desire to drink another cup—what was it?
1118. Describe and name the three types of crosses used in the days of our Lord—which was used with our Lord?
1119. Over what robe did the soldiers gamble? What did they use in "casting lots"?
1120. Please notice how remarkable a prediction is Psa. 22:16. Remember—crucifixion was a Roman form of capital punishment.
1121. Mark says "the third hour"—John says it was "the sixth hour." Cf. John 19:14—how reconcile these times?
1122. "No serious and sensible writer would dream of talking about a discrepancy in the different versions of the title on the cross" —why not?
1123. The chief priests did not like the title—why not?
1124. Show how Jesus touched life at its lowest point.
1125. Why leave out vs. 28? Isn't it true?
1126. Why would some folks be passing by the scene of the crucifixion?
1127. Was the expression "save thyself" ironical?
1128. The men who lied when they told the truth—who were they? Cf. vs. 31.
1129. What shows a true index of the religious ideas of the chief-priests?
1130. How does Augustine explain the thought that Mark says both thieves reviled Jesus?
1131. How do we know the darkness was not an eclipse of the sun?
1132. How account for the darkness? Was the darkness confined to Judea?
1133. What is "the finest thing in all this dear history of Immanuel"?
1134. What could have been a sarcastic denial of His Messiahship?

1135. Did Jesus control His own death? i.e., choose the time His spirit would depart His body? Discuss.
1136. Show how beautifully symbolic was the tearing of the temple veil.
1137. Why did the death of Christ have more effect on the centurion than on the Pharisees?

7. WOMEN WATCHING. DESCENT FROM THE CROSS. THE BURIAL. 15:40-47

TEXT 15:40-47

And there were also women beholding from afar: among whom were both Mary Magdalene, and Mary the mother of James the less and of Joses, and Salome; who, when he was in Galilee, followed him, and ministered unto him; and many other women which came up with him unto Jerusalem.

And when even was now come, because it was the Preparation, that is the day before the sabbath, there came Joseph of Arimathea, a councillor of honourable estate, who also himself was looking for the kingdom of God; and he boldly went in unto Pilate, and asked for the body of Jesus. And Pilate marvelled if he were already dead: and calling unto him the centurion, he asked him whether he had been any while dead. And when he learned it of the centurion, he granted the corpse to Joseph. And he bought a linen cloth, and taking him down, wound him in the linen cloth, and laid him in a tomb which had been hewn out of a rock; and he rolled a stone against the door of the tomb. And Mary Magdalene and Mary the mother of Joses beheld where he was laid.

THOUGHT QUESTIONS 15:40-47

917. What purpose did Mark have in mentioning the women of vs. 40?
918. Have we heard of Mary of Magdala, or Magdalene, before?
919. Please attempt to identify the persons here mentioned—i.e.: (1) James the less, (2) Joses, (3) Salome.
920. What is the meaning of the expression—"ministered unto him"?
921. Why the many women who followed Jesus i.e., why were they there?
922. Can we definitely identify Friday as the day of the crucifixion?
923. Are we to understand from vs. 43 that Joseph of Arimathaea was a member of the Sanhedrin?
924. Just what was involved in "looking for the kingdom of God"?
925. What could Pilate learn from the centurion he could not have found out from Joseph?
926. Why use a linen cloth for the body?
927. To whom did the tomb belong?

COMMENT

TIME.—Friday.

PLACE.—Calvary or Golgotha—the tomb.

PARALLEL ACCOUNTS.—Matt. 27:45-66; Luke 23:49-56; John 19:28-42, 15:40-47.

OUTLINE.—1. Women watching, vs. 40, 41. 2. The descent from the cross, and the burial of Jesus, 42-47.

ANALYSIS

I. WOMEN WATCHING, VS. 40, 41.
   1. Watched from a distance.
   2. They were: Mary Magdalene, Mary the mother of James the less, and of Joses and Salome.
   3. Earlier they had followed Him and ministered to Him in Galilee.
   4. There were many other women present who had followed Him to Jerusalem.

II. THE DESCENT FROM THE CROSS, AND THE BURIAL OF JESUS, VS. 42-47.
   1. Joseph of Arimathaea came in the late afternoon of the day before the Sabbath to ask of Pilate the body of Jesus.
   2. Pilate was surprised Jesus was already dead—he confirmed the report by asking the centurion.
   3. Upon a sure knowledge of the death of Jesus, the corpse was given to Joseph.
   4. Joseph bought linen in which to wrap the body of Jesus—Jesus' body was taken down from the cross and laid in a rock-hewn tomb—a stone was rolled against the door of the tomb.
   5. Mary Magdalene and Mary the mother of Joses noticed the place of His burial.

EXPLANATORY NOTES

I. WOMEN WATCHING.

"All the synoptists mention this group of women, Luke without enumeration of their names. Luke has a similar group (or, more strictly, the same) at chap. 8:2,3, with some names enumerated. Here three are mentioned as belonging to the company that *followed him, when he was in Galilee, and ministered unto him* (Luke 8:3, "ministered to him of their substance"), and *many other women* are mentioned (by Mark alone) as having come up *with him unto Jerusalem.*—They stood *afar off* (so all the synoptists), looking on, and with them (Luke) were "all his acquaintance"—i.e., the group contained generally those of his friends who were present in Jerusalem. Of course the mention of this group, being introduced after the record of his death, relates to no single moment, and does not imply that the same persons were together during the whole time of the crucifixion. John has already spoken of all whose names are given here as standing earlier "beside the cross." It is a touching fact that the mother of Jesus appears only there, beside the cross, and not among those who stood *afar off*. — *Mary Magdalene.* Now earliest mentioned, except in Luke 8:2. Her connection with her Lord began, as that passage leads us to believe, with his act in casting out of her "seven demons"—i.e., in relieving her of some specially severe form of demoniacal possession; for there is no good reason to spiritualize the healing, as James Freeman Clarke has done (*The Legend of Thomas Didymus*) into the deliverance from falsehood, murder, pride, luxury, selfishness, unbelief, and despair. There is no evidence for identifying her with any other Mary of the Gospels or to cast doubt on the purity of her life. The most probable derivation of her name is from "Magdala," or "Migdol," "the watchtower," a town on the shore of Lake Gennesaret. After the healing she became one of the "ministering women"; but her recorded connection with her Lord has to do mainly with the scenes of his death and resurrection.—*Mary the mother of James the less,* or the little. Probably a descriptive name, given because he, like Zacchaeus, was small of stature.—*And of Joses.* (See Mark 3:18). There are unanswered questions about this family group, but it seems most probable that the James and Joses here mentioned are not to be identified with those who appear among the "brethren of the Lord" at Mark 6:3.—*Salome* is to be identified with "the mother of Zebedee's children" in the parallel passage in Matthew, and probably with the sister of our Lord's mother in John 19:25.

Between the record of the death and that of the descent from the cross John inserts the narrative, which he alone has preserved, of the breaking of the legs of the two robbers, in order to hasten their death before the beginning of the Jewish Sabbath, and of the piercing of the side of Jesus with the soldier's spear, in order to test the reality of his death, or rather to decide the question, if there was any doubt. It is from the outflow of "blood and water" that the inference is drawn respecting the physical cause of his death.

II. THE DESCENT FROM THE CROSS AND THE BURIAL OF JESUS.

42. The natural inference is that the death occurred not long after the ninth hour—i.e., at between three and four o'clock by our reckoning. The Sabbath would begin at sunset. It was common enough for the Romans to leave the bodies of the crucified on the cross—indeed, they often remained there till they were devoured by birds or fell to pieces in decay—but this execution had taken place under Jewish auspices, and the Jews would not be willing, in view of the prohibition in Deut.

21:23, that the body of Jesus should remain all night on the cross, and still less over the Sabbath, which as the Sabbath of the passover week, was "a great day" (John 19:31).—*The Preparation, that is, the day befor the sabbath.* A valuable definition, because it removes the suspicion that the same word may elsewhere mean the day before the passover.—The time, *when the even was come,* cannot be more closely defined, but it cannot have been long after the death of our Saviour.

43. *Joseph of Arimathaea,* or "who was from Arimathaea." Mentioned on this occasion only, his name and residence being given by all four evangelists. Arimathaea is of uncertain site. It is commonly identified with Ramah, or Ramathaim-zophim, the home of Elkanah, the father of Samuel (1 Sam. 1:1; 2:11)—a place which is known in the Septuagint as "Armathaim." The identification is probably correct, but the site of Ramah has long been in doubt. The best modern theory follows a somewhat ancient tradition in locating it at *Neby Samwil,* about four miles north-west from Jerusalem. This site would satisfy all the requirements of the history, and may be regarded as probably the true one. Concerning Joseph himself, we learn from Matthew that he was a rich man; from Mark, that he was *an honorable counsellor,* or, more probably, "a counsellor of honorable estate," a rich and prosperous man. Luke as well as Mark calls him a counsellor, which means, here, a member of the council, or Sanhedrin, of the Jews. Luke further calls him "a good man and a just," and adds that "he had not consented to their counsel and deed." Apparently, he had been absent from the meeting; perhaps intentionally omitted from the call, perhaps absent at daybreak, when the meeting was held, at his home in Arimathaea. Concerning his relations to Jesus, we have in Mark and Luke that he *waited,* or was looking, *for the kingdom of God* (compare Luke 2:25, 38), by which is meant that he was a devout Jew who delighted in the promises of God concerning his coming kingdom and was expecting their early fulfillment. The phrase does not declare that he was a disciple of Jesus, but it does represent him as one of those who were ready for discipleship. Matthew says, however, that he "was a disciple of Jesus," and John says the same, adding, "but secretly, for fear of the Jews." Thus he belonged to the class mentioned in John 12:42, 43. Not until now, apparently, had his convictions in favor brought him to frank confession. His position was a trying one, and he had not had moral power to conquer its difficulties. But now, "the Lord being merciful unto him," as he was to Lot in Sodom (Gen. 19:16), he was brought forth out of his false position, love and sorrow being the messengers that led him forth. He *came*—i.e., to the place of crucifixion. Perhaps the word, standing where it does, indicates that he arrived at the place when Jesus was dying or

dead, having only then come into the city from his home. If he had been at Arimathaea since the night before, he may have known nothing of what was going on; in which case the sudden amazement would swell the tide of his indignation and horror, and easily lead him beyond his former self in devotion to the Crucified one. The participle does not merely mean *boldly;* it means, "waxing bold," coming to new boldness. The word is peculiar to Mark. In this new boldness he *went in unto Pilate,* to his house or place of judgment, whither the chief priests would not go for fear of defilement (John 18:28). There he *craved*—or, literally, "asked"—*the body of Jesus.* So, identically, the synoptists; John, "asked that he might take away the body of Jesus."

44, 45. The mention of Pilate's wonder and inquiry is peculiar to Mark. Plainly, Pilate did not know of the breaking of the legs of the robbers. Only a few hours had passed, and it seemed impossible that Jesus was dead. Not improbably, there was a shock to Pilate's mind in the tidings: he had honestly wished to save him, and so soon all was over! *Calling unto him the centurion, he asked him whether he had been dead* long (palai), not *any while.* There is a certain rough tenderness in Pilate here; he would do what he could to preserve the Crucified One from insult and help him to honorable burial; so, the death being officially confirmed, *he gave the body* (or, rather, "granted the corpse") to Joseph. So the best text: *ptoma,* instead of *soma.* Here John adds, "he came therefore, and took away his body." Here, also, John tells of the coming of a helper to Joseph—a man of the same class, a fellow-member of the Sanhedrin, another secret disciple—Nicodemus, who came to Jesus by night (John 3:1). His accession now is a surprise to us, but it may not have been to Joseph. He has appeared before only in that nightly conversation, and as pleading for candor in the judgment respecting Jesus, and taunted by his companions as if they already suspected him of a kind of discipleship (John 7:50-52). He now brought "a mixture of myrrh and aloes"—i.e., of the aromatics used in preparing the dead for burial—"about a hundred pounds weight." This was not necessarily bought beforehand; speedy burials were common in that land, and rapid preparation must have been common too. Moreover, there is no reason to doubt that Nicodemus knew all the day what was going on. He may have been preparing while Jesus was dying. So there is no reason to suppose, as some have done, that his preparation was parallel to that of Mary of Bethany, made beforehand (Mark 14:8). There is something extremely touching about the coming of these two men to bury the body of him whom they had not publicly confessed when he was alive. The shock of sorrow and indignation quickened love and rendered secret discipleship no longer possible. If the two men were thus drawn to Jesus in his extremest humiliation, it seems likely that by his resurrection their faith would be confirmed and rendered permanent.

46. The fine linen was the *sindon,* the same as that mentioned in Chap. 14:51—a foreign fabric, probably Indian, said to have been used in Egypt as a wrapping for mummies. In later Greek, however, the word means "linen." It can scarcely be said to define positively the nature of the cloth. Mark alone says that it was *bought* now, at the very time it was to be used. *Wrapped him in the linen.* The wrapping in this cloth was not a mere enfolding of the body, but, at least in part, the closer wrapping or binding (John, "they took the body of Jesus, and wound it in linen clothes with the spices") which was customary among the Jews. When Lazarus came forth, he was "bound hand and foot with grave-clothes" (John 11:44), each limb wrapped up by itself. This wrapping, however, in the case of Jesus, was left unfinished because of haste, the Sabbath coming quickly on. Observe that the very thought of preparing the body thus for burial was inconsistent with all thought of a resurrection. Of the site and ownership of the sepulchre Mark tells us nothing, saying merely that it *was hewn out of a rock,* or rather, "out of the rock"—i.e., not a natural cavern, such as were frequently used for tombs. Matthew and Luke note the same fact, Luke using a word (*laxeutos*) that points a little more definitely to the skillful workmanship of which the tomb gave evidence. It was no rude cave in which he was laid, but a carefully-made *sepulchre.* Luke and John tell us that it was new and had never before been used; Matthew, by a single word, that it was the property of Joseph. From John we learn that it was in a "garden" or orchard, an enclosed and cultivated place—the same word that is used of Gethsemane—and that the garden was "in the place where he was crucified"—i.e., close at hand. The nearness of the spot is given by John, who says nothing of Joseph's ownership as the reason for selecting it, the approach of the Sabbath requiring haste. Having thus placed the body, Joseph *rolled a stone unto,* or against (epi), *the door of the sepulchre.* Matthew, "a great stone." Visualize the tomb described in the following passage: "In Jerusalem has been found a peculiar tomb. The sloping ground has been cut down perpendicularly and the rock is cut out, so that the front wall is perpendicular rock. There is a chamber within, containing a table of stone on which to prepare the body for burial and a stone bowl for water. Within this is the tomb itself, an inner chamber, with shelves to receive the bodies. The entrance to this is an opening in the upright rock-wall three feet square. Running across before this opening, at the foot of the wall in which it is made, is a groove in the floor, one foot deep and six inches wide. In this groove is a round stone, six inches thick, just fitting the groove, and four

feet or more in diameter—a stone like a grindstone. This runs in the groove, and can be rolled up before the square opening so as to cover it, and rolled away from it so as to give entrance. It is so heavy that the full strength of a man is required to roll it away. If Joseph's new tomb were like this, the women might well ask who should roll away the stone for them." The date of this tomb, however, seems to be unknown, and so high an authority in Jewish customs as Dr. Edersheim appears to know nothing of such structures. (See *Bible Educator,* vol. iv., p. 332.) It is certain that rock-hewn tombs usually had doors of stone that turned on hinges. (See Hackett's *Illustrations of Scripture,* p. 108; Van Lennep's *Bible Lands,* p. 580.) If Joseph's new tomb, perhaps unfinished, had such a door, with its fastenings yet uncompleted, he may, for additional security, have caused a stone so large as to be moved only with difficulty to be rolled up against it, on the outside.

47. The women had remained at the cross when no apostle was there, and now they followed to the sepulchre, where new friends were doing the work that belonged to old. Only two are mentioned here and in Matthew; in Luke, the women generally who had followed from Galilee. Matthew shows them "sitting over against the sepulchre"; Mark says that *they beheld where he was laid;* and Luke shows them present and watchful during the entombment. He also shows them going home and preparing spices to finish the embalming, but not till after the Sabbath. (See the true division of paragraphs in Luke, in the Revision.) That Sabbath was to be "a high-day" with the Jews; to the disciples it was a day of despair. In truth, it was the turning-point of time, though neither Jews nor disciples knew it. The crime of the Jews and of sinful humanity was completed; the revelation of God as Saviour had been made; the work of preparatory dispensations was ended; all was ready for the breaking forth of the new power of God unto salvation. But that Jewish Sabbath before the dawning of the first Lord's Day was the time of pause and silence: the Prince of Life lay dead, and all hopes seemed disappointed; the new power was as yet unknown and undreamed of in the world. No day was ever like that, or ever shall be.

Matthew adds the record of what was done after the night had passed: the enemies of Jesus secured the placing of the official seal of the governor on the door of the tomb and the setting of a guard there, under the pretence of fear that his friends might steal his body and declare that he had risen." (*W. N. Clarke*)

FACT QUESTIONS 15:40-47

1138. What purpose was there in mentioning the women who followed and ministered to Him of their substance?

1139. What touching fact is mentioned about the mother of Jesus?
1140. What was the first mention of Mary Magdalene?
1141. There is no reason to associate Mary Magdalene with some special acts of sinfulness—why do some do this?
1142. Identify Mary the mother of James the less—who was Joses and Salome? (Cf. John 19:25; Mark 3:17.)
1143. John alone records an incident between the record of the death and the descent from the cross—what was it?
1144. Is it true that Jesus died of a literal, physical "broken heart"? Discuss.
1145. What Jewish law forbid bodies to be left on the cross overnight—what was the practice of the Romans?
1146. Why refer to one sabbath day as "a great day"? (Cf. John 19:31.)
1147. What is meant by "The Preparation,"?
1148. Give three facts about Joseph of Arimathaea.
1149. Where is Arimathaea?
1150. What was Joseph's attitude toward the condemnation of Jesus?
1151. What is meant by the expression "he waited, or was looking, for the kingdom of God"?
1152. Joseph was a disciple of Jesus—but what kind?
1153. When did Joseph arrive at the crucifixion? Show the boldness in the act of asking for the body of Jesus.
1154. What "certain rough tenderness" is seen in the actions of Pilate?
1155. What was probably a shock to Pilate? Why had Jesus died so soon? What had hastened the death of the robbers?
1156. Who came to help Joseph in the burial of Jesus—what did he bring.
1157. What was it that "quickened love and rendered secret discipleship no longer possible"?
1158. Did Nicodemus know of the events on the day of the crucifixion?
1159. What type of cloth was bought for the body of Jesus?
1160. Was Jesus bound in the cloth even as Lazarus?
1161. Give three facts about the tomb where Jesus' body was laid.
1162. What should we understand in the fact that a stone was rolled in front of the door of the tomb?
1163. How were doors usually fastened to the rock-hewn tombs?
1164. "New friends were doing the work that belonged to old"—what was it?
1165. What day was the "turning point of time"? Explain.
1166. What was done after the night was passed?

F. SUNDAY:

1. JESUS RISEN 16:1-13

TEXT 16:1-13

"And when the sabbath was past, Mary Magdalene, and Mary the mother of James, and Salome, bought spices, that they might come and anoint him. And very early on the first day of the week, they come to the tomb when the sun was risen. And they were saying among themselves, Who shall roll us away the stone from the door of the tomb? and looking up, they see that the stone is rolled back: for it was exceeding great. And entering into the tomb, they saw a young man sitting on the right side, arrayed in a white robe; and they were amazed. And he saith unto them, Be not amazed: ye seek Jesus, the Nazarene, which hath been crucified: he is risen; he is not here: behold, the place where they laid him. But go, tell his disciples and Peter, He goeth before you into Galilee: there shall ye see him, as he said unto you. And they went out and fled from the tomb; for trembling and astonishment had come upon them; and they said nothing to any one; for they were afraid.

"Now when he was risen early on the first day of the week, he appeared first to Mary Magdalene, from whom he had cast out seven devils. She went and told them that had been with him, as they mourned and wept. And they, when they heard that he was alive, and had been seen of her, disbelieved.

"And after these things he was manifested in another form unto two of them, as they walked, on their way into the country. And they went away and told it unto the rest: neither believed they them."

THOUGHT QUESTIONS 16:1-13

928. Identify the particular time the women came to the sepulchre.
929. What was the purpose in anointing the body?
930. Why did the women come to the tomb if they knew they could not roll away the stone?
931. Where were they that they could look up?
932. Describe in your own words the thoughts of the two Mary's as they approached the open tomb.
933. Why especially mention Peter in the message to the disciples?
934. Why call Him "Jesus, the Nazarene, who hath been crucified"?
935. Why promise to meet them in Galilee? When was this promise kept?
936. How long were the women quiet? i.e., as indicated in vs. 8?
937. Who did Mary Magdalene tell about His resurrection? Why didn't they believe? Discuss.
938. Please read the fuller accounts of His post resurrection appearances.

939. What are the evidences in these accounts that show them to be genuine?

COMMENT

TIME.—Sunday morning, April 9th, A.D. 30; the third day after the crucifixion and burial of the Lord.

PLACE.—The place of the burial was in a new made tomb, hewn out of the rock, belonging to Joseph of Arimathea. It was in a garden not far from Calvary, but the precise location of Calvary or the sepulcher is unknown to man. It is almost certain, however, that it was not where here now stands the "Church of the Holy Sepulcher."

PARALLEL ACCOUNTS.—Matt. 28:1-8. Luke 24:1-11. John 20:1-21.

INTERVENING HISTORY.—Soon after the Lord's death the chief priests came to Pilate, requesting that the bodies might be taken down before sunset, because the next day was the Sabbath. Obtaining their request, the legs of the two malefactors are broken to hasten their death; but Jesus, being found already dead, is pierced with a spear in the side. At this time Joseph of Arimathea goes to Pilate, and informing him that Jesus was already dead, asks his body for burial; and Pilate, after satisfying himself that he was actually dead, orders the body to be given him. Aided by Nicodemus, Joseph took the body, and winding it in linen cloths with spices, laid it in his own sepulcher, in a garden near the cross and shut up the sepulcher. Some women beheld where he was laid, and, returning home, prepared spices and ointments, that they might embalm him after the Sabbath was past. During the Sabbath the council obtains permission from Pilate to seal up the sepulcher, and to place a watch, lest the disciples should steal the body.—*S. J. Andrews.*

OUTLINE.—1. The Women at the Sepulcher. 2. The Angel's Message. 3. The Risen Saviour.

ANALYSIS

I. THE WOMEN AT THE SEPULCHER, VS. 1-4.
   1. The Women Come with Spices. Mark 16:1; Luke 24:2.
   2. Visit to the Sepulcher Sunday Morning. Mark 16:2; Matt. 28:1; Luke 24:1; John 20:1.
   3. The Stone Rolled Away. Mark 16:4; Matt. 28:2; Luke 24:2; John 20:1.

II. THE ANGEL'S MESSAGE, VS. 5-8.
   1. The Angel in the Sepulcher. Mark 16:5; Matt. 28:2; Luke 24:4.
   2. The Angel's Message. Mark 16:6; Matt. 28:5; Luke 24:6.
   3. The Women Flee from the Sepulcher. Mark 16:8; Matt. 28.8; Luke 24:9.

III. THE RISEN SAVIOR, VS. 9-13.

1. The Lord Appears to Mary Magdalene. Mark 16:9; Matt. 28:9; John 20:14.
2. The Unbelief of the Disciples. Mark 16:11.
3. Appears to two Disciples. Mark 16:12; Luke 24:15.

INTRODUCTION

Nothing stands more historically certain than that Jesus rose from the dead and appeared again to his followers, or than that their seeing him thus again was the beginning of a higher faith, and of all their Christian work in the world. It is equally certain that they thus saw him, not as a common man, or as a shade or ghost risen from the grave; but as the Only Son of God—already more than man at once in nature and power; and that all who thus beheld him recognized at once and instinctively his unique divine dignity, and firmly believed in it henceforth. The twelve and others had, indeed, learned to look on him, even in life, as the True Messianic King and the Son of God, but from the moment of his reappearing, they recognized more clearly and fully the divine side of his nature, and saw in him the conqueror of death. Yet the two pictures of him thus fixed in their minds were in their essence identical. That former familiar appearance of the earthly Christ, and this higher vision of him, with its depth of emotion and ecstatic joy, were so inter-related that, even in the first days or weeks after his death, they could never have seen in him the Heavenly Messiah, if they had not first known him so well as the earthly.—*Ewald*.

EXPLANATORY NOTES

I. THE WOMAN AT THE SEPULCHER.

1. *When the sabbath was past.* The seventh day of the week, Saturday, the Jewish Sabbath. The first day of the week, Sunday, is never the Sabbath in the Scriptures, but the "Lord's day," or the "first day." The Sabbath ended at sunset according to Jewish ideas. Much as these women loved the Lord they waited until the Sabbath was over before they come to the sepulcher. *Mary Magdalene.* We find that Mark mentions Mary Magdalene, Mary mother of James, and Salome. Luke mentions Mary Magdalene, Mary mother of James, and Joanna, "and others with them." John mentions Mary Magdalene only. What shall we conclude from these discrepancies? Do the evangelists speak in general terms, giving the names of certain prominent members only of the party, without designing to enumerate all; or do they refer to two or more distinct parties, who visited the sepulcher at different times? The former is much the more probable. *Had bought sweet spices.* Consisting of myrrh, aloes

and other preventives of putrefaction, ond odorous perfumes. These spices had been prepared upon the previous Friday evening.—*Whedon. Anoint him.* This had not been done as yet. Nicodemus (John 19:40) had only wrapped the body hurriedly in the spices with the linen cloths. —*Alford.* It was customary among the Jews, as a mark of honor to the deceased, after washing the corpse, to anoint it with certain perfumes, or to enclose them in the grave-clothes in which the body was wrapped. They were sometimes also burned as an incense. The hurried burial had not permitted this anointing to be completed; it had been commenced by Nicodemus at the time of the interment (John 19:39, 40). Perhaps the women were ignorant of that; perhaps they wished to add their own offerings. The aromatics employed for this purpose appear from John to have been aloes and myrrh.—*Abbott.*

2. *And very early in the morning.* All the four accounts agree that the visit of the women was very early Sunday morning, about dawn. The spices had probably been gathered in the night, after the Sabbath had ended. *Came unto the sepulcher.* Salome, the wife of Zebedee, had a home in Jerusalem; Joanna, the wife of Chuza, Herod's steward, had her home doubtless in Herod's palace on Mount Zion. These and the two Marys seem to have gathered the spices in concert and to have come together.

3. *Who shall roll us away the stone?* They seem not to have known of the deputation of the Jewish rulers, which had gone to Pilate, and secured the sealing of the stone and the setting of the watch over the tomb (Matt. 27:62-66). Hence, their only anxiety was how they should get the great stone removed from the mouth of the sepulcher. Keep in mind that the tomb was not a grave, but a cavity hewn in the side of the rocky cliff, with a door that was closed with a stone.

4. *The stone was rolled away.* Matthew says that an angel came and rolled it away, and that there was an earthquake; but the grave was not opened by the commotion or earthquake, but the commotion or earthquake accompanied the rolling back of the stone. It is not necessary to suppose that the resurrection accompanied the earthquake. It was not for him, to whom (John 20:19, 20) the stone was no hindrance, but for the women and the disciples, that it was rolled away. Often the difficulties we picture before us in the path of duty are removed. "The stone is rolled away."

II. THE ANGEL'S MESSAGE.

5. *And entering into the sepulchre.* Mary Magdalene seeing the stone rolled away, and supposing the body had been removed by the Jews,

runs to find Peter and John (John 20:1, 2). The other women proceed to the sepulcher, and enter. *Saw a young man.* Matthew calls him an angel. Luke says that there were two who stood; i.e., appeared suddenly. Besides, they might easily have both sat and stood during the interview; might have been both outside and inside at different moments; and they might have been seen both singly and together in the sudden and shifting apparition.—*Jacobus. Sitting on the right side.* As they entered, apparently. He might be sitting on one of the ledges or platforms which are common in the Oriental sepulchres, and which are convenient for the accommodation of the body during the process of anointing.—*Morison. In a long white garment.* Matthew says it was white as snow, and his countenance was like lightning. The white raiment was a symbol of purity and of fellowship with God (Rev. 3:4, 5, 18; 4:4; 6:11; 7:9-13). *Affrighted.* Rather filled with awe and amazement.

6. *Ye seek Jesus of Nazareth.* "Jesus the Nazarene, the crucified," is not a mere description of the person, but a pointed allusion to his extreme humiliation, summed up in the name *Nazarene* (Matt. 2:23), and terminating in his crucifixion. *Behold the place where they laid him.* Pointing, doubtless, to the particular cell in the wall of the tomb. This implies that the angel was in the tomb.

7. *Tell his disciples and Peter.* Observe, that as Christ's first appearance is to Mary Magdalene (John 20:18), out of whom he had cast seven devils, so his special message is to Peter, who had denied him.—*Abbott.* A touching commentary on our Saviour's saying that he came to save sinners. Tell Peter, for it will be news more welcome to him than to any of them; for he is in sorrow for sin, and he will be afraid lest the joy of this good news do not belong to him.—*Matthew Henry. He goeth before you into Galilee.* Where the Lord had promised just before his death to meet his disciples after the resurrection. Indeed (Matt. 26:32) he used almost this very language in his prediction, "After I am risen, I will go before you into Galilee."

8. *Neither said they anything to any man;* i.e., on their way to tell the disciples. "For," says Dr. Wells, "they were afraid to stay, and not to hasten all they could to the apostles." They were in a tumult of commotion, and could not pause by the way to speak to any. Observe, in their haste here to tell the story of the resurrection, an illustration of the spirit which should always actuate the disciples of Christ.

III. THE RISEN SAVIOR.

9. *He appeared first to Mary Magdalene.* This appearance is described more fully in John 20:11-17. Mary Magdalene, on finding the tomb empty, went away immediately to inform Peter and John, leaving the

other women at the tomb. Soon after these had left, Peter and John arrive in haste, followed by Mary Magdalene. The disciples examine the tomb, and depart, leaving Mary near the sepulchre. While weeping there she looks in, and sees two angels, who speak with her; then, turning back, she sees Jesus himself, whom she thinks to be the gardener, for the tomb was in a garden. She recognizes him by the tone in which he speaks her name. *Out of whom he had cast seven devils.* Recorded in Luke 8:2.

10. *And she went.* While she was going to tell the disciples, Jesus appeared to the other women, who had started before on the same errand (Matt. 28:9, 10). Possibly Mary had joined the others by this time. *As they mourned and wept.* It seemed to them that not only had their Friend gone, but every hope of salvation, and of the promised coming of the kingdom of God, had departed with him.

11. *They . . . believed not.* Perhaps the fact that he had not appeared to any of the apostles had something to do with the incredulity of the latter, for it is natural to suppose that he would first manifest himself to them. Accordingly we find that it was the testimony of Peter that convinced them (Luke 24:34). In the entire remainder of the chapter Mark gives three appearances of our Saviour which illustrate the matter of the unbelief which his resurrection had to overcome in the minds of the apostles. First of all, to Mary Magdalene, whose narrative was discredited; "after that" to the two from Emmaus, whose account was also disbelieved; and "afterward" (or rather, finally, v. 14) to the whole eleven, whom he "upbraided with their unbelief."

12. *After that.* This second appearance of Jesus is more fully described in Luke 24:13. The place in the country was Emmaus, some eight miles from Jerusalem. Dr. Thomson identifies Emmaus with the present Kuriet el' Aineb, situated on the road to Joppa, on the dividing ridge between plain and mountain.

13. *Neither believed they them.* Their skepticism affords just ground for our belief. Their testimony is the testimony of incredulous and scrutinizing witnesses. They seemed to have forgotten that he said he would rise again. It was while they were discussing the story of the two disciples who had seen him at Emmaus that the Lord appeared in their midst and "upbraided their unbelief" (Luke 24:36).

FACT QUESTIONS 16:1-13

1167. Wherever Calvary was located we are sure it is not in one place —where?
1168. Who started the action in getting the bodies down from the cross before sunset? Why pierce the side of Jesus?

1169. When was the watch set at the door of the tomb?
1170. Is it ever proper to call Sunday "the Sabbath"?
1171. How shall we account for the differences in the records of the evangelists as to who came to the tomb?
1172. What was the purpose in the custom of anointing the body?
1173. It would add reality to this account if you knew the particular fragrances from each of the perfumes and ointments. Look it up in a Bible Dictionary.
1174. Who among the women lived in Jerusalem—and could thus conveniently gather the spices?
1175. What didn't the women know about the tomb? Was this providential.
1176. How was the stone rolled away? Did the earthquake accompany the resurrection?
1177. Jesus did not need the stone rolled away to rise from the dead—why, then, was it?
1178. Mary Magdalene does not go all the way to the sepulchre—where does she go?
1179. Show how the accounts of the appearing of two angels can be harmonized. How was the angel dressed?
1180. What implied the angel was in the tomb?
1181. What is "a touching commentary on our Saviour's saying that He came to save sinners"?
1182. Read Matt. 26:32 and show its connection with the words of the angel.
1183. What is meant by the expression "neither said they anything to any man"? What example is in this for us?
1184. Describe in your own words the activity of Mary at the tomb—i.e., from her first visit until Jesus appeared to her.
1185. When and where did Jesus appear to the "other women" including Mary Magdalene?
1186. The fact that Jesus did not first appear to the apostles affected the women—how?
1187. Jesus had much unbelief to overcome in the minds of His apostles—show examples.
1188. What was being discussed by the apostles when the Lord appeared to them in the upper room? (Cf. Luke 24:36.)

2. THE GREAT COMMISSION ACCORDING TO MARK 16:14-20

TEXT 16:14-20

"And afterward he was manifested unto the eleven themselves as they sat at meat; and he upbraided them with their unbelief and hardness of heart, because they believed not them which had seen him after he was risen. And he said unto them, Go ye into all the world, and preach the gospel to the whole creation. He that believeth and is baptized shall be saved; but he that disbelieveth shall be condemned. And these signs shall follow them that believe: in my name shall they cast out devils; they shall speak with new tongues; they shall take up serpents, and if they drink any deadly thing, it shall in no wise hurt them; they shall lay hands on the sick, and they shall recover. So then the Lord Jesus, after he had spoken unto them, was received up into heaven, and sat down at the right hand of God. And they went forth, and preached everywhere the Lord working with them, and confirming the word by the signs that followed. Amen."

THOUGHT QUESTIONS 16:14-20

939. Is this the first and only time Jesus appeared to the eleven apostles at a meal?
940. Give your definition of the word "upbraided".
941. Are unbelief and disbelief the same?
942. How does hardness of heart relate to unbelief? Please define "hardness of heart."
943. Please mention at least three different persons or groups of persons who had seen Him after He was raised from the dead.
944. Why was there a hesitancy in believing the report of those who had seen Him?
945. When and where did our Lord give the commission as recorded in vs. 15 and 16?
946. What is meant by the word "world" as here used—i.e., does this refer to all the world as we know it—or as the apostles knew it—or as our Lord knew it?
947. What is included in "the whole creation"?
948. Are we to understand "the gospel" to be preached is something different than "the faith" of Jude 3—or "the whole council of of God of Acts 20:27? Cf. Acts 20:25; 8:4.
949. Are we to equate "Shall be saved" in vs. 16 with "the remission of sins" in Acts 2:38; "washing away of sins" Acts 22:16; "putting on Christ" of Gal. 3:27? Discuss.
950. Is a lack of baptism included in the condemnation of 16b? Discuss. "And these signs shall accompany *them that believe*"—who is involved in *them* that believe? Please note in vs. 14 who was lacking in faith.
951. Read the following references and note who performed the signs: (1) Acts 8:7, 16:18; (2) Acts 2:4-11; (3) Acts 28:5; (4) Acts 3:7, 5:15, 9:34. What is the meaning of the word "sign"?

952. Were miracles ever performed as an end in themselves or always as a means to an end?
953. Is there a time or place in the mind of Mark as he speaks of the ascension?
954. Cf. Psa. 110:1 and show its fulfillment.
955. Show how verse nineteen seems to be a most fitting close to the gospel of Mark.
956. Verse twenty summarizes the theme of which book in the New Testament.
957. Who went forth everywhere preaching? Who used the signs of vs. 17? For what purpose? Were the signs performed without faith?

COMMENT

TIME.—Sometime after the resurrection—no definite time is indicated. PLACE.—At a meal of the apostles—no definite place indicated for vs. 19, 20.

PARALLEL ACCOUNTS.—There are no parallel accounts. There are some similar references—i.e., Luke 24:36-43; Matt. 28:16-20; I Cor. 15:6; Luke 24:47; Matt. 28:19; Acts 1:9.

OUTLINE.—1. The place of the great commission, vs. 14. 2. The great commission, vs. 15, 16. 3. The promise of signs to confirm the commission, vs. 17, 18. 4. Jesus went to heaven, the apostles went into the world accompanied by the promised signs, vs. 19, 20.

INTRODUCTION

How should we regard the last twelve verses of the gospel of Mark?

"By the revisers these verses are set by themselves with the remark, 'The two oldest Greek manuscripts, and some other authorities, omit from verse 9 to the end. Some other authorities have a different ending to the Gospel.' Doubtless the revisers would not be understood to mean that the 'different ending' was of any value. They would only cite its existence in some ancient authorities as a sign of uncertainty as to the genuineness of the present ending. The majority of modern authorities regard these verses as the work of some other person than Mark. The most elaborate defense of their genuineness is by the Rev. J. W. Burgon (*The Last Twelve Verses of St. Mark's Gospel Vindicated*). The argument in their favor may be found clearly stated in Scrivener's *Introduction to the Criticism of the New Testament* (second edition, pp. 507-513). Dr. J. A. Broadus has argued on the same side in the *Baptist Quarterly,* July, 1869. The reasons for regarding the passage as the work of another hand than that of Mark are given by Alford in his *Commen-*

tary, and by Meyer. The possible conjectures as to the history of the passage are given by Dr. Plumptre in Ellicott's *New Testament Commentary for English Readers.* It is to be noticed that the revisers do not enclose the passage in brackets as they do John 7:53-8:11, evidently regarding the argument against it as less conclusive than the one against that passage.

The reasons in favor of the passage are as follows: (1) It is contained in all the ancient manuscripts except two, and in all the versions. (2) The nineteenth verse is quoted by Irenaeus (about A.D. 170) with the introduction, "Mark says, at the end of the Gospel." From that time on the passage is freely cited by Christian writers generally, who treat it as they do other Scripture. (3) It has a place in the lectionaries, or selections of Scripture for public reading, which were in use in the Eastern Church "certainly in the fourth century, very probably much earlier" (*Scrivener*). It held a place of honor, indeed, in being taken as the Scripture for a special service at matins on Ascension Day. There is no question that the passage came down, to say the least, from very nearly the same date as the Gospel of Mark, or that it was generally, though not universally, accepted in the church as a part of that Gospel." (*W. N. Clarke*)

ANALYSIS

I. THE PLACE OF THE GREAT COMMISSION, VS. 14.
   1. After several other appearances.
   2. To the eleven as they were eating.
   3. He reproved them sharply for their lack of faith in the report of those who had seen Him after His death.

II. THE GREAT COMMISSION, VS. 15, 16.
   1. Go into all the world preaching the good news to the whole creation.
   2. He that believes the good news and is baptized shall be saved.
   3. He who disbelieves will be condemned.

III. THE PROMISE OF SIGNS TO CONFIRM THE COMMISSION, VS. 17, 18.
   1. Promised upon the basis of faith.
   2. Accomplished by the authority of Christ.
   3. Cast out demons.
   4. Speak with new languages (i.e., new to the speaker).
   5. Handle serpents without harm.
   6. Suffer no ill effects from poison.
   7. Heal the sick by the laying on of hands.

IV. JESUS WENT TO HEAVEN, THE APOSTLES WENT INTO ALL THE WORLD ACCOMPANIED BY THE PROMISED SIGNS, VS. 19, 20.

1. Jesus taken up into heaven by the power of God.
2. Sat down at the right hand of God.
3. The apostles went forth to preach everywhere.
4. The Lord worked with them confirming the truthfulness of their message by the promised signs.

EXPLANATORY NOTES

I. THE PLACE OF THE GREAT COMMISSION.

14. *as they sat at meat.*—The circumstance that the disciples "sat at meat" when Jesus appeared to them, as recorded in this verse, seems to identify this appearance with that recorded in Luke 24:36-43, at which he called for food and ate it in order to convince them that he was not a spirit. And as that appearance occurred on the evening of the first day of the week, this identifies it with that recorded in John 20:19-23.

because they believed not.—Mark has thus far mentioned only such testimony to the resurrection as had been discredited by the disciples, and it is true that to the extent of this testimony "they believed not them who had seen him after he was risen." Yet, as we learn from Luke, this discrediting of the testimony was not universal, for they did believe the testimony of Peter (Luke 24:33, 34, and comp. note on verse 13).

II. THE GREAT COMMISSION.

15. *And he said unto them.*— Here there is a silent transition from the interview on the evening after the day of the resurrection, which is the subject of verse 14, to one which occurred on the day of the ascension (verse 19), forty days later (Acts 1:3). From Mark's narrative alone we would not be able to discover this transition, but would suppose that the words of Jesus in verses 15-18 were spoken at the time of the appearance mentioned in verse 14 but this is only one among many instances in which details not essential to an understanding of the chief thought to be conveyed, are omitted from one narrative but found in another.

Go ye.—Here begins the Apostolic Commission, as given by Jesus on the day of his ascension. It had already been given, as recorded by Matthew, on the mountain in Galilee (Matt. 28:16-20), and now it is repeated in a slightly different form. It is properly called a commission, because it committed to the apostles what they had not before received, the authority to preach the gospel, and to announce the conditions of salvation. Hitherto they had been forbidden even to tell any man that Jesus was the Christ. (See Matt. 16:20; 17:9). Now their lips are unsealed, with this only limitation, that they are to tarry in Jerusalem until they are "endued with power from on high." (Luke 24:47-49; Acts 1:7,

8). Then they are to "go into all the world, and preach the gospel to every creature."

16. *He that believeth.*—That is, he that believeth the gospel (verse 15). It was to be preached in order that it might be believed, and belief, both on this account, and because it is, from the nature of the case, a prerequisite to repentance and obedience, is the first act of compliance with its demands.

and is baptized.—The collocation of the words, and the fact that baptism is an act of obedience, which could not be without faith, shows that baptism is to be preceded by faith. This commission both authorizes the apostles to baptize believers, and restricts them to believers as the subjects of baptism. No comment can make this clearer than it is made by the words of the commission itself. It is impossible, therefore, that the apostles could have found authority in their commission for baptizing infants, and it is equally impossible for modern Pedobaptists to find it (Comp. Matt. 28:19).

shall be saved.—To be saved is to be made safe. It implies that the person saved was in danger, or in actual distress, and that the danger or the distress is removed. When the term refers to the eternal state it includes the resurrection from the dead, and perpetual safety from sin and suffering. But death and all suffering are but the consequences of sin, and therefore to be made safe from sin exhausts the idea of the salvation provided in the gospel. When the term "saved" is used in reference to the state of the Christian in this world, as it frequently is (Acts 2:47; I Cor. 1:18, 15:2; Eph. 2:5; Tit. 3:5), it means that he is made safe from his past sins, which is effected by pardon and can be effected in no other way. If it be said that when a man is once saved he is saved forever, because he can not fall away, still it must be granted that the salvation affirmed of him includes the present forgiveness of his past sins. Consequently, in the statement, "He that believeth and is baptized shall be saved," the salvation promised must include at least the forgiveness of sins, whatever it may be supposed to include in addition to this. It really includes no more than this, and is equivalent to the promise of pardon to all who believe and are baptized. If any man's mind revolts at the idea of placing baptism in such a connection with salvation or the forgiveness of sins, let him remember that it is Jesus who has placed it in this connection, and that when our minds revolt at any of his words or collocation of words, it is not his fault but ours. It is always the result of some misconception on our part. If one should be tempted to say, True, he that believes and is baptized shall be saved, but he that believes and is not baptized shall also be saved, let him ask himself why Jesus in this formal commission, says, "He that believeth *and is baptized* shall be saved," if the same is true of him who is *not* baptized. Men do not, on solemn occasions, trifle with words in this way. If the Executive of a State should say to the convicted thieves in the penitentiary, He that will make a written pledge to be an honest man, and will restore fourfold what he has stolen, shall be pardoned, there is not a man in any penitentiary who would expect pardon without the restitution required; and if it were ascertained that the Executive meant by these words to promise pardon to all who would make the pledge, whether they would, being able, make the restitution or not, he would be justly chargeable with trifling, and also with offering different conditions of pardon to the same class of criminals. So in the present case. If he that is not baptized, being capable of the act, is as certainly saved as he that is baptized, the Saviour spoke idle words in the commission, and he offers two plans of pardon to the same class of sinners, showing partiality by offering to release one on easier terms than another. Such is the absurdity in which we are inevitably involved if we allow not the words in question their proper and natural force. When the apostles went out to preach under this commission, they knew only from its terms to whom they should promise pardon, and consequently they never encouraged any person to hope for it previous to baptism, nor gave any unbaptized person reason to think that his sins had already been forgiven. If any of the unbaptized, therefore, are pardoned, it is because God has granted to them more than he has promised. This he may unquestionably do, if the circumstances of individuals shall make it right in his eyes to do so, but of these circumstances He alone can judge, who knows all things and whose judgments are guided by infinite wisdom.

he that believeth not shall be damned.—The term "damned" has no more reference to the eternal state than the term "saved" in the preceding clause. They both have primary reference to the present state, and the former is the exact counterpart of the latter. The original term means "condemned," and this should be its rendering. Condemnation already rests on those who believe not (John 3:19), but the apostles are here told that it shall especially rest on those who *hear* the gospel and believe it not. It rests on them now, and it must, of course, rest on them forever unless, at some subsequent period of life, they shall become believers. In this way the state of condemnation which now exists will reach forward into eternity, unless its cause be removed, in like manner as the state of salvation enjoyed by the baptized believer will reach into eternity, unless it be forfeited by subsequent apostasy. It has frequently been observed, that though Jesus says, "He that believeth and is baptized shall be saved," he does not, in stating the ground of condemnation, mention the failure to be baptized as part of it, but simply says, "He that believeth not shall be condemned." From this it is again inferred that baptism is not one of the conditions of pardon. But the conclusion does not follow; for the fact that baptism is not mentioned in stating who shall be condemned, can never remove it from the place it occupies in stating who shall be saved. In the supposed case of the convicts above mentioned, if, after saying to all the convicted thieves, "He that will make a written pledge to be an honest man, and will restore fourfold what he has stolen, shall be pardoned," the Governor had added, "but he that will not make this pledge shall serve out his time in prison," none but a crazy thief could think that because restitution is not mentioned in the latter instance he would be pardoned without making restitution. Equally unreasonable is the conclusion in question. The leading thought in the commission is to state the ground on which men would be saved, and not that on which they would be damned. The apostles were to be concerned with saving men, not with damning them; consequently, Jesus tells them in detail on what ground they are promised salvation; but as damnation is his own work, not theirs, he speaks of that comprehensively by naming the one sin of unbelief which renders all acceptable obedience impossible, and is the chief cause of all condemnation. A man should come to the commission, then, not to learn how he may be damned, but how he may be saved; and this it teaches him right plainly.

The assertion, "He that believeth not shall be condemned," implies that all who hear can believe—that no innate or acquired incredulity can justify unbelief of the gospel. This is asserting the highest possible claim in behalf of the evidences of Christianity, and he who makes the claim is He who will judge the world at the last day. If, in the face of this declaration, any man will venture to the judgment in unbelief, alleging that the evidence is not sufficient for him, he must settle the issue with Jesus Himself."

III. THE PROMISE OF SIGNS TO CONFIRM THE COMMISSION.

"17, 18. *these signs shall follow.*— The promise is, not that these signs shall follow for any specified time, nor that they should follow each individual believer; but merely that they shall follow, and follow "the believers" taken as a body. They did follow the believers during the apostolic age—not every individual believer, but all, or nearly all, the organized bodies of the believers. This was a complete fulfillment of what was promised. He who claims that the promise included more than this, presses the words of the promise beyond what is necessary to a full realization of their meaning; and he who affirms that the signs do yet follow the believers, should present some ocular demonstration of the fact before he asks the people to believe his assertion. Signs were intended to convince the unbelievers, and they were always wrought openly in the presence of the unbelievers: let us see them, and then we will believe. Paul's expectation was that prophesying, speaking in tongues, and miraculous knowledge, would vanish away (1 Cor. 15:8); and so they did with the death of the apostles and of those to whom they had imparted miraculous gifts."

IV. JESUS WENT TO HEAVEN, THE APOSTLES WENT INTO ALL THE WORLD ACCOMPANIED BY THE PROMISED SIGNS.

"19. *after the Lord had spoken.*—The statement that "after the Lord had spoken to them he was received up into heaven, and sat on the right hand of God," establishes a close connection in time between the close of the speech and the ascension of Jesus. The same connection is indicated by Luke both in his gospel and in Acts, where, although he quotes none of the words reported by Mark, he reports a conversation quite similar to it which occurred on the same occasion and was immediately followed by the ascension. (See Luke 24:49-51; Acts 1:4-9.)

20. *And they went forth.*—In this sentence Mark overleaps the stay of the apostles in Jerusalem, and reaches forward to the period of their greatest activity, when "they went forth and preached every-where, the Lord working with them, and confirming the word with signs following." Thus he brings to a most appropriate termination his narrative of those events that had gradually prepared the apostles for the mission of mercy on which they were sent forth, and which, when recited in their preaching, led men to believe in Jesus, and to accept the offered salvation." (*J. W. McGarvey*)

SUMMARY
15:16—16:20

This closing section of Mark, like the corresponding section in Matthew, contains two proofs of the divinity of Jesus. The first is found in the darkness that covered the earth during three hours of his suffering. It is common, when we would make a comparison to indicate the impossibility of an undertaking, to say that you may as well attempt to blot the sun from the heavens. But this, God did, in effect, when the noonday sun was shining on the dying agonies of Jesus. It was accomplished by no natural eclipse, for the moon was on the opposite side of the globe (the moon was always full at the Passover); but it was done by the simple fiat of Jehovah. No stroke of His almighty hand since the sun was created has been more wonderful. It finds its only conceivable explanation in the fact that Jesus was dying. Was Jesus, then, an imposter? Or was he, what he claimed to be, the Son of God? Let a man stand, by imagination, for three hours amid that awful gloom, as did the Roman centurion, and then answer the question.

But the crowning proof in the grand series which Mark has presented, is the resurrection of Jesus from the dead. No power but God's could have raised him from the dead, and this power could not have been exerted in behalf of a pretender. That he was raised from the dead, then, is proof demonstrative that he was all that he claimed to be—the Christ, the Son of the living God.

It has sometimes been admitted, that to prove so extraordinary an event as the resurrection of one from the dead, would require most extraordinary evidence; and certainly it would in the case of any ordinary person; but in the case of Jesus, who had wrought so many miracles in proof of his divinity, who had repeatedly declared that he would arise from the dead, and who had died amid the most astounding manifestations of the divine displeasure toward his murderers, his resurrection was an event most reasonably to be expected, and it ought to be believed on the most ordinary testimony. Indeed, after having lived as he did, and having died as he did, his failure to arise from the dead would have been the most astonishing circumstances in his wonderful career. Such a life ending in the unbroken slumber of the grave, would have been an everlasting puzzle to the world. But such a life, followed by a glorious resurrection from the dead, attains a fitting consummation, and rounds out to completeness the most extraordinary personal history known in the annals of earth or heaven. The proofs of this event, furnished by Mark, are briefly these—that an angel appeared to a company of women in the empty sepulcher, and told them that Jesus had arisen; that he himself appeared alive that morning to Mary Magdalene; that he appeared the same day to two male disciples as they walked into the country; that he appeared afterward to the eleven as they sat at meat; and that, having given them a commission to preach salvation through him to every creature, he ascended up to heaven, and subsequently worked with the disciples by "signs following," as they went everywhere preaching the Gospel. Closing his testimony in the midst of a world which at the time of his writing was being filled with these last-mentioned signs, and which was still able to disprove by living witnesses all that he had written, if it were not true, he laid his pen aside, and sent forth his graphic narrative to challenge contradiction, and to do its part in the regeneration of mankind. We thank God that it has lived and come down to us; and as we pass it on to generations which shall come after us, we smile to think of the blessings it will bear to millions yet unborn, and of the undimmed radiance with which every sentence in it will shine when the sun shall have been blotted out forever, and the harvest of God shall all be gathered in. (*J. W. McGarvey*)

FACT QUESTIONS 16:14-20

1189. Why have authorities referred to the "different ending" of Mark?
1190. What authority is opposed to the genuineness of the last verses? What authority is in favor of their genuineness?
1191. Please state the three arguments in favor of the passage—are these conclusive?
1192. Show how Luke 25:36-43 and John 20:19-23 relate to Mark 16:14.
1193. In what limited sense are we to understand the phrase "they believed not"?
1194. What is the silent transition of vs. 14 to 15? On what two days do these events occur?
1195. State the two places where the great commission was given.
1196. What one limitation was involved in preparation before giving the great commission?
1197. How does the commission both authorize and restrict?
1198. It is impossible to find authority to baptize some persons—who are they?
1199. What is promised in "the salvation" of vs. 16?
1200. The understanding of some persons would involve Jesus in partiality—explain.
1201. Show how the use of the term "condemned" or "damned" has reference to the present and not the future.
1202. Indicate how unreasonable it is to conclude that baptism is not necessary for salvation because it is not necessary for condemnation.
1203. What is implied as to the ability to believe?
1204. When and how were the words "these signs shall follow" fulfilled?
1205. Do signs follow believers today? Discuss.
1206. Show the close connection of Luke 24:49-51, Acts 1:4-9, and Mark 16:19.
1207. Show how vs. 20 is an appropriate termination of Mark's narrative.

SPECIAL STUDIES

by Seth Wilson

THE RESURRECTION OF JESUS

Proclaim the good News! Tell the facts! Carry the message to all the world! Jesus has risen from the dead! This was the apostles' assignment; and to it they applied themselves as men possessed of a magnificent obsession. They knew by tremendous and triumphant experience the reality of the death and resurrection of Jesus.

Under the teaching of Jesus during his resurrection appearances, the apostles began to see the significance of these facts in the plan of God for all men. They began to feel the transforming power of this great manifestation of God's might and mercy. They felt the obligation to carry out Jesus' urgently repeated command to tell everybody these facts by which men are brought to salvation and new life and without which men have neither hope nor light in a world of darkness and death.

Far too much, we take it for granted that men do know these facts when in reality they do not. Many, many people have heard something about the resurrection of Jesus. But they think of it as a religious doctrine which some men believe. They do not actually know it as a fact. We must proclaim the resurrection of Jesus not as part of a philosophical ideal, nor as our opinion or a corollary of hopeful dreams for the future, but as certainty of what God has done in the past. Jesus has commanded us to make it known "to the whole creation." For by this knowledge men are saved through believing and obeying the risen Lord.

THE CENTRALITY OF CHRIST AND HIS RESURRECTION

Christianity is Christ! It is confidence in Jesus Christ as the divine Son of God, having all authority and absolute trustworthiness. Christianity becomes a matter of doctrines and practices simply because Jesus taught and commanded. Its doctrines are His teachings; and its practices are obedience to His commands.

Our Christian faith is faith in Christ and the divine revelation of which He is the source and center. It certainly is not a philosophy or a system of reasonings about realms beyond our experience. It is following Him wherever He leads and trusting Him for all our needs. The whole validity of Christianity and of the Bible depends upon who Jesus is — upon His personal merit and power.

Because He put His stamp of approval upon the Old Testament, and said that it could not be broken (John 10:35) and that none of it shall pass away until all be fulfilled (Matt. 5:18; Luke 24:44), therefore we believe that the Old Testament scriptures are inspired, authoritative and divinely dependable. Because Jesus promised to give to the apostles the Holy Spirit to guide them into all truth as well as to remember all that He taught them (John 14:26; 16:12-14), we believe that the New Testament scriptures are inspired of God and possessed of divine accuracy and authority.

The evidence that Jesus is the Son of God is shown:

1. in many O.T. Phophecies (e.g. Isaiah 9:6; Micah 5:2-4; Psalm 110:1; 45:6, 7; etc.)
2. in His supernatural birth;
3. in the direct testimony of angels (Luke 1:30-35);
4. in the witness of John the Baptist (John 1:33, 34);
5. in the confession of demons (Mark 5:6, 7);
6. in the testimony of the voice of God at His baptism and on the Mount (Matt. 3:16, 17 and 17:5);
7. in Jesus' sinless life, in which all His deeds and motives were of God;
8. in His superhuman wisdom and insight into the nature and needs of men;
9. in His miraculous works, showing both the power and the merciful character of God;
10. in His persistent and positive claims to be one with God (See Matt. 11:27; 28:18; Mark 2:10; Luke 22:69-71; John 8:58; 10:30; 14:6-11; etc.).

But the death and resurrection of Jesus are the facts that reveal most clearly and conclusively His person and character, as well as His purpose and His ministry to us.

In the New Testament the resurrection is made the chief evidence upon which faith in Christ is to be based. It is the fitting climax of every account of His life. The key-note of Peter's sermon on the day of Pentecost was: "This Jesus hath God raised up, whereof we are all witnesses" (Acts 2:24-32). "With great power gave the apostles their witness of the resurrection of the Lord Jesus" (Acts 4:33). It was the major item of testimony in all their preaching (See Acts 3:15; 4:2; 5:31, 32; 10:41-42; 13:30-37; 17:31, 32; 26:8, 23; Romans 1:4; I Cor. 15:1-18). It is continually emphasized in the epistles as the basis of our faith and hope, and as a motive to holy living (See Rom. 6:4-11; 8:34; I Cor. 15:58; Eph. 1:19-23; Phil. 2:9-11; Col. 2:12; 3:1-4; I Thess. 4:14; I Peter 1:3-7; Heb. 13:20, 21).

Jesus Himself often predicted His own resurrection and considered it the greatest sign of His authority and truthfulness (See Matt. 12:38-40; 16:21; 17:9, 23; 20:19; John 2:19-21; 10:17, 18). His enemies noticed His predictions of His resurrection and even the time that He set for it (See Matt. 27:63). In their blindness they tried to stop the power of God with military might and the authority of a Roman seal. They only provided circumstances that contributed to the proof of the resurrection.

The guard they placed to watch the tomb stands guard today against false objections and foolish doubts that would try to explain away the empty tomb.

Many people who are misled by scientific talk of unvarying uniformity in nature, and who therefore doubt miracles, speak in glowing praise of Jesus' teachings. But they overlook the fact that Jesus' teaching was much more than a set of rules for conduct. He taught much about the life to come and insisted that faith in Him is the only way to life. He taught men to put their trust in Him because of His works which demonstrated that the power of God was with Him. He emphasized the importance of the resurrection as the sign of His authority and dependability. There is no honest or intelligent way to separate something called "Jesus' Teachings" from His words recorded in the New Testament which emphasize repeatedly the supreme importance of every man's definite commitment of self to Him by faith and obedience to His authority (See Matt. 7:21-27; 10:32-38; 11:27; 12:30-42; 16:15-28; 21:37-45; 22:41-46; 26:63, 64; 28:18-20; John 3:36—as properly translated in most versions: "He who doth not obey"—; 5:22-29; 6:29, 53-57; 8:24; 10:24-30; 12:46-48).

Confession of Christ and belief in the resurrection go together to obtain salvation: "Because if thou shalt confess with thy mouth Jesus as Lord, and thou shalt believe in thy heart that God raised him from the dead, thou shalt be saved" (Rom. 10:9). Denying the resurrection of Christ is the same as denying His authority and power to save: "If Christ hath not been raised, your faith is in vain; ye are yet in your sins" (I Cor. 15:17).

DIRECT EVIDENCE FOR THE RESURRECTION

The resurrection of Jesus is not a matter of hope for what will happen, or a faith in what should happen, but knowledge of what did happen. It is not a compelling feeling, or reasonable philosophy, but it is a fact. If the events of the past recorded as history can be known, then we know that Jesus arose from the dead.

The chief proof of the resurrection is *Testimony*. The testimony for Jesus' resurrection is the kind that all experience proves to be reliable—the kind that is acceptable to establish the truth in any court or in any matter of history.

The witnesses are *sufficient in number* — eleven apostles, five or six women (at least), some other disciples, James, Paul, and more than five hundred at one time. These saw Jesus alive after His death again and again, singly and in groups, indoors and outdoors, by day and by night. All were brought to one conviction. Their united, active witnessing and their convincing testimony produced thousands of believers within a few days in the very city where it happened, less than two months after Jesus was in the tomb. The testimony of some of them and the experience of all of them is recorded by at least six writers in different accounts that show all the variations of independent testimonies and all the harmony of truth.

The witnesses were *competent* — men of intelligence (read their classic writings); of mental balance before and after; well prepared by long and intimate acquaintance with Jesus; of a mental attitude requiring proof; having personal interest in knowing the certainty of these things. They, at least the leading ones, repeatedly saw the risen Christ and listened to extensive teaching from Him, walked and talked with Him, touched Him, and saw Him eat in their presence, discussed His death and resurrection and plans for the future.

> "To whom also he showed himself alive after his passion by many proofs, appearing unto them by the space of forty days, and speaking the things concerning the kingdom of God" (Acts 1:3).

They even saw Him ascend into heaven. There was no mistaking His identity. They told of such detailed experience with Him. The circumstantial details of their accounts show that they were not trying to tell of an inner conviction but of real physical experiences. This destroys the supposition that they could have been honestly mistaken. If Jesus did not actually arise and appear as they said, then they knew their testimony was false.

But they were *honest* men. They had been trained in righteousness, in both reverent fear and loving devotion toward the God of truth. Their lives show no tendency to dishonesty. Their teachings and their examples have had the greatest power in the world to make other men honest. They had nothing to gain by spreading a false report; but rather suffered much affliction and even death for their witnessing. Some men might die for what they believed and be mistaken. No such group of men will devote years of life and accept death for what they know to be false. But these apostles lived and died for what they knew to be true; if it had been false they most surely would have known that it was.

But there was other testimony, of unusual quality and force, to support the testimony of the eye-witnesses. The *prophecies of the Old Testament testify* of the coming of this unique event in the life of the promised Messiah (Psalm 16:10; Isaiah 53:10-12). As we have noted above, Jesus Himself predicted it, and it cannot be destroyed without destroying His integrity.

The testimony of the New Testament has been subjected to centuries of unfriendly criticism and scrutiny. Many objections have been made to various details; but no one has been able to deny that the apostles and the *early church honestly and firmly believed that Jesus* arose bodily from the grave. And no one has ever given a satisfactory explanation of how this firm and persistent belief could have arisen without the reality of the resurrection. Surely no one can deny that the church came into existence and Christianity became a force in the world, beginning with and growing because of the firm conviction and the convincing testimony of the resurrection.

The resurrection is confirmed by the *Holy Spirit,* who came upon the apostles as Jesus had promised (Luke 24:49; John 15:26; 16:7-14; Acts 1:5, 8), and who bore witness with them concerning the resurrection (Acts 2:33; 5:32).

The testimony is confirmed by *perpetual observances* which are based upon the fact of the resurrection. The form of baptism pictures both Christ's burial and resurrection, and their significance in our lives. The practice of worship on the first day of the week instead of the seventh, and that in a church which was at first Jewish, explicitly and pointedly commemorates both the resurrection of Jesus and its importance in their sight.

The resurrection of Jesus Christ from the dead is a fact made known to us by such an array of testimony and effects that it is more than what is usually called faith. Conviction based on testimony of facts frequently reaches the point at which it is called knowledge; for we speak of knowing many things that happened in the past which are made known to us through testimony and effects. The resurrection of Jesus is a matter of knowledge as much as any other fact in history is a matter of knowledge. At least, it is surely clear that to the eleven apostles the resurrection was not merely a belief, but knowledge of the greatest possible certainty. To us it is not only a part of the doctrine of Christ; but a proof of the authority of all His doctrine—not so much a belief, but a firm basis for faith in Him and hope of that which He has promised.

CONSIDER WHO IT WAS THAT AROSE!

The resurrection of Jesus was not merely an unexplained appearance of some unknown or ordinary man from the grave. His resurrection was in perfect harmony with His manner of life, His unique birth, His unparalleled works, His distinctive death, and with the prophecies that prepared the way for Him. The resurrection of Jesus is made both more readily believable and much more meaningful when we consider the following facts:

1. He fulfilled the promises and predictions of the prophets; His resurrection is a victory for revealed truth.

2. He is the One who lived in perfect righteousness; He arose as victor over great powers of wickedness.

3. He was the One who had raised others and promised to raise all men; His resurrection gives assurance that He still gives life to whom He will.

4. He is the One who predicted His own resurrection and claimed to speak the truth; it is proof that His words are infallibly true and all His claims are valid.

5. His death was declared to be an offering for our sins (Matt. 20:28; 26:28). His resurrection is our own victory over sin and death if we join our lives with His. His rising proves that His death was adequate and acceptable for our redemption.

6. He is the One who said that all judgment was given unto Him and who read men's hearts with unerring accuracy. His resurrection is positive proof that we all shall stand before Him to be confessed by Him or to be condemned by Him.

We might be interested in what Lazarus would tell of his experience in four days of death and in living again, but we could not have much assurance that Lazarus could deliver the rest of us from death and all its terrors. We should indeed be students of everything Jesus has to say; for He is the author of a divine covenant by which we all may have eternal life, and He is the judge to whom we all must give account.

We can be sure that Jesus is the Lord of life and death. Let us serve Him with glad assurance that our labor is not in vain in the Lord.

Let every man acknowledge Him as Lord—*admit* who He is, *submit* to His commands and the control of His Spirit, and joyfully *commit* to His keeping all that we are or hope to be.

We must either acknowledge and serve Him as our Lord here on earth, or confess Him as Lord hereafter to our everlasting shame and condemnation (Philippians 2:9-11).

WHAT THE KINGDOM IS LIKE

The chief emphasis in the preaching of John the Baptist was that the kingdom of God was close at hand and men should prepare to meet the King (Matthew 3:2-12). Then Jesus and His disciples went throughout the land teaching as if the chief aim in anyone's life was to enter into the kingdom (See John 3:3, 5; Matthew 4:17, 23; 5:3, 10, 20; 6:10, 33; 7:21; Luke 4:43; 7:28; 8:1).

Jesus had preached in Judea about eight months (until He was leading more to baptism than John was—John 4:1-3). After that, He had preached in Galilee at least eight months or more. About half of His entire ministry was past. Many miracles had been wrought. Great throngs of people were following Him, so that He had not time to eat and sleep. Some of the Pharisees were trying desperately to combat His popular influence. His family sought to take Him home for a rest. That was the time when Jesus taught the sermon all in parables about the kingdom (just before He left on a boat trip during which He was so tired that He slept right through a terrible storm).

The people were excited about the kingdom message, but they did not understand it. The Jews expected a kingdom of military power and material wealth. They were not listening well to Jesus' teaching about true religion and obedience to God. When Jesus taught them about the kingdom of God, they did not understand or even realize that He was talking about it. They thought of the kingdom as a form of national power, a relationship between their own nation and other nations. But Jesus thought of it as a relationship between each individual and God. They thought of it as the possession of material security and power to rule over others; but He spoke of it as the possession of God's word and as submission to God's rule over one's own life.

To help them overcome their habitual, mistaken ideas of the promised kingdom and to show how near it was to each of them, Jesus told these simple illustrations, which were called in Greek, "parables." Jesus is famous for His parables on various subjects. Some notable ones had been told before the time recorded in Matthew 13. But on this occasion He spoke nothing but parables! An immense crowd was gathered on the shore of Galilee, so that Jesus got into a boat in order to speak to them all. He taught "many things in parables," perhaps more than are recorded in the combined accounts of Matthew 13:1-53; Mark 4:1-34; and Luke 8:4-18. But all that are recorded are comparisons to describe and identify the kingdom. Instead of defining or explaining the kingdom in abstract terms, Jesus pictured it in concrete comparisons. They were pictures to show the characteristics of the kingdom which the Jews had not seen or had never expected it to have.

Jesus was asked by His disciples why He spoke only in parables to this crowd. He said it was because the crowd did not know the secrets which He had been revealing about the kingdom, as the apostles knew them. The "mysteries" of the kingdom meant simply the things about it that were revealed and which could not be known unless they were learned by revelation. Jesus had been revealing them in His teaching, but the people did not give as much attention or have as much faith as the apostles did, and their old mistaken notions were very much in the way. Even in this sermon, if He spoke in plain terms about the kingdom without parables, they would not perceive what He meant.

No doubt the picture stories which He used left many of the people wondering and unconvinced; but they also left them with some clear and easily remembered pictures to refer to frequently until their minds were able to accept the truths of the kingdom to which they pointed.

We are helped in understanding the parables by the explanations which Jesus gave of two of the most complex ones to His disciples that very day. His interpretations of the soils and the tares give us a guide to the meaning of all the parables. The interpretation is also helped by the fact that two or more parables point to the same feature of the kingdom. Two or three illustrations of the same thing make one more sure of the point of each illustration.

LIKE THE PRODUCT OF SEED GROWING IN SOIL

The first parable shows that the kingdom is like the results obtained when seed is sown on various kinds of soil. In explaining this one, Jesus said, "The seed is the word of God" (Luke 8:11).

Some hearers of the word are like the soil of the beaten path, not receptive to the word, and Satan takes it away from their consciousness, as birds eat the seed off the roadway.

A second class of hearers is like the thin soil over a slab of rock. The word gets from them an immediate response. They make a good start in letting the word of God live in them. But when trials and hardships come because of the word, their citizenship in the kingdom immediately withers away. They are not the stable kind of people who endure steadfast in what they know is right, but are like plants without roots deep enough to endure when the sun is hot.

A third kind of hearer includes those who have too much else occupying their minds and affections. They are like good soil with the seeds or roots of thorns in it. The word is received, but the cares of this world and the enticements of riches soon outgrow the desire to do God's will. The Lord's control is choked out by other controlling interests as wheat is choked out by Johnson grass.

The fourth class of hearers is like the good soil that bears much fruit. They hear the word of the Lord, understand it, and hold it fast in a good and honest heart (See Luke 8:15), hence they bring forth the fruit of living faithfully according to the will of God.

Another short parable, which is recorded only in Mark 4:26-29, says that the kingdom is like the growing of seed in the ground. The sower, having sown the seed does no more work on it, and does not know how it grows. But the earth produces of itself, first the blade, then the ear (or head of wheat), then the full grain in the ear. So the kingdom does not come like a finished product delivered from the factory, or like ruling power is seized in a revolution, but it grows by the effect of God's word in each person's mind and heart.

LIKE WHEAT IN A FIELD WITH WEEDS

Again (in Matthew 13:24-30) the kingdom is pictured as good seed growing in a field, but an enemy has sown tares (weeds that look like wheat) in the same field. Some servants suggest pulling out the weeds. But the owner said that wheat might be pulled up with them, therefore both would be allowed to grow together until the harvest, when they would be separated and the weeds would be burned.

Jesus explained this parable, being asked by His disciples, so we do not have to guess at its meaning. The field is the world. The good seed, or the plants that grow from it, represent the people of His kingdom, planted in the world by Christ. The devil is the enemy that sowed the tares, which are the people who serve the devil. Jesus did not say who the servants were that suggested pulling the weeds; perhaps they might be men who propose to serve God by killing off wicked men. But in the harvest, which comes at the end of this age, the reapers will be the angels, who will gather all the wicked to be burned. Notice that He said they will be gathered "out of His kingdom"! He had said before that "the field is the world" and the plants from the good seed are the sons of the kingdom. Either this views the whole world as the realm of His rule, potentially His kingdom, or the angels are to gather some wicked ones from among those who were the kingdom.

Then the righteous shall shine as the sun *in the kingdom* of their Father, when the kingdom apparently will be free from all offenses and evils.

LIKE A NET FULL OF FISH, GOOD AND BAD

Another parable pairs with the one about the tares to picture the fact that some unacceptable persons are to be sorted out of the kingdom at the end of the age. In this one the kingdom is compared to a dragnet gathering all kinds of fish. It is brought to shore, and the bad ones are thrown out, which represents the work of angels at the end of this age, separating the wicked from the just and casting then into fire (Matthew 13:49, 50).

The parables reviewed thus far show that the kingdom is not national and material, but spiritual and individual; also that it is not all glory and success, but some people start in it and fail, some are cast out at last, and others are unaffected by it though in contact with it. These comparisons indicate that the kingdom is not a time when the Lord forces His rule upon all, but those who accept His word yield to His rule and are the kingdom while they live on this earth in the midst of the ungodly.

LIKE THE BEST KIND OF GROWERS

Jesus said the kingdom is like a seed of mustard and like leaven. Both of these picture its growth. The mustard seed, though very small, produces a large plant, sometimes fifteen feet high, in one year. The leaven may not look like much alive and may be only a little bit hidden in a large batch of meal, but quietly and unnoticed it multiplies itself. Thus Jesus' kingdom, beginning with twelve humble men (or even 120, or 500) looked insignificant, but by a spiritual vitality put into it by the Lord it had power to grow and encompass the earth.

The parables were not intended to be prophecies, but illustrations. The parable of the leaven represents the growth of the kingdom without noise or show, by transfer of transforming faith from one person to another; it probably does not predict the complete transformation of the world by the growth of the church or (as some say who consider leaven always a symbol of evil) the complete corruption of the church by evil growing in it. There are predictive elements in Matthew 13:41-43 and 49, 50, but these are subordinate parts of comparisons which describe the nature of the kingdom in pictures rather than telling the high points of its history in predictions.

LIKE THE MOST PRECIOUS THING KNOWN

Two other parables picture the kingdom as having greater value than everything else combined that any man can have.

It is like a treasure lying hidden in a field. Whoever finds it will joyfully sell all he has to buy that field.

It is like one priceless pearl so precious that the owner of a great collection of prize gems will give all that he has to buy it.

Whether to the poor laborer, working in another man's field, or to the rich merchant admiring his collection of jewels, to everyone the kingdom of God is the opportunity of a lifetime. Perhaps by this we should test the reality of our faith in Christ's words:—Are we eager to sell all else to have Him rule in our lives? And how great is our joy at the opportunity to make the transaction?

TREASURES OF THE KINGDOM

"The kingdom of heaven is like unto a treasure hidden in the field; which a man found, and hid; and in his joy he goeth and selleth all that he hath, and buyeth that field.

Again, the kingdom of heaven is like unto a man that is a merchant seeking goodly pearls: and having found one pearl of great price, he went and sold all that he had, and bought it." (Matthew 13:44-46)

Of all the precious things that the thoughtless crowd casts aside or ignores as valueless, none is so greatly and so generally underestimated as the kingdom of Christ. Not only the majority of Americans, who take no active part in any church, prefer a mess of pottage to their birthright in Christ; but a large percentage of church members cannot tell what Christ means to them. Indeed their lives testify that He means less to them than many mundane things. How does it go in your personal market? Are you selling everything else to buy Him? And—(don't answer out loud)—how great is your joy at the opportunity to make the transaction?

Jesus told two parables to emphasize the fact that whether to the poor laborer, working another man's field, or to the rich merchant, admiring his great collection of prize gems, to everyone the kingdom of heaven is the opportunity of a lifetime — literally! No man has so many worthy attainments and personal powers, such great wealth, such varied and important interests that he should regret losing every one of them to be a humble disciple of Jesus. It is easier for the poor and oppressed to realize that in coming to Christ they have nothing to lose and everything to gain. The rich and self-righteous, the proud and powerful are very hard to bring to that realization. Even when they see value in Christ their hearts are often "joined to their idols." "How hard it is for them that trust in riches" (Mark 10:24) "How can you believe, who receive glory one of another, and the glory that cometh from the only God ye seek not" (John 5:44). Those who are wise in their own conceits have these things "hid from them" (Matthew 11:25). Compare I Corinthians 1:26-31. Still it *is* true that *any man* giving up all to have Christ has *nothing to lose and everything to gain!*

In Philippians 3:4-14 Paul tells of his own experience as a "merchant seeking goodly pearls." Compared with others he had made a good showing of things gained outside of Christ, but he counted them all loss to gain Christ. He actually suffered the loss of all things but counted them mere rubbish compared with the excellency of Christ.

LET'S TAKE AN INVENTORY

What are the treasures that the Saviour sets above the sum of all that the best-favored life can assemble? What is the preciousness that so satisfies the great apostle and makes all his former attainments as rubbish? It is evident that many of us do not value the kingdom as Jesus and Paul did. Surely we have not known what riches abound there. Jesus spoke as if any man in his right mind would joyously part with everything he had to get that supreme treasure as soon as he saw it. Paul and many others did just that. But today people are putting off accepting Christ, and are afraid to part with anything to gain Him.

What makes Christianity precious? One thing—it cost an infinite price: time and sacrifices, life and blood, heartaches and struggles of men and God. Nothing else in history compares with it. Another thing—it is rare, the only thing of its kind and nothing else approaches it or can substitute for it. But Jesus was thinking of its value to us for what we may find in it and receive from it.

It is possible to expect the wrong thing and, being disappointed, to turn away and lose all. The crowd that Jesus fed miraculously tried to turn His beneficent powers to political and material purposes. They would take Him by force and make Him their king to satisfy their own ambitions and desires, but Jesus would not consent. (John 6:15). Then Jesus, the following day, rebuked them for seeking the bread that perishes and tried to give them the Bread of Everlasting Life, but they had expected the wrong thing and when they found it not they forsook Him (John 6:26-66). Paul writes of those, "corrupted in mind and bereft of the truth, supposing that godliness is a way of gain" (I Timothy 6:5). So do not follow those false prophets abroad today who promise all the material things you want if you buy their religio-psychology course. But Paul did go on to say: "But godliness with contentment is great gain: for we brought nothing into the world, for neither can we carry anything out; but having food and covering we shall be therewith content" (I Timothy 6:6-8). In the same letter he said: "Godliness is profitable for all things, having promise of the life which now is and of that which is to come" (I Timothy 4:8).

FOR THE LIFE THAT NOW IS:

(Note: Do read the scriptures cited. Look into the catalogue of the products of God's love with at least as much interest as you look at Montgomery Ward's catalogue of products of American industry. This is merely an index held to a minimum of space.) We should expect and find:

1. Justification, the burden of sin removed, conscience relieved (Romans 8:1, 33, 34; I Corinthians 6:11; Hebrews 10:19-23)
2. The burdens we bear (e.g., responsibility) lightened by love and by the strengthening the Lord gives (Philippians 4:13; II Timothy 4:17; II Corinthians 12:9).
3. A sure and steadfast hope (Hebrews 6:17-20).
4. Peace (Romans 5:1; John 14:27; Philippians 4:9), freedom from anxiety, fear and despair (Philippians 4:6; Matthew 6:33).
5. Self-mastery, Christ dwelling in us (Galatians 5:16; Ephesians 3:14-19; James 1:2-4; Galatians 2:20).

6. True liberty (Galatians 5:13; John 8:32, 36).
7. The unshaken life (Matthew 7:25; Romans 8:37-39; Hebrews 12:28; I Corinthians 15:28; Philippians 4:12).
8. The best of human fellowship, refinement of every social relationship (Colossians 3:8—4:16).
9. Comfort (II Corinthians 1:3-5; I Thessalonians 4:18).
10. Increasing joy and satisfaction out of life (Philippians 4:4; Galatians 5:22).
11. Partaking of the divine nature, its beauty and poise, its radiant righteousness (II Peter 1:3, 4); chastisement (Hebrews 12:5-11); correction, instruction (II Timothy 3:16, 17); improvement—the discipline of a loving Father, building us up to a wonderful and beautiful ideal (Ephesians 4:13).

FOR THE LIFE THAT IS TO COME:

1. Eternal life (I John 5:11, 12).
2. Transformation (Philippians 3:20, 21; I Corinthians 15:50-54).
3. Being with the Lord (John 14:3; II Corinthians 5:8). Divine fellowship unhindered.
4. Being like the Lord (I John 3:1, 2).
5. Joint-heirs with Christ, Heir of all things (Romans 8:17).
6. Divine power's sure victory (Galatians 6:9; II Timothy 2:12).
7. Rest (Matthew 11:28; Hebrews 4:9-11).
8. New heavens and new earth, wherein dwelleth righteousness (II Peter 3:14).
9. The glory of God and of the children of God (Romans 5:2; 8:18-20; II Timothy 2:10; II Corinthians 4:17; I Peter 5:10; Revelation 21:11).
10. A kingdom that cannot be shaken (Hebrews 12:28).

REFLECTIONS

These treasures are chiefly personal. "I am thy shield and thy exceeding great reward." (Genesis 15:1). They are not in things, but in the realm of spirit and persons. Therefore they are not seen and appreciated by the profane eye of Esaus. Even the practical providence is the Lord's personal care. He is able to provide for all out of little or nothing. The feeding of the multitudes, miraculously, demonstrates Jesus' teaching that God knows our needs and cares about them. He will add all these things if we seek first the kingdom (Matthew 6:33; Philippians 4:19). To have the Lord is to have everything! "The Lord is my shepherd; that's all I want," said the little girl who had the words mixed, but the idea exactly right. We may have Him who makes "all things work together for good" (Romans 8:28) and who is "able to do exceeding abundantly above all we ask or think" (Ephesians 3:20). His best gifts to us are what He creates in us personally, not material stores.

Cleansing! *Righteousness!* Priceless goal of the awakened soul! We who know not the curse and shame and defilement of sin do not appreciate the cleansing from sin. We who believe not the written sentence of doom and damnation upon sinners care not for deliverance. We are so prone to have such low standards, such trashy ideals, as to be satisfied with a little self-righteous respectability of works of the flesh, even in pride; but Paul sought not a righteousness of his own, of law and flesh, but sold everything to gain the righteousness of God, given by faith in Christ through His blood.

"He is so precious to me!" In a burning building a fire escape is the most precious thing—no matter if the crown jewels of Russia and England combined be there. Dear brother, are you ashamed of this phase of our precious faith?

It is desirable to be healthy, wealthy and wise. These proverbial prizes are the object of most of men's daily efforts. In Christ we have: *wisdom* exceeding the greatest education; *security* exceeding the greatest wealth, the *"unspeakable riches"* administered for us now by a loving Father and reserved for us unto the day of inheritance; *health* of mind and soul, rightly affecting the body, renewing within though the outward man decay, lasting beyond the putting off of the flesh.

The greatest treasures are yet to come. We "who have the first-fruits of the Spirit . . . groan . . . waiting for our adoption, to wit, the redemption of our body. For in hope were we saved" (Romans 8:18-25). "If we have only hoped in Christ in this life we are of all men most pitiable" (I Corinthians 15:19). "In due season we shall reap, if we faint not" (Galatians 6:9). "In the world ye shall have tribulation" (John 16:33). The whole New Testament emphasizes that we are to invest this life in securing that one which is final and eternal. The blessings of God we receive here are to prepare us for and to lead us to that limitless blessedness there. "A tent or a cottage, why should I care? They're building a palace for me over there."

WHAT DOES CHRIST MEAN TO US?

Are we living up to the privileges of the Kingdom? A man paid for first class passage on a steamship and took along a lot of cheese and crackers to eat for the whole trip. One day another passenger too sick to eat found him off by himself eating his cheese and crackers. "If you can eat, why don't you go eat that fine fare they are serving in the ship's dining room?" He answered, "The ticket for this trip cost so much I couldn't afford to eat that kind of meals." "Man, you paid for it in your ticket. You are not getting all that's coming to you."

Are we continually living such rejoicing, thankful, and victorious lives that other people may see how valuable Christ is to us and desire what they see that we have?

OUTLINE OF MATTHEW 24:1-51 (Cf. Mark 13 and Luke 21)

I. vv. *1-3*—THE OCCASION AND THE QUESTIONS. (Mk. 13:1-4; Lk. 21:5-7).

1. Observing the magnificent buildings of Jerusalem. v. 1.
2. Jesus' dire prediction: "There shall not be left here one stone upon another, that shall not be thrown down." v. 2.
3. The disciples' questions:
   (1) *"When shall these things be?"* (Destruction of Jerusalem).
   (2) *"What shall be the sign of thy coming,* and of the end of the world?" v. 3.

II. vv. *4-31*—ANSWERS TO THE QUESTIONS.

1. *Answers to first questions,* concerning Jerusalem. (Matthew 24:4-28; Mark 13:5-23; Luke 21:8-24).
   a. Warning of preliminary troubles—"the beginning of travail." (4-14; 5:13; 8-19).
      (1) False Christs, wars, rumors of wars, famines and earthquakes do not indicate the end: be not troubled.
      (2) Persecutions, apostasies, false prophets, shall afflict the church: "take heed to yourselves"; endure to the end; trust God for help; the gospel testimony shall go into all the world. (9:13-14; 12-19) cf. Col. 1:6, 23; Rom. 1:8; 10:18; 16:19.
   b. The sign of Jerusalem's end, and how to escape the woes of that terrible time. (15-28; 14-23; 20-24).
      (1) "The abomination of desolation standing in a holy place" is "Jerusalem compassed with armies"; "then know that her desolation is at hand."
      (2) Let those in Judea flee to the mountains without delay. Pray that the hardships of flight may be lessened; but the unprecedented afflictions of the city must be escaped at all costs. Believe no false prophets, signs or promises; I have forewarned you; the Christ will not return at this time, or at any time without being seen from east to west.
      (3) The tribulation shall be excessive, shall threaten extinction of the Jewish people, shall take them captive to other nations, shall leave Jerusalem to the Gentiles, "until the times of the Gentiles be fulfilled."
2. Answer to the second question, concerning Christ's coming. (29-31; 24-27; 25-28)
   a. The time is purposely indefinite; but the event is to be watched for at all times ("immediately"—Matt. 24:29), after a terrible and extended (see Luke 21:24) tribulation.

b. The event itself shall be unmistakable; accompanied by tremendous sights and sounds in all earth and heaven, the Lord Himself shall be seen by everyone, coming in the clouds with power and great glory.

c. The angels shall gather the elect from everywhere: look up, your redemption draws near. (31; 27; 28)

III. vv. *32-36*—THE ANSWERS REVIEWED IN CONTRASTING SUMMARY.

1. Parable of the fig tree: signs are easily recognized. Watch for *all these things*—wars, persecutions, false Messiahs, the desolation of Jerusalem, and great tribulation, to come to pass in this generation. (32-34; 28:30; 29:32).
2. Solemn affirmation of unfailing certainty of His words. (35; 31; 33).
3. But of *that day,* Jesus' coming, no one knows. The time cannot be told, even by the Son of God. (Matt. 24:36; Mark 13:32).

IV. vv. *37-51*—PARABLES AND EXHORTATIONS TO BE READY AT ALL TIMES.

1. As in the days of Noah the flood came suddenly upon those who had been warned but believed not, so shall the coming of the Son of man be without any immediate forewarning signs. (Matt. 24:37-39).
2. In the midst of daily work, suddenly one shall be taken and another left; *watch* for you know not the day. (Matt. 24:40-42; cf. v. 31; I Thess. 4:16, 17; I Cor. 15:52.)
3. Parable of a householder unprepared for a thief who came when he was not expected. Be ready, for when you think not, the Son of man comes. (43, 44)
4. The servants of the absent Lord have each one his own work (Mark 13:34) to be faithful until He comes. He may not come as soon as they imagine; but if they think that He tarries and they can take advantage of His delay to indulge in sin, He will come when they least expect it and will punish them. (45-51; 33-37; 34-36). *"Watch at every season"*—Luke 21:36.

(Christ continued the same lessons in the 25th chapter—1. in the parable of the ten virgins waiting for the bridegroom, 2. in the parable of the talents committed to servants until the Lord's return, and 3. in the scene of judgment that shall take place when the Son of man shall come in His glory.

(In these additional prophetic pictures, He emphasizes that the servants must be prepared to wait patiently and to serve faithfully even though the Master may not come for "a long time" (see v. 19); also that His coming will bring strict judgment and swift vengeance upon all who have not used the intervening time in His service.)

NOTES ON DEMON POSSESSION

One of the four following conclusions must be true concerning the reality of demons as mentioned in the Gospel accounts. No other is possible, and only one of these can be true.

Either, 1, Jesus did cast out real demons as represented;

or, 2, Jesus did no such things but the accounts are entirely false;

or, 3, Jesus did go through the motions and the pretense of casting them out, while He knew there were no real demons;

or, 4, Jesus was as ignorant and superstitious on this subject as the people and honestly thought He cast out spirits in healing sickness.

Which of these views fits the facts and the testimony? The true meaning of a word or an expression may be put into its place in any account; and the definition will fit as well as the word it defines. Just read the accounts of Jesus' intelligent conversations with demons, supplying the word "disease" as the explanation for the word "demon."

I. MEANINGS OF THE WORD "DEMON."

1. Not the same as "devil." There is only one devil but many demons.
2. Oldest meaning: divine power, deity. Homer (c. 850 B.C.) used it interchangeably with (God). Cf. Josephus, *wars,* 1, 2, 8. Acts 17:18. See A. Campbell in *Popular Lectures and Addresses,* pp. 379-397, for older uses.
3. A being between man and God. Plato attempted to fix this definition. Used in both good and bad sense. Plato held that they included departed spirits of good men. Socrates spoke constantly of his "demon." Ignatius (*Epistle to Smyrna* 3, 2) says that Jesus told His disciples after the resurrection, "I am not a disembodied demon." This shows his way of expressing what Luke 24:37-39 says. Cf. also Luke 4:33, "spirit of an unclean demon."
4. Elsewhere in the N. T. demons are always evil spirits, messengers and ministers of Satan.
   a. Heathen deities, Acts 17:18; I Cor. 10:20; Rev. 9:20.
   b. Ones who believe and tremble (or bristle) but are lost, James 2:19.
   c. They recognize Jesus as Son of God, Matt. 8:29; Mark 1:23, 24, 34; 3:11; Luke 4:41.
   d. Agents of Satan, Matt. 12:24-26; Luke 10:17, 18; 11:15-22.

II. EVIDENCES THAT THEY ARE IMMATERIAL, INTELLIGENT BEINGS, NOT TO BE CONFUSED WITH DISEASES OR FIGURES OF SPEECH.

1. The O. T. legislation proceeded upon the assumption that there is such a thing as a "familiar spirit." Lev. 19:31; Deut. 18:9-14.
2. In the N. T. they are regarded as personalities. e.g. James 2:19, believing Rev. 16:14, working signs. Jesus founded a parable on their conduct, Luke 11:24-26.
3. Jesus distinguished between them and diseases. So did His disciples. Matt. 10:8; Luke 10:17-20.
4. Jesus addressed them as persons and they answered as such, Mark 5:8; 9:25.
5. They manifested desires and passions, Mark 5:12, 13.
6. They showed superhuman knowledge of Jesus, Mark 1:24, 34; Matt. 8:29, and of His apostles, Acts 16:16; 19:14.

III. VIEWS OF THEIR IDENTITY AND ORIGIN.

1. *Plato*; Departed men, some good. (*Symposium*, p. 202).
   Josephus: Spirits of evil men who have died. (Wars, 7:6:3).
   A. Campbell (Lect. on Demonolgy in *Popular Lectures and Addresses,* pp. 384-389) holds firmly to the view that they are (or were) the ghosts of dead men. He says all pagan writers, the Jewish historians, and the Christian fathers express this opinion. He thinks it is implied in Scripture (I Tim. 4:1).
2. *The book of Enoch* says demons are fallen angels. Consider II Pet. 2:4 and Jude 6 on "angels who sinned." Matt. 25:41—"the devil and his angels." Eph. 6:11, 12—"We wrestle not against flesh and blood, but against principalities, against powers, against rulers of the darkness of this world, against spiritual wickedness in high places." Cf. Eph. 3:10; Col. 1;16; Rom. 8:38; Col. 2:15.
   Their immediate recognition of Jesus might indicate former acquaintance with Him or supernatural knowledge. In the Bible they do not seem to be confused with ghosts; but in the one case of a dead man reappearing (I Sam. 28:11-19) he does not act as a demon.
3. Other spirits, neither human, nor of the rank of angels. Cf. Judges 9:23; I Sam. 16:14; 18:10; 19:9; I Kings 22:19-23.

Note: the word might be used of a combination or all of these. See *Vocabulary of The Bible,* ed. by J. J. Von Allmen, pp. 83-85.

IV. RATIONAL SUPPOSITIONS OF PROBABILITY. (See Balmforth's Com. on Luke, ref. to in R. C. Foster's *Studies In Life Christ,* vol. I, pp. 211, 212).

1. Any non-materialistic (idealistic or spiritual) view of the universe makes it likely that man is not the only product of the cosmic process.

2. Experiences of missionaries may be best explained by assumption of demon possession.
3. Lack of experience with demons in Christian countries may be explained.
4. The mysterious hinterland beyond surface consciousness is hardly known at all, so we cannot rule out the possibility of spiritual intelligences being able to affect it by entry from without.
5. It is common experience (as well as teaching of Scripture) that the powers of darkness and evil do influence our moral freedom. Then it is just possible that they may act through man's physical nature upon his rational, or vice versa.
6. It is well-ascertained fact physiologically that the conditions of a man's mental and spiritual nature exert influence upon the body and are influenced by the body: e.g. fever produces delirium; dyspepsia, despondency; etc.
7. If effects between man and man can be produced by animal magnetism or by hypnotism, so might demons influence and disturb both the physical and rational natures.

V. EFFECTS OF POSSESSION, OR ACCOMPANYING CIRCUMSTANCES.

1. Physical ills or diseases:
   a. Matt. 9:32,33, "dumb man" spoke when the demon was cast out.
   b. Matt. 12:22, "blind and dumb"
   c. Matt. 17:15, "epilepsy"; but Mark 9:25, "deaf and dumb spirit".
   d. Mark 5:15, wildness.
   e. Mark 7:25; Matt. 15:22ff, "greivously vexed" literally, "badly demonized" with no specific disability indicated.
   f. The woman "whom Satan had bound" (Luke 13:16) "had a spirit of infirmity" but is not said to have been possessed. Deformity of the back.
2. There are cases in which no physical ill is attributed to the demon (Mark 1:21; Luke 4:31ff. Jesus was charged with demon possession when no malady was apparent, but simply because of His speech and mental attitude. John the Baptist was similarly charged because of his manner of life. See John 7:21; 8:48,52; 10:20; Matt. 11:18.

Note that all these same physical ills, except the being "bowed together", are represented in the Gospels as separate from demon possession in other cases. Deaf and having impediment, Mark 7:32; Dumb, Matt. 15:30,31; Blind, Luke 18:35ff; John 9; Epilepsy (KJV-lunatics), Matt. 4:24 literally "moonstruck", meaning epileptic, not insane.

3. Effects other than disease.
   a. Superhuman knowledge, Mark 1:24; 5:7; 3:11,12; Luke 4:41; Acts 16:16-18
   b. Fear of torment, Luke 4:33,34; 8:28-31; Matt. 8:29
   c. Conversation as of third person, Mark 1:24,25; Luke 4:34,35
   d. Manner of departing (convulsions), Mark 1:26; 9:20; Luke 4:35
   e. Extraordinary strength, Mark 5:3,4; Acts 19:13-16
   f. Fierce wildness, Matt. 8:28; Mark 5:4,5; Luke 8:29. Cf. John 10:20.
   g. Desire to enter into some body, Mark 5:12,13; Matt. 8:31; Luke 11:24,25
   h. Multiplicity, Mark 5:9; 16:9; Luke 11:26; 8:30

VI. NATURE OF PERSONS POSSESSED

1. Mostly grown men, but two were children, Matt: 17:15; Mark 7:25-30; 9:21; Matt. 15:22. Some were women, Mark 16:9; Luke 8:2,3.
2. Some made very faithful helpers of Christ after they were released, Mark 5:20; Luke 8:2,3.
3. They always appear to be pitied rather than blamed, treated as unfortunate rather than immoral. Jesus was interested in the persons, not the demons. At least their demons are something else than unbreakable bad habits.

VII. OTHER REFERENCES TO THE WORKING OF DEMONS.

1. I Tim. 4:1, doctrines of demons and seducing spirits.
2. James 3:15, factious wisdom is demoniacal ("devilish"),
3. Rev. 16:14, "working signs" and going "forth unto the kings of the whole world, to gather them unto the war of the great day of God."
4. I Cor. 10:14-22, involved in idolatry and heathen worship.

FOR FURTHER READINGS ON DEMONS, see the following:

1. Articles in *I. S. B. E.* on "Demons" and "Exorcism"
2. Articles in *Unger's Bible Dict.* on "Demons" and "Demoniac"
3. *Biblical Demonology,* by M. F. Unger, book pub. 1953.
4. Lecture on 'Demonology" by Alexander Campbell, in POP. LECT. & ADD. pp. 379-397.
5. *The Vocabulary of the Bible* (also called *Companion to the Bible*), ed. by J. J. von Allmen, see article on "Demons" pp. 83-85.

6. Discussion in Cremer's *Biblico-Theological Lexicon of N. T. Greek,* pp. 168-171.
7. *Life and Times of Jesus The Messiah,* by A. Edersheim, vol. I, pp. 479-485; 607-613; and on Jewish notions and traditions, vol. II, pp. 755-763; 770-776.
8. Halley's *Bible Handbook,* pp. 428.239.
9. Vin's *Expository Dictionary of N. T. Words,* p. 291.
10. Baker's *Dictionary of Theology,* p. 163 on "Demons"; p. 206 on "Exorcism"
11. *Dictionary of Christ and The Gospels, Hastings,* pp. 438-443.

THE PURPOSE OF MIRACLES
The Reason Jesus Healed

In New Testament times, miracles had a distinct purpose, as stated and shown in various ways in the Word.

Jesus said, "The works which the Father has given me to accomplish, the very works that I do, bear witness to me that the Father has sent me" (John 10:25). See also John 10:38; 14:10, 11.

A DEMONSTRATION

A very clear example is given in Mark 2. When the paralytic was let down through the roof for Jesus to heal him, Jesus said, "Son, your sins are forgiven." Scribes who were in the crowded house thought Jesus was blaspheming in claiming to forgive sins.

Jesus answered their thoughts: "Why do you reason these things in your hearts? Which is easier, to say to the sick of the palsy, Your sins are forgiven, or to say, Arise, take up your bed and walk? But that you may know that the Son of man has authority on earth to forgive sins, (he said to the sick of the palsy) I say unto you, Arise, take up your bed and go to your house." And he did!

MIRACLES CONFIRM

The book of Hebrews reports that this great salvation, "having at the first been spoken through the Lord, was confirmed unto us by them that heard; God also bearing witness with them, both by signs and wonders and by manifold powers, and by gifts of the Holy Spirit, according to His own will."

John regularly called Jesus' miracles "signs." In the 21 chapters of his gospel account, he refers to them as "signs" 14 time. As Nicodemus saw, and as Jesus said, they were signs that God was with Jesus and was doing His works in Him. Peter preached on Pentecost that Jesus was "approved of God unto you by mighty works and wonders and signs which God did by him in the midst of you, even as you yourselves know" (Acts 2:22).

When the apostles worked miracles in Jesus' name, they gave evidence that Jesus was at the right hand of God (Acts 2:33), evidence of the power of His name (Acts 3:16), evidence that God was with them and their message was from God (Acts 13:9-12). Their miracles gave boldness and strength to the few witnesses faced by overwhelming opposition (Acts 4:29, 30).

They gave proof that the Gentiles were to be accepted in Christ through obedience to the gospel, the same as the Jews (Acts 10:9-16, 44-47; 11:15-17; 15:8, 9, 12). This was proof, even to the elders and the church at Jerusalem, that the preaching of Paul and Barnabas among the Gentiles was according to God's will (Acts 15:12-22).

The great miracles of God, wrought through the apostles and some on whom they laid their hands, were so clear and so certain that even sorcerers and people who practiced magical arts saw the proof of real truth and gave up their superstitions and trickery (Acts 8:6-14; 19:11-20).

MIRACLES WERE NOT ALWAYS FOR COMPASSION

The miracles of the Bible taught God's power and authority, sometimes His love and goodness, sometimes His righteous and fearsome judgments.

Consider the deaths of Uzzah (II Sam. 6:6, 7), Nadab and Abihu (Lev. 10:1, 2), and of Ananias and Sapphira (Acts 5:1-11); the leprosy. of Gehazi (II Kings 5:27) and of Miriam (Numbers 12:9-14); the blindness of Elymas (Acts 13:8-12) or of the Syrian band (II Kings 6:18-20); the destruction of armies (I Kings 20:30; II Kings 19:35) or of cities (Gen. 19:24, 25; Joshua 6:20).

Although such miracles as healing and feeding people did show the merciful goodness of God and did express the compassion of Jesus, the accounts show that they were not worked merely to relieve suffering.

Physical healing, material blessing, or the prolongation of this earthly life, are not the real purposes of God's grace toward us. He did these things sometimes as visible examples of His power and loving goodness, to encourage faith.

But miracles have always been limited to few and special cases. Never have they been used to relieve suffering or prolong this life for all of God's people impartially. Their benefit was usually temporary and only a demonstration to engender and support an abiding faith.

All who were delivered from sickness or affliction had other times to suffer and to die. All who were raised from the dead had to die again. Once and again Peter was delivered from prison and from persecutors; but another time he was left to die, when God was no less compassionate and Peter was not less believing. So it was also with Paul.

Some received no miraculous deliverance here, but a better resurrection for the life hereafter (Heb. 11:35-40). John the Immerser, greatest of the prophets, worked no miracles, nor was he miraculously delivered from prison and death (Matt. 11:7-11; John 10:41).

Jesus could have healed all the sick or raised all the dead. But he did not and would not. Many were healed by Paul, but Trophimus and Timothy were not (II Tim. 4:20; I Tim 5:23). A multitude of sick and afflicted lay by the pool at Jerusalem, but Jesus healed only one man (who did not know Him or ask Him to) and then hid Himself from the others. But later He sought the healed man again to teach him and to meet the debate which the Sabbath miracle had aroused with the Pharisees.

Miracles form part of the foundation of our faith, being divine demonstrations witnessing to the origin of the message we have believed. But they are not part of the faith or part of its practice in the lives of obedient believers. The miracles wrought by the messengers of God while the faith was being "once for all delivered to the saints" are still effective evidences to establish the truth and authority of that faith.

MODERN MIRACLES

Miracles claimed by preachers today do not clearly confirm the message of ancient apostles and prophets; they seem instead to have the opposite effect. They are not the conclusive and undoubtable kind that established the faith in the beginning. They are claimed by men whose message does not altogether agree with the sure Word of God as given in the Bible.

Even if true miracles were worked today by men who taught the truth of God's word, they would add little or nothing to the proof of that divine revelation. In fact, they would make men tend to depend upon continual miraculous demonstration rather than upon the unchanging power and veracity of God. They would tend also to make men overly eager for physical and material aid instead of concerned for spiritual and eternal salvation.

The spiritual transformation of a sinner through birth of water and the Spirit and the reality of Christ dwelling in him through faith is a greater work than even the mightiest miracles Jesus wrought in Galilee. This is surely what He meant in John 14:12. Compare John 16:7 and Eph. 3:10.

BLIND MAN OF BETHSAIDA

"And he cometh to Bethsaida; and they bring a blind man unto him, and besought him to tough him."

—Mark VIII:22

From the book JESUS LOVED THEM by Sam Patrick and Omar Garrison, copyright 1957 by P-G-Service, Los Angeles, Calif. Published by Prentice-Hall, Inc., Englewood Cliffs, New Jersey.